A History of Malaysia

A History of Malaysia
Second Edition

Barbara Watson Andaya

and

Leonard Y. Andaya

palgrave

First Published 1982
Reprinted 1995, 1996 Published 2001 by
PALGRAVE
Houndmills, Basingstoke, Hampshire RG21 6XS
Companies and representatives throughout the world

PALGRAVE is the new global academic imprint of
Palgrave Publishers Ltd (formerly Macmillan Press Ltd).

ISBN 0–333–94503–4 hardback
ISBN 0–333–94504–2 paperback

This book is printed on paper suitable for recycling and made from fully managed and sustained forest sources.

A catalogue record for this book is available from the British Library.

10   9   8   7   6   5   4   3
10   09   08   07   06   05

Printed in China

Again, for Elise and Alexis
Then little girls,
now young women

Contents

Contents

Acknowledgements

We would like to acknowledge our debt to several individuals and institutions who have assisted us in completing the revisions for the second edition of *A History of Malaysia*. In the first place, we wish to thank again Wang Gungwu and Khoo Kay Kim for the encouragement they gave to the writing of the original edition. A summer in Malaysia during the rewriting process was made possible by the Faculty Exchange Program between the Business Schools of the University of Hawai'i at Manoa and the Universiti Kebangsaan Malaysia. This was supported by a grant from the United States Information Agency, College and University Affiliations Program, administered by the Pacific Asian Management Institute (PAMI) at the University of Hawai'i College of Business Administration. We are grateful to the director, Shirley Daniel, and to Jack Godwin of PAMI who made this fruitful summer possible. Additional financial assistance was received from a University of Hawai'i National Endowment for the Humanities grant under the University Research Council, and from the Research Relations Fund of the University of Hawai'i. Again we express our thanks for this show of confidence.

In Malaysia, the Business School of Universiti Kebangsaan, particularly the Department of Management, welcomed two historians with great warmth and generosity. Our colleagues were invaluable in helping us understand not only the economic developments in the country, but various aspects of contemporary Malaysian society. Other faculty members in the History Department and the Institute of Malay World and Civilization (ATMA) were extremely generous with their time and knowledge. We wish to thank in particular Takiah Iskandar, Mohd Ezani Mat Hassan, and Rozlan Othman of the Business School; Nabir Haji Abdullah and Yahya Abu Bakar of the History Department; and Shamsul A.B. and Jim Collins of ATMA.

We benefited from seminars held at the National University of Singapore (NUS), the Universiti Malaya, and Universiti Kebangsaan Malaysia. We would like to express our special thanks to Edwin Lee, head of the NUS History Department, who made our stay in Singapore both fruitful and enjoyable.

Acknowledgements

Geoffrey Benjamin spent considerable time with us discussing his thoughts on aspects of early history. In Universiti Malaya, Shaharil Talib of the Asia-Europe Centre, Mohd Noor bin Othman of the Economics Department, and the members of the History Department further contributed to the rethinking of our ideas on Malaysia. To all of them we are most grateful. In this new edition we have attempted to incorporate more about Sabah and Sarawak into the general history of Malaysia. The task was made infinitely easier through the guidance of Khoo Kay Jin, Callistus Fernandez, Welyne Jeffrey Jehom and Michael Leigh, currently director of the Institute of East Asian Studies at Universiti Malaysia Sarawak. Finally, we would also like to thank the History Department, Universiti Sains in Penang, for their invitation to a most useful conference on Southeast Asian history where we had a valuable opportunity to discuss Malaysian history with our Malaysian colleagues.

There are numerous other individuals who have been kind and generous to us over the years and whom we have not mentioned here. However, they have not been forgotten and we will always remember them with fondness.

Preface to the Second Edition

Revisiting work that belongs to a much earlier period of one's career is a sobering but interesting experience, especially for a historian. As we worked on the revisions to this new edition, we were made aware of the passage of time not only in Malaysia, but also in the historical discipline and in our own approach to the subject. The first edition of this book was written in 1980, when our understanding of Malaysian history was shaped both by our own academic training and by our experience of living in Kuala Lumpur between 1972 and 1974. Returning to undertake revisions in the summer of 1999, we were constantly struck by the changes which were visible everywhere, and which were particularly evident in our immediate environment. When we were in Malaysia nearly 30 years ago we lived in a largely English-speaking enclave near the University of Malaya, where our neighbours were virtually all expatriates or of Chinese or Indian descent. As a result of the New Economic Policy (NEP), Malay students were beginning to enter higher education in large numbers, but they were most noticeable in the Arts faculty. In 1982, when the first edition was published, Dr Mahathir Mohamad had only just come into office. Despite the NEP's lofty objectives, few observers anticipated any rapid shifts in the association between ethnicity and occupation that seemed so embedded in Malaysian society.

The atmosphere in which the revisions were completed was very different. Though faced with a strong political challenge, Datuk Seri Dr Mahathir Mohamad maintained control of government in the elections of November 1999, and will thus become the longest-serving prime minister in the nation's history. The goals of the New Economic Policy (1970–90) and the National Development Policy (1990–2000) have not been totally achieved, but evidence of their impact is apparent everywhere. Living in Bangi, on the campus of the Universiti Kebangsaan Malaysia, we found the Malay entry into education as both staff and students especially impressive. Elsewhere – using the internet, enjoying the convenience of commuter train and light rail, wandering through some new shopping mall – we were very much aware of the extent of change which Malaysia has experienced over the last three decades. We of course realize that this development has been uneven and that it has not been without costs, and in the final chapter we have tried to give due weight to the social and economic problems that the country now faces. And even when surrounded by change, we have tried to view Malaysian history in terms of the continuities that bind its peoples to their various pasts.

From the very outset of this project some 20 years ago we were well aware that ours was an outsider's view. The proliferation of historical writings in Malay over the last generation is a very specific reminder of the relocation of both audiences and practitioners to Malaysia itself. None the less, it has been tremendously gratifying for us to see that shops still stock our book and to learn that it continues to be used in courses on Malaysian history. More than anything else, it is this response that persuaded us to embark on the task of revising. After some thought, we decided to retain the basic structure of the original edition, while incorporating new material that has appeared since its publication. These changes are probably most evident in Chapter 8, which discusses the period from 1969 to 1999, and thus covers the two decades which have elapsed since the first edition was written. But in the earlier sections, too, the research of colleagues has necessitated numerous changes, and the careful reader will find evidence of rewriting throughout the text. Sometimes this represents simply attention to stylistic lapses, or a refinement of the previous argument; sometimes, however, we have found it necessary to reshape entire sections in the light of new theories or historical interpretations.

We must emphasize, however, that the present work is a revision rather than a recasting. As before, our major theme remains the tracing of Malaysia's development from early times through the period of colonial rule to the creation of an independent nation. Like its predecessor, this edition falls naturally into three divisions, which represent significant periods in Malaysian history. Chapters 1–3 examine the social and economic bases of the 'traditional' society that evolved along the Melaka Straits and in Borneo prior to the nineteenth century. Chapters 4–6 continue the story from the founding of Singapore in 1819, which initiated colonial rule and in consequence a new type of economic and political organization which brought far-reaching changes to local society and the traditional Malay polity. Chapters 7 and 8 discuss the modern Malaysian nation as the heir to earlier maritime states and the colonial past, but also as the architect of a new kind of society. The conclusion then attempts to highlight significant patterns that can be traced in Malaysian history from early times to the present day.

Note on Spelling and Currency

The most notable feature of Malay romanization is the use of 'c' and 'sy' to indicate English ch and English sh. However, names of people and places often follow earlier systems, and it is therefore impossible to be completely consistent. The spelling of titles in Malaysia has not yet been standardized. In this book most honorifics have been rendered according to modern usage (thus Syah, not Shah, and Datuk, not Dato). Although we have tried to follow current practice in the spelling of Malaysian place names, these are not uniform and one frequently finds variation in words such as Baru, which can also be rendered Bharu or Bahru.

With the exception of historical (often non-Mandarin) terms and personal names that are well established in publications on Malaysia and that have been romanized according to the Wade-Giles system or some other form, we have used pinyin to romanize Chinese words.

Throughout the text the term 'Thai' refers to the ethnic group which came to settle in present-day Thailand, as well as to the citizens of that state, which was officially decreed as Thailand in June 1939. Before that date the various Thai kingdoms are called by their specific names, such as Sukhothai and Ayudhya. The terms 'Siam' and 'Siamese' are used for the Thai kingdom and people reunified under the Chakkri dynasty in 1782 until the official name change in 1939.

All dollar figures quoted are in Straits (later Malay/Malaysian) dollars or *ringgit*. In the nineteenth century the value of the Straits dollar fluctuated, but in 1904 it was pegged to sterling at the rate of M$1.00 to 2s. 4d. (about US$40–60 in pre-Second World War terms). From 1947 to 1974 M$3.00 was equal to about US$1.00. In 1973 Malaysia opted out of the sterling area and floated the *ringgit* against the US dollar and the British pound. In 1997, in the wake of the region's economic downturn, the Malaysian dollar was fixed at M$3.80 to US$1.00, but allowed to float against other currencies.

Abbreviations

ABIM	Angkatan Belia Islam Malaysia (Islamic Youth Movement of Malaysia)
AMCJA	All-Malaya Council of Joint Action
BCE	before the common era
BEFEO	*Bulletin de l'École Française d'Extrême-Orient*
Bhd	Berhad = Ltd
BKI	Bijdragen tot de Taal, Land- en Volkenkunde
BP	before present
CCP	Chinese Communist Party
CE	common era
Cod. Or.	Codex Orientalis
DAP	Democratic Action Party
EIC	East India Company (English)
FAMA	Federal Agricultural Marketing Authority
FELDA	Federal Land Development Authority
FMS	Federated Malay States
FSGCP	Fort St George Council Papers, British Library
FWCP	Fort William Council Papers, British Library
Gerakan	Gerakan Rakyat Malaysia (Malaysian People's Movement)
GLU	General Labour Unions
HICOM	Heavy Industry Corporation of Malaysia
IMP	Independence of Malaya Party
INA	Indian National Army
JMBRAS	*Journal of the Malayan (later Malaysian) Branch of the Royal Asiatic Society*
JSBRAS	*Journal of the Straits Branch of the Royal Asiatic Society*
JSEAH	*Journal of Southeast Asian History*
JSEAS	*Journal of Southeast Asian Studies*
JSS	*Journal of the Siam Society*
KMM	Kesatuan Melayu Muda (Young Malay Union)

KMT	Kuomintang (Chinese Nationalist Party)
KRIS	Kesatuan Rakyat Indonesia Semenanjung (Union of Peninsular Indonesians)
MARA	Majlis Amanah Rakyat (Council of Trust for Indigenous People)
MAS	Malay Administrative Service
MBRAS	Malaysian Branch of the Royal Asiatic Society
MCA	Malayan (later Malaysian) Chinese Association
MCP	Malayan Communist Party
MCS	Malayan Civil Service
MDU	Malayan Democratic Union
MIC	Malayan Indian Congress
MNP	Malayan Nationalist Party (Partai Kebangsaan Melayu Malaya)
MPAJA	Malayan Peoples Anti-Japanese Army
MPHB	Multi-Purpose Holdings Bhd
MRLA	Malayan Races Liberation Army
MSC	Multimedia Super Corridor
NAP	National Agricultural Policy
NCC	National Consultative Council
NDP	National Development Policy
NEP	New Economic Policy
NGO	non-governmental organization
PAP	People's Action Party
PAS	Parti Islam Sa-Melayu (Pan-Malayan Islamic Party)
PETA	Pembela Tanah Air (Defenders of the Fatherland)
PKMM	Partai Kebangsaan Melayu Muda
PMFTU	Pan-Malayan Federation of Trade Unions
PPP	People's Progressive Party
PUTERA	Malay Pusat Tenaga Rakyat (Centre of People's Power)
RISDA	Rubber Industry Smallholders Development Authority
SCO	Sarawak Communist Organization
SFR	Sumatra Factory Records
SITC	Sultan Idris Training College
SSR	Straits Settlements Records
UMNO	United Malay National Organization
UMS	Unfederated Malay States
VOC	Vereenigde Oostindische Compagnie (the United East India Company) (Dutch)

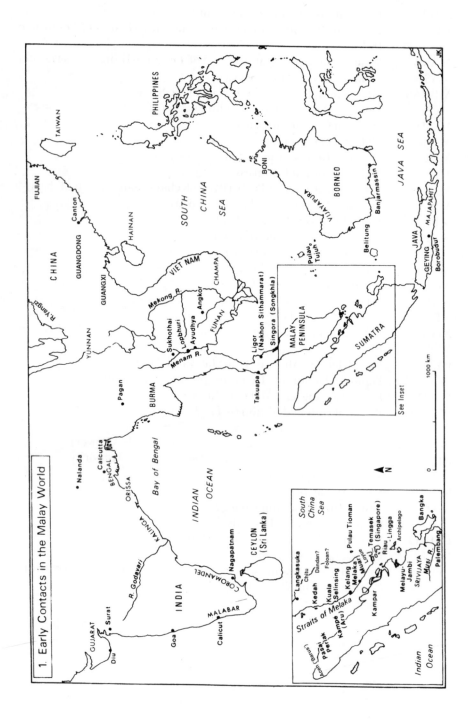

1. Early Contacts in the Malay World

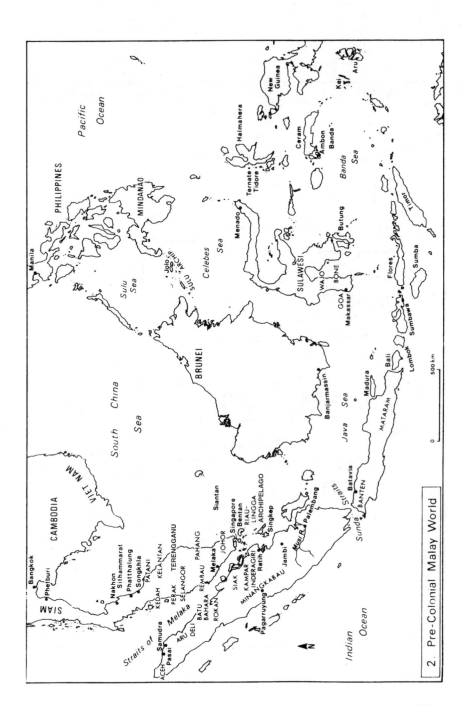

2. Pre-Colonial Malay World

3. Peninsular Malaysia

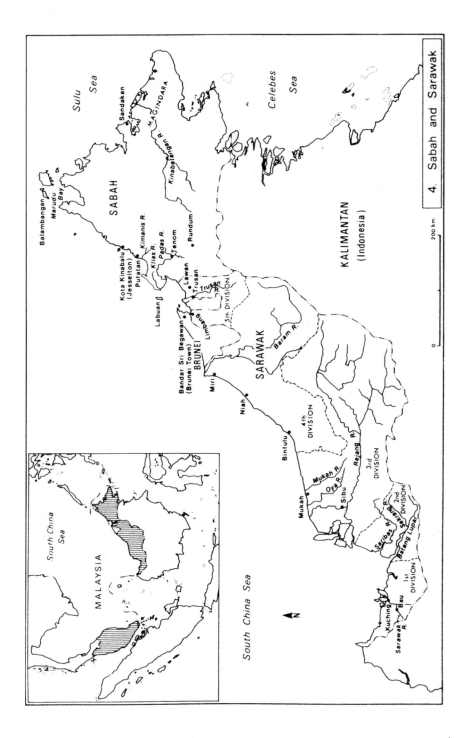

4. Sabah and Sarawak

Introduction: The Environment and Peoples of Malaysia

Established in 1963, the Federation of Malaysia comprises the long peninsular land mass which separates the Indian Ocean from the South China Sea, together with the northern quarter of Borneo but excluding the small state of Brunei. Peninsular Malaysia, covering 131 573 square kilometres (sq km), is made up of eleven states: Perlis, Kedah, Penang, Perak, Selangor (with the Federal Capital Territory of Kuala Lumpur), Melaka, Johor, Negeri Sembilan, Pahang, Terengganu and Kelantan. At 795 sq km, Perlis is the smallest state, while Pahang (35 964 sq km) is the largest after Sarawak. The island of Singapore, which was part of Malaysia between 1963 and 1965, is independent. The Borneo territories, Sabah (formerly British North Borneo), Sarawak, and the Federal Territory of the island of Labuan, together cover roughly 198 000 sq km, but are separated at the closest point from the Peninsula by over 530 kilometres (km). Kota Kinabalu (previously Jesselton), the capital of Sabah, is 864 km from Kuching (Sarawak's capital) and more than 1600 km from Kuala Lumpur.

The terrain of both the Peninsula and Borneo is characterized by coastal plains giving way to a rugged mountainous interior. The spine of the Peninsula is the Main Range, running roughly north–south for 483 km and varying from 914 metres to 2134 metres (m) above sea level. A further block of highland, covering most of Kelantan, inland Terengganu, and Pahang, includes the Peninsula's highest peak, Gunung Tahan (2207 m). A continuous alluvial plain, 960 km long and at places 60 km wide, stretches along the west coast from Perlis to Johor. Another lowland plain occurs on the east coast, but this is narrower and interrupted by the Terengganu highlands. Because the interior mountains have historically impeded trans-Peninsular movement, the focus of settlement has been the coastal lowlands. Early political centres were established on the rivers which have their headwaters in the inland ranges, and it is from their principal river that most Peninsular states derive their name. Of these the Pahang river (447 km) is the longest.

1

In Borneo, low-lying, often swampy, alluvial plains also form a belt along the coast, narrowing considerably when they reach Sabah, where larger but isolated plains occur in the north and east. Behind these plains are the foot-hills leading inland up to a mountainous mass through which runs the border between Malaysia and Indonesian Borneo (Kalimantan). The imposing Mount Kinabalu (4101 m) in Sabah is the highest point in Southeast Asia outside New Guinea. From the highlands of the interior the great rivers of Borneo flow down to the sea, the largest in Malaysian Borneo being the Rejang in Sarawak (563 km) and the Kinabatangan in Sabah (560 km).

Both Peninsular Malaysia and the Borneo states lie between 2° and 6° north of the equator. The climate is uniformly warm and humid, with temperatures ranging from 25.5° to 33°C, except at high altitudes where the nights are considerably cooler. The passing of the seasons is not marked by variations in temperature but by changes in rainfall, which in turn are related to the cycle of the monsoonal winds. However, variations in this pattern have periodically been recorded due to the El Niño effect. The northeast monsoon, a steady strong wind sweeping down across the South China Sea, is the dominating air stream from November to January. It then gradually decreases in force, with a transitional period in April–May followed by the southwest monsoon. Another transitional period occurs in October–November, and the whole cycle starts again, once more made apparent by changes in rainfall. Throughout most of Malaysia the rainfall averages from 2000 millimetres (mm) to 4000 mm per annum, but there is considerable variation between different regions. Nowhere is there a true dry season, but in most areas certain periods in the year are predictably wetter than others. For much of the Peninsula and northwest Borneo the wettest season coincides with the northeast monsoon.

Although Malaysian soils are not generally fertile, the heavy rainfall and warm temperatures provide almost perfect conditions for the growth of equatorial rainforests. Along the coastal lowlands most of the original forest cover has been removed since the nineteenth century to make way for settlements, road and rail communication, and the development of commercial agriculture and industries. The remaining jungle areas have been substantially reduced by heavy logging over the last two decades, particularly in Sabah and Sarawak. While a national total of around 19.4 million hectares is covered with natural or planted forest, the primary rainforest is increasingly confined to national parks and reserves and to areas so inaccessible or at such high altitudes that they will probably remain uncleared.

A very different type of vegetation, but one equally characteristic of the region, are the mangrove swamps. These border the sheltered shores and estuaries along the western coasts of the Peninsula and Borneo, sometimes reaching inland for 20 kilometres. Shorelines more exposed to the open sea, like those along the east coast of the Peninsula, are edged by long sandy beaches backed by low heath. The attractiveness of this environment has been a prime factor in tourist promotion.

In 1998 Malaysia's population was estimated at 22 179 000, although this will be adjusted when the figures from the census of 2001 become available. It is already obvious, however, that there has been a significant demographic expansion from around 13.46 million in 1980, partly because of natural growth and partly because of migration, notably from Indonesia and the Philippines. In Sabah, for example, migrants are largely responsible for the dramatic rise in population between 1980 and 1991 of 5.5 per cent annually. The increase here and elsewhere may be even greater, owing to the numbers of unregistered non-citizens. These are officially estimated at 1 554 200, but because of the likelihood of a significant undercount in this and other categories, demographers have urged caution when citing the available figures.

The varied composition of Malaysia's population remains one of its most distinguishing features. The dominant ethnic group is the Malays, who in 1991 comprised 58.3 per cent of Peninsular Malaysia's population. Because Malays have a higher fertility rate than other groups, this figure will probably show some increase in the next census. Furthermore, the legal definition of a Malay – one who habitually speaks Malay, adheres to Malay customs, and is a follower of Islam – has readily permitted the inclusion of migrants from Indonesia and the southern Philippines, and even individuals from other groups. Population figures can thus be misleading. In the 1991 census tabulations, for example, many Indonesians who had recently become citizens were classified as Malays, while their non-citizen fellows were categorized as 'other'. In the past it has also been common to associate ethnic groups with specific economic occupations, but this is increasingly changing. Malays still predominate in government service, the army and the police force, but over the last 30 years many have moved from rural areas to the city, and Malays can now be found in all sectors of the economy.

As well as Malays, the category of 'Bumiputera' (sons/daughters of the soil) in Peninsular Malaysia includes other numerically small but historically important indigenous groups, now collectively known as Orang Asli (literally, original people or aboriginals), a term coined during the 1950s. In 1994 they were numbered at 92 203, much less than 1 per cent of the population, although an increase on the 1980 estimate of 83 453.[1] Few live any longer in the deep jungle, which has been severely diminished through logging and the spread of urban and industrial development. Numerous Orang Asli settlements are instead found around forest fringes, and it has been estimated that around 40 per cent are lowland and coastal dwellers. There are officially 19 different Orang Asli subgroups, commonly divided into three broad divisions. However, the merging of Orang Asli with other groups, notably Malay, and their increasing choice of marriage partners outside their own communities, is blurring categories which academics and administrators continue to use. The first division is the northern Orang Asli, to whom the unfortunate term 'Negritos' was applied by early anthropologists because of their relatively darker skin and smaller stature. Scattered across the northern and central areas, they numbered less than 2700 in 1994, with some very

3

small groups, like the Mendriq of Ulu (upstream) Kelantan, estimated at fewer than 150, and the Kensiu of Kedah around 230. The second division is the Senoi, who were found in the central part of the Peninsula and who in the past were largely shifting cultivators. They include some of the largest groups, such as the Temiar (15 122) and the Semai (26 076). The third division is the southern Orang Asli, who have been burdened with the labels 'aboriginal Malay' and 'proto-Malay'. This is partly because communities like the Temuan (16 015) and the Jakun (16 637) have had close associations with coastal Malays for several generations, and in many cases have adopted a sedentary farming life and have become Muslim.

Among the Peninsula's non-indigenous population, which includes a range of different groups such as Arabs, Armenians, Eurasians, Filipinos and so on, the main communities are the Chinese, estimated at 29.4 per cent in 1991, and the Indians, including individuals of Pakistani, Bangladeshi and Sri Lankan origin (9.5 per cent). Chinese and Indians are mainly descendants of migrants who arrived from the mid-nineteenth century to work in the colonial economy. Although Chinese have historically been associated with urban centres, there is a significant if overlooked rural Chinese population. The urban Chinese tend to be employed in the professions and the business sector. Indians are prominent in the bureaucracy and professions, and in certain government departments such as railways. In the past many were employed on rubber estates, but plantation closures over the last 30 years have resulted in a drift of poor and largely unskilled Indians to urban areas.

The demographic picture changes considerably when Sarawak and Sabah are taken into account. Classification of local peoples, problematic enough on the Peninsula, has in Borneo posed enormous difficulties for census makers. Attempts to construct a simple Bumiputera category to include Malays and all other indigenous groups have not been sucessful in Sabah and Sarawak because the term subsumed so many ethnic categories, which are in turn simplifications of earlier and much longer lists. A comparison of these simplified Borneo groupings makes apparent the increase in population over the last 30 years as well as the changing percentage distributions, often because small communities have been included in larger ones. In Sarawak (1.7 million) the mainly urban and coastal Malay population, placed at 129 300 (17.4 per cent) in 1960 rose to 360 400 (21 per cent) in 1991. The Iban, formerly referred to as Sea Dayak, still outnumber Malays, but at 506 500 have fallen from 31.9 per cent to 29.5 per cent of the total. They are more homogenous than other groups and in many cases have adopted Christianity. Other indigenous groups are the Bidayuh (formerly Land Dayak) at 140 700 (8.2 per cent) who are also largely Christian, and the more diverse Melanau (97 100 and 5.7 per cent), who live in Bintulu and Miri and along the lower reaches of the Rejang, and who are approximately 65 per cent Muslim; remaining indigenous groups together number 104 400 (6.1 per cent). The last is the most varied category, including among others the Kayan, Kenyah, Kajang, Lun Bawang, Kelabit, the Bisaya, Tagal,

Kedayan, Penan and Punan. Even in this listing there are subdivisions: the peoples classed as 'Kenyah', for example, include a number of other smaller groups. Development has also brought marked changes in lifestyle. The Penan, who speak a language related to Kayan and Kenyah, were previously forest dwellers, but only around 400 are still hunter-gatherers. In addition, Sarawak also has a significant Chinese population of 475 800, amounting to 27.7 per cent of the total.

In Sabah (1.8 million), the Malays (123 800 or 6.6 per cent of the population) are outnumbered by the Kadazan/Dusun, who were formerly classified together simply as Kadazan (343 400 and 18.4 per cent). While the Kadazan tend to be Christian, the Dusun are generally Muslim. Today they are referred to jointly as Kadazandusun. Another large group is the Muslim Sama-Bajau of the east and west coasts (212 000 and 11.4 per cent), who were formerly boat dwellers. The more rural Murut groups amount to 2.9 per cent (53 900), while other Bumiputera communities account for around 14.5 per cent. The Chinese community of 218 200 comprises 11.7 per cent of the population; as in Sarawak, they can be roughly divided into urban dwellers, predominantly merchants and middlemen, and rural agriculturalists. There are also large numbers of Filipinos from Mindanao and Sulu, who together with recent Indonesian migrants make up 24.9 per cent of Sabah's inhabitants.

Incorporating this range of humanity under one national flag has meant that no single group in Malaysia has a total majority. In the 1998 estimates, the Bumiputera category, including Malays and other indigenous groups, was placed at 57 per cent (12 842 800). With a total of 5 515 400 according to the 1998 figures, the Chinese population is currently reckoned at 24 per cent, and the Indian population of 1 562 300, concentrated almost totally on the Peninsula, at 7 per cent. At 3 per cent the category of 'Other' has increased slightly from previous years, and to this should be added an uncertain number of non-citizens, amounting to around 7 per cent or more.

Facility in the national language, Malay, has been seen as the most important means of linking the nation together. At the end of the twentieth century, most people between the ages of 7 and 30 have been educated almost exclusively in Malay. None the less, English is widely used, and the opening of numerous English-language colleges may suggest some shift in favour of English. A number of other languages are also commonly spoken, notably those from South China (Hakka, Teochiew, Hokkien, Cantonese and Hailam) as well as Mandarin. Among the Indians Tamil is most common, but numerous other regional languages from the subcontinent are also found. Though increasing Malay education is making inroads on other indigenous languages, the linguistic diversity of Bumiputera groups in the Peninsula and Borneo makes this region a fertile area for research.

The linguistic complexity is matched by the range of religious and cultural traditions within Malaysian society. The state religion is Islam, and virtually all Malays are Muslim. While some other indigenous groups have adopted Islam or Christianity, a significant number have retained their indigenous religions. Some Chinese are Muslim, but the majority are Christian, Buddhist, Confucianist, Taoist or a combination of these. Hinduism and Christianity are common among Indians, but a minority are Muslim.

Malaysia and Singapore are the only two countries in Southeast Asia that have held elections at regular intervals since they became independent. Malaysia's ethnic composition has contributed to a political structure that combines some of the features of the parliamentary system with the practical realities of the local situation. The head of state, the *yang dipertuan agung*, is a position that rotates among the sultans of the Peninsular states. Though Malaysia is a Federation, the Borneo territories have special rights which were granted when they joined. The governing Barisan Nasional, or National Front, is a coalition of 14 parties, the most important of which claim to represent the interests of specific ethnic groups. The Barisan is overwhelmingly dominated by UMNO, the United Malay National Organization.

Occasionally the assumptions and compromises underlying this structure have been questioned, as in May 1969 when ethnic disturbances broke out. In general, however, Malaysia has successfully maintained co-operation if not harmony among its different communities at a time when the world has witnessed disturbing racial and ethnic violence. Part of this success has been due to the fact that Malaysia has been able to support a formidable economic growth rate. Whether it will be able to sustain this record into the twenty-first century will hinge on its bold economic venture into high technology and its ability to reconcile the often competing demands of its ethnic groups for equitable sharing of resources and equal access to political power.

The Heritage of the Past

Until the beginning of the fifteenth century CE, the history of what is now Malaysia is difficult to reconstruct with any certainty. Because of this lack of information, historians have tended to regard the rise of a great entrepôt, Melaka, on the west coast of the Malay Peninsula as an identifiable starting point for Malay history. There is a consequent inclination to consider the centuries before 1400 – the 'pre-Melakan period' – as being of relatively little importance in the evolution of modern Malaysia. But Melaka's development from a quiet fishing village to a world-renowned emporium and centre of Malay culture cannot be explained unless one realizes that behind the splendour of its court and the vigour of its commerce lay traditions of trade and government that had evolved over centuries. The story of Malaysia does not therefore begin at Melaka but stretches back deep into the past. An examination of Melaka's heritage not only provides the context essential for an understanding of later events, but throws up themes that continue to be relevant as Malaysian history unfolds.

Reconstructing early Malaysian history: historiographical considerations

In Malaysia today tangible evidence of the past is far less obvious than in most Southeast Asian countries. There are no great temple complexes such as Angkor in Kampuchea or Borobodur in Java, no impressive array of inscriptions as in Burma's Pagan, no chronological continuity like that provided by the Vietnamese court annals. Painstaking research has unearthed numerous references to the Malay world before 1400, scattered through Indian, Chinese and Arab sources, but the linguistic skills required to exploit these are daunting. The Chinese records are the most promising for a historical reconstruction of the early history of the Malay region, yet they also present the historian with specific problems. Imperial dynastic chronicles usually devote one section to foreign countries, but these sections were often compiled years later from notes and are thus subject to error. Descriptions by Buddhist pilgrims of their voyages to India, navigational guides for mariners and accounts by travellers are also important Chinese sources. But here too questions of chronology and veracity may arise because supposedly eyewitness reports could incorporate much earlier material or be based on second- or third-hand information.

More problematic than the Chinese sources are the Arab travel accounts, which purport to contain an accurate picture of far-flung places in the then known world. Until the mid-fourteenth century, however, none of the more frequently quoted authors had ever been to Southeast Asia, and their collections often deteriorate into a farrago of highly imaginative sailors' tales, emphasizing the incredible and miraculous.

Archaeological research also offers limited possibilities for illuminating Malaysia's early history. The rapid decay of most material in a tropical climate means that only the most durable objects of stone or metal have survived, and many discoveries have been purely accidental because written evidence provides few clues as to the location of early settlements. It is quite possible that some sites have been permanently lost as a result of geological and environmental change. Around 11 000 years ago, for example, the sea level along the Peninsula's east coast was about 68 metres below the present level, and any evidence of human habitation there would now be submerged. Even in more recent times alluvial deposits have considerably altered the shape of some coastlines. In some places remains of boats have been found several miles inland, in almost inaccessible jungle or along creeks now unnavigable because of river silting. It is also unfortunate that the bulk of metal antiquities on the Peninsula were unearthed before the introduction of scientific archaeological methods. Important finds made in the last century, like 'the relics of a Hindoo colony' discovered in Kedah by James Low, were naturally not subjected to the kind of rigorous investigation that would be employed today.[1] Epigraphic evidence, too, has been disappointingly sparse, apart from a few remains such as the famous Terengganu Stone. Erected by an unknown Muslim ruler some time in the fourteenth century, this is the earliest example of Malay written in Jawi, a modified Perso-Arabic script. The contents (difficult to read because of damage to the stone's surface) enjoin obedience to God's law and prescribe punishments for certain crimes.

The relative dearth of monuments and inscriptions in Malaysia gives added importance to the material that has been located. During the colonial period the Museums Department pioneered archaeological excavation, providing a basis for later work by the National Archaeological Survey and Research Unit, established in 1969. Under the leadership of trained professionals the progress over the last decade has been particularly striking. Several exciting discoveries have been made, including early human remains in Perak, new slab graves in Bernam, cave paintings in Kedah and Kelantan, as well as further finds of ceramics, beads and other items in Kedah's Bujang valley. Even the modern development normally seen as hostile to preservation has had its uses: during the construction of the Sungai Muda irrigation project in Kedah, for example, the remains of a stupa were found when a canal was cut through the middle of a village.

None the less, with limited funds and a small number of experts, archaeological investigation can proceed only slowly. Even with the combined skills of historians, archaeologists, linguists, anthropologists, art historians and geographers, the material does not permit more than a general picture of developments in the Malay archipelago before about 1400. Yet this broad canvas in itself generates a certain energy, since speculation on many aspects of early Malaysian history is still rife, and long-standing theories can well be challenged on the basis of fresh evidence. Indeed, one authority contends that the results of archaeological and linguistic research since the 1970s have 'revolutionized' scholarly understanding of Peninsular Malaysia's prehistory.[2]

One of the most contentious topics still concerns the chronology of human habitation and the history of language development. In Peninsular Malaysia, the reasons for the cultural, linguistic and biological differences between contemporary Malay, 'Aboriginal Malay', Senoi and Negrito have been debated for almost a century. Stone tools found in Perak may be around 34 000 years old, and there is a possibility that other more recent discoveries may be considerably earlier. However, the bulk of prehistoric tools recovered in cave sites like those in Perak and Kelantan are more recent, dating from around 13 000 to 2000 years ago. They include the 1990 discovery of what is thus far the oldest Peninsular evidence of human burial, a complete skeleton now termed 'Perak man'. Scientific analysis of other skeletal remains suggests that early inhabitants of the Peninsula were genetically linked to the smaller and darker northern Orang Asli (the so-called Negritos) of contemporary Malaysia, who would thus appear to have a truly local ancestry, and with the Senoi, who display stronger connections with Neolithic societies in southern and central Thailand. But explanations for the variations in appearance and lifestyle of Peninsular populations are divided between those who see cultural and biological shifts as occurring locally, and those who place greater emphasis on immigration from elsewhere in the region.

Proponents of the latter view feel that the linguistic differences between Malay and Orang Asli provide convincing evidence of external origins for most groups, with the probable exception of the Negrito. Among the Orang Asli at least twelve languages have been identified, collectively termed 'Aslian'. Though diverse, Aslian languages are all related to Mon-Khmer which is found in mainland Southeast Asia, and are thus included in the Austroasiatic family. On the basis of these findings, it has been concluded that the ancestors of today's Aslian-speaking Orang Asli moved down the Peninsula from southern Thailand in Neolithic times. The Aslian languages they introduced were then absorbed by the existing Negrito populations.

Between 4000 and 3000 BCE, speakers of proto-Austronesian languages settled in Taiwan from southern China. It is generally believed that between about 2500 and 1500 BCE they migrated outward through the Philippines,

9

the northern half of Borneo, Sulawesi, central Java and then to eastern Indonesia. From about 1500 to 500 BCE there was a further movement southward in Borneo, then out to the western half of Java and westward to Sumatra and the Malay Peninsula. This slow filtering into the archipelago occurred over a long period of time, and was combined with continued movement back and forth between islands and along coasts. Settling in riverine and coastal areas in the Peninsula, these migrants displaced or absorbed Austroasiatic speakers and adapted their own lifestyles to suit environments which ranged from the deep jungle to the open seas.

Some scholars feel that explanations of the diversity of Peninsular populations should give more attention to factors other than migration. In certain situations, it has been argued, Malays developed from the same genetic pool as the Orang Asli, with the presence or absence of specific biological characteristics attributed to a variety of factors, including adaptation to local conditions. The Malay language began to be used among the forest and sea-dwelling Aslian-speaking groups who lived along the Straits of Melaka, and gradually spread northwards, eventually displacing Austroasiatic languages. In the Kedah area, for example, an Orang Asli population speaking an Austroasiatic language had by the twelfth century become linguistically and culturally Malay. The strength of the immigrant Malay presence in the south would explain why some Aboriginal Malay groups in Johor and Pahang speak dialects of Malay, while Aslian is more clearly associated with central and northern groups.[3]

The influence of migration is generally accepted in the case of Borneo, which has a special place in Malaysia's demographic history. Although the previous dating of 38 000 BP is now being revised, the so-called 'deep skull' found in Sarawak's Niah Caves may still be among the earliest examples of modern human remains found in Southeast Asia. It is currently thought that from about 40 000 to 2000 years ago the Borneo region was inhabited by Austro-Melanesian populations, related to the peoples of New Guinea and Australia. However, all languages spoken in Borneo today belong to the Austronesian family, and no groups similar to the northern Orang Asli ('Negritos') have ever been recorded here. The only hunter-gatherer group remaining, the Penan of Sarawak, belong to the same biological pool as other Borneo populations and their lifestyle reflects an adjustment to a specific rainforest environment. The filtration of Austronesian speakers into Borneo probably dates from around 3000–4000 years ago. This migration would have involved not only movement along the coast, but also along internal river systems in a manner similar to the migrations of Borneo peoples documented in modern times. The cultural and linguistic patchwork so characteristic of Sabah and Sarawak can be attributed primarily to adaptations to different ecological environments, although similarities in vocabulary and morphology reflect a substratum of a basically shared heritage. In recent years more systematic work has attempted to compare and classify the numerous indigenous languages and dialects, although much remains to be done. Arguably the most significant claim of recent linguistic research is that 'Proto-Malayic', from which Malay and a number of other related languages evolved, originated somewhere in western Borneo.

While the nature and extent of demographic movement into and within the region remains unresolved, scholars generally agree that variations in language, appearance and culture among the peoples of the Peninsula and Borneo have been accentuated by environmental adaptation and social development. It is also recognized that the activities of all communities, from the coast to the deep interior, overlapped to some degree with their neighbours, so that no cultural feature was completely unique. In some cases the lifestyle of one linguistic community was virtually indistinguishable from another with which it commonly interacted; in others, distinct cultural characteristics persisted although the groups might live in close proximity. Selective transfer of technology also reflects continuing interaction between groups. In more recent times the Punan of Sarawak, for instance, have acquired boat making and blacksmithing skills from their Kayan neighbours. But even when differences appeared pronounced, certain societal traits were shared because all groups were responding to a similar physical environment and had in common a world-view in which animism and ancestor worship were entwined with a veneration for the forces of regeneration and fertility. The significance of rock carvings dispersed over northeast Sarawak, for example, awaits investigation but it is already clear that they were executed by people who were products of similar cultural traditions. On the other hand, the dolmens, megaliths and menhirs found throughout Malaysia performed a variety of functions which differed according to the locale. Thus, although the prehistory of Malaysia remains a subject for debate, the differences and the links between the indigenous peoples both remain important lines of enquiry.

Early trade and the products of the Malay archipelago

A major theme that does emerge as we move from prehistory into the historic period is the importance of trade in shaping the region's history. By the time Melaka was founded, around 1400, the Malay archipelago had for hundreds of years been part of a complex trading network threading through the entire Southeast Asian region and stretching from Africa to China. During the first millennium CE the skills of merchants, sailors and suppliers from India, the Arab lands, China and Southeast Asia's maritime world had been brought together in a close-knit commercial relationship.

The geographic position of the Malay archipelago was fundamental in this development. Located on the convergence of two major sea routes, it was linked to the great markets of India and China by the annual monsoon wind systems. Although the all-sea route between China and India did not come into use until the fifth century, trading links between India and the Malay world were well established at least 200 years before that.

A second factor in the growth of trade to and within the Malay archipe-lago was the richness of its natural resources, which provided a multitude of products for sale or exchange. The most important resource in early times was the jungle-covered landscape itself, since it was the trees of the rainforest that supplied the aromatic woods, resins and rattans for which the Malay world became justly renowned. But while Malays may have been responsible for the eventual sale and distribution of forest products, they were not the principal gatherers. Malay settlement had developed along the rivers and coasts rather than the hinterland, and Malays themselves rarely ventured beyond the fringes of the jungle. To them the forest remained an alien realm, the haunt of demons and spirits which must be propitiated by offer-ings and warded off by charms. They were content to barter goods such as salt and iron with the forest-dwelling nomads who remained the primary collectors and who made the jungle their natural habitat.

The antiquity of hunting and gathering in the region is still a matter for discussion. Some groups, like the Negritos, have probably inhabited the jungles of Peninsular Malaysia for at least 10 000 years. Others, like the Penan of Sarawak, probably moved into the rainforest at a later stage. What is impressive among all forest dwellers is their successful adaptation to a unique environment, where the unparalleled variety of trees and plants rep-resented a virtual sea of resources. Generation after generation, each group came to know its own locality in intimate detail, as research on one Orang Asli group, the Temuan, suggests. Undertaken in the early 1970s, this study found that by late adolescence every Temuan could identify several hundred plant species from his or her particular environment. To move to a different locality would demand an almost impossible task of relearning a great number of unfamiliar types.[4] Such specialized knowledge was a vital element in jungle collecting because, despite the enormous range of botanical types, many forest trees were found only in certain areas and even there in limited numbers. A locality that might otherwise have been considered a backwater could thus assume significance as one of the few sources of a valued product.

The collection process required that the collector be attuned to specfic clues which signalled that a particular jungle product was ready for harvest. The aromatic *gaharu* wood, for example, is in fact the diseased core of a particular tree, but only certain indications such as peeling bark and falling leaves betray the presence of the valuable heart. Camphor, which takes the form of small grains inside the tree trunk, must be detected by specific signs like the smell of the wood when chipped. Even more important for the extraction of forest products was a mastery of the secret and esoteric know-ledge needed to facilitate the search and placate the spirits of the plants concerned. According to accounts from the late nineteenth century, these beliefs were so ingrained that collectors employed a special language and observed rigid dietary restrictions while gathering certain jungle products.

The available sources do not explain how early collectors brought their valuable supplies to the Malay coasts, although one must assume the existence of an internal trading network that connected the periphery of the rainforest with the hinterland. By this means goods were bartered and passed from one group of jungle dwellers to another. Sometimes this traffic went overland along forest tracks but more frequently it was along the rivers, where skilfully paddled rafts and canoes negotiated upstream rapids and the currents in the estuaries. Finally forest products were brought to a central collection point that acted as a subsidiary market, and also fed larger ports nearby. The discovery of imported bronze drums along the west coast, and more recently in Terengganu, points to trans-Peninsular trade relationships that were tied to a larger network oriented towards the outside world. The Middle Eastern pottery, shell bracelets and beads found at Kuala Selinsing in the Larut area of Perak have been dated between 200 BCE and 1000 CE, and it apparently served as an intermediary link with neighbouring centres in Kedah.

Apart from the wealth of the jungle, the Malay lands were fortunate in being located along a highly mineralized belt reaching from Yunnan in southwestern China to the islands of Bangka and Belitung in contemporary Indonesia. Like particular trees or plants, the presence of certain metals, base and precious, provided opportunities for relatively isolated regions to develop their trading potential. Excavations in northwest Borneo, for example, indicate that from the seventh century the Sarawak delta, known to the Chinese court only through hearsay, was actively involved in the export of smelted iron and gold to other places within the archipelago.

It may have been for its gold deposits that the Malay Peninsula was best known in early times. Although Malaysia and Sumatra are not today considered important sources of this metal, the region's reputation was once sufficient to warrant the appellation 'Golden Khersonese' by Greek geographers. Early human habitation seems to be linked with gold-bearing locations, and the widespread use of gold for decoration and ornament in early Malay courts is almost certainly linked to the tradition of yellow as a royal colour.

Less valuable than gold, but far more extensively found, was tin. The world's largest tin fields are located on the Malay Peninsula, and the richness of the deposits is apparent when one recalls that even after at least 1500 years of continual extraction, tin mining was until recently one of Malaysia's foremost industries. It is not known when Malay tin first became desired overseas, but from the fifth century CE it may have been shipped to India to be used in alloys like bronze for the manufacture of religious images. Because the tin was washed down from the granite ranges of the interior and deposited on the coastal riverbeds and alluvial plains, mining was not a complicated procedure. Even with primitive techniques it could be a profitable supplement to agriculture and collecting, and the local people could pan tin from nearby rivers without venturing far beyond their settlements. The method of washing tin-bearing soils to extract the tin as well as the simple

13

smelting described by a fifteenth-century Chinese visitor to Melaka had probably remained unchanged for centuries. Sinking shallow shafts to gain access to veins below the surface, mentioned in seventeenth- and eighteenth-century Dutch sources, was probably a relatively recent development.

The hinterland of the Malay areas thus offered minerals and jungle products; equally important was the rich harvest of sea products possible along the coasts and the oceans. The mangrove forests that border the west coast of the Peninsula and the river deltas of western Borneo are as much a specific ecological zone as the rainforest, and those who lived there also selected from a multitude of resources those which were economically profitable. To outsiders the labyrinth of mangroves rooted in alluvial mud and washed by the saltwater tides was as mysterious as the jungle, the haunt of man-eating monsters like the dreaded crocodile. But to the Orang Laut, the 'strand and sea peoples' who made this region their home, the creatures of the mangrove swamps aroused respect rather than terror. Gliding on dugout canoes along the natural waterways formed by tidal channels and depressions, they sought out from the very limited species here those that had a specific value. Mats could be woven from the leaves of the *nipa* palm, a fermented drink distilled from its fruit; the bark of certain mangrove trees yielded tannin, and the timber provided excellent firewood.

Along the east coast of the Malay Peninsula where the wave action is more vigorous, the shore is edged not with mangroves but with stretches of beach fringed by plants resistant to salt spray and capable of growing in sandy soil. Over time the peoples here had discovered uses for the numerous types of shellfish in the rock pools and could recognize the types of edible seaweed cast up on the sand at low tide. Offshore, plant and animal life was even richer, especially along the coral shelves formed by strong winds and currents as in the Riau-Lingga archipelago and the Pulau Tujuh area of the South China Sea. Here warm shallow waters, rarely more than 60 metres deep, provided an environment ideal for the evolution of a variety of sea life. Along reefs at low tide molluscs and bivalves could be found, with pearl oysters deep in the coral sand below. And although the origins of Orang Laut culture and sea nomadism remain obscure, recent excavations at Bukit Tengkorak in eastern Sabah point to communities of able seafarers at least 3000 years ago. Evidence from several areas of the use of boat-shaped coffins for burial also suggests this sea-going orientation. Shell items, widely used for barter before coins became common, may have helped such communities initiate early exchanges; by the fifth century CE Chinese sources provide evidence that tortoiseshell and cowries were a well-established component in Malay trade.

Later the list of sea products grew as the Chinese market developed, including such items as the rare black branching coral known to the Malays as *akar bahar* and the famed *teripang* or sea slug, used as an ingredient in Chinese cooking and medicinal preparations. Again it was the Orang Laut, the sea nomads, who could locate with unerring accuracy the desired products. Equipped with an intimate knowledge of local conditions, they could safely navigate their dugouts around the perilous sand banks and coral reefs where an unwary sailor might well founder. Without their swimming skills it would have been impossible to dredge up the shells and corals from the ocean floor. Something of the respect these abilities aroused in China is suggested in a twelfth-century mention of slaves from the Malay lands, that 'variety of wild men from near the sea which can dive in water without closing the eyes'.[5]

Thus, from a very early point in historical time, the inhabitants of the Malay world not only came to appreciate the wealth of the jungles and oceans that surrounded them, but also learned to combine their different skills to exploit the environment. The expanding lists of marketable products, the experimentation that must have preceded any appreciation of new uses for specific plants and animals, and the development of more efficient trading and collecting techniques, could only have occurred in response to the demands of a lively and growing market. But this market could not be just a local concern, for the potential buyers of camphor and lakawood, incense and gold, were far away. Furthermore, it was goods from distant lands – cloth, copper and ironware, drums and musical instruments, beads, pottery, glass – that were desired in the Malay region. The resulting development of an international exchange trade, its changing patterns and its effects on local society, provide the key to understanding early Malaysian history.

Indian influence in 'the land of gold'

Although no definite evidence dates the first Indian voyages across the Bay of Bengal, archaeological investigation points to trading contact between India and Southeast Asia as early as 200 BCE. The geographical location of the Malay Peninsula meant it was inevitably caught up in this early trade. Blown by the westerly winds, shipping made landfall in the isthmian region, north of Kedah, from whence passage down the Straits would have been a logical development. However, while the routes of Indian traders can be reconstructed, it is not known if the products they took back from the Malay archipelago were essentially the same as those in the later China trade. We do not know precisely what early Indian merchants most desired from the Malay areas. Despite vague references to a 'land of gold' that have been linked with the Peninsula, Indian sources have yielded little tangible information. There are no Indian navigational guides, lists of products or travellers' itineraries like those from China. Before the extension of maritime communications to China, Indian traders may have been drawn to the Malay region principally in search of gold, aromatic woods, and spices such as cloves.

For indisputable evidence of Malaya's centuries-old relationship with India, which trade initiated and sustained, one must look at the influence of

15

the subcontinent on Malay culture. The growth of trade with India brought the coastal peoples in much of the Malay world into contact with two major religions, Buddhism and Hinduism, and with concepts of political power well established in India.[6] Without the physical testimony of monuments or inscriptions, it is not possible to discuss the effects of Indian influence in any depth. The major foci of influence were undoubtedly coastal settlements along the Melaka Straits; a notable example is Kedah, where there is unambiguous evidence of early Indian contacts. Seventh-century inscriptions in Old Malay found in Sumatra and the Peninsula are also heavily Sanskritized, and much of the ritual, vocabulary and notions of kingship still preserved in Malay courts is Indian in origin. Royal genealogies preserved in classical Malay texts enhance the ruler's status by drawing ancestral connections to the kings of Kalinga, a semi-mythical kingdom once situated on India's east coast. Key terms – for example, *bahasa* (language), *negeri* (district, country) and *raja* (ruler) – are all loan words from Sanskrit.

The process by which early societies adopted and absorbed Indian motifs into an evolving Malay world-view is similarly a matter for speculation. At the village level powerful Hindu gods like Shiva and Vishnu were incorporated into a pantheon of supernatural beings, and individuals and episodes from Indian epics such as the *Ramayana* became an integral part of the Malay cultural heritage. It is also likely that Indian icons, votive tablets and other religious items were regarded with veneration and assumed some value in trade and for the protection of individuals. A terracotta statue of a goddess carrying a child found in the Bujang valley is thought to be a locally made image of Hariti, and may have acted as a talisman against disease. It is not surprising that numerous Malayized Indic words, such as *dosa* (sin), *jaya* (success), *merdeka* (powerful, independent), *puasa* (to fast), *neraka* (hell), reflect an interest in tapping supernatural powers. However, Malay legends hold no memories of a Hindu or Buddhist 'conversion' like the dramatic depictions of Islam's adoption, nothing that conveys any sense of a cultural watershed. The localization of Indian influences by early Malay communities proceeded imperceptibly, deepening and enriching an already vital culture. While the later trade with China introduced a wide range of objects and some technological skills, the relationship with India was in many ways richer. Not only did it provide local élites with a more refined and elaborated version of a fundamentally similar outlook on life; it also laid the groundwork for the transference of Islamic beliefs which were indeed to transform Malay society.

The contact with India stimulated other responses among the peoples of the region, encouraging them to recognize the rewards that came to those willing to participate in maritime trade. The longevity of Malay engagement with the seas is attested by archaeological and linguistic evidence, and by the range of indigenous nautical terms and a variety of boat types that defy English translation. While foreign models may have been readily copied or adapted, the acquisition of seafaring skills was primarily a local accomplishment. One of the few specifically Malay terms in the seventh-century inscriptions found in the Palembang region of Sumatra is *puhavam*, meaning shippers, and the first mention of a vessel making the journey from Sumatra to India comes from the same period. The influence of Malay on a language as far distant as Malagasy is an impressive testimony to these intrepid voyagers.

Early trade with India must also have made apparent the commercial potential of collecting points along the Melaka Straits. Vessels that came from India on the southwest monsoon were forced to remain in the archipelago for several months until they could sail back with the northeast winds towards the end of the year. During this period they needed a place to discharge their cargoes, to refit vessels, replace masts and purchase enough to make a profitable sale on their return. They required a permanent base where they could obtain credit, lay up surplus and return again the following year. Numerous local harbour chiefs would have been ready to fulfil the requirements of a stapling port in the hopes of reaping the benefits of a growing ocean-borne trade. One of these ports, Geying (Ko-ying), is mentioned in Chinese sources in the third century CE as a terminus port for Indian shipping, and was apparently located somewhere near the Melaka Straits or possibly western Java.

With the development of sea communications between these regions and China from the fifth century CE, trade with India received further impetus. To service this trade, numerous small settlements began to spring up along the archipelago's principal maritime routes. Excavations at Takuapa on the Kra isthmus have shown that between the seventh and tenth centuries this was a flourishing entrepôt connecting the ports of the Indian Ocean and the South China Sea. It was in such coastal ports that the infusion from India was most pronounced, and in Takuapa a ninth-century inscription and the remains of a temple indicate that the Tamil trading community there was affiliated with a South Indian merchant guild.

As might be expected, most of the Indianized archaeological discoveries have been along the west coast of the Peninsula which provided a landfall for shipping from India. There have been significant finds in Kedah and Perai (Province Wellesley), including fragmentary Sanskrit inscriptions as well as Hindu and Buddhist images. The earliest of these has been attributed to the fourth century. The links with maritime trade are especially evident in the so-called Buddhagupta Stone, which dates from about 400 CE and expresses the hope that the sea captain Buddhagupta and his fellow travellers will be successful in their voyage. Further south, later mining activities also unearthed considerable evidence of Indian connections. Recovered statuary includes a Buddha image dating from the late fifth or early sixth century in the Gupta style of North India (*c*.319–500 CE) and various Buddha images from the eighth to tenth centuries.

The vitality of the commercial exchange with India meant that the coastal peoples probably had some knowledge of changes in the intellectual and religious environment in the subcontinent. It has been tentatively proposed, for instance, that the ritual deposit boxes found in Kedah and the Sarawak delta bear some relation to the Tantric Buddhism gaining favour in India from around the sixth century. But while receptivity to new ideas became a hallmark of Malay society, there is also very early evidence of adaptation of outside influences to suit the local environment. This is well illustrated in the reconstructed temple of Candi Bukit Batu Pahat in the Bujang valley in Kedah, apparently erected to the memory of a deceased ruler or official. Dating from about the tenth century, it blends Hindu and Mahayana Buddhist elements in a manner that has no exact equivalent in India. Although it bears some similarities to Sumatran finds as well as to a *candi* (temple) in the ancient iron-smelting centre of Santubong (Sarawak), there is also a clear retention of a local architectural style.

This kind of adaptation indicates that local people themselves played an important role in spreading Indian cultural ideas beyond the entrepôts where the connection with outsiders was most pronounced. It is hard to imagine that a trader who regularly frequented ports with his cargoes of tin, beeswax, woods and rattans, who waited while they were graded and priced, who then purchased another cargo for the homeward trip, would have been untouched by the stories of the foreigners to whom he sold his goods. Although direct ties with India were stronger on the west coast, seventh-century Chinese itineraries testify to the strength of Indian religions in courts along the east coast of the Peninsula, and it would seem unrealistic to deny local traders a place in the transmission of these new ideas. Local participation in the gradual Indianization process also meant that ideas about human relations and the nature of the universe remained basically similar throughout the region. What ultimately helped sustain this similarity of outlook was the interaction resulting from trading exchanges. Indian images discovered on the Peninsula can be compared with similar statuary in India and Sumatra; it is also significant that the mercury found in a chemical analysis of remains in the Bujang valley appears to have come from the Sarawak delta. Such evidence suggests that the oceans did serve to link a world that reached from the east coast of Sumatra to western Borneo, and that that the peoples who lived here shared in a common cultural environment.

Chinese trade and the rise of early Malay-Indonesian entrepôts

Prior to the fifth century Chinese sources contain few references to the Nan Yang, the Southern Ocean, which was the general term used to refer to the Southeast Asian region. Interest in the Malay Peninsula probably stemmed initially from Chinese relations with an area they termed 'Funan', believed to have been located near the lower Mekong river. From 200 CE ambitious chiefdoms here began to extend their influence into the northern Malay Peninsula, and Chinese envoys make vague references to 'Funan's' subjugation of 'ten kingdoms', tentatively located in the isthmus region. While at this stage the Chinese were already aware of some Indonesian products such as the clove, the foreign goods they desired most were the luxury trade items from western Asia. Before the fifth century, goods typical of what Chinese sources term the 'Persian trade' were carried overland from western Asia to northern China, and only subsequently did merchants begin to use the maritime routes.

The reason for this shift to the sea was political events in southern China. In 420 a new dynasty, the Liu Song (420–78), gained control in southern China but it did not have access to the overland trade route in the north. As communities in the Yangzi river area in southern China became more prosperous, the demand for luxury goods from western Asia rose. These developments made participants in the 'Persian trade' look more closely at the possibilities of shipping goods previously sent by land. China itself, however, did not begin to develop ocean-going vessels until the eighth and ninth centuries and it was thus not the Chinese who acted as shippers. It has been argued that, with the incentive of rich profits, 'Persian' goods were taken by sea across the Bay of Bengal to the Malay archipelago and then trans-shipped in 'Nan Yang' vessels to China. Non-Chinese shipping, including that of the coastal peoples in the Malay regions, was therefore vital in bringing valuable cargoes to Chinese ports and maintaining trans-Asiatic trading links.

From the fifth century CE onwards, the increasing use of the sea to transport goods between western Asia and China created an environment well suited to the rise of ports in numerous places in the Malay archipelago. But harbours along the Melaka Straits and its approaches had a distinct advantage because of their geographical location at 'the end of the monsoons', where all ships had to await the change of winds to continue further or return homeward. Unlike the west coast of Borneo, which was somewhat isolated from the main maritime routes, the Melaka Straits was 'a gullet... through which the foreigners' sea and land traffic in either direction must pass.'[7] Moreover, the Straits provided a refuge from the buffeting of the oceans beyond. Along the east coast of the Peninsula the seas were almost impossible to navigate during the northeast monsoon, but the Straits were so sheltered that they were frequently compared to an inland lake. Even though violent storms, which later European sailors termed 'Sumatras', could spring up, these were confined mainly to the stretch between Selangor and Singapore, and in any event were seasonal and therefore predictable.

The calmness of the Straits waters also facilitated transport of cargoes. Local traders were able to carry goods between Sumatra, the Peninsula and the small islands of the Riau-Lingga archipelago with boats that depended only on paddles and the simplest of mat sails. Jungle products could be brought down to the coast along any of the numerous rivers that disembogue on both sides of the Straits. Many of the tidewater bays and inlets into which these rivers flow could potentially serve as collection and distribution as well as trans-shipment points. It has been suggested that gradually some local

19

jungle products were drawn into the China trade and accepted as substitutes for 'Persian' frankincense, bdellium and camphor. In time the variety and versatility of marine and jungle produce from the Malay areas assumed great value in China in its own right. When a king of Melaka went to China in 1411 a selection of these local products was considered a fitting gift even for the emperor.

It is possible that Gantuoli (Kan-t'o-li), a toponym occasionally mentioned in fifth- and sixth-century Chinese sources, was the first port in the Straits vicinity to exploit the growing Chinese market for local products. Gantuoli has been tentatively located on Sumatra's southeast coast, at the eastern approaches to the Melaka Straits. In this area several species of jungle trees are found that could have provided the resins accepted in China as substitutes for those of India and Persia. It is known that Gantuoli's trade was based not only on the cartage of overseas goods but on the export of forest products, perfumes and drugs for the Chinese market. Because of the advantages of its location and its access to desired items, Gantuoli for a brief period came to dominate other collecting points that were contenders for the position of entrepôt. The suggestion has been made that Gantuoli was a predecessor of the famed Srivijaya that arose in the Palembang area of southeast Sumatra in the late seventh century.

The mention of Srivijaya brings us to what was one of the most long-standing controversies in Southeast Asian studies. In 1918 George Coedès published a learned discussion of a place termed 'Shilifoshi' in Tang Chinese records (619–906 CE). Transcribing the Chinese characters as 'Srivijaya', he located the kingdom in southeast Sumatra on the Musi river in Palembang. In the reconstruction offered by Coedès and other scholars, Srivijaya was presented as the earliest of the great maritime kingdoms, arising some time in the seventh century and lasting until the end of the thirteenth. It was argued that Srivijaya came to exercise suzerainty over the Melaka Straits, the numerous islands that dot the approaches, and the shores on either side. It developed into a prosperous emporium for local products as well as those from India, western Asia and China, and was renowned for its patronage of Mahayana Buddhism.

Until relatively recently, this reconstruction was subject to challenge because of the very limited evidence on which it was based. From the late seventh century comes a description by a Chinese monk, Yiqing (I Ching), written after a period studying Buddhism in Srivijaya, and several inscriptions in Old Malay from Palembang, Jambi, Lampung, the island of Bangka and the Peninsula that date from roughly the same period. Records of missions from Srivijaya to the Chinese court and notes by Chinese geographers also begin in the late seventh century and, with a break in the ninth century, continue on through to the thirteenth century. The Chinese sources are supplemented by scattered inscriptions invoking the name of Srivijaya at Nalanda and Coromandel in India, and by isolated references in Arab writings.

Because the evidence did not appear conclusive, some scholars, while accepting the existence of Srivijaya, expressed doubts about its longevity and even its location in southeast Sumatra. These debates encouraged further archaeological and historical research that has ultimately strengthened Palembang's credentials as a location and supported the claims made on Srivijaya's behalf. In 1985, for example, a beautiful statue of the elephant-god Ganesa, dating from the eighth century, was unearthed during the construction of a building in the very centre of modern Palembang. From the late 1980s systematic excavations were also carried out in the Palembang area by combined French and Indonesian teams, and in 1990–1 more than 55 000 artefacts were itemized. The cumulative results of ten years' work are indeed impressive. Fragments of inscriptions, statuary, evidence of bead manufacturing, remains of boat timbers, evidence of large reservoirs linked by canals, new temple surveys and site excavations have generally confirmed earlier reconstructions. In particular, the volume and character of Chinese ceramics point to a vibrant local and overseas trade at least from the tenth century. The dates ascribed to these finds confirm an uninterrupted occupation of the Palembang area for 700 years between the eighth and fourteenth centuries.

While the historical record for Srivijaya still leaves many questions unanswered, scholars are now more confident in their interpretations of available evidence. Of special significance in terms of Malaysian history is the argument that Gantuoli, Srivijaya and the type of settlement that grew up in Melaka after 1400 can be seen as a continuum. It seems that these places satisfied the criteria of entrepôt and in that capacity serviced maritime trade in the western archipelago. Srivijaya, in short, was not a parvenu, and in understanding the reasons for its success we can more readily appreciate what contributed to the prestige not only of Melaka but of the latter's eventual successor, Johor.

Srivijaya and its rivals

From its appearance on the historical scene in the late seventh century Srivijaya conveys the impression of a state anxious to establish its pre-eminence. One of the early inscriptions found in Palembang commemorates a mighty expedition of 682 that brought 'victory, power and wealth' to Srivijaya. Four years later another force was sent against 'Java'. But if Srivijaya was attempting to impose its authority in southeast Sumatra, fragmentary references to blood and battle suggest considerable resistance; indeed, in later Malay writings the theme of warfare dominates the mythical pre-Melakan past. Furthermore, Srivijaya was by no means the only port in the region that could attract traders, for the jungle and ocean products that drew merchants there could also be carried to numerous other places. Several of these were also able to offer good anchorage and harbour facilities, and had a reputation overseas which may well have predated that of Srivijaya. A place called Melayu, apparently located on the Jambi river just north of Palembang, sent a mission to China in 644, several years earlier than Srivijaya's first mission around 670. But between 672 and 692 Melayu was incorporated into Srivijaya, perhaps by conquest, perhaps by marriage between two ruling families. This was a significant development because although the toponym of Melayu is less well established than Srivijaya in the scholarly literature, the name itself suggests its contribution to the shaping of Malay traditions.

Tang dynasty records also show that across the Melaka Straits and on the Peninsula's east coast other kingdoms had developed. Quite possibly these areas had once been dominated by an overlord in the Cambodian region (the 'Funan' of Chinese sources), but had gained a degree of autonomy with the lessening of this influence around the sixth century. Their exact locations remain conjectural, since several transcriptions bear no relation to contemporary Malay place-names, and the sites of others must be calculated from the often vague geography of Chinese sources. While there is understandably more information about the east coast, which was better known to Chinese travellers, available sailing directions and itineraries provide sufficient guide for modern historians to make a broad sketch of Peninsular settlements during Tang times. At least seven states have been proposed in the isthmian region, with a possible eighth in Johor.

What were they like, these early kingdoms that shared the same commercial world as Srivijaya but were eventually overshadowed, though not eclipsed, by it? Like Srivijaya, their rulers were clearly aware of the importance of cultivating good relations with China. By the sixth century Langkasuka in the Patani region was sending envoys to the Chinese emperor, and was well known in China as a religious centre. In the later seventh century several Buddhist monks specifically made voyages there. Approaches to China also came from Chitu, the 'Red-earth land' tentatively located in Kelantan, and Dandan, which some scholars, again with reservations, place on the east coast in the vicinity of present-day Terengganu. The Chinese did not by any means regard these places as insignificant. In 607, several decades before we first hear of Srivijaya, the Sui dynasty (CE 590–618) decided to 'open up communication with far-distant lands', and honoured the court of Chitu with an embassy carrying over 5000 gifts. Indeed, Chinese records show that these small states could conduct diplomatic affairs with the aplomb of their larger neighbours. When the Chinese envoys entered Chitu waters, a leading court figure whom they called a 'Brahman' was sent with a fleet of vessels to meet them. On their arrival at the upriver capital a month later, the king's son himself came down to greet them with suitable gifts. The hospitality extended to foreign visitors and missions that was to become a feature of Malay court protocol is clearly evident. The Chinese monk, Yiqing, records that Buddhist pilgrims *en route* to India were treated in Langkasuka 'with the courtesy appropriate to distinguished guests'.

These kingdoms were not mere collecting centres that had sprung up under the leadership of some enterprising chief. They were states that stood in a tradition of government. In the seventh century Langkasuka already claimed to have been in existence for 200 years, and when the ruler of Chitu gave up the throne in favour of the religious life the succession passed peacefully to his son. Nor was their territorial control inconsiderable. It reputedly required 30 days to cross Langkasuka from east to west, and the Lion City, the capital of Chitu, was a month's journey inland. From their forested interior came the jungle products that were so prized in the markets abroad, and it was from the trade in items like gold and camphor that these kingdoms drew their wealth. The king of Chitu had 30 ocean-going vessels presumably used to carry cargoes to other countries, and the Chinese envoys sent there in 607 were obviously impressed by the richness of the court. 'The king sits on a three-tiered couch, facing north and dressed in rose-colored cloth, with a chaplet of gold flowers and necklaces of varied jewels. Four damsels attend on his right hand and on his left, and more than a hundred soldiers mount guard.'[8]

These kingdoms also maintained well-ordered governments. Officers of the state were appointed to oversee matters such as criminal law, and in Chitu each settlement had its own district chief. Within the court the king was actively involved in administering the realm, and Chinese visitors specifically recorded that the ruler of Dandan held audience twice a day. With the treasury under royal control, the king could both reward powerful families and keep them in check. As in later Melaka, one way to achieve this was to limit the display of wealth. In Chitu, the Sui envoys noted, although the Chitu nobles were largely independent of the ruler's authority, they were permitted to wear gold lockets only at his discretion. Even at this early date we thus catch a glimpse of a familiar theme in Malay history – the potential challenge to royal power from high-ranking families. If a ruler disregarded the code of conduct considered appropriate for kingship, he could not expect to maintain the support of the leading court figures. In Langkasuka one king was said to have exiled a popular 'man of virtue', but the latter fled to India and there married an Indian princess. The Chinese envoys were told that shortly afterwards, following the death of the Langkasuka ruler, the chief ministers 'welcomed back the exile and made him king', thereby initiating a new dynasty.[9]

Early trading kingdoms along the east coast of the Peninsula thus flourished with the growth of commercial exchange between India and China, and within the archipelago. In this context, the recent discovery of Mahayana Buddhist votive tablets and amulets in caves in Ulu Kelantan, where Chitu was possibly located, acquires additional significance.

Other ports that sprang up along the maritime route to China are also briefly mentioned in Chinese sources. For example, Loyue, which has been located in Johor, is described in the ninth century as a place 'where traders passing back and forth meet'. In the same period Pulau Tioman, off Pahang, was another well-known port of call, where over the last 30 years finds of ceramics and stoneware have confirmed the evidence of Arab and Chinese sources.

It therefore appears that from the seventh century the expansion in maritime communications and the increasing value placed on products from the Malay archipelago created new economic opportunities. This impression becomes greater when it is recalled that written sources supply only part of the picture. Vijayapura in west Borneo was a major port that apparently coexisted with Srivijaya, yet it did not send envoys to China and therefore attracted scant attention in imperial records. The failure to send missions may simply indicate a healthy local trade and freedom from external or internal threats, eliminating any need to court China's favour. Similarly, Kedah receives little mention in Chinese sources except as an embarkation point for India. However, the excavation of over 30 local sites in the Bujang valley has resulted in finds that may date from as early as the eighth century and has provided strong evidence of a thriving economy based on agriculture, trade and the distribution of local products. None of these places could have attracted merchants unless they could offer a whole range of facilities that became typical of Malay trading states – a hospitable attitude to foreigners, efficiency in discharging cargoes, desired products available for purchase, and an enlightened and co-operative administration.

It is a measure of Srivijaya's achievement that it was recognized as suzerain over many of these ports, some long-established kingdoms. A stele found in Ligor dated at CE 775 indicates that Srivijaya had by this time extended a loose overlordship to the Malay Peninsula. At the beginning of the eleventh century Chinese records note that 'fourteen cities' paid tribute to Srivijaya, which was called the 'uncontested master of the Straits'. It seems, however, that the nature of this control was not onerous and that despite early references to conflict, vassal chiefs were in fact left to rule in virtual independence. The question then arises as to why Srivijaya could maintain its pre-eminent position in the Straits, and what its prestige contributes to an understanding of later Malaysian history.

The bases of Srivijaya's power

In trying to understand the nature of the Srivijayan state scholars have again been faced with a paucity of information, although there is growing agreement regarding the significance of what is disparate and sometimes contradictory evidence. In particular, academic research has been concerned with identifying the reasons behind Srivijaya's emergence as a major emporium, the bases of its power, and why its name disappears from the records in the fourteenth century. How can we explain the developments which would have led a Srivijayan ruler to become so confident that he could proclaim himself 'sovereign over all the kings in the entire earth'?[10]

According to the generally accepted interpretation, Srivijaya owed its initial rise and its later success primarily to the development of a special relationship with Chinese emperors. First, it was well placed to benefit from the maritime trading route to China. Located on the path of the northeast monsoon, it held an advantage that other kingdoms could not match as long as ties with China determined a port's international standing. Secondly, the maharajas of Srivijaya fully understood the value of the tribute system that involved a recognition of China as overlord. Because Chinese emperors until the Southern Song period (CE 1127–1279) refused to countenance private Chinese trade, overseas goods could be accepted only if they came in the guise of tribute missions. Although other Malay kingdoms were also aware of this, Srivijaya was the most successful in manipulating the system to its benefit. Its rulers were willing to acknowledge China's suzerainty in order to ensure that a profitable trade continued. Between 960 and 983, for instance, no less than eight missions from Srivijaya presented themselves at the imperial court. Nothing was permitted to interfere with the health of this relationship. When the Buddhist pilgrim Yiqing arrived at the Srivijaya capital, he was received with due hospitality, but after the ruler realized his visitor came from China this show of respect doubled. During the following centuries the same pattern continues. In 1003 Srivijayan envoys arrived in China with the flattering information that their ruler had built a temple to pray for the emperor's well-being. In compliance with their request, the Chinese emperor then bestowed a title on the temple and presented it with a bell. The prestige acquired by Srivijaya in such an exchange must have been considerable.

Another reason behind Srivijaya's dominance was the ability to maintain a supply of local products for its own market as well as the China trade. Not only was it easily accessible by river from jungle areas in Sumatra and the Peninsula, but the Riau-Lingga archipelago and the nearby coastal mangroves were also under its jurisdiction. In the estuary of the Musi river, where cargoes were probably unloaded, one can visualize the dugouts arriving with the *nipa* mats, tortoiseshell, beeswax and aromatic woods for which the country was justifiably renowned. A story related in an Arab travel account of the ninth century suggests that the maharajas fully appreciated their debt to the sea. It was said that the ruler daily propitiated the spirits of the ocean by throwing a gold brick into the water, saying as he did so, 'Look, there lies my treasury.'[11]

In this favourable commercial environment an entrepôt economy would have been readily established. Here, in the lull between the monsoons, exotic cargoes from overseas could be unloaded – pearls, frankincense, rosewater, gardenia flowers, myrrh, amber, silks, brocades. Here local products could be sorted, graded, blended and loaded, with the surplus stored for other buyers. Here could be found the array of skills necessary to refit and provision ships for the voyage home. In sum, Srivijaya could well satisfy the demands of an international market. An Arab source in the early tenth century notes that the bulk of Srivijaya's wealth came from tolls and harbour dues, a testimony to the number of ships it attracted. Two hundred years later Srivijaya was still famous as a place where a merchant could rely on justice, correct commercial behaviour and all the business facilities expected of an entrepôt. When troubles disturbed trade in India and China, Chinese merchants are said to have transferred their activities to Srivijaya. The consistency with which foreigners comment on the vitality of its trade is impressive. As one Chinese official wrote in 1178, '[Srivijaya] is the most important port of call on the sea routes of the foreigners from the countries of Java in the east and the countries of the Arabs and Quilon [on the Malabar coast] in the west; they all pass through it on their way to China.'[12]

A basic factor in Srivijaya's strength was the symbiotic relationship that developed between its rulers and the Orang Laut, the sea and riverine people. From early times it seems that Orang Laut groups tended to regard passing ships as another economic resource and readily incorporated raiding practices into their lifestyle. Early sources make it clear that sea travel through archipelago waters was beset with dangers; in CE 413, for example, the Chinese Buddhist pilgrim Faxian remarked following a voyage to India that the oceans were 'infested with pirates'. The most dangerous area was the southern approaches to the Melaka Straits, the haunt of many Orang Laut groups whose raiders lurked amongst the numerous islands and rocky outcrops. A Chinese itinerary dated about CE 800 directs mariners' attention to an island to the northeast of Srivijaya where 'many ... people are robbers and those who sail in ships fear them.'[13] Only limited types of Chinese stoneware from before the tenth century have been found in Palembang, suggesting that when the situation was especially dangerous foreign traders may even have preferred to use the old trans-isthmus routes. In this context, seaborne trade in the Melaka Straits could only flourish if the Orang Laut were made to feel part of the overlord's enterprise.

Srivijaya's great triumph was to control piracy in the surrounding waters by commanding the loyalty of the Orang Laut. Intimately acquainted with the treacherous shoals and sandbars, understanding local wind conditions, they protected Srivijaya's sea lanes from other raiders and thus increased its attractiveness to foreign traders. The Orang Laut were a formidable fighting force, and their paddling skills made them the obvious choice as crews for Srivijaya's fleets and thus the backbone of its navy. The 'harladj' mentioned in tenth-century Arab sources, 'who gave his name to an island and was head of the ruler's army', may have been the predecessor of the Raja Negara, the Orang Laut leader in seventeenth- and eighteenth-century Johor, who commanded the sea people throughout Singapore waters. Living in the islands and coast off Palembang and Jambi, the Orang Laut could have responded readily to the ruler's call in time of crisis. Of them it was said that 'in facing the enemy and braving death they have not their equal among other nations'. When the maharaja of Srivijaya styled himself 'King of the Ocean lands', it was thus no meaningless honorific.

Srivijaya's prestige in the area would also have been due to the fact that its rulers had succeeded in creating a society which, by the standards of the time, was cultured and civilized. As a result of its trading connections, Srivijaya had become a centre of learning that could hold its own against far older kingdoms. A Chinese source mentions that the people there were skilled mathematicians and were able to calculate the eclipses of the sun and moon. Perhaps the greatest indication of the respect given to scholarship in Srivijaya was the strength of religion. When the Chinese pilgrim Yiqing went there in 671 he found a community of over 1000 Buddhist monks, and in his own writings he commended the city as a place to study the Buddhist scriptures. With the wealth brought by trade, Srivijayan rulers could sponsor religious studies and maintain religious foundations. One maharaja endowed a Taoist temple in Canton while another rebuilt a Buddhist sanctuary in India's great pilgrimage centre of Nalanda. Although the nature of Buddhism in Srivijaya is not totally clear, several different schools, including Tantrism, coexisted. When the history of Buddhism in the archipelago is understood more fully, Srivijaya may assume even more importance as a dissemination point for religious ideas.

A number of factors thus contributed to Srivijaya's emergence as a leading entrepôt in the archipelago, a position that it apparently sustained for six centuries. It was able to maintain this dominance because harbour chiefs along the coasts of Sumatra and the Peninsula were willing to accept Srivijaya's overlordship so that they could share in its prosperity and take part in its thriving trade. Such ties could only survive if local lords saw advantages in recognizing a higher authority. However, available sources also hint at the underlying tension in the ruler–vassal relationship. Ideally, a chain of command stretched down from the Srivijayan ruler to his chiefs and vassal princes, binding him to his lowest subject. The administration of the realm was based on the concept of unquestioning loyalty to one's leader, and nowhere was this better exemplified that in the fidelity of the Orang Laut.

Despite the great riches which the ruler of Srivijaya had at his disposal and the honours he could heap on his faithful servants, rewards could not have been a guarantee of unfailing allegiance. It was perhaps to remedy this weakness that *derhaka*, a word found repeatedly in Srivijayan inscriptions and meaning 'treason to the ruler' was adopted from Sanskrit to denote what became a heinous crime. Srivijaya's court may also have propagated the belief in a special force possessed by the ruler, perhaps by invoking the Hindu concept of a God's *sakti* (later expressed by the Arabic term *daulat*). This force would strike down the disobedient vassal, the subject guilty of *derhaka*. Local inscriptions, notably the Telaga Batu of 686, are replete with threats against those who betray the ruler and his appointed officials: 'If you behave like a traitor, plotting with those who are in contact with my enemies, or if you spy for the enemy, you will be killed by the curse.'[14] It was possibly the maharajas of Srivijaya who first built up the idea of the devoted subject willing to die for his lord, a frequent theme in later Malay texts. So entrenched was this concept in Srivijayan statecraft that in the thirteenth century the Chinese customs official Zhao Rukua believed that the personal followers of the maharaja commonly killed themselves when their master died.

Evidence of the early origins of basic Malay cultural ideas in turn raises the fundamental question of Srivijaya's place in the evolution of Malay society. As we have seen, it is in the written sources associated with southeast Sumatra and Srivijaya that the term 'Melayu' first emerges, and it is here that Old Malay was first written in the courtly Pallava script introduced from India. Although apparently incorporated into Srivijaya in the late seventh century, the association of Melayu with the Straits was such that an Arab text dating from around CE 1000 notes that travellers bound for China sailed through 'the sea of Melayu', while a Cola inscription talks about 'the ancient Malaiyur'.[15] Of particular significance is the suggestion that local people were themselves adopting the term 'Malay' as a self-referent. A copper plate inscription found in Palembang, dated between the thirteenth and fifteenth centuries, uses the angular *rencong* script once found over much of interior Sumatra to record a story in Old Malay in which the hero is likened to 'former kings of the Malay people' (*ba[ng]sa Melayu*). The association of a prestigious port like Srivijaya with notions of Melayu makes it possible to see how the process of Malay acculturation along the Straits of Melaka was encouraged as lesser centres modelled themselves on the Srivijayan example.[16] Influences from Srivijaya can even be seen in Old Malay inscriptions, dating from between the seventh and tenth centuries, found in Java. Much further afield, another tenth-century inscription which was discovered in southern Luzon in the Philippines points to the use of a localized form of Old Malay in commercial transactions.

The weakening of Srivijaya's authority

Srivijaya's commercial and political dominance in the Melaka Straits ultimately depended on its ability to tie a large number of scattered harbours to an acknowledged centre. Neither force nor rewards nor threats of divine retribution could achieve this unless local chiefs recognized that allegiance was in their own interests. As long as they were convinced that a powerful and prosperous capital was to the benefit of all, they remained the maharaja's loyal vassals and sent their products to be sold in his port. 'Empire' or even 'kingdom' may thus be a misleading translation of the Old Malay compound *huluntuhanku* (hulun – slave; tuhan – lord; ku – my). In the view of one authority, the very looseness of these vassal–lord ties may have allowed Srivijaya 'to survive for more than five hundred years and to outlive many more centralized "empires"'.[17] However, the centrifugal forces which continued to pose a challenge to central authority throughout Malay history eventually undermined Srivijaya's hold over its dependencies and its position as *primus inter pares*. The natural wealth so freely available, the favourable position of the

Malay world on the maritime trading paths, and the profits to be drawn from this commerce made the lure of independence great. From the twelfth century Srivijaya's vassals became increasingly less amenable to its authority.

The basic reason for this seems to have been a weakening in the centre itself. Several seemingly unconnected pieces of evidence suggest a kingdom undergoing severe internal tensions as well as challenges from outside. Historians believe that in the mid-ninth century a marriage alliance joined the royal family of Srivijaya with the Sailendra dynasty of central Java. An inscription from Nalanda in India dated about 860 refers to a younger son of the Sailendras who was then ruling in Srivijaya. These ties, however, did not make for continued harmony. In 992 envoys from Srivijaya told the Chinese court that the Javanese had invaded, and asked the emperor for protection. In the same year a Javanese mission claimed that the two countries were continually at war, and less than three decades later, in 1016, Srivijaya retaliated in a campaign against Java. At the same time Srivijaya was also challenged from India, although here again information is fragmentary and therefore conjectural. One brief episode refers to hostility between Srivijaya and the Cola dynasty of southern India (tenth–twelfth centuries), perhaps because of disputes over the passage of trading ships through the Melaka Straits. In about 1025 it is thought that the Cola ruler attacked Srivijaya, capturing the maharaja himself. Several other states in Sumatra and the Malay Peninsula were also raided, including Srivijaya's vassal Kedah. Although the long-term effects of these raids appear slight, memories of conflicts with Cola forces may underlie accounts of battles waged by mythical Indian kings in the later Melaka court text, the so-called *Sejarah Melayu*.

Between 1079 and 1082 there was another significant development in Srivijaya when the centre of power moved from Palembang to Melayu, customarily located in the lower reaches of the Jambi river. Although Palembang apparently remained an important place of trade, there was apparently some decline, since a recent analysis of around 1500 ceramic sherds revealed that well over half were pre-eleventh century. Though the reasons behind the shift to Melayu are unclear, available evidence suggests that it came at a time when Srivijaya's dominance in the Melaka Straits was weakening. From this period it seems that Srivijaya was increasingly compelled to rely on Orang Laut patrols to maintain its hold over passing trade. As one twelfth-century Chinese observer remarked, 'If some foreign ship passing Srivijaya should not enter the port, an armed party will certainly board it and kill the sailors to the last man.'[18] But it also appears that Srivijaya's authority even over the Orang Laut was gradually diminishing and that much wealth was passing into hands other than the maharaja's. At times Srivijaya itself was forced to stretch an iron chain across the harbour to prevent pirates from entering, raising it only to permit the passage of merchant ships. The danger to shipping was greatest among the islands around Singapore which were the domain of several pirating Orang Laut groups. In the words of a Chinese who himself knew the southern seas,

29

When junks sail to the western ocean the local barbarians allow them to pass unmolested but when on their return the junks reach the Karimun [islands]...of a certainty two or three hundred prahus will put out to attack them for several days. Sometimes the junks are fortunate enough to escape with a favouring wind; otherwise the crews are butchered and the merchandise made off with in quick time.[19]

Malay legends also comment on the increase in piracy at this time, attributing it to Orang Laut raiders sent out by the Javanese minister Gajah Mada (1330–64) to attack Palembang.

In such disturbed times those archipelago ports which could guarantee their sea lanes would have presented a real alternative to Srivijaya. The unlocated Foloan (possibly Kuala Berang, Terengganu) was purportedly protected from pirate raids by the compassionate Bodhisattva Avalokitesvara who sent fierce winds to drive enemies away. It is not surprising that with this reputation traders from Arab lands found Foloan as attractive a market as its overlord Srivijaya. Another dependency, Kedah, strategically located on the trans-isthmus route, had already demonstrated a desire for greater economic and political freedom. Between the tenth and twelfth centuries commercial activities expanded, possibly due in part to the development of wet rice (*padi*) on Kedah's alluvial plains. The vast amount of trade debris found along the banks of the Bujang river testifies to the existence of an established entrepôt. Over 10 000 sherds of Chinese ceramics have been found near the village of Pengakalan Bujang, and a variety of glassware from India and the Middle East, including more than 4500 beads. There are also extensive earthenware finds from other places in Southeast Asia. Pangkalan Bujang clearly served as a major port, obtaining jungle and marine products from subsidiary collection centres like those in the Larut area of Perak. It may well have supplied storage facilities so that the Kedah ports could act as a trans-shipment centre between monsoons. Excavations have shown that another trading port was located a little further south, at the mouth of the Muda river. This flourishing commercial environment presumably enabled local chiefs to marshal their own manpower, and an eleventh-century Cola inscription mentions 'Kadaram [Kedah] of fierce strength'.[20] Even after the devastation of the 1025 Cola raid, Kedah was apparently able to make a bid for independence, although the language employed in Cola inscriptions makes it difficult to be certain about subsequent events. It is possible that Kedah's ruler rebelled in 1068 and that Srivijaya then called in Cola assistance to bring its vassal to heel; an alternative reading suggests that a Cola ruler acted as viceroy in Kedah before returning to India.

Although Cola power declined from the twelfth century, Srivijaya faced a progressively greater challenge from neighbouring ports and its own dependencies. Indeed, the growing involvement of other centres in regional trade was probably the greatest single cause of Srivijaya's decline. While undoubtedly commerce within the archipelago and to the west was expanding, a prime factor in this increased traffic was a change in Chinese policies. During the Late Song and Mongol periods (late twelfth to mid-fourteenth centuries) the restrictions which permitted foreign trade only in the guise of tribute missions lapsed. Srivijaya, which had gained recognition of itself as the regional overlord and the rightful bearer of tribute to China, had prospered under the tributary system. Now, however, private Chinese trade flourished. These traders began going to the sources of supply, rather than to the central entrepôt, and therefore fostered the development of the many small but attractive ports within the Malay world which now found it more profitable to buy and sell without reference to Srivijaya. Some of these ports are known through Chinese court records or archaeological excavations, but others have left almost no concrete evidence. Little is known, for instance, of the north Sumatran kingdoms of Po-lo, Kampé (Aru) and 'Barus' (a vague term apparently referring generally to the later Aceh), which may have posed the most serious challenges to Srivijaya. By the thirteenth century Kampé had proclaimed its independence and was sending its own ships to southern India. Further north along Sumatra's coast the kingdoms of Perlak and Pasai were also thriving. During the thirteenth century they were being drawn into the fold of Islam, although the full impact of this would not be felt for another hundred years. Srivijaya's hold over the Peninsula was similarly lessening. The revitalized settlements in Kedah's Bujang valley were also dealing directly with China, and an inscription from the Ligor area dated to 1230 makes no mention of its former overlord and presumably represents a local claim to autonomy.

Throughout the Malay world the benefits of economic independence continued to grow as Chinese trade with the Malay world increased. In return for ivory, tortoiseshell, aromatic woods, wax, resins, rattans and tin, Chinese merchants supplied basic items like pottery and luxury goods such as silk and lacquerware. Fourteenth-century Chinese sources comment that all the Malay states along the Peninsular east coast 'acknowledged a ruler', indicating a tradition of settled government and stable administration which was an inducement to foreign merchants. Chinese travellers were also struck by the ease with which trade was conducted, the inhabitants' honesty, and the calibre of those in control. One account mentions Terengganu in particular: 'The present ruler is capable, forbids greed and encourages diligence and frugality.' From this report it seems that life there was relatively comfortable: 'The fields are middling to poor, but even the poorest folk have enough food.'[21]

The benefits which came as a result of private Chinese trade were not limited to the Melaka Straits region. Elsewhere other ports were thriving, among them Boni (P'o-ni) in northwest Borneo. First mentioned by the Chinese in the ninth century, the toponym continues to recur in Chinese sources until the fifteenth century. Some historians have consequently seen Boni as a rendering of 'Brunei'. Although it can probably be regarded as the forerunner of Brunei, 'Boni' is in all likelihood a general term used by the

31

Chinese court to refer collectively to Borneo's northwest coast. Archaeological work near Brunei's present capital suggests a continuous occupancy of the region from Tang times (618–907) onwards and it probably drew trade away from the Sarawak delta where pottery findings are virtually all earlier than Ming (1368–1644). By the twelfth century Boni's trade was flourishing and in 1225 Zhao Rukua, the inspector of foreign trade at Canton, depicted it as a state of some territorial power. According to his account, the capital had a population of 10 000 people and the country itself comprised 14 districts. His informants were clearly impressed by Boni's wealth and fighting power. 'The ruler', Zhao wrote, 'has for his protection over a hundred fighting men and when they have an engagement they carry swords and wear armour.' Court protocol was well established and no maharaja of Srivijaya could have extended greater hospitality to merchants than did the court of Boni, where 'traders are treated in high regard'. From the Chinese this was high praise indeed.[22]

The rise of Boni represents part of a recurring pattern in the Malay archipelago. As trade in the ports of its vassal states and other rival kingdoms expanded, Srivijaya was less able to impose recognition of itself as the region's principal market. Although its prestige as a major entrepôt was still considerable, Srivijaya's previously dominant position was now open to challenge. So vulnerable had it become that in 1275 the ruler of the Javanese kingdom of Majapahit, Kertanegara (1268–92), launched an attack against Melayu-Jambi and also laid claim to Pahang, a dependency of Srivijaya on the Peninsula. From the thirteenth century Java regarded itself as the rightful overlord in southeast Sumatra. It seems that around this time Melayu-Jambi's ruling family moved to the upper reaches of the Batang Hari river, foreshadowing the upstream and downstream settlement pattern typical of Sumatran kingdoms in later times. Although 'Melayapura' was subsequently recognized by Java, its more immediate overlord was the ruler of the interior kingdom of Minangkabau.

On the Peninsula other developments undermined Srivijaya's former authority. In the late thirteenth century the chiefs of Ligor in southern Thailand were extending their control over the northern Malay Peninsular states which then became vassals of the Thai rulers of Sukhothai. Thai ambitions became greater after 1351 with the rise of an energetic new kingdom, Ayudhya. Pushing down into the Peninsula, the kings of Ayudhya demanded a closer relationship, a more formal mode of homage from their Malay vassals, thus initiating a tradition of tension that was to endure for centuries afterwards. It was probably Thai pressure which led Pahang, a port that rivalled Patani in importance along the east coast, to send envoys to China between 1378 and 1416.

On the basis of this evidence it seems that by the fourteenth century there was no longer any acknowledged centre of the once mighty Srivijayan empire. Perhaps even more significant is the suggestion that this was a period of growing rivalry between Melayu, with its Minangkabau connections, and the former capital of Palembang. As in the past, one key to an enhanced position was the favour of China and its recognition as the leading power in the Straits. When the first Ming emperor, Taizu, came to the throne in 1368 he restored the old tributary system and forbade the private trade which had previously contributed to the growth of Srivijaya's rivals. From 1371 to 1377 leaders in both Melayu and Palembang sought to reassert their former status by sending official missions to take both tribute and cargoes of goods to China. In an attempt to renounce Java's claim to suzerainty, the ruler of Melayu in 1377 asked to be invested by China and to become its vassal. The Chinese emperor agreed because he was unaware that Java now claimed overlordship in southeast Sumatra. The Ming Annals then record how the Javanese prevented the Chinese envoys from reaching Sumatra by 'enticing' them to Java, where they were killed. Learning of what had happened, Emperor Taizu was incensed that 'Srivijaya' (by which he meant both Melayu and Palembang) had deceived him. In the Chinese view, Srivijaya had not only defied its Javanese overlord but had flouted Chinese policies which did not favour a proliferation of regional power centres. Taizu therefore decided to punish this rebellious vassal by refusing to receive further tribute missions.

This reconstruction of events further suggests that the Malays of southeast Sumatra saw their banishment from the imperial court and the consequent loss of trade as unfortunate, but not catastrophic. They fully believed that, given time, the attitude of Chinese emperors would change, and that the traditional relations between Srivijaya and China would be restored. In a context where the sources indicate continuing rivalry between Melayu and Palembang, the real question was the location of any new centre, and the kind of claims it could make to the Srivijayan past. In 1391, in an effort to revive Palembang's claims to leadership in the region, the ruler there apparently declared himself independent of Java and overlord of the Malays. But this was too much for the Javanese, and they invaded, expelling the rebel. As the records of the Ming dynasty noted in 1397, 'At that time the Javanese had already destroyed Sanfoqi...[i.e. Srivijaya]. Consequently Sanfoqi was a ruined country. Great unrest existed there.' Ten years afterwards, when an official naval expedition from China reached Sumatra, the harbour of Palembang, though still a busy port, was controlled not by Malays but by a Chinese pirate chief.

From Srivijaya to Melaka: two differing accounts

Both Malay and European accounts of Melaka's early years attribute its establishment to a refugee prince from Palembang. But in attempting to understand something of the circumstances surrounding his flight, historians have again been faced by problems inherent in the sources. This time it is not so much a dearth of information as a conflict between historical traditions.

We now have two exciting, even gripping, versions of Melaka's founding, each of which was a conscious effort to record past events in a coherent form. The difference between them, however, becomes more understandable when we appreciate why each was written.

The first is the *Suma Oriental* (*Complete Treatise of the Orient*), the work of Tomé Pires, a Portuguese apothecary sent to Melaka in 1512 after its conquest by Portugal. Pires was to act as accountant and supervisor of drug purchasing, but he was also regarded as a skilled diplomat of studious tastes and an enquiring mind. After two and a half years in Melaka, during which time he made several trips within the archipelago, Pires had amassed sufficient information to compile his 'complete treatise'. The sixth book, based on Pires's own observations and 'what the majority affirm', deals with Melaka, its origins, administration and trade. Pires intended the *Suma Oriental* to be an authentic account of Melaka's history which could serve as a reference book for its new Portuguese masters.

The second source stems from a very different tradition – the practice in Malay courts of recording the names of successive kings and the important events of their reigns. Indeed, what later generations have termed the *Sejarah Melayu* or the 'History of the Malays' was originally entitled simply *Sulalat Us-Salatin*, meaning 'Genealogies of the Sultans'. Its stated aim was 'to set forth the genealogy of the Malay rajas and the ceremonial of their courts so that this can be heard by [the king's] descendants, and so they can derive profit therefrom'.[23] Generally regarded as a literary masterpiece and the foremost example of classical Malay prose style, the *Sejarah Melayu* has been handed down in a number of versions, the earliest of which is now dated from the early seventeenth century. It is clear, however, that many of the stories it contains had been part of Malay culture for generations. On the basic framework of royal succession are ranged a series of highly entertaining episodes (*kisah*) which trace the origins and descent of Malay kings from mythical ages until just after the fall of Melaka in 1511. But although the narrative moves through time, the *Sejarah Melayu* does not purport to adhere to a strict chronology or provide a precise rendering of events in the past. It has provided historians with a rich mine of information, but it was not written according to the Western conception of a historical document, and to treat it as such is to misunderstand its fundamental aims. Like other Malay court annals, the *Sejarah Melayu* should be regarded as a particular genre of Malay literature, the primary concern of which was the edification of future generations.

The *Suma Oriental* and the *Sejarah Melayu*, despite their differing purposes, contain a core of similar information concerning the founding of Melaka. Both trace the Melaka line to an individual ruling in Palembang; both mention his special status; both describe his departure for Singapore, where he sets up a settlement. They relate how the settlement was later moved to Muar, about 8 kilometres from Melaka, then to Bertam, being finally established at Melaka itself, the site of which was chosen because of a mousedeer's peculiar behaviour. Apart from this basis of shared information, however, the two accounts differ markedly. Pires's narrative is presented in a relatively straightforward manner which to Western ears has a ring of authenticity. A Palembang prince, here termed Paramesvara, leaves Sumatra because he realizes that his standing in 'the neighbouring islands' makes his subservience to Java intolerable. As a sign of his new status he takes a title which Pires translates as 'The Great Exempt'. Following an invasion by a Javanese army he flees to Singapore with a following that includes 30 Orang Laut. After eight days in Singapore he kills the local chief there, an Ayudhyan vassal, and sets himself up as lord. In Singapore he and his followers eke out a living by growing rice, fishing and piracy, but after five years a force from Ayudhya drives them out and they flee to Muar. After another five years the Orang Laut discover an attractive site for a settlement at Bertam where Paramesvara moves. He rewards his faithful followers with noble titles, and his son marries the daughter of their leader, who then becomes chief minister.

One day this son, Iskandar Syah, is out hunting, but as he approaches Melaka Hill the mousedeer his dogs are chasing suddenly turns on them. Attributing this strange behaviour to the fact that the sea is so close, or to some quality in the hill itself, Iskandar Syah asks his father's permission to settle there. 'And at the said time, he built his house on top of the hill where the Kings of Melaka have had their dwelling and residence until the present time.'

The Malay version, the *Sejarah Melayu*, begins with an impressive genealogy which traces the line of Melaka kings back to Alexander the Great (Iskandar Zulkarnain) who assumes in the text the status of a glorious Muslim king. It follows the fortunes of Raja Iskandar's line in India and the Malay world until three of his descendants miraculously appear on Bukit Siguntang, a sacred hill in Palembang. Their heavenly descent acknowledged, the princes are hailed by the rulers of Sumatra, and one, Seri Teri Buana, is made ruler of Palembang. After vainly seeking a consort who can cohabit with him, Seri Teri Buana finally weds the daughter of his chief minister, Demang Lebar Daun, who had been Palembang's former ruler. Minister and king then conclude a solemn covenant which ensures that Malays will always remain loyal to their kings, who must repay them by just rule. In search of a suitable place to build a city, Demang Lebar Daun and Seri Teri Buana leave Palembang. When their fleet arrives at Bintan in the Riau-Lingga archipelago, the queen there takes Seri Teri Buana as her son.

Some time afterwards, seeking a suitable site for a settlement, Seri Teri Buana sees across the ocean the island of Temasek. With the help of the queen of Bintan, he establishes a city on Temasek which he calls Singapura, the 'Lion City', after glimpsing a strange beast there, which he takes to be a lion (*singa*). His descendants rule in Singapura (Singapore) for another five generations. Under their rule it becomes a great city which will not accept Java's attempt to impose overlordship and even withstands an assault by the ruler of Majapahit. However, when the fourth king unjustly punishes one of his subjects, contravening the contract made between his forebear and Demang Lebar Daun, Singapore is attacked by swordfish. The attack is repelled by a stratagem suggested by a child, who in turn is killed by the ruler, apprehensive of some future challenge. 'But when this boy was executed the guilt of his blood was laid on Singapore.' The next ruler, Sultan Iskandar Syah, publicly humiliates the daughter of a treasury official because he believes the unjustified slanders against her. The wronged father then invites the Javanese to attack, and this time they are successful. Sultan Iskandar flees to Muar, but here he is attacked by monitor lizards; he flees yet again, but his fort collapses; he finally moves up the coast to a river called Bertam. As the king is out hunting, one of his hounds is kicked by a white mousedeer. 'And Sultan Iskandar said, "This is a good place, where even the mousedeer are full of fight!"' Because he was then standing under a *melaka* tree, he decides that the new settlement should bear that name.

Recited aloud in public gatherings, these detailed and elaborated episodes would have been highly dramatic. At the same time, passages which have in the past been regarded simply as literary hyperbole may in fact encode valuable historical information. The Singapore period, for instance, receives considerable attention and is attributed a length of a hundred years prior to the founding of Melaka. Previously these claims were discounted because of the lack of evidence from other sources, and because the Pires version accords Singapore little importance. However, although memories of a great city recorded in the *Sejarah Melayu* may have been embellished by Malay memory, archaeological work in Singapore since the 1980s has yielded firm evidence of a fourteenth-century trading settlement, but has recovered no material from the fifteenth. This would be totally explicable in terms of Melaka's founding, believed to be around 1400.

In the larger historical framework, rather than being distracted by differences between the two versions, it is more useful to concentrate on the similarities. Above all, both see Melaka's origins in Palembang, where scholars believe a great entrepôt called Srivijaya once flourished. Available evidence and Melaka's subsequent history support the suggestion that its rapid rise and great self-confidence were due to a direct connection with the legendary Srivijaya. This link would provide Melaka with the background which it hitherto seemed to lack and which has represented an unexplained gap in our understanding of the period. The movement from Palembang to Melaka can then be seen as part of a continuum with no significant break in the momentum of Malay history.

Melaka's heritage

This chapter has drawn together some of the scattered evidence relating to the Malay world before the founding of Melaka. Far from being merely a prelude to the period of great Malay power, these early centuries established a context which makes later Malaysian history more explicable. The Malay archipelago came to the attention of the outside world because of the great natural wealth of its jungles and oceans. The area was doubly fortunate in being placed midway on the sea route between China and India and linked by a wind system with these two great markets of the early Asian world. But even more importantly, the peoples of the area were ever ready to respond to the demands of international trade. Because the long coastlines surrounding the Malay archipelago provided many natural harbours which could act as collecting points, rivalry inevitably grew up between different ports vying for trading supremacy. Periodically one would establish itself as a regional entrepôt with the right to command the patronage of foreign merchants. As such a port asserted commercial hegemony, its neighbours had to accept their position as subsidiary collection centres feeding the entrepôt.

The maintenance of this relationship depended on the ability of the centre to hold together a number of scattered harbours by loose political and economic ties which both vassal and overlord recognized as mutually advantageous. When the vassals began to question the value of the benefits they received, links with the overlord were weakened. The region would then break up into a number of small kingdoms competing for supremacy until one again succeeded in asserting its pre-eminence. It is this ebb and flow of power which has been called the 'rhythm' of Malay history.[24]

In the continuing contest to gain and maintain hegemony, a port along the Melaka Straits or its approaches had the advantage. Favourable geographic conditions and the availability of desired products led to the development of Gantuoli, arguably the first important Malay entrepôt, which was probably located somewhere in southeast Sumatra. Though virtually nothing is known of Gantuoli, it was highly successful in exploiting trade with India and China, and in commercial terms can be regarded as the predecessor of the greatest of the early Malay maritime kingdoms, Srivijaya.

Emerging in the seventh century in southeast Sumatra, Srivijaya was apparently able to maintain its economic and political superiority in the region until about the thirteenth century. Though many questions about Srivijaya remain unanswered, its claim to be the wealthiest and most prestigious of the early harbour ports now seems confirmed. It is also reasonable to suggest that traders were not drawn only by the ready market in jungle and sea products, or by the exotic goods brought from overseas by foreign merchants; they also appreciated the regulated government and the smooth functioning of commercial transactions. The prosperity that came to Srivijaya through international trade made possible a refined and cultured society that could hold its own even when compared with the great civilizations of India and China. Yet the association of Srivijaya with Palembang may hide other important loci of identity. Scholarship has accorded relatively little attention to the kingdom termed 'Melayu' by the Chinese and its connections with Minangkabau, but the Melayu-Minangkabau contribution to Malay cultural traditions may be more significant than previously thought. While the name of Srivijaya may have disappeared from the Malay mind, the Palembang-Melayu heritage was subsumed in memories associated with the Musi river region. In the words of the *Sejarah Melayu*: 'According to the account we have received, the city of Palembang which has been mentioned was the same as the Palembang of today. Formerly it was a very great city, the like of which was not to be found in the whole country of Andelas [Sumatra].' It was the Palembang-Melayu tradition to which the rulers of Melaka laid claim. To quote the *Sejarah Melayu* once again: 'From below the wind to above the wind Melaka became famous as a very great city, the raja of which was sprung from the line of Sultan Iskandar Zul-karnain [Alexander the Great]; so much so that princes from all countries came to present themselves before [the ruler].'

Chapter 2 . . . .

Melaka and its Heirs

During the fifteenth century Melaka rose to become, in the words of Tomé Pires, 'of such importance and profit that it seems to me it has no equal in the world'. Melaka's great success and its honoured place in Malay history were not only due, however, to its prosperity and renown as a trading centre. Building upon an illustrious past, it established a pattern of government and a lifestyle which was emulated by subsequent Malay kingdoms and became the basis of what was later termed 'traditional' Malay culture and statecraft. Local pride in these accomplishments was still evident in the late sixteenth century, when Malays told Europeans that their forebears had built a world-famous city from 'seven or eight fishing huts' and had there developed 'a language named Malay' that was regarded as 'the most courteous and refined in all India'.[1] So imposing was Melaka's reputation, and so clearly did it establish the criteria for Malay leadership, that its successors were in a sense condemned to the task of attempting to emulate its formidable achievement. However, the restraints imposed on international commerce by the trading policies of the Portuguese in the sixteenth century and the Dutch in the seventeenth meant that it was all but impossible for a Malay emporium in the tradition of Melaka to re-emerge. Nonetheless, while no Malay kingdom succeeded in recreating the greatness of Melaka, it remained an inspiration and a source of strength to all those states that considered themselves its heirs.

The sixteenth and seventeenth centuries: historiographical considerations

Although historians generally agree that Melaka was founded somewhere around 1400, the evidence for its subsequent history remains relatively sparse. Apart from the two major sources relating to the late fourteenth and fifteenth centuries, the *Suma Oriental* and the so-called *Sejarah Melayu*, information regarding the hundred years of Melaka's greatness is limited to an occasional mention in Chinese imperial histories and isolated comments in Portuguese documents. This means that only a few of the dates commonly assigned to rulers and events can actually be corroborated.

The capture of Melaka in 1511 by Portugal meant the sixteenth-century Malay world received greater Portuguese attention, and their subsequent records are thus more informative than previously. The *Sejarah Melayu* also continues to provide material unavailable elsewhere about the fortunes of the refugee Melaka princes until their descendants eventually established the kingdom of Johor. But no existing Malay texts describe events from the mid-sixteenth century to the end of the seventeenth, and the historian is again forced to fall back on European accounts. The Portuguese material is primarily concerned with the numerous wars waged against Johor and Aceh, reflecting the serious dislocation which occurred after Melaka's fall. This mirrors the fact that the Portuguese chronicles and letters were mainly intended to glorify Portuguese deeds in these distant lands, and to advance the interests of the writer. While it is certainly possible to add kernels of additional information to the chronology constructed from archival material, in general the surviving Portuguese sources reveal little of the lives of ordinary people. The most that can be established is that the local population gained their livelihood from agriculture, fishing and petty trading, and that they rendered their services to the ruler in times of war and during major celebrations. Because Christian missions in the rest of the Malay world were short-lived, we do not find the kind of documentation available for eastern Indonesia, although it is possible that the archives of the religious orders may yet yield new material. Failing the discovery of significant Portuguese sources, it is unlikely that future research will greatly change the existing picture.

The arrival of the Dutch in the Malay areas in the late sixteenth and early seventeenth century brought another European power to the scene, bequeathing data that has proved invaluable to the modern historian but has not yet been fully exploited. The formation of the Dutch East India Company (VOC) in 1602 was followed in 1619 by the establishment of Batavia (modern Jakarta) as the seat of the Company's government in Asia. To ensure the success of VOC trade, Batavia needed to understand the political as well as the economic policies of native kingdoms, since only with this information could its vast resources be effectively deployed. In order to compile accurate political and economic details, Company officials all over Asia were required to submit reports to Batavia.

In the Malay Peninsula the chief VOC outpost was at Melaka, captured from the Portuguese in 1641. From here missions were regularly sent to the various Malay kingdoms to gather information, while in Melaka itself local traders and envoys kept the Dutch informed of significant happenings in the area. Letters were also exchanged with native rulers and officials, providing yet another important source for historians. Ultimately this material was brought together and summarized by Melaka's Dutch governor in his monthly missive to Batavia, with many of the original documents appended for further perusal by the VOC leaders. It is these sources which form the basis for reconstructing events in the Malay world during the seventeenth and eighteenth centuries.

Detailed though the VOC records are, their nature still determines the kind of historical writing possible for this period of Malaysian history. They were intended primarily as a means of furthering VOC commerce, rather than aids to government or records for later administrations. Since some knowledge of politics in local kingdoms was vital for ensuring the Company's trading profits, Dutch attention focused on the governing classes. Even then on many occasions only a minimum of information was considered necessary for Dutch purposes. It is thus futile to expect VOC sources to yield the same kind of data about local society as do the colonial records from the late nineteenth and twentieth centuries. The lack of information concerning the common people is compounded by the fact that the available Malay texts (most of which date from the eighteenth century) emanate from the courts. They therefore deal almost exclusively with the ruler, the nobles, and the events that impinged on court life. Failure to appreciate these fundamental differences between the nature of modern records and those stemming from earlier times has led some scholars better acquainted with later Malaysian history to set unattainable goals for their colleagues working on the precolonial period. The Dutch sources can be immensely helpful in establishing a chronology and identifying the major political and economic developments, but many matters of interest to modern historians are mentioned only briefly, if at all.

In the tradition of Srivijaya

The previous chapter has described the period of rivalry in the thirteenth and fourteenth centuries when neighbouring ports in the Straits of Melaka sought to inherit Srivijaya's political and economic status. These harbours flourished with the patronage of foreign traders, who no longer found it practicable, profitable, or even safe to conduct their business at the central marketplace in Srivijaya. With merchants from both East and West now electing to patronize ports near the source of particular products, ambitious rulers saw opportunities for transforming their estuarine settlements in emulation of great entrepôts of the past.

An area which never totally relinquished its ability to provide alternative ports to Srivijaya was northern Sumatra. From the twelfth century two regions were particularly prominent: Samudra-Pasai, near the northern tip of Sumatra, and Aru, located to the south close to the former port of Kampé and in the area later known as Deli. Both states are mentioned in thirteenth-century Chinese sources, but their prestige increased during the fourteenth century after their adoption of Islam. While the reasons for Islam's success here and elsewhere in the archipelago have long been debated, historians generally agree that proselytization was closely linked to trade, which in this period was dominated by Muslims from India. Samudra-Pasai's fame as a trading port is well documented, and preliminary archaeological evidence suggests that during the twelfth and thirteenth centuries Aru too was a prosperous commercial state.

Thus, when Melaka was established around the turn of the fourteenth century, two well-established entrepôts already existed across the Straits, as well as at Kedah on the Peninsula. The evidence suggests that the founder of Melaka consciously set out to surpass his potential rivals, first by his careful choice of a site for his new capital. Situated on the convergence of the sea lanes from India and China, the Melaka harbour was sheltered and free of mangrove swamps, with approaches sufficiently deep to allow large vessels safe passage. A short distance to the south was the Muar river, which led to the Pahang river through a short land-portage area known as the Penarikan. River connections provided access into both Ulu Pahang and Ulu Kelantan (possibly the Chitu of early Chinese sources), an area that produced much of the Peninsula's gold and which may have had a long history of trade with China.

With an abundant supply of fresh water and timber, Melaka was ideally placed for international trade. But the decisive factor in its favour was probably its naturally defensible position. While Muar was a promising trading site, it was more vulnerable to attack than Melaka, where a prominent hill overlooked the estuary. As a further precaution the refugee Palembang prince Paramesvara (equated with Seri Teri Buana in the *Sejarah Melayu*) decided to build his residence upstream from Melaka, at Bertam. Here he could receive ample warning of any impending danger, which would allow time to escape to the interior. Although Paramesvara's successors maintained a residence on Melaka Hill, they too lived mainly in Bertam, going to Melaka only to arbitrate disputes or dispense justice. In its early years Melaka proper was thus a settlement of traders, where the ruler was represented by his Orang Laut retainers and guards, and by various nobles appointed to administer the city's affairs.

Once the site had been determined and a settlement founded, Paramesvara began systematically creating the conditions necessary for the establishment of a major trading centre. An unexpected opportunity arose with the installation of the Ming Emperor Yongle (Yung-lo) in July 1402. Following the same policies as his father, the new Chinese emperor forbade all private commerce overseas, re-established the Bureau of Maritime Trade, and encouraged state trading on a large scale. In early October, in order to proclaim his accession and his policies, envoys were dispatched to the Nan Yang ('the Southern Ocean'), the term the Chinese used to designate the Southeast Asian region. Because of the information then available in the imperial court, Samudra was the only port in the Melaka Straits visited by the Chinese mission. Less than four weeks later, however, on hearing of

Melaka's existence from Indian Muslim traders, Emperor Yongle immediately sent out a further mission. These envoys arrived in Melaka in the middle of 1404, and were accompanied on their return to China in early 1405 by a delegation from the new settlement. When presented to the Chinese court, the Melaka ambassador appeared with representatives of Samudra and Calicut (southwest India), two older and well-established kingdoms. Evidence of the emperor's favour was shown by the promulgation of an edict appointing all three rulers as 'legitimate' kings. Shortly afterwards another signal honour was bestowed on Melaka when it became the first foreign nation to receive the emperor's inscription. This inscription contained the moral and political philosophy of the Ming dynasty and was to be placed on a hill to the west of Melaka, which the emperor designated as its 'State Mountain'.

Behind Emperor Yongle's fostering of a special relationship between China and various Asian kingdoms lay his desire to expand official Chinese trade overseas. The selection of Melaka for particular honours may be explained by China's need for a convenient trading centre in the Straits somewhere at the 'end of the monsoons'. Imperial interest in Melaka in these early years imparted a prestige and respectability to the new entrepôt and a guarantee of protection from the Thais. Nonetheless, the ports along the northern Sumatran coast did not willingly relinquish their position. Unable to draw international trade away from Melaka and Samudra-Pasai, Aru mounted attacks on shipping destined for the other two ports. But though this piracy was irritating, it never seriously jeopardized the trade which was the source of Melaka's wealth and power.

Samudra-Pasai, on the other hand, remained Melaka's greatest rival for many years. Though increasing numbers of merchants flocked to Melaka under its second ruler, Megat Iskandar Syah, Tomé Pires was told that 'this was not felt in Pase [Pasai] because of the large number of people who were there'. A major Muslim port, Pasai was also distinguished because during the early fifteenth century it was under two female rulers. It is possible, indeed, that Pasai's prosperity under these queens can be traced to a more harmonious relationship with the largely male trading aristocracy, without the rivalry that often put kings and nobles at odds. Only towards the latter part of the fifteenth century did Pasai feel the effects of its neighbour's success. 'At this time,' wrote Pires, 'there was a large number of merchants of many nationalities in Malacca [Melaka], and Pase was already beginning to be less great than it had been.'[2]

Melaka's efforts to assert its position in the Straits were evidently successful. At the very inception of the settlement its rulers had solicited vassal status from China, and in becoming the recipient of Chinese favour they had gained the assurance of protection and status. Melaka also took the precaution of acknowledging the sovereignty of two powerful and much closer neighbours, the Tai-speaking kingdom of Ayudhya and Majapahit in Java. The advantages of this move were not purely in terms of protection, for

Melaka petitioned its two overlords to send people and foodstuffs to support the growth of the new settlement. Undeterred by the prosperity of rival Straits ports, an early ruler of Melaka was sufficiently confident to inform Pasai that all its needs could be provided by Melaka's markets.

Reasons for Melaka's success

Melaka continued the traditions of its predecessor, Srivijaya, in ensuring the success of international trade. In the first place, it was generally able to guarantee the safety of its sea lanes. The rulers of Melaka, like those of Srivijaya, commanded the allegiance of various Orang Laut groups who protected Melaka's clients and wreaked havoc on shipping making for rival ports. These safeguards (and the threat of attack for those who passed Melaka by) were an important element in the decision of traders to frequent the new settlement in preference to other ports in the Straits.

Secondly, Melaka was attractive to traders because of its commercial facilities. High priority was given to security within the town and to the protection of foreign merchants and their goods. For example, underground warehouses were constructed where stored goods would be less vulnerable to fire, damage or theft. Such measures were necessary because departures, arrivals and the exchange of goods were all governed by the monsoon winds. Between December and March, the period of greatest activity, vessels reached Melaka from western Asia and the Far East; it was not until May, however, that ships from Java and the eastern Indonesian archipelago began to arrive. All traders, especially those from China and eastern Indonesia, had some time to wait before the change in monsoon winds made their homeward voyage possible. Secure storage facilities were therefore a significant factor in Melaka's ability to attract an international clientele.

Third, and most important, was Melaka's efficient legal and administrative machinery, which provided a predictability essential for the long-term plans of foreign traders. The *Undang-Undang Melaka* (Melaka Laws), initially compiled under the third ruler, devote considerable attention to the regulation of commercial matters. A separate codification of maritime laws concentrated specifically on matters concerned with sea-going trade, such as the collection of debts, shipboard crimes, and the duties of captain and crew. The recognition that an effective judicial system could promote commerce was exemplified by one sultan who was said to have preferred roaming city streets to hunting 'so that he could hear and decide about the abuses and tyrannies which Melaka creates on account of its great position and trade'.[3]

Melaka's administrative system also directly responded to the needs of a growing trading community. Four *syahbandars*, or harbour masters, were appointed, each one representing different ethnic groupings. One was in charge of the Gujarati from northwest India, who were the most numerous, being estimated at around 1000 in 1509; another was appointed for Indians from southern India and Bengal, together with traders from Pegu in Burma and from Pasai; a third for those from Java, Maluku, Banda, Palembang, Borneo and the Philippines; and a fourth for traders from Champa (central Vietnam), China and the Ryukyu Islands (probably including Japanese). Each syahbandar was required to oversee the affairs of his particular group; to manage the marketplace and the warehouse; maintain a check on weights, measures and coinage; and to adjudicate in any disputes between ship captains and merchants. The Melaka ruler was the final arbiter in all quarrels between the different trading communities.

Whenever a ship arrived in port, the captain reported to his particular syahbandar, who in turn referred him to Melaka's principal minister, the *bendahara*. The syahbander then supplied elephants for the captain to transport his cargo to a warehouse assigned for the temporary storage of his goods. Before trading could be conducted, customs duties were paid in accordance with the value of the merchandise and the area from which a trader came. In addition, it was necessary to present gifts to the ruler, the bendahara, and the *temenggung* (the Melaka official principally involved in the collection of import and export duties), as well as to the appropriate syahbandar.

A much simpler procedure was used for large ships, notably those from Gujarat. A flat 6 per cent of the value of the cargo was paid, eliminating any necessity for separate gift-giving. Once the duties had been paid, the merchandise could be sold. Usually a group of Melaka merchants would reach a price with the ship's captain or the merchants on board, and then the goods would be distributed in proportion to the contribution made to the total price. This method disposed of a ship's merchandise quickly and efficiently, and since cargoes were customarily handled in order of arrival, traders could normally depend upon fair and rapid transactions. Speed was highly desirable because merchants were often working against time, aiming to complete their business in order to catch the right monsoon winds back to their homelands. The Malay traders of Melaka then took the goods which they had bought, and either sold them in the marketplace, in the booths set up on the bridge and in the streets in front of houses, or else brought them to various parts of the archipelago to barter for other products. It was this middleman role played by the Melaka merchants which served to strengthen Malay as the language of trade throughout the archipelago. Malay was the language of Srivijaya, and would have accompanied its traders to distant areas in the archipelago; a tenth-century Malay copper inscription from southern Luzon in the Philippines provides evidence of this early spread of the language. During the heyday of the Melaka kingdom, however, Malay extended through the archipelago and eastward to the Spice Islands, establishing itself as the incontestable *lingua franca*.

Melaka's reputation for security, a well-ordered government and a cosmopolitan and well-equipped marketplace all attest the priority its rulers placed on creating the conditions for safe and profitable commerce. But these facilities alone would not have automatically attracted traders. The fundamental element in Melaka's success as an entrepôt was the dual role it played as the principal collecting point for cloves from Maluku and the nutmeg and mace of the Banda Islands, and as an important redistributing centre for Indian textiles from Gujarat, Coromandel, Malabar and Bengal. Indian cloth was carried mainly by Malay traders from Melaka to various parts of the archipelago and bartered for spices, aromatic woods, sea products, and other exotic items highly prized by traders from both East and West. Without the Indian cloth or the spices, Melaka would have been simply one of a number of other ports in the area specializing in a few local products.

In his *Suma Oriental*, Tomé Pires estimated that 2.4 million cruzados' worth of trade passed through Melaka in 1510. This figure takes on greater significance when compared with the total value of imported goods entering Seville, one of the wealthiest ports in Europe, which at the end of the sixteenth century was reckoned at about 4 million cruzados. There was some royal trade, but in terms of the kingdom's total revenue this was eclipsed by the customs levied on trading ships now flocking to its port. At any one time there were upward of 2000 boats lying at anchor in the harbour. By the beginning of the sixteenth century, the population of Melaka, swelled by foreign traders, numbered perhaps as many as 100 000.

The nature of the Melaka state

One of the most impressive achievements of the Melaka court was its articulation of basic concepts regarding the nature of the state and how it should ideally function. Clearly expressed in the *Sejarah Melayu*, these concepts became an integral part of the Malay world-view and remained basically unchallenged until the nineteenth century. Even today elements of earlier statecraft can be discerned in modern Malay political relations and in Malay society itself. Although the earliest known version of the *Sejarah Melayu* was composed in the early seventeenth century, it is likely that some sections were written down nearly 200 years before, in the days of Melaka's greatness. These probably reflect traditions of government that arose even earlier, possibly in the court of Srivijaya.

For Malays, the structure of government was justified by its intimate ties with the kingdom's origin myths. At the apex of the state, the ruler claimed descent from the Palembang prince, Seri Teri Buana, who had miraculously appeared on Bukit Siguntang and whose line itself threaded back to Raja Iskandar Zulkarnain ('Alexander of the Two Horns', that is, Alexander the Great). In keeping with this exalted lineage, Malay subjects were bound to their rulers in a social covenant described in the *Sejarah Melayu* which makes the ruler responsible solely to Almighty God, who will mete out both rewards and punishments:

46

If any ruler puts a single one of his subjects to shame [*memberi aib*], that shall be a sign that his kingdom will be destroyed by Almighty God. Similarly it has been granted by Almighty God to Malay subjects that they shall never be disloyal or treacherous to their rulers, even if their rulers behave evilly or inflict injustice upon them.

In the system of Malay governance as conceptualized in the *Sejarah Melayu*, the ruler stood at the heart of all meaningful activity. It was the ruler with his impeccable ancestry and unique 'Melayu' heritage who brought Melaka the prestige that distinguished it from surrounding states. In both the *Sejarah Melayu* and another Malay epic, the *Hikayat Hang Tuah*,[4] the word Melayu is clearly linked to Sumatra and, as we have seen, early Chinese sources mention a Melayu believed to have been in the Jambi region. Other sources locate Melayu more specifically: the *Sejarah Melayu* records that 'Melayu' was the name of a river flowing near the sacred hill of Bukit Sigun-tang in Palembang, and Pires identifies 'tana Melayu' (the land of the Malays) with an area near present-day Palembang. This association was clearly a prestigious one. A close examination of the *Sejarah Melayu* indicates that 'Melayu' was a mark of distinction initially used to denote those descended from Palembang forebears, and the Palembang connection remained an important element in the dynastic claims of Melaka kings. Paramesvara's apparent anxiety to reassert control in Palembang suggests the continuing identification of Melaka's rulers with their ancestral homeland, and significantly, when Sultan Mansur (d. 1477) visited Java, he was escorted by several rulers from Sumatra, including the raja of Jambi and 'people of Palembang'.

The ruling dynasty's association with its sacred Palembang origins formed the basis of its exclusiveness, which was further reinforced by the concept of *daulat/derhaka*. Traces of these ideas can be discerned in earlier sources from Srivijaya, and they were to reach their full potential in Melakan conceptions of the ruler–subject relationship. At the heart of Malay governance was the ruler, a concept encapsulated in the Malay term for government, *kerajaan*, literally, the condition of having a raja. The famous Melaka hero Hang Tuah says categorically that treason (*derhaka*) towards the ruler is tantamount to a sin against God, and so heinous was this crime that the retribution meted out by the forces of kingship (*daulat*) entailed far more than simple punishment. Over the centuries a storehouse of legends was built up recording the fate of those who had transgressed. In the early nineteenth century Sultan Husain of Singapore was merely repeating a traditional prescription in the *Sejarah Melayu* when he said that a man guilty of *derhaka*, along with his family, would be killed, his house uprooted, and the soil on which it stood thrown into the sea.

This emphasis on the inviolability of ties between king and subject may have been prompted by a need to assert the standing of Melaka's rulers in the eyes of nearby communities, who were mainly of Orang Laut and Orang Asli origin. With only a small contingent of Melayu newcomers, it was

vital that the Melaka dynasty be confirmed and accepted. Only by incorporating local groups into the Melayu system of governance and society and
persuading them to accept the authority of its rulers could the early kings of
Melaka establish a secure position and ensure the prosperity of their young
settlement.

It was this assimilatory aspect of Melaka society that struck Portuguese
observers. Paramesvara had been accompanied in his flight from Sumatra by
a number of Orang Laut followers, but according to Barros, a sixteenth-
century writer, these 'Celates' (from Strait – *selat*) and the 'people of the land'
(*gente da propria terra*) already spoke a mutually intelligible form of Malay.
Initially the local inhabitants, whom Barros termed 'native Malays' (*Malaios
naturaes*), had kept their distance from the newcomers, but a shortage of
women among the migrant community brought them together. They then
formed one settlement, with the Celates collecting the products of the sea
and *Malaios* those of the jungle as they had been accustomed to do. Ties
established through women also enabled Paramesvara to strengthen his links
with Orang Laut leaders in the Melaka vicinity. His marriage to the daughter
of a Singapore Orang Laut chief is mentioned by Tomé Pires, and it was the
son of this union who succeeded as Melaka's second ruler. The close family
ties by which Melaka kings maintained the relationship established much
earlier between the sea people and the rulers of Srivijaya were extremely
significant. Because of their relatively large numbers and maritime skills, the
Orang Laut were essential allies for any lord aspiring to political hegemony
in the Straits. Furthermore, their cargoes of sea products were acknowledged as being vitally important in attracting the traders who became the
source of Melaka's wealth. For several hundred years the Orang Laut
remained 'loyal friends' (*fieis amigos*) of the Melaka rulers, and their devotion
was a crucial factor in maintaining the kingdom and ensuring its prosperity.

Like later migrants to the Peninsula, the Sumatran settlers also readily
accepted wives from local Orang Asli groups. Barros specifically comments
on this intermarriage, remarking that 'from [the] Celates and native Malays
came all the nobles who are now Fidalgos in Melaka'.[5] Forest dwellers were
apparently willing to become associated with the new regime because this
gave them access to a profitable market and the added status of ties to the
prestigious Melayu rulers. For its part, Melaka gained obvious commercial
benefits. Although forest-dwelling groups were never populous, their ability
to deliver the jungle products valued in international trade must have been
a major impetus towards their inclusion in Melaka's evolving society. The
kinship links mentioned by Barros were important because even at the
beginning of this century Orang Asli groups such as the Jakun were still
regarded by the people in the hinterland of Melaka as the original lords of
the soil. Furthermore, their familiarity with the spirit-haunted jungle meant
they were regarded with great respect. In the seventeenth century the
'benuas' who lived around Melaka were known for their ability to invoke
supernatural powers and their intimate knowledge of plant medicines.

This close relationship between the Melaka court and Orang Asli groups is suggested in several Malay sources. The *Hikayat Hang Tuah*, which brings together numerous Malay oral traditions, notes that after Melaka's fall to the Portuguese in 1511, the queen flees for safety into the jungle. Here she becomes a member of one of the northern Orang Asli groups, the Batek. Meanwhile, Hang Tuah himself retreats upriver to Perak where he is accepted as ruler by another Orang Asli people, the Orang Biduanda (literally, palace servants). Although the latter are now referred to as Orang Temuan, the older terminology suggests the close relationship between the Melaka court and the Orang Asli. A Malay text, the *Hikayat Deli*, originating from east coast Sumatra, describing how Melaka people flee to the jungle after an attack to became Jakun, or forest dwellers, similarly suggests the ease of movement in and out of Malayness.

The porous nature of an evolving Malay identity made possible the creation of a new élite that linked the Sumatran settlers with the aboriginal population of neighbouring coastal and riverine areas. This interaction recalls the association described in the *Sejarah Melayu* between Seri Teri Buana, the prince who appeared on Bukit Siguntang, and the local head of Palembang, Demang Lebar Daun. The Melaka dynastic line was descended from the union between the daughter of Demang Lebar Daun and Seri Teri Buana, and the two men were buried together on Singapore Hill. The legendary contract between them, guaranteeing the rights of ordinary people, permeated Malay understanding of the ruler–subject relationship. As Demang Lebar Daun reminded Seri Teri Buana, a king's exalted position was no licence for arbitrary government, and while subjects should render unquestioning loyalty, they in turn should not be bound or hanged 'or disgraced with evil words'. The *Sejarah Melayu* records the dying words of one Melaka ruler: 'subjects are like roots and the ruler is like the tree; without roots the tree cannot stand upright; so is it with rulers and their subjects ... If you put them to death when they have done no wrong, [the] kingdom will be brought to nought'. The *Hikayat Hang Tuah* specifically points to the rights of Malay subjects when describing the hero's visit to Siam. Malays, Hang Tuah assured his hosts, were not required to crawl before their sovereign, and Malay protocol permitted men to wear a *keris* (Malay dagger) in the royal presence. Thus, although the sources reveal little of the lives of ordinary people, it is clear that the the *kerajaan* concept could only operate if it was accepted by the *hamba Melayu* ('servants of the Melayu' or 'Malay subjects').

The same comments can be applied to the court, where the support of wealthy and high-ranking nobles was vital for effective government. The *Sejarah Melayu* is insistent that 'no ruler, however great his wisdom and understanding, shall prosper or succeed in doing justice unless he consults with those in authority under him. For rulers are like fire and their ministers are like firewood and fire needs wood to produce a flame.' As the practical administrators, wise ministers were essential. By faithfully executing their duties, they helped distance the ruler from the mundane tasks of government so that the more sacred functions of royalty could be preserved untarnished. The ministers and the rulers thus had specific complementary functions, which merited mutual respect and trust. As one minister in the *Sejarah Melayu* explained: 'What we think should be done we do, for the ruler is not concerned with the difficulties we administrators encounter, he only takes account of the good results we achieve.'

An examination of the *Sejarah Melayu* in conjunction with other sources, particularly the *Suma Oriental* of Tomé Pires, conveys some idea of how such concepts functioned in practice. The most important minister in Melaka was the bendahara, the arbiter of disputes among Melaka residents, and between them and foreigners. Though himself a noble, the original bendahara was not of royal birth. As time passed, however, it became customary for a daughter of the bendahara to become the ruler's consort, and because of this intermarriage the bendahara family came to wield great power, frequently acting as kingmaker. So important was the position of bendahara that in the *Sejarah Melayu* even a queen dowager intervenes to ensure that a candidate she favours is installed. But no matter how influential his patrons, the bendahara, like the lowest commoner, was in theory subject to the strictures governing the relationship between ruler and ruled. The *Sejarah Melayu* thus presents the ideal picture of a powerful bendahara who refused to commit treason against the ruler, despite being unjustly accused; only God Almighty, the text reminded Malays, could punish a wicked king.

According to the *Sejarah Melayu*, the next prominent official in Melaka was the *penghulu bendahari*, who was head of all the syahbandars and controlled all state revenues. In addition, he was responsible for the ruler's servants and clerks. The third-ranking official in the Melaka hierarchy was the temenggung, who later became more important than the penghulu bendahari and was considered to be the bendahara-designate. His principal concern was Melaka's security, and he was therefore in charge of the police and acted as chief magistrate. The fourth minister was the *laksamana*, who headed the military administration and was commander of the ruler's bodyguard. Since the most effective arm of Melaka's forces was the navy, the post of laksamana became equated with the leader of the fleets.

These four ministers were the most prominent in the Melaka period. Below them were various titled nobles whose positions stemmed from their territorial holdings or from a privileged association with the royal family. Little is known about individual functions, but it is apparent that Melaka rulers considered these men worthy of consultation in any important decision affecting the people. A meeting of the nobles constituted a form of council or assembly (*mesyuarat bicara*) in which all views could be heard and then a decision taken by consensus (*muafakat*). It was this collective decision-making process which normally prevented arbitrary acts by a ruler and guaranteed that a resolution taken would be faithfully implemented. Although there were ways in which shrewd rulers or nobles could circumvent decisions made by the council, in most cases this form of government, which was found in all later Malay states, functioned well.

The success of *muafakat* is the more impressive because the ruling élite in Melaka contained many men of wealth, ambition and ability. The ruler was by no means the only recipient of the riches which flowed into the coffers of the Melaka court; indeed, the Malay phrase commonly used for a noble in Melaka, *orang kaya*, simply means 'rich man'. Malay officials such as the bendahara and temenggung were presented with princely sums through the traditional practice of submitting a certain percentage of a cargo's value in gifts. As the noble class gained increasing wealth from customs and their own private trade, it thus became necessary to reinforce the ruler's place at the apex of the state. To accentuate his distinctiveness in relation to his nobles, certain royal privileges were instituted. The colour yellow was reserved for the exclusive use of royalty; white umbrellas were to be used only by rulers, and yellow umbrellas only by princes; gold anklets could be worn only by royalty; no one, 'however rich he might be', could wear gold unless it had been presented by the ruler, in which case it could then be worn 'in perpetuity'; 'enclosed verandahs, pillars that hung down not reaching to the ground, posts that went right up to the roofbeam, or summerhouses' were the preserve of royalty; only royalty could have windows and reception cabins on boats; and no commoner could have a metal casing on the sheath of his *keris*. Such visible manifestations of the ruler's unique position were a continual reminder to Melaka nobles of their rightful place in the hierarchy.

Nonetheless, a recurring problem in Melaka, as in subsequent Malay states, was court conflicts between royal children born of relationships with *gundik*, or secondary wives, and the offspring of fully royal wives. The degree of intermarriage between the nobility and the royal family also increased the potential contenders for power. The possibility of a successful challenge to a ruler was always present because royal privileges were at times insufficient to deter a high-ranking prince or official from aspiring to greater authority and prestige. One bendahara in the *Sejarah Melayu*, for example, was 'so clever in his handling of foreigners and skilled in conciliating the good will of the populace' that masters of ships bound for Melaka would invoke a prayer before weighing anchor which concluded: 'May we reach Melaka safely and see Pisang Jeram, the stream of Bukit China, and Bendahara Sri Maharaja.'[6] Such rich and famous men could attract a large following, and in the Malay context followers have always meant strength. During the reign of the last Melaka ruler, accusations that the bendahara intended to usurp the throne seemed so credible that the minister was executed by royal command.

In the relationship between the ruler and his nobles, the wealth of international trade was thus a mixed blessing. While it enriched the ruler, it also swelled the coffers of the local aristocracy and provided them with the means to oppose royal authority. It is therefore not surprising that Malay court traditions continued to stress the *daulat* vested in the ruler and the dire retribution visited upon those committing treason. Reinforced by rigid

51

sumptuary laws, these traditions became part of the mystique that surrounded the Melaka rulers descended from the Palembang line. For many years they served either to discourage would-be usurpers, or to compel them to mask their activities by outwardly acknowledging the formal relationships that tradition dictated.

Melaka's territorial expansion

The increased revenue from trade transformed Melaka from an insignificant backwater into a bustling international emporium with political ambitions. Under Paramesvara (d. 1413–14), Melaka comprised the small settlement at the port itself and the royal residence upriver at Bertam. During the reign of his successor, Megat Iskandar Syah (d. 1423–24), the boundaries of Melaka expanded to include all lands between Kuala Linggi and Kuala Kesang (the borders of the modern Melaka State). The extension of its authority into what became Naning, Sungai Ujung and Rembau was highly significant. None of these names occurs in the *Sejarah Melayu*, but it is believed that Minangkabau were already settling in the Melaka area. In a society where matrilineal ownership of land and houses encourages male migration (*merantau*), the rivers of east coast Sumatra, which originated in the Minangkabau uplands, provided a ready access out to the Straits and from thence to the Peninsula. In this new environment, as migrant leaders established their claims to land through intermarriage with local Orang Asli groups, a system of government developed that was distinct from that in Minangkabau. What these migrant communities did retain, however, was the Minangkabau concept of the *suku*, or clan, in which descent and inheritance was reckoned through the maternal line. Though areas retained strong connections with Minangkabau, they were also readily brought under Melaka's umbrella. This was undoubtedly facilitated by Minangkabau–Melayu cultural connections; in one version of the *Sejarah Melayu*, for example, the rulers of Minangkabau are descended from one of the Bukit Siguntang princes. According to another tradition, a sultan of Melaka appointed a leading member of this migrant community, the son of a Minangkabau chief and a Jakun woman, as supreme law giver or *undang* of Rembau.

In this early period of consolidation, Melaka was still smaller than its principal rival, Pasai. However, its territorial expansion resumed under Sultan Muzaffar Syah (d. *circa* 1459), who incorporated the Dindings, Selangor, Muar, Singapore and Bintan into the kingdom. Pahang, which fourteenth-century Chinese sources depict as a thriving port on the east coast of the Peninsula, was similarly forced to acknowledge Melaka's suzerainty. Muzaffar also successfully extended Melaka's authority across the Straits into Inderagiri and Kampar, which controlled access to the rich pepper and gold of the Minangkabau interior. Sultan Mansur Syah (d. 1477) added Bernam and Perak on the Peninsula to the Melaka kingdom, while Siak on Sumatra's east coast became another vassal area. On succeeding his father, Sultan Alauddin Riayat Syah (d. 1488) extended Melaka's conquests southward 'to the many islands belonging to the Celates [Orang Laut]', that is, the Riau-Lingga archipelagos. By the reign of the last ruler, Sultan Mahmud Syah (1488–1530), the kingdom had grown to include Pahang, the west coast of the Malay Peninsula from Perak to Johor, Singapore, the Riau-Lingga archipelagos, much of east coast Sumatra, and the islands of the South China Sea.

Melaka's vassal rulers were generally willing to accept subordinate status because they recognized the benefits of trading access and enhanced status that came from acknowledging a wealthy overlord. Yet several who could look back on past independence were always restless. Siak was only overcome by force, and when Kampar and Inderagiri attempted to assert their autonomy they were subdued. The same punishment was meted out to Pahang, where control was vital to ensure Melaka's authority in the South China Sea and its domination of the sea route to China. Although tensions periodically surfaced, especially in east coast Sumatra, the use of force was to some extent ameliorated by royal marriages, which created a network of family connections linking the Melaka domains. By the end of the fifteenth century Melaka had become so powerful and so confident that Sultan Mahmud rejected the overlordship of both Ayudhya and the weakened kingdom of Majapahit while continuing to acknowledge the more distant and less obtrusive suzerainty of China.

Melaka's territorial control, however, was never as extensive as that credited to Srivijaya at the height of its power. The northern Malay states of Patani, Kelantan, Terengganu and Kedah still acknowledged Ayudhya as overlord, and Melaka's influence was only felt here towards the end of the fifteenth century. Even on the opposite side of the Straits the suzerainty of Melaka was incomplete. Pasai, though suffering from Melaka's increased international trade, remained an independent port able to satisfy foreign traders, and Aru too retained its autonomy. With both Pasai and Aru continuing to exercise freedom of action in local waters, and Ayudhya still a major threat on its borders, Melaka, unlike Srivijaya, never succeeded in making the Straits its private lake.

Islam and the spread of Melaka culture

Melaka's territorial ambitions may have been checked, but its cultural influence spread beyond the immediate vicinity of the Straits throughout the Malay-Indonesian archipelago. A principal factor in the transmission of Melaka-Malay culture was its association with Islam. By the ninth century Arab traders were acquainted with much of Southeast Asia but appear to have neglected this area in favour of the lucrative China trade. Although

Arab sources mention the northwest and east coasts of Sumatra, the Melaka Straits down to Palembang, Johor, part of the Riau-Lingga archipelago and Pulau Tioman, there is no evidence of organized Arab trade here until the mid-tenth century. It is certainly possible that settlements of Muslim traders may have developed in this early period, like 'Kalah', which has been located tentatively somewhere in the northern part of the Malay Peninsula. Since Muslim merchants did not travel with their families, the gravestone of a Muslim woman found in Brunei dated 1048 CE suggests a continuation of old patterns whereby foreign traders married local women. The latter would then have been given Muslim names and become at least nominal Muslims. However, the first clear reference to an established Muslim community in the Straits is Marco Polo's account of 1292, which notes that the town of Perlak in northern Sumatra had adopted Islam.

A source of Islamic influence which is only recently receiving attention is China, where trade with Persia and central Asia had led to the growth of Sino-Muslim coastal communities, notably in Canton (Guangzhou). From the twelfth century the closing of overland routes across central Asia spurred these communities to expand their maritime trade into Southeast Asia. Islam was already in high favour in the imperial court, and when the Ming emperor sent a fleet through Southeast Asia in the early fifteenth century he chose a Chinese Muslim, Zhenghe (Cheng Ho, 1371–1435), as his emissary. The Islamic connections with China assume added importance in view of the fact that the Terengganu Stone, like gravestones found in Champa, is located on the trade route followed by Chinese shipping. However, the most important Islamic influence in the thirteenth century undoubtedly came from Muslim Indian traders, who by this time had largely superseded their Arab brethren. It is to Muslim Indians, therefore, that the spread of Islam through the archipelago is generally attributed.

Although the ongoing debate as to which Indian group was responsible for the conversion of island Southeast Asia may never be resolved, the direct relationship between trade and the spread of Islam is undeniable. After the fall of Baghdad and the destruction of the Abbasid Caliphate by the Mongols in 1258, the spice route from the east through the Persian Gulf up to the Levantine coast and thence to northern Europe was effectively closed. A new route now went from the east to India, then to Aden in southern Arabia, through the Red Sea up to Alexandria and thence northward. Since the caliph in Egypt allowed only Muslim shipping through Alexandria, the Muslim ports of Cambay, Surat and Diu in Gujarat province (northwest India) acquired great importance as trans-shipment centres for spices. In addition to the thousand or so Gujarati merchants resident in Melaka, there were about three to four thousand others always *en route* between this port and those in Gujarat.

Growing demand for Eastern spices by a prosperous Renaissance Europe and the cessation from the fourteenth century of direct Chinese trade to India brought the Gujarati merchants into greater prominence as intermediaries in the spice trade. They also became more important in Melaka after the Chinese emperor banned private Chinese trade in 1433. Their sizeable numbers in Melaka, the pre-eminent market in the Malay-Indonesian archipelago, facilitated the work of Muslim missionaries in spreading the ideas of Islam to Melaka and elsewhere in the region. But the Gujarati merchants did not have the exclusive trade to Southeast Asia. There were substantial numbers of other Muslim Indian traders from the Malabar and Coromandel coasts in south India, as well as from Bengal in northeast India. All these groups at one time or another would have played their part in familiarizing the island peoples of Southeast Asia with Islam, not necessarily with any of its dogma but with attitudes, values and a way of life.

The manner in which Islam took root within Malay society is still a matter of speculation. It is often suggested that Sufism, which flourished in Aceh in the sixteenth and seventeenth centuries, was a factor.[7] A mystic stream of Islam which at various periods verged on heterodoxy, Sufism's particular attraction lay in its readiness to incorporate a number of indigenous pre-Islamic beliefs. It is possible that Sufi notions of the perfect man, developed in Persia, were also appealing to Melaka rulers. However, although the Sufi connection can be established for Aceh, parts of Java and even south Sulawesi, the intriguing hints of Sufi theology in the *Sejarah Melayu* may represent a seventeenth-century interpolation of ideas borrowed from Aceh. That is, they do not necessarily demonstrate that Melaka Malays had a strong familiarity with Sufi doctrine. Furthermore, it is unlikely that one method or one particular school of Islam would have found uniform acceptance throughout the varied societies in the archipelago. It is evident that Muslim traders, principally from India, were responsible for introducing local societies to Islam, but the process by which ordinary people became Muslim is still unclear.

Although contradictions in the sources allow for debate, modern scholars generally ascribe Melaka's adoption of Islam to the third reign. The *Sejarah Melayu* rightly sees the ruler's conversion as a watershed in Melaka's history, an inspired event which confirmed the kingdom's superior status. But while the doctrinal simplicity of the new religion and its stress on the individual worth of all men were appealing, it seems clear that the temporal benefits were equally apparent. Melaka's rulers had only to look across the Straits to see the advantages of adopting the new religion. Pasai had accepted Islam towards the end of the thirteenth century and had consequently been favoured by large numbers of Muslim Indian traders. Its prosperity had demonstrated that any port which obtained the patronage of these Muslim Indian cloth merchants could be certain of attracting other merchants, since Indian textiles were the basic item of trade. As we have seen, the Patani-Kelantan-Terengganu region was closely linked to maritime and overland trading networks, and the hope of emulating Pasai's success may have been one factor in prompting a local ruler in Terengganu to proclaim his Islamic credentials by erecting the renowned Terengganu Stone. Because the text is only partly legible, the Muslim date could correspond to either 1303 or 1387 CE. Apart from an injunction to obey the law of God, the edict deals with debt relationships and punishments for perjury and sexual transgressions.

In using what would have been more familiar Sanskrit terms, such as referring to the Supreme God as Dewata Mulia Raya, the Terengganu Stone also supplies evidence of the localization process which underlay the acceptance of Islam. On the other side of the Peninsula, in what is now Negeri Sembilan, the mixture of Javanese and Arabic script and Islamic dates corresponding to 1467–8 on what is obviously an ancient megalith emphasizes the palimpsest nature of a developing Malay culture. This adaptation also became a vehicle which established links between local Muslims and a wider world. Thus, while Muslim rulers could display the attributes culturally expected of leaders, they also became members of a great Islamic community. It is likely that stories of the fabled Rum (Turkey), which Hang Tuah himself is said to have visited, were already filtering into the archipelago, and its prestige would have risen further after the capture of Constantinople in 1436. Such examples were reinforced by the new Islamic ideology that depicted a Muslim ruler as the 'Shadow of God upon Earth' and made him the head of a religious network which could extend to the village level. The strengthening of kingship, implicit in the teaching propagated by Muslim scholars, was almost certainly a factor in persuading one of Melaka's earliest rulers to embrace the new faith. According to both the *Sejarah Melayu* and the *Suma Oriental* the decision was made with the encouragement of the ruler of Pasai, which may have hoped to confirm its position of superiority as the older Islamic centre.

Once the Melaka court had accepted Islam some time in the early fifteenth century, the kingdom became transformed. As Melaka expanded territorially, its rulers in turn persuaded or compelled their vassals in the Straits area to adopt Islam, while its prestige and commercial success also reinforced the process of self-Islamization in the archipelago. Local traders who brought their products for sale in Melaka markets would have witnessed Islam at work and seen the added status accruing from the new titles and pretensions assumed by the Melaka sultan and his nobles. Such changes would have been reported to their own rulers who, eager to emulate the wealthy Melaka court, would have been receptive to proselytizing efforts by Muslim missionaries. Undoubtedly some rulers were sincerely attracted by the doctrine of the new faith, but the practical advantages that had earlier appealed to the Melaka court were equally evident. Perhaps the deciding argument would have been the assurance that Muslim traders from India and Melaka would favour their ports because of the protection they could expect from a fellow Muslim and because of the presence of a mosque where they could worship without interference.

Throughout the fifteenth century Melaka's reputation as a commercial and religious centre established it as the yardstick by which other Muslim kingdoms in the archipelago were measured. Although Melaka society was highly cosmopolitan and incorporated influences from a number of sources, its style of government, courtly titles, literature, music, dance, dress and amusements came to be regarded as distinctively 'Malay'. But though customs associated with the prestigious name of Melaka were all consciously imitated in courts ranging from Aceh in the west to Ternate in the east, the clearest evidence of Melaka's influence was undoubtedly the widespread use of Malay. As one sixteenth-century Portuguese observer remarked, 'Though the heathen [on Sumatra's east coast] differ from one another in their languages, almost all of them speak Malayo de Malaca [Melakan Malay] because it is the language most used in the whole region'.[8] So identified was language with the entire gamut of Malay culture that the word *bahasa* (literally, language) came to subsume correct behaviour, appropriate speech and knowledge of Malay custom or *adat*.

None the less, the spread of Malay culture, like the development of Melaka itself, should be viewed in perspective. The Malay cultural heritage did not originate in the fifteenth century, and neither Melaka's great reputation nor the ubiquity of its traders fully explains Malay influence in the Indonesian archipelago. It is more revealing to look beyond Melaka to the period of Srivijaya's dominance in the Straits. Scholars have noted that the oldest evidence of the Malay language comes from the seventh-century inscriptions found in Palembang, Jambi and Bangka. It would appear, therefore, that the language of the government and court of Srivijaya was an early version of the Malay spoken in Melaka. Malay legends of Melaka's founding by a Palembang prince give further weight to the argument that its language and culture were based upon that which flourished in Srivijaya. The extension of Malay culture thus built upon much earlier traditions. Because of its prestige and commanding position, Srivijaya's cultural influence would have been disseminated throughout its extensive though loosely governed empire. Smaller kingdoms would have adopted Srivijaya's lead, including the use of an early form of Malay as the language of the élite.

Melaka's main contribution to the evolution of Malay culture was the incorporation of Islamic ideas. Though Islam had been promoted earlier by Samudra-Pasai, the new religion became so closely identified with Malay society that to become Muslim was termed *masuk Melayu*, 'to enter [the fold of the] Melayu'; one ruler even boasted that Melaka could become an alternative to Mecca as a place of pilgrimage. Melaka continued earlier traditions by providing a cultural yardstick for areas formerly under Srivijaya's influence. Aru, for instance, had originated as a Batak state but by the mid-fifteenth century had adopted many of the trappings of a Malay kingdom, including the use of Malay titles for its officials. It had also become Muslim, although the *Sejarah Melayu* is quick to point out that the people of Aru could not read the Koran. At the height of Melaka's power in the fifteenth century, Malay culture spread eastwards beyond the Straits to areas in eastern Indonesia which had never been influenced by Srivijaya and were far beyond Melaka's political sway. But Melaka's period of greatness was already drawing to an end with the arrival of the Portuguese in Asia.

The Portuguese conquest of Melaka

Fifteenth-century Portugal was unique in Europe in having suffered no debilitating internal strife. Freed from civil wars and major intrigues, Portuguese rulers from the time of Infante Dom Enrique (better known as Prince Henry the Navigator (1394–1460)), initiated a number of reconnaissance missions by both land and sea. The fifteenth century thus became known as Portugal's Age of Discovery. The motivation for Portuguese expansion beyond their tiny kingdom to the far corners of the globe represented a mixture of different aims: an anti-Muslim crusading spirit; a hope for Guinea gold; a search for the mythical priest-king Prester John ruling over a powerful kingdom in 'the Indies'; and a desire for Asian spices.

This last goal assumed greater prominence with the accession of Dom João II in 1481, when Portugal became seriously interested in tapping the sources of the lucrative Asian spice trade. Until this time it had been content, as were other European kingdoms, to purchase Asian spices from the Venetians, who in turn obtained them from the Muslim Mameluke empire in Egypt and Syria. In order to investigate commercial possibilities Dom João sent an agent overland to the Persian Gulf area and the east coast of Africa. It is doubtful, however, whether the agent's report of 1490–1 ever reached Lisbon because Vasco da Gama was unprepared for Calicut's commercial sophistication when he reached the west coast of India by sea in 1498. Elated by da Gama's achievement, Portugal's king announced that he intended to divert the Asian spice trade away from the Muslims by establishing a new spice route around the Cape of Good Hope.

It was with this avowed aim that the Portuguese came to Asia. The principal architect of their expansion in Asia was Afonso de Albuquerque, who became the second Portuguese governor or viceroy of the Estado da India, Portugal's Asian empire. During his tenure of office (1509–15) Albuquerque sought to dominate the key points in the Muslim trading network through which Asian spices reached Europe. With this goal in mind, he seized the island of Goa off the west coast of India in 1510, Melaka in 1511, and Hormuz, at the mouth of the Persian Gulf, in 1515.

As the collecting point for the valuable spices of Maluku in eastern Indonesia, Melaka was a prime target for the Portuguese, and Albuquerque personally led an expedition which succeeded in capturing the city on 10 August 1511. Although Portuguese eyewitness accounts comment on the fierceness of hand-to-hand fighting, Melaka fell after little more than a month's siege. Undoubtedly the superior firepower and military tactics of the Portuguese were decisive factors, but palace factionalism may also have made Melaka particularly vulnerable. According to the *Sejarah Melayu*, rifts within the court deepened when Sultan Mahmud Syah ordered the execution of his bendahara. The unspoken condemnation of his queen, the bendahara's daughter, eventually compelled Sultan Mahmud to abdicate in favour of his son Sultan Ahmad Syah, who was ruling at the time of the attack. With Melaka's fall, both fled into the interior. When it became apparent that the Portuguese had no intention of abandoning their new conquest, the two rulers went their separate ways to Muar and then to Pahang, finally settling on the island of Bintan in the Riau-Lingga archipelago. The extent of the divisions within the Melaka court were evident a short time later, when Sultan Ahmad was murdered at the instigation of his father, who then resumed the throne.

As had been the case a hundred years before in relation to Melaka, Sultan Mahmud's choice of Bintan as the location for a new capital was well calculated. The *Sejarah Melayu* depicts the island as a friendly area, and its sheltered harbour was well suited to the disbursement of cargoes. It was also the home of one of the largest Orang Laut groups in the Riau-Lingga archipelago, who would be able to guide incoming ships through the shallow and sometimes treacherous waters. From this base Sultan Mahmud hoped to oust the Portuguese from Melaka. Though attacks in 1517, 1520 and 1521 were unsuccessful, Orang Laut support made possible the re-establishment of Sultan Mahmud's court and the resumption of trade at the new site. Its success led to a Portuguese punitive expedition which destroyed Bintan in 1526.

With Orang Laut assistance Sultan Mahmud Syah escaped and fled to Kampar in east coast Sumatra, where he subsequently died. He was succeeded by his son, Sultan Alauddin Riayat Syah, who married the sister of Pahang's ruler and at some point between 1530 and 1536 established his royal residence at Pekan Tua in the upper reaches of the Johor River. He therefore became the first of the Melaka dynasty to rule in what became known as the kingdom of Johor. Excavations here in the 1950s recovered evidence of both fortifications and international trade, and projects currently under way may reveal more about the layout of Johor Lama ('old Johor'). Significantly, it seems that in this new environment a process of interaction with local Orang Asli groups occurred, resembling that in Melaka a hundred years earlier. This in turn laid the basis for a relationship that was still apparent in modern times, when some Jakun regarded the Johor ruler with great respect and saw Malay culture as imparting special insight into spiritual matters.

Meanwhile, the Portuguese, who aimed to control maritime trade not only in the Straits but throughout the region, were determined to annihilate their rivals. In Melaka they proclaimed their triumph by evicting Muslim traders and destroying the great mosque. On the same site they built their impressive fort, which they aptly named 'A Formosa', the famous. For nearly a hundred years, relentlessly pursued by the Portuguese fleet, the descendants of the Melaka rulers and their Orang Laut followers were repeatedly forced to seek some safe haven where they could once again begin the task of attracting traders and establishing their credentials.

Responses to the fall of 'Melayu' Melaka: Brunei, Perak and Aceh

So decisive was the Portuguese victory that the fall of Melaka in 1511 has usually been seen as the end of a chapter in Malay history. Attuned to identifying supernatural intervention in any cataclysmic event, many Malays would have seen the Portuguese attack as divine retribution for the ruler's execution of his own son and his injustice to the bendahara. From a modern vantage point, it could be argued that this period represents another episode in the changing fortunes of entrepôt states in the western half of the Indonesian archipelago. In the late thirteenth century a beleaguered Palembang prince had abandoned his former domains for Melaka; now again a prestigious centre was able to reconstitute itself under a new name in another part of its extensive territories. But Johor's assertion of its position did not go unchallenged, for it was not accepted as the automatic heir of Melaka and the Melayu heritage. The very success with which Malay culture had spread meant that a number of ports on both sides of the Straits and beyond could stand as exponents of Malayness. The rivalry that would determine who eventually emerged as the acknowledged Malay leader absorbed the energies of several of the stronger kingdoms for much of the sixteenth century. This rivalry was complicated by the presence of the Portuguese. Several Malay kings proved ready to court the favour of Melaka's new rulers in their bid to enter the lists as contenders for the position of pre-eminent Melayu state.

An example of an emerging claimant to Malay leadership can be seen in Brunei, on the northwest coast of Borneo, an area which was an ideal landfall for ships participating in the China trade and which was apparently well known to sailors at least from the fifth century. Although there is still some debate as to its location, it is generally believed that the place the Chinese called 'Boni' (P'o-ni) was the predecessor of the sixteenth-century kingdom of Brunei. In the early fifteenth century, Boni appears to have been an independent state of some consequence. Envoys were exchanged with China, and in 1405 Boni, like Melaka, became one of only four countries to receive an imperial inscription for the State Mountain. In a special ceremony the ruler of Boni was invested as king with 'a seal, a commission and silks of various colours'. Three years later the ruler even made a personal visit to the imperial court. Missions from Boni to China remained fairly regular until 1425, from which time they became less frequent.

With an extensive hinterland and its own populations of Orang Laut, Boni's successor Brunei was well equipped to service international commerce. Like Melaka, its commerce operated in tandem with the prevailing wind system. Traders bound for Chinese ports on the southwest monsoon could harbour here before resuming their journey, while ships coming from China followed a route to the Vietnam coast and could then sail south to northwest Borneo with the northeast monsoon. Brunei was also an important port of call for Chinese shipping between the northern Philippine Islands and the Sulu archipelago. From Brunei they could return to China or sail to other parts of Southeast Asia on the appropriate monsoon winds.

Having long been a part of the international trading network, Brunei was frequented by Muslim merchants and therefore came into contact with Islamic teachings. The flight from Melaka of Muslim traders and possibly high-ranking Malays after the Portuguese conquest in 1511 also laid the groundwork for Brunei's conversion. Its ruler finally adopted Islam some time between 1514 and 1521. The association between Melayu culture and Islam brought Brunei within the ambience of the Melayu world, although, in a pattern familiar from Srivijaya and Melaka, its early rulers were probably closely related to local groups such as the Bisaya and Muruts. According to Brunei tradition, it was around this period that the sultan of 'Johor' (that is, Melaka) presented the Brunei court with various items of its royal regalia and granted it rights over certain rivers along the northwest coast.

In accepting Islam, Brunei sultans, like other archipelago rulers, gained in prestige, acquired the services of a new religious hierarchy and benefited from increased trade. When the survivors of an expedition led by the Spanish explorer Ferdinand Magellan arrived in Brunei in 1521, they were impressed by the splendour of the court and by evidence that its influence extended northward to Luzon in the northern Philippines. But the consequent establishment of a Spanish post in Cebu in 1565 signalled the beginning of Muslim–Christian rivalry. After the Spaniards conquered Muslim Manila in 1571, they directed their attention southward. Here the potential obstacles to Spanish dreams of control were more formidable because of the protection and support Brunei could offer neighbouring Muslim rulers. The ruler of Sulu, for example, was a vassal of Brunei and had himself originated from that kingdom. In 1578, however, the Spaniards successfully attacked Brunei and installed two officials as puppet rulers. What they found there confirmed earlier sixteenth-century Spanish reports of Brunei's importance. Its ports were patronized by traders from China, Vietnam, Cambodia, Ayudhya, Patani, Pahang, Java, the Moluccas, Mindanao, Sumatra and elsewhere, and religious and commercial links with the southern areas of the Philippines were especially strong.

The Spanish hold on Brunei was soon undermined by European susceptibility to tropical disease. Regarding Brunei as unhealthy, the Spanish abandoned their post there, despite the goal of colonization. None the less, their campaigns in the south did have far-reaching consequences, for they provided Sulu with an opportunity to assert its independence from Brunei. While the latter kingdom revived, maintaining an independent but cautious relationship with Spanish Manila, its political hegemony had been severely curtailed and was now limited to the regions of northern Borneo. Only its position as a vital link in the northern trade route to the Spice Islands assured it a source of revenue and hence the hope of re-establishing its former strength in the area.

The subsequent history of Brunei and northern Borneo in the seventeenth century became closely linked to that of Sulu. Their fortunes had been interwoven even earlier, since together they produced many of the exotic sea and jungle products sought by traders, especially those from China. During its period of dominance, Brunei became the central collecting point for these valued items and thus the focus of international commerce. Sulu later came to challenge Brunei's position, and in the seventeenth century attained the upper hand by intervening in a succession dispute in Brunei. In return for supporting the successful claimant, Sulu obtained suzerainty over the territories north of Brunei Bay. These concessions, which were soon disputed by later Brunei rulers, comprised almost half of Brunei's territories on Borneo. More importantly, they consisted of the coastal waters and the areas along the Marudu, Magindara and Tirun rivers in northeast Borneo which yielded the forest and sea products so much desired by foreign traders. By the eighteenth century the growing economic and political strength of Sulu was clearly seen in the allegiance it could now command from many of the Orang Laut groups formerly responsive to the Brunei court. Brunei, which had seemed ready to claim a new ascendancy after Melaka's fall, had now been eclipsed by its northern neighbour.

Westwards, Johor's claim to be the rightful heir to Melaka was complicated because the extensive network of royal marriages meant several other kingdoms could also trace their descent from the Melaka line. A particular instance was the case of Perak, previously much coveted by both Ayudhya and Melaka because of its extensive tin deposits. Perak's prestige rose considerably when a new dynasty was established by Sultan Muzaffar Syah, a son of Sultan Mahmud Syah, the last ruler of Melaka. In the eyes of some, Sultan Muzaffar was in fact the rightful heir to the Melaka throne, having been designated *raja muda* ('young king', normally given to the next in line) by his father. Sultan Mahmud had subsequently favoured a younger son by another wife. This prince was accorded the title *sultan muda*, and succeeded his father to become Sultan Alauddin Riayat Syah, the first ruler of Johor. In the *Sejarah Melayu*'s account of this episode, the elder prince, Muzaffar, left Melaka and went to Siak and then to Kelang. A trader from Perak invited him to come to Perak, where he was installed as ruler.

This event marked a significant change in Perak's status. No longer was it merely one of the western territories (*rantau barat*) on the fringe of the Melaka empire; it was now a respectable kingdom ruled by a prince from the prestigious Melaka dynasty. The founding of Perak also signified a further extension of Melaka Malay culture, for the reign of Sultan Muzaffar Syah (1528?–1549?) brought not only refugee members of the Melaka court, but also its customs and traditions. Established some 80 kilometres from the mouth of the Perak river, Muzaffar's court was organized following the Melaka model. The influence of Melaka continued under its second ruler, Sultan Mansur Syah (1549?–1577?), who had been raised in the Johor court and was sent back to Perak to rule after his father's death. As part of his policy of extending Perak's boundaries into the mountainous interior, Mansur established his capital further upstream, not far from modern-day Kuala Kangsar.

Slowly wealth began to flow into the new kingdom. By the second half of the sixteenth century, Perak was able to profit from an increasing demand for tin from European traders now filtering into Southeast Asia via the Cape of Good Hope. Tin was not only sent back to Europe but also used as a medium of exchange for the inter-Asian trade. Europeans and Indians began purchasing directly in Perak, encouraging a more extensive mining of the rich alluvial tin deposits along the Perak river and its tributaries. As the market expanded, more people were attracted to participate in the tin mining and to share the state's new-found prosperity. In the early sixteenth century Pires estimated that there were around 200 people in Perak's major settlement, fewer than in nearby Bernam, Beruas and Manjung, but a hundred years later it had grown to a kingdom of some standing with a population numbering more than 5000.

While never sufficiently powerful to rival its stronger neighbours, Perak's prestigious genealogy could not be discounted. Like many other smaller states in the Malay world with little or no pretensions to regional overlordship, its primary concern after Melaka's demise was the preservation of its independence and security. Yet Perak rulers also held firm to the idea that they were guardians of the Melayu heritage. Court manuscripts laid out a genealogy that reached beyond Melaka to Iskandar Zulkarnain and the Palembang heritage, and related how Demang Lebar Daun himself had helped his grandson establish the kingdom. Even in the early nineteenth century one sultan told the British that although his kingdom might be weak and vulnerable, he was descended from the 'ancient race' connected with Bukit Siguntang. As he put it, 'I am the oldest of all the kings in these parts, such as the kings of Siak, Selangor, Riau [i.e. Johor], Kedah and Tereng-ganu'.[9]

Despite these prestigious connections, Perak never harboured any ambitions for economic and political hegemony in the Straits of Melaka. Its relatively small population was scattered over a considerable expanse of often inaccessible terrain, which made it difficult to marshal human resources or impose any form of royal control. Since some of the richest tin veins were located in the remote upstream tributaries of the Perak river, interior chiefs were easily able to avoid royal tolls and retain revenue for themselves. This fragmentation meant that Perak remained basically a collecting point for local products, notably tin, and its rulers never aspired to the status of an international entrepôt like Portuguese Melaka, Johor, or the newly emergent Aceh in north Sumatra.

It was Aceh, in fact, which represented the most serious challenge to Johor and which in different circumstances might well have become a new cradle of Melayu culture. Like Brunei, Aceh had reaped the benefit of Muslim trade following the fall of Melaka. In addition, many scholars from Pasai were attracted after that port was conquered by Aceh in 1524. Aceh soon developed into a wealthy kingdom, able to sponsor Muslim scholars whose erudition was famous throughout the Muslim world. Such scholars played an important role in propagating the Malay language through Malay versions of popular Islamic stories and especially through translations of Arabic and Persian texts. In the Acehnese context the identification of 'Malayness' with Islam was given a new emphasis. A Malay translation of an Arabic work dated 1590, for example, specifically links the concept of *kerajaan* with the application of Islamic law, together with the view that *derhaka* is disobedience not just towards the king but towards God Himself.[10] Although Sultan Iskandar Zulkarnain, (Alexander the Great) had been incorporated into Melaka's royal genealogy, the rulers of Aceh depicted this legendary figure, regarded by Malays as a great Muslim prophet, as the absolute progenitor of their line. This prestigious genealogy was further enhanced through linkages to the royal genealogy of Melaka. Aceh's abortive attempts to capture Melaka in 1558, 1570 and 1575 were followed by an attack on Perak, which may have been motivated by more than a desire to dominate the tin trade. According to a Perak source, the widow of the ruler and her children were brought back to Aceh and her eldest son taken as a husband by the Acehnese queen. Four years later this prince – himself descended from the Melaka line – succeeded to the throne of Aceh and sent his younger brother back to Perak to be installed as ruler.

Relations between Aceh and Perak remained amicable until the early seventeenth century, when Perak's decision to allow the Portuguese to establish a factory and thus gain direct access to its tin supplies met with the disapproval of Aceh's powerful ruler, Sultan Iskandar Muda ('Young Alexander', (1607–36)). His attempt to extend Acehnese authority across the Straits came at a time when Johor, reeling from repeated Portuguese assaults, was quite unable to offer Melaka's former vassals the protection expected of an overlord. Beginning in 1620 Iskandar Muda launched a series of attacks along the east coast of Sumatra; Deli was conquered, and further south Jambi and Palembang readied themselves for an Acehnese onslaught. Though this did not happen, Sultan Iskandar wreaked havoc in Kedah, Perak, Johor and Pahang. In Kedah the ruler fled to Perlis where he placed himself under the protection of Ayudhya. However, his country and capital city were ravished, and about 7000 people brought as slaves to Aceh. Other Malay areas experienced a similar fate, and according to a European observer some 22000 slaves captured in these invasions were taken to Aceh. Of this number only about 1500 survived their ordeal.

Aceh's confidence and its claims to leadership in the Malay world are clearly expressed in the reports and correspondence of English and Dutch traders in the early seventeenth century. The grandeur of Aceh only served to highlight the parlous condition of Johor, while its sponsorship of Malay literature underscored the extent to which the courts of Palembang and Jambi had adopted the language and customs of their Javanese overlord. Aceh's position seemed unassailable, and it is surely no coincidence that this period saw the composition of the famed *Hikayat Aceh*, a celebration of Acehnese achievement. But the failure of Sultan Iskandar Muda to take Portuguese Melaka in 1626 and the massive naval defeat by Portuguese forces in 1629 were a fundamental blow to Aceh's standing. Perak's rulers, for example, displayed progressively greater defiance and were openly hostile to an Acehnese contract with the VOC that gave the latter a monopoly of the tin trade. Eventually the Dutch too turned against Aceh. As we shall see, it was their arrival in the region that was instrumental in enabling Johor to regain much of its former prestige. Though Aceh remained an important place of commerce, from the late seventeenth century the Melayu heritage here was increasingly diluted by a more localized and 'Acehnese' identity.

Thai influence in the northern Malay states

It is significant that an episode in the *Hikayat Aceh* describing the arrival of a Siamese delegation provides an opportunity for the scribe to emphasize Sultan Iskandar Muda's achievements. While Javanese influence was pressing the Malays along the southeast Sumatran coast, in the northern Peninsula the Thai presence was also increasingly evident. Though Ayudhya had laid claims to overlordship in this region since Melaka times, historians believe that the presence of Thai-speaking peoples in the isthmus is a relatively recent occurrence. Beginning perhaps about the seventh century, Thai groups had slowly trickled southwards from their homelands between the upper part of the Mekong river and the tributaries of the Menam river. Though originating from the same general area, they followed different routes and settled in widely scattered areas. These Thai settlements formed the nucleus of independent kingdoms like Sukhothai and Ayudhya which were to emerge in later centuries.

During the thirteenth century princely leaders and their followers migrated southwards from an early Thai state at Phetburi to clear forests, establish ricefields and form organized communities in the isthmus. According to one version of the *Ligor Chronicle*,[11] the Thais then began moving into the Peninsular region, incorporating areas inhabited by Malay-speaking peoples. Two descendants of the Phetburi royal family who became lords of one southern region were responsible for appointing Malays to govern Malay lands now under Thai control. Among the places mentioned in this chronicle are Pahang, Kelantan, Patani and Kedah. Ligor or Nakhon Sithammarat became the major Thai centre in the south through which Ayudhya was able to supervise its Malay vassals. In the early sixteenth century Pires speaks of the 'viceroy' of Ligor who controlled territories from Ayudhya to the Malay Peninsula, including Pahang, Terengganu and Patani, 'all [of which] have lords like kings, some of them Moors [Muslims], some of them heathen'. Each area was required to send about 600 grammes of gold as tribute, the collections being supervised by two Ligor officials. Although Pires also mentions Kelantan, local tradition suggests that in this period Kelantan consisted of two countries. Historians have inferred that the chiefs west of the Kelantan river offered allegiance to Patani, and those east of the river to Terengganu.

From this early period, therefore, Ligor came to exercise a specific form of control over the northern Malay states. A principal reason was its favourable strategic and economic position. In the second half of the thirteenth century, Ligor had already developed into the maritime outlet for the Sukhothai kingdom and was thus well placed for any Thai penetration into the Malay Peninsula. So serious were incursions from Ligor into the Malay areas in the thirteenth century that Srivijaya sought the Chinese emperor's intervention to prevent further Thai aggression. By the mid-fourteenth century, however, Ligor had acknowledged its vassal status to Ayudhya, now the dominant Thai power, whose overlordship of many Malay areas became an established fact. In turn, Ayudhya's ambitions initiated a long period of rivalry with Melaka and later Johor concerning hegemony in the Peninsular region. Melaka was at first willing to recognize Ayudhya's suzerainty in order to obtain both protection against more powerful rivals in the Straits and trade from its wealthy Thai overlord. But although Ayudhya had granted Melaka vassal status, it was apprehensive about the prospects of a new entrepôt in the Straits which could well challenge its own ambitions of becoming a major international trading port. In the early fifteenth century Muslim merchants from the West were already going directly to Ayudhya, auguring well for its commercial future. Delayed by its political manoeuvres against Sukothai, Ayudhya finally launched an attack against Melaka in the mid-fifteenth century in an effort to destroy this budding emporium.

Both Thai and Malay sources mention a major Thai campaign which the *Sejarah Melayu* says was under the command of a provincial lord who led his troops overland through Pahang and cross the Penarikan route to Muar. It seems reasonable to accept the *Sejarah Melayu*'s assertion that the Thais were repulsed, especially since Thai chronicles, though precisely dating the expedition at 1455–6, are silent on the outcome. None the less, Thai aspirations to overlordship in the southern Peninsula were not forgotten, and an Ayudhyan Palatine Law of 1468 alludes to the campaign to justify its purported suzerainty over Melaka. Periodically in later centuries ambitious Thai kings such as Narai (1657–88) and Rama I (1782–1809) revived the old claims.

Ayudhya dispatched no further expeditions to the Peninsula for some years because of its increasing involvement in the affairs of Sukhothai. For the greater part of the fifteenth century these two kingdoms were locked in a struggle for dominance of the Thai-speaking world and could not disperse their scarce resources in a prolonged campaign so far from home. Only during the reign of Sultan Mahmud Syah, the last ruler of Melaka, did the Thais again intervene in the Malay states, apparently responding to Melaka's perceived defiance. Shortly after his accession, Sultan Mahmud attacked Kelantan, one of Ayudhya's vassals, and brought three of its princesses back to Melaka. The challenge to Ayudhya's overlordship apparently did not stop at Kelantan, for the *Ligor Chronicle* mentions an attack in 1497 from 'Ujung Tanah', a term later used for Johor but in this context obviously referring to Melaka.

Other Malay states which recognized the sovereignty of Ayudhya appear to have noted Sultan Mahmud's ambitions and taken appropriate action for their own preservation. According to the *Sejarah Melayu*, a Thai prince defeated a Malay ruler of Patani and became a Muslim in fulfilment of his vow to embrace Islam if given the victory. He then selected a new site for his capital and went to Melaka where he acknowledged Melaka's suzerainty and received in turn from its ruler the *nobat* or 'drums of sovereignty'[12] and the title Sultan Ahmad Syah. The sultan of Kedah likewise requested and received the *nobat* from Sultan Mahmud Syah of Melaka, as well as the traditional robes of honour reserved for individuals the ruler favoured. When the sultan of Pahang died, his successor was installed by a Melaka official sent especially to supervise the beating of the drums of sovereignty during the ceremony.

Despite Ayudhya's preoccupation with Sukhothai, it could not ignore these challenges in the south, and soon retaliated through the medium of its vassal, Ligor. The *Ligor Chronicle* records that in 1500 a Thai force penetrated as far south as Kelantan but soon retreated via Patani because of rumours of yet another invasion of Ligor by Ujung Tanah (that is, Melaka). The *Sejarah Melayu* also records an attack by Ligor on the northeast states which occurred some time prior to the first appearance of the Portuguese in Melaka in 1509. This may have been the same expedition mentioned in the *Ligor Chronicle*, but according to the Malay version the Thai army went beyond Kelantan to Pahang. No further mention is made of Thai involvement in the Malay Peninsula until 1535, some 25 years after the fall of Melaka. In that year, says the *Ligor Chronicle*, the 'enemy' again came from Ujung Tanah. The reference is clearly to Johor, whose forces would have come from the new capital – destroyed by the Portuguese later that same year – in the upper reaches of the Johor river

Ayudhya's continued expansion down the isthmus in the first half of the sixteenth century had thus impinged upon areas that had previously been under Melaka but where Johor, harassed by the Portuguese, was unable to enforce its claims. Although Johor had to accept a temporary extension of Ayudhya's suzerainty into the Peninsula, its ties with Pahang remained close, particularly since several past rulers of Pahang had been princes from the Melaka dynasty. In the late sixteenth century Johor was again able to assert overlordship over Pahang because of Ayudhya's preoccupation with the threat from the Burmese kingdom of Taung-ngu. In 1564 and 1569 Ayudhya was defeated by Taung-ngu, and for the rest of the sixteenth century it was subject to repeated invasions from both Taung-ngu and Cambodia.

Ayudhya's wars with its two neighbours diverted attention from the Malay vassals, with predictable results. Patani, the dominant Malay state in the north, seized the opportunity to attack the weaker Kelantan and extend its own territory. Only with the accession of Narai (1657–88) as ruler of Ayudhya were the Thais able to reimpose their former suzerainty over the northern Malay kingdoms. In applying the traditional overlord–tributary (*prathesaraj*) relationship, they were essentially insisting on Malay recognition of Ayudhya's dominance in a hierarchical and unequal association.

Malay states were periodically willing to accept Thai conditions, since protection from a powerful and prestigious Ayudhya enhanced their status and offered some guarantee against an outside attack. Nevertheless, there was a price. When Ayudhya was strong, it was more likely to demand subservience from its Malay vassals, and also more likely to challenge its own traditional enemies – Burma, Cambodia and Vietnam. The prolonged warfare which resulted meant that Ayudhya's tributaries, whether in Lower Burma, Laos or the Malay Peninsula, were expected to demonstrate their loyalty by willingly dispatching men, food and weapons to service Ayudhya's large armies. Even in times of peace Malay states found the tribute demanded by Ayudhya was considerable. Submitted triennially, this tribute was known collectively as the *bunga mas dan perak*, 'the gold and silver flowers'. It consisted of two small trees, meticulously fashioned from gold and silver, and standing about a metre high. Accompanying the trees were other costly gifts, weapons, cloth and slaves for both the ruler of Ayudhya and the provincial governor at Ligor, who was in charge of escorting the tribute to the Thai capital. Although the value of the *bunga mas* in earlier times is uncertain, its total worth in the nineteenth century was in the vicinity of 1000 Spanish dollars.

The necessary funds for the *bunga mas* were raised by the imposition of a poll tax, which local chiefs, both Malay and Thai, at times abused to enrich their own coffers. But even prompt payment of the *bunga mas* did not relieve the Malay states of their vassal obligations. Ligor, Ayudhya's principal administrative centre in the south, could and did demand burdensome corvée duties and tributary gifts. In 1821, for example, an English envoy to the Thai court remarked that Kelantan, Patani, Kedah and even Pahang had contributed to the cost of constructing a great Buddhist reliquary in Ligor. Thus, while Malay court chronicles gloss over the deep resentment which Thai overlordship aroused among the peasants, it is small wonder that at the village level tales abound of the greed of Thai kings.

Little is known of the origin of the *bunga mas dan perak*, or its precise significance. Although the practice is found elsewhere in Southeast Asia – Perak, for example, had sent 'gold and silver trees' to Aceh in the seventeenth century – this form of tribute became particularly associated with Thai over-lordship. Terengganu Malays attribute the first sending of the golden flowers to the late eighteenth century when the king's own merchant suggested this as a suitable present for the Thai king. In Kelantan, too, the custom appears relatively recent, and a Thai chronicle notes that tribute had only been sent regularly since the early nineteenth century.[13] In Kedah and Patani, however, it had become an established custom around 200 years earlier. According to one legend recounted in a Kedah court text, the *Hikayat Marong Mahawangsa*, the royal families of Kedah and *negeri Siam* (that is, Ayudhya) had in the past been closely related; the *bunga mas*, originally sent as a gift from the Kedah court, was intended as a plaything for a Thai prince. But whereas Ayudhya saw the dispatch of the *bunga mas* as Malay recognition of its suzerainty, a seventeenth-century Kedah ruler claimed that it was a demonstration of friendship and alliance rather than an acknowledgement of vassal status. When Ayudhya was weak, some Malay kings delayed sending the *bunga mas*, perhaps for several years. But at the first sign of a revival of Thai power, missions were quickly dispatched with the *bunga mas* for their overlord. Had it not been for Dutch intervention, in the late seventeenth century even Jambi in Sumatra would have offered Siam the *bunga mas*. This unique practice was only ended with the extension of British control over most of the northern Malay states in 1909.

The great strength of the Thai–Malay relationship was the mutual understanding that, however onerous Thai demands might be, the Malays would be left to conduct their own affairs and be treated with the respect due to independent kings, not simply provincial governors. In 1645 when the Kedah ruler was uncharacteristically summoned several times to Ayudhya, he feigned illness and did not go. It would have been humiliating for a Malay ruler to have submitted to the prostration ceremony customary at the Thai court and demanded of all other vassals. But rather than sending an army to punish the Kedah ruler, the king of Ayudhya found an acceptable solution by sending a statue of himself to Kedah with instructions that the entire court should pay it homage twice daily.

Ayudhya was thus willing to allow Malay kings to rule with minimum interference as long as they duly submitted their tribute. This factor, combined with their distance from the Thai capital, allowed Ayudhya's Malay vassals considerable political flexibility. In effect, they were able to operate within two distinct geopolitical spheres, each with different sets of rules. One sphere was that of Ayudhya, where certain obligations were demanded in return for protection and patronage, and where unwritten rules governing interaction between overlord and vassal helped define unacceptable demands by the one or intolerable defiance by the other. The other sphere was that of the Malay world itself, where relationships were expressed in terms of kinship, but where a more equal status encouraged constant vying for greater prestige in the area. And though the Thai influence that was absorbed into local Malay customs and dialects attests the dexterity with which the northern Malay states moved between these spheres, their position between two cultural worlds was not without its complications. These are well illustrated in the history of Patani.

The gradual extension of Thai control during the nineteenth century and Patani's incorporation into Siam proper in 1909 often lead modern historians to overlook its role as another node of Melayu culture and a leader in Malay resistance when Thai overlordship proved onerous. During the latter part of the sixteenth century Patani had been relatively free from Thai restraints and developed into an important trading centre, drawing considerable wealth from local commerce in pepper, gold and foodstuffs. Unchallenged by any other Malay kingdom, Patani was able to assume a prominent place in Malay affairs. Aceh was only beginning to emerge as a major power in the Straits, and Johor had been effectively checked by the Portuguese in Melaka. Through marriage between a Patani princess and a Pahang ruler, Patani became increasingly involved with Pahang and through Pahang with Johor. By 1620 marriage alliances and practical politics had pushed Patani to attempt a balance between the influence of Ayudhya and Johor by endeavouring to maintain friendly relations with both.

In 1628, however, the outbreak of disturbances in Ayudhya coincided with threats of an invasion by Aceh, which had already attacked Pahang. In this situation Patani's court decided to link its fortunes firmly with Johor. Raja Ungu, queen of Patani (1623–35), refused to follow customary practice and use the Thai title *chao phraya*, which Ayudhya normally bestowed on a high-ranking vassal. She also provoked Ayudhya by marrying her daughter Raja Kuning to the ruler of Johor, although the princess's former husband, a Thai officer (probably the eldest son of the governor of Ligor) was apparently still alive. When a Thai prince, Prasat Thong, usurped the throne of Ayudhya in 1630 he met open defiance from Patani, which attacked Ligor and Phattalung. Ayudhya did not react immediately to these challenges because it was preoccupied by problems with Cambodia, Burma, and the Japanese community in Ayudhya itself. Finally in 1634 a Thai punitive expedition of some 30 000 troops was sent, whereupon Patani sought and received help from the Malay kingdoms in the south, including 50 ships and 5000 men from Johor and Pahang. Patani and its Malay allies succeeded in repulsing the invaders, but another Thai expedition was under way when Raja Ungu died. Her successor prudently sought the mediation of the ruler of Kedah in order to bring about a reconciliation with Ayudhya. Prasat Thong accepted this peace offer, and subsequently Patani resumed its *bunga mas dan perak* tribute to Ayudhya, while its new ruler, Raja Kuning, once again assumed the Thai title of *chao phraya*. However, Patani's ties with Johor were also undergoing some strain, despite Raja Kuning's marriage to the younger brother of the Johor ruler. The increasing arrogation of power by the Johor prince and his entourage aroused so much disaffection in the Patani court that in 1645 the nobles instigated a massacre of many of the Johor people, including the prince's mother. A mission of reconciliation sent to Johor by Patani towards the end of that year averted war, but relations between the two states remained cool.

Patani's history exemplifies the dilemma faced by the northern Malay states. The very independence permitted by Thai overlordship often tempted Malay rulers to repudiate some of their vassal obligations, in turn incurring harsh retribution. The relationship between Thai and Malay kingdoms was thus never static, but was constantly undergoing reassessment according to historical circumstances. Even so, the northern Malay states during this period were never able to conduct their affairs with the independence and confidence of the other Malay kingdoms further south. Johor, for example, was able to seize the new opportunities presented in the seventeenth-century Malay world and by this means become the most powerful state in the Straits of Melaka. In so doing it reasserted its claim to be the heir of Melaka and all that the Melaka heritage implied.

The Dutch and Johor's ascendancy

Although historians have been divided about the emphasis that should be accorded the Dutch presence in the Straits of Melaka, there is no doubt it served to redirect historical events. In part this was because so much was at stake in the Dutch enterprise. The appearance of the first Dutch trading ships at Banten in west Java towards the end of the sixteenth century was simply one facet of Dutch commercial activities that were expanding to the Mediterranean, the Levant, the South Atlantic and the Indian Ocean. The profits gained from the sale of pepper obtained at Banten spurred the development of a number of trading companies in the various Dutch port cities. But it soon became evident that the rivalry among these companies was commercially damaging, and in 1602 they were amalgamated into the United Netherlands Chartered East India Company, often referred to as the VOC (Vereenigde Oostindische Compagnie). In its charter the VOC was given wide-ranging sovereign powers, such as the right to enter into treaties and alliances, wage war, levy troops, erect forts and appoint governors and judicial officers. These powers, coupled with a substantial operating capital and the blessings of Dutch government leaders, many of whom were Company directors as well, made the VOC a formidable organization in Asia. In the last quarter of the seventeenth century the Company was further strengthened by its decision to retain a percentage of its profits in Asia. This financial resource was used judiciously at selected times and places to ensure a continuing maximization of returns on various commercial ventures. Overseeing this vast trading empire in Asia was the VOC's Supreme Government, composed of the governor-general and the Council of the Indies based in Batavia (present-day Jakarta). Founded in 1619, Batavia became the nerve centre of the VOC in Asia, assimilating reports from various outposts and factories and making decisions

71

based on the interests of the Dutch trading network as a whole rather than on the immediate concerns of any individual area.

It was Johor which was to draw greatest benefit from the association with the Dutch, and its position in the Malay world improved in almost direct proportion to the growing influence of the VOC. From the first contact at the beginning of the seventeenth century, Johor saw the Dutch as a potential ally against its two most hated enemies, Aceh and the Portuguese. For nearly a hundred years it had suffered from devastating raids by both these powers as they aspired to dominate economic and political affairs in the Melaka Straits. It seems that the Dutch were well aware of Johor's desire to reclaim its former standing in the Malay world. As early as 1606 the VOC and Johor negotiated an alliance whereby the Dutch would control Melaka, while Johor would control the Riau-Lingga archipelagos and surrounding islands. Though subsequent attacks on Melaka (in 1606, 1608 and 1615) were unsuccessful, Malay expectations of a return to their ancient capital may have motivated the compilation of a new text of the *Sejarah Melayu* that accorded particular attention to genealogical links through Melaka to the semi-divine ancestor of all Malay rulers. The doyen of Malay studies, Sir Richard Winstedt, even argued that the scribe deliberately omitted references which might have emphasized the Perak line.

In 1636 the death of Aceh's aggressive ruler, Sultan Iskandar Muda, opened up further opportunities for Johor. The new Acehnese ruler was ambivalent about joining the Dutch in attacking Portuguese Melaka, and, in search of a local ally, the VOC again turned to Johor. Their siege of Melaka commenced in August 1640 and ended successfully in January 1641. Although Johor's forces did not participate in any major fighting, they played an important supporting role in transporting material, constructing batteries and trenches, preventing the enemy from fleeing into the jungle and, most importantly, in lifting sagging Dutch morale at a very crucial time during the siege. In 1643 Governor-General Antonio van Diemen, writing to the VOC directors, clearly expressed this sense of indebtedness: 'We must continue to remember that the Johor people contributed substantially towards the conquest of Melaka. Without their help we would never have become master of that strong place.'[14]

The *Hikayat Hang Tuah*, the best-known version of which probably dates from the seventeenth century, presents a Utopian picture in which Malays and Dutch jointly governed in Melaka. While this may represent a thwarted dream rather than actual fact, Johor was indeed able to re-emerge as the foremost patron of Malay culture, primarily because of the new prosperity it now enjoyed. In acknowledgement of its assistance, the Dutch granted Johor certain trading privileges at Melaka which were denied all other local kingdoms. They also assured Johor of protection against its great rival, Aceh. Through Dutch mediation Johor and Aceh signed a peace treaty in 1641 in which the two powers agreed that 'each occupy his own kingdom ... and all hostile actions be stopped'. The VOC conquest of Melaka and its involvement in local politics thus meant that Johor was freed from Portuguese and Acehnese threats which had plagued it for more than a century. Shortly afterwards a bolder Johor removed Aceh's presence from Pahang and again reasserted its control there. With renewed vigour and a revived sense of purpose, Johor's status in the Malay world continued to rise. Attracted by the greater variety of goods and cheaper prices, traders flocked to Johor, while Dutch Melaka soon became simply one of a number of archipelago ports helping to fuel the bustling Johor entrepôt. Dutch officials in Melaka continually begged Batavia to destroy Johor so that Melaka's trade could revive, but their pleas were rejected. The VOC leaders had already decided to make Batavia the centre of all economic operations in the Company's vast Asian trading network. Melaka's task was henceforth to be a guardpost protecting shipping through the Straits and not an international emporium as it had been in the past.

Johor soon realized that the VOC's wider interests would override Melaka's parochial concerns, and regularly sent missions directly to Batavia whenever there was a difference of opinion with Dutch officials in Melaka. In Batavia its envoys subtly indicated that any Dutch punitive measures against Johor would result in the flight of the court and re-establishment at another site, probably in the islands among its Orang Laut subjects. From here the Orang Laut would be sent to harass ships passing through the Straits and to divert them from Dutch ports. Apprehensive of such a prospect, Batavia often sided with Johor at Melaka's expense.

Although Johor's revival was due in part to the benefits accruing from its alliance with the Dutch, there were other Malay kingdoms which had recognized the significance of the new regional alignments. Within a year of the conquest of Melaka, nearly all Malay rulers in the Straits area had sent congratulatory letters to the VOC, and victories over Aceh further enhanced Dutch standing. In some cases the possibility of friendship with a militarily powerful ally compensated for the restrictions of VOC monopoly contracts. In Perak, where the connection with Aceh had fallen away, a small faction within the court argued that a Dutch contract would provide protection against the ambitious Ayudhya ruler, Narai (1657–88), whose demands were already being felt in Kedah. The Dutch themselves were anxious to pursue this because of their hope of acquiring a monopoly of Perak's tin. Rumours of an imminent Thai invasion in 1674 and 1677 made Perak more receptive to the re-establishment of a Dutch post on Pangkor Island, opposite the Dinding river. But as soon as the danger from the north diminished, opposition to VOC commercial controls resurfaced. In 1685 and again in 1689 attacks were made on the Dutch and their employees, and consequently the VOC withdrew its garrison. It says much for the lure of Perak's tin that the VOC was still willing to negotiate a new contract. When agreement with the Perak nobles proved impossible, ties with the Dutch were essentially severed for another 50 years.

Across the Straits, in another former locus of Malay culture, Jambi also saw opportunities in a Dutch alliance. Having thrown off Javanese overlordship, emboldened by a new prosperity derived from its pepper trade, and supported by their own Orang Laut fleets, Jambi's rulers clearly felt their star was in the ascendant. But the VOC was not anxious to become involved in Johor–Jambi rivalry and did not interfere when war broke out between them in 1673. The frustration of Jambi ambitions redounded to the fortune of Johor, whose success and enhanced position can be traced less to VOC influence than to the services of its powerful ministers and their families, especially that of the laksamana.

The influence wielded by individual ministers, which had been very obvious in Malay Melaka, was made possible because Malay conceptions of statecraft envisioned the ruler as remaining above the mundane affairs of state while his ministers were responsible for the actual administration. Their position as mediators between the ruler and the world beyond the court allowed great scope for personal aggrandizement and in periods of crisis ministers frequently assumed considerable authority. In the seventeenth-century version of the *Sejarah Melayu*, the activities of the bendahara overshadow all other ministers, indicating that it may have been commissioned by a member of that family. Nonetheless, the importance of the laksamana's office cannot be ignored, especially in times of war, for it was he who commanded the Orang Laut fleets so vital for the defence of the kingdom. The closeness of the laksamana–Orang Laut association is suggested by the legend that Hang Tuah, the most famous laksamana in Malay folklore, was himself of Orang Laut background.

The laksamana family rose to prominence in the sixteenth century during the dislocation resulting from the Portuguese conquest of Melaka when Johor was repeatedly forced to move its capitals because of attacks from Aceh and the Portuguese. Led by the laksamana, the Orang Laut were responsible for establishing Johor's ruler at a new site and then redirecting trade to its port. In so doing, they ensured the preservation of the kingdom and the international trade which was its lifeblood. Not surprisingly, on numerous occasions a new capital was located among the islands of the Riau-Lingga archipelagos in the Orang Laut heartland. Under these circumstances, the laksamana's duties became far more vital to the kingdom than those of the bendahara.

The individual perhaps most responsible for Johor's rise in the seventeenth century was Laksamana Tun Abdul Jamil, who succeeded his father some time in the 1640s. The opportunity to serve his kingdom while furthering his own ambitions came following an attack by Jambi on Johor, and the destruction of the capital on the Johor river in 1673. Sultan Abdul Jalil (1623–77) took refuge in Pahang, but instructed the laksamana to re-establish the kingdom. It was the laksamana, therefore, working from a secure base among Johor's Orang Laut in Riau, who succeeded in wreaking vengeance on Jambi, restoring Johor's status in the Malay world, and establishing his family in the most influential positions in the kingdom.

None the less, the wars with Jambi had taken their toll, for the razing of Johor's capital weakened its authority over its dependencies, especially the

Minangkabau-settled areas around Melaka. In capturing Melaka, the Dutch also claimed authority over nearby Naning, but adjacent districts such as Rembau were increasingly indifferent to Johor's overlordship. This assertion of independence became more evident from 1667, when the VOC forcibly eliminated the control of Aceh on both the east and west coast of Sumatra. As a result, the long-bridled traffic from the Sumatran interior to the east coast began to expand as Minangkabau traders brought their gold, pepper and tin down the rivers of Jambi, Siak, Rokan, Kampar and Inderagiri to the foreign ships in the downstream ports. Within a short time large numbers of Minangkabau began to move eastward into the *rantau* (areas of Minang-kabau settlement outside their heartland in central Sumatra). The expansion of existing Minangkabau settlements in Naning, Rembau and Sungai Ujung was a logical development; indeed, the Sumatra–Peninsula connections were so close that an area in upstream Jambi was even termed 'little Melaka'.

Growing Minangkabau migration to the Straits in the second half of the seventeenth century coincided with a renewed vigour within the Pagar-ruyung court, the Minangkabau capital in the mountains of central Sumatra. With both the east and west coasts of Sumatra freed from Aceh's control, Pagarruyung's spiritual influence over its subjects was restored. During the late seventeenth and early eighteenth centuries, Pagarruyung was often invoked by Minangkabau leaders to impart legitimacy to their cause and to attract support from all Minangkabau in the *rantau*.

The strength of these Minangkabau links provided an important focus of solidarity as areas drawn into the VOC orbit fretted against Dutch demands for taxes and the imposition of trading restrictions. In 1677 Sungai Ujung, Naning and Rembau collectively requested a representative from their spiritual Minangkabau overlord at Pagarruyung to rule the three settlements as one entity. But although it is understandable that this repres-entative, known as Raja Ibrahim, should be readily acknowledged by Minangkabau migrants, other groups long exposed to Minangkabau-Malay traditions were equally ready to accept him as leader. While Minang-kabau were considered to have access to magical skills that could even tame wild tigers, Raja Ibrahim was also invested with the extraordinary powers associated with his Pagarruyung overlord, such as the ability to produce a bountiful harvest. So great was his appeal that numerous Orang Laut were willing to join 3700 Minangkabau in an abortive attack on Melaka. For the first time in the history of Minangkabau settlement on the Malay Peninsula, a broad-based Minangkabau movement had appeared, one which was now directed against the alien Europeans.

Raja Ibrahim was the most successful of a succession of Minangkabau leaders who appealed to the migrants of Rembau, Sungai Ujung and Naning on the basis of their common culture and overlord in Pagarruyung. Mean-while, another Minangkabau ruler in upriver Inderagiri was urging his people to rise against the Dutch. However, the two Minangkabau causes were never co-ordinated, and Raja Ibrahim was forced to broaden his search for allies. He therefore called on all fellow Muslims to combine in a holy war (*jihad*) against the infidel Dutch, hoping to attract the support of Bugis and Makassar settlers in nearby Kelang. But these migrant groups, whose origins lay in distant Sulawesi, found little compelling in the invocation of the Bukit Siguntang ancestry. Nor did the summons of Islam prove sufficient to overcome the Bugis/Makassar suspicion of Minangkabau intentions. In the event, even the Minangkabau themselves did not support Raja Ibrahim wholeheartedly, and in 1678 he was murdered, apparently by a Bugis in the pay of some people from Rembau. With Raja Ibrahim's death, any possibility of a coalition between the Minangkabau settlements on the Malay Peninsula faded, and shortly afterwards they reverted to their Malay and Dutch over-lords.

Although the Bugis and Makassar settlements had not responded to Raja Ibrahim's call, the Dutch were concerned at the increasing numbers of Bugis/Makassar migrants from south Sulawesi fleeing from the civil wars in their homeland. The VOC alliance with several Bugis leaders from Bone and Soppeng and their defeat of neighbouring Goa in 1669 led to a wave of refugees from the vanquished kingdom and its allies. Wars continued to plague south Sulawesi for the next decade, and the unrelenting overlordship of the Bugis prince Arung Palakka and the VOC further contributed to a steady outflow of people seeking refuge. Moving westwards, bands of Bugis and Makassar led by some prince or noble began settling in Java, Jambi and Palembang. Here they frequently came into conflict with local authorities, and subsequently Bugis leaders preferred uninhabited lands where they could be guaranteed a certain amount of autonomy. The southwest and east coasts of Borneo and the sparsely populated but economically valuable tin areas of Selangor, Kelang and Linggi on the Peninsula suited them admirably, and it was here that pockets of Bugis/Makassar settlements began to grow.

In the late seventeenth century, Johor had become the pre-eminent power in the Straits and felt little threatened by the small Bugis and Makassar communities which had sprung up in its Peninsular dependencies. Through the perseverance of the skilled laksamana, it had succeeded in wreaking vengeance on Jambi and restoring Johor's trade and prestige in the Malay world. So powerful had the laksamana become that Sultan Ibrahim, who succeeded Sultan Abdul Jalil in 1677, was wary of his influence. Accordingly, the new ruler initiated steps to curtail the laksamana's authority by encouraging other nobles to take a more active role in the kingdom's affairs. Only Ibrahim's unexpected death in 1685 prevented a potentially dangerous confrontation. But by the time the five-year-old ruler, Sultan Mahmud Syah, came to the throne, the laksamana's family was securely ensconced in power. The young ruler sat on the lap of his mother, the laksamana's daughter, and was surrounded by the laksamana and his six sons, who all held important posts.

The laksamana family appeared unassailable, but its strength was dependent on its ability to demonstrate that it was governing on behalf and with the blessings of the ruler. Sultan Ibrahim's death, under extremely suspicious circumstances, eliminated the only potential challenge to the influence of the laksamanas for nearly a century. The succession of a child ruler under the tutelage of the laksamana family seemed to reinforce its position as guardian and yet servant of the king. But the other nobles and the bendahara family understood full well the reasons for the influence of the laksamana and took measures to undermine it. One fateful day they snatched away the young ruler, breaking the association between him and the laksamana and demonstrating to the Orang Laut that the supposedly all-powerful minister no longer had royal sanction. This move was sufficient to draw the Orang Laut away from the laksamana to the camp of the plotting bendahara and nobles. Within a day the laksamana family had to flee to safety, bereft of their armed following and the authority which they had so long wielded. Though some of the laksamana's sons escaped to Patani, the laksamana himself died fighting.

The demise of the laksamana family saw the restoration of established roles within Johor. The offices formerly held by the laksamana's sons once again reverted to the nobles, while the bendahara assumed his traditional position as the principal minister of the kingdom and rightful role as regent for the young ruler. During this regency period, Sultan Mahmud remained quietly in the background. But with the death of the bendahara towards the end of the century and with Sultan Mahmud's coming of age in 1695, there were noticeable changes in Johor. The new bendahara, Tun Abdul Jalil, was unable either to control the excesses of Sultan Mahmud and the atrocities he committed against his subjects, or to direct royal attention to matters of government. With no leadership from the capital, the Orang Laut began to prey on passing ships for their own profit. The lack of security in the Straits and the absence of leadership in Johor led to a sharp decline in Johor's international trade. Fearing further cruel or unpredictable actions by Sultan Mahmud, and resenting their loss of revenue as trade in Johor's ports dwindled, the nobles finally felt impelled to act.

The nobles' decision to end the life of Sultan Mahmud was made with deliberation and yet with apprehension. Despite the Sultan's cruel and unjust deeds, court traditions firmly upheld the view that only God Almighty could punish rulers, especially those descended from the Palembang-Melaka dynastic line. But as Sultan Mahmud, borne on a servant's shoulders, passed through the market on the way to the mosque, one of the nobles stabbed him. No sooner had he fallen to the ground than he was set upon by the other plotters and killed. This regicide in 1699 undermined a very basic assumption about the relationship between Malay rulers and their subjects, and also severed the bonds of allegiance that had bound the Orang Laut to all previous rulers of the Melaka dynasty.

From the establishment of Melaka at the beginning of the fifteenth century until the assassination of Johor's Sultan Mahmud in 1699, Malay kingdoms had operated very much in the tradition of Srivijaya and earlier ports along the Straits of Melaka. Attracting international commerce was crucial for the continuing well-being of such kingdoms, and the whole governmental apparatus and rationale for rule were therefore directed towards the smooth functioning of trade. The memories of a mighty kingdom in Palembang served as an inspiration to Melaka, whose founders appear to have been well versed in the requirements of an entrepôt, prompting one scholar to remark that 'Melaka was founded as, rather than developed into, a trading port'.[15]

While Melaka established new standards for Malay achievement, its fall to the Portuguese in 1511 brought a reversion to the situation which had followed the demise of Srivijaya. Smaller states enjoyed a period of political and economic independence rarely possible under a strong regional overlord, but more powerful kingdoms along both sides of the Straits and even beyond sought to strengthen their claims as entrepôts. The stakes were high, for although Melaka retained a special status, the assimilatory aspects of Malay culture meant that a number of states could lay claim to be patrons of Malayness. Furthermore, unlike the earlier period, there were now two new actors on the scene: the Portuguese and the Dutch, both seeking to dominate trade in the area. Despite the considerable power they exercised, at the end of the seventeenth century these newcomers were still unable to monopolize trade in the same way that Melaka and Srivijaya had previously done. Yet their restrictive practices, plus the restraints placed on the Malay states by their ambitious Thai neighbours, served to prevent the rise of another Malay kingdom which could emulate its great predecessors. Certainly, as Aceh's star waned, and as other claimants were eclipsed, Johor could proclaim its direct links to Melaka, and it did succeed for a time in becoming a port of importance. However, the regicide in 1699 changed the nature of power in Johor and made it vulnerable to new external pressures which came to redirect the entire course of Malay history in the eighteenth century.

Chapter 3 . . . .

The Demise of the Malay Entrepôt State, 1699–1819

The decline in Johor's standing in the Malay world after the events of 1699 led to the rise of a number of newly independent states, several of which had been vassals of the old Johor. No kingdom emerged immediately as a dominant force in the Straits, able to maintain a degree of order in regional trade and politics, and to take on a leading role as exemplar of Malay culture. Without an acknowledged overlord, individual states now had greater freedom in seeking their own political and economic goals. To nineteenth-century observers, however, a situation where various rulers were attempting to assert their independence or supremacy appeared 'chaotic' and symptomatic of the 'decay' besetting the Malay world. It was therefore with the claim of 'restoring order' to the area that the British came to justify their intervention in Malay affairs. But an examination of events in the Malay world in the eighteenth century indicates that such rationalization ignores the cyclical pattern of alternating unity and fragmentation which had characterized Malay-Indonesian commerce and politics for well over 1000 years.

The eighteenth century: historiographical considerations

The primary source material for the eighteenth century, both European and Malay, is unevenly distributed, and some areas are particularly ill-served. The history of the east coast Peninsular states may never be adequately reconstructed because of the paucity of both of European trading records and relevant Malay texts. Events in what is now Sabah and Sarawak are even more obscure. Court dynastic lists from Brunei, the nominal overlord in the area, and isolated commentaries by Western visitors convey only a broad outline of developments. In the early eighteenth century the Spanish renewed their efforts to subdue and Christianize the southern Philippines, but were never successful. The rising economic and political power in the northern

Borneo region was the sultanate of Sulu, which continued to expand in response to both the Spanish advance and to Brunei's decline. Conflicts between the Brunei ruler and some of his nobles had earlier resulted in Sulu's control over the northeast coast of modern Sabah, while Brunei itself slowly relinquished authority over the Bajaus, the local sea people, and lapsed into a collection of riverine territories ruled by semi-autonomous chiefs. The inadequacy of written sources from northwest Borneo in this period has frustrated Western-trained historians, who have only recently begun to develop methodologies that incorporate indigenous oral material like the chanted genealogies of the Sarawak Ibans. It is a sobering fact, however, that opportunities to access this material are already disappearing as traditions which contribute to the retention of local memories retreat before the forces of modernization.

When we turn to Johor and the west coast of the Peninsula, we find that a basic chronology is still provided by VOC records, supplemented towards the end of the century by those from the English East India Company (EIC) from their bases in India and the island of Penang. Though more limited in scope and detail than those of the Dutch, they have been particularly valuable in the reconstruction of the history of Kedah and adjacent areas. There are also several works written in Malay. Frequent reference will be made to the *Tuhfat al-Nafis* (The Precious Gift), written in the mid-nineteenth century by Raja Ali Haji, a Riau prince of Bugis descent whose aim was to explain the relationship between his Bugis forebears 'and the kings of Johor and Sumatra'. Another text from Siak, which has been called the *Siak Chronicle*, gives a different view of events as perceived by the Malays of east Sumatra, with their strong Minangkabau links. Added to these are notebooks of daily happenings in the Johor court, collections of treaties signed with the Dutch, and compilations of customary laws. In the eighteenth century one Perak ruler commissioned a court work, the *Misa Melayu*, and fragments of texts and recorded legends have also survived from Selangor and Kedah. Certainly many valuable manuscripts have been lost, and many questions remain about life outside the courts, which are the focus of Malay and European sources alike. Nonetheless, enough remains for the modern historian to discuss the political history of Johor and the west coast during this period with some confidence.

The consequences of regicide in Johor

One striking feature is the degree to which so many of these sources, whether indigenous or European, confirm the shattering effects of Sultan Mahmud's murder in late July or August 1699. A hundred years afterwards a Dutchman was told that Malays considered Mahmud the last direct descendant of Raja Iskandar Zulkarnain (Alexander the Great) and Seri Teri Buana, the prince who had miraculously appeared on Bukit Siguntang in Palembang. He was therefore remembered as Sultan Berdarah Putih, the King of the White Blood, to distinguish him from his successors who lacked this same evidence of true royalty. Even a nineteenth-century Thai chronicle considers the death of Mahmud to be a momentous event, for after that 'his lineage disappeared and was never heard of again'.[1]

At the time, eyewitnesses informed the Dutch that the assassination had been carried out by a group of nobles, which included the bendahara. Malay histories single out the individual responsible for the fatal blow, a man called Megat Seri Rama whose pregnant wife had been disembowelled at Sultan Mahmud's orders. But though contemporary European accounts corroborate Malay texts in describing the Johor ruler as a vindictive sadist, Malays found the regicide difficult to condone; it was, after all, *derhaka*, treason, which merited the most terrible of punishments. According to the *Siak Chronicle*, Megat Seri Rama was struck on the foot by the ruler's spear. Because of *daulat*, the spiritual powers associated with kingship, grass began to sprout in the wound, and for four years Megat Seri Rama suffered agony before he finally died. The text goes on to describe how one of the nobles denounces those guilty of murder and delivers an impassioned speech, reiterating a subject's duties and the obedience he owes his lord. But his words go unheeded, and he is killed. The most vehement condemnation of the regicide came from the rulers of Palembang and Perak, who shared with the kings of Melaka-Johor a common tradition of descent from the sacred princes of Bukit Siguntang. They appealed to the VOC to wreak vengeance upon those responsible for this heinous crime, but to no avail.

The gravity of the deed was accentuated because the assassinated Sultan Mahmud had no direct heirs, thus enabling the conspirators to appoint a new ruler. In September 1699 the bendahara was chosen as ruler of Johor with the title Sultan Abdul Jalil Syah. Some texts attempt to justify this by pointing out that the kings and bendaharas of Johor had intermarried and that custom decreed a bendahara should succeed if there were no suitable royal princes. Other manuscripts invoke the Islamic ruling that it is permissible to depose an insane ruler. But Malay society, imbued for centuries with concepts of the divine status of the kings of Bukit Siguntang, could not easily accept the changed order. Nowhere was the animosity towards the new regime greater than among the Orang Laut, whose role in Melaka and Johor had been traditionally linked to their special relationship with the ruling dynasty. Several groups now claimed that 'there were no more descendants of the old royal house [that is, of Bukit Siguntang] and therefore there could no longer be a ruler of Johor'. Others said publicly that they would rather serve the sultan of Palembang than a usurper, and there were even rumours of an Orang Laut invasion of Johor. But despite their initial revulsion, most Orang Laut groups realized that they would have to reconcile themselves to the new regime or be excluded from the influential association they had maintained with the Melaka-Johor kingdom for over 300 years. Although the majority of Orang Laut eventually resumed their former functions under the bendahara dynasty, their ties with it were always tenuous.

Elsewhere in Johor territory the legitimacy of the bendahara line was also challenged. In the ensuing years revolts continually disturbed the peace along the east coast of Sumatra, in Deli, Rokan, Batu Bahara and Inderagiri, and in Johor's Peninsular dependencies of Selangor, Kelang and Rembau. Inevitably this disturbed situation discouraged commerce, and VOC officials noted with pleasure the degree to which Dutch Melaka had benefited from traders seeking an alternative market. Added to these internal troubles came news of Ayudhya's advance down the Peninsula in 1709. Temporarily halted at Patani, the Thai army invaded Johor's dependency of Terengganu in the following year. Johor made preparations for a possible attack, but fortunately Ayudhya's forces were withdrawn and deployed eastwards because of Vietnamese incursions into Cambodia. Nonetheless, Ayudhya remained a potential danger. The new regime in Johor was thus confronted with the task of rebuilding a state which was divided from within and threatened from without. One of the first steps it took under the dynamic leadership of Sultan Abdul Jalil's brother, the raja muda, was to move the capital away from the Johor river to the island of Bintan (more commonly termed Riau), the home of those Orang Laut groups who had returned to serve the new regime. Here the raja muda began to re-create an entrepôt, exploiting Johor's privileged status with the Dutch, a result of their 1641 alliance, to divert trade away from Melaka. VOC officials looked with envy towards the port of Riau, which became a magnet for Chinese junks and was crowded with 'Moors, Armenians, English, Danes, Portuguese and other nations'. In the words of the *Tuhfat al-Nafis*, 'Johor prospered, and was famed not only for the refinement of its customs, but also for its culture [*bahasa*]'.[2]

Johor's ability to revive an entrepôt economy so rapidly in the wake of regicide is a tribute both to the determination of its leaders and its long experience in international trade. Situated at the strategic crossroads of maritime traffic, the Riau harbour offered the same attractive environment that had drawn trade in the past – an international market, good portage and stapling facilities, readily available credit, and an administration which welcomed foreign merchants. In the well-established Melayu tradition, Johor's new capital at Riau also became an important Islamic centre, attracting and sponsoring scholars from Gujarat and the Arab world. For the first two decades of its existence, therefore, the bendahara dynasty conducted itself according to established traditions and appeared no different from its predecessors. In other circumstances, Johor's increasing wealth and prestige as a centre of Malay-Muslim culture might have compensated for the manner in which the new regime had gained power. But the enormity of the crime of *derhaka* had opened deep wounds within the kingdom which no riches or status, however great, could heal. This crack in the façade of unity and well-being was quickly detected and exploited by two migrant groups in the area: the Bugis of south Sulawesi and the Minangkabau of Sumatra. In the development of Malay history, the consequences were far-reaching.

Bugis influence in the Malay states

The migration of different groups into the Malay world is a theme that threads through Malaysian history, and movement between Sumatra, Borneo and the Peninsula had been occurring since very early times. Internal migration was also significant. From the sixteenth century, groups of Iban, whose slash-and-burn agriculture required access to large tracts of forest, began expanding into present-day Sarawak from what is now Kalimantan (Indonesian Borneo). Most smaller interior societies they encountered were overrun or absorbed, but others posed a greater challenge. In these areas competition became much greater, with a consequent increase in raiding and internecine warfare. About the middle of the eighteenth century Iban contact with coastal groups began to increase as they moved into what later became Sarawak's Second and Third Division. It is a tribute to their fighting skills, and the respect with which they were regarded, that they were able to establish not merely compromises but alliances with Malay leaders of raiding expeditions.

Historical sources, however, are preoccupied with the migration of another Indonesian people, the Bugis of Sulawesi; indeed, the eighteenth century has often been called 'the Bugis period' of Malaysian history. As we have seen, Bugis and other south Sulawesi groups had been arriving in the Malay areas since the last quarter of the seventeenth century. Leaving south Sulawesi in the wake of protracted civil wars, they had attempted unsuccessfully to settle in such places as Sumbawa, Lombok, Bali and Java. Conflicts with local authorities led to further Bugis migrations westwards in search of areas which would be free from the exactions of an overlord. Relatively unpopulated and lightly governed areas in Sumatra and the Malay Peninsula provided an ideal refuge. During the late seventeenth century a number of Bugis settlements had sprung up along the west coast of the Peninsula in the Johor dependencies of Selangor, Linggi and Kelang. For a brief period a Bugis dynasty even ruled in Aceh.

The Dutch in Melaka made little distinction between these migrant communities, ignoring the fact that they were from different groups (*suku*) and kingdoms, and were sometimes mutual enemies. Quarrels among their leaders were by no means rare, and they were never the monolithic force depicted by both European and Malay observers. But in time the Bugis did develop a remarkable cohesion and an intense loyalty to their cultural heritage, which may have both fostered and fed an increasing assertiveness in expressions of Malay identity. New waves of migrants from south Sulawesi and frequent contacts with the homeland helped the Bugis sustain a pride in their origins which is still found in Malaysia among those of Bugis descent.

At first Malay kingdoms did not regard the Bugis as a threat, since they could be an asset to rulers aspiring to greater economic and political power. Bugis navigational and commercial skills were highly valued, for the widely flung Bugis trading connections stretched from the Spice Islands in the east across the entire Indonesian archipelago and beyond. As Francis Light, the founder of Penang, wrote in 1794, 'They are the best merchants among the eastern islands...The great value of their cargoes...make their arrival wished for by all the mercantile people.'[3] Bugis patronage of a port could be a key to its success.

The Bugis appeared equally useful as fighting men, a commodity always in great demand in the Malay world. Their renown as formidable warriors, their awe-inspiring chants and war dances, and their chain-mail armour, injected a new element into the conduct of warfare in the area. The support of Bugis mercenaries in conflicts between Malay princes could in many cases help tip the balance in one combatant's favour. In the later seventeenth century, for instance, one Kedah prince declared that with 'two ships and three or four hundred Bugis he could set himself up as king of Kedah',[4] and in 1710 the raja muda of Johor employed Bugis troops to help suppress a revolt in Batu Bahara. The Dutch, too, recognized the fighting skills of Bugis warriors and they were an important component in the VOC's armies.

An alliance with a Bugis migrant leader could thus make a significant contribution to the economic and political strength of a Malay ruler. As time went on, however, the very presence of these semi-autonomous communities raised fundamental questions about their acceptance of the traditional ruler– subject relationship which lay at the heart of the Malay polity. Although the Bugis paid a nominal allegiance to their Malay overlord, they were governed by their own Bugis leaders. Initially they were able to exist on the periphery of Malay society, but as the migrant Bugis communities expanded this separate existence was no longer possible.

The first event to test the Bugis relationship to a Malay king occurred in 1715 following a succession dispute in Kedah. The details are not altogether clear, but it seems that a younger brother of the Kedah ruler recruited the assistance of the Selangor Bugis, promising them a certain quantity of tin for their services should he be the victor. When the prince failed to fulfil his promise, the Bugis responded by invading Kedah, razing the countryside and seizing a great deal of booty. Malay custom decreed that in such a case half the spoils of war should be surrendered to the overlord, in this case Johor. Conflicts developed after the Bugis refused to comply, not because they denied the ruler's right to a share, but because in their homelands Bugis were traditionally required to give up only a tenth. An angry raja muda, acting on behalf of the Johor ruler, immediately sent troops to attack the Bugis strongholds of Selangor and Linggi, but this force was soon repelled.

The Bugis refusal to bow to Johor's demands was only one of several revolts against the new regime which had broken out in Johor territories since Mahmud's death in 1699. This particular confrontation was significant, however, first because it was based on a cultural misunderstanding, and secondly because it demonstrated that Johor's armies, though numerically superior, were no match for the Bugis. Campaigns continued for another two years and invariably Johor's forces were defeated. The raja muda was finally forced to acknowledge that he no longer wielded any authority over the Bugis areas in Selangor.

The unsuccessful wars fought by Johor and its loss of the Bugis-occupied territories on the Peninsula were but the prelude to further developments which divided not only Johor but the entire Malay world on both sides of the Straits and beyond. In 1717 a certain Raja Kecil appeared in Siak, one of Johor's outlying territories in east coast Sumatra, claiming to be the posthumous son of Sultan Mahmud, assassinated in 1699. Far from dismissing such claims, many Johor subjects saw in Raja Kecil a long-awaited sign that Johor's fortunes would be renewed and its former strength and prestige restored. The kingdom had been riven with enmity and distrust following the 1699 regicide and was now facing defiance from its Bugis subjects. The arrival of Raja Kecil raised widespread hopes that the rightful dynasty would return and harmony would again prevail. The Orang Laut flocked to Raja Kecil in their hundreds, accepting him as the miraculously preserved son of their murdered lord, a prince of the old Melayu line come to avenge his father's death. With the Minangkabau spiritual overlord in Pagarruyung providing his blessing to Raja Kecil, the latter's claim was also cloaked with a legitimacy Malays appreciated. Legends that invoked an ancient Melayu–Minangkabau connection exerted a powerful hold on Malay society. According to one tradition, the kings of Minangkabau were descended from one of the princes who had appeared on Bukit Siguntang, and therefore shared similar origins with those who came to rule in Melaka.

Raja Kecil appeared in the Riau river in early 1718 with a large Minangkabau force and was met in battle by the Johor fleet. But, in the initial encounter between them, the Orang Laut, who formed the backbone of the Johor navy, deserted to Raja Kecil and were joined by a number of other prominent Johor nobles. With all resistance overcome, Raja Kecil was able to capture the Johor capital on Riau and proclaim himself ruler. He then married one of the daughters of Sultan Abdul Jalil, whom he demoted to his former position of bendahara. The latter, finding this new situation intolerable, fled to Terengganu where he set up an alternative court composed of local nobles as well as others from Pahang and Kelantan.

There were now three loci of power in the Malay world: Raja Kecil in Riau, Sultan Abdul Jalil on the Peninsular east coast, and the Bugis in Selangor and Linggi. Ultimately, however, it was the Bugis who were to emerge triumphant. Raja Kecil lost much support, not only by inexplicably killing some of the principal Orang Laut leaders but also by having Sultan

Abdul Jalil murdered. He then proceeded to attack the Bugis in a number of sea battles in which his opponents' mastery of maritime warfare became obvious. As the *Tuhfat al-Nafis* explains, many of Raja Kecil's men were from the Minangkabau interior, accustomed to river paddling rather than the ocean. Their actual fighting ability could not match that of the Bugis, and the latter were soon able to force Raja Kecil out and become masters of Johor.

The Bugis leaders realized the need to re-establish a measure of royal authority in Johor as a focus for Malay loyalty. As outsiders they would be unacceptable, and so in 1721 they installed as ruler the 20-year-old prince Sulaiman, son of the assassinated Sultan Abdul Jalil. By this act they laid the grounds for the later Bugis 'justifying myth' – that is, that they had been recruited by Sulaiman and had come to his assistance when he was abandoned by other Malay kings. Having had no part in Sultan Mahmud's murder, and without the same cultural abhorrence of *derhaka* as Malays, the Bugis found no difficulty in giving Sulaiman their support. But the guilt of Sulaiman's father was still fresh in the mind of many Malays, who also realized that Sulaiman now had little influence in Johor. The Bugis had all assumed exalted honorifics and one, Daeng Marewa, had even been named *yang dipertuan muda* (shortened by the Bugis to *yamtuan muda*), a title meaning 'junior ruler' which Malay courts traditionally gave to the heir to the throne. Daeng Marewa had then married the virgin widow of the murdered Sultan Mahmud.

It was very evident, however, that Sulaiman resented his position as a figurehead. A little over a year after Daeng Marewa's installation, Sulaiman wrote to the governor of Melaka asking to be 'rescued' from the Bugis. The extent to which he had been deprived of all effective power is aptly summed up in an eighteenth-century Bugis chronicle from Johor. 'The Yang Dipertuan Besar ['great king', that is, Sultan Sulaiman] is to be like a woman: When food is given to him, he may eat; and the Yang Dipertuan Muda ['young king'] is like her husband. Should any question arise, it is he who is to decide it.'[5] During the 1720s and 30s a more mature Sultan Sulaiman was occasionally able to assert his authority, but it was patently clear that Bugis influence had extended to all areas of government. Even allowing for the antipathy towards the Bugis evident in Melakan reports, their dominance in Johor's affairs was patently evident. A Dutch governor writing in the mid-eighteenth century thus described Sultan Sulaiman as 'a puppet, who must dance to the piping of the yamtuan muda and his Bugis following'.[6]

While the Bugis were consolidating their hold in Riau-Johor, they were subject to periodic attacks from Raja Kecil from his base in Siak, in theory still Johor territory. But the Bugis managed to maintain their position, eventually forcing Raja Kecil to abandon any hopes of recovering the kingdom. Meanwhile, leadership of the Bugis in Riau-Johor came under the control of a small group of closely related men. In 1728 when the Bugis prince Daeng Marewa died, the post of yamtuan muda passed without opposition to his brother, Daeng Cellak (1728–45). Gradually other contending Bugis factions in the Malay Peninsula were pushed aside, despite their efforts to withstand those in power in Riau. In Linggi, Topassarai, an uncle of the queen of Bone in Sulawesi, had attempted to strengthen his position by assuming the title of sultan. In 1732 he even offered the VOC all Linggi's tin if it would support his bid for power. Another prince from the kingdom of Wajo, also in Sulawesi, joined Raja Kecil's son, Raja Alam, in an effort to assert authority over Selangor. Through the 1730s the battle lines between different Bugis groups moved back and forth contending for control of the rich tin areas of Selangor, Kelang and Linggi. By 1743 these were all firmly in the hands of the Riau Bugis, with Selangor itself regarded as the appanage of the yamtuan muda family.

In less than three decades after Mahmud's death the nature of power in Johor had again been fundamentally changed. In virtually all matters, Sulaiman had to yield to Bugis wishes, and the Malay nobles found that unless they were willing to co-operate with the Bugis leaders they too had little influence in government affairs. It is understandable that this situation aroused intense Malay resentment, the greater because it could not be expressed openly. It was probably the Orang Laut, however, who were most affected by the Bugis presence. From the days of Palembang they had always held a privileged and valued place not only in the actual economy but also in the administration of the realm. Honoured with titles, entrusted with duties such as leadership of the war fleet and guardianship of the ruler's chambers, they now found themselves replaced by the Bugis seamen whose navigational and fighting skills quickly made redundant most services the Orang Laut could render. The only area in which they still played a vital role was in the procurement of sea products. Even more significant was the fact that Johor's Orang Laut no longer had a specific focus of loyalty. Some followed Raja Kecil to Siak, but others could not accept a move away from their familiar haunts in the Riau-Lingga archipelagos to the mangrove swamps of east Sumatra, which were already the home of other Orang Laut groups. Accordingly, some again submitted to the new Johor dynasty, and a court notebook records numerous occasions when Sulaiman personally sailed out to encourage the Orang Laut to return. Yet others simply retreated to the periphery of Johor's territories, to islands like Siantan in the South China Sea. Here, bereft of their former functions, they took to raiding passing ships outside the authority of any court. For all Orang Laut, however, their proud and ancient status had gone. Whereas the founder of Melaka had been pleased to marry his son to the daughter of an Orang Laut chief, at the beginning of the nineteenth century a Malay writer described them as filthy, repellent, little better than animals.

The changes which had taken place in Johor meant that there was no longer the same reason for Malays to ascribe to its rulers a special status because of their descent from the semi-divine prince who had appeared on Bukit Siguntang in Palembang. The new dynasty's direct links with the old Melaka line had been for ever severed, weakening Johor's formerly exalted status among Malay kingdoms. The Malay world by the 1750s was in some ways reminiscent of other periods like the early seventh or fourteenth centuries, when the direction of an overlord was lacking and a number of states had the opportunity to assert their own individuality. Although the loosening of ties with a central authority has led some to describe the period as one of 'fragmentation', this process did not necessarily entail a loss of morale or purpose, as is apparent from an examination of developments outside Johor.

Developments in the Peninsula outside Riau-Johor

Though the sequence of events in other Malay states during the first half of the eighteenth century is not as well documented as in Johor, it is obvious that for some this was a significant period in their history. At the time of Mahmud's murder Terengganu had no fleets and only 500 fighting men, but it had a well-established reputation as a supplier of pepper to junks from China and *perahu* from the eastern archipelago. Terengganu's status as one of Johor's more valuable dependencies was enhanced in 1718 when Sultan Abdul Jalil fled there from Riau to escape further humiliation at the hands of Raja Kecil. Defiantly setting up his own court, Sultan Abdul Jalil distributed many titles among local nobles, bringing Terengganu into the centre of Johor politics and giving its chiefs a greater sense of participation in Malay affairs. Terengganu continued to receive the attention of Johor even after the Bugis were established on Riau. The installation of Zainal Abidin, a brother of the late Sultan Abdul Jalil, as the first ruler of Terengganu in 1722 may have been intended to strengthen ties with Johor. Following Zainal Abidin's death eleven years later, his youngest son, Raja Mansur, was taken under the protection of Sultan Sulaiman of Johor. Raja Mansur was brought up in the Johor court and later married Sulaiman's daughter. When the young prince came of age in 1741, Sulaiman installed him as Terengganu's second ruler.

Little is known of events within Terengganu during this period. The sources focus primarily on the activities of Sultan Mansur (1741–93) who lived on Riau from 1750 to 1760, leaving Terengganu's administration in the hands of his uncle. We can infer something, however, about Sultan Mansur himself. As a king of impeccable Malay pedigree who was both cousin and son-in-law to the Johor king and whose mother was a Patani princess, Sultan Mansur was implacably hostile to the Bugis arrogation of power in Riau-Johor. During his ten years' residence on Riau he led Malay opposition to the Bugis, staunchly defending the interests of what he called 'the Malay nation'. Even after his return to Terengganu in 1760 he actively sought to unite all Malays against the Bugis.

At the same time, Sultan Mansur obviously had personal ambitions for a greater role in Malay politics. At one stage he was intent on assuming the throne of Johor itself and wresting it from Bugis control. At home, he extended his influence northwards into a weak and divided Kelantan, which he attacked in 1764. Initially he attempted to support Kelantan princes as his representatives, but after continuing resistance he eventually installed his own son, married to a Kelantan princess, as Kelantan's ruler.

The effectiveness of Sultan Mansur's government depended on strong central control, for the possibility of opposition from chiefs in the isolated areas of Besut and Kemaman, or in the interior region, was always present. Contemporary European accounts praise Sultan Mansur's well-ordered administration and the respect in which his subjects held him, and his personal stamp on Terengganu's history is attested by the legends about him which still survive. Even as a child, it is said, he demonstrated remarkable powers. According to one story, a learned man of religion officiating at Sultan Mansur's birth predicted that he would be a famous ruler who would rid the seas of pirates. Had it not been for the renewed Thai threat after 1782, Terengganu might have moved to fill the political vacuum left when Johor lost its position of leadership, and in so doing have advanced its standing as a regional focus for Malay culture.

With the rise to power of another dominating and equally long-lived ruler, Sultan Muhammad Jiwa (d. 1779), Kedah also took a more active part in Malay affairs. Events immediately prior to his reign are impossible to reconstruct in detail, but it is apparent that civil war in Kedah had been endemic since the late seventeenth century. The confusion of these decades is reflected in the conflicting accounts found in Dutch and Malay sources. Both the *Tuhfat al-Nafis* and the *Siak Chronicle* mention a prolonged war between the king and his younger brother, while VOC sources record two major conflicts, one in 1715 involving the Bugis and another in 1723–4 which drew in both Bugis and Minangkabau. It is unclear whether the protagonists were the same on both occasions, for neither Dutch nor Malay sources give their names. It is possible that Sultan Muhammad Jiwa was involved in the second war, for some time around the middle of the eighteenth century he emerged from the background of civil strife to become ruler of Kedah. A coin minted in his reign has been found with the Muslim date 1154 (1741–2 CE), customarily denoting the year of accession. In any event, it seems that success in battle did not come easily, and the victor may, as the *Tuhfat* claims, have initially relied on Bugis arms. The internal conflicts in Kedah at the beginning of his reign presaged the periodic outbreak of short-lived rebellions led by rival princes which are briefly mentioned in VOC records.

Despite undercurrents of opposition, Sultan Muhammad managed to retain control of his throne until his death. He is remembered in Kedah tradition as a hero in the classical Malay image, a man of great courage who in his youth journeyed to Palembang, Java and India with a learned teacher. Returning in triumph to Kedah, he reputedly established customary and Islamic law codes, organized an administrative hierarchy, and laid the basis for organized government. European sources depict him as a man of independent mind who, in order to maintain an open port, persistently refused to sign a commercial contract with the Dutch. With its direct trading links to India, Kedah's economy thrived, supported by its brisk trade in pepper and its exports of rice in a rice-deficient Peninsula. Nineteenth-century Kedah Malays recalled that Sultan Muhammad Jiwa was also able to alleviate the burden of tribute to Ayudhya by reducing the amount of gold used in the *bunga mas* and limiting the accompanying presents. His independent policies were probably encouraged by Ayudhya's weakness. Occupied by protracted wars with Burma, Thai kings did not press their claims to overlordship in the northern Malay states until the 1770s.

The status of Perak's ruling house was enhanced by the 1699 regicide since, as a court text implies, Perak could now be regarded as the sole heir to old Melaka. But Perak could never lay claim to the wealth, power and prestige possessed by either Melaka or Johor. The kingdom was torn by civil war in the first four decades of the eighteenth century, with rival princes supported by different chiefs hoping to seize the throne and thus gain control of revenue from the lucrative tin trade. These quarrels were complicated by the ambitions of the Selangor Bugis and the Minangkabau. Both groups were willing to assist one or another of the warring factions in order to extend their influence into Perak. In 1743 dissatisfied Perak chiefs allied with the Selangor Bugis to oust the reigning Perak ruler, Sultan Muzaffar (d. 1752). In his place they installed the raja muda, who was in reality manipulated by his son, the dominating Raja Iskandar.

In the wake of this conflict, Perak was effectively divided into two. Retreating inland, Sultan Muzaffar retained control over the *ulu* (upriver) districts, leaving the lower reaches of the Perak river to Raja Iskandar. Attempting to reassert his position, Sultan Muzaffar recruited Minangkabau help, but he still could not dislodge Raja Iskandar and his Selangor Bugis allies. With Muzaffar denied access to the sea, and Iskandar unable to reach the tin-bearing highlands, both sides reached a reluctant reconciliation. Yet Sultan Muzaffar remained adamantly opposed to Iskandar's eventual succession as ruler and therefore secretly contacted the VOC. In return for a VOC tin monopoly in Perak, Muzaffar wanted Dutch assurance that his daughter and Raja Kecil's son, who were betrothed, should accede to the Perak throne after his own death. It was on this understanding that a contract was signed in 1746, permitting the Dutch to construct a lodge and maintain a small garrison in lower Perak to supervise tin deliveries. From the outset, the contract was under fire from Perak chiefs and princes wishing to sell their tin for higher prices elsewhere. However, the majority of the court valued the prestige and protection which came from Dutch friendship. Despite recurring tensions in VOC–Perak relations, such as the threat by one ruler in 1773 to join with Selangor, the alliance endured until the British assumed control of Melaka in 1795.

A major beneficiary of the Dutch alliance was Raja Iskandar himself. When Raja Kecil's son fell from grace, Raja Iskandar married Sultan Muzaffar's daughter and was reinstated in royal favour. Although he had initially opposed the contract, he decided to renew it after his accession in 1752. His reign was a time of unprecedented peace in Perak, for the VOC alliance guaranteed protection from outside attack and strengthened the ruler's hand against potential rivals. Sultan Iskandar was also able to take advantage of opportunities provided by the prosperity deriving from uninterrupted trade. He travelled widely throughout Perak, appointing his personal representatives in isolated areas like Larut and Kuala Kangsar and giving the kingdom a sense of royal authority it had never before known. A significant development in his reign was a shift of power away from the ministers to the royal princes. It was Sultan Iskandar who made the position of bendahara a prerogative of the prince third in line to the throne, rather than of a noble family. The sources also suggest that such actions were not undertaken lightly and that Sultan Iskandar saw himself as part of the continuum of Malay history. The court text he commissioned, the *Misa Melayu*, tells the story of his rule, but it was obviously modelled on accounts of great Malay rulers in the past like the king of Aceh, Iskandar Muda (1607–36). Even Sultan Iskandar's adoption of the honorific Iskandar Zulkarnain (Alexander the Great) was a reminder that Perak kings claimed descent from the princes of Bukit Siguntang. His reign stands out as a high point in Perak history and in Perak today is still remembered as a *zaman mas*, a golden age.

The importance of leadership in providing a focus for government becomes apparent in Perak's history after Iskandar's death in 1765. The two brothers who succeeded him in turn were not of his calibre and under them the challenge to royal power resurfaced. Now princes and even the principal ministers became involved in the smuggling of tin, bypassing not only the Dutch monopoly but also royal tolls.

More telling examples of the effects of weakened rule are found in Patani and Kelantan, where the eighteenth century could well be regarded as a period of fragmentation. From about 1688 a dynasty originating from Kelantan ruled Patani, but factional disputes continued to undermine stable government, driving away the traders who had formerly brought Patani such wealth. Conflicts worsened as differing royal groups sought to curry favour in Ayudhya or to gain assistance from one of the Thai governors in the southern provinces. By 1730 central control had collapsed, the gravity of the situation eliciting a terse comment in the *Hikayat Patani*: 'Patani has been in great confusion and its people suffer from many ills, while rules and customs are no longer observed.'[7] Despite a proud sense of its Malay identity, Patani at the end of the eighteenth century was in no position to withstand the revitalized and belligerent Siam, successor to Ayudhya.

In Kelantan too there were continuing problems of leadership. For the greater part of the seventeenth century Kelantan was divided into small districts controlled by chiefs. In about 1730 a move towards greater unity was made when a royal family with strong Patani connections attempted to extend its rule over the state. But rebellions persisted, and even though the exploits of individual princes are recalled in Kelantan legends, the country was ill-prepared to deal with the threat of invasion. In 1746, when a Thai attack was believed to be imminent, a Riau text notes the arrival of envoys from Kelantan requesting Riau-Johor's assistance. Any temporary unity this impending danger might have brought to Kelantan was soon dispelled when the renewal of Burmese power in 1752 under the Konbaung dynasty diverted Thai attention. Continual warring amongst Kelantan's princes co-incided with incursions from Patani chiefs to the north, making outside intervention almost inevitable. In 1764 Sultan Mansur of Terengganu, allied with a force from Siak, launched what was probably the first of several campaigns into Kelantan. Subsequently he installed his protégé, a Kelantan prince named Long Yunus, as raja muda. His own son, married to a daughter of Long Yunus, was made ruler of Kelantan.[8]

This occurred some time before Sultan Mansur's death in 1793, and not until the end of the century did a son of Long Yunus, with the aid of Chinese from one of the mining settlements, oust the Terengganu faction. Under the aegis of Siam, he then assumed the throne as Sultan Muhammad I (*c*.1800–35). A Chinese description from the 1780s indicates that the local economy, based largely on gold-mining, was not markedly affected by the conflicts within the ruling class. None the less, Kelantan's political history during most of the eighteenth century is an example of the vulnerability of a state caught up in continuing internal strife.

Economic and political challenges in the eighteenth century

Economically, the eighteenth century is more appropriately regarded as a time of new opportunities and challenges rather than of decline. The prospects for international trade had rarely been better. In 1727 the Chinese emperor lifted the oft-flouted prohibitions against junk traffic between south China and Nan Yang ports, and the expanding China trade reflected the great demand for the region's forest and marine products. The revenue Malay rulers derived from the China trade is evident in the numerous royal monopolies, ranging from rattans to the more exotic birds' nests used in Chinese soups.

Trade with China was made even more profitable because of the growing European participation, primarily due to the popularity of Chinese tea in Europe. By the beginning of the eighteenth century tea, like coffee, had become a social beverage and the demand seemed almost insatiable. Europeans had difficulty in acquiring sufficient quantities of tea because they found Chinese merchants uninterested in the goods Europe could offer in exchange. Silver was naturally acceptable, but this was a heavy drain on bullion. Another solution was to transport cargoes of Indian cloth and opium to the Malay world, and barter these for tin and spices, which were valued items on the China market. The Malay world had long been an important trans-shipment area, but to Europeans in the eighteenth century it became a linchpin in the valuable China tea trade.

Europeans preferred to deal in tin and spices because, unlike the Chinese, they did not have sufficient specialized knowledge to select high quality cargoes of forest and marine products. Furthermore, Malay tin was preferred in China to that from England since it was more malleable and could be beaten to the fine foil required for lining tea chests and for ritual burning. With large quantities of tin available, especially in the west coast Peninsular states, virtually every estuary from Kedah down to Singapore was a potential supply point for passing European traders seeking to overcome the VOC's monopoly treaties with the tin-producing states of Perak, Rembau and, across the Straits, Palembang.

Malay pepper also had a high reputation abroad and became another important item in European trade with China. Because of Dutch monopolies, the pepper of Borneo and the Peninsula was one of the few spices available outside the sphere of VOC control. Kedah, with access to the 'pepper island' (Pulau Lada) of Langkawi, had been frequented for generations by traders coming from India. Terengganu pepper was especially favoured in China, being considered superior to any other in the archipelago and cheaper than that from Malabar. Not surprisingly, both Sultan Muhammad Jiwa of Kedah and Sultan Mansur Syah of Terengganu actively sponsored trading ventures, sending out cargoes of pepper on their own ships.

The expanding international market stimulated a widening search for fresh sources of tin and gold, the most valuable of the local products. In Rembau in 1769, for instance, gold mines were opened, while a contemporary Chinese work entitled *Hai-lu* (Record of the Seas) mentions several gold-producing settlements in the Kelantan and Pahang interior, accessible only by braving treacherous rapids and swift-flowing mountain streams. There are good reasons to suggest that the old Penarikan trade route across the Peninsula remained an important means by which gold and jungle products were carried to both the east and west coasts. During the latter half of the century major tin deposits were also discovered on the island of Singkep in the Lingga archipelago, on the Perak–Patani border, in Larut, and elsewhere in Perak and Selangor. Throughout this period one has the impression that slowly but inexorably hitherto little-frequented areas are becoming known as sources of some valued product.

But developing economic opportunities often opened the door to unforeseen political and social problems, especially in terms of royal authority. As settlement fanned out to develop natural resources in the hinterland, Malay rulers encountered in a more urgent form the whole question of territorial control. Many of the valuable gold mines and rich tin lodes of the isolated mountain regions were located in areas between states where forest dwellers moved freely back and forth and where only legend established the limits of control. When the economies of neighbouring states began to expand in response to growing commerce, disputes over territory inevitably arose. Malay rulers were entitled to a percentage of profits from mining or agriculture, and it was therefore important that any claim to territory be publicly recognized. A long-standing conflict, for instance, arose between Perak and Kedah regarding ownership of the Kerian river, a valuable tin area, and it was not settled in Perak's favour until the middle of the nineteenth century.

Obviously it was not sufficient merely to claim suzerainty over large tracts of land, especially if these were far removed from the royal residence. Effective territorial control demanded a stable administration and officials who would loyally represent a ruler they might not see for a year at a time. On the calibre of these district chiefs could hang the allegiance of an entire local population which in terms of manpower was an economic resource as valuable as the richest tin mine. In Kedah alone, the collection of birds' nests from Langkawi was said to require 1000 *perahu* and 4500 men annually. Elephant-trapping in the northern states involved huge numbers of men to clear the jungle for an enclosure, drive the animals towards it, and subsequently tame them. A useful measure of the manpower required simply to build an elephant enclosure is suggested by the eighteenth-century *Hai-lu*'s account of elephant-trapping in Terengganu: the text mentions the necessity of 'clearing out the big trees in a ten mile [16 km] circle and building a fence around this area'.[9]

It was of prime importance for a Malay ruler to harness these human resources. Economic expansion, therefore, was normally closely followed by extension of political authority aimed at tying distant settlements more closely to the centre. Malay and Dutch records from Perak contain a detailed and probably typical account of the appointment of *ulu* chiefs who, entrusted with wide administrative powers, were also charged with the general supervision of local tin collections. Contact between forest-dwelling Orang Asli and Malays may have been expanding during this period as Malays became increasingly active as middlemen in the transport of jungle products. In Selangor, says the *Hai-lu*, mountain aborigines were 'controlled by the king of the country' and took their goods to trade with the Malays; according to the same text, contacts between some Orang Asli and Malays in Kelantan were such that the former were even prepared to bring their disputes to the ruler for adjudication.

Undoubtedly, in most cases local administration functioned smoothly, but the tension between the centre and periphery which recurred in the archipelago on a wider scale was also prevalent in smaller territorial units. Local revenues, frequently considerable, made it possible for an ambitious chief to acquire a fair degree of independence, and geographical distance enabled him virtually to ignore the existence of his suzerain. As a result, the potential foci of allegiance for the peoples of the Malay world multiplied. An Orang Laut headman of an island like Siantan could essentially operate as an autonomous chief, while in northwest Borneo nobles could oppose the

Brunei ruler with impunity, especially as royal authority in districts where property was inherited (*tulin*) was strictly limited.

The difficulties involved in asserting central control were compounded in border areas where inhabitants had traditionally learned to reconcile the often conflicting demands of two masters. As links with local centres became stronger, such compromises were less feasible, and border disputes were commonly expressed in terms of regional rivalries – Patani men against those of Kedah, Kelantan against Terengganu. The recognition of a shared Malay heritage with its roots in the Melaka kingdom did not displace strong regional affiliations and local identifications with variant versions of Melayu culture. It was not necessarily easy, therefore, for a Malay ruler to impose his political authority over an area where the population saw him as an outsider. Thus in 1764, when Sultan Mansur of Terengganu invaded Kelantan, he purportedly said that he had not come as a conqueror but to place 'a prince of Kelantan' on the throne. In Perak, after a district head from Patani usurped control over lucrative tin mines near the northern border, Sultan Alauddin (1774–92) explained that he himself could do nothing because the person involved was 'not a Perak man but from Patani'. By the same token, the lengthy correspondence about piracy carried on between the Dutch and Malay rulers often hinged on the origins of the raiders themselves, for only thus could they be brought to justice.

There were always those who disclaimed association with any court, and such individuals, often likened by Malays to migratory birds, posed particular difficulties. A feature of the Malay world during this period is the number of wandering *anak raja* (sons of princes) who for various reasons rejected the authority of their rulers. Too numerous to be absorbed into the court administration, the extensive royal offspring resulting from the custom of polygamy had been an endemic problem in Malay courts. In the eighteenth century they attracted greater attention because widespread succession disputes, especially in Siak and Kedah, led to a marked increase in dispossessed *anak raja*. In this situation, a long-standing custom in Malay courts suffered serious abuse. For generations it had been accepted that princes unable to support themselves on the ruler's bounty (*kurnia*) could take to sea raiding, while observing royal guidelines as to what ships they could attack and where. Now, however, many princes were roaming the seas as independent pirates. In the eighteenth century the growing Orang Laut piracy, which had been an indirect consequence of the Johor regicide in 1699, was augmented by the raiding of undisciplined *anak raja* beyond the reach of a responsible ruler. Their activities did not stop at piracy, and many were ready to act as the focus for other discontented elements. They and their followers were ripe for conspiracy or revolt. Previously such princes could have found few allies willing to risk men and arms on some dubious adventure, and rarely were rebellions against an established ruler successful. What now made these fugitive princes a far greater threat was the Bugis who, as in Kedah and Perak, could be enticed to lend their fighting skills in return for promises of material and/or political rewards.

The eighteenth century thus presented Malay states with economic opportunities, yet at the same time also witnessed the proliferation of challenges to political authority that often defied solution. But one continuing feature was still the strength of Melayu culture which, despite regional variations, bound the Malay states of the Peninsula and east Sumatra together. The individual experiences of each Malay area had inevitably meant local adaptations of customs, dress and dialect, but such differences were still incorporated in the concept of Malayness. Whatever the difficulties faced by Malay rulers in exercising political control over other Malays, there was at least a shared language, religion, belief system and an acceptance of the traditions governing ruler–subject relations. This did not exist in the same way for non-Malays who, in response to expanding economic prospects, were now much more evident in the region.

The growing influence of non-Malay groups in the Peninsula

Most Malay states had a growing Indian population, many of whom were Muslim traders from the Coromandel coast. Among them were men who moved easily between the two cultures, and the case of an Indian trader mentioned in the *Misa Melayu* who had 'one wife in India and one in Perak' was by no means uncommon. Some of these traders were incorporated into Malay courts, taking up influential intermediary positions such as royal merchant, scribe or interpreter, and thus serving to reinforce the key role of Indians in Malay commerce. In several states, and especially Kedah, the wealthy Indian community formed a powerful faction whose interests were not always in accord with those of the ruler.

Another influential group was the Arabs, particularly those from the Hadramaut, where land was in short supply. They traded extensively in the archipelago and were granted commercial privileges because they were of the same race as the Prophet; those bearing the title Sayid were even of the same lineage. They were particularly welcomed as husbands for Malay princesses and towards the end of the century a prince of mixed Malay-Arab descent, Sayid Ali, became ruler of Siak. Europeans, however, viewed Arab influence with concern, and in 1750 a Dutch governor of Melaka complained at the extent to which they had penetrated Malay society. He would probably have agreed with a later comment by Francis Light that the Arabs were 'unwilling to yield to any authority . . . Good friends and very dangerous enemies'.[10]

Economic opportunities in the Malay states also attracted large numbers of migrant Chinese, swelling the small existing Chinese communities, some of which could date their predecessors to the Melaka period. They had intermarried with Malays, producing a mixed Sino-Malay or Baba society with its own distinct characteristics and a specific form of Malay. By 1750 the 'Chinese' population of Melaka, largely of Malay-Hokkien descent, had increased to 2161 (over one-fifth of the total population), although very few were China-born. The Chinese communities each had their own Kapitan China, appointed by the Dutch in Melaka and elsewhere by the Malay rulers. Though control generally presented no problem, the seeds of change can be seen as Chinese migration increased, their settlements became larger, and newcomers moved into occupations formerly dominated by Malays. In earlier times most Chinese migrants had been traders or shopkeepers, but now there was a growing emphasis on miners and agriculturalists. Terengganu's pepper plantations were by the middle of the century largely in the hands of Chinese who, according to a Thai chronicle, had been encouraged to settle there by the ruler. In the 1730s Daeng Cellak, the second yamtuan muda, brought Chinese coolies to Riau to develop gambier, a tanning agent also used in medication. The gambier plantations there became almost totally a Chinese concern. Large numbers of Chinese had come to Riau after the Chinese uprising in Batavia in 1740, and 40 years later the population included at least 4000 Teochiew and 1000 Hokkien. Elsewhere the Chinese population was also growing. The *Hai-lu* notes that in Kelantan there were Chinese gold miners from Guangdong and traders and pepper growers from Fujian, while English reports from the same period mention a settlement of Chinese pepper planters in Brunei. In Selangor, Fujian and Guangdong settlers worked in tin mines, and from 1777 the ruler of Perak and the Dutch collaborated in recruiting indentured Chinese labourers from Melaka to exploit newly discovered tin fields. It was not long before these Chinese miners themselves introduced innovations in mining and smelting techniques which were to give them a tight grip on the industry in later years. Already there were complaints by Europeans of the secret society and clan rivalries which became enmeshed with Malay politics in the nineteenth century. The recent discovery by Sabah Museum staff of around 100 apparently Chinese coffins in a limestone cave points to the likelihood of overseas Chinese settlements even further afield.

The Minangkabau were yet another group to respond to the economic opportunities in the Malay Peninsula in the eighteenth century. There were already sizeable settlements of Minangkabau who in earlier centuries had selected the Peninsula as an area for *merantau*, the Minangkabau practice of temporary or permanent residence abroad for a spiritual or economic purpose. The focus of their migration remained the *rantau* districts of Naning, Sungai Ujung and particularly Rembau. This was the nucleus of what later came to be called Negeri Sembilan, the Nine Lands.[11] Until ceded to the Dutch in 1758, Rembau remained in theory under Johor, but in fact only paid nominal allegiance to its Malay overlord. Despite the renewal of an ancient contract between the Minangkabau ruler in Pagarruyung and Johor in 1725–6, in which the former relinquished authority over his subjects in the *rantau* areas, the Minangkabau settlements on the Malay Peninsula retained strong cultural links with their homeland in Sumatra. Although it is evident that they were bound together by a loose affiliation, there is little information in Dutch sources about the development of their varying political systems, which were superimposed on a complex social system based on matrilineal descent. The customs associated with matrilinearity were known as *adat parapatih* (Malayized to *adat perpatih*), while those practices more closely related to Islamic laws of inheritance and succession, particularly with regard to royalty, were codified in the *adat katumanggungan* (Malayized to *adat temenggung*). Within the Minangkabau states the strong influence of the clans (*suku*) meant that rivalry for leadership was often bitter. After Raja Hadil of Rembau died in 1778, the territorial heads and clan leaders attempted to govern 'Rembau' (then meaning much of present-day Negeri Sembilan) jointly, but by 1780 hostilities between two factions over the choice of a new *datuk penghulu* (principal chief) had broken out. The disruption to the tin deliveries was so great that, notwithstanding their reluctance to interfere, the Dutch in their role as overlord felt compelled to send an investigative mission. At one point the Melaka governor even contemplated persuading some Minangkabau prince from Sumatra to come to Rembau as ruler, to ensure greater co-operation. It has not yet been established whether Sultan Ahmad ibni Raja Bayang, elected as paramount ruler (yang dipertuan besar) in 1785, was from Sumatra or locally born. As yet no individual has emerged in VOC sources who can be definitely identified with the legendary Raja Melewar, popularly believed to have been installed in 1773 as the first ruler of Negeri Sembilan. But it is perhaps premature to suggest that this folk hero arose from myths surrounding Daeng Marewa, the first Bugis yamtuan muda (1721–8), despite the similarity in names. By the end of the eighteenth century the Minangkabau areas on the Peninsula, while developing their own version of Melayu culture, had also became so politically distinct that there was no way in which the former relationship with their Johor sovereign could have been reforged.

In the same period the Bugis in Selangor broke away from Johor and set up an independent state. During the 1730s the Riau Bugis had asserted control in Selangor and had made it the special appanage of the acknowledged heir to the yamtuan muda post. From 1740 to 1760, when relations between Malays and Bugis in Riau were often extremely tense, Selangor was a convenient place of retreat where local Bugis welcomed their compatriots from Riau. Daeng Kamboja, the successor to Daeng Cellak, spent a number of years here before his eventual return to Riau. By the middle of the century Selangor's administration had taken on a character of its own, with a form of government which borrowed certain aspects from south Sulawesi. Considerable power lay with a small group of nobles, the *orang tua* or elders, resembling the Hadat or governing council of the Bugis state of Bone rather than the large assembly of nobles as in other Malay states. The office of *suliwatang*, which in the Bugis homelands was a military title, became in Selangor a senior position of great influence.

In 1745, when Yamtuan Muda Daeng Cellak died, his son Raja Lumu was designated as Selangor's future ruler, but during his minority a regent was appointed. For nearly two decades, until Raja Lumu came of age, this regent and the *suliwatang* controlled Selangor's affairs. In 1766, together with his nobles, Raja Lumu took the momentous step of declaring Selangor independent of Riau-Johor. To signify his independence, the new ruler, now called Sultan Salehuddin (1766–82), requested the sanction of the sultan of Perak, acknowledged to be a descendant of the old Melaka line. The Perak ruler then presented him with the Malay mark of royalty, the *nobat* or drum of sovereignty, to signify his new status. Selangor had by no means set aside its Bugis cultural heritage, but its leaders had clearly seen the need to reach some accommodation with the Malay environment of which they now formed a part.

Despite the persistence of enmity among the Bugis, Malays and Minangkabaus, the distinction between their ruling classes became increasingly blurred. Migrant groups gradually adopted Malay, and Malay titles were used rather than Bugis or Minangkabau honorifics. One recension of the *Sejarah Melayu* even cast the Malay hero Hang Tuah as a Bugis warrior. This merging was reinforced because from time to time political alliances sealed by marriage were made among the three groups. The intricacies of the blood ties which had developed a generation after the Bugis installation in Riau in 1721 are well illustrated in Siak. Because Raja Kecil and several Bugis leaders had married daughters of Sultan Abdul Jalil of Johor, they were, though sworn enemies, also brothers-in-law. Raja Kecil later established his own dynasty in Siak, but after his death some time in the 1740s the throne was disputed between his two sons, each of whom could draw on differing sources of support. One, Raja Alam, could appeal to the Bugis through his marriage to the sister of Daeng Kamboja, the Bugis yamtuan muda from 1745 to 1777. Raja Alam also retained links with the old following of his father, Raja Kecil, and was able to appeal not only to the Minangkabau of east coast Sumatra and Rembau, but also to several Orang Laut groups. Raja Muhammad, Raja Kecil's other son, was more closely associated with the Malays because his mother was Sultan Sulaiman's sister. Inevitably, these bonds of blood and marriage conflicted with the obligations imposed by other alliances.

Extensive intermarriage meant that the conflicts in the area cannot be characterized as simply one ethnic group versus another. Some Riau Malays, like the Temenggung, had acquired Bugis relations through marriage and therefore felt bonds of loyalty pulling them in opposing directions. The children of Bugis–Malay unions also gave rise to an increasing number of so-called *peranakan* Bugis whose allegiance was similarly divided. Nor was Malay leadership itself in complete agreement. Although Sultan Mansur Syah of Terengganu saw a sharp division between Bugis and Malays, several other Malay nobles were willing to seek accommodation with the Bugis because they resented Sultan Mansur's arrogation of power in Riau and the influence of Terengganu Malays at court. Since the third yamtuan muda, Daeng Kemboja, remained in Selangor for some years, Sultan Mansur had been able to assume considerable authority. During his residence in Riau from 1750 to 1760, he dominated the Assembly of Nobles, taking unilateral actions which ignored long-standing precedent that all government decisions should be the result of *muafakat*, consultation between the chiefs and senior ministers. Discontented Riau nobles found allies among the Bugis leaders, many of whom were convinced that Sultan Mansur had poisoned the second yamtuan muda, Daeng Cellak, who died unexpectedly in 1745.

Expansion of Bugis influence

The marriage ties linking the Bugis and several Malay leaders notwithstanding, in Riau the struggle for power was still perceived as one between two distinct cultural groups. In fact, it is probably fair to say that the sense of being 'Malay' had been considerably sharpened by the Bugis presence in the region. In the Riau court the most public reminder that the origins of the Bugis lay outside the fold of Melayu was the formal oath of loyalty sworn on the death of any Malay ruler or Bugis yamtuan muda. During the ceremony every member of the court had to decide whether he would swear as a Bugis or as a Malay, and those of mixed descent thus openly made known their allegiance. The very oath itself, which solemnly spelt out dire punishments for any Bugis or Malay who harmed each other, revived memories of how the Bugis had become part of the Johor polity. During the 1750s the *Tuhfat al-Nafis* graphically describes how *fitnah* (malicious rumour) circulated unchecked, thrusting the two groups even further apart. This estrangement was not confined to Johor, for Malays elsewhere were increasingly resentful of the rapidly expanding Bugis influence. In the words of Sultan Muhammad Jiwa of Kedah: 'Riau, Johor, Selangor and Kelang [were] formerly governed by Malay kings and are inhabited by Malays ... the Bugis came and settled at Riau and from thence to Selangor and from Selangor to Kelang. From what pretensions the Bugis derive their authority in these areas we know not.'[12]

A crisis was reached in 1754 when the entire Bugis community left Riau for Linggi. In the wake of this development, Malays must have been shocked to see how heavily Johor's economy had come to depend on Bugis commercial acumen. Dutch sources note the 'desolation' of Riau, the total lack of trade, while the *Tuhfat al-Nafis* describes in more human terms the pitiful attempts of the Orang Laut to fend off starvation. The parlous state of Riau's economy was also due to a lessening of access to the rich resources of Siak, where control was contested between Raja Kecil's sons. A decade earlier Sultan Sulaiman had attempted to gain Dutch support for an attack here, and it must have been with some relief that he learned of the VOC's successful attack in 1755 after a decade of indecision. It was now apparent that the Dutch had abandoned any pretence of neutrality and had thrown in their lot with Sultan Sulaiman and his ally Sultan Mansur. At the latter's urging, Sulaiman signed a treaty with the VOC in 1756, in which the Dutch promised to bring all the territory occupied by Bugis and Minangkabau 'under Johor's authority again'. In return, the VOC was promised toll-free trade throughout Johor and monopoly of the tin from Selangor, Kelang and Linggi – areas which Bugis settlers had come to regard as their own. Naturally this move infuriated the self-exiled Bugis in Linggi, and they too began making preparations for a confrontation.

Despite the general VOC policy of remaining neutral in local disputes, the possibility of confrontation with the Bugis had been threatening since the 1740s. The Dutch saw Bugis raids on shipping and refusal to abide by the Dutch pass system as a direct challenge, and reiterated the belief that Bugis migrants from Sulawesi were rejects from their own society, 'pirates and riffraff'. In both Batavia and Melaka there was a growing conviction that VOC interests would be best served if some way could be found to drive the Bugis from the Straits without great outlay of men and materials. Thus, when Sultan Sulaiman in 1756 promised substantial economic benefits if the Bugis were crushed, and agreed to assist the Dutch with fleets from Riau, Terengganu and Siak, the Melaka government was willing to launch an attack on the Bugis stronghold of Linggi. Though defeated in this engagement, the Bugis yamtuan muda, Daeng Kamboja, quickly retaliated. In alliance with Minangkabau groups from Rembau, Bugis forces converged on Melaka, burning houses in the suburbs and even raiding into the town itself. In the ensuing siege the inadequacy of Melaka's defences was embarrassingly obvious, and Dutch reports describe with awe the Bugis military equipment and their stockades, the largest of which could hold up to 2000 men. Only in mid-1757, with the arrival of a Dutch fleet, was Melaka able to make plans to avenge its humiliation. In December an attack on Linggi was launched, catching the Bugis off guard. Under pressure, Daeng Kamboja then agreed to a peace treaty by which Johor ceded suzerainty over Kelang, Rembau and Linggi to the VOC, with the stipulation that there was to be no interference in Islamic practices. The Bugis, for their part, promised to acknowledge Dutch authority and to recognize the ruler of Johor as their sovereign. Sultan Mansur of Terengganu, however, would have willingly seen the implementation of stronger measures to control his enemies. Though basically opposed to a monopoly treaty with the Dutch, he even expressed his willingness in 1759 to grant the VOC all Terengganu's pepper if they would help oust the Bugis from Johor territories and grant Riau protection from any Bugis attack. Negotiations abruptly broke down when the VOC decided that the commercial inducements he offered would be insufficient compensation for the costs such a campaign would involve. Besides, even in Riau, Malay support for continuing the confrontation was vanishing. Trade there had deteriorated to such an extent after the Bugis departure that one influential faction felt it was crucial to persuade them to return. In 1760, when Sultan Mansur Syah was absent in Terengganu, the principal nobles took the opportunity of bringing about a reconciliation with the Bugis.

Following the return of the Bugis leaders to Riau, several factors guaranteed that they would not only regain but intensify their former influence in Johor. First, Sultan Mansur decided to remain in Terengganu, where the government had suffered during his ten years in Johor. Second, in 1760 Sultan Sulaiman died and was followed in rapid succession by his son and elder grandson. The Bugis then nominated as king a small boy, Mahmud, also Sulaiman's grandson, whose mother was a daughter of Daeng Cellak. Third, several Malay nobles were willing to co-operate with the Bugis, and the Temenggung and his father-in-law Daeng Kamboja were named as joint regents for the young ruler. It was not long before the Malay component of this partnership was submerged, so that Daeng Kamboja could rightly term himself 'Yang Dipertuan Muda, who occupies the throne of Johor and Pahang and all their dependencies'. Dutch comments at this time confirm the reality of Bugis power in Riau which 'increases from day to day, the Malays no longer having any influence in the government'.[13]

English–Dutch rivalry and the impact on Malay trade

Two years after Melaka's near-capture by the Bugis, questions about the VOC's military preparedness were again raised. In 1759 Raja Muhammad, Raja Kecil's son and ruler of the new VOC possession of Siak, routed the Dutch post on Pulau Gontong, an island at the mouth of the Siak river. Not until 1761 were the Dutch able to mount a punitive expedition which avenged the massacre and placed Raja Muhammad's brother Alam on the Siak throne, ignoring his past alliance with the Bugis. This was to be the last active Dutch campaign in the Malay world until 1784. The decade before 1760 had seen the VOC deeply and uncharacteristically involved in Malay politics, prepared to take the part of any ruler who held out sufficiently enticing economic offers. But the Dutch were to find that they had gained little by their activities, and they now stood to benefit by a continuance of the status quo. From 1760 permission was granted for Melaka to dispose of surplus tin in direct sales to passing ships, and the town's finances showed a noticeable improvement as the revenue collected from duties and tolls increased.

Despite the improvement in Melaka's trading figures, the growing weakness of the VOC as a whole was slowly becoming obvious to Malays. Hamstrung by financial difficulties and problems in VOC organization, Dutch administrators faced almost impossible odds in any attempt to keep pace with rising prices. By the middle of the century officials were publicly commenting on the 'disadvantageous aspect' of the VOC's fortunes. A contemporary observer compared the VOC to a man infected with a creeping disease which, if not cured in time, would prove fatal. The erosion of its trade was so marked that during the 1750s new measures had been introduced to force ships to dock at Melaka or Batavia. Particular efforts were made to prohibit 'smuggling', the secret transport of goods from places governed by Dutch monopoly contracts to areas outside VOC control. Naturally, Malays everywhere resented the increasing restrictions on trade, especially the diversion of Chinese junks to Batavia. In the past the dubious economic benefits derived from a contract with the VOC were balanced by the recognition throughout the Malay world of Dutch prestige and military superiority. The attacks on Melaka and Pulau Gontong brought even this assumption into question.

Malay awareness of Dutch decline was heightened by the increasing presence of their major competitors, the English private 'country' traders, called such because they did not take cargoes to Europe but carried out port-to-port commerce east of the Cape of Good Hope. At a time when official English interest in the Malay world was minimal, these men had formed close associations with Malay courts. They sometimes acted as advisers on political and military matters and were often on intimate terms with the ruler. Speaking fluent Malay and sometimes related to local Malays through liaisons with their womenfolk, the influence of such traders was considerable. Although Malays still viewed the Netherlands as the most powerful European state, they were becoming conscious of Britain's mounting prestige. The British were able to gain a dominating commercial position over other Europeans in the Malay areas for several reasons. First, by the middle of the eighteenth century the English East India Company (EIC) had gained a tighter control over the cloth-producing areas of India. With access to steady supplies of cloth, British traders were able to squeeze out most of their Indian rivals in the vital piece-goods trade.

Secondly, the British also controlled the principal poppy-growing areas of India and could thus dominate the supply of opium to Southeast Asia and China. Malays had been smoking opium mixed with tobacco since the seventeenth century, when the Dutch began importing the drug into the area. A hundred years later their consumption had reached such heights that the governor of Melaka could tell his superiors that 'the people of Rembau, Selangor and Perak, like other natives, cannot live without opium', while Chinese accounts show that east coast Malays were equally addicted. No entrepôt could compete in this new economic environment unless it had ready supplies of opium, and in 1786 Francis Light was to recommend the import of large quantities of the drug to Penang specifically to attract merchants.

Thirdly, through improved maritime techniques British shipping was fast overtaking that of other Europeans. As early as 1714 the British navy was larger and better administered than any other in Europe, and Britain was also superior in skills such as shipbuilding and cartography. Whereas in

1754 the Dutch had to postpone a mission to Terengganu because available maps were totally inadequate, British sea captains, though relative new-comers to the area, had by 1788 charted the east coast sufficiently well for maps to be used as a guide for navigation. The eighteenth century saw the development of the great India-built East Indiamen, which in the 1780s averaged 600 to 800 tonnes and were capable of transporting extremely large cargoes.

Finally, British country traders had no compunction about selling armaments, which had been strictly forbidden by the VOC. It is significant, for instance, that when a French crew went ashore to trade in Terengganu in 1763, they took 'two cases of muskets, two cases of opium, and some knives'. British adventurers were also willing to trade their knowledge of the manu-facture of gunpowder and cannon, and thus exploit the Malay desire for acquisition of arms denied them by VOC policies.

The growing numbers of British traders added to the importance of those ports free of Dutch control along the maritime routes to China. There was now an even greater need for places to refit vessels and buy up supplies for the trip to Canton, and with this new impetus, Kedah, Selangor and Terengganu continued to flourish. The greatest beneficiary, however, was undoubtedly Bugis-controlled Riau, which one English country trader called 'the key to the Straits'. Here vessels from Cambodia, Siam, China, Vietnam and all over the archipelago, including the Bugis homelands, flocked to trade. With Yamtuan Muda Daeng Kamboja firmly in control, Riau became an integral part of an extensive Bugis trading community which stretched like a giant web across the entire region. Bugis ships had made Riau a prin-cipal point of exchange for smuggled spices from the eastern archipelago; here could be found all the features typical of a Malay entrepôt, including the various items in demand in the China market – forest and ocean products, tin, pepper and locally grown gambier – which were readily bartered for cloth and opium. Duties were low and cargoes could be discharged or stored easily. Traders also reported that there was little need to extend credit, a common practice in smaller ports with less access to funds. Looking back in later years, says the *Tuhfat al-Nafis*, old people simply said, 'those days in Riau were good'.

The similarity between Riau under the Bugis and earlier Malay entrepôts, like seventeenth-century Johor, Melaka and the legendary Srivi-jaya, was not limited to trade. Like its predecessors, Riau's fame as a centre for religious scholarship continued. Muslim scholars from India and the Islamic heartlands were maintained in special religious hostels, while devotees of Sufism, the mysticism at the margin of orthodox Islam, could seek initiation into one of the many *tarikat* or Sufi brotherhoods which flourished on Riau.

There was, however, one significant difference between Riau and the great ports of former days. Although there was indeed a Malay king, the young Sultan Mahmud, effective control was no longer in Malay hands but in those of outsiders.

The curtailment of Bugis power and the decline of Riau

In Terengganu, Sultan Mansur found the Bugis prosperity particularly galling. Although he had returned home, he did not forget his campaign to oust the Bugis from Riau even without VOC support. For a time he hoped to achieve his goal by allying with Raja Kecil's grandson, Raja Ismail of Siak, to whom he gave his daughter in marriage in 1765. Two years later a fleet under Raja Ismail left to attack Riau. Remembering the events of 1699 in Johor, several Orang Laut groups, especially those from Singapore, flocked to Raja Ismail's cause, but the Bugis successfully drove them off and Raja Ismail was forced to return to Sumatra.

The abortive Malay attack on Riau came at a time when, for a brief period, a chink appeared in the Bugis armour. Following the installation of Sultan Salehuddin of Selangor in 1766 and his declaration of independence, a rift developed between the Selangor and Riau Bugis. Daeng Kamboja, the yamtuan muda, was furious at Selangor's rejection of Riau–Johor overlordship, and for a few years Malays witnessed a return to the Bugis divisions which had characterized the early years of the eighteenth century. The alienation between Selangor and Riau in turn made Sultan Salehuddin anxious to strengthen his ties with his Malay neighbours. He entered into an alliance with Kedah, which was sealed by a betrothal between his daughter and Tunku Abdullah, son of Sultan Muhammad Jiwa. By this arrangement Selangor hoped for respectability and acceptance among Malay rulers by establishing a *berbisan* relationship (that is, one between those whose children wed) with an acknowledged Malay leader. Sultan Muhammad Jiwa, for his part, hoped to guarantee assistance for Kedah should Burmese forces, already deep into Ayudhya's territory, move down the Peninsula. He also hoped that Tunku Abdullah's new relatives would eventually ensure his succession to the Kedah throne in the face of claims from several other princes. A few days after Ayudhya fell to the Burmese in April 1767, the wedding between the Kedah prince and his Selangor bride took place.

The Thai recovery, however, was rapid. In December 1767 a minor provincial official, Phraya Taksin, was crowned king, and soon demanded the traditional token of submission, the 'gold and silver flowers' (*bunga mas dan perak*) from Ayudhya's former Malay vassals. Although Malays saw Taksin as a usurper, a man of inglorious genealogy, they could hardly refuse to comply. Sultan Mansur of Terengganu had even been told to expect annual raids. Kedah was particularly vulnerable because its alliance with Selangor had lasted less than three years, and it was now bereft of allies. Both VOC records and Bugis texts mention the announcement of a divorce in 1769, which Bugis historians attribute to Sultan Salehuddin's anger at his son-in-law's prolonged absences in Kedah.

Bugis resentment at this slight led to the mending of the rift between Riau and Selangor through the mediation of Raja Haji, son of Daeng Cellak and brother of the ruler of Selangor. He was a charismatic adventurer whose exploits had become legendary and who even in his own lifetime was regarded as imbued with magic power (*keramat*), often associated with saints. Under his leadership the Bugis of Selangor and Riau soon demonstrated how quickly they could avenge wounded pride, and in 1770 they formed a secret alliance with some of the discontented Kedah princes opposed to Tunku Abdullah's succession. Their consequent attack on Kedah later the same year was brief, for the Bugis found greater opposition than they had expected. When they retreated in early 1771 Sultan Muhammad Jiwa was still in power. Nevertheless, they so devastated Kedah that it was to be many years before it showed signs of returning to its former prosperity.

Once again a single incident served to highlight the Bugis–Malay enmity which permeated Malay politics of the period. Neither Sultan Muhammad Jiwa nor his son, the future Sultan Abdullah (1779–1802), ever forgot what the Bugis had done. In alliance with Sultan Mansur of Terengganu, they were determined to make yet another effort to drive the Bugis out of the Malay world. According to this new plan, Selangor and Riau-Johor would be invaded and Raja Ismail of Siak would then be installed as ruler in the latter kingdom. Sultan Muhammad Jiwa later declared that 'the whole coast of Malaya and Sumatra would be well pleased to see Raja Ismail on the throne of Riau as he was descended from all their ancient kings'.[14] For a short period it appeared that he might have found an ally in the English East India Company, to whom he promised the cession of the coast near Kuala Kedah in return for support in an attack on Selangor. However, when it became clear that any assistance the British could give would be insufficient, Sultan Muhammad Jiwa refused to continue the association, and in the middle of 1772 the EIC post in Kedah was withdrawn. When it also became obvious that Raja Ismail was more interested in returning to Siak than in setting himself up in Riau, talk of a Malay invasion was quietly dropped.

The short-lived association between Kedah and the EIC in 1770–1 is noteworthy because it represented part of the ongoing British quest for a place on the China sea route which would also give them access to Malay products. Riau and the Redang Islands, off Terengganu, had already been considered, but tentative British approaches to the Malay rulers concerned had been inconclusive. In 1759 the British discovered the existence of an eastern sea route to China, which enabled ships to reach Canton even when the adverse monsoon was far advanced. As a result, British interest in the Borneo region grew. By an agreement in 1762 with the sultan of Sulu, the EIC acquired the island of Balambangan, off Borneo's northern coast, as a trading post. In 1773 a factory was established there but was abandoned two years later following an attack by Sulu raiders. Efforts in 1774 to reach an agreement with Brunei which would provide access to local pepper supplies proved no more successful than the negotiations with Kedah.

For Sultan Muhammad Jiwa of Kedah, the collapse of his brief alliance with the British meant the loss not only of a potential ally against the Bugis but the end of his plans for an attack on Bugis-controlled Selangor and

Riau. The eventual elimination of the Bugis as a serious threat in the region can be attributed not to Malay action but to the deteriorating relations between Britain and the Netherlands, and to the repercussions in Riau's dealings with the VOC. In 1780 the British declared war on the Dutch Republic to prevent its joining the Russian-sponsored League of Armed Neutrality. To VOC employees in Asia the news of war in Europe seemed merely an extension of the long years of bitter commercial rivalry between British and Dutch traders in the Asian areas. What became known as the Fourth Anglo-Dutch War (1780–4) intensified this rivalry, feeding rumours that the British were planning an attack on Melaka itself. Such rumours were taken seriously by VOC officials and Riau leaders alike. Raja Haji, who had succeeded as yamtuan muda in 1777, in evaluating the possible effects of European rivalry, decided that Riau's interests would be best served through improved relations with the Dutch. Accordingly, in 1782, when a British merchant vessel loaded with opium appeared in Riau's harbour, Raja Haji approached Melaka with a secret offer: the ship would be surrendered to the Dutch, with the understanding that he would receive a share of the confiscated cargo. But though the ship was duly seized, Raja Haji was denied his promised rewards, despite extended negotiations. Angry and humiliated, he began massing troops in Muar to the south of Melaka, and rumours of an impending assault, possibly with British help, circulated wildly. Years of suspicion of Bugis intentions fed the Dutch belief that Riau should be 'chastised and humiliated'. But although a VOC fleet was dispatched to blockade Riau, its performance was mediocre, and an attempted landing in January 1784 failed miserably. Two weeks afterwards, despite efforts at mediation by the ruler of Perak, Raja Haji and his allies attacked Melaka.

At first the Dutch governor fully expected he would reap the benefits of Malay–Bugis hostility and be able to rally the assistance of neighbouring Malay kings. Most did send letters of encouragement, but the two from whom Melaka had expected most, Kedah and Terengganu, were themselves occupied with preparations for a possible confrontation with the reunified Thai kingdom of Siam. In addition, the influence of British traders in both places probably strengthened beliefs that the VOC was a crumbling edifice. The only Malay state which actually dispatched ships and men was Siak, but the prince in command, Sayid Ali, was well known in the Straits for his raiding activities, and the governor was therefore wary of placing too great a reliance on his loyalty. In any event, the Siak fleet did not reach Melaka in time to repel the Bugis forces which placed the town under siege for five weary months. Had it not been for the arrival of a large Dutch squadron and the death of Raja Haji in a subsequent assault on the main Bugis fort, Melaka would almost certainly have fallen.

For a short time after the relief of Melaka, the VOC was able to press home its military advantage. A fleet was quickly sent to capture Riau, and by the end of 1784 Sultan Mahmud of Riau-Johor had reluctantly agreed to a treaty in which he formally announced his 'eternal gratitude' to the Dutch who had freed him from 'the Bugis yoke'. Riau-Johor was to become a Dutch vassal state, a *leenrijk*, where Malays would rule only at the VOC's pleasure. All Bugis except those actually born in Riau were expelled, and the Dutch stipulated that no Bugis was ever again to hold the position of yamtuan muda. Control of all trade was placed firmly in VOC hands. In the face of the Dutch victory over Riau, the Selangor ruler, Sultan Ibrahim (1782–1826), fled to Pahang, and the VOC immediately sent a force to claim Selangor. As a reward for their loyalty to the Dutch, the former ruler of Siak, Muhammad Ali, together with his nephew Sayid Ali, was placed in charge of Selangor, now subject to VOC sovereignty.

As a result of these developments, the VOC came to exert greater territorial control in the Straits and Peninsular states than ever before. Naning had been a VOC possession for more than a century, with its chief required to accept a Dutch-appointed head 'without demur'; Siak, Rembau, Kelang and Linggi had been ceded by Riau-Johor in the 1750s; now the VOC had become the lord not only of Selangor but of the entire kingdom of Riau-Johor, from Sumatra to Pahang. The Bugis pennants and banners captured in Riau, which were now proudly displayed in the Knights' Hall in The Hague, appeared to signal a new era of VOC domination. But if any Dutchman had entertained visions of a re-energized trading empire, he would have been quickly brought back to reality. The last decade of the eighteenth century saw the VOC slide rapidly into bankruptcy, a major factor being the settlement with Britain in 1784, which permitted free navigation in the eastern seas. As Dutch seaborne trade faced unprecedented competition, the VOC position as overlord in Selangor and Riau was also called into question. In Selangor, the rapacious rule of the Siak princes proved totally unsatisfactory, and when Sultan Ibrahim returned overland from Pahang with a large band of followers, he easily persuaded most of the Selangor district chiefs to join him. In June 1785 his forces overran the Dutch defences at the mouth of the Selangor river, forcing the occupants to flee. Although the subsequent Dutch blockade had disastrous effects on Selangor's economy, Sultan Ibrahim would not surrender, and in 1786 the Dutch reluctantly concluded a treaty, reinstating him as their *leenman* or vassal. But while these months of conflict and the consequent depopulation represented a considerable setback for Selangor's economy, the VOC contract brought little fundamental change. As one scholar has put it, 'Prior to 1784 the Company had never set foot in Selangor, and after August 1786 they were never to return.'[15]

In Riau, the challenge to the Dutch was even greater and the economic repercussions especially far-reaching. Contrary to Dutch expectations, Sultan Mahmud did not prove a grateful recipient of Dutch favours, especially when further measures were introduced which made the VOC Resident the virtual ruler of Riau. Resentful and humiliated, Sultan Mahmud recruited the assistance of the Ilanun from the Sulu archipelago, whose formidable slave-raiding fleets had begun appearing regularly in Malay waters since the early 1780s. The Ilanun quickly established a reputation for navigational ability and fighting skill, while the sheer ferocity of their attacks struck terror into coastal villages. In May 1787 a huge Ilanun force of around 90 vessels and 7000 men appeared off Riau on the pretext of sheltering from bad weather. With Sultan Mahmud's secret assistance they entered the Riau river by stealth and overcame the Dutch garrison, most of whom were killed or captured. Interested only in booty, the Ilanun left in June, and shortly afterwards Sultan Mahmud, who apparently feared Dutch reprisals, moved to the neighbouring island of Lingga. Except for the Chinese, Riau was depopulated, with the Malays following Sultan Mahmud to Lingga, Terengganu and Pahang, and the Bugis dispersing to Selangor, Siantan and Borneo. The Dutch recaptured Riau in late 1787, but only in 1795 did they reach an agreement which permitted Sultan Mahmud to return. The catastrophic effects of these years, when the Malay ruler exercised little authority and the economy was moribund, ended any hopes that Riau might once again assume its former position in the Malay world.

As so often in the past, however, another Malay state seized the opportunity to move into a political and economic vacuum. This time the pendulum swung once again to the Sumatran side of the Straits, to the area of Siak that had been so closely associated not only with Riau-Johor but with the family of Raja Kecil. Offering access to an extensive and resource-rich hinterland, the Siak river was more easily navigated than many Sumatran rivers, and from the late seventeenth century the Dutch had frequently sought to extend their influence in this important Johor territory. Since its incorporation into the Melaka empire in the fifteenth century, Siak leaders had been ambitious for a greater role in the Malay world, but although they had attempted to establish a base in various areas, including Siantan, they had been effectively restrained. For much of the eighteenth century the potential of Siak was kept in check because of continuing conflicts between the sons and grandsons of Raja Kecil, but in 1791 a new ruler of part-Arab descent, Sayid Ali, came to power. Well known to the Dutch as a former 'pirate' and occasional ally, he incorporated much of his raiding experience into his style of government. Allying with the dreaded Ilanun, he mounted periodic attacks on neighbouring ports and rival shipping. By the early nineteenth century, Riau had become a commercial backwater, whereas Siak, noted one Englishman, was 'at the summit of prosperity'. It is surely significant that in the early nineteenth century the Siak royal family also produced a version of the *Sejarah Melayu*, tracing its origins back to Melaka and beyond to the sacred hill of Bukit Siguntang in Palembang. The same text points to the continued standing of Raja Kecil's line among Orang Laut and Orang Asli groups, and recalls that Sultan Mahmud, the ruler of Riau, 'was not descended from the line of Sultan Iskandar Zul-karnain, but from the bendahara who committed *derhaka* against the ruler of Johor.... This is the true origin of the present rulers of Lingga.' Yet Siak's attempt to make a bid for the Melayu heritage faced obstacles, for many Malays regarded its *kacu* (mixed) culture as inferior to that of Riau-Johor, and saw its rulers as upstarts. Such attitudes were clearly evident when Sultan Mahmud himself reminded a delegation departing for Siak that no special obeisance should be made to the Siak ruler.

The political and territorial manoeuvring of Malay kings should not distract the historian from other significant developments in the Malay world, most notably the resurgence of Islamic literature in Malay. From early times Malay port cities had been a focus for Muslim teaching, and in the latter part of the eighteenth century the traditions of Aceh and Riau were found again in the prosperous court of Palembang. Here, despite Javanese influence, Malay continued to be used for much court writing, especially dealing with religion. Palembang produced a number of Islamic scholars, but undoubtedly the most famous was 'Abd al-Samad al-Palimbani (d. 1785), who had studied with a number of notable teachers in Mekka and Medina. His commentaries and translations of Arabic works made a significant contribution to the corpus of Islamic texts used by students and teachers across the Malay-Indonesian archipelago. Through this network connections were maintained between the Melaka Straits and other centres of Islamic scholarship such as southeast Borneo and Patani, where the proximity of Thai Buddhism had long injected a special intensity into religious life.

The resurgence of the Thais and the establishment of Penang

The revival of Islamic debate in the Malay world coincided with important shifts of power in the northern Malay states. In 1782 a dynamic general in the Thai army, Chakri, subsequently known as Rama I (1782–1809), seized the throne and established a new dynasty at Bangkok. This revitalized kingdom of Siam resumed hostilities against the Thais' traditional enemy, Burma, with renewed vigour. But whenever the Thai army was assembled, it boded ill for the Malay vassals who were required to contribute their quota of men and weapons. The northern Malay rulers therefore waited apprehensively for indications of what their new overlord would require. The demands surpassed their worst expectations. Not only were they ordered to submit greater material assistance than ever before, but the rulers of Kedah, Patani, Kelantan and Terengganu were also commanded to leave their capitals and make personal obeisance (*tawai bangkom*) in Siam.

The Malays were outraged: 'from time immemorial' such a thing had never been asked. The sending of supplies, expensive gifts, arms and men was as much as any overlord should properly demand. No Malay ruler should be required to prostrate himself before the Siamese king as Thai court protocol required. Every Malay would have been familiar with the story of how Hang Tuah, the legendary hero of Melaka, had refused to crawl on his hands and knees when visiting Ayudhya because this was totally opposed to the dignity of a Malay subject. How then could a king accept such humiliation? Sultan Abdullah of Kedah side-stepped the issue by sending his brother-in-law and son in his stead; Sultan Mansur dispatched a Portuguese envoy to placate the Siamese king while continuing his negotiations with Goa and Macao for a Portuguese post in Terengganu. The ruler of Patani flatly refused, returning 'a very rude answer', and suffered the most terrible consequences. Patani, it was said, was razed by the Siamese, 'all the men, children and old women . . . [being] tied and thrown upon the ground and then trampled to death by elephants'.[16] But unrest continued in Patani, and after three major rebellions in 1789, 1791 and 1808, Rama I deposed the ruler. Stripped of its status as a semi-independent vassal (*prathesaraj*), Patani was divided into seven separate jurisdictions, known as *Khaek Jet Huamuang*, under the control of the southern Thai province of Songkhla (Singora).

By 1809 the Siamese tributary system had been forcibly reimposed over all the northern Malay states, and it seemed that Bangkok's control here was firmly in place. It is not surprising that Malay *prathesaraj* rulers had looked with hope towards the British, whose representatives, the country traders, had been specifically advised 'to conciliate the esteem and affection of the natives and to teach them to look up to the English as their friends and protectors'. Little wonder, too, that Sultan Abdullah of Kedah, pressured by Burmese demands as well as Siamese, offered to lease Penang to the EIC. He hoped by this means to gain protection against possible attacks from Siam or Burma and from any future uprisings by his own relatives. In August 1786 Francis Light, a country trader entrusted with the negotiations, took formal possession of Penang in the name of King George III of Britain.

For Malays, the establishment of Penang transformed the EIC into a territorial power with an obvious stake in the security of the area. Only a year after its founding all Malay rulers of standing had written to Light in an effort to gauge British willingness to lend them material aid. Perak saw the British as a potential ally against the Bugis of Selangor; Terengganu and Kedah hoped for assistance against the continuing demands of Siam; Sultan Ibrahim of Selangor, Sultan Mahmud of Riau-Johor and the new Bugis yamtuan muda, the exiled Raja Ali, all anticipated support against the Dutch. Disenchantment, however, quickly set in. Whatever verbal promises Light may have made, whatever hopes he may have encouraged, it soon became clear that his superiors were as unwilling as the Dutch to enter into any contract which might in the future involve them in warfare with another power, whether Siam or the Netherlands. Sultan Mansur of Terengganu, having failed in his efforts to gain Portuguese help, now found that the most the EIC was willing to offer was a post with 12 men. In Kedah, Sultan Abdullah discovered that the compensation he was to receive in return for the British occupation of Penang was far less than he had been led to expect. The sense of disillusion was complete. In the words of the Kedah chiefs, 'Now these English will not submit to the King's demand, therefore we have written to the English to go away from Pulau Pinang in the name of peace, for when they first came it was with a good name'.[17] When Sultan Abdullah's efforts to effect a financial settlement with Light failed, he recruited some Ilanun raiders roaming the Straits and attacked Penang in March 1791.

The attack itself, while unsuccessful, is intriguing because for the first time since the Minangkabau-led movements of the late seventeenth century there was some effort to rise above ethnic divisions and to forge a unity based not on a sense of being Malay but on being Muslim. In writing to the native population of Penang to arouse support, the Kedah nobles addressed themselves to 'all Muslims, that is, Bugis, Acehnese, men of Minangkabau, Malays and Chulias [Indians from Coromandel] who dwell at Pulau Pinang ... God will assist us and our Lord Muhammad the Guardian of the Muslims and the last of all the Prophets'.[18] The following month the British attacked the Kedah placements on the shore opposite Penang, dispersing the Kedah forces and removing the immediate threat to the island. The British occupation of Penang was subsequently confirmed in a treaty with Kedah in 1791.

Britain's supremacy in the area seemed total four years later when it assumed direct control of several VOC possessions in the Malay Indonesian archipelago. This move was part of a general policy intended to prevent any Dutch possession in Asia falling into French hands after Napoleon conquered the Netherlands in January 1795. After the Dutch *stadthouder* fled to England, he asked the British government to take control of Dutch territories in the East until his own restoration to power. Technically speaking, therefore, Melaka remained Dutch, but the subtleties of the European situation were lost on Malays, who could not understand why the 'Kompeni Wolanda', the Dutch Company, which had existed for so many years, had capitulated without a struggle. With their base in Penang, the British had no interest in reviving Melaka's position, nor in encouraging the development of an entrepôt at Riau. Now the epitome of commercial success was represented not by a Malay port but by the British town of Penang. In his reminiscences, one Chinese merchant later recalled how 'the English called in traders and it gradually became more prosperous. The clothing, food and houses there [were] all magnificent, and horses and carriages [were] used for travelling.'[19] In 1800 the ruler of Kedah also leased the district of Prai (Province Wellesley) on the coast opposite Penang to the EIC in return for an increased pension.

The demise of the Malay entrepôt state

The legacy of generations of hostility and division, combined with economic weakness, meant that in Riau Sultan Mahmud could exert little influence over his chiefs or principal ministers. The bendahara in Pahang and the temenggung at Singapore became to all appearances independent rulers. Numerous Malay leaders, notably the temenggung, desperately in need of an income which Riau-Johor could no longer provide, financed and equipped Orang

Laut raids as a source of revenue. It was in fact the prevalence of piracy that prompted some Englishmen to write of the Malay kingdoms in terms of 'decay'. They blamed the Dutch monopoly treaties which, by disrupting traditional trading patterns, had weakened Malay states and caused a breakdown of authority on the oceans. However, other factors also contributed to the increase in Orang Laut and *anak raja* piracy. First, the ties between Johor and many Orang Laut groups had been irrevocably damaged after the regicide of 1699, and this had been compounded by the weakening of central control in Riau after 1784. Secondly, succession disputes, especially in Kedah and Siak, had led to a rise in the number of pirating princes operating outside the restraints of any court. Thirdly, since the 1790s a different type of raiding had come to exist together with the plundering of the Orang Laut and *anak raja* of the Malay world. Requiring virtually unlimited supplies of manpower to service the lucrative China trade, the chiefs of the Sulu sultanate were now raiding throughout the archipelago specifically for slaves. Their attacks on the Borneo coast had become so frequent that the pepper plantations lay untended and junks no longer called there. Regularly with the northeast monsoon they surged out into Malay waters, even establishing a permanent base at Retih, on the east Sumatran coast. Throughout the archipelago coastal settlements came to dread the 'pirate season', the *musim Ilanun*.

From the end of the eighteenth century continuing disputes over succession racked the Malay world. In the Minangkabau states of later Negeri Sembilan struggles between branches of the ruling families pitted faction against faction. Perak, disrupted after 1792 by battles between contending heirs and without the protective mantle provided by the VOC contract, was a tempting lure to ambitious neighbours because of its tin. In 1804 forces from Selangor attacked and for some years occupied the downstream area. The withdrawal of Selangor did not end Perak's troubles, for Bangkok and its provincial government in Ligor revived Thai claims to suzerainty. In 1814, when the Perak ruler flatly refused to send tribute to Bangkok, invoking his proud descent from Bukit Siguntang, Siam ordered its vassal, Kedah, to invade. Troops from Kedah moved into Perak in 1816, and three years later Perak acknowledged the overlordship of Siam. In Kedah itself succession disputes took a different turn. One prince, seeking support for his bid for the throne, turned in 1803 to Bangkok. He was duly installed as Sultan Ahmad (1803–21, 1842–5), with the deposed ruler being made raja of Perlis. There was, predictably, a price. In addition to the traditional levies of men and supplies demanded by its Siamese overlord, Kedah was now expected to act as its agent when force was required in the Peninsula.

Though conflicts within the Malay states were extensive, it was events in the kingdom of Riau-Johor which were to have the most far-reaching ramifications. The last years of Sultan Mahmud's life had been relatively peaceful, and in the words of a Malay account, 'in justice, equity and mercy he cherished all his people'.[20] None the less, it is also clear that the old Bugis–Malay conflicts simmered even after the reinstatement of a Bugis yamtuan muda in

Riau in 1804. Neighbouring princes were all too ready to take up the quarrel on the side of one or another party, and there was thus no possibility of any succession dispute remaining purely an internal affair. This became apparent in 1812 when Sultan Mahmud died leaving two sons, both born of commoner mothers. The Bugis faction, led by the yamtuan muda, favoured the younger, Raja Abdul Rahman; while the Malays, under the bendahara of Pahang and the temenggung, supported the elder, Raja Husain. In 1818 the Dutch signed a treaty with Abdul Rahman recognizing him as sultan in return for the re-establishment of the Dutch post on Riau.

The Dutch action was a bald challenge for those Englishmen who were convinced that Britain must control the maritime route to China. Sir Thomas Stamford Raffles, the greatest exponent of this view, had strongly opposed the return of Dutch possessions in the East after the Napoleonic Wars. Britain, he felt, was destined to take on the role of overlord in the archipelago in the tradition of great kingdoms of earlier times. Raffles was convinced of the need to establish a British entrepôt somewhere in the region which could become another staging post along the maritime route to China. Previous hopes of developing an entrepôt in the Borneo area had failed when Balambangan, re-established in 1803, was abandoned two years later. However, another opportunity came when Raffles was ordered to set up a post in the southern approaches to the Melaka Straits. Raffles had hoped to use Riau, but found the Dutch already entrenched there. An alternative site was soon found. On 30 January 1819 Raffles signed a treaty with the temenggung of Riau-Johor, the territorial chief of Singapore, which gave the British the right to establish a factory on the island.

Singapore had an abundance of drinking water, a natural sheltered harbour and was conveniently placed as a centre for trade with China and the eastern archipelago. All it needed to fulfil the classic role of a Straits entrepôt in the tradition of Srivijaya and Melaka was a ruler. To impart legality to the rights he had acquired on Singapore, Raffles recognized Husain, elder son of Sultan Mahmud, as the legitimate successor in Riau-Johor. On 6 February 1819 a financial settlement was made and a formal treaty signed with 'Sultan Husain Syah of Johor', together with the temenggung. Four months afterwards the new ruler took up residence in Singapore in his own settlement, known as Kampung Gelam. Both he and the temenggung continued to live in Singapore, although in 1824 they formally agreed to give up their authority there in return for a pension. But without the regalia and the backing of the Riau-Johor court, which remained with his younger brother in Riau, Sultan Husain could never claim any great prestige among Malays. In practical matters he was always eclipsed by the more dominating temenggung, whom the British saw as the stronger of the two. Indeed, his status had not been diminished but had on the contrary been enhanced by his association with Raffles and the new European power in the area. Sultan Husain, on the other hand, was treated by the British as 'a legal necessity' and with the passing of time faded into the background.

While there are identifiable continuities between Singapore and previous entrepôts, its establishment ushers in a new period in Malay history because it confirmed the dominance of British commercial interests in the region. This process had begun in 1786 with the occupation of Penang, but although Penang was founded, like Singapore, on the principles of free trade, it did not make the same impact. In the latter part of the eighteenth century the British still had to contend with the Dutch, whose prestige, even when the VOC was crumbling, was still great. Furthermore, Penang was not on one of the major routes between China and the archipelago. Though its trade flourished, it was generally focused on the region of the Straits and southern Thailand rather than drawing shipping from all over the island world. When Java was taken by the British in 1811 during the Napoleonic Wars (1795–1815) to prevent its falling to the French, Batavia was opened to country traders, and its position as the dominant centre in the archipelago was strengthened. All this was changed after 1819. Singapore was better sited than Penang and its free trade policies drew commerce away from Batavia, where the Dutch, returning in 1816, had reimposed their old tariff restrictions. Moreover, the great days of the Netherlands were past; Singapore, by contrast, was linked to the growing industrial power and prestige of Britain, which in the nineteenth century came to eclipse all other nations. As a contemporary Chinese traveller, marvelling at Singapore's prosperity, remarked: 'There has never been a country as powerful as England.'[21]

In terms of Malay history, Singapore signalled the end of the entrepôt under Malay rule or even, as Riau, functioning under Malay auspices. With two British ports, Penang and Singapore, in the area there was now no need for British traders or Chinese junks to frequent Malay harbours. The response of Malay traders on both sides of the Straits to Singapore's founding provides ample evidence of their continued willingness to patronize a convenient and well-regulated Straits port which could provide a meeting place for local and foreign merchants. But an entrepôt such as Singapore, controlled by Europeans and maintained primarily for their benefit, was very different from those which had previously existed in the area. Its impact on Malay history was to reflect that difference. The musings of Raffles's Malay scribe capture something of this sense of change:

> Singapore at that time was like the sun when it has just risen, waxing stronger and stronger as it gets higher and higher ... I am astonished to see how markedly the world is changing. A new world is being created, the old world destroyed. The very jungle becomes a settled district and elsewhere a settlement reverts to jungle.[22]

In many ways one could argue that the eighteenth century was a low point in Malay history. The murder of Mahmud of Johor in 1699 set in motion a chain of events which resulted in the usurpation of effective power in that kingdom first by Minangkabaus from Sumatra and then by Bugis from

Sulawesi. Although these were indeed traumatic events, it is possible that in time the rifts in Malay society would have healed, and that the new arrivals would have been absorbed. The Dutch presence, however, precluded the emergence of a new Malay centre on the old Melaka-Johor model. Dutch victories in the battles with Malay-Bugis forces during the 1780s were a massive blow to the standing of Riau-Johor, and any further hopes of commercial revival were dashed by the founding of a British entrepôt at Singapore in 1819. No other Malay kingdom succeeded in challenging this new port, nor in re-establishing the tradition of Malay commercial hegemony in the Straits. Many of the Malay states were preoccupied with succession disputes and wars which increased in intensity and complexity as outsiders became involved. Siam was quick to exploit the situation and within a short time reasserted Thai overlordship in the northern Malay kingdoms. Perhaps the break with the past was most evident in 1809 when the British, during a temporary occupation, destroyed the great Melaka fort. As Munshi Abdullah put it, 'After its destruction, [Melaka] lost its glory, like a woman bereaved of her husband, the lustre gone from her face. But now by the will of Allah it was no more, showing how ephemeral are the things of this world.'[23]

But the picture is not as bleak as the broad outline of events might indicate. The history of individual states shows that for some the eighteenth century could be remembered with pride. Terengganu and Selangor were formally established as independent kingdoms; other states, like Kedah and Perak, also threw up their share of able leaders. A shadow of the great economic developments of later years is discernible as both Malays and newcomers moved to take advantage of changing international trade and the growing demand for Malay products, especially for the China trade. The very concept of what 'Melayu' signified had broadened far beyond the narrow definition of Melaka's early days. The language and culture of the Riau-Johor court was still held up as a model, but 'Malayness' had grown to incorporate the whole range of regional variations from Patani to east Sumatra. Beyond the Peninsula and the Melaka Straits other foci of Malay culture like Brunei helped sustain a healthy Malay commercial diaspora which had established fruitful linkages with other indigenous groups. In such places the Malay language and customs were both adopted and adapted so that the epithet 'Malay' could apply as easily in west Sumatra as in southeast Borneo. Europeans were themselves struck by the extent to which Malay culture had spread throughout the archipelago, and in an essay published in 1816 Raffles even spoke of the 'Malayu Nation'. Although a new generation of European scholars had already begun to depict Malay history in terms of decline, the evidence indicates that in a difficult period the Malay world did not stagnate and the legacy of past achievements was still honoured. However, transition to the changed political and economic environment of the nineteenth century required time, and it was one of the ironies of history that this is precisely what Western imperialism could least afford to give.

'A New World is Created', 1819–74

The most colourful description of life in the new British settlement of Singapore is contained in the *Hikayat Abdullah* (The Story of Abdullah), the autobiography of the noted teacher of Malay who was also scribe to Stamford Raffles. One of Abdullah's main concerns is the change brought about by the European presence, 'the destruction of the old world and the creation of a new'. He is understandably less interested in the historical continuities which, despite the overriding sense of change, can still be discerned. The very readiness of Malay rulers to establish links with British officials in Singapore and Penang was in keeping with previous Malay diplomacy. Like the Dutch and Portuguese, the British simply represented a new and powerful element whose friendship was desirable. Nor was Singapore's commercial success unprecedented. In the tradition of earlier entrepôts such as Melaka and Johor, its prosperity owed much to its unrivalled geographic position, to which was added the attraction of free trade in an age when tariffs and protection were almost universal. The initial acceptance of the British was also aided by the fact that the areas involved – Penang, Singapore, Province Wellesley and Melaka – had not been forcibly taken from any Malay power, and at least the trappings of legality surrounded their transfer. Well before the Anglo-Dutch Treaty of 1824, the British appeared the legitimate heirs to the prestige formerly accorded the VOC. Melaka continued under British rule from 1795, except for a brief period of Dutch control from 1818 until 1824, and Munshi Abdullah remembered how those people of Dutch extraction 'changed their customs and language, their clothing and habits of their race, men and women alike copying English ways of life'.[1]

It is not 'change' as such which makes the nineteenth century of special significance. The Malay world had, after all, been absorbing and responding to outside influences for hundreds of years. What characterizes this period is rather the pace of change, itself part of a global phenomenon. 'The world,' as one Englishman wrote in 1864, 'moves faster and faster'.[2] The Malay archipelago, always sensitive to the shifts of international trade, was now caught

117

up by far-reaching economic and political forces which were drawing Europe and Asia ever closer. Developments such as the expansion of Western technology, the tightening relationship between European government and commerce, and the shrinking of distance through improved communications began to transform the nature of Malay society. International agreements saw the establishment of political boundaries which became the basis of modern Malaysia; the growing association with industrializing Britain strengthened the role of the Malay Peninsula as a supplier of raw materials; unprecedented Chinese and Indian migration encouraged growing socio-economic distinctions between the major ethnic groups. Against this background the meaning of 'Melayu' again became the subject of debate.

The nineteenth century: historiographical considerations

In the historiography of Malaysia, the period from the founding of Singapore until the signing of the Pangkor Treaty in 1874 represents a new phase. The principal sources are no longer the commercial reports of European trading companies but those of the local British administration in the 'Straits Settlements', concerned as much with the problems of governing as with revenue. An important supplement to official documents is the contemporary commentary provided by locally printed English-language newspapers and scholarly publications, as well as an increasing number of personal memoirs and travel writings. Many of these sources, official and unofficial, contain useful statistics, the most frequently cited being those for population. However, while the figures for the Straits Settlements are probably reasonably accurate, those for the Malay states must be treated as estimates until 1891, when the first official census was carried out.[3] There are other significant historiographical developments: in Borneo the inception of 'white raja' rule in Sarawak in 1841 has spawned a voluminous body of literature, while the expansion of a Thai bureaucracy helped generate a growing mass of documentation which provides important insights into the nature of Thai–Malay relations.

In terms of indigenous material this period is noteworthy because for the first time many oral sources were being committed to paper, either by Europeans or at their behest, and a large number were published in newly established scholarly journals. In Sarawak and Sabah these records have been indispensable in understanding how local groups understood many of the changes in which they were involved. At the same time writing in Malay was itself passing through a transitional phase. Chronicles in the classical literary style persisted, but now personal accounts were reaching a wider audience through lithographing and vernacular publishing houses. Yet although the corpus of data is far larger than in earlier periods, many questions remain unanswered. There are still glaring gaps in our knowledge of vital subjects such as the implementation of Islamic law and the life of the

Malay peasant. Nonetheless, the relatively greater amount of information available makes historical reconstruction in the nineteenth century more practicable than in earlier periods.

Relations between Siam and the northern Malay states

In their anxiety to ensure the commercial success of Penang and Singapore, East India Company (EIC) authorities were willing to recognize Thai suzerainty in the northern Malay states, and even at times to support it; at the same time, they did not wish to see Thai power extend further down the Peninsula. This somewhat ambiguous attitude had important repercussions as the notion of 'spheres of influence' began to shape international relations. As a new dynasty in Bangkok once again begun to push southwards, some of Siam's Malay tributaries began to see Britain as a potential friend.

The reassertion of Thai overlordship over the northern Malay states after 1782 was the more onerous owing to the relative freedom they had enjoyed for much of the eighteenth century. As Sultan Mansur Syah of Terengganu had put it, 'The previous king was content when I sent him the *bunga mas dan perak*, but the present King [Rama I, 1782–1809] thinks only of ruining me.'[4] The end of the wars between Siam and Burma after 1810 brought no respite from Bangkok's demands and in 1819 Kedah, acting under Siamese orders, helped reduce Perak to vassal status. Continuing Thai aggression here was largely due to the ambitions of Ligor, whose traditional autonomy was sufficiently great for its governor to declare himself king after the destruction of Ayudhya by the Burmese in 1767. In 1811 a new governor had been appointed whose status was so high that some European visitors assumed Ligor was not a province but an independent vassal of Bangkok. His ambition was clearly evident when he helped initiate an attack on Perak in 1811, demanding that Kedah assist with troops and supplies. In his administration of Kedah and Kelantan, however, the Ligor governor had a rival in the other major Siamese provincial centre, Songkhla (Singora), which was responsible for Terengganu and Patani. Jealously guarding his prestige, the new appointee was extremely sensitive to anything which undermined his own standing. According to one account, he was particularly annoyed when Sultan Ahmad of Kedah (1803–21, 1842–5), his presumed subordinate, was awarded the superior title of *chao phraya*[5] by the Siamese king as a reward for assistance in the campaigns against Burma.

The animosity of the Ligor governor was a potential danger for Kedah. Although Bangkok assumed general responsibility for any moves in the south, the Siamese administrators there had great influence in formulating policy and were given considerable latitude in its execution. The Ligor family had powerful relatives at court, and in 1820 the governor's accusation that Sultan Ahmad refused to recognize his authority and was conspiring with both the Burmese and the English coincided with other allegations of misgovernment from a rival Kedah prince. Tensions were exacerbated when Sultan Ahmad failed to submit the *bunga mas*, and refused to present himself at the Siamese court. The future Rama III, who had been accorded wide-ranging powers owing to his father's ill-health, saw this as rank defiance. Suspicious of British aims in the region and determined to maintain Siam's hold in the strategically important Peninsula, he could not countenance any suggestion of disloyalty. A Siamese fleet was made ready and in November 1821 the invasion of Kedah began. The Siamese were met by a strong Malay force, but when the Kedah laksamana and temenggung were killed and the bendahara captured, Malay resistance collapsed.

Hoping to receive British help, Sultan Ahmad fled to Penang where his plight aroused some sympathy among the European community, particularly as British commercial interests in Kedah appeared endangered. However, although loud voices were raised locally in support of intervention, the EIC government in India persistently refused to condone any confrontation with Siam, regarding such a prospect as 'an evil of very serious magnitude'. The question of Kedah's future became more problematic because Bangkok's decision to exercise direct control through the Ligor governor and his appointees was not successful. A major difficulty was the proximity of Sultan Ahmad, whom the British, somewhat reluctantly, maintained in Penang. His presence provided Kedah Malays with a focus for conspiracies directed against Siamese rule.

Bangkok rewarded the Ligor governor for his part in the subjection of Kedah by bestowing on him the title of *chao phraya* in 1822. Two years later Rama III ascended the throne fully prepared to continue the expansionist policies he had pursued as prince regent. In their correspondence with EIC authorities, the Malay rulers liable to be directly affected made clear their apprehension. Already in 1822 Kelantan had unsuccessfully petitioned the British to be accepted as a vassal state. Perak, which had expelled the occupying Siamese with Selangor's help, was in 1825 again reduced to a Siamese vassal under Ligor's control. In appealing to Penang for assistance, the Perak ruler expressed his feelings simply: 'I am afraid, for this country is part of the same continent as Siam.'[6] In the light of developments in Perak, argued the governor of Penang, a further extension of Siamese influence into Selangor seemed imminent.

This possibility finally aroused the EIC authorities in India to respond to Penang's appeals. Like the VOC before them, the British were always anxious to avoid direct conflict, but they agreed that some kind of agreement was necessary to exclude Siam from Perak and Selangor, where prospects for British investment in the tin trade seemed bright. In 1826 the military secretary at Penang, Henry Burney, was sent to Bangkok. After lengthy discussions a treaty was concluded by which Siam agreed not to attack either Perak or Selangor, with the provision that the Perak ruler could, if he wished, send the *bunga mas dan perak* to Bangkok. But although Kedah was clearly acknowledged to be 'a territory subject to Siam', the English wording of the Anglo-Siamese Treaty left the status of Kelantan and Terengganu ambiguous. Burney was careful to obtain a guarantee of British trade in these areas, for Singapore's commercial links with Kelantan and Terengganu had alerted Straits business interests to the attractiveness of the east coast, where the estimated populations were higher than other Malay states. While no British military involvement was permitted in Kelantan and Terengganu 'on any pretext whatever', the treaty did not formally recognize Siamese overlordship. Even at this stage British policy-makers realized the advantage of such an omission if British 'protection' were to be eventually extended over the Peninsula. But this ambiguity existed only in European eyes. From Bangkok's point of view, Kedah, Kelantan and Terengganu were all vassal states who acknowledged their tributary status by sending the *bunga mas dan perak* every three years. The northern Malay states were an important source of rice and manpower, and the new Bangkok dynasty was not willing to allow them the kind of autonomy they had enjoyed for some decades.

In Perak, where Ligor's interests had always been greater than Bangkok's, the ties with Siam were also renounced in 1826. Captain James Low was sent to Perak by the Penang authorities and on his own initiative concluded a treaty by which the EIC recognized Perak's sovereignty and promised help in case of attack. Although the governor-general in Calcutta refused to ratify this agreement, it was never explicitly abrogated and thus allowed the continuation of a vague relationship between Perak and the British. With Penang's encouragement the Perak ruler formed a new administration free of any pro-Ligor officials and publicly announced that he would no longer send the gold and silver flowers to Bangkok.

In a situation where Malay rulers took an active role in resistance, the experience of Thai overlordship may well have promoted the *kerajaan* attachment. In Perak, for instance, one group of Semai still recall that it was during this period of Siamese incursion that the ruler promised them access to land in return for support. Among the northern states Thai retribution for perceived disloyalty undoubtedly sharpened the sense of Malay identity. Stories of carnage, looting and rape had become so closely associated with Thai armies that the first reports of Siam's advance on Kedah in 1821 were sufficient to cause a terrified flight of refugees to the safety of English protection in Penang and Province Wellesley. Such punitive expeditions served to widen the gulf between the overlord and vassal, prompting Rama III's comment that Thais and Malays were so different in attitudes and way of life that they resembled oil and water, 'which cannot be made into one'. Although the changed tenor of Bangkok's rule through the nineteenth century recast Thai–Malay relations in a more tolerant mode, Patani lullabies (*lagu dodoi*) still recall the hardships Malays suffered at the hands of Siamese armies.[7]

Nevertheless, centuries of contact between the two cultures were also reflected in a distinctive northern Malay culture which owed much to Thai influence. This interaction was the more obvious because the court language and customs of Riau-Johor, with their links to Melaka, were regarded as 'pure' Malay. Munshi Abdullah in his travel accounts thus contrasted the dialect of Kedah, Kelantan and Terengganu with 'the Malay language' and drew a distinction between *joget Melayu* and the Thai-influenced dances of Kelantan.[8] Forms of dance drama, like the *makyong*, in which the main roles are played by women, are still regarded as unique to Patani and Kelantan. At the same time, despite these regional differences, Malays living under Thai suzerainty still remained firmly rooted in the Malay world and shared a common heritage with their southern brethren. They too acknowledged the same traditions, the same set of norms governing interpersonal relations subsumed in the word *bahasa* (language, etiquette), the same perception of the world and above all the same adherence to the faith of Islam. The degree to which Siam's Malay vassals were drawn together by their sense of belonging to a different culture from their overlord is seen in the *Hikayat Sri Kelantan's* description of the king of Siam as 'an infidel [who] does not know correct behaviour [*bahasa*]'.

In the nineteenth century the role of religion in shaping Malay relations with outsiders, and particularly Siam, took on a new character because of a marked change in Islam's doctrinal mood. In 1803 a puritanical sect, the Wahabi, had succeeded in capturing Mecca, and the wider Muslim community reverberated to their call for a purification of the faith and a return to the Koran's basic teachings. A feature of this reforming wave was the rising influence of religious teachers as both spiritual and temporal leaders and the increased stress on Islam as a militant religion. In the archipelago the impact of such doctrines was apparently first felt in Minangkabau, but their influence soon extended to the Peninsula. The ongoing process of translating and interpreting Arabic works for Malays gained added impetus through access to lithographing and the printing press, which provided an effective vehicle for the spread of reformist teachings. Working from Mecca, the Patani scholar Shaykh Dawud (1740?–1847) was particularly prolific, and several of his publications circulated in the *pondok* (literally, hut) schools for which Patani was famous. Another medium for propagating Wahabi ideas were the the influential Sufi *tarikat*, or brotherhoods. Some of the most prestigious, like the Naksyabandiyyah, which had been influential in the region since the early seventeenth century, were quick to respond to Wahabi condemnations of moral decay and embarked on a process of self-purification.

The new resurgence in religious militancy with its call for Islamic unity was particularly appealing in Kedah after the Siamese conquest. The efforts by Sultan Ahmad and other *anak raja* to regain possession of Kedah took on the character of a holy war (*jihad*) against a regime which was not only non-Malay but *kafir* (infidel). For nearly two decades Kedah princes and Islamic leaders joined in a resistance to the Siamese which held the attention of Malays everywhere. Muslim merchants in the Straits Settlements and even some Europeans lent covert support, and it was probably about this time that the Penang-based Red Flag society was formed as a rallying point for Islamic opposition. It is noteworthy that Patani Malays were particularly supportive. In 1831, Tunku Kudin, Sultan Ahmad's half-Arab nephew, actually succeeded in capturing Kedah and held it for six months before Siamese rule was reinstated. Anxious to maintain friendly relations with Bangkok, the Penang government had already run a naval blockade to prevent supplies reaching what were described as Malay 'pirates', and Sultan Ahmad was forcibly moved to Melaka to discourage further resistance. In 1838, however, another Kedah prince expelled the Siamese from Kedah, and Malay forces pushed northwards to Patani and Singora, sacking Buddhist pagodas as they went. Supported by Penang's blockade of the Kedah coast, the Siamese were able to reassert their control of Kedah and Patani in a few months.

The intensity of anti-Siamese feeling in Kedah caused Bangkok some concern. When the Ligor governor died in 1839 it was decided to end the experiment with direct ruler. Muang Zaiburi (Kedah) was divided into four regions – Setul, Perlis, Kabang Pasu and Kedah proper (the last two being combined in 1859). Each of these was governed by a Malay chief who was simultaneously a Siamese official, his appointment dependent on his willingness to work with Bangkok. In 1842, following pressure from British officials anxious to see peace in Kedah, Sultan Ahmad was restored to his throne and died three years later.

The legacy of the conflict between Kedah and Siam was evident for some time. Population loss had been considerable during the years of hostilities, and, although refugees trickled back, the previously thriving economy was not fully restored until the 1870s. Politically, while Kedah's subordinate status in relation to both the British and the Siamese had been reaffirmed, its survival depended on a delicate balancing act between the two. In 1848 Penang invoked Low's 1826 engagement with Perak, forcing Sultan Ahmad's successor to transfer the disputed border district of Kerian to Perak. But at the same time the Kedah court so feared Bangkok's wrath that it refused to cede to Penang another small district adjoining Province Wellesley.

Bangkok's concern to safeguard its interests in the Peninsula was similarly apparent in Terengganu and Kelantan, where there had also been rumblings of discontent. Rulers in both states sent troops to assist a Patani uprising in 1831 and sheltered fugitives fleeing from avenging Siamese forces. Yet after witnessing Patani's total subjection by Siam, neither Sultan could realistically contemplate renewed resistance. A further argument for appeasing Bangkok was the assurance of support against rival claimants to the throne. These considerations moved Sultan Muhammad I of Kelantan (c.1800–37) to reaffirm his loyalty as a vassal to his Siamese overlord and pay a substantial indemnity, thus enabling him to survive the Patani crisis. On his death a civil war broke out, but another Siamese-backed prince, Sultan Muhammad II (1838–86) was eventually restored as ruler. His long reign was due not only to his strong personal control but to the support of Bangkok, a powerful deterrent to other contenders for the throne. In turn, Sultan Muhammad earned this support by punctiliously fulfilling his vassal obligations.

The situation in Terengganu, too, illustrates the readiness of Siam to manipulate local politics. Unlike his neighbour, the Terengganu ruler had been reluctant to make his peace after his involvement with Patani, and Bangkok took advantage of a succession dispute to unseat him. Another claimant to the throne, Baginda Umar (1839–76), then living on the island of Lingga, was encouraged to return to Terengganu. With only a small force he succeeded in seizing power and exiling the former ruler to Kelantan. When Baginda Umar showed signs of resistance to Siamese authority, he was made aware that Bangkok was quite willing to appoint an alternative ruler, like the deposed Sultan Mahmud of Riau. Sharply brought to heel, Baginda Umar, like his neighbours in Kelantan and Kedah, reconciled himself to Bangkok's overlordship and carried out the duties expected of a *chao prathesaraj* (tributary ruler).

With the northern Malay rulers accepting their tributary status, and with King Mongkut of Siam (Rama IV, 1851–68) and his son Chulalongkorn (Rama V, 1868–1910) anxious to avoid tension, Siamese–Malay relations from the mid-nineteenth century onward improved markedly. Provided a Malay vassal was loyal and dependable, and conditions in the state were stable, Siamese interference was minimal. Malay rulers of talent and ambition were able to exploit their situation, creating legends which assured them a place in Malay history. Baginda Umar of Terengganu is remembered as a devout ruler, a man of exceptional ability who devoted his energies to the promotion of trade and ordered government. According to local memories, he lessened the possibility of chiefly challenge by making village administration directly answerable to himself. He also travelled extensively within the state, extending his authority over outlying areas like Kemaman and supervising the prospecting of tin and gold in the interior. So free was his reign of Siamese intervention that he was later erroneously believed to have refrained from sending the *bunga mas*.

The nineteenth century was a formative period in the history of the northern Malay states. Previously, Thai control on the Peninsula had waxed and waned in proportion to the strength of successive Thai kingdoms, but the 1826 treaty signed between Britain and Siam placed the Malay *prathesaraj* within an internationally recognized 'sphere of influence' that permitted far less manoeuvrability than hitherto. They now had little choice but to acknowledge Siamese overlordship. It was clear, as Governor Ord of Singapore remarked in 1868, that the Siamese 'assumed the right to act for the [Malay] Rajas without asking their consent and that they anticipated no difficulty or defection on the part of these rulers'. The traditional Malay policy of countering Thai strength by enlisting a powerful ally was rendered ineffective because both Siam and Britain were anxious to preserve peace in the Peninsula. Thus in 1867 when Singapore merchants complained of trading restrictions in Kelantan, the Siamese government quickly took steps to ensure the compliance of its Malay vassal. Two years later, apparently without realizing the futility of such a gesture, Baginda Umar sent a deputation to

London to negotiate directly about possible protectorate status. But these approaches met only a cool response, since the British government was not anxious to incur Bangkok's displeasure. Without any formal declaration, London had acknowledged that Terengganu was a Thai vassal.

The treaty of 1824 and the division of the Malay world

In the nineteenth century the 'sphere of influence' concept became a cornerstone of British diplomacy, serving to limit the commercial or political ambitions of rival powers while avoiding the expense of establishing additional outposts of empire. As we have seen, in the northern Peninsula the 1826 treaty between Siam and Britain provided a vague but acceptable delineation of their respective areas of interest. Further south, another highly significant 'sphere of influence' had also been negotiated. While British officials in Penang and Singapore regarded Siam with disquiet, in London the principal concern was the possible expansion of other European nations, notably France, into the archipelago. It was the hope that the Malay Peninsula could be reserved for British interests that underlay London's successful negotiation of the Anglo-Dutch Treaty with the Netherlands in 1824. In retrospect, the signing of this agreement stands as one of the key events in the shaping of modern Malaysia. According to its terms, islands south of Singapore, including Java and Sumatra, were to remain the preserve of the Dutch, while the Peninsula would be a British 'sphere of influence'. Melaka would pass to the British in exchange for Bengkulen, on Sumatra's west coast. Although at this point no mention was made of Borneo, the Anglo-Dutch agreement signalled to other European powers the possibility of future British and Dutch accommodation in this area as well.

At the most obvious level, the division of the Malay world down the Melaka Straits laid the basis for the contemporary boundary between Indonesia and Malaysia. But there were other and even more far-reaching ramifications, as centuries of history were set aside without a qualm. Without consulting any Malay ruler, the Riau-Johor kingdom was irrevocably divided and the cultural unity of east coast Sumatra and the Peninsula arbitrarily severed. Ties between individuals and communities remained close but the division into 'Dutch' and 'British' spheres meant that the easy movement of Melayu leadership back and forth between the Peninsula and east coast Sumatra was now a thing of the past. What were effectively political divisions also affected academic scholarship as a new generation of British 'orientalists' concentrated on collecting and compiling Malay texts associated with the Peninsula, leaving the study of Malay culture in Sumatra and southwest and southeast Borneo to their Dutch counterparts. But the latter, with some notable exceptions, were not drawn to the study of coastal Malays. In Sumatra their descriptions of 'Minangkabau' or 'Aceh' tended to accentuate differences

rather than similarities with Melayu traditions, while in Borneo Dutch scholarship focused largely on the Dayak groups of the interior. The increasing
British arrogation of the role of interpreters of Malay society was foreshadowed by John Leyden's 1821 translation of the *Sulalat Us-Salatin*, which he
entitled *Sejarah Melayu*, the 'history of the Malays'.

When the 1824 treaty was signed, the British government had no stated
intention of territorial expansion beyond their existing settlements; indeed,
the aim of guarding Britain's interests while avoiding direct commitment was
to dominate imperial policy for the greater part of the century. Nevertheless,
this policy was persistently challenged by men on the spot who pressed for an
extension of British political control in order to guarantee trade. The most
vocal exponent of this view, Stamford Raffles, died in 1826 but his writings
continued to inspire other Englishmen with a vision of empire. Compromises
between these two opposing views are apparent in the wording of almost
every treaty concluded by Britain relating to the region. Whether it was with
a small Malay state or a major power, such agreements were carefully
phrased to minimize involvement while keeping open the possibility of an
extension of interests in the future. In 1826 Singapore, Melaka, Penang and
Province Wellesley (modern Perai) were formed into a single administrative
unit called the Straits Settlements which remained under the control of
British authorities in India until 1867, when it was transferred to the Colonial
Office. It was to become the base from whence British influence was gradually extended throughout the Peninsula.

The formation of the Straits Settlements coincided with a period of
expanding trade and a growing population in all three ports. In Singapore
alone Chinese migration pushed the population, estimated at 10 000 in 1824,
to nearly 18 000 five years later, and in 1832 Singapore replaced Penang as the
capital of the Straits Settlements. But this rapid development did not herald
British movement into the Peninsula, as some vociferous empire-builders
had hoped. The debates continued between those who proclaimed the benefits to be gained from commercial exploitation with official British protection, and those who maintained that further involvement would be disastrous.
The first test of these differing views came in 1831 in Naning, long an area of
Minangkabau migration and settlement. The energetic governor of the
Straits Settlements, Robert Fullerton, considered Naning part of Melaka and
attempted to impose Melaka's land and judicial system and to collect a full
tenth of local revenue to which Melaka was in theory entitled by earlier VOC
treaties. The British move met strong opposition from a local *penghulu*
(district head), Abdul Said, who saw British demands as a deliberate humiliation. In the tradition of Malay folk heroes Abdul Said was credited with
supernatural abilities, and the titles he used invoked memories of the rulers
of ancient Melaka. His resistance to the British, however, was complicated by
another local dispute concerning the installation of a yang dipertuan besar
from Minangkabau as overlord of Sungai Ujung, Johol, Naning and Rembau.
A decisive point in the conflict came when powerful chiefs, anxious to obtain

support in the succession quarrel, defected to the British side. Despite the final British victory, the year-long Naning War aroused strong criticism in London because of the expense entailed and the dubious rewards. To officials in Singapore, Naning remained a sensitive reminder of the complexity of Malay politics and the unforeseen dangers of involvement in Malay affairs.

The arguments of those who opposed any further acquisition of territory gained further ammunition in 1833 when the EIC lost the monopoly of the China trade which had hitherto alleviated the costs of maintaining the Straits Settlements. Like the VOC a century before, the EIC found itself in possession of strategically valuable ports that were not self-supporting and were a drain on financial resources. There was thus no temptation to embark on any further extension of territonal control. If Sultan Husain, created sultan of Singapore by Raffles, had been a more impressive figure he might well have been able to form a new centre of power as a rival to the old kingdom of Riau-Johor. He was, however, a pathetic personality who proved incapable of arousing the admiration of either British or Malays. Living in obscurity in Melaka, he appeared, remarked Munshi Abdullah scornfully, 'like a tiger without teeth'.

The situation was otherwise with the Riau-Johor ministers, for whom the 1824 treaty offered new opportunities. During the latter part of the eighteenth century the independence of the bendahara family and its hold over its appanage of Pahang had increased markedly. Bendahara Ali (1806–41) was quick to perceive the possibilities created by the division of the Riau-Johor kingdom and British anxiety to sever links between the Peninsula and Dutch-controlled Riau. At first he refused to acknowledge Sultan Husain on the grounds that his principal allegiance was to Riau-Johor, but as time passed he became aware of potential advantages brought about by the Anglo-Dutch Treaty. The Riau-Johor court could no longer become involved in Pahang affairs without incurring European displeasure, and in effect the bendahara was able to conduct himself as an independent king. By 1853 he was sufficiently confident to declare his autonomy, and in 1881 his son, with the support of the Pahang chiefs, assumed the title of sultan. The nineteenth-century *Hikayat Pahang*, written in the classical Malay court style, serves not merely to glorify and legitimize this new royal house, but to demonstrate Pahang's status as a distinct political unit.

But the greatest beneficiary of the new boundaries established by the English and the Dutch in 1824 was undoubtedly Riau-Johor's temenggung family, who prospered as Singapore grew. When Sultan Husain died in 1835 no influential voice was raised in support of the succession of his son Ali, then a child of ten. The governor of Singapore in fact commented that now 'no reason exists for the recognition of a mere titular prince'. Political wrangles about Ali's status continued, but in 1855 it was finally agreed that he could be installed as sultan of Peninsular Johor, with authority only in the small area of Muar. All administrative powers in Johor proper would be ceded to the more energetic Temenggung Ibrahim (1841–61), whose father had been instrumental in the acquisition of Singapore. Although British officials regarded Ibrahim with some misgivings because of his reputation as a pirate, he was still the best candidate for paramount chief. Gradually the temeng-gung came to realize the benefits which would accrue to him personally by co-operating with the Singapore government, and with general British approval he governed mainland Johor until his death. The links with Riau gradually weakened or were ignored, and by 1885 the position of the temenggung family was so secure that Ibrahim's son, Abu Bakar, was able to take on the title of sultan. In so doing he, like Bendahara Ali, formalized an independence from Riau which had effectively existed for over 60 years. The Anglo-Dutch Treaty of 1824 thus indirectly opened the way for the emergence of modern Johor and Pahang as independent states.

The creation of new political units in Borneo

There were other areas on the periphery of the Malay world where the weakening of central authority also created opportunities for ambitious men. The Anglo-Dutch Treaty did not mention Borneo and thus left its relation-ship to the Dutch and British spheres of influence ambiguous. The Dutch had signed treaties with several small sultanates in southeast and southwest Borneo, but had not made any move up the northwest coast where the hold of the Brunei court was purely nominal. Because Batavia was reluctant to assume the financial burden of further expansion, the British were not yet seriously concerned about a Dutch challenge in this area. In any event, for the first half of the century British policy was firmly wedded to the EIC's view that 'trade, not territory' was the goal east of the Melaka Straits. The likeli-hood of future involvement in the Borneo region became much greater from the 1840s after Sarawak developed as an identifiable political unit.

Sarawak owes its inception as a state to the ambition of a middle-class English adventurer, James Brooke (1803–68). Brought up in India, Brooke was fascinated by life in the East and was also imbued with Raffles's vision of a benevolent English administration which protected the trader while foster-ing native welfare. Brooke's attention was particularly caught by Borneo which seemed to hold out the promise of adventure, a place where his dreams of 'reforming' Malay states might become reality. Arriving in Singapore in 1839 *en route* to northern Borneo, Brooke was entrusted with a message from the Singapore governor to the raja muda of Brunei. When he reached Borneo, Brooke found the raja muda struggling to preserve a semblance of authority over Malay chiefs in the Sarawak river area whose independence had grown as Brunei's power declined. The rebellion was still in progress when Brooke returned to Sarawak a year later. As a reward for assisting the raja muda to suppress the uprising, and in return for an annual payment of £500, Brooke induced the Brunei sultan to grant him as a personal fief the area later known as the First Division. Accorded the title raja of Sarawak in 1841, Brooke set up his capital on the coast at Kuching, a small Malay village, and established a dynasty of 'White Rajas' which was to rule Sarawak until the Second World War.

In a remarkably short space of time Brooke was able to consolidate his authority along the Sarawak river. He pardoned rebellious Malay chiefs and gave them positions of some administrative authority, while at the same time limiting their power. The interior tribal people of what became administered as the First Division, the so-called Land Dayaks (Bidayuh), were generally willing to accept the new order and presented Brooke with little overt opposition. Many apparently saw Brooke as imbued with *semangat*, the special powers associated with indigenous leadership, which could be absorbed by association. But when Brooke attempted to press his authority into the Batang Lupar, Saribas and Sekrang rivers, the home of the 'Sea Dayaks' or Ibans, he faced greater problems. Here authority was fragmented and localized, usually vested in Malay or Arab/Malay chiefs established along the rivers. Their power rested on the ability to extract revenue from passing trade and to organize Iban groups to defend their interests against rival claimants. The importance of headhunting in Iban culture and their love of travel and warfare prompted the more aggressive groups to join Malays in expeditions against shipping and coastal villages. Iban traditions also fostered continuous retaliatory raiding for heads and for slaves between different Iban communities.

The espousal of a cause popular in Singapore and London – the suppression of piracy and the slave trade, and the extension of a benign British influence – became the justification for Brooke's expansion into Iban territory. Classifying virtually all Iban raiders as pirates, Brooke argued that 'nothing but hard knocks' could convert them into 'honest people'. Assisted by the Royal Navy, Brooke was able to make some impressive displays of force, but he was also able to exploit local rivalries to attract Iban allies. With their help he put down other Iban groups who opposed him, together with their Malay leaders. In one engagement a squadron that included four British ships and 2500 Iban recruits in 70 *perahu* killed around 800 'pirating' Ibans. Through the 1840s and 1850s European-manned forts along the Batang Lupar, Saribas and Sekrang rivers stood as evidence of Brooke's authority in areas nominally subject to Brunei. Combined with the enforced resettlement of nearby Malay communities, these forts denied Ibans access both to the sea and to the Malay leadership that had formerly provided a basis for raiding.

Merchants in the Straits Settlements naturally assumed that the rule of a European in Sarawak would open the door to business enterprise. Brooke, however, believed that the development of 'free trade', a goal he espoused, should not be at the expense of the indigenous people. Commercial growth should come gradually, and should not entail large capital investment which would almost certainly undermine local lifestyles (and could present a challenge to his own position). But in the face of vocal criticism from Singapore merchants and a rapidly depleting treasury, James Brooke was forced to modify his stance. In 1856 he permitted the establishment of a Borneo Company which would take over the mining of antimony and other minerals, and organize trade in sago, primarily with Chinese labour. In its early years this enterprise yielded few financial benefits to Sarawak, although the economy did improve under the second raja, Charles (1868–1917). But wealthy Singapore businessmen like W.H. Read, who saw Sarawak as another field for investment in mining and plantation agriculture, were disappointed. Certainly Sarawak's trade with Singapore became the mainstay of its economy, but these links rested primarily on the skills and experience of the growing Chinese community. Indeed, both James and Charles Brooke saw Chinese labour and commercial acumen as the hope for Sarawak's future development.

A recurring question in the first two decades of Brooke's rule was the relationship of the White Rajas to Britain, for the informal connection was indisputable. Even when adverse publicity attached to Brooke's anti-piracy campaign led to a lessening of British support, officials in London acted on the assumption that they were Englishmen dealing with an Englishman. Dutch suspicion that Sarawak was operating simply as an extension of the British empire was not completely unjustified, for White Raja rule was seen as one way to secure British domination of an important trade route to China. In 1846 London officially informed the Dutch that, although there were as yet no plans to colonize the area, Britain reserved the right to do so. The following year a treaty was concluded with Brunei, stipulating that all cessions of territory had to receive British approval. By the same treaty Brunei ceded the island of Labuan off the Brunei coast to Britain as a coaling station for steamships and, it was hoped, as a future centre for regional trade. James Brooke became the first governor of Labuan, and he acted as British Agent to the Brunei court until 1853. In that year Brunei formally transferred to Raja Brooke the major Iban-occupied districts of what later became the Second and Third Divisions in return for a yearly payment of $1500. Even when relations were strained, Brooke continued to draw benefits from his links with the British government. In 1860, for example, a Brunei noble attempted to deny Sarawak traders entry to the sago rivers of the Mukah region, which was in Brunei territory. The stakes in this contest were high, for sago had ceased to be simply a food product and was now in demand as a cheap industrial starch to service growing textile industries in Europe and America. Brunei appealed to the governor of Labuan, but British non-intervention enabled Brooke to annex valuable sago-producing areas of Mukah and Oya and the territory comprising the Third Division for an annual payment of $4500.

During the last years of James Brooke's life the British government placed even greater value on Sarawak as a prop to the British sphere of influence. Dutch authority was expanding in southwest Borneo and there was also a growing apprehension of intrusion by France, the United States or Germany. The presence of an English raja in Sarawak seemed particularly advantageous as France moved to consolidate its position in Vietnam and thus dominate another flank of the sea route to China. Despite years of uncertainty about the precise relationship between Sarawak and Britain, after 1863 London essentially recognized Brooke's independence from Brunei. Although Britain persistently refused to extend protectorate status because of Dutch opposition, the shadow of empire was cast across the Sarawak landscape.

The association between Britain and the Brookes also helped reinforce the connection between northwest Borneo and the Malay Peninsula. Despite Brunei's status as a centre for the dissemination of Islam and Melayu culture, Malay society there had absorbed so many local features that the *Hikayat Hang Tuah* had even described Brunei as a *negeri asing*, a foreign country. Yet at the beginning of the nineteenth century Europeans and Peninsular Malays had little hesitation in categorizing its court as 'Malay', and legends of links with Johor were found not only in Brunei chronicles but among the Bajau, the local sea people. However, the use of 'Malay' as a general term for Muslims in mid-nineteenth century Sarawak was probably strengthened by Brooke usage. Though the people the Brookes termed Malays were genetically closely related to other Borneo groups such as Bisayas or Ibans, they were differentiated by their Islamic faith. When coastal peoples like the Melanau adopted Islam and a sedentary lifestyle, they became almost indistinguishable from Malays, with whom they often intermarried. The propensity to characterize 'Malays' of Borneo and the Peninsula together was increased because the creation of the Brooke dynasty linked Sarawak, albeit loosely, with the British presence in the Straits Settlements and later the Peninsular states. In the words of the second raja, 'Wherever the Sarawak flag is planted, there English interests will be paramount.'

The Brooke style of government, the personal nature of authority and the opposition to major change, helped establish a unique identity for Sarawak. However, some aspects were shared with the later colonial administrations in the Peninsular Malay states, most significantly the tendency to view the population in terms of ethnic communities. The Brookes divided the range of linguistic and cultural groups in Sarawak into three basic categories, each with distinct roles. To initiate economic activity, Chinese migration should be encouraged and the Chinese would then trade, cultivate or mine. Under Charles Brooke the Chinese community grew considerably, and without any European competition they were able to assume a dominant position in Sarawak's economy. This development was encouraged because of the nineteenth-century British view that commercial activities were inappropriate for anyone involved in government. The Brookes therefore believed that Malays employed in the administration should abstain from trade. Malay peasants should take on the roles for which they were deemed best suited, and become agriculturalists and smallholders rather than

131

traders. The Brookes may even have recruited the assistance of their employees to mount this campaign. The *Hikayat Panglima Nikosa*, published in 1876 by the former secretary of James Brooke, extols the joys of settled life: 'When you are old and your bones are no longer strong, you will be happy to watch your land, and it will be an inheritance for future genera-tions'.[9] Like the Malays, other indigenous groups were also encouraged to grow rice and cash-crops. A special place, however, was reserved for the Ibans; from their ranks came the special fighting forces known as the Sarawak Rangers, which were under the raja's personal command. The personal relationship Charles Brooke fostered with the Ibans and their specific niche in the administration went far towards creating a feeling of 'Ibanness' in place of the customary fragmentation between longhouse communities.

Another feature characteristic of both Sarawak and the later colonial administrations on the Peninsula was the incorporation of native officers into the government while retaining almost all real authority in white hands. The linchpin of Sarawak's government was the White Raja, who at monthly meet-ings discussed policies and government action with his Supreme Council, which, formed in 1855, included several leading Kuching Malay chiefs. Decisions were then relayed to the European Residents, who were required to be fluent in Malay and sometimes Iban. They presided over their own divi-sional councils and passed down orders to their European district officers and native officers. The latter were normally Malay chiefs who continued to exercise authority in their own region and served as liaison with the head-men of different ethnic communities. The headmen represented their people in any dealings with the raja or his officers. In 1867 Charles created the Council Negeri, comprising Iban leaders as well as senior European and Malay officials. It had only vague consultative powers, since Brooke believed that native leaders should be guided by the 'superior intelligence' of Euro-peans; none the less, it did become an instrument by which policy could be discussed and explained. If the Brooke administration did not train the local peoples for self-government, it did foster some notion of allegiance to a central authority alongside the traditional identification with a longhouse, a family group or a river system.

The mid-nineteenth century also saw the first hesitant steps towards the eventual incorporation of present-day Sabah into the Malaysian rather than the Philippine political orbit. Some British officials felt that the north-ern tip of Borneo, where authority was ill-defined and overlordship claimed by both Brunei and the Sulu sultanate, might provide a means by which Spain would extend her territory southwards. In 1861 the British consul at the Brunei court was even prepared to predict the eventual eclipse of British interests in Borneo unless definite action were taken. Although reiteration of Sulu's independence was the furthest extent to which London would go, this declaration was important because it implicitly denied Spanish authority over Sulu and thus set aside any rights which Spain through Sulu might assert along Borneo's north coast. In 1865 the British government demonstrated a more positive interest in northern Borneo when it learned that the American consul in Brunei had leased a large tract of land there. Later that year the American Trading Company established a settlement on the Kimanis river, about 96 kilometres from Brunei Town. British enquiries in Washington, however, confirmed that the United States was not officially involved, and in any event the American settlement was abandoned in November 1866, while the American consulate in Brunei was withdrawn two years later. By 1868, when James Brooke died, there was a tacit understanding in London that Britain, with a minimum amount of commitment, had made clear her interests in northern Borneo, which was now included in the British 'sphere of influence'.

By the middle of the nineteenth century, the Malay world, whether viewed from Bangkok, London, The Hague or Singapore, could be seen as a varied assortment of colonies, vassal states and independent kingdoms divided between separate 'spheres of influence'. To a historian the outlines of modern Malaysia are slowly becoming identifiable. At the time the effects of the new alignments were experienced most keenly by Malay rulers, whose family ties represented loyalties that could rarely be contained within precise political boundaries. In 1837, for instance, the sultan of Riau felt obliged to lend assistance to his cousin, Baginda Umar, in the latter's bid to return to power in Terengganu. These plans were quickly squashed by the Dutch, who feared British reaction to any encroachment over the 'boundaries' established by the Anglo-Dutch Treaty of 1824.

For the majority of peoples in the Malay world the political regroupings as such were not as significant as the social and economic changes which, however imperceptible, were beginning to impinge on their lives. Long before the formal imposition of colonial rule, the Western presence had begun to affect the patterns of traditional society, and in this sense justified Munshi Abdullah's perception of a 'new world'.

The campaign against piracy

In their desire to safeguard the vital seaborne trade centred on Singapore, the Straits Settlements government placed great emphasis on the elimination of piracy. They were thus pitting themselves against a Malay tradition which had created a distinct cultural niche for pirating activities. As noted in earlier chapters, piracy in the Malay world had played a varied role, whether as a means of forcing trade into local ports or as a source of income for impoverished but ambitious princes. Much of this heritage lingered on into the nineteenth century. The plundering and the savagery of pirate attacks did not detract from the respect accorded a successful raider. Stories abound of local heroes in buccaneering escapades, and the prestige of one Orang Laut group from the island of Galang rested mainly on their reputation as pirates.

Sultan Husain of Singapore could thus speak with confidence when he assured Raffles that 'piracy brings no disgrace'.

From the end of the eighteenth century, however, the nature of piratical activity had begun to change. The breakdown of centralized Malay authority in the region and the participation of so many local princes and chiefs removed whatever restraints had existed in the past. The Riau court seemed unwilling or unable to control piracy in neighbouring waters, and its authority over Orang Laut in the British sphere was substantially lessened after 1824. To a greater extent than before, Orang Laut piracy had become simply a variation in seasonal occupation. Many Orang Laut groups had attached themselves to Malay chiefs who, in return for a percentage of the profits, helped outfit fleets and supplied the Orang Laut with provisions. From February to early May the latter were principally occupied in collecting sea products for the China trade, but with the southwest monsoon in June they began to move up the Melaka Straits, attacking passing vessels and particularly native craft. In addition, new elements had appeared in the Malay piracy pattern. There was a seasonal raiding fanning out from the Borneo coasts and the Sulu sultanate in search not only of booty but of slaves, preying on shipping along the 2400 kilometres of ocean between Singapore and Canton. Even more significant than European indictments is the fact that the two major Malay texts of the period, the *Hikayat Abdullah* and the *Tuhfat al-Nafis*, both agree on the unprecedented piracy in the early nineteenth century.

In the past the VOC had waged a wearying and unsuccessful battle against piracy, but had never possessed the means to make any lasting impact. From 1824 the perennial campaign assumed another dimension when the Anglo-Dutch Treaty pledged European co-operation. Although anti-piracy patrols were not co-ordinated effectively until 1835, the combination of European resources, albeit short-lived, was to have significant results. The British and Dutch not only had the advantage of steam-powered gunboats and superior artillery; they were also determined to stamp out a practice which they felt was incompatible with 'civilized' government and of inestimable harm to maritime trade.

A major step in the elimination of piracy came when the Europeans realized the necessity of gaining support from Malay chiefs who were sponsoring local piracy. One of the principal objects of British attention was Temenggung Ibrahim of Johor. Like his father, he had used his authority over a number of Orang Laut groups to organize pirate expeditions in return for a share of the booty. Constantly under pressure from the Singapore government, Temenggung Ibrahim was eventually persuaded to lend his support to the campaign. His changed attitude seems primarily due to his recognition of the benefits of maintaining British approval in his effort to strengthen his hold over mainland Johor and enhance his standing among other Malays. From the 1840s, he, like the leaders of Riau, was probably sending out his own boats to patrol neighbouring waters, joining the small British force which from 1837 was stationed in the Straits. These patrols often met fierce resistance, but the combination of persuasion and force was effective against both Orang Laut and the more formidable Sulu raiders. By the 1870s piracy in Peninsular waters had been essentially eradicated.

The eventual success of the protracted European campaign had far-reaching effects on many of the archipelago's maritime peoples. It dealt a severe blow to Malay chiefs for whom piracy was an important source of revenue that enabled them to retain a large following, an acknowledged index of power in the Malay world. It was now much less possible for a member of the ruling class whose fortunes had reached a low ebb to 'seek his fortune' at sea while waiting a chance to make a bid for power. In another sense, the elimination of 'pirates' was also a means of putting down any resistance to Europeans or any authority they supported. Because piracy was regarded as a legitimate way of obtaining revenue, prestigious leaders in the archipelago were frequently involved in raiding activities. It was thus all too easy to see a man like Tunku Kudin, who led Kedah Malay resistance against the Siamese in 1831, as a 'pirate' who deserved punishment. Accusations of 'piracy' to justify often savage attacks on pockets of opposition were most clearly demonstrated along the Borneo coasts. Some of the greatest heroes of Iban culture are the nineteenth-century leaders who, as 'pirates' and 'rebels', resisted the Brooke advance and the anti-piracy patrols of European ships.

The campaign against piracy may also have been a factor in the declining proportion of native shipping in the overall trade of Singapore. In 1829–30, 23 per cent of this trade was carried by native *perahu*, and 77 per cent by square-rigged vessels; by 1865–6 the figures were 8 per cent and 92 per cent respectively. Quite frequently, as the Straits Settlements Governor, Robert Fullerton, remarked in 1828, a man could be both a trader and a pirate as the occasion warranted, and we have seen that for many Orang Laut 'piracy' represented merely a change in their seasonal occupation. The European attacks on 'pirates' involved immediate pursuit and shelling of suspected native vessels and the complete destruction of any settlement believed to be a pirate lair. Some abuse of these tactics was undoubtedly encouraged by the monetary payments for pirates killed, captured or present during an engagement which Britain authorized between 1825 and 1850. In the space of a few years during the 1840s, for example, Royal Navy and EIC ships received over £42 000 for actions against piracy. Perhaps not surprisingly, the main Singapore newspaper commented on the decline in native trade between Singapore and Borneo caused by the 'war-like operations' of British gunboats. The experience of one Orang Laut, recorded in the *Tuhfat al-Nafis*, eloquently sums up the bewilderment of a people who were the hapless victims of European determination to safeguard commerce: 'An English warship fired on me, and my *perahu* was smashed to smithereens by bullets as big as husked coconuts.'[10]

Some of the dislocation which must have occurred in the lives of many sea people, for whom trading and raiding had coexisted as part of a cultural heritage, has been documented in Sabah during the late nineteenth century.

Here specific policies of taxation, licensing and resettlement instituted by the British North Borneo Company finally forced the Bajau community to move to the land to seek other forms of subsistence, and thus brought about lasting changes in Bajau society. The elimination of piracy undoubtedly made the seas safer, but also came at a time when native shipping was facing increased competition from Chinese, Indian and Arab as well as European seaborne trade. The introduction of steamships in the 1840s foreshadowed the gradual decline of all sail-powered traffic, and even the great fleets of the Bugis became a thing of the past. Maritime trade had always been the lifeblood of the Malays, the basis of the pre-colonial economy. By the mid-nineteenth century Malay and Orang Laut participation in this seaborne trade had been all but eliminated. In the Singapore region the Orang Laut were fast disappearing as an identifiable group, while in the opinion of contemporary observers Malays were hawkers rather than traders. 'Their one day of glory', remarks a modern scholar, 'was the New Year's sports [in Singapore] when the Malays and Orang Laut in boats of their own design invariably triumphed over European, Chinese, Bugis and all other competitors.'[11]

Changing patterns of trade in the Malay states

The far-reaching impact of the Western presence on regional trading patterns was disguised to some extent because of the expanding trade with China. Although Raffles had originally hoped that Singapore would become a conduit for channelling British goods, especially textiles, to China, his hopes remained unrealized. Chinese traders were still drawn to Singapore primarily by what the British called 'Straits produce', marine and forest products such as camphor, beeswax, dragon's blood (a resinous gum from the rattan palm), birds' nests, *agar-agar* (seaweed), and so on, which had established the reputation of the Malay world in centuries past. Initially, the trade in Straits produce was given a new stimulus by the growing number of junks arriving in Singapore. For over 100 years direct trade between China and the Malay world had been limited by VOC demands that all junks make straight for Batavia. The attractiveness of Singapore's free port, however, was quickly recognized by Chinese merchants. In 1821 four large junks docked in Singapore; in 1856–7 the number was as high as 143.

All over the archipelago the demands of the China market encouraged the gathering of local products and closer co-operation between the collector and middleman. Nineteenth-century sources provide further evidence of how the trading environment served to strengthen links between Melayu and Orang Asli groups. Slave raiding by interior Malays, sometimes for arduous mining activities, represents the darker side of this relationship, but in all cases increased contact helped to 'Malayize' many forest dwellers. During a trip to Pahang, Munshi Abdullah in 1838 saw Jakun bringing resins, rattans and aromatic wood to trade with Malays, and also working in Malay gold mines; some groups had adopted Malay dress and had begun to speak Malay. Differences between isolated Orang Asli and others more closely associated with Malays grew, as Malay rulers, hoping to tap reserves of manpower, fostered connections between Orang Asli leaders and Malay government. In 1844, for example, Bendahara Ali of Pahang appointed an Orang Asli headman as his representative over all Orang Asli in the Endau river area in southern Pahang, while Temenggung Ibrahim of Johor posted agents at numerous aboriginal settlements to supervise forest collection. Numerous Orang Laut groups, especially around Singapore, who had been relocated on land and forced to abandon many of their maritime activities, turned to gathering forest products for their livelihood. One such group was the *suku* Galang, among the most prestigious of the Orang Laut, who previously had a reputation of being fearsome pirates. In 1837, after the anti-piracy campaign was under way, they asked the Temenggung of Johor if they might settle in Singapore under his protection. Traditionally Orang Laut had rarely ventured far from the shore because they feared the jungles, but by the mid-nineteenth century a considerable number had adjusted to their new environment and were actively collecting forest products for the China market.

But despite the impressive growth of the China trade, the percentage of overall trade was slowly shifting in favour of Europe. In 1848–9 Britain and Continental Europe accounted for 16 per cent of Singapore's total trading revenues as against 19 per cent for China, by 1868–9 the figures were 25 per cent and 12 per cent respectively. A reflection of these trends can be discerned in the trade in local products as European industrial development found new uses for the natural resources of the Malay region. Antimony, for example, had only a limited market in parts of the eastern archipelago, where it was used for painting decorations on cloth; in Europe, however, it was in great demand as a component in certain alloys. Deposits had been found in Sarawak in 1824, and Malay chiefs using Dayak labour were quick to open mines and exploit the profits offered by Singapore's prices. It was not long, however, before Chinese miners came to dominate production of this mineral. So associated was antimony with this area of Borneo that Malays termed it *batu Sarawak* (Sarawak stone), and Sarawak remained Europe's main source of antimony until the end of the century.

A more dramatic instance of the influence of Europe on the trade in local products was the meteoric rise in the market for gutta percha (*pallaquium gutta*), previously regarded by Malays simply as one of a number of rubber-like forest resins. Gutta percha's importance increased in the 1840s when Europeans, noting that Malays used it to manufacture buggy whips, realized the potential of a product which could be moulded into any shape by heating and would harden on cooling. With the development of submarine telegraphy, gutta percha was also found to be the only substance which protected cables under water. A Malay chief with access to large tracts of jungle where gutta percha trees grew and with the ability to attract the services of Orang Asli collectors could thus prosper. Temenggung Ibrahim found his monopoly of gutta percha in Johor a welcome substitute for income previously obtained through piracy, and under his leadership the skills of Malays and Orang Asli were combined to bring once again a valued forest product to port. Elsewhere in the Malay world the response to the gutta percha boom was similar. Though the headiness of the early days died as supplies were depleted, gutta percha continued to be an important source of revenue for many Malaysians until it was superseded by other rubber-like products towards the turn of the century.

Even so, the collecting of forest and marine products could not expand indefinitely to meet increased demands. For centuries part of their very value had lain in their scarcity and their limited natural occurrence in certain areas of the jungle. No forest product was cultivated, and collection was attended by strict adherence to certain prescribed formulae which would appease the spirits of the items being gathered. It was believed that the spirits would be angry if the quantities gathered were too great. With the rising profits in Singapore, many of the age-old strictures were ignored by the Malay and (increasingly) Chinese middlemen who bartered with the Orang Asli and who stood to gain from greater sales of Straits produce. The recruitment of larger numbers of Orang Asli collectors and the demands of middlemen placed in jeopardy the delicate balance which for hundreds of years had allowed harvesting to proceed without endangering the ecology of the jungle. Towards the end of the century, as far away as Sarawak, the Kenyahs of the Baram river area complained that Iban incursions into their territory were denuding the country of jungle produce.

The fate of gutta percha was a sobering example of the new strains on the environment. Though it is possible to tap gutta percha resin without damaging the tree, the process was extremely slow and it became common practice to cut the tree down and bleed the trunk at regular intervals by ringing. Even by what has been called a 'predatory' method, ten full-grown trees were still needed to supply enough resin to make one pikul (about 62.5 kg) of gutta percha. But between 1848 and 1866 the value of gutta percha exports from the Peninsula to Singapore rose from $5239 to $139 317, and in the rush for profit the wholesale destruction of trees went on unchecked. As the species of trees yielding gutta percha virtually disappeared in more accessible areas, notably Johor, Singapore firms looked to Borneo. Many Singapore Chinese already had personal and business connections with their counterparts in Kuching, and it was therefore Sarawak which became the main source of gutta percha for the Singapore market. With few restrictions on collection it is estimated that around three million trees were felled in Sarawak between 1854 and 1875, a sobering example of the strains placed on the environment and on the traditional economy by the search for commercial profit.

The problems of locating specific jungle products, the intermittent nature of collection, and the dependency on a personal relationship between collector and middleman imposed obvious restraints on the future of forest collection as a revenue earner. Orang Asli co-operation was critical for access to most jungle areas, and Malay efforts to recruit their labour by force could severely jeopardize this relationship. Because forest collection remained largely in indigenous hands and continued to function along traditional lines it was not an attractive field for investment. Singapore merchants, both Chinese and British, were anxious to find profitable avenues for capital investment which would complement their trading activities and offset losses. They were therefore looking for activities where the injection of finance would guarantee expansion and good returns. In the opinion of Straits business interests, the only really potentially rewarding areas for investment, able to service both the China trade and the growing markets in Europe, were commercial agriculture and tin mining. It was to these that they turned their attention.

Chinese domination of commercial agriculture and mining

In the early years of the nineteenth century Europeans in the Straits Settlements had embarked on some experimental plantation agriculture, hoping to exploit the European market. Coffee, cotton, tea, tobacco and spices had all been planted but none had yielded the anticipated profits. Chinese agriculturalists, on the other hand, had greater success. It was they who pioneered sugar planting in Province Wellesley and thus encouraged later efforts by Europeans. Chinese achievements were most apparent in their three favoured crops – tapioca (especially in the Melaka area), pepper and gambier. There was a steady demand for tapioca in flake, pearl or flour form and, like gambier, it ensured rapid returns because of a relatively short life cycle. Pepper was seasonal and slower to mature but it could be combined profitably with gambier, which was harvested the year round. Gambier acted as a cover for the pepper vine and also helped reduce erosion, while the residue remaining after the gambier leaves had been boiled in preparation for processing could be used as fertilizer. Chinese migrants had already developed extensive pepper and gambier estates in Singapore by the mid-1830s, initially feeding the China trade but increasingly drawing their profits from Europe. In Britain gambier was widely used in dyeing and in the tanning of leather, and the attraction for investors was enhanced after the abolition of duties on gambier in 1834.

Profits from tin also increased. Until the 1850s the principal markets for Malay tin were still India and China, but with the expansion of British tin plate manufacturing and the repeal in 1853 of all duties on tin imported into Britain, sales there leapt ahead. The technological advance of the steamship meant that Singapore and London were now only five weeks apart by sea, and after the opening of the Suez Canal in 1869 the passage was reduced even further. The continuing improvement in communications enabled Straits merchants to take greater advantage of favourable prices in England and Europe.

Chinese participation in plantation agriculture and mining was already apparent in the eighteenth century, and in the nineteenth they came to dominate production in these two industries. Many arguments have been advanced to explain the displacement of Malays in the local economy during this period. Inherent cultural attitudes may well have been a contributing factor, since although Malays had traditionally been noted as energetic traders, they seemed unwilling to work for wages on estates or in mines. But there were other more specific reasons for the tightening Chinese economic hold in the mid-nineteenth century, such as an available labour force, ready capital and an effective business organization.

In the first place, the pool of Chinese manpower in the region was rapidly increasing. By 1827 the Chinese were the largest single community in Singapore, and by 1845 they formed more than half its population. In a less spectacular fashion, the same pattern was repeated in urban centres elsewhere. Kuching, a Malay village in 1840, had by the end of the century become a predominantly Chinese town. Active encouragement was given to this migration by both the Straits Settlements and the Sarawak governments, for Chinese energy and enterprise were widely acknowledged. A Chinese community was also valuable because it provided the European administration with a guaranteed source of revenue through taxes levied on opium, pork, pawnbroking and the sale of spirits. The administration itself was freed from the burden of collecting taxes since this was rented out to other Chinese, either an individual or a syndicate. As Francis Light had perceptively remarked in 1794, 'The Chinese ... are the only people of the east from whom a revenue may be raised without expense and extraordinary efforts of government.'[12]

Unsettled conditions in South China, and especially the outbreak of the Taiping rebellion in 1851, acted as a stimulus to migration, mainly from the southeast provinces of Guangdong, Fujian and Guangxi. As a consequence, the Chinese population in the Malay areas during the nineteenth century comprised five major socio-linguistic groups: Teochiew and Cantonese from Guangdong; Hokkien (Fujian); Hakka from the mountain areas of Guangdong, Guangxi and Fujian; and Hainanese from the island of Hainan. There were also numbers of Kwongsai, Henghua, Hok Chiu and Hok Chhia people. Within these groupings there were several different dialects, often mutually incomprehensible. Some workers paid their own passage, bribing local officials in order to bypass Manchu restrictions against emigration, but the majority came under the iniquitous credit ticket system. Sometimes voluntarily, sometimes compelled, the *sinkheh* (new man) bound himself to a Chinese employer in return for his passage from China. Enduring the appalling conditions of shipboard existence, these men were put ashore in Singapore to become a key ingredient in the labour force in the urban centres, the agricultural estates and the Peninsular tin mines. Until they had worked off their term of service they received no wages apart from maintenance, but after this they were in theory free to choose another occupation or find a different employer.

The Chinese who came to the Malay world were intent on one thing: to escape the life of grinding poverty they had known at home. The hopeful could always point to successful merchants like the famous Hoo Ah Kay, more commonly known as Whampoa after his birthplace. A Cantonese who had migrated to Singapore in 1830 as a youth of 15, Whampoa made his fortune in business and land speculation. As one of the few Singapore Chinese who spoke fluent English, he was able to mix socially with Europeans and even acted as Russian vice-consul. Although only a minute percentage of the Chinese migrants could ever hope to attain such wealth, the lure of riches continued to draw them in their thousands. Demographic changes rapidly extended beyond the Straits Settlements to the Malay states. In the 1830s the small Chinese mining communities scattered through the Peninsula rarely numbered more than 500; by 1870 there were about 10 000 miners in Sungai Ujung alone. Even on the east coast, where the rise in the Chinese population was far less dramatic, immigration continued steadily and small communities began to grow. Bereft of women, Chinese miners in inland areas initially obtained wives from local Orang Asli populations, sometimes through payments to their families but sometimes acquired as slaves from Malays. Though most *sinkheh* were already accustomed to harsh conditions and backbreaking work, the rigours of existence on the edge of the jungle and the depredations of tropical disease took their toll, the death rate in some areas being estimated at 50 per cent. Those who survived exhibited a competitive spirit and determination to succeed which could not but affect the pace of change in the Malay world. It was the Chinese whose experimentation revealed many of the potentialities and limitations of the Malaysian economic environment.

A second factor in Chinese dominance of planting and mining was their access to the capital necessary for development on any substantial scale. Such finance became increasingly necessary as surface deposits were gradually exhausted, necessitating excavation at deeper levels. It became common for a Malay wishing to open a tin mine to borrow the necessary money from a Chinese merchant in the Straits, and to then recruit Chinese labour and management. The tin was sold back to the creditor at a fixed sum, usually considerably below the market value. Initially, much of the capital was supplied by the Baba or Malay-Chinese society of Melaka and Penang, men whose wealth was acquired from land speculation, trading profits and their position as revenue farmers (collectors of taxes for the Straits government). Speaking the Baba Malay which was the language of business in the Straits Settlements, these traders and businessmen maintained residences and business houses in Singapore, were well acquainted with the local situation, knew some English, and could draw on years of experience in dealing with a European administration. Early census figures do not give the precise numbers of Baba in the Straits Settlements, but they must have formed a sizeable portion of the Straits-born Chinese community, who in 1881 made up 14.53 per cent of the Chinese population. Within the Baba category were subtle statements of local affiliations: for example, Penang Baba continued to speak a Malay/Thai-influenced form of Hokkien, and although Baba women usually wore Malay-style dress, three hairpins were typical of Melaka and six small ones of Penang.

Whether Baba or 'pure' Chinese, Chinese merchants in the Straits Settlements were set apart from traditional Malay traders by their access to credit, either supplied from their own resources or from wealthy European merchant firms in the Straits Settlements. Over the centuries outsiders had often commented on the lack of liquid capital even among rich Malays. Available funds were usually expended quickly on an open display of wealth and on the maintenance of a large following, the cultural indices of a great man. The inability of most Malays to call on reserves for immediate investment was to have obvious effects even where Malay interests were well established. In Sarawak, Malays in the Mukah river area had been extracting sago for generations. They found it impossible, however, to compete with local Chinese who were able to process their own sago using modern equipment bought with credit obtained from Singapore merchants.

The Chinese also had a concept of business organization which gave them a further advantage in comparison with Malays. Their expertise is clearly seen in the *kongsi*, an association of individuals from the same dialect group and the same area of China who held shares in a co-operative venture. In South China elements of the *kongsi* system had been in existence from the fifteenth century, but refinements had been introduced over the years, especially by Hakka communities in the copper mining areas of Yunnan. In the Yunnan *kongsi* organization, a man with capital brought together a group of men from the same clan or dialect group who, whether managers or wage labourers, were willing to share in the gain or loss of a common endeavour. The idea of partnership between miners was also closely linked to the notion of a brotherhood, a *hui* or union. It was this experience and this tradition, characterized above all by group cohesiveness, which the Chinese introduced to the Malay world. An added strength of the *kongsi* system was its ties to other major commercial centres of Southeast Asia, a network that was unfettered by political boundaries. Thus the extensive gold-mining settlements of Bau on the upper Sarawak river, already well established when Brooke arrived, had been founded by a Hakka *kongsi* which was a branch of a much larger parent body in Dutch West Borneo. *Kongsi* names such as *Shiwufen* ('Fifteen Shares') and *Shisanfen* ('Thirteen Shares') attest their small-scale beginnings, but by the nineteenth century they had developed into a highly sophisticated organization with central and district branches, each comprising an ordered hierarchy of clerks, overseers, accountants, inspectors and labourers.

Chinese–Malay relations

With a ready pool of labour, access to capital, long experience in mining, and a business organization to absorb temporary losses, the Chinese were well equipped to seize opportunities in a rapidly changing economy. The expertise they brought from China was particularly important at a time when surface tin mines were less productive than previously. Up to this point Malay methods of sluicing and the construction of vertical shafts had been effective, but more complex techniques were required to gain access to richer deposits that were often seven or more metres below ground. Drawing on their knowledge of mining techniques, the Chinese began to open more extensive pits that could be enlarged sideways to follow ore deposits. The Chinese were additionally advantaged because such mines demanded continuous maintenance to prevent flooding, which was rarely compatible with Malay agricultural and trading activities.

The concentration of Chinese settlement around often isolated mining areas minimized their interaction with Malay villagers, and consequently cases of Chinese–Malay clashes in the first half of the nineteenth century were infrequent. There were, of course, some perceptive Malays who were able to take advantage of the new resources the Chinese represented and to work with them in a true partnership. One of these was Raja Juma'at (d. 1864), son of a Riau prince, who had been granted the district of Lukut by Sultan Muhammad of Selangor (1826–57) in 1846. Because of his disciplined government, Chinese merchants in Melaka were willing to advance capital for the development of Lukut mines in return for a share of the profits. One of Raja Juma'at's backers was Chee Yam Chuan, a fifth-generation Baba Chinese who was head of Melaka's Hokkien community. A genuine trust seems to have existed between these two men, and Raja Bot, a son of Raja Juma'at, lived with Chee in Melaka for some time, acting as his business intermediary with other Malays. Raja Juma'at's brother, Raja Abdullah, had been given control of the Kelang valley, and in 1857 the two men borrowed $30 000 from Chee Yam Chuan and other Melaka merchants to open up mines in Ulu Kelang, using Chinese labour. The success of these mines at Ampang and Kuala Lumpur soon attracted other Chinese traders and shopkeepers, so that before long the isolated jungle settlement became a small town.

The best example of Malay co-operation with Chinese investors and labourers was undoubtedly in Johor, where Temenggung Ibrahim encouraged extensive Chinese cultivation of pepper and gambier plantations. From the mid-1840s Chinese began moving to Johor as the estates in Singapore were exhausted, but by controlling the system of land grants Ibrahim was able to maintain active Malay involvement in Chinese economic enterprises. In the system he devised, a Chinese headman, called the *kangchu* ('lord of the river'), was placed in charge of each river where plantations were developed. He received a written authorization, initially similar to the old *surat kuasa* or letter of authority given to a Malay *penghulu* (district headman). This document empowered the holder to open up plantations, supervise cultivation and act as a revenue farmer. The last-mentioned privilege, the right to collect taxes, was potentially even more lucrative than agriculture

Ibrahim's son, Abu Bakar (1862–95), further refined the *kangchu* system. The *surat sungai* (river documents) he issued became more closely modelled on a European-style contract, and they were usually given to individual merchants resident in Singapore or to a *kongsi* made up of a group of businessmen. The *kangchu* now became simply the manager for the absentee holder of the *surat sungai*. The Chinese community in Johor was responsible to a Kapitan China, but ultimate authority was still vested in the Temenggung, who could at any time withdraw his support from a *kangchu* or a Kapitan. Abu Bakar actively encouraged good relations with the Chinese. In the 1860s when no British official was proficient in any Chinese dialect, Johor had at least one able Malay administrator who could speak Teochiew and write characters. Two Chinese were members of Abu Bakar's 24-member advisory council, while prominent Malays in his bureaucracy were shareholders in some of the *kongsi*.

By the mid-nineteenth century the results of Johor's policy were evident in the expansion of plantation agriculture and the increase in the Chinese population. When Temenggung Ibrahim took office Johor was covered with jungle, and the settlement was limited to scattered Malay villages along the rivers. In the 1860s there were 1200 gambier and pepper plantations in Johor, employing about 15 000 labourers. Ten years later, though an estimated 100 000 Chinese were living in Johor, friction with the Malay government was rare. A major factor in this situation was the restraints placed on Chinese secret societies. Only one, the Teochiew-dominated Ngee Heng (Ghee Hin), was permitted to operate in Johor, and until disbanded in 1916 it maintained a close association with the Malay government.

Johor's control over the Chinese, however, was exceptional. On the whole, Malay rulers were content to let the Chinese community exist outside centralized authority as long as the revenue due to the local authority was paid. Chinese investors in the Straits soon found it more efficient simply to advance finance directly to the mineworkers, bypassing the local Malay chief. This trend was to have far-reaching effects. First, it hastened the rate at which Chinese tightened their grasp of economic resources; secondly, the independence of the Chinese settlements undermined the authority of the Malay chiefs and hence their ability to maintain order. Divisions within local Chinese society complicated matters further. Rivalries and hostilities between dialect and clan groups were imported from China and frequently formed the basis for quarrels among migrants in the Malay world. Troubles, for instance, often involved Hakka, who originated from the mountain areas of south China and were frequently ridiculed by other Chinese for their distinctive customs and language.

Dialect divisions were accentuated since they roughly corresponded to differences in occupation. The Cantonese dominated mining and crafts,

Hakka were miners, the Hokkien and Teochiew were agriculturalists, small shopkeepers and boatmen. In Sarawak, where Hakka controlled the mining industry but where most Kuching Chinese were Hokkien, Teochiew or Cantonese, cultural differences were to have a significant effect on local politics. In the Malay states even the affinity between Hokkien and Teochiew in occupation, speech and customs was undermined because the Hokkien community was more prominent in urban Baba society and had closer links with Europeans. Chinese of the same surname or clan but speaking different dialects also clung to their own dialect group. To complicate the picture further, other rifts were introduced by the conversion of some Chinese to Christianity and by the rivalries between old Chinese communities and more recent arrivals.

The absorption of the Chinese into the existing Malay political and social system was hindered by the so-called 'secret societies'. In China these organizations had begun as a form of mutual-aid society with all the trappings of a quasi-religious group. From the seventeenth century they assumed a political role as well, advocating the overthrow of the foreign Manchu dynasty in China. When the Chinese migrants came to the Malay world, the concept of a *hui* or union based on clan or dialect appeared to be an indispensable organization affording protection and assistance in an alien and often hostile environment. Such associations were also of fundamental importance in maintaining links with China and in preserving Chinese values and culture. Although such societies had existed earlier in Dutch Melaka, they were strictly controlled and appeared to have limited their activity to mutual aid and rituals related to ancestor worship. There is no record of any open Chinese defiance of Dutch rule, and the Melaka societies, whose members were drawn from the local Chinese élite, were more in the nature of exclusive clubs. In Penang and Singapore, however, where the immigrant community was larger and where there was no long-established tradition of leadership, the societies from the beginning had a reputation for fomenting dissent.

By 1825 there were at least three large *hui* in the Straits Settlements: the Ghee Hin, the Ho Seng and the Hai San, which may all have been offshoots of the Triad Society in China. Other societies mushroomed, and their complexity makes generalizations difficult. Though termed secret, they often operated openly apart from matters connected with oaths and ritual. Some societies were small and exclusive, others numbered thousands and could even include Malays, Portuguese, Indians or *Jawi Peranakan* (Indian/Malay). Sometimes local chapters were controlled by one speech group or a clan, but leadership could pass into different hands with the passage of time. Nor was each society a united and monolithic group. The possible permutations are illustrated by the Singapore Ghee Hin, which had five subdivisions corresponding to each of the major dialect groups. The Hakka Ghee Hin in Singapore was further split along clan lines. Chinese from one area and one dialect group might well divide their allegiance. In one mining area of Selangor,

Hakka from Kah Yeng Chew (a prefecture in Guangdong) belonged to three different societies. However, a feature common to all the societies was their covert but strong relationship with the Chinese business community. A society was often virtually synonymous with a *kongsi*, and most *hui* were wealthy because the members included successful businessmen. Not infrequently, these connections with prominent individuals allowed secret societies to control major tax farms, such as opium and rice wine or *arak*. Added to these profitable ventures were more sinister activities such as gambling and prostitution and the accompanying extortion and blackmail which brought the societies into such disrepute and provided an umbrella for the criminal elements among them.

Because of the recruitment, sometimes forcible, of all new arrivals into one of the secret societies, they gained a dominant position in most areas where Chinese settled. While they could provide the migrant with assistance in a strange land, they could equally demand his services in any capacity, particularly in the recurring conflicts with rival societies. In a monotonous and exacting life it was not uncommon for thousands of men to be sworn foes because of an isolated dispute involving only a few society members over a woman, or rights to a watercourse, or because of some event as far away as Rangoon or Saigon.

Very little in their culture equipped the Malays to deal with this kind of independent organization. Traditionally Malay rulers dealt with the Chinese as a whole through the Kapitan China, normally a man of standing among both Malays and his own people. For its part, the Chinese community had in the past recognized the right of the Malay sultan, in consultation with the Kapitan, to adjudicate disputes. As the Chinese population expanded in the nineteenth century these customs no longer applied. Usually the Kapitan China was himself a leading member of a secret society and subject to loyalties and obligations to his own *hui*. This was a major change in the nature of a post which had previously functioned as an extension of the Malay court hierarchy. Furthermore, the growth and increasing diversity within the Chinese population required more than one individual to represent their interests. In Sungai Ujung in the early 1870s, for instance, there were at least five different Chinese headmen. No longer was it possible for the Malay sultans to exercise the same authority over the proliferating numbers of Chinese headmen as they had done in the past with a single acknowledged Chinese leader.

With the competing interests of dialect, clan, *kongsi* and secret societies, only a rare Kapitan could have exerted authority over all Chinese in his area. Kapitan Yap Ah Loy, who was to oversee the development of the tin mines in the Kuala Lumpur region during the 1870s, was one such figure. A Hakka, he was elected Kapitan in 1868 by the headmen of local Hakka, Cantonese and Hokkien groups, and confirmed in his position by Raja Mahdi, then head of Kelang. But even Yap Ah Loy, for all his prestige, could not ultimately prevent quarrels erupting between different Hakka clans. The system was also vulnerable because no rules governed succession to the Kapitan post. As the economic rewards for control over a district became greater, conflicts among the Chinese became more frequent. Now the death of a Kapitan could herald the outbreak of a prolonged power struggle between opposing Chinese groups.

The challenge secret societies presented to established government was evident in the street fights between *hui* in Singapore and Penang, and in the rioting which occurred when some unpopular law was promulgated or when underlying tensions were ignited by economic downturns. In 1846, following a decline in gambier prices and the consequent closure of many plantations on both sides of the Straits, hundreds of impoverished Chinese arrived in Singapore seeking employment. In a situation where many Chinese were living on the brink of starvation, attempts by a wealthy Hokkien *kongsi* to move into plantation agriculture (previously dominated by the Teochiew) acted as a catalyst in the eruption of serious riots. On this occasion, and during subsequent riots in 1851, 1854 and 1861, it is possible to discern growing socioeconomic cleavages in Chinese society. The interests of individuals and *kongsi* who were closer to the British authorities were often quite distinct from those of poor and often rural Chinese labourers, and membership of syndicates that had purchased the right to sell opium or spirits gave almost unlimited access to resources for recruitment and control of manpower.

Economic considerations were also a factor in the Chinese uprising in Sarawak in 1857, where a *kongsi* of Hakka gold miners was established at the interior settlement of Bau well before Brooke's arrival. Operating quite outside Brooke's authority, the Hakka of Bau were also in competition with the Cantonese and Teochiew of Kuching to control the lucrative trade of the Sarawak interior; in effect, Bau and Kuching were political and economic rivals. In a bid to assert their independence, Chinese from Bau attacked Kuching, reducing much of the town to ashes. But Brooke's ability to recruit help from a British steamship in the vicinity, from Kuching Chinese, from Sarawak Malays, and above all from his Iban levies, enabled him to suppress the uprising and assert control over Bau. Strong leadership was a decisive factor in the White Raja's success, and in the British view it was precisely this element which was most lacking in the Malay states. The need to establish law and order became the rationale for British involvement in the Peninsula.

Malay conflicts and Straits Settlements involvement

For much of the nineteenth century the 'decay' of Malay society was implicitly accepted among Europeans in the Straits Settlements. Nowhere did this decay seem better demonstrated than in the civil wars which divided so many Peninsular states. But though quarrels over succession and territorial rights were particularly widespread in this period, they were by no means uncommon in earlier times. They could even be said to have played a purifying role in traditional politics. Normally Malay conflicts did not entail great loss of life and were exercises in insult and skirmish rather than full-scale battle. The outcome brought a rearrangement of the power structure at the top rather than a change in the policy or style of government. The typical civil war threw up a powerful man who commanded the loyalty of most influential chiefs, and a period of fighting was then followed by a relatively stable reign.

The ultimate victor in Malay wars was usually one who could rally the strongest or most prestigious allies. In previous centuries ambitious *anak raja* had bought the assistance of Portuguese, Minangkabau, Thai, Bugis or Dutch with promises of future rewards should victory be attained. Nineteenth-century diplomacy, however, had lessened the possibility of gaining support from powerful nations in the region. First, the treaties of 1824 and 1826 restrained Siam and the colonial Dutch government at Batavia from interference in the British sphere of influence. Secondly, the East India Company and, after its demise in 1858, the British government, was adamantly opposed to any involvement in Malay quarrels. It was considered vital to keep any Malay dispute a local matter so that it did not have repercussions in neighbouring spheres of influence. Britain believed its trade and investment in the area could be adequately safeguarded without any formal commitment to a Malay prince.

The application of this policy can be seen in the Pahang Civil War (1858–63). In many ways it was a classic Malay conflict. Two brothers, Mutahir and Ahmad, both sons of Bendahara Ali, disputed the succession when their father died. In the customary manner, both princes sought to recruit support. Mutahir became allied with Temenggung Ibrahim of Johor, while Ahmad was able to obtain support from Sultan Ali of Muar and from Rembau, Terengganu and Kelantan. Sultan Mahmud of Riau, who had been deposed by the Dutch in 1857 but still claimed to have inherited the rights of Riau-Johor along the east coast, also associated himself with Ahmad. In former times such a dispute might well have drawn in rulers throughout the Peninsula and east coast Sumatra. Now the Singapore government, anxious to localize the Pahang conflict, at first forbade Ibrahim to lend Mutahir direct assistance. It was understandably disturbed to hear that Sultan Mahmud of Riau had gained Siam's sympathy. After a trip to Bangkok in 1861 Mahmud arrived in Terengganu escorted by a Siamese ship, and there were widespread rumours that he might be installed as ruler in Pahang or Terengganu. Fears of increased Siamese influence on the east coast and pressures from Singapore merchants who had invested in Pahang finally convinced Governor Cavenagh (1859–67) to support Mutahir's claim. In November 1862, as a warning to Bangkok and to force Sultan Mahmud to leave, Cavenagh ordered a warship to shell Kuala Terengganu.

This episode did not signal the installation of Mutahir as bendahara in Pahang, for an outraged British government considered Cavenagh's action far too extreme. Prevented from taking further steps which would directly

involve Britain, Cavenagh could only encourage the alliance between Mutahir and Singapore's friend, the new Johor Temenggung Abu Bakar. Despite
military assistance from Johor, Mutahir could not defeat Ahmad. The latter,
supported by powerful Pahang chiefs, gained prestige from his links with
ex-Sultan Mahmud of Riau and the memories of ancient loyalties this partnership invoked. In 1863 Ahmad successfully invaded Pahang from his
Terengganu base. Shortly afterwards Mutahir and his son both died, and
Ahmad then became bendahara. He lost no time in making his peace with
Singapore, where the government was pleased simply to see order restored.
As Governor Blundell (1855–9) had earlier remarked, 'It matters not who
rules [Pahang], but it is of importance that its trade and general prosperity
should not be destroyed.'[13]

Though Malay diplomatic traditions always favoured an ever-widening
alliance system, the Pahang conflict had been successfully contained. The
most powerful European states in the region – Britain and the Netherlands –
were unwilling to be directly drawn into local quarrels, and Siam's influence
had been confined. On the west coast, however, there were many other
potential sources of support for ambitious princes. Not only was the Chinese
community large, but it was already divided into society and clan factions
which were often bitter enemies. Furthermore, Straits Settlements investment in the tin mines was considerable, and the merchants concerned were
naturally anxious that the Malay prince who gained power should be amenable to further economic development. These factors had played a relatively
minor role in Pahang, where less extensive tin deposits had attracted only
limited Chinese migration and outside capital. But in Perak, Selangor and
Negeri Sembilan, as Malay chiefs fought for political control to ensure their
prestige and revenue, Chinese mining groups and Straits merchants alike
were determined that the victorious Malay faction should favour their
particular interests. Solicited by one or other Malay leader, the Chinese clans
and societies contributed money, supplies, arms and fighting men, while in
the Straits Settlements both British and Chinese merchants gave financial
backing.

The extent of local non-Malay involvement made the character of
nineteenth-century Malay conflicts on the west coast different from those of
the past. The supply of funds from the Straits and the pool of fighting men
among the Chinese groups prolonged quarrels in a manner hitherto impossible. Because of the numerous vested interests, any Malay disputes in the
tin-producing states had ramifications stretching far beyond the local issue
itself. As the fighting became more widespread through the 1860s and early
1870s, the Straits government was subject to increasing pressure from various
lobbies, ranging from individual merchants and shareholders in important
companies to English legal firms employed by Chinese secret societies.
Through public meetings, the press, petitions and personal connections,
these interest groups argued that Britain must take steps in the Malay states
to create a climate more conducive to investment and trade.

The leader of the mercantile community and the most outspoken advocate of British intervention was W.H. Read (1819–1909). Connected with several leading Singapore companies, he was president of the Singapore Chamber of Commerce and senior non-official member of the Legislative Council. He had been a supporter of James Brooke in the 1840s, and also had long-standing business connections with several Malay states. Read's partner, Tan Kim Cheng (1829–92), was a noted Singapore-born Hokkien merchant whose commercial interests extended throughout the Peninsular states as far as Saigon and Bangkok. This partnership was to play a crucial role in the complex events leading to British intervention in the west coast states in 1874.

The core of the civil wars in the tin areas was the continuing struggles between members of the Malay ruling class. In the Negeri Sembilan confederacy this had a long history. The death in 1824 of the yang dipertuan besar, a prince brought from Minangkabau, initiated a decade of rivalry among contending heirs. Indeed, one could argue that it was in Negeri Sembilan that the nineteenth-century erosion of Sumatra–Peninsula links became most evident. Another prince from Minangkabau who attempted to assume the office in 1826 was also unsuccessful, leaving the field open for further fighting among local princes. These prolonged conflicts meant repeated blockades of river traffic as chiefs attempted to extend their control of revenue or levy new customs duties. Hostilities were most pronounced between the Datuk Kelana, the territorial chief of Sungai Ujung, and the Datuk Bandar, who controlled the middle reaches of the Linggi river. Their quarrels severely hampered Melaka's economy, which was dependent on the tin trade from Sungai Ujung and Linggi. In 1857 the Singapore governor even dispatched an expedition to destroy toll stations erected along the Linggi river, but the effects were short-lived. Local trade received a further setback when Chinese–Malay violence erupted in 1860 after the Datuk Kelana attempted to increase taxes imposed on the Chinese community. The pattern of succession disputes, wars and disrupted trade was repeated in 1869 after another yang dipertuan besar died. Under pressure from Straits merchants, the Singapore government began considering the appointment of a British Agent in Linggi to act 'as a referee upon all matters appertaining to the commerce between our merchants and the native traders'.[14]

In Selangor the seeds of conflict were sown during the reign of Sultan Muhammad (1826–57). Since he was not the eldest son, nor was his mother the principal consort, his position as ruler was never completely accepted by the numerous *anak raja* who vied with each other for authority over profitable mining districts. In 1849 or 1850 Sultan Muhammad had transferred control of the rich tin area of Kelang, previously held by his own son, to Raja Abdullah, brother of Raja Juma'at of Lukut. Raja Mahdi, Sultan Muhammad's grandson, had expected to receive Kelang as his appanage and never reconciled himself to its loss. In other parts of Selangor enterprising *anak raja* were also carving out lucrative holdings, drawing their income from levies made on goods passing along their river and from a share in the profits of Chinese-worked tin mines. By the time Abdul Samad (1859–93) came to the throne, Selangor was effectively divided into five different territories, corresponding to each of the major river systems – Lukut, Kelang, Langat, Bernam and Selangor proper. The princes controlling these districts were prepared to use force to counter any attempt to undermine their authority or wealth.

In 1866 the head of Kelang, Raja Abdullah, granted the Read-Tan syndicate the right to collect tax revenues in his district in return for 20 per cent of the profits. The following year Raja Mahdi, whose father had once ruled Kelang, disputed the payment of taxes to the Read-Tan group. Fighting broke out and soon Raja Mahdi succeeded in establishing himself in Kelang. However, the Selangor ruler, Sultan Abdul Samad, saw Raja Mahdi's continuing refusal to remit revenues as rank defiance. The Sultan recruited the support of his son-in-law, a Kedah prince called Tengku Kudin (Ziauddin) who had no appanage of his own and was therefore interested in gaining control of Kelang. Meanwhile, Abdullah had died, but Kudin found an ally in Abdullah's son, Ismail, who also had ambitions of regaining hold over Kelang.

Like rival Malay princes in centuries past, both sides sought to marshal their allies, forming alliances with local chiefs, leaders of migrant communities and adventurers who could call on large supplies of manpower. The presence of rival Chinese clans and societies in Selangor offered the possibility of further extending these alliances. The Hakka community in Selangor was already split by bitter quarrels between two major clans, the Fei Chew and the Kah Yeng Chew, each linked with separate secret societies. The noted Kapitan Yap Ah Loy, leader of the Fei Chew, was a member of the Hai San while most of the Kah Yeng Chew belonged to the Ghee Hin society. From the end of 1869 Yap Ah Loy and the Fei Chew supported Tengku Kudin, who had successfully taken Kelang; their rivals, the Kah Yeng Chew, joined forces with Raja Mahdi's supporters.

By 1871 the search for powerful allies had gone further, as Raja Mahdi turned to Maharaja Abu Bakar of Johor and Tengku Kudin looked to Rembau and his relations in Kedah. Influential interests in the Straits Settlements had also become involved. In order to strengthen their position, Raja Mahdi and Raja Ismail obtained financial support from Chinese merchants in Melaka, while Tengku Kudin borrowed money from several Singapore financiers. Notable among his creditors was the Read-Tan Kim Cheng syndicate, which had earlier leased the Kelang revenue farms. Another was James Guthrie Davidson, whose family had developed the powerful merchant firm of Guthrie & Co. and who was himself a well-known lawyer and secretary of the Singapore Chamber of Commerce. What had begun as a quarrel over territorial rights in Kelang now touched the nerve centre of economic and political influence in the Straits Settlements.

During the first stages of the war the two sides seemed evenly matched, but the Tengku Kudin/Raja Ismail alliance eventually gained the advantage.

In March 1870 Tengku Kudin captured Kelang and the retreating Raja Mahdi then established himself at the mouth of the Selangor river. Through personal connections in Singapore, Tengku Kudin was able to convince the Straits authorities that his rule in Kelang would encourage peaceful trade. The capture of a Penang Chinese merchant vessel at Kuala Selangor seemed convincing evidence of Raja Mahdi's piracy, and he was forcibly driven out by British troops who had come to seek restitution. In 1871 Singapore's colonial secretary, J.W.W. Birch, visited the Selangor capital at Langat and officially promised future support to Kudin, formally acknowledging his position as Sultan Abdul Samad's 'viceroy' in Selangor and lending him a British man-of-war to enforce his position.

By throwing its weight behind Kudin, the Singapore government had stepped beyond London's policy of non-intervention and in so doing had prevented the expected *dénouement* in a traditional civil war. The local British authorities, like the Dutch before them, had been drawn inexorably into Malay politics as they came to believe that only an amenable ruler could assure the continuing profitability of trade. Kudin was not liked by the Selangor chiefs and could not have maintained his position without continued outside help. By 1872 the war had already swung back in Mahdi's favour, but Governor Ord (1867–73) encouraged offers of help from the bendahara of Pahang. With Pahang's assistance the Kelang and Selangor rivers were again brought under Kudin's control. The outcome of the Selangor wars demonstrated to Malays that even an unpopular or weak prince could gain power with British assistance. This lesson was quickly learned and applied by other Malay factions in the internal disputes which beset Perak.

Here also quarrels over succession were recurrent. A system of rotating the rulership between three different branches of the royal family, instituted at the beginning of the century, had been intended to prevent disputes but had never functioned perfectly. Problems were bound to arise if a prince were for any reason unacceptable as a ruler. Although the dearth of sources makes reconstruction of events in the 1850s difficult, it is clear that the system was undergoing strain. Sultan Abdullah (1851–7) faced a serious challenge from other princes, led by the raja muda. An appeal to Siam in 1854 was unsuccessful because Bangkok accepted the intent of Low's (unratified) treaty in 1826 which removed Perak from Thai influence. Abdullah then appealed to Singapore, an admissible recourse because the treaty had assured Perak of British protection. This move apparently checked the rebellious faction, and when Sultan Abdullah died in 1857 the raja muda was duly installed as sultan. The chiefs, however, refused to appoint Sultan Abdullah's son, Raja Yusuf, to the third royal position of bendahara because he had opposed many of them in the recent conflict. He was also likely to be an autocratic ruler when his turn came to succeed. Instead, a prince of lesser birth, Raja Ismail, was chosen as bendahara, leaving Yusuf resentful and humiliated.

The enmity of several princes was cause enough for hostility within the ruling class, but in Perak the ambitions of powerful chiefs further increased the possibility of conflict. Aided by geographical isolation and with access to extensive tin deposits, they could maintain themselves economically and become independent of royal authority. The district of Larut, separated from Perak proper by a range of hills, became a particular trouble spot. In 1848 Long Ja'afar, the territorial chief of Larut, had invited Chinese miners to develop the tin deposits there. When he died in 1858 his son, Ngah Ibrahim, inherited Larut's considerable wealth as well as its large Chinese population. The majority of these were Chen Seng Hakka who were members of the Hai San. Fighting broke out in 1861 when another Hakka group from the Fei Chew clan, most of whom were Ghee Hin adherents, attempted to gain control of a watercourse feeding the mines of both factions. Since each group had strong ties to societies and business interests in Penang, and since many Larut Chinese claimed to be British subjects from the Straits Settlements, it was impossible to confine the quarrel to Larut. Penang merchants were also eager to influence the outcome of the disputes, seeing their rewards not only in tin mines but in domination of the Larut opium tax farms.

Initially, the group backed by the Hai San succeeded in expelling its rivals, but the Ghee Hin faction drew on its Straits connections, persuading the Penang government to demand compensation from Perak for the loss of their mines. A British gunboat was consequently sent to blockade the Larut river. Ngah Ibrahim then paid the amount demanded from his considerable tin revenue. In 1863 the Perak ruler rewarded him with the title of Orang Kaya *Menteri* (Minister) and confirmed his authority over Larut.

Feuding between the hostile Chinese groups simmered after this episode, but soon boiled over again because of the favouritism shown by Ngah Ibrahim to the Chen Seng Hakka and their allies. It is even likely that he had become a member of their supporting society, the Hai San. By 1865 the Ghee Hin group had been forced out of Larut, but the fighting spread into the rest of Perak. Serious riots also erupted in Penang in 1867, the involved alliances between different clans and societies reflecting the complexities of local Chinese politics. At the height of the struggles in Larut, one side consisted largely of Fui Chew Hakkas and San Neng Cantonese from the 'Four Districts' (Si Kwan) region of southwest Guangdong who belonged to the Ghee Hin and Ho Hup Seah societies; while the other side comprised mainly Chen Seng Hakka from the 'Five Districts' (Go Kwan) who were members of the Hai San society. By 1870 the Ghee Hin grouping had become sufficiently strong to move back into Larut again, and although the Hai San formed an alliance with two other societies, the Penang-based Hokkien Toh Peh Keng and the Ho Seng, the conflict in 1872–3 was still unresolved. The protracted fighting between the Chinese in Larut soon became deeply enmeshed in the festering succession quarrels in Perak itself.

For several years deteriorating relations between members of the ruling class had threatened to bring about civil war, and matters finally came to a head after the death of Sultan Ali (1865–71). Raja Muda Abdullah was the obvious candidate for succession, but he did not appear at the funeral where custom dictated the election should take place. In his continued absence the chiefs elected Bendahara Raja Ismail as ruler. Ismail's genealogy was less prestigious than Abdullah's, and he had already been passed over twice for the office of raja muda. Now, however, he had the advantage of support from powerful members of the ruling class. Foremost among these was Ngah Ibrahim, who had quarrelled with Abdullah some years earlier and who himself had aspirations towards the position of ruler. In the following months Raja Abdullah enlisted the help of Ghee Hin, while Ngah Ibrahim vacillated between several Chinese societies, finally opting for his old friends, the Hai San, in late 1872. In the same year Raja Abdullah openly assumed the title of sultan, to which he claimed a greater right than Ismail. He could justifiably argue that this claim, if recognized, gave him the state's revenues and resources to bestow as he wished. Having failed to arouse official interest either in Penang or in Bangkok, Sultan Abdullah approached Tan Kim Cheng, W.H. Read's partner and a member of the Ghee Hin, and offered him the Larut tax farms in return for assistance.

The debate on 'civilization'

Raja Abdullah's decision to solicit Tan Kim Cheng's aid came at a time when the Straits merchants were as never before convinced of the need for British intervention in the Peninsula. In the late 1860s tin prices in Britain had risen dramatically, a trend stimulated when the opening of the Suez Canal in 1869 further shortened the voyage to Europe. The commercial community in the Straits Settlements were adamant that the disturbances in the Malay states not only endangered trade and capital investment, but also inhibited future economic opportunities. Whipped up by the editorials of influential newspapers, public opinion in the Straits was agreed that drastic changes were necessary to halt the 'decay' in Malay society. The transferral of the Straits Settlements from the India to the Colonial Office in 1867 had not brought any change in the official policy of non-intervention, and it seemed clear that outright annexation would not be countenanced. However, London might be more amenable to the notion of some kind of British Agent, whose advice would encourage a Malay ruler to govern in a 'civilized' manner, creating an environment in which commerce could thrive.

The acceptance by Malay rulers of 'civilization' was the keynote of this proposal, first put forward by Straits merchants in 1871. 'Civilization' naturally meant the adoption of English law, English government and, as far as possible, an English way of life. It was felt that no prince could do better than model his rule on that represented by a 'superior' culture. Indeed, in the Malay states several examples could be cited of princes who had established good relations with Straits merchants and officials, and in so doing had bettered their own position. Raja Juma'at of Lukut had become a close friend of the Resident Councillor of Melaka, who acted as guardian for Raja Juma'at's son (Raja Bot) during a period of English schooling in Melaka. He worked closely with the Straits government, donating land for the construction of a lighthouse, co-operating in the campaign against piracy and helping to apprehend fugitive criminals. Under Raja Juma'at's rule Lukut had appeared a model state, and his willingness to 'introduce our modes of government' raised him high in British esteem. 'Raja Juma'at', said the governor of Singapore, was 'perhaps the most intelligent of the Malay chiefs and one moreover who has invariably shown a disposition to cultivate our alliance and to be guided by our advice'.[15] The ability of Tengku Kudin of Kelang to rally support in Penang and Singapore was equally due to his willingness to adopt English ways. After taking control of Kelang in 1871 he made some efforts to reorganize the administration, even giving the streets English names. His desire to foster a 'civilized' reputation in the Straits Settlements is suggested by his ostentatious sherry drinking and the pack of dogs he maintained in defiance of Islamic prohibitions. The benefits both he and his English friends drew from their association were obvious. In 1873 Tengku Kudin used his influence in Selangor to grant concessions to the Singapore Tin Mining Company for exploitation of most of the state's undeveloped mining land. Both J.G. Davidson and W.H. Read were closely linked to this company.

To many Malay princes it would have seemed that the cultivation of Western acquaintances and the adoption of a European style of living made the difference between political success and relegation to the backwaters of power. The prime example of the advantages accruing to a ruler who had received the stamp of British approval was undoubtedly Abu Bakar of Johor, son of Temenggung Ibrahim, who had taken office in 1862. Educated at a mission school in Singapore and speaking English well, Abu Bakar became a leading figure in Singapore society. He was a hospitable host, who not only followed horse racing but could hold his own in such civilized pastimes as billiards and cricket. 'In his tastes and habits', wrote Abu Bakar's friend, Governor Ord, 'he is an English gentlemen.' Abu Bakar made several trips abroad and was received by a number of monarchs, notably Queen Victoria and the emperor of Japan. In 1866 the flourishing port on the northern shore of the Johor Strait was renamed 'Johor Baru' ('New Johor') and made the state capital, and the royal residence there equipped with every European comfort. The government of Johor likewise assumed a form familiar to a Western observer. The bureaucracy was built around an élite of loyal and able Malays, most of whom were descended from the old Riau-Johor nobility. Appointed as Abu Bakar's representatives throughout the state, these men successfully combined English notions of a 'modern' civil servant with the best features of traditional Malay government. By the 1870s Johor's administration comprised numerous departments, among which were land and public works. To this was added a functioning treasury, judicial system, police force and some secular education. In short, Johor so resembled a Western-style government that Ord considered Abu Bakar 'the only raja in the whole Peninsula or adjoining states who rules in accordance with the practice of civilized nations'.[16]

A major reason for the generally high opinion of Abu Bakar was his willingness to see Johor operate as an economic extension of Singapore. He went out of his way to attract investment by Singapore merchants and employed English lawyers to minimize the legal differences between Johor and the Straits Settlements. On the very few occasions when Abu Bakar attempted to assert Johor's economic independence from Singapore, he was subjected to such pressure that he eventually capitulated.

For most of his reign, Abu Bakar epitomized the kind of Malay ruler who would best serve British interests, leaving Singapore with no convincing justification for extending control into Johor. Abu Bakar was fully aware of his delicate relationship with the Singapore authorities, and his skilful political manoeuvring and innovations at all levels of government enabled Johor to retain its sovereignty. His achievement is a tribute not only to his personal ability but to the heritage of his forebears who had also skilfully manipulated changing situations to assure the continuing viability of the Johor kingdom. In 1868 the Riau court recognized Abu Bakar's success when it granted him the right to assume the title maharaja, once used by the rulers of Melaka.

Abu Bakar, however, was not without his critics in contemporary Malay society. His influence in Singapore and London, and acceptance in European circles, aroused disapproval from some Malay rulers who took exception to his favoured position. It was not easily forgotten that his father had been simply temenggung, and Abu Bakar's apparent efforts to stake out a claim as heir to the status of the old Johor kingdom did arouse resentment. The announcement in 1885 that he was henceforth to be termed sultan was an occasion for caustic comment, and one *pantun* of the period was a pointed jibe at Abu Bakar's pretensions:

> A gaudy lantern is bound in rattan
> A wooden sheath holds the keris
> The Temenggung has become a Sultan
> Through his royal forebears the Bugis.[17]

Abu Bakar's position raised new and disturbing questions concerning the relationship between 'civilization' as it was defined by the West, and what it was to be a Malay. The adoption of much that was foreign to Malay custom had certainly contributed to Abu Bakar's achievements, as it had to those of other princes like Tengku Kudin and Raja Juma'at. But how far could an individual go along this road without jeopardizing his 'Malayness'?

The clearest articulation of this problem came from Riau, long a centre of Islamic scholarship and still regarded as the arbiter of Malay culture. Court writings expressed concern at the decline of traditional custom, especially among the youth, and urged Malays to maintain the purity of their language by eliminating accretions which had crept in through association with other races. To the Islamic-educated élite, the insidious influence of Western ways appeared a direct threat not only to their religion but to Malay culture itself. The respected Riau scholar, Raja Ali Haji, was openly critical of Malays who dressed in the European or Chinese manner, wearing trousers, socks and shoes, 'so that at night one would not know they were Malay'.[18] In Penang, young Muslims educated in European schools asserted their Malay identity by wearing Arab-style tunics and turbans over their shirts, trousers and boots.

Such discussions gained additional stimulus during the second half of the nineteenth century because everywhere Islam seemed to be retreating before the advance of the Christian West. Debates in the Islamic heartlands about the state of the Faith assumed a new immediacy for Malays as improved communications, notably the Suez Canal, made the pilgrimage to Mecca easier. Malay newspapers, journals and religious teachers fostered the view that self-strengthening and reform within Islam was the only solution to the Western challenge. The Muslim community could undoubtedly learn from Western technology, but to adopt Western values unquestioningly would undermine the health of Islam and strike at the essence of Malay culture. Yet some Malays, especially in the Straits Settlements, while expressing impatience with the assumptions and practices associated with the Malay *kerajaan*, saw the European example as a persuasive model.

Varying styles of government among Malay rulers mirror differing perceptions of the most appropriate road towards the future. In Kedah, Kelantan and Terengganu the nineteenth century saw religious bureaucracies developing in response to royal encouragement, and an expansion of Islamic education. Johor during the same period presents something of a contrast. Abu Bakar, a product of a Christian mission education, set up a school in 1865 but it was based on an English-type syllabus rather than the Arabic grammar, logic and Koran reading of the Islamic schools. In 1863, at a time when Baginda Umar in Terengganu was laying the basis for an expansion of the Islamic judicial system governed by *syariah* law, Abu Bakar wrote to the Singapore governor to say that he had revised the Islamic code, making it 'more conformable to European ideas'. Yet despite the very real differences between these approaches to government, the aim was the same: the maintenance of meaningful Malay political control when it was apparent that economic initiatives were passing into alien hands.

The Pangkor Treaty

Until the 1870s the full impact of the Western presence was kept at bay. Despite the continual petitions and memoranda from the Straits merchant community, London remained adamant that there was to be no further British involvement at an official level. At this point, however, commercial interests in the Straits Settlements discovered a source of ammunition which was far more effective than complaints about Malay government and Chinese fighting. They began to realize the potential of exploiting London's fear of the intrusion of another power, particularly Germany, into the Peninsula. So effective was this approach that the mood in London showed a marked change.

In November 1873 a new governor, Andrew Clarke, took up his duties with the impression that he could act on his own initiative to settle disputes between Chinese secret societies and among Malay princes, even to the extent of appointing a British officer in the Malay states. Briefed on his arrival by W.H. Read, Clarke came to the conclusion that the assertion of British control was the only possible solution. His first step was to arrange a ceasefire between the Chinese factions fighting in Larut and to request the leading Perak Malays to meet him on Pangkor Island off the Perak coast in order to settle the succession question. In the meantime, Raja Abdullah, still hoping to be recognized as sultan of Perak, had followed the advice of his business associates, Read and Tan Kim Cheng. He had written to Clarke inviting him to send a Resident to Perak and asking in return for recognition as sultan. It was this offer which resulted in the Pangkor Treaty of 20 January 1874, which recognized Abdullah as sultan in return for his agreement to accept a British Resident. According to Article Six in the English version, the Resident's advice 'must be asked and acted upon on all questions other than those touching Malay religion and custom'. In this context, the British saw Abdullah's apparent predisposition to rule 'in an English fashion' as a virtue; by contrast, his principal rival, Sultan Ismail, was dismissed as an 'impracticable Malay of the old school' known to be suspicious of British policy.[19]

While the Pangkor Treaty accelerated the process of British involvement in the affairs of the Peninsular states, the initial impetus had come from the establishment of Singapore in 1819. Singapore was unique not just because it had been founded by the European nation destined to build the greatest empire that the world had yet seen, but because it would become an important instrument of that imperial expansion. The British presence in Singapore initiated a new kind of diplomacy in the region, reflecting the mood of the imperial age. Colonies might be, in Disraeli's oft-quoted phrase, 'a millstone round our necks', but there was a continuing growth of informal European empires of trade, investment and influence. The Malay world was divided among Siam, Britain and the Netherlands, and the new boundaries fixed by international agreement. Singapore, the central point of this redrawn map, was from the first envisaged as a great trading port which would further the commerce of its British rulers.

Britain's increasing interest in the area inevitably affected the lifestyle of the local inhabitants. The campaign against piracy undoubtedly made the seas safer for trade, but for some maritime peoples it removed an accepted source of livelihood. Steamships improved communications, but provided stiff and often fatal competition to native shipping. The ties with Europe opened up new markets, but those who benefited were principally Europeans and the ever-increasing migrant Chinese population. Most traditional forest and sea products of the Malay Peninsula were not sufficiently profitable to entice outside capital investment. Instead, European and Chinese investors encouraged new commercial crops and more intensive mining of tin, especially along the west coast. As financial backers of several Malay princes and as investors in the Malay states, Straits merchants became intimately involved in Peninsular affairs. When continual fighting among Malays and Chinese threatened local trade, their lobbying for a greater British supervisory role intensified. The letter from Sultan Abdullah was the 'key to the door' which in 1874 finally led to political intervention.

The British presence in the nineteenth century brought the peoples of the Malay world into contact with a self-confident culture, convinced of its superiority and its 'civilized' status. The success of Johor's rulers, entailing a partial adoption of this culture, raised the still-debated question of what constitutes 'Malayness'. Could Malay society incorporate the advantages of Western civilization without jeopardizing the centuries-old Melayu heritage? With the beginning of colonial rule, this question was to assume a new urgency.

The Making of 'British' Malaya, 1874–1919

Although commonly accepted as a convenient means of demarcating the beginning of Malaysia's colonial period, the Pangkor Treaty does not signify a radical change in British imperial policy. Governor Andrew Clarke may have concluded the treaty on his own initiative, but it did not cause great consternation in the Colonial Office, where the possible appointment of a British Agent in the western Malay states had been under discussion for some time. Nor does the Pangkor Treaty stand as a clear break between two different phases of economic development. Despite the expectations of the commercial community in the Straits Settlements, European enterprise was only slowly established in the Peninsula. Chinese predominance continued in both tin mining and most forms of plantation agriculture, and not until the 1890s did the initiative pass to Europeans.

The significance of the Pangkor Treaty lies in the fact that it represented a turning point in the formal relationship between Britain and the Malay states. Arguments for and against expansion of British control had been tossed back and forth since Singapore's founding, but once the Pangkor Treaty had been concluded it essentially became a question of how and when British rule would be extended across the entire Peninsula. Over a period of about 50 years British authority, whether represented by governor, agent, resident or adviser, was to be formalized in several separate administrative units which became known by the deceptively unified term 'British Malaya'.

Historiographical considerations

For a historian one redeeming feature of colonial rule in Malaya is the extent to which government was conducted on paper, especially with the bureaucratic expansion from the 1880s. Regardless of the administrative centre to which they were dispatched – Bangkok, London, Singapore, Kuching –

nineteenth-century officials generated innumerable documents that were in turn filed, duplicated, and incorporated into further reports. Improved communication between Europe and Malaya, and between outlying areas and capitals, facilitated the transmission of the vast amount of information on which the colonial enterprise relied. Though intended primarily for administrative purposes, historians have shown that this material can reveal much about social history as well, and lends itself to many different interpretations. The production and storage of written material became a personal preoccupation as well, particularly for Europeans. The nineteenth-century practice of preserving correspondence and diaries, for example, often provides information unavailable elsewhere. The presence of European women as wives and travellers offers a new and different perspective on events normally seen from the male point of view. Publishing in Malay, notably newspapers, also gathers pace with the establishment of lithographic and printing presses, and with output in Malay from government agencies. Writing in Chinese similarly flourished, especially from 1881 when a Straits-born Chinese founded the first modern Chinese newspaper. Together with visual material like maps and photographs, the preservation of so many different kinds of documents in archives and libraries has bequeathed a bank of priceless data on which historians can continue to draw.

The extension of British control

Governor Clarke was quick to seize the long-awaited opportunity provided by the signing of the Pangkor Treaty in January 1874. In Larut, where fighting had been most extensive and the tin trade most disrupted, the former commander of Menteri Ngah Ibrahim's forces, a colourful adventurer called Captain Speedy, was installed as Assistant Resident. Three commissioners, including Frank Swettenham, a young civil servant qualified in Malay, and William Pickering, who was fluent in Chinese, were dispatched to Larut to supervise the dismantling of the Chinese stockades, organize the return of women captured in the fighting, and resolve the disputes over mines and watercourses which had fuelled the conflicts. In early November, pending his official posting as Resident, Singapore's colonial secretary, J.W.W. Birch, took up residence on the Lower Perak river.

Meanwhile, Clarke was ready to exploit the unusually amenable mood in London in order to extend British influence in Selangor. A case of 'piracy' in Selangor waters in November 1873 gave him the justification he needed to open negotiations with Sultan Abdul Samad. Although no formal agreement like the Pangkor Treaty was signed, the young Frank Swettenham went to live at the royal capital, Langat, as Assistant Resident. Tengku Kudin's financial associate, J.G. Davidson, who was already assisting in the administration of Kelang, was officially appointed as Resident. A final posting was made in

Sungai Ujung, where Clarke gave the newly appointed Datuk Kelana, the territorial chief, 'the protection of the British Government' as well as arms and ammunition. In return, the Datuk Kelana promised to keep the Linggi river open to trade and to charge reasonable duties. This association with the British gave the Datuk Kelana a decided advantage over his rival, the Datuk Bandar, who had come to be regarded as the Kelana's equal. Fighting between the two factions had been protracted, but now, in an ensuing quarrel between them, the Datuk Kelana unilaterally hoisted the British flag and asked for troops to reinforce his position and an officer to live with him. In granting both requests, British control was effectively extended in Sungai Ujung, despite the lack of any formal treaty.

By the beginning of 1875, the first steps had thus been taken in the development of what came to be called the residential system. It is striking how ill-prepared the British were for the role they had assumed. Only some time after the meeting at Pangkor, for example, did Swettenham learn of the existence of Raja Yusuf who would have succeeded to the Perak throne in 1857 and 1865 had it not been for his unpopularity with the Malay chiefs. If the men on the spot were often surprised by some new disclosure, it was immeasurably more difficult for decision-makers in London to conceive of what Malaya was like. To them, the way in which Malay culture was intertwined with its politics was a continual puzzle. As one exasperated official in London sighed in 1878, 'Malay modes of election, Malay customs as to inheritance and relationship and purity of blood etc. are incomprehensible to us.'[1]

In 1875 there was no long-term plan as to how the British should proceed, and the difficulties which developed were almost inevitable in view of the lack of thought which had gone into the precise nature of 'intervention'. There had as yet been no formulation of the specific duties of a Resident or a clear statement of the way in which he would 'advise'. It is doubtful whether Perak Malays fully understood that the British conceived of powers far more extensive than the purely commercial role of the Dutch Resident in Perak 80 years earlier. Although there is no fully authenticated Malay version of the Pangkor Treaty, a possible copy of the original speaks not only of advice (*nasihat*) from the Resident but of discussion (*bicara*). Unlike the English original, the Malay rendering of the critical Article Six obliges the ruler to listen to the Resident's advice, but not necessarily to act on it. Malays would have been justified in assuming that decision-making would continue to be collective, following the same process as in their traditional *mesyuarat bicara* (meetings for discussion). In these assemblies a general consensus was necessary before any action could be taken, and debates might continue for several days. A Malay ruler could rarely impose his will arbitrarily on his court or his chiefs, since the enforcement of obedience was beyond royal powers. The Pangkor Treaty, however, presupposed not only that the ruler himself would be receptive to the Resident's 'advice', and would help to implement any measures advocated, but that he had the ability to ensure acceptance by his court. In the most peaceful situation this would not necessarily have been the case, and now the Residents also had to deal with the aftermath of years of hostility between members of the ruling class. In Perak, despite Birch's efforts to effect a reconciliation, Sultan Ismail refused to sign the treaty and he, like Raja Yusuf, the third claimant to the throne, was supported by his own coterie of chiefs. Repeatedly in their dealings with the Dutch in past centuries, Perak rulers had insisted that the approval of the assembly was required to make any contract binding. By refusing to sign the Treaty several prominent Perak chiefs were denying its legality.

In cultural terms, moreover, the Pangkor Treaty drew distinctions which were meaningless to Malays but which continued to emerge as contentious issues in British–Malay relations. 'Religion and custom' was to be excluded from British control, but 'the general administration of the country' would be conducted in accordance with the Resident's advice. Yet religion and precedent were the fundamental and frequently the only justification for Malay political action. The division between religious and secular, so clearcut to Europeans, was simply an alien concept to Malays. Perhaps the most problematic area involved state finances. According to Article Ten of the Treaty, the 'collection and control' of revenue was to be regulated by the Resident. Though resentment at the levying of tolls or taxes by an overlord was nothing new, the nineteenth century had seen a widespread tendency to ignore royal prerogatives as district chiefs and princes established centres of economic independence. These men were understandably hostile to the notion of a central treasury which paid out salaries and was subject to the Resident's control. In 1858 the Selangor princes had already rejected similar proposals put forward by Raja Juma'at of Lukut. In 1874 the threat to a much-valued independence was heightened because now the state revenues would be under non-Malay authority. Realizing full well that the promised salary could always be withheld from those who failed to please, chiefs were not willing to surrender their right to collect taxes in exchange for placement on a 'civil list'.

As contentious as revenue collection was the question of slavery, which after a long and acrimonious battle had finally been abolished throughout the British empire in 1833. The Pangkor Treaty made no reference to slavery, but it was regarded by Straits Settlements authorities as repugnant to the 'civilized' government they proposed to initiate. Clarke himself specifically stated that 'no slavery could be permitted to exist in any state under British protection'. Given this adamant attitude, it was inevitable that difficulties would arise because in the Malay world the human resources represented by slaves were as important to the status of rulers and the chiefly class as revenue itself. In Perak, slavery was more of an issue than in Selangor, since the Perak ruling class was considerably larger: here, slaves and debt bondsmen numbered an estimated 3000 in a total Malay population of perhaps 50 000 (approximately 6 per cent).

Europeans tended to define this slavery in Western terms and to see slaves as an undifferentiated group of people condemned to lives of unrelenting misery. But among Malays, slaves were generally divided into two classes: slaves in the Western sense, and debt bondsmen. Debt slavery usually occurred when an individual voluntarily 'mortgaged' himself in return for some financial assistance from his creditor, frequently his ruler or chief. In times of hardship, after a bad harvest or when a trading venture had failed, debt bondage might be the only means for a peasant to raise finances. If after a prescribed time such an individual was unable to redeem the debt, he or she was absorbed into the creditor's household. They were then obliged to carry out any order the lord might give until the debt was repaid. Through debt bondage the ruling class gained followers to increase their status and an economic asset which could be transferred, if need be, to some other creditor. Nor was this a matter which concerned only men. Many female domestic servants were bonded through debt, and in 1874 the largest investor in debt bondage was a woman, the wife of the menteri of Larut.

Local attitudes were largely ignored by the newly appointed British Residents, who were all unanimous in their condemnation of slavery. Admittedly the lot of many was indeed deplorable. Slaves proper were often subject to rank exploitation because they were usually non-Muslim Orang Asli and were therefore considered outside the pale of the Melayu. It is indicative, for instance, that a Malay term for slave, 'Semang', is still used to refer to certain Orang Asli groups. Among debt slaves there were certainly cases of cruelty and other abuses, especially in the treatment of women. At the very least, a chief could simply refuse to accept payment from a debt-slave when the debt fell due. Because slavery was so bound up with a chief's prestige, British enquiries into alleged mistreatment aroused considerable resentment among Malay nobles. Sultan Abdul Samad of Selangor was so incensed by the intrusive questions that he refused point-blank to permit his slaves to be counted.

As Clarke realized, the questions of revenue collection and the abolition of slavery were potentially explosive. To challenge established custom would obviously demand Residents with sensitivity and discernment who were knowledgeable about Malay society. The difficulty in finding men sufficiently fluent in Malay to take up the new postings is a sobering comment on the lack of British interaction with Malays since the founding of Singapore in 1819. However, the newly created Straits Civil Service had established language requirements, and one of its products, Frank Swettenham, spoke good Malay. He quickly succeeded in winning Sultan Abdul Samad's approval. But there were others whose shortcomings in administrative ability or temperament endangered British–Malay relations. Speedy's regime in Larut had aroused criticism, and Sultan Abdul Samad had already been offended by Birch's abrupt manner at a meeting in 1871. It was in fact with some reservations, and after some delay, that Governor Clarke posted Birch to Perak as Resident.

His misgivings were justified. Birch soon aroused the hostility of the Perak chiefs, not merely because he had come to initiate the new system of tax revenue and centralized collection, but because he employed public humiliation to enforce his authority. What Birch called 'a good dressing down' aroused as much resentment among recalcitrant chiefs as the burning of their homes and the forced surrender of arms. The Resident's attitude to slavery and his willingness to provide a sanctuary for fugitive debt-slaves, especially women, was regarded by Malays as simple theft. The menteri of Perak, Ngah Ibrahim, although a signatory to the Pangkor Treaty, was in the forefront of the nobles critical of Birch and the new state of affairs. He was especially humiliated because his territory of Larut was now administered by his former employee, Captain Speedy. This displacement of an established chief, the menteri argued, augured ill for Perak's future. In a conversation with Sultan Abdullah, the menteri reportedly said:

> I think bye and bye Mr Birch will keep many more Europeans to take charge of the country and have stations and sepoys and police. After a few years they will surely drive us out of the country . . . I have considered many days upon this case. It is improper for Your Majesty to follow the Resident, for his rank is only that of a Datuk[2]

The tension was heightened by the animosity between Birch and Abdullah. The delay in Birch's appointment had allowed the Perak ruler to function virtually independently, and he resented the restrictions imposed by the Resident's presence. The manner in which he tried to resolve the situation is a curious mixture of traditional and modern which helps highlight the cultural changes taking place. On the one hand, Sultan Abdullah addressed a formal petition to the Singapore governor, asking that the Resident be placed under him; on the other, he called in the services of a spirit medium to help rid himself of Birch and other 'light-eyed men'.

For his part, Birch not only considered Abdullah 'eminently silly and foolish . . . an arrant coward', but maintained that Ismail was more widely acknowledged as ruler and was therefore a more legitimate successor. By June 1875 the new governor, Sir William Jervois, was already contemplating the removal of Abdullah, and the rumours flying around Penang and Singapore rapidly spread to the Malay states. Apprehension was heightened when Jervois himself raised the possibility of annexation with the Perak princes and chiefs. From Singapore's standpoint this would simply formalize the existing arrangement whereby the west coast states, though considered 'but tributary to the British Government . . . are absolutely and virtually annexed except in name'.[3] In September Jervois sent an ultimatum: either Sultan Abdullah agree to greater British administration over financial and judicial matters, or he would be deposed. As a concession, Abdullah was assured that he would be consulted 'whenever possible'.

This measure, a fundamental departure from the terms of the Pangkor Treaty, seemed to Jervois necessary because Perak was already indebted by $18 000 to the Straits Settlements treasury. In his opinion, there was little chance of regaining this sum unless the British tightened their control. This exposure of the fiction of Malay rule with British advice was the final insult, and it was the unpopular Birch who bore the brunt of Malay anger. On 2 November, while posting notices of the controversial enactment, Birch was killed; Swettenham, who was also in Perak, escaped downriver.

The precise motives for Birch's murder are still debated. Popular interpretations of his death have seen it as an outburst against British authority, the first stirrings of an incipient nationalism. Certainly, the sense of being Malay against a European, an infidel, did play a part, as had attacks on Dutch officials in Kedah and Perak in the seventeenth century, and in Siak in the eighteenth. More significant is what the British represented: a departure from tradition and custom, a new and alien government which would destroy established privileges. But though the Perak ruling class presumably envisaged a return to something resembling the old order, the anger the British had aroused was not a Malay preserve. In 1878, for instance, members of the Ho Seng secret society killed the superintendent of the Dindings district as a reprisal for their loss of revenues.

On hearing of Birch's death, the British authorities anticipated a general uprising, and steps were immediately taken to quash any possible resistance. In Johor, Raja Mahdi of Selangor, who had purportedly been planning an attack on his old appanage of Kelang, was arrested. Skirmishes occurred through November and December in Sungai Ujung, where British troops supported the Datuk Kelana against rivals bitterly hostile to those who had 'brought the white men into the country'. On one occasion armed bands were seen carrying the Turkish flag, a counter to the Datuk Kelana's Union Jack and a reflection of the Pan-Islamic movement being sponsored by Turkey. The greatest attention was focused on Perak, but here the British clearly overreacted. The call for troops from as far afield as India and Hong Kong proved quite unnecessary, and one observer commented that there were probably no more than 300 Malays under arms. However, for several months those pronounced guilty of conspiracy against Birch, including Sultan Abdullah and Sultan Ismail, were pursued. For the individuals captured, justice was summary. Three were hanged, while Abdullah, Ismail and several major chiefs were exiled.

In retrospect, Swettenham regarded this harsh retribution as having served the new order well. By removing most of the first-ranking chiefs, the British had eliminated the principal obstacles to the changes they proposed to make. For over 15 years these positions remained unfilled, allowing for the creation of a very different type of administration. 'The state of Perak,' Swettenham wrote, 'gained in twelve months what ten years of "advice" could hardly have accomplished.' But for Malays, the punishment meted out was a blatant demonstration of European ability to enforce their demands. Sultan Abdullah was never permitted to return to Perak, and years later the sultan of Kedah stressed his anxiety to remain on good terms with the British because he well remembered the Perak ruler's fate. In Malay society where rebellions were traditionally led by some chief or *anak raja*, the British power to punish even the highest-born, coupled with the knowledge that open resistance had little hope of success, goes a long way towards explaining Malay quiescence.

For those who co-operated with the British, the rewards were high. Raja Yusuf of Perak was appointed Regent since he had been absolved of implication in the conspiracy. Despite his known unpopularity with the Malays, he was installed as sultan by the British in 1887. In Sungai Ujung the new Datuk Bandar, successor to the old enemy of the British, accommodated himself so successfully to the changed order that the British began to favour him above the Datuk Kelana.

Resumption of the 'forward movement'

The events of 1875–6 meant that what has been called the British 'forward movement' received a temporary check. In London the Colonial Office was appalled, and its recriminations stilled for the moment any talk of further annexation which would entail increased expenditure. But exponents of expansion in the Straits Settlements remained undaunted. Although Birch's death was a timely reminder of the need to tread carefully and choose Residents wisely, it was not long before the attention of Jervois and his supporters turned to the Melaka hinterland. Here it is not easy to locate a straightforward economic motive for expansion, and indeed no British official ever argued that control in this area would bring great financial rewards. One study of the period has spoken of the imperialists' desire to quell the 'turbulent frontier' so close at hand, and certainly politics in what later became Negeri Sembilan were nothing if not turbulent. British assistance to the Datuk Kelana of Sungai Ujung had merely introduced an added complexity into the already protracted disputes among the leaders of Sungai Ujung, Jelebu, Johol and Rembau. In order to restore peace while strengthening British influence, Governor Jervois resorted to a device which had been considered successful in other areas of the British empire – the use of a friendly and influential chief who would act as a medium through which subtle pressure could be exerted on his peers.

Abu Bakar, the maharaja of Johor, seemed ideally suited to this role. He himself was ambitious and, as his previous involvement in the Pahang Civil War suggests, was anxious to extend his hold over territories that had in centuries past acknowledged the suzerainty of the old kingdom of Riau-Johor. In addition, he was already regarded with respect by most leaders in the quarrelling states. As far as Jervois was concerned, his prime qualification was his reputation as a willing recipient of Singapore's advice. So convinced was the governor of the maharaja's suitability as Singapore's representative that he aimed eventually to make Abu Bakar overlord of the entire Negeri

Sembilan area. In 1876 Jervois was even willing to see not the British choice but Abu Bakar's own client, Tunku Antah, assume the contested position of yamtuan over a number of small states (Sri Menanti, Jempul, Terachi, Gunung Pasir, Ulu Muar, Johol and Inas) which would now become the Sri Menanti confederacy. The Sri Menanti group agreed to permit peaceful trade through their territories and to refer disputes among themselves to Abu Bakar. The underlying assumption in Singapore was that the maharaja would then consult British authorities over any future course of action. The following year a similar arrangement was made with the penghulu of Rembau and with Jelebu. When Sultan Ali of Johor died soon afterwards, Abu Bakar was made guardian of Muar, Sultan Ali's fief, in preference to either of Sultan Ali's sons. By 1878 Abu Bakar had thus become adviser to all the Negeri Sembilan states except Sungai Ujung.

The manoeuvring which this had involved on the maharaja's part, and the maintenance of credibility both in Singapore and the Negeri Sembilan states, is a testimony to Abu Bakar's political dexterity. While his achievement brought him an enhanced status and a prestige enjoyed by no other Malay ruler, it also served the Singapore government, which in effect hoped to exploit Abu Bakar as a substitute Resident.

From the 1880s the 'forward movement' gained further momentum, a development attributed to the growing fear in London of threats to Britain's paramountcy in the Peninsula. German activity in the Pacific was disturbing, while the French continued to consolidate their hold over Vietnam, Cambodia and Laos. The future of Siam, now caught between British Burma and French Indochina, was not at all clear. King Chulalongkorn's recruitment of European specialists to assist in his modernizing programme was a source of unease, and the possibility of Siam falling under French or German control could not be discounted. In London, therefore, officials began to listen more seriously to arguments advocating an extension of British power in the Malay region.

Simultaneously a number of strong personalities were emerging as guiding forces behind public opinion in the Straits Settlements and the tiny European population in the Malay states. Among the most forceful was another admirer of Raffles, Frank Swettenham, who throughout his life argued that expansion was not only in British interests but would also benefit Malays. Frederick Weld, governor from 1880 to 1887, was also an influential figure whose stated ambition was to extend British control as far as possible over the Peninsula south of Siam during his term of office. Such men were far less amenable than Jervois to sponsoring Abu Bakar's influence in Negeri Sembilan. The maharaja's loyalty to British interests, they claimed, was suspect, and he seemed unwilling or unable to settle the recurring quarrels between Negeri Sembilan chiefs. The peace of the other protected Malay states stood in marked contrast to the Melaka interior, where a complex system of inheritance and succession, adapted from Minangkabau custom, imparted a unique character to local disputes. What would happen, it was asked, when Abu Bakar died? Would his heir be able to claim the same standing as his father?

With London's encouragement, Governor Weld began to press his views by slowly whittling away at Abu Bakar's position in Negeri Sembilan. There was, however, a distinct difference between 1874 and 1880 in the manner in which the Residents were posted. In the former case, speed was essential in order to seize the long-awaited opportunity in the major tin areas. Now, because of the lack of significant tin deposits, the belief that non-British intrusion in this area was unlikely, and the inability of most of these states to support a full Residential system, Weld could afford to bide his time. A process which took just months in Perak and Selangor was in Negeri Sembilan stretched over years. In 1881 Weld met the Sri Menanti heads and spoke of the advantages of dealing directly with Singapore rather than through the maharaja. Then, between 1883 and 1887, British officers were appointed in Jelebu and Rembau, their powers slowly extended to resemble those of Residents elsewhere. There was sufficient time to ensure that the local chiefs were men who would willingly accept British advice, even if this entailed a manipulation of the electoral system by which leaders were chosen. The difference in Perak and Selangor is well illustrated when one realizes that the requests of Yamtuan Antah of Sri Menanti for a British Resident were in fact rejected until Weld considered the time appropriate.

In 1885 a British officer was stationed in Sri Menanti, without any treaty basis, and performed duties similar to those of a Resident. Supervision over external affairs was also transferred to the British government. Four years later, in 1889, a new confederacy of Negeri Sembilan was formed, excluding only Sungai Ujung and Jelebu, which were eventually included in 1895. In 1898 the British were able to bring about the election of Yamtuan Antah's son as yamtuan besar of this reconstructed Negeri Sembilan, under the authority of a Resident. Despite the persistence of many local customs traceable to Minangkabau, the new administrative unity contributed to gradually lessening local differences in governments and *adat* which had characterized the small Negeri Sembilan states prior to colonial control.

In contrast to Negeri Sembilan, the extension of British control into Pahang is a prime example of the way in which economic concerns could shape policy. Malay memories of Pahang as a land of gold, combined with its relative isolation, had given rise to stories depicting it as 'the richest and most favoured state in the Peninsula'. These accounts were widely accepted, though the reality was less exciting, for gold and tin deposits were limited to small pockets in the interior near the Selangor and Terengganu borders. However, reports of Pahang's 'great wealth' from Swettenham, who travelled across the Peninsula in 1885, served to reinforce the general belief. In Singapore, London's growing sympathy with the ambitions of colonial expansionists did not go unnoticed. As the price of tin rose to unprecedented heights, so too did the sense of urgency among the Straits business community. Weld's conviction that Pahang's touted storehouse of minerals should be brought under British control established a primary goal for his administration.

Commercial appetites were whetted because Bendahara Ahmad of Pahang, who had previously rebuffed attempts by both Clarke and Jervois to extend Singapore's influence, now seemed more receptive to the notion of closer relations. From 1880 Ahmad made several trips to Singapore as the guest of Abu Bakar, whom he had forgiven for supporting Ahmad's brother Mutahir in the Pahang War of 1858. The example of Johor apparently convinced him that European investment need not necessarily entail surrender of sovereignty. Ahmad subsequently sold mining concessions to a number of individuals and companies in Singapore, many of whom were merely speculators hoping to profit from a predicted treaty between Pahang and Britain. The personal nature of these transactions was to have serious implications, since there were no legal controls over the transfer of concessions; some were later bought up by the Pahang Corporation, whose directors included prominent men in London, one a member of parliament. Several concessions were apparently sold without any consideration of the territorial rights of Pahang chiefs or recognition of the fact that certain areas were already being worked by local Malays or Chinese.

To Weld's disappointment, Ahmad did not ask for a Resident; on the contrary, he sought to prevent British political intervention following hard on commercial investment. Clearly intent on strengthening his own authority, Ahmad assumed the title of sultan in 1881, and was acknowledged as such by most of his chiefs. From a Malay point of view he could now claim an even higher position than Abu Bakar of Johor, still only a maharaja. Arguments in favour of a British alliance put forward by Weld and his silver-tongued spokesman Swettenham met strenuous resistance, and in 1885 Ahmad stated point-blank that he simply did not want a Resident. But by October 1887 the combined influence of Weld's nephew, Hugh Clifford, and the mediation of Abu Bakar finally persuaded Ahmad to sign a treaty with the British similar to one concluded two years before between Britain and Johor. Under immense pressure, he accepted a document that acknowledged Pahang's standing as a 'sovereign state' while providing for a British Agent who would help open up the country to 'commerce and civilization'.

While the affirmation of Pahang's sovereignty was immensely significant to Ahmad, Hugh Clifford, the first Agent, found the restraints on his powers a constant irritation, since he was unable to introduce desired reforms, especially regarding slavery, or control the granting of concessions. Pahang's government at the time, he afterwards claimed, was 'a disgrace to the Peninsula'. Neither Ahmad nor his chiefs would willingly relinquish their rights, and the former even said he would rather see Pahang revert to a jungle than let it be governed by the British. He himself was determined to govern 'as long as life lasted'.[4] At the same time, Ahmad's unilateral leasing of land to European investors and the consequent disruption of the local economy fed a growing pool of hostility among his subjects.

The atmosphere in the royal capital, Pekan, grew ugly. Rumours circulated of a possible British shelling of the ruler's palace, with panic-stricken Malays recalling Singapore's action against Kuala Terengganu in 1862. Given the generally held belief in Singapore that Pahang was a land of untold wealth, Weld's own ambitions, and the involvement of commercial interests able to manipulate Colonial Office apprehension of German or French speculators, extension of British control into Pahang was a foregone conclusion. In 1888 the murder of a Chinese British subject provided the Straits government with the excuse to act. Fearing armed intervention, and remembering what had happened in Perak, Sultan Ahmad was finally induced to write a letter in which he asked for a British Resident who would help govern Pahang in the same manner as the other Malay states. His only conditions were that his own privileges and powers be protected and that customs which had 'good and proper reason' be guaranteed. The Resident was duly appointed, but no guarantees were made. As one study of the period has pointed out, the request and the accompanying proviso were incompatible.[5]

Realizing the extent of opposition, the first Resident moved slowly, but historical circumstances made conflict almost inevitable. Even before any British Agent arrived, the political system in Pahang was undergoing considerable strain. Some of the interior chiefs, whose territories included rich mining districts, had gained their positions as rewards for helping Bendahara Ahmad come to power. In 1884 other nobles who resented the royal favourites had conspired with Ahmad's brother in an abortive attempt to attack Pahang through Selangor. The independence of interior chiefs had been strengthened during Ahmad's prolonged visits to Singapore, while the links of blood, marriage and economic interests which often drew them to Selangor undermined any sense of allegiance to the distant capital in Pekan. When representatives of European and Chinese firms to whom Ahmad had sold mining and timber concessions arrived to stake their claims, they were confronted by angry chiefs who regarded these areas as their rightful holdings.

Changes subsequently introduced by the British created further grounds for discontent. Regarding the Pahang chiefs as 'an ignorant body of men', the new Resident set up courts of justice, a small police force and a State Council, but the issuing of jungle passes, restrictions on carrying weapons, corvée duties for road building, registration of slaves and the centralization of finances met considerable hostility. In particular, the chiefs objected to the payment of salaries which denied them the right to collect revenue in their districts. The omission of several from the state's 'civil list' effectively left them without any source of income, while other chiefs found their revenue dropped substantially. The syahbandar, for example, had previously raised about $1200 annually, but now received only $720. New regulations regarding the treatment of debt-slaves and limitations on their use of forced labour (*kerah*) were also perceived as a direct attack on the traditional privileges of chiefs and princes. The Orang Kaya (district chief) of the *ulu* district of

171

Semantan, Abdul Rahman, was so enraged by the decline in his revenue that he even asked for Semantan to be transferred to Selangor. It was Abdul Rahman, commonly known as Datuk Bahaman, who was the spearhead of opposition to the changes the British had introduced. In 1891, as punishment for his continued defiance, the Resident persuaded Sultan Ahmad to sign a decree depriving Bahaman of his title. Towards the end of that year the latter declared his open rebellion, setting in motion a protracted series of skirmishes, ambushes and occasional engagements which became known as the Pahang War.

In terms of British policy, these disturbances strengthened the uneasy feeling that extension of control into Pahang might have been a mistake and forced a reassessment of Pahang's real worth in relation to Britain's interests. But for modern Malays the Pahang War, like that in Perak, has come to symbolize the struggle to safeguard Malay tradition, Malay values, the sense of Malay independence, against outside intrusion. The rebellion of the Orang Kaya of Semantan and his allies created the opportunity for leaders to emerge and legends to be created. Like other leaders of local resistance, the deeds of the famed fighter, Mat Kilau, during the Pahang War have gained him a place in popular memory as one of the heroes of Malay nationalism.

Throughout the conflict, the rebellious chiefs always claimed that they were defending the ruler's interests. Initially Sultan Ahmad gave his tacit support, and the strength of the resistance also owed much to the role of Bahaman's Orang Asli supporters. Bahaman's own origins are obscure but he was reported to be partly Jakun, and his own knowledge of the jungle and ties with Orang Asli enabled him and his followers to elude capture for some time. Another story claimed that he was descended from a royal family of Sumatra. The perception of Bahaman and his allies as guardians of the Melayu heritage was heightened during the dying stages of the campaign when the remnants of the rebels became associated with a Terengganu holy man who infused their cause with the spirit of *perang sabil*, a holy war against infidels. The resistance, however, had already begun to weaken when Sultan Ahmad was pressured by the Resident into aligning himself with the British. It was his Malay following which pursued the rebels and only when the situation seemed more serious were small companies of Sikh troops brought in from Selangor and Perak. A general amnesty was issued in 1892 and the majority of the chiefs and their following surrendered. The remainder fled to Terengganu where they were treated sympathetically by local Malays, but in 1895 a force led by Hugh Clifford pursued them across the Terengganu boundary into Kelantan. The leaders were arrested by the Siamese authorities and exiled to Chiang Mai, being permitted to return to Pahang only in 1913. Sultan Ahmad's son Tengku Mahmud, who had been educated in Singapore and had long entertained hopes of succession, was rewarded for his co-operation with the British and confirmed as Sultan Ahmad's heir.

The Pahang War represented only a brief setback to the British 'forward movement'. Johor was now encircled by the Protected States and from the

1890s Abu Bakar's support in Singapore and even in London declined as the existence of a state governed completely by Malays came to be considered an anomaly. Prior to 1880 Abu Bakar had been able to maintain his high standing through his carefully cultivated relationship with the British authorities. While personally disapproving of many aspects of British policy along the west coast, he had become the linchpin of British influence in the Negeri Sembilan region, and had been instrumental in the extension of the Residential system to Pahang. However, rather than being held up as a model government, Johor was now suffering by comparison with Perak and Selangor. In Singapore it was claimed that the administration of justice was haphazard and the revenue unregulated, with far too much spent on Abu Bakar's 'extravagances' such as overseas travel. In London too the feeling grew that indirect rule as exemplified in the Residential system more effectively promoted 'peace, commerce and civilization'. Abu Bakar's insistence on Johor's status as a foreign state and his visits to foreign capitals aroused particular concern because it raised the bogey of French, Dutch or German intervention.

Abu Bakar was fully aware of the attitude of Governor Weld and his circle, and seized every opportunity to counter their complaints. In 1885, during Weld's absence, Abu Bakar invited the acting governor to inspect Johor. As a result of the visit a report praising government in Johor and Muar and commending the maharaja's receptiveness to British suggestions was submitted to the Colonial Office. Abu Bakar himself went to London the same year and received a personal assurance that no Resident would be placed in Johor. But although a new treaty was negotiated, granting him the title of sultan and recognizing Johor as a sovereign state, it none the less hinted at future developments. Johor's foreign affairs were to be under Singapore's control, and Abu Bakar agreed not to interfere in the affairs of other states or to grant concessions to foreign Europeans. One clause in the treaty also made provision for the appointment, should the need arise, of a British Agent. Admittedly this Agent was to have only consular powers, but events in Pahang three years later showed how easily such functions could be converted into a more stringent type of 'advice'. In 1888, when an Agent was in fact proposed, Abu Bakar had to call on all his political adroitness and personal charm to convince Weld's successor of the value of direct relations between Johor and Singapore. Though he was successful, the treaty remained, and British officials quietly assumed that the situation would be re-evaluated when Abu Bakar died.

In his final years, Abu Bakar attempted to ensure that Johor's special status would in fact endure. In London he instituted a Johor Advisory Board made up of several prominent Englishmen to communicate directly with the Colonial Office. In April 1895 he promulgated a written Constitution which spelt out Johor's separate identity. Islam was specified as the state religion; the duties of the cabinet ministers and the legislative council were laid down; and most importantly, it was stipulated that no part of Johor's territories could ever be alienated to any European power.

The Johor leaders who were to live on after Abu Bakar's death to become advisers to his son realized the strength of the expansionist lobby in Singapore. Despite Johor's long record of economic prosperity and sound administration, the Singapore governor in 1893 claimed that 'progress' there was less evident than in any state under a British Resident. When Abu Bakar died in June 1895, Johor's position was less secure than 20 years earlier. Its independence was under increasing threat as advocates of a 'British Malaya' that would include the whole Peninsula gathered strength. Yet Abu Bakar's reign had bequeathed to Johor a tradition of sovereignty which was not easily set aside. Skilled diplomats, like the Chief Minister Datuk Ja'afar, whose forebears had served the temenggung family since Singapore's founding, realized that this tradition must be reconciled with reality. As the twentieth century dawned it was obvious that the relationship between Johor and Britain would require reshaping to meet the demands of a changing political environment.

The Residential system

The cornerstone of the Residential system was the concept of indirect rule, vigorously enunciated by Frank Swettenham in 1876: 'To preserve the accepted customs and traditions of the country, to enlist the sympathies and interests of the people in our assistance, and to teach them the advantages of good government and enlightened policy.'[6] As it evolved in the Protected Malay States, the Residential system owed much to Hugh Low (1824–1905), whose successful administration of Perak (1877–89) became the yardstick by which other Residents and their achievements were measured. Low had spent 30 years in the Borneo region and was a close friend of both James and Charles Brooke. He admired their creation of a government which seemed eminently suited to the local scene, being shaped by a genuine respect for many indigenous customs and by a limited budget which precluded a large European establishment. Based on a modified version of the Brooke model, Low's administration was a highly influential example in the evolution of colonial rule in the four Protected States.

The co-operation of the Malay ruling class, initially the most hostile towards the British arrogation of power, was essential for the success of indirect rule. As important as the rulers themselves were the nobility, and Swettenham later acknowledged that one of the principal British goals had been to 'conciliate or overawe' the chiefs, many of whom were more powerful than the rulers.[7] A primary means of gaining the desired co-operation was to compensate the ruling class for income they had lost through the abolition of slavery and the introduction of a central treasury. The major beneficiaries were unquestionably the sultans, who were given liberal allowances enabling them to enjoy a far more comfortable lifestyle than other members of the élite. They also gained in other ways. Though they lost most of their former powers, British support gave them security from potential challengers. In the Protected Malay States the days of civil war were gone, for no *anak raja* could now muster the strength necessary to topple a British-backed sultan. This new confidence was manifestly apparent in the installation of Sultan Sulaiman of Selangor in 1903, the first time since 1826 that the state had mounted such a ceremony. Envoys were dispatched to Riau to determine the ceremonial appropriate for a ruler of Bugis descent, and new and splendid items were crafted for the royal regalia.

Co-operative princes and important chiefs were also rewarded. A considerable number were incorporated into the bureaucracy in positions such as native magistrate, and state allowances for this type of work relieved many from dependence on the all-too-fickle royal bounty. As another generation grew up under the British umbrella, and as the immediate benefits of complying with the system became apparent, murmurings of discontent faded away. In 1878 Raja Bot, son of Raja Juma'at of Lukut, had objected to the loss of his appanage and accused the Residents of 'usurping the position of rulers, acting so as to make the rajas small and of no account in the eyes of the people'. Yet he apparently appreciated his own schooling in Melaka and in 1890 he sent his son to the newly established Selangor Raja School for an English education.

The appearance of British 'advice' to a ruler and his court was created by the institution of a State Council, which became the sole legislative body. It consisted of about ten individuals: the ruler, selected princes and chiefs, a restricted representation from the Chinese community and the Resident. But it was the Resident who nominated the members, who were then approved by the governor and then formally appointed by the sultan, usually for life. The Council met only about seven times a year. While the regent or sultan formally presided, the Resident, in consultation with the governor, proposed the legislation to be discussed, and prepared the agenda. Although the Council did provide a useful sounding board for public opinion, especially on matters affecting the Malays, its direct influence on legislation was limited. Furthermore, as time went on and administration became more involved, even the consultative function of the Council was ignored. Once the government had decided on a particular course of action, there was little the Council could do. Increasingly, the Councils simply approved decisions which had already been made. By the 1890s agenda for Council meetings were more detailed and meetings fewer; anything but the most perfunctory discussion would have been impossible. The process of governing was thus very different from the traditional assemblies, where several hundred members of the ruling class would gather in a meeting open to the public, and decisions were reached after debates which could last several days. The only area which remained under effective Malay control was the administration of religious law and the appointment of religious officials, responsibility for which was left in the sultan's hands. Even here the definition of what was 'religious' was not uncommonly redefined when the British felt it intruded into the sphere of civil law.

Local administration was under the general supervision of the British district officer, a post apparently modelled on the examples of Sarawak and British India. The district officer functioned as a Resident on a smaller scale, and the area under his control could reach up to 3800 square kilometres or even more in Pahang, and include as many as 20 000 people. The district officer was responsible for such matters as the district treasury, land rents, justice, revenue collection, law and order, public health and the supervision of the Malay establishment. The latter was based on the penghulu, who were in charge of *mukim*, an administrative division consisting of a main village or township and a smaller number of other hamlets or villages. The Malay penghulu under the British were drawn principally from well-connected families and received state salaries and perquisites. As agents of government, with jurisdiction over 500–3000 peasants scattered through several villages, they were charged with the collection of rents, the administration of local justice, and the maintenance of order.

Despite the retention of a shell of the traditional governmental struc-ture, the nature of British rule was very different from that of the former Malay administration. Those most obviously affected by the changed order were the commoner chiefs who, unlike the princely class, were not accorded the privileges the British felt were due to royalty. Only a few chiefs could be included in the new-style Councils or be appointed as penghulu. With the authority they had once held in the countryside relinquished to the district officers, the chiefs lost control over the peasants from whom they had formerly exacted labour and revenue. Many found it impossible to live within their state allowances, and without rights of taxation were perpetually in debt. The maintenance of a large following, previously a sign of high status, was no longer possible because from 1882 measures were taken to abolish slavery and debt bondage. Corvée was henceforth restricted to state works, and was limited to a few days a year which could be commuted to a monetary payment. In eradicating these practices, the colonial government removed the credit relationship between chief and villager which, with all its inequalities, had in the past created a mutual dependency between the two. The traditional role of the chief as a link between court and *kampung* was also undermined. While the penghulu still owed fealty to the sultan, he was no longer directly responsible to a chief but to his British district officer. Furthermore, those chosen as penghulu were no longer the chief's clients but were recommended by the district officer and appointed by the Resident and Council.

A more subtle change was the widening gap between the topmost levels of the Malay ruling class and the rest of Malay society. British rule entailed a continuing association between the colonial power and members of the Malay élite. Traditionally the life of the sultan and court had in most essentials paralleled that of the peasants, with whom they shared the same perception of the world and interacted at the most mundane levels. In the eighteenth century a Dutch envoy to Perak had chanced across the raja muda personally supervising the laying out of new rice fields. A hundred years later observers commented how Sultan Abdul Samad of Selangor mingled freely with his people, whether watching a cockfight, chatting in the market or taking his daily walk. The Western ambiance into which the ruling class was being slowly drawn was quite foreign to Malay villagers. In the *kampung*, boys still sought to excel at *sepak raga*, Malay football, but the new generation of Malay aristocrats played tennis and polo. While village lifestyles remained unchanged, many members of the Malay élite were adopting Western dress, living in Western houses and even taking trips to London in emulation of the colonial official. By its very presence the new regime had helped foster a cultural cleavage between the Malay aristocracy and the peasants, which helps explain their often different reactions to the colonial presence.

To a considerable extent this association between the Malay ruling class and the colonial authorities served to disguise the fact that real power ultimately resided with the British. Though the latter were in theory teaching Malays to administer their states, the nature of colonial rule did not encourage political initiative or provide an education in concepts of popular government that by the late nineteenth century had taken root in Britain. The State Councils were never seen as a transition to a greater Malay voice in the administration. Weld, indeed, expressed the general British view that the status quo should continue indefinitely

> Nothing we have done has taught them to govern themselves; we are merely teaching them to co-operate with us ... I doubt if Asiatics will ever learn to govern themselves; it is contrary to the genius of their race, of their history, of their religious system, that they should. Their desire is a mild, just and firm despotism.[8]

The 'plural society'

Weld's comment opens up another perspective on the colonial period, for what the British had done was to introduce their own perception of what constituted the 'Melayu'. To the administrators of the Protected States, over-whelmingly middle-class, there was much in Malay society which touched an empathetic chord. A whole genre of literature grew up, vignettes of 'life in the East', reinforcing the British stereotype of the true Malay. As Swettenham put it:

> The real Malay is courageous; ... But he is extravagant, fond of borrowing money and slow in repaying it ... He quotes proverbs ... Never drinks intoxicants, he is rarely an opium smoker ... He is by nature a sportsman

... Proud of his country and his people, venerates his ancient customs and traditions and has a proper respect for constituted authority ... He is a good imitative learner ... [but] lazy to a degree ... and considers time of no importance.[9]

By contrast, there developed a whole list of 'unMalay' qualities which were exemplified by other races. In British eyes the foremost of the unMalay traits was industry. Malays, it was widely accepted, were lazy, unwilling to work for wages and therefore could not be considered a potential pool of labour in the colonial economy. The measure of their lack of industry was provided by the Chinese, who laboured in tin mines and on plantations and operated the tax farms. As a rule of thumb, the British believed, the rate of migration and the numbers of Chinese settlers were a reliable index of economic progress. During a trip to Perak in 1875 the secretary of Jervois could thus assert that 'the introduction of a quarter of a million of these hard working frugal subjects would completely change the face of the country'.[10] His words were prophetic: in 1890 the Chinese community indirectly provided 89 per cent of Selangor's revenue. Chinese continued to come as labourers to the Malay states under the credit ticket system, but there was an ever-growing number of assisted migrants sponsored by family or friends, especially after the Chinese government abolished restrictions on emigration in 1893. Until the twentieth century no attempts were made to stem this flow and, despite the relatively high death rate and the numbers returning home, the Chinese population grew steadily. In 1891, when the first official census was taken, about half the total population of Perak, Selangor and Sungai Ujung was Chinese.

Several factors served to maintain the cultural and economic gap between Malays and Chinese. Although some certainly gravitated to rural areas, Chinese were for the most part drawn to the new towns developing around tin mines. In 1891 Kuala Lumpur, with a population of 43 786, was thus 79 per cent Chinese. In this type of environment intermarriage with non-Chinese began to decline. In remoter areas, like interior Pahang, Chinese often took wives from among the Orang Asli, and in Sarawak Chinese–Dayak marriages were common. But although Chinese women were always in short supply, and prostitution consequently flourished, from the mid-nineteenth century a growing number were being brought out as wives. The arrival of 'several Chinese ladies with small feet' in 1853 aroused some amazement in Singapore, but by 1881 British officials estimated that there were 14 195 Chinese women as opposed to 72 571 men, and by 1893 almost 5 per cent of all Chinese migrants were female. In Kuala Lumpur there were even sufficient Chinese children for Kapitan China Yap Ah Loy to press the government to finance a Chinese school.

In the mining towns the infusion of fresh arrivals from China also fostered the process by which the Chinese community functioned as a self-contained unit; in Kuala Lumpur, Yap Ah Loy was said to employ hundreds of men in his various mines, plantations and shops. Lacking the personnel necessary for policing Chinese activities, the British depended on the co-operation of men like Yap because of their strong ties with the secret societies which both recruited and controlled the majority of Chinese migrants. In Perak, for example, the leaders of both the Ghee Hin and Hai San were appointed to the State Council.

Gradually, colonial authorities began to frown on secret societies because of their obvious involvement in so many nefarious activities. A more formal means of dealing with the Chinese was instituted in 1877, when a Chinese Protectorate was set up in Singapore under William Pickering. In the ensuing years other officials fluent in at least one Chinese language and familiar with Chinese customs were also appointed to the Malay states. It consequently became accepted that a Chinese could more readily appeal to his 'protector' than to his district officer, who usually spoke only Malay. Yet though even registered societies were suppressed in the Straits Settlements after 1890, and secret associations were theoretically illegal in the Protected States from the inception of British control, the colonial government was not interested in rigorously policing the Chinese community as long as the general peace was not disturbed.

Chinese secret societies thus persisted, despite official disapproval. The Ghee Hin and Hai San remained strong, and in the Kinta district (Perak) in 1896 it was estimated that about 70 per cent of the Chinese mining population of nearly 14 000 were members. Nevertheless, the role of the societies was undergoing change, principally because they no longer had a monopoly on force. British access to superior arms, including the awe-inspiring Sikh police, quickly brought society-inspired riots under control. In addition, Chinese leaders themselves were concerned to keep the peace because their co-operation was frequently rewarded by a grant of profitable state revenue farms. While the societies did not disappear, many of their activities were diverted into more socially acceptable forms, and in the late nineteenth century there was a blossoming of dialect associations and mutual aid societies which filled many of the functions formerly the preserve of the secret *hui*.

With the gradual demise of the Kapitan China system, the Chinese Protectorate became the medium through which the colonial government hoped to oversee the Chinese community. One of Pickering's original briefs had been to address himself to abuses of the credit ticket system, the living conditions of Chinese labourers and their exploitation at the hands of mine owners or plantation managers. Ordinances were introduced to register labour contracts, to explain the law to new arrivals, and to make undue cruelty a punishable offence. Subsequently steps were taken to limit the number of days any labourer worked and to restrict his working day to nine hours. Laudable though such enactments were, it is difficult to assess the effectiveness of enforcement, despite periodic inspections, since the recruitment and supervision of Chinese labour remained largely in Chinese hands. Many iniquities persisted. Labourers were often paid by the truck system, by which goods, especially liquor and opium, were given in lieu of money. Addiction to alcohol and opiates among Chinese workers was high, and the cycle of constant indebtedness all too common. Reforms were hindered because the government was always open to pressure from employers and mine-owners who presented the worker in a poor light. Government officials themselves were not anxious to change the cost structure and thus endanger the supply of cheap labour for mines, plantations and public works. Many of the ordinances, like those penalizing absconders, were in fact intended to keep Chinese workers from moving to areas such as Sumatra, outside British jurisdiction.

Because the British assumption of responsibility for the Chinese tended to lessen meaningful contact between Chinese and Malays, both groups became increasingly bound by stereotyped perceptions. The Chinese saw the Malays as a race dominated by more energetic and sophisticated peoples, causing one Malay-language Baba Chinese newspaper in 1894 to ask, 'Why are the Malays inert?' For the Malay villager, the Chinese was a shopkeeper or a moneylender, often someone to whom a debt was owed. Cultural interaction between the two groups was also lessened as the slow marginalization of the Malay–Chinese Baba community helped to define the boundaries of 'Chineseness' more sharply. By 1891 China-born migrants to the Peninsula outnumbered Baba Chinese by three to one, and by the early twentieth century Hokkien was replacing Baba Malay as the language of business. It was increasingly more difficult for individuals of mixed Chinese-Malay descent to maintain their identity in a colonial framework where they were identified as 'Chinese'. Furthermore, even though growing numbers of Chinese migrants elected to stay in the Malay states, the British regarded them as transient, and there seemed no need to foster greater co-operation with Malays. Some were employed in the lower ranks of the administration as clerks, surveyors and interpreters, but there was little involvement in government apart from the inclusion of prominent Chinese on State Councils. Several colonial officials argued that Malay–Chinese separation was unavoidable. The Chinese Protector, Pickering, for example, considered Malays incapable of governing Chinese: to the latter, he said, it would seem 'like the white settlers of America submitting to the rule of Indian chiefs'.[11]

The success of Chinese–Malay relations in Johor belies the simplistic categorizations which underlay colonial attitudes and which accentuated the cultural divide between the two groups. Abu Bakar, recognizing that Johor's population was largely Chinese, incorporated Chinese into the highest levels of the bureaucracy. The Ghee Hin was permitted to function openly, despite British objections, because it was a useful means of maintaining order. In 1894 the Manchu emperor even awarded Abu Bakar a decoration for his services to the Chinese. Chinese–Malay relations in Johor were exemplified by the Datuk Bentara Luar, who spoke Teochiew and had studied Chinese music, art and literature. 'My life,' he said, 'was enriched by the fact that I made many Chinese friends and acquaintances'.[12] But in the Protected

States the introduction of the Chinese Protectorate meant it was far less important for Malay chiefs and rulers to interact with Chinese leaders.

The British creation of a dual system of government to administer the two major ethnic divisions made no provision for the growing Indian community. Indians had been migrating to the Malay areas for generations, but under the British their numbers increased markedly. Moneylenders from the Chettiar subcaste were a familiar sight in the Straits Settlements, as were the Sikhs recruited as police and guards. Indians were also very visible in the lower ranks of the colonial bureaucracy. For well over 20 years after the introduction of British 'protection', the numbers of English-educated Chinese and Malays were simply insufficient for effective administration. British civil servants in Malaya were often seconded from Ceylon (Sri Lanka), and in their wake came a steady stream of Jaffna Tamils from northern Ceylon who were proficient in English and accustomed to the workings of the British system. Indeed, they so dominated junior and technical ranks in the Federated Malay States that in the view of one leading official, 'the Government was dependent upon the Jaffeness'.[13] By the end of the century, however, the need for cheap labour meant that most Indian migrants were labourers. A fall in tin prices led to a decline in Chinese migration, and the consequent shortage of workers pushed wages higher. In earlier times the Government of India had restricted migration from India to the Straits Settlements and the Malay states, but in the face of Singapore's arguments a compromise was reached. Indian migration to the Straits Settlements was legalized in 1872 and to the Protected States in 1884, and was further encouraged by subsidized steamship fares introduced in 1887.

Since the British Indian government was willing to condone labour migration only from South India, most migrants came from Tamil areas. This policy was supported by European planters in Malaya, many of whom had previously worked in Ceylon and were accustomed to Tamil workers. Recruited from the lowest levels of society, Tamil were considered more accustomed to British rule, more amenable to discipline than the Chinese, and more willing to work for wages than Malays. These views were shared by the colonial government, which needed a constant supply of workers for public projects, municipal services and road and rail construction. South India came to be regarded as a 'natural source' of labourers for the Malay states.

Indians came to Malaya by two means: the indentured and the *kangani* systems. By the former, the organization of migrants in India was in the hands of private recruiting firms in Madras or Nagapatnam. This system was never popular, either with Indians themselves or with employers. For Indians, the poor working conditions on many Malayan plantations, the prevalence of disease and the distance from home made Malaya far less attractive than either Burma or Ceylon, especially as the minimum contract was three years. Large numbers of recruited Indians were urban dwellers, unaccustomed to estate work, and there was a high rate of sickness and desertion.

181

While government ordinances stipulated that an estate must provide medical care, enforcement of such measures was frequently resented by planters
and seen as interference. In 1907, through the co-operation of government
and planters, the Tamil Immigration Fund was set up to maintain recruiting
depots in India and underwrite the expenses of Indian migrants who were
then free to sell their labour where they wished. However, although the
indentured system was maintained in principle until 1910, it did not succeed
in attracting sufficient workers to satisfy the demand.

The *kangani* system, by which the *kangani* (overseer) became the
recruiter, originated in the late nineteenth century when coffee planters,
again drawing from the Ceylon experience, sought to replace indentured by
'free' labour. The *kangani*, usually a former estate worker, was licensed by the
colonial governments and agents of the rubber estates to sign up men (and
often their womenfolk) from his own village in India. He was then paid a
commission for each labourer. This personal association was more successful
in recruiting workers, and after 1884 the net increase in the Indian labour
force was rapid. While Chinese migrants still surpassed all others in total
numbers, between 1891 and 1901 the Indian population in the Protected
States rose to 58 211. Representing an increase of 188 per cent, relatively far
greater than that of the Chinese in the same period (83.4 per cent), this was a
pleasing development for those who supported Indian migration in order
that the colonial economy would not be unduly dependent on Chinese.

Malaya's access to the continuing supply of cheap labour provided by
Indian migration ensured the later success of the rubber industry, when
virtually the sole source of Indian labour was via the *kangani* system. Since
there was work for wives and older children on the rubber estates, Indian
migration included whole families who were then housed on the plantations
in barrack-like labour 'lines'. But these new Indian migrants, unlike those of
past centuries who had often found high places in Malay courts, had little
chance of venturing outside the narrow boundaries imposed by their social
and economic status. Low wages, indebtedness, poor social status and physical isolation kept estate Indians apart. As a result, they exercised little influence on Malayan society at large. No individuals emerged during this period
to represent the interests of plantation labourers, and although the government made sporadic efforts to improve their working conditions, planters
usually raised objections when reforms involved additional expenditure.
Without leadership, and with wages strictly controlled by agreements between
government and private enterprise, it was not possible for Indians to exploit
the chronic shortage of labour and the consequent competition between
plantations and public works. They were probably relatively better off than
in their villages at home, but poverty among estate workers remained high,
a depressing contrast to the wealthy Indian merchants in the urban centres.

At the turn of the century even the term 'Indian community' is misleading. The category 'Indian' included not only Ceylonese (Sri Lankans) but
disguised a whole range of subcastes, as well as language and occupational

groups from different areas of the subcontinent, whose historical and cultural links were often minimal. On the estates Asians in supervisory positions were predominantly Malayalam or Ceylonese, while the labourers were largely Tamil and Telegus. Although the latter two groups, like the Malayalam, were from South India, their languages were mutually incomprehensible. The Ceylonese Jaffna Tamils also saw themselves as far superior in class and education to Indian Tamils. State governments in search of an Indian representative often chose a Jaffna Tamil, but the latter's ability or even desire to speak for estate workers was doubtful.

The plural society which evolved to service the developing colonial economy thus consisted of three generalized ethnic divisions: Malay, Chinese and Indian. Though simplistic and ill-defined, these were the categories by which the British administration perceived and governed local society. No real thought was given to the marginalized category of 'Others', which included groups like the *anak awak* of Penang, the children of Siamese or Burmese fathers and Chinese or Baba mothers. British suspicion of the 'half-breed' was evident in their attitude to the Eurasians. Usually of mixed Portuguese or Dutch descent, they were relegated to secondary positions such as senior clerks, overseers and engineers in private firms or state bureaucracies. Another group which did not fit easily into British categories were the Jawi Peranakan, individuals of Malay-Indian or Malay-Arab descent. Their exclusion from the upper levels of the Malay administration ignored the fact that their skills had often gained them positions of honour in traditional Malay society. In urban areas like Penang and Singapore, however, Jawi Peranakan assumed a prominent role in vernacular education, in the Malay language press, and in local Islamic leadership.

While the British categorization of Malayan society ignored demographic nuances, its very simplicity served to extend the boundaries of Melayu. The first formal colonial definition of a 'Malay' was made in the Malay Reservations Act of 1913, classifying as a Malay 'any person belonging to the Malayan race' who habitually spoke Malay or 'any other Malayan language' and who professed Islam. Even these boundaries were flexible. In the 1911 census the government eliminated the category of 'Sam-Sam'[14] (Thai-speaking Muslims and Malay-speaking Thais, found mainly in Kedah, Perlis and Perak), with the result that in 1921 over 14 000 Kedah Sam-Sam (around 7.5 per cent of the population) were counted as 'Malay'. Orang Laut and Orang Asli are largely invisible in early colonial sources, but those long associated with Malays could also satisfy the 'Malay' criteria, especially as the declining importance of forest and sea products encouraged some to adopt a more sedentary existence. The most significant contribution to the growing Malay population, however, was immigration from the Netherlands East Indies. Many of those termed simply 'Other Malaysians' in the census count were from Sumatran societies with their own distinctive cultural identities. In some areas recent arrivals – Minangkabau, Rawa, Mandailing, Acehnese and Batak – could even outnumber the older population. Large gangs of

Javanese also arrived to work as coolie labourers on government schemes such as canal or road construction, especially in Johor and Selangor. In the latter state, for example, the Javanese population was numbered at 1111 in 1891 but, despite considerable transience, had risen to 33 412 forty years later.

Typically, the first generation of immigrants clustered together and for a time preserved something of their own identity, as testified by the numerous Kampung Jawa, Kampung Bugis, Kampung Kerinci and so on scattered through the Peninsula. Malays distinguished between foreigners from the Netherlands East Indies, the *anak dagang* ('child of traders') and the locally born, the *anak negeri* ('child of the country'), but the distinction disappeared for the migrants' descendants. A report on the 1931 census, for instance, noted that most local-born migrant offspring referred to themselves as 'Malay', although this seemed to take a generation longer for Javanese. This shifting self-identity and the British tendency to group 'Malays' together was made possible because of a basic similarity of appearance, the use of Malay as a common language, and above all a shared religion. By 1931 as many as 244 000 of the 594 000 Malays living in the former Protected States were either first generation arrivals from the Netherlands East Indies or descendants of Indonesian migrants who had arrived after 1891. The continuing absorption of Indonesian migrants into Malay society meant that the limits of Malayness were cultural and emotional rather than ethnic. When a man of Bugis origin saw himself as Malay, then that indeed he was.

Differing rates of development in the Protected States

Within the Protected States, British interest focused on Selangor and Perak, where an infrastructure was developed around the mining centres. Roads were built to the mining towns and later the plantation areas. In 1885 the first railway line was opened in Larut between Port Weld and Taiping, and in 1893 Ipoh and Teluk Anson (now Teluk Intan) were connected. By 1910 railways joined Johor Baru to Province Wellesley (Perai) on the mainland opposite Penang. Simultaneously, existing towns grew larger. It was here, where population was concentrated and where the revenue was largest, that social amenities were introduced. The first government hospital, for example, was opened in Taiping in 1878. In the towns other innovations – paved roads, lighting, sanitation, the piping of water – continued to improve the quality of life. Already the disparity between the urban environment and that of the village had become marked.

On a wider scale, a similar disparity was evident in the economic development of Perak and Selangor as opposed to Negeri Sembilan and Pahang. A prime reason for the latter's failure to demonstrate the same material progress was the lack of resources, especially widespread tin deposits. Negeri

Sembilan, by virtue of its proximity, did participate to a limited degree in the wealth of its neighbours, but Pahang's economy continued to flag. Specific geographic problems, such as the closure of the coast during the northeast monsoon and the high range separating Pahang from the west coast, impeded development. Only through bitter experience did European mining companies realize the greater difficulties involved in mining Pahang's lode tin as opposed to alluvial deposits on the west coast. The importation of sophisticated machinery which would have facilitated mining was impracticable because of poor communications. Rivers were still the main means of transport, and a trip from Pahang's new capital of Kuala Lipis to Singapore took over a fortnight by boat. Even when a road was built from Kuala Lumpur over the mountains to Kuala Lipis, the 130-kilometre journey could only be made by bullock cart. Until the introduction of the motor car Pahang was effectively cut off from the other British-ruled areas.

Having to contend with such disadvantages, Pahang's production could not begin to equal that of Perak and Selangor. At no time did the mining revenue exceed 5 per cent of the total from the four Protected States, and it was never sufficient to meet Pahang's needs. It is not surprising, therefore, to find that in 1895 Perak had 15 hospitals, Selangor 14, but Pahang only two. Finances showed no signs of improvement, and fiscal difficulties were exacerbated by the uprising of 1891–5. By the time peace was restored, Pahang's official expenditure was two and a half times greater than its income. The development of local rubber plantations at the beginning of this century did bring financial benefits, but by then in terms of economy and social services Pahang had been far outstripped by the west coast states.

Demographically, too, Pahang was more like Kelantan and Terengganu, since the limited tin and gold deposits attracted considerably fewer Chinese. The Malay character of the state remained, despite strenuous efforts by successive Residents to encourage Chinese enterprise. Reckoned at about 6 per cent of the total in 1891, the Chinese population did reach 22 per cent by 1911, but Pahang could still be popularly described as 'the one real Malay state' under British influence.

The creation of the Federated Malay States

At the beginning of the nineteenth century the east coast of the Peninsula had been more prosperous and more populous than the west. By the 1890s, however, the British had come to associate the largely Malay states of the east coast with lack of development. It was partly to lessen the differences between Pahang and the west coast that the four Protected States were grouped into a Federation in 1896. But the notion of a common purse which would, it was hoped, solve Pahang's indebtedness was only one reason behind the Federation decision. Proposals for some kind of union had been made through the 1880s, reflecting a trend towards larger administrative units already apparent in Negeri Sembilan and elsewhere in the British empire. Although administrative differences between the states were probably exaggerated, the call for uniformity in such matters as communication, taxation and justice found many supporters, including Swettenham. In 1895 Swettenham, then Resident of Perak but with ambitions of gaining a higher post in the new Federation, was assigned the task of obtaining the rulers' approval.

From the Malay viewpoint, it seems fair to say that the implications of the scheme were never fully explained. The longest discussion between Swettenham and a Malay ruler took only four hours, and there was no consultation with the leading chiefs or princes. The Treaty of Federation was worded so ambiguously that years later Sultan Idris of Perak complained he could not understand how Federation functioned. But Swettenham's arguments were persuasive, and in July 1896 the Federated Malay States (FMS) came into being, with its capital at Kuala Lumpur in the heart of the tin-mining region. The Federal Secretariat was to be headed by a Resident-General with jurisdiction over all the Residents and authority to represent the Federation's interest to the Singapore governor, who was also high commissioner for the Malay states. Departments of police, public works, posts, telegraph and railways were now placed under a single director; a unified civil service was set up, and tentative proposals were made for a common treasury. To assure uniformity, all laws except those of a purely local nature and all financial measures were drawn up in Kuala Lumpur.

The British had thus brought together four states in an administrative entity which had no historical antecedents. A significant step had been made in the centralizing process and the creation of what was to become British Malaya. It had, however, little obvious effect on Malays at large. Despite plaudits from the British, Federation brought no tangible benefits to the people and was a disappointment to the rulers who had hoped they might regain some of their lost authority. In a grandiose fashion, the Federation Treaty had guaranteed that they would 'not in the slightest degree be diminishing the powers and privileges which they now possess nor be curtailing the rights of self-government which they now enjoy'.[15] In fact, after 1896 more administration than ever before was carried out by the Residents in consultation with the Resident-General, without any reference to the ruler or the State Council. Official conferences of rulers, or durbars, were convened in 1897 and again in 1903 to bring the four rulers together, but despite the panoply surrounding them the durbars had only vague advisory powers. It was the realization of the extent to which Malay rulers had relinquished their powers to outsiders that prompted Sultan Idris to express public concern at the loss of state individuality and the lack of Malay participation in government. The very real possibility that Malays might one day become 'strangers in their own land' led, as we shall see in the following chapter, to the establishment of a Malay College at Kuala Kangsar in Perak.

In 1909 a further move towards centralization and uniformity was made with the creation of a Federal Council. It was to be headed by the high commissioner based in Singapore, assisted by the Resident-General in Kuala Lumpur. The sultans had agreed to the Council on the condition that their prerogatives were reduced no further, but the Council proceeded to assume the few financial and legislative powers still remaining in the hands of the State Councils. The sultans had no power of veto and in reality the Council, which included Europeans and Chinese representatives of planting and mining interests, became a vehicle for an extension of the authority of the high commissioner/governor of Singapore. Governor Anderson (1904–11) was known to favour an amalgamation of Singapore and the Malay states, so that income from the FMS could help shore up Singapore's finances at times of recession. Since the FMS made use of Singapore's facilities, it was felt that they should also make a contribution to its revenue. Anderson's own goal of reinforcing Singapore's position in relation to Kuala Lumpur was achieved when the position of Resident-General was formally changed to that of chief secretary. Previously, the Resident-General had to some extent been considered the champion of state interests, but the chief secretary became more of an officer subordinate to the high commissioner/governor. The development was certainly a major constitutional change in the FMS administration. From the standpoint of the Malay rulers, however, the rivalry between Singapore and Kuala Lumpur merely diverted attention from a further diminution of states' rights.

The expansion of British interests in Borneo

The reality of British control in the newly Federated Malay States was clearly visible in the extent and growing complexity of the colonial administration. In Borneo, on the other hand, the British government seemed far more reluctant to become directly involved. The only Malay sultanate along the northwest coast was the weakened state of Brunei, and until 1868 Sarawak had been able to push northwards, absorbing Brunei's territory in return for agreed payments. This created a dilemma for Britain, which was at least partly committed to Brunei because the 1847 treaty provided that any territorial cessions should be approved by the British government. In order to obviate the possibility of future intervention in conflicts between Sarawak and Brunei, Britain in 1868 invoked the 1847 treaty and refused to permit Sarawak to purchase the Baram district from Brunei. The second raja, Charles, who succeeded his uncle the same year, was not easily deterred and for several years continued to press for the Baram cession. Eventually Britain agreed, basically because after 1881 it became involved in sponsoring an equally expansionist Trading Company in North Borneo and could not logically permit it to expand without granting the same approval to Sarawak.

The emergence of this Trading Company was a relatively late development. Until the 1870s there had seemed no necessity for the British to assert
their position along the far northern coast of Borneo, which had remained
under the nominal control of the sultan of Sulu. From fortified coastal
villages, high ranking Sulu chiefs, who had been granted revenue rights over
local jungle and sea products, wielded a fragmented and intermittent
authority. By the last quarter of the nineteenth century, however, this area
was attracting greater interest in Britain. The passage between Sulu and
North Borneo was important because it provided a trading route between
Australia and China. It was therefore necessary to ensure that it would not
fall under the control of any other European power, especially as France was
moving to consolidate its position in Vietnam and thus dominate another
flank of the sea route to China. Furthermore, the Dutch had for several years
been expanding in southwest Borneo and there was also some British apprehension of intrusion by Spain, the United States, Germany and even Italy
into the Borneo region. In the Peninsula such fears had already given an
impetus to Britain's 'forward movement', and in a less direct fashion they
were also to influence developments in Borneo.

In 1877, an Englishman, Alfred Dent, advanced capital enabling the
Austrian consul-general in Hong Kong, Baron von Overbeck, to purchase
the unexploited American concessions in North Borneo, soon due to expire.
With the active support of William Treacher, the young acting governor of
the British colony of Labuan (and later second Resident-General of the
FMS), Overbeck negotiated a new cession of 17 252 000 hectares from the
Brunei sultan for an annual payment of $15 000. A significant feature of
the agreement was that North Borneo would be in all essential respects independent of Brunei. Shortly afterwards, followed by Treacher, Overbeck
went to Jolo where the sultan of Sulu also ceded his rights in North Borneo
for a rent of $5000 yearly and made Overbeck 'supreme and independent'.
Under Treacher's supervision a treaty was drafted with Sulu stipulating that
this territory could not be alienated to any other nation without Britain's
acquiescence. In February 1878 a Resident was appointed in the port of
Sandakan, where the Union Jack was hoisted alongside Dent's own standard.
Other representatives of the Dent-Overbeck partnership were subsequently
landed along the west coast.

Officially, Britain could disclaim any responsibility for this activity
in North Borneo but, though informal and personal, the links between London and the new order in North Borneo were real. Treacher did not act
simply from a sense of patriotism, but had received indirect intimations from
the Foreign Office as to how the North Borneo grant should proceed. Dent,
who soon bought out Overbeck's share in the venture, had an influential
friend in the Foreign Office, the permanent under-secretary. Protests from
Singapore and Sarawak against the grant of such a large block of land to
a private concern met the response that it was 'truly a British undertaking'.
When the Philippine authorities attempted to raise the Spanish flag near

Sandakan, a British warship with Treacher aboard was sent to forestall any future intrusion.

Dent's London connections also helped him gain support for the formation of a company under government auspices. In 1881, after protracted discussion, a British North Borneo Company was chartered in London and thus gained from the British Crown a degree of protection. The Company was bound to remain 'British in character', to relinquish foreign relations to Britain, and to submit the names of proposed governors for London's approval. In the same year Treacher was seconded from the Civil Service to become North Borneo's first governor, further strengthening the links with colonial authorities on the Peninsula. In 1885, England, Germany and Spain signed a convention recognizing Spanish sovereignty over Sulu; in return, Spain withdrew its former claims to North Borneo. Thus, though the British government had somewhat reluctantly felt compelled to stake its claim along Borneo's northern coast, it had avoided unwelcome administrative expense and deflected expected objections from other European countries by the useful expedient of a chartered company.

Both Sarawak and North Borneo were eager to expand their territories further. Charles Brooke's publicly stated goal of incorporating all Brunei into Sarawak expressed both his personal ambitions and economic reality, for much of Sarawak's revenue came from jungle produce, requiring still greater tracts of forest. For their part, Company officials in North Borneo argued that expansion was justified because the large land areas ceded by Brunei were not all coterminous. In some districts Company concessions were separated by rivers controlled by independent chiefs, and these the Company was anxious to acquire. At the same time it also hoped to expand southwards, persisting in the belief that the forbidding jungle interior of Borneo was a storehouse of untapped wealth. Each additional river brought under Company control, it was felt, was a source of revenue – immediate in terms of taxes and customs duties, and potential in terms of land sales and possible mineral exploitation.

This expansion could take place only at the expense of Brunei, whose sultan was painfully aware of the cessions made to Sarawak and North Borneo. 'Formerly,' he wrote to Charles Brooke in 1881, 'the territory of Brunei was united like unto a man with all his members complete. At present his arms are lost to him, leaving only his head and feet.'[16] The appointment of a British Resident to Brunei would have stopped its dismemberment, but although this proposal was discussed several times in the 1880s, it was for the time set aside. Ironically, in view of later oil discoveries, the British Foreign and Colonial Offices believed that Brunei could not support the cost of a European establishment. Another common view was that Brunei could not long survive as an independent state and that partition between Sarawak and North Borneo was the best solution. Only rarely did the British government raise objections to cessions by the impecunious Brunei sultan and his nobles, for continued encroachment by Sarawak or North Borneo at least excluded the intrusion of any other nation. From the outset, therefore, both Brooke and the Company saw themselves as engaged in some kind of contest to absorb as much territory as possible, often using highly questionable methods to gain or force Brunei's consent. Some of the North Borneo Company's most valuable acquisitions were along the west coast, like the Putatan area and the Klias peninsula, both rich rice-growing areas, and by 1901 Company territory included most of the modern state of Sabah.

Meanwhile, Brooke was attempting to anticipate the Company. In 1882 and 1884 he acquired the Baram and Trusan rivers, and in 1890 he seized the Limbang river, Brunei's last remaining territory of importance. In 1905 the final cession was made when the North Borneo Company transferred the small district of Lawas to Sarawak In the following year a British Resident was appointed to Brunei as an alternative to total absorption by Sarawak, ending for ever the Brookes' cherished ambition. Nonetheless, Sarawak was now over twenty times its original size and its dominant ethnic group, the Ibans, had come to occupy many areas traditionally inhabited by peoples like the Kayans, Kenyahs and Muruts.

The rivalry between Sarawak and North Borneo, the question of Brunei's future, and the possibility of foreign intrusion in Sarawak after Raja Brooke's death all fuelled discussion of a closer association between the three states and Britain. Singapore was the obvious point of linkage, and even in 1881 Weld spoke hopefully of one day becoming high commissioner for Borneo and the Malay states. Seven years later, in 1888, protectorate status was negotiated with all three states, by which they surrendered to the British government responsibility for foreign policy and were in turn guaranteed protection from the threat of outside attack. The Brunei sultan, Brooke and the Company all welcomed the security promised by the new arrangement, symbolized in the person of the governor of the Straits Settlements, who was now also high commissioner to the Malay states and consul-general for the Borneo states. An agreement between Britain and the Netherlands in 1891 legalized the interior boundary between Dutch and British Borneo and settled disputed border claims. Subsequent surveys provided more precise topographical detail, resulting in amendments to the boundary in 1915 and again in 1928. An arbitrary division which had no meaning to the interior peoples, and which has still not been completely surveyed, this line nonetheless provided the basis for the Borneo frontier between modern Malaysia and Indonesia.

By the last years of the nineteenth century, northwest Borneo was thus so closely linked to British interests that an official in the Colonial Office could anticipate a future administration in North Borneo and Sarawak 'on much the same principles as the native states of the Malay Peninsula'.[17] Such predictions made little allowance for the very different character of the Borneo territories, not only from the Peninsula but also from each other. The development of Sarawak and North Borneo had thus far followed separate paths despite some superficial similarities. Though the North Borneo

Company was a governing concern, and not directly involved in commerce, it developed no real administrative policy to match the often perceptive views of the Brookes. Whereas the latter justified the lack of economic development by arguing that the spread of Western 'civilization' would be harmful to indigenous society in Sarawak, the lack of Western influence in North Borneo was more a function of faltering Company finances. There were scattered settlements along the coast, but only Jesselton (Kota Kinabalu) on the west coast and Sandakan on the east showed any signs of growing into large towns similar to those on the Malay Peninsula. For the first decade of its existence, indeed, London fully expected the North Borneo Company to collapse. It was only saved from bankruptcy by revenue and export taxes derived from the local collection of jungle and sea products destined for the China trade. However, with the development of timber and tobacco in the 1890s, North Borneo's income steadily improved. The revenue rose from £37 075 in 1895 to £62 392 in 1900 and the flourishing timber and rubber industries in the early years of this century established the economy on a healthier footing. None the less, North Borneo was not considered a wealthy state, and over-ambitious projects such as a west coast railway absorbed much of its income.

The Company also had less success than the Brookes in fostering a general recognition of a white overlord. The administrative structure, incorporating many features found in Sarawak and the Peninsula, had little meaning for the local populace. At the apex was the governor, responsible to the Court of Directors in London, but with his brief term of office no governor could ever assume the charisma of a Charles Brooke. From 1895 to 1910 the most dominant figure in North Borneo affairs was not a man on the spot but the Company's managing director in London, W.C. Cowie. While Sarawak could claim some local participation in government through the Council Negeri, in North Borneo the governor's Advisory Council included no non-whites except an occasional Chinese merchant. North Borneo was divided into two Residencies, the West Coast, controlled from Jesselton, and the East Coast, with its headquarters at Sandakan. Further administrative subdivisions were under district officers. From economic necessity, North Borneo's civil service remained small, numbering only 28 Europeans in 1895. Many did not speak Malay, the only lingua franca along the coast, until several months after their arrival; knowledge of Malay was not required for promotion until 1892, and Hugh Clifford remarked at the time that not a single European in Company employ was familiar with the language of any of the interior or coastal tribes.

Although Charles Brooke himself always emphasized the difference between his style of government and that of Brunei, he did exploit many elements of the old system to the advantage of his regime. The North Borneo Company was impressed by the cheapness and effectiveness of Sarawak's administration but was far less successful in adapting pre-existing forms of authority to its own ends. Until the second decade of the twentieth century the Company relied heavily on the assistance of traditional leaders who were recruited as 'Company chiefs'. However, by depending on feudal-type relationships between these leaders and their retainers, the Company was perpetuating the fragmentation of North Borneo society. A monthly salary of five Straits dollars might claim the support of a Sulu chief in the short term, but it could not guarantee his allegiance when new duties conflicted with a leader's traditional obligations. The lack of any heritage of wider loyalty beyond the purely local scene was exacerbated by the tribal and ethnic divisions within North Borneo which Company officials only vaguely understood. The administrative division of interior peoples into two general categories 'Dusuns' and 'Muruts' subsumed a large number of groups whose language and culture were often very different. A further distinction was made between these generally animist inland peoples and the Muslim-influenced coastal groups, but the latter category also included several distinct ethnic communities. From necessity or ignorance the Company frequently placed native officers from one group over others with whom they had little in common, which in itself could be the basis of conflict. The influx of Chinese, Indians, Peninsular Malays and other groups from elsewhere in the archipelago compounded the demographic complexity of the local population; in 1871, for example, it was estimated that there were 7156 Chinese in North Borneo, but by 1911 the number had risen to 27 801.

In both Borneo territories, as in the Peninsula, revenue collection was a common cause of complaint against white rule. Yet in Sarawak, while many an Iban legend lauds the resistance of those who refused to pay the White Raja's dues, Charles Brooke was relatively successful in perpetuating the notion that tax remittance symbolized service to the ruler. Those who failed to pay, he said, were in a state of rebellion and justly deserved punishment. Without a personality like Brooke, and without access to a fighting force like the Ibans, the Company found the collection of taxes difficult, and yet they were an important source of revenue. A particular local grievance was the poll tax and the rigidity of its application. As one Bajau remarked, 'Although the Brunei *pangiran* [nobles] fine people tens and hundreds of piculs, it is all mere words, they can give what they have, but the white man's two dollars is two dollars and no less.'[18] So often, it seemed to the interior people, the acquisition of a river by the Company simply meant an increase in revenue collection. Established economic patterns were also changed by the Company's trading posts which often diverted commerce away from a previously prosperous river.

Undoubtedly some individual Residents administered wisely, and fostered harmonious relations with the local population, but local distrust of alien rule was widespread. The Company encountered recurring resistance which generally took the same form as past responses to encroachments by Brunei or Sulu overlords. At the time the Company was chartered, one young chief in the Putatan area commented that he 'had heard dreadful accounts of the white man's government, that the police interfered in everything and that men were shut up in prison and that revenue was required in cash instead of kind'.[19] A generation later such suspicions had not been laid to rest. Sometimes involving a few hundred people, sometimes widespread, such disturbances reflected the fragmented nature of North Borneo's population, which at the Company's own count included 39 different groups. Periodic attacks on Company posts and its officers brought harsh retribution, and through the 1880s several expeditions were sent to bring hostile groups to heel by burning villages and imprisoning or hanging rebel leaders.

It is often difficult to see the reason behind individual uprisings; perhaps it was a disputed judgment of a native magistrate, some European officer's ignorance of a past agreement, rumours of some new tax, a bad harvest, changes in land registration, resentment at the imposition of corvée or simply a generalized fear of change. One of the more intriguing of these occurred among west coast Muruts in the Padas and Tenom districts in 1891. Called the Malingkote Revolt, it was initiated by an individual who dreamed that an angel had given him powers of flight and invulnerability in return for the destruction of animals and crops. The cult spread across large areas of the interior, uniting many groups across traditionally hostile lines and sustaining its hold for nearly a year. A similar pattern could be seen in the so-called Rundum Revolt among the interior Muruts in 1915, which was a direct outcome of Company policies and the adverse effects of social and economic innovation. Combined with the Company's attempts to eliminate headhunting practices were other unwelcome intrusions into Murut life: the use of Dayak as police officers, the demand for Murut labour in clearing jungle paths, the imposition of taxes on liquor, the restriction of shifting cultivation and the registration of land titles.

Company reaction in 1915 may point to greater co-ordination between Murut groups than has been previously thought; in one engagement, for example, over 300 Murut were killed. However, the most extensive movement against the Company was the Mat Salleh rebellion, which erupted in 1895 and was not fully quelled until 1905. Mat Salleh's grievances were never totally clear, although it seems that the introduction of a new tax on imported rice and another to help finance a cross-country railway exacerbated general discontent. Mat Salleh himself was an impressive man of mixed Bajau and Sulu parentage, who could draw on a combination of Muslim and indigenous symbols of authority. His mouth, it was said, produced flames and his *parang* (curved cleaver) lightning; Muslims saw him as the Mahdi, the coming saviour. His use of flags, Islamic standards and the umbrella of royalty accorded his cause a wider appeal than more localized uprisings. In addition, his wife Dayang Badang, herself of royal background, was credited with the gift of clairvoyance. Although Mat Salleh was eventually killed in 1900, jungle warfare continued for another five years and today he is still regarded as one of Sabah's great heroes. Significantly, Sabah women activists have also begun to invoke Dayang Badang as evidence of women's participation in the nationalist story.

By the first decade of the last century the effects of Western penetration in northwest Borneo reflected the nature of the separate administrations. When Charles Brooke died in 1917 he left behind an economically undeveloped Sarawak but one in which there was some sense of allegiance to a central authority. However, in creating this entity he had assigned specific functions to the three major communities – Malays, Ibans and Chinese. In a society already ethnically fragmented, this policy merely heightened the natural tendency of the local peoples to view themselves communally.

In North Borneo, although the Company had become more willing to employ negotiation rather than confrontation, they had been unable to instil among the disparate population any significant feeling of loyalty to a greater political unit beyond individual groupings. One early official, W.B. Pryer, used considerable poetic licence when he eulogized that 'men from far off colder lands' had brought 'religion, enterprise and law' to 'an unclad tawny race [who] age after age/ had roved the woods and waters, all unchanged.'[20] Apologists for Company rule pointed to the gradual abolition of slavery following edicts in 1881 and 1883, an improvement in communications and medical services and the establishment of vernacular schools after 1911. But evidence that the Company was slowly assuming the responsibilities of a colonial government was apparent only in the towns. Thirty years after the inception of Company control, inhabitants of North Borneo had received few tangible benefits apart from the effective elimination of headhunting. Yet officials in the British Colonial Office remained undaunted by these realities and already there was talk of extending colonial control. A Resident had been posted in Brunei, and one official commented confidently that 'British North Borneo, possibly also Sarawak, will fall to us within a measurable time'.[21]

The incorporation of the northern Malay states into British Malaya

Separate though they were, North Borneo, Sarawak, the FMS and the Straits Settlements at least shared some experience of Western rule, something which did not apply to the northern Malay states under Siam's suzerainty. Towards the end of the nineteenth century Siamese overlordship here became more formal, reflecting not only the development of a modern bureaucracy in Siam itself but also Siamese awareness of Britain's expansion in the Peninsula. Siamese leaders and the European advisers they employed realized that the division laid down in the 1826 treaty was being questioned by British expansionists. Consequently, Siamese interest in all the northern Malay states became more pronounced. One indication was the compilation during the 1880s of various chronicles (*phongsawadan*) describing Siam's dealings with its Malay vassals, although officials found it necessary to refer to Malay accounts such as the *Hikayat Marong Mahawangsa* for their reconstruction of early history. The contrast between the detailed Siamese knowledge of nineteenth-century events and the vagueness of information relating to anything before about 1800 clearly shows the changed tenor of Siamese–Malay relations.

Several royal visits made by Chulalongkorn to the Malay states, the first ever made by a Thai king, were a further sign of renewed Siamese interest in the northern Peninsula. In the 1890s there was a general reorganization of all provincial government in Siam, including the Malay *prathesaraj*. The latter now fell under the direct control of the Ministry of the Interior and were grouped into circles (*monthon*), each with a superintendent commissioner (*Khaluang Thesaphiban*) appointed by the ministry. Under this new system Patani was under Ligor, Kelantan and Terengganu were controlled jointly from Phuket, while Kedah was placed over another circle which included Perlis and Setul.

In contrast to the British, the Siamese placed no great value on uniformity, and the differing degree of centralized control reflected Bangkok's view of local politics. Kedah (Muang Zaiburi), by the 1826 treaty a 'territory' of Siam, had since 1842 been generally willing to submit the *bunga mas dan perak* and comply with Siam's periodic requests for corvée labour for projects such as road building. As a result, its rulers had been supported against challengers and honoured with special privileges. The tone of the relationship was clearly established by Sultan Ahmad Tajuddin (1854–79). Awarded the high title of *chau phraya*, he was considered 'more loyal and closer to Bangkok than any other ruler of Siamese-Malay tributaries'. His son Abdul Hamid (reigned 1882–1943) was accorded similar favour. Chulalongkorn had been actively involved in a resolving a potential dynastic crisis between 1879 and 1882, when three princes had agreed to act jointly as regents for the young prince. The position of trust Abdul Hamid received in the *thesaphiban* system indicates the value Bangkok placed on his diligent maintenance of peace. Kedah had also fulfilled its role as a loyal vassal by sending guns to assist Siam in a border dispute with the French in Laos. Links with Siam were reinforced through frequent trips to the Bangkok court by Kedah princes, some of whom pursued their studies there. Of all the Malay states finally ceded to the British in 1909, Chulalongkorn regretted most the loss of Kedah.

Kedah's excellent relations with Siam are all the more remarkable because Kedah was increasingly involved with the British. Sultan Abdul Hamid actively sought to incorporate many aspects of Western government, and in 1885 he visited Perak and Singapore to examine their administration. In Kedah itself he established the nucleus of a bureaucracy, including departments dealing with posts and telegraphs, lands and a treasury. Kedah was also fortunate in possessing several able court officials, among whom was Menteri Besar (chief minister) Wan Mohamed Abdul Saman, still considered one of the state's most outstanding administrators. As an observer remarked in 1900, 'It is interesting to see how a purely Malay government without European interference or guidance has endeavoured to model the administration on colonial lines, even to the appointment of an Auditor General.'[22]

Economically, too, Kedah had been closely linked to the Straits Settlements from the early nineteenth century. Kedah's revenue farms were controlled by Hokkien merchants in Penang, and from 1887 the same concern leased the principal farms, opium and spirits, in both places. Canals were built with loans from Penang, the most successful stretching for 33 kilometres, connecting Alor Setar and Kedah Peak and opening up new areas for rice production. With Penang serving as an conduit to outside markets, Kedah began growing some commercial crops such as tapioca, nutmeg, cloves and coffee in addition to the staple crop, rice. Land registration was introduced in the 1880s, giving rise to a more prosperous Malay peasant class, while the Chinese were beginning to develop rice milling and marketing.

Thus, in the face of potential intervention from Siam and the British, Kedah had succeeded in maintaining considerable freedom of action, establishing a reputation for responsibility and initiative. Even an avowed advocate of British expansion like Swettenham considered Kedah 'exceptionally well-governed'. Towards the end of the twentieth century Terengganu resembled Kedah in presenting no problems to Bangkok. In 1897 and again in 1902 the ruler made personal visits to Siam, and on at least one occasion he was said to have performed the *tawai bangkom*, prostration in the Thai style, at which Malay rulers had traditionally balked.

In Kelantan the Siamese saw little reason to interfere during the long reign of Sultan Muhammad II, who came to power in 1838. Although he abdicated in 1877, he continued to provide a guiding hand during the reign of his son, Tuan Long Ahmad. Royal authority was extended through land registration and the expansion of parishes or villages (*mukim*). A new office was created, with the Siamese title of 'To' Kweng', as *mukim* head. As a link between village and court, they coexisted with local imam, who also acted as *mukim* leaders, although the influence of each varied according to the locality.

While the rivalry among Kelantan princes and nobles was contained by this more rigorous administration, dynastic troubles again surfaced after Long Ahmad's death in 1890, as high-ranking individuals and their supporters jockeyed for access to greater wealth and influence. Aggrieved *anak raja* who objected to the new ruler's arrogation of power became open advocates of friendship with Britain.

The stance of the dissident Kelantan *anak raja* undoubtedly made Bangkok nervous, but the way in which Siam emphasized its position as overlord along the east coast was very different from the actions of Rama I a hundred years earlier. Beginning in 1889, King Chulalongkorn made the first of several state trips to Kelantan and Terengganu; in both states the institution of a postal service which issued Siamese stamps was a quiet but unequivocal statement of suzerainty. In Kelantan, a Siamese officer was appointed to the court, and efforts were made to reorganize state finances and tighten the centre's hold over village administration. Such measures were intended to prevent disturbances and thus forestall any British intervention. More administrative changes followed, including the establishment of a Land Office and a Public Works Department. Sikhs recruited from Selangor made up a small police force, and other signs of 'progress' were apparent in the small printing press for government notices and the beginnings of a telephone system. In 1899, in response to an appeal from an aspirant ruler beleaguered by rival claimants, Bangkok despatched a Siamese commissioner who took up residence in Kota Baru, the royal capital. The hoisting of a Siamese flag and the garrison of Siamese soldiers was evidence of Bangkok's concern to maintain its authority.

Unlike Kedah, however, the economies of Terengganu and Kelantan displayed few signs of economic development. Rumours of great mineral wealth circulated in the Straits Settlements, but the Europeans who made their way to the east coast found that they were not made welcome, apparently on Siam's instructions. Demographically, Kelantan and Terengganu remained heavily Malay, and the traditional trading and agricultural economy had altered little. There were certainly some prominent Chinese entrepreneurs, but at the time of the first official census in 1911 the Chinese population here numbered less than 14 000, or about 2 per cent of the Peninsula's total. Despite limited mining and commercial agriculture, the two states were barely rocking in the wake of the changes along the west coast. If anything, the power of the aristocracy was more entrenched than ever, and most of the land and resources were locked up in concessions granted by rulers to members of leading families. In Perak and Selangor, a communications network was slowly lessening the historical and geographic separateness of the upriver (*ulu*) areas. In Kelantan and Terengganu, by contrast, roads outside the principal settlements were virtually non-existent, the only access to the interior being by rivers and jungle tracks.

It was not by the criteria of economic development, which to the Westerner represented 'civilization', that the Malays of Kelantan and Terengganu measured their great achievements; rather, it was by standards which lauded Islamic learning and scholarship. Terengganu and Kelantan were already known for the vitality of their *pondok* schools, and the movement of Islamic teachers through the region and their contacts with scholars in the Holy Land strengthened an established tradition of religious education. Wealthier individuals made the pilgrimage to Mecca, and a rest house for travellers in Mecca and another in Jeddah even bore the names of the Terengganu merchants who had donated them. There is little doubt that Islam here had benefited from Asian rather than Western overlordship, for, unlike the British, the Siamese perceived no division between the secular and the religious. The influence and vigour of Islam had not been dissipated by the British partition of 'civil' and Islamic courts found in the FMS. In Kelantan and Terengganu, efforts to enforce Muslim precepts and eliminate 'unIslamic' practices were accorded continuing priority. Legal administration was brought more closely under the supervision of Muslim law courts, presided over by experts in Islamic law. Compliance with the outward forms of Islam, such as mosque attendance, were made obligatory, while stress was also laid on correct dress and strict observance of the fasting month. Admittedly, the enforcement of such statutes in areas away from the capital was difficult. The *Hikayat Sri Kelantan*, for instance, acknowledges that in the villages old customs were still current. But even if ineffectual, bans on popular amusements such as *menora* and *makyong* dance dramas gave rulers a widely respected reputation for piety.

Even within the Siamese ambit, therefore, differences between the east and west coast were apparent. Although the Kedah court also acted as a sponsor of Islam, the links with Penang meant it was economically and administratively more like Johor than Kelantan or Terengganu. But one thing which all the northern Malay states had in common was a sense of pride in preserving more independence than their counterparts in the FMS. It was precisely this relative freedom that was slipping away as Bangkok sought to tighten its hold over the *prathesaraj*. In the words of King Chulalongkorn,

> We have no particular interest in the Malay States ... If we lost them to England we would miss only the *bunga mas*. Apart from this there would not be any material loss. However, it is bad for the prestige of a nation. That is why we have to strengthen our hold over this territory.

In the late nineteenth century this view was obviously at odds with the opinions of Singapore and FMS officials. Constantly pressing for the inclusion of the 'independent' states under the colonial umbrella, they were also indefatigable in fanning London's apprehension about German and French interest in the Kra Isthmus. In 1897 Britain and Siam concluded a Secret Convention, by which Siam's suzerainty over Terengganu and Kelantan was recognized on the condition that no territory be alienated to a third power. Accordingly, Siam refused permission to German firms that applied for prospecting licences on islands off the Kedah coast, even though these lay within the border of 'Siamese' Malaya established by a Boundary Agreement in 1899. But the fact that Siam was attempting to preserve national pride while defending its record as overlord meant that the often secret negotiations were bound to focus on sensitive issues.

One recurring problem in the northern Malay states was monetary. Whereas Johor had been able to finance much of its development through Chinese revenue, neither Terengganu nor Kelantan had a sizeable Chinese population and even in Kedah the Chinese numbered less than 8 per cent. Unlike the FMS, there was no watchful British Resident with his budget, carefully monitoring income and expenditure, nor was there a ready source of credit which in time of trouble could shore up the treasury. A glance at Pahang helps make the point more clearly. Here, even with the most stringent fiscal controls the expenditure between 1904 and 1908 still exceeded revenue by 100 per cent, and the state was heavily dependent on loans from its FMS neighbours. There was no such safeguard for the states outside British control. In Kedah during 1904 the expense of five royal weddings brought the state to the brink of bankruptcy, with its debts reckoned at four times the annual income. Kedah's credit in Penang was exhausted and as a final resort the ruler turned to Siam. A substantial loan was made, but only on condition that a financial adviser would be appointed. The discussion between the Siamese government and the British about who should fill this role demonstrates the intensity of colonial interest. The first Adviser, an Englishman in Siamese employ, arrived in Kedah in 1905 but was replaced soon afterwards by a British officer seconded from the Indian Civil Service. Advisers were also placed in Perlis and Setul in 1907.

Meanwhile, financial problems in Kelantan had also provided the opening for the appointment of a British Agent, although here the State Council also hoped that British enterprise might provide support against closer Siamese supervision. In 1900 a certain R.W. Duff, newly retired from the state administration in Pahang, came to Kota Baru with the aim of acquiring mining concessions. Backed by Straits Settlements firms, he was able to reach an arrangement with the raja of Kelantan without any application to Siam. By the terms of his grant, Duff secured an absolute monopoly of mineral, trading and other rights over 777 000 hectares (about one-third of Kelantan), together with an assurance that no further land would be alienated to Chinese. In return, the raja received $20 000 and 2000 shares in the Company.

Although the British government had not lent Duff official support, Bangkok not unreasonably saw this transaction as an indirect extension of British influence, aided by active Malay collaboration. It was only after extensive appeals and litigation that Bangkok finally agreed to the Duff Company's concessions. Through 1901 tension escalated as Sultan Muhammad IV (1899–20) was summoned to Bangkok to explain his actions, and as he himself tried to forestall Siamese assumption of greater control. During these meetings, one of which included the rulers of Kedah and Patani, the Malays were told firmly that all contacts with foreigners should be channelled through Bangkok. The forcible removal of the Tuan Besar ('Great Lord') of Patani in February 1902 following an uprising was a telling reminder that Siam would not condone disobedience from its Malay vassals. Nevertheless, the following May a defiant Sultan Muhammad made the trip to Singapore and in a meeting with Swettenham, now governor, asked for British protection and a British Resident.

For proponents of British expansion over the entire Peninsula these developments opened up new opportunities for a possible transfer of sovereignty. In 1902 Swettenham proposed that in return for a clear statement of Bangkok's suzerainty over Kelantan and Terengganu the two states should accept a Siamese Adviser appointed by Bangkok but of British nationality. A principal factor in Siam's acceptance of these conditions was the influence of the American General Adviser to the Siamese Government, who regarded the Malay states as the cause of 'irritations and difficulties' and thus of little value. In October 1902 an Anglo-Siamese Treaty was signed, and the Malay version presented to the Kelantan ruler as a *fait accompli*. Although any opposition would have been futile, he agreed to sign on condition that Kelantan fly its own flag, that the Siamese garrison leave, and that the ruling dynasty would be secure. In 1903 an Adviser, W.A. Graham, was sent to Kelantan, his staff subsequently augmented by other Englishmen.

The success of this appointment, which had encouraged Bangkok to appoint Advisers in Kedah and the other *prathesaraj* on the western seaboard, also foreshadowed their integration into the British administrative system. Graham always saw himself as an employee of Siam, but his duties were defined in precisely the same terms as the FMS Residents, and the small bureaucracy he built up was modelled on that of Perak and Selangor. Judicial reforms were instituted, the police force reorganized, the powers of the Islamic court delineated, roads constructed, the treasury regulated, medical services developed, and some secular education introduced. Telling terms such as 'new order' were employed in official correspondence, and efforts were made to remove individuals 'too hopelessly imbued with the spirit of the past'. As in Kedah, however, state finances were insufficient to fund even fairly modest reforms, the situation being aggravated by the debased currency. In 1906 further loans were necessary to ward off impending bankruptcy.

Several factors hastened the final transferral of the northern Malay states to Britain in 1909. In Bangkok, Chulalongkorn still felt humiliated by the terms of the 1897 Secret Convention, which had essentially placed Siam's dealings with the Malay states under British control. Another source of shame was British extraterritorial rights in Siam which prevented the Siamese from bringing to court any Asian or European claiming to be a British subject. There was also a growing suspicion of Malay loyalty, particularly in light of the 1902 Patani rebellion and rumours that Malay rulers were cultivating the favour of the British Agents.

On the British side, men like Swettenham were simply impatient at delays to what they considered the inevitable extension of British control. The pressure was equally strong from the commercial community. In Kelantan, for example, Duff argued that if Britain did not move into Kelantan, 'the rich commercial advantage to be gained in the development of the state would fall to the Germans'. Such threats found a receptive audience in London because of the growing tension in Europe; the British had noted with concern the growing numbers of Germans working in Siam, especially in departments dealing with railways. To undermine German interests, the British agreed to relinquish their extraterritorial rights in Siam and to provide a generous loan from FMS revenues for railway construction. In return, the Siamese should withdraw from the northern Malay states.

Rumours about a legal transfer had in fact been circulating for some time, especially as the Duff Company had been advised to remain in Kelantan. Nonetheless, the Malay rulers received little information through official channels. In 1908, through his Penang lawyers, Sultan Abdul Hamid of Kedah specifically asked the British to be consulted on any future changes, and in all states it was clear that the more rigorous nature of British control was not something the old aristocracy welcomed. The Kelantan ruler sent a special deputation of ministers to present his case in Bangkok, while Terengganu dispatched the *bunga mas* as a reminder of their long-established ties. In Siam itself objections were also raised at the loss of prestige which the surrender of territory entailed. A treaty was nonetheless concluded in March 1909, and in November of that year a probably bemused Edward VII was presented with the time-honoured symbols of overlordship, the *bunga mas dan perak*, from Siam's former Malay vassals.

The treaty of 1909 was seen by many northern Malays as a betrayal, and the ruler of Kedah purportedly said that his country had been 'bought and sold like a buffalo'. In drawing an international boundary between Siam and 'British' Malaya, the 1909 treaty finds a direct parallel in that between Britain and the Netherlands in 1824. Patani, which had been one of the most important Malay kingdoms in the seventeenth century and had remained a centre of Islamic scholarship, was now severed from the rest of the Malay world. Though Britain had initially pressed for the cession of Patani as well, the Siamese considered this too great a sacrifice. By insisting on the retention of Patani, Siam bequeathed to future governments the problem of absorbing the ethnically and culturally distinct Malay Muslims into the modern Thai state.

In Kedah and Kelantan, where British Agents had already paved the way, the appointment of a British Adviser went relatively smoothly, although in each case any suggestions of incorporation into the FMS were vehemently opposed. As a result, the 'Unfederated Malay States' were able to retain a greater sense of local identity than was the case in the more uniformly administered FMS. Kedah, for example, attained a reputation for the independence of its Malay Council, and in Singapore it was said that Kedah was a state 'where the black man rules the white'.[23] For Kelantan, so long a pawn in the rivalry between larger powers, symbols such as state postage stamps and the elevation of the raja to sultan were particularly meaningful. The retention of a sense of Malayness was encouraged because Malay remained the official language and the lack of economic development precluded the importation of Chinese and Indian labour. The construction and maintenance of roads and public buildings was undertaken with Malay labourers, patently disproving the old adage that Malays would not work for wages.

In Terengganu Malay resistance to the changed order was more difficult to overcome. Sultan Zainal Abidin (1881–1918) bitterly condemned the Siamese as thieves who gave away what did not belong to them. He was only persuaded to agree to the 1909 treaty after an assurance that the British Agent assigned to Terengganu would only have consular powers. For the sultan, the difference between an Agent and Adviser was an important legal distinction that he jealously guarded as a guarantee of his kingdom's independence and of the few freedoms still remaining to him. The 1911 Constitution, with its insistence on Islam as the 'State and Official Religion', was an important manifestation of Malay identity. Modelled on that of Johor, this Constitution allowed for a cabinet, a State Council, ministerial departments and district officers – the outward trappings of a modern sovereign state. But the economy could not support the expenses involved in this degree of change, and in 1914 the Terengganu government was forced to request a loan from the Straits Settlements. The British Agent also complained about other factors, such as the judiciary, the nature of land concessions, currency problems and above all lack of access to the treasury. The discovery of wolfram, a valuable component in some alloys, intensified the argument for extending the Agent's powers. Had it not been for the outbreak of the First World War in August 1914 an Adviser might have been forced on Terengganu much earlier. As it was, the declaration of war and the Malay belief in an impending victory by Turkey, still regarded as the champion of Islam, hardened resistance. But it was only a matter of time before Terengganu succumbed to unrelenting pressure from Singapore. A British commission, dispatched in 1918 to investigate local administration, the police and the granting of concessions, predictably recommended the appointment of an 'Adviser' whose counsel 'must be asked and accepted in all matters except religion'. The new ruler, who had been one of the most forthright opponents of the British Agent, was forced to abdicate, ostensibly on grounds of ill-health

The inclusion of Johor under British rule

Meanwhile, British control had also extended into Johor. Abu Bakar, who had repeatedly diverted any attempts to modify the relationship between Singapore and Johor, realized the changes his death might bring. As we have seen, a constitution expressly affirming Johor's sovereign status had been promulgated in 1895; just two months later Abu Bakar died, to be succeeded by his son Ibrahim, a young man of 22. Though inexperienced in administration, the new sultan was at ease in Western society, had been educated in English and was a good horseman, cricketer and tennis player. But he acceded at a time when colonial authorities were increasingly anxious to expand Britain's hold over the entire Peninsula. It is unlikely that any Malay ruler could have held out against the imperialist conviction that direct political control of Johor was vital to British interests in the area. Maladministration, however, could not be a justification. Anxious though he was to oversee the formation of 'British Malaya' before his retirement as governor, Swettenham could find no reason for intervention during a tour of Johor in 1903. Abu Bakar's legacy was evident in a well-ordered government and an economy which, like the road system, was integrated with that of Singapore and the FMS.

In this situation, advocates of intervention found ammunition in Ibrahim's personal life and attitude towards the colonial power. Unlike his father, Ibrahim never gained the friendship of powerful individuals in the

British government, and his lavish lifestyle, depleting a treasury already drained by Abu Bakar's frequent travels, aroused considerable criticism. Swettenham also objected to the influence in Johor of 'clever' Malays like Ibrahim's English-educated secretary who was accused of encouraging German and Dutch financiers. More serious in British eyes were the number of occasions when Ibrahim ignored colonial wishes, thus rejecting the implicit assumption that Johor should effectively operate as part of the FMS. The most contentious issue was Ibrahim's determination to maintain control over proposed railway links between Singapore and the FMS which was only settled when the FMS took over construction in 1904. In exasperation, Swettenham criticized Ibrahim for lacking 'good Malay qualities'.[24]

By 1905 Ibrahim had lost much of the privileged position for which his father had fought. Colonial Office opposition to private enterprise in Johor thwarted his attempts to found an independent Johor State Corporation for economic development. Even members of the Johor Advisory Board in London were working closely with the British government, and Ibrahim's efforts to constitute a new board in 1907 were blocked. Under the constant threat of British intervention and more aware of the seriousness of Johor's debts, he finally agreed to consult the British government on important matters and to obtain permission before making any trips abroad. In 1909, after the Siamese cession of the northern Malay states, Ibrahim himself proposed that a financial adviser be appointed to Johor. A British officer duly arrived the same year with instructions obviously not limited merely to financial affairs. More Europeans were appointed to the growing Johor administration, and after 1912, all such officers were seconded from the FMS.

To those anxious for the 'ripe plum' to fall into British laps, the delay in assuming full control was irritating in the extreme. Ibrahim struggled to protect his shrinking independence, but several matters, notably his alleged extravagance and the condition of the Johor prison, finally provided the British with sufficient justification for intervention. In March 1914 Johor's General Adviser was legally made responsible to the high commissioner (that is, the Singapore governor) rather than the sultan. But in the last weeks of Johor's independence, Ibrahim showed that he was still his father's son. His final acceptance of an Adviser with extended powers was made with the proviso that certain privileges be maintained in Johor, such as the wearing of a Johor uniform and the preference for Johor Malays in government appointments. Something of the unique place gained for Johor in British Malaya has lingered to the present day.

The new 'British' Malaya

A process which stretched back to the early nineteenth century had thus reached its conclusion. Though the Peninsula was divided into the Straits

Settlements, the FMS and the Unfederated Malay States (the four northern states plus Johor), though Borneo consisted of three protectorates, and though there was an uneasy division of power between Singapore and Kuala Lumpur, British paramountcy was to all appearances complete. However, while covering much of the territory of previous empires such as Melaka and Johor, the areas under British purview excluded some places which were culturally Malay while including others that had only marginal associations with the Melayu core. The boundaries reflected no sense of common allegiance to any centre, and the social and economic differences between the component parts were often extreme.

Within the domain broadly defined as 'British' the process of territorial delineation which was everywhere intrinsic to the colonial project continued. While Malays conceived of a ruler's authority in terms of his control over people and resources, the British related it to control over land. As Malay rulers were progressively drawn under the British umbrella, there was normally a period of sometimes painful negotiation by which colonial administrators established the territorial boundaries between neighbouring states. Sometimes these settlements simply made ancient understandings explicit, but on other occasions decisions were based on compromises that had little to do with local loyalties; several offshore islands, for example, were 'shared' between Johor and Pahang. Censuses and land registration helped the colonial regime further define the space it now occupied and classify the people who lived there. In 1906 Frank Swettenham could thus write confidently about 'British Malaya', while acknowledging that in the 1870s the Peninsula had been a 'closed book' to him.

Even more insidious, however, was the British mapping of an intellectual terrain that came to be called 'Malay Studies' and their arrogation of a special position in overseeing that terrain. Officials who spoke good Malay and who had lived for many years in the region had no doubt of their ability to expound on the world of the 'real Malay'. Not only could they decide what was best for Malays, but definitions of 'Malay culture' should also rest in British hands. Young British officials could best learn about Malays from their more experienced countrymen, and from the publications on Malay history, society, customs, literature and law which they had produced. Perhaps the most telling example of this confidence was the reinterpretation by colonial officials of the Malay past and its presentation in a standardized form modelled on English-style textbooks. In 1918, in collaboration with a Bugis-descended Malay, R.O. Winstedt published his *Kitab Tawarikh Melayu* ('The History Book of the Malays'), intended for use in the training of Malay teachers.

The inclusion of Chinese, Indians and 'Others' in the process of classification and counting, but their exclusion from works intended to inform either colonial officials or Malay teachers, already points to an indifference to the ethnic divisions which colonialism had created. In 1902 Hugh Clifford saw the recruitment of 'alien races' as justified because it enabled Malays to lead their own lives undisturbed in a fashion 'which completely commends

itself to them'. As invidious as racial stereotypes was the way in which colonialism maintained and encouraged class difference. It is clear that those of
high rank, whatever their ethnic affiliation, shared an interest in maintaining
a status quo where a privileged minority enjoyed wealth and influence possible only because of a quiescent labouring and agricultural class. Sanctified
by tradition, the social distinctions between the ruling class and Malay peasants
had many parallels with English society, and in the colonial mind this relationship was often translated into something approaching the squire–tenant
relationship with which they were familiar. But although British officialdom
saw Malay rulers as the natural spokesmen for their subjects, under colonial
rule the interests of aristocrat and peasant rarely coincided. In the past,
dissatisfied peasants had often given expression to discontent by rallying
around some forceful *anak raja*; by the early twentieth century, however, the
position of the upper classes had been so strengthened by the British presence that such alliances were now unlikely.

The few occasions when peasants allied with dissident elements among
the traditional élite were quite unsuccessful in reversing the tide of change.
In Kelantan, for example, several princes were involved in an uprising in
1915 under a local leader named To' Janggut which focused on issues
related to land reform. Members of the royal family were antagonistic to any
diminution of their appanage privileges; peasants resented colonial reforms
intended to provide security of tenure, but which attempted to enforce rice-
growing by stipulating that land rent be paid even when plots were uncultivated. Although this disturbance was short-lived, the British were were well
aware of the *haji*-led disturbances which broke out in Patani between 1910
and 1919, and past experience had shown the potential of opposition that
linked princes and subjects. It is not surprising to find, therefore, that in
1920 the uncooperative ruler of Terengganu was effectively deposed.

It is a measure of peasant resentment that even without royal leadership
a rebellion broke out in Terengganu in 1928, led by one Haji Drahman,
whose appeal in many respects resembled that of To' Janggut. Both men
laid claim to spiritual powers, attracting followers who believed in their supernatural abilities and the invulnerability imparted by special objects such
as a charmed kris. Haji Drahman even developed the notion that the land
belonged to the people, for whom infidel government was improper and
unnecessary. Although this peasant resistance has been a source of pride to
later Malays, the muting of upper-class resistance testifies to their realization
that survival depended on co-operation. As the government steadily worked
to minimize friction between rulers and colonial officials, the interests of the
Malay aristocracy and British colonizers drew steadily closer.

The special place of the Malay élite in the colonial system mirrored the
class hierarchy within the British community, which placed colonial officers
above merchants and planters. These social distinctions became more significant as the numbers of Europeans increased and as more women joined
their menfolk. In Selangor, for example, the figure of 487 Europeans in

1901 had nearly trebled 10 years later. As a result, they were no longer forced to associate with non-Europeans for relaxation or entertainment. Clubs reserved exclusively for whites had been formed, and in the major towns European residences clustered in recognized areas. During Anderson's term as governor (1904–11), non-Europeans were excluded from the civil service, although in 1910 a separate arm was created for Malays. This latter group, of minor aristocratic and well-born commoner descent, in turn became co-opted into the British system. Lacking any ability to influence the nature of government, they nevertheless had a high status among other Malays, in part because of their ability to emulate the lifestyle of their British counterparts.

As we have seen, class combined with caste and ethnicity to produce major divisions in the Indian community; the emergence of class was also increasingly apparent among the Chinese population. In the Straits Settlements Chinese spokesmen had long been drawn from a cohort of wealthy merchants, some with old Baba roots; by the early twentieth century a similar pattern of class differentiation was also emerging among *sinkheh* descendants who were slowly displacing the old Baba élite. As wealthier Chinese gained access to English education and emulated the lifestyle of British colonials, their links with poorer Chinese labourers and shopkeepers weakened. This process was also hastened because of changes in the colonial administration. After 1909 the practice of farming out revenue was ended, so that the government itself now assumed responsibility for tax collection. Not only did this sever the old link between Chinese tax collectors, who had often acted as agents for Malay rulers; it also lessened the hold of leading Chinese over the mass of their countrymen, from whence many of the tax payments originated.

The 'King's Chinese' (a term coined in 1906), who were largely Straits born, wealthy and English-educated, were especially hard hit by the increased exclusiveness of colonial society. Inevitably, many were disappointed and resentful at the dichotomy between the belief in equality acquired through Western education and the barriers to their own advancement. Drawn together by common interests, rich Chinese found solace among their own kind in clubs like the Weld Hill Club. The latter was modelled after the European clubs but was reserved for Chinese and had the highest subscription in the FMS. But although the lifestyle of upper-class Chinese thus became an amalgam of Oriental and Western customs, the very process of exclusion helped reforge some links between the richer Chinese and the mass of the Chinese population. For example, it was often English-educated Chinese who had excelled academically and had been sent to Britain for further study who were most active in sponsoring Chinese-language schools. For them the survival of classical Chinese literature and culture was critical as a reminder of China's ancient civilization and an antidote to daily reminders of the inferior status of the Chinese in colonial society.

An even more important development that fostered links within the Malayan Chinese community was the new nationalism now sweeping through

China. In the late nineteenth and early twentieth century the whole question of what constituted a Chinese had come under fire because of challenges to the old order in China. In 1909 the Manchu government announced the principle of *jus sanguinis*, claiming as Chinese citizens those of Chinese descent through the male line, irrespective of where they were born or how long their forebears had lived outside China. In their struggle to retain power, the Manchu called on the loyalty of the Nan Yang Chinese, urging them to return to China or remit funds for the imperial cause. In order to reach the overseas Chinese community, from 1905 Manchu officials encouraged the formation in Malaya of Chinese Chambers of Commerce, which also promoted a sense of unity across dialect boundaries.

Other groups in China also recognized the financial resource represented by the overseas Chinese, and the value of fostering greater communal unity. Reformers exiled from China were active in soliciting support, and Sun Yat-sen, the revolutionary leader, visited Malaya eight times between 1900 and 1910. After 1906 branches of the T'ung Meng Hui, the Chinese Revolutionary League, began to spring up. Sometimes, it is true, these were simply former secret societies in a new guise whose presence merely served to fan old feuds between clan and dialect groups. On the whole, however, the formation of a republic in China in 1911 engendered among overseas Chinese a widespread sense of pride in China's achievement, and ideological divisions were submerged until the rise of the Chinese Communist Party in the early 1920s.

If events in China helped stimulate a pride in being Chinese, it is not surprising that it was within the Islamic context that new questions were raised regarding wider Malay loyalties and the position of the faith under an alien government. Islam had always been an integral part of Malayness, but its egalitarian and universal message had often been overshadowed by the particularities and hierarchies inherent in Malay *kerajaan* culture. Now, from the Islamic heartlands of the Middle East, revitalized notions of Pan-Islam infused with the concept of *jihad*, the holy war, were filtering down to the village level. In Kelantan and Terengganu, where Muslim traditions were particularly strong, and where the adverse effects of colonial rule were increasingly evident, such messages were especially attractive. Branches of the Sarikat Islam, a modernist Islamic association which in Indonesia provided a basis for later nationalist movements, developed all along the east coast, deriving support from a sense of Malay injury at increased taxes, changed tenancy regulations, interference with accepted agricultural customs, and the powers given to Malay officials imported from other parts of the Peninsula.

In the Straits Settlements a younger generation (*kaum muda*) of the urban Islamic élite had also begun to address the whole issue of the Malay condition in response to the reformist teaching emanating from great Islamic universities such as Al-Azhar in Cairo. According to this new creed, if Islamic society were to throw back the advance of the Christian West, Muslims everywhere must work to improve their situation. 'Verily, Allah does not change the condition of a people until they change their own condition' (Koran, surah 13:11). With a heavy component of Arab and Indian blood, and linked to the wider Islamic community, they saw themselves operating in a domain where Muslims could relate to each other as equals on the basis of shared religious beliefs. Throughout the Malay world, wherever educated Muslims gathered, study clubs were formed to discuss some of the issues facing Muslims and particularly why Malays had apparently failed to attain *tamadun*, the newly coined word for a technological civilization. Similar questions were debated by the vernacular press. Because of their failure to grasp *tamadun* and acquire *ilmu* (knowledge), said a modernist Islamic journal published in Singapore, *al-Imam* (1906–8), Malays had been subdued by an alien white race. In urging the need for Malay action and unity such editorials were implicitly critical of the Malay rajas and the tenacity with which they clung to traditional privilege. While the Malay ruling class accepted the British notion that English education should be limited to boys of good birth, *al-Imam* urged the nurturing of a new generation of Malays through reforms in Islamic education that would incorporate the skills necessary to compete in a modern world. Indeed, such reforms should extend further, into the social realm: *al-Imam* championed property rights for women, criticized polygamy, and was guardedly supportive of women's education.

In this chapter we have traced the political formation of British Malaya from its beginnings in indirect rule in the Protected States to its final assertion of control over the entire Peninsula. Northwest Borneo still stood somewhat apart, but in the Colonial Office the view that Britain would soon assume a more direct role there was frequently expressed. Much has been written about the aims and motivations of British policy. It has been argued here that although there was never any blueprint for the extension of British control, a line of continuity does seem to stretch back beyond 1874 to the Anglo-Dutch Treaty of 1824 and the founding of Singapore in 1819. The endpoint of a process by which the British had helped separate Peninsular Malay society from Sumatra was symbolized in 1906 in the publication of Swettenham's eulogy to colonialism, entitled *British Malaya*, and two years later by R.J. Wilkinson's *History of the Peninsular Malays*.

The perceived unity of the Malay Peninsula is, of course, deceptive, for the piecemeal nature of colonial expansion meant that some areas were always more directly exposed to the effects of Western influence. Within the Federated Malay States the development of Perak and Selangor, where tin deposits were rich, was very different from that of Pahang, from the outset an economic disappointment to the colonial government. In the Unfederated States the experience of Terengganu and Kelantan, many miles from any British-controlled city, bore little resemblance to that of Johor or Kedah, each separated from a Straits Settlements town by only a narrow stretch of water. The character of the Straits Settlements differed again, and the disparity between the Borneo states further complicated the picture. Despite the many differences so evident to a modern observer, the Peninsula and in effect the Borneo protectorates had now been brought together under the colonial umbrella. Yet while drawing the disparate groups together adminis-tratively, the British presence in Malaya and the Borneo protectorates con-tributed to the hardening of ethnic divisions. Though the labour of Malay farmers, Indian estate workers and Chinese miners was vital to the capitalist economy, the physical and cultural distance which separated them precluded any sense of common exploitation. Furthermore, the maintenance of a class structure in which the élite of all races co-operated with the British to ensure their own access to privilege, rank and wealth was central to the colonial enterprise. In the evolution of Malaysia these developments were to cast a long shadow.

The Functioning of a Colonial Society, 1919–41

By 1919 the entire Malay Peninsula had come under some kind of British control. The Straits Settlements and the Federated Malay States (FMS) had the longest history of British influence, and consequently their institutions were more closely co-ordinated than those of the Unfederated Malay States (UMS). Despite colonial pressure to accept incorporation into the FMS, the Unfederated States, demographically heavily Malay, continued to maintain separate systems of governance until the outbreak of the Second World War. Yet even within the more uniform FMS there were differences, especially between Pahang and the west coast states. Loyalties to specific rulers and localities also retained an emotional hold that was not easily transferred to the larger administrative units the British had created.

Although the Borneo protectorates were geographically and administratively separate, they too had become incorporated into the colonial project and could not fail to be affected by prevailing attitudes in Singapore and Kuala Lumpur. Fundamental in such attitudes was the belief that Malay rulers needed to be 'conciliated' for their loss of power, and that Malay peasants should suffer 'minimal interference' from the colonial presence. With the conflicts of the nineteenth century behind them, the British justification that they were simply 'advising' the rulers helped to disavow discussions of political change. As late as 1927 a seasoned colonial like Hugh Clifford, the first Agent in Pahang, declared that 'no mandate has ever been extended to us by Rajas, Chiefs or People to vary the system of government'.[1] Such a statement belied the far-reaching changes which the British had long since introduced into the Malay states in order to provide European capital with a supportive and attractive investment environment.

Sources for the later colonial period

The vast and growing corpus of information produced by federal, state and local administrations means that it is possible to take almost any subject which attracted British attention – immigration, mining, agriculture, sanitation, railway development, education – and follow its history in considerable, sometimes exhaustive, detail. It is useful to remember, however, that generalizations about 'British Malaya' draw heavily on material from the Straits Settlements and the FMS, where the records are most dense. But while Borneo and the Unfederated States did not produce the same mass of data as the FMS, published and archival sources are sufficiently informative for twentieth-century developments to be traced in a manner not previously possible. Nevertheless, the historian still encounters frustrating gaps. In Sarawak, for example, much of the documentation for the 1920s and 30s was lost or destroyed during the Second World War.

From the late nineteenth century a number of important articles and books on Malay history and culture were published by colonial administrators who were scholars in their own right. But invaluable as these studies were in recording many aspects of Malay culture, they paid little attention to current events. The academic development of Malay Studies was very much in the 'Orientalist' tradition, and very few Malays contributed to these scholarly publications. A more revealing gauge of local attitudes towards the changes occurring in Malaya in the first half of the twentieth century is found in the vernacular newspapers and journals, and the growing body of Malay literature. Another resource, but one which is truly endangered, is human memory. Though individual scholars and students have shown the potential of oral sources for the reconstruction of Malaysian history, there remains a continuing need to record and catalogue recollections of the colonial period as it slips further away. This is especially true for Sabah and Sarawak, where it seems unlikely that the oral heritage, once so rich, will be retained by future generations.

Establishing the framework for an export economy

The almost unchallenged power of Malaya's new rulers had made possible the rapid introduction of specific changes considered necessary to facilitate the development and continuing profitability of the export economy. In a relatively short space of time the colonial regime had achieved its goal of constructing a 'congenial political and administrative framework' in which private enterprise could flourish. Without the resistance of strong local interest groups, the British were free to embark on restructuring Malayan society by regulating relations among groups of people and reorganizing resources for the greater aim of economic progress. By 1919 the socioeconomic landscape of the Malay Peninsula had been transformed. It was appropriate that the term 'British Malaya' now began to gain currency, for in terms of social and economic goals Malaya had indeed become 'British'.

Since the frequent wars between Chinese secret societies and their Malay allies had been one of the reasons for intervention in 1874, a prerequisite to economic development was the assurance of law and order. Indeed, the maintenance of peace was always an important justification for the colonial presence, and access to an armed force continued to uphold British authority. The physical appearance of the Sikh soldiers and policemen so prominent in colonial troops was itself intimidating, and in Ulu Pahang the conflicts of the 1880s are still known as the 'Sikh War' (Perang To' Sik). No private entrepreneur, whether a European or a Chinese capitalist from the Straits Settlements, could be persuaded to invest in Malaya unless the colonial authorities demonstrated their ability to enforce the law. By 1919, despite occasional challenges, this ability was widely acknowledged.

A second priority in Malaya's socioeconomic transformation was the establishment of an infrastructure which would underwrite a new communications system. In 1896, as Resident-General of the FMS, Swettenham stated categorically that Britain's duty was 'to open up the country by great works: roads, railways, telegraphs, wharves'.[2] Initially roads were built to connect tin mines, principally owned and operated by Chinese, with navigable rivers, where the tin was then transported to the coast. But between 1885 and 1895 four short railway lines were constructed, each connecting a coast port with a tin field in west coast Malaya. Roads were then built to link mines with the new railways, which were amalgamated in 1901 to form the FMS Railways, and placed under the Malayan Railway Administration. Two years later a north–south trunk line joined the mining towns, and by 1910 it reached from Perai (Province Wellesley) in the north to Johor Baru in the south. The line was extended in 1918 from Perai to the Siamese border, in 1920 from Gemas to Kuala Lipis (Pahang) and finally in 1931 from Kuala Lipis to Tumpat (Kota Baru, Kelantan). In 1923 new sections were also added further southward to link Johor with Singapore across the causeway. In this same period a direct road link, completed in 1928, was constructed between Johor Baru and the Siamese border. In the 1930s a spate of road building in the east coast states and Johor, mainly in areas not served by railways, enabled many export products to be transported by road.

A third and major change instituted by the British in their aim to develop a profitable export economy in Malaya was the establishment of an effective legal and administrative system. One of the first acts in this regard was to repudiate Malay customary land rules and to formulate a Western-style tenure system that would help bring to fruition the colonial vision of vast plantations replacing Malaya's virgin forests. Between 1887 and 1904 favourable land regulations were enacted in order to encourage Western planters to open up and settle the country, and surveys were conducted so that leases could be accurately demarcated. Information on mineral deposits was made easily available, and regulations were introduced to expedite export activities. In the early years these dealt principally with tin mining, and concerned matters such as the use of streams and watercourses, the disposal of tailings and the treatment of silt. By the same token, the clearing of rivers, the repair of railway lines and roads and the provision of adequate port facilities all became the duty of the colonial government.

Perhaps the most significant service provided by the colonial government was the organization of manpower. As indicated in the previous chapter, Chinese and later Indian migrant labour had been permitted to enter Malaya primarily to assist the various export industries. Between 1911 and 1931 the government encouraged unrestricted immigration from India, China and the Netherlands East Indies to provide much-needed workers for the still considerable tin-mining enterprises, and especially for the booming rubber industry. Only when world prices in tin and rubber fell during the Depression of the early 1930s did the government favour the repatriation of alien labour. A restricted immigration policy was in force between 1931 and 1947, and was then relaxed for the next decade as production was restored to prewar levels. Over the years, the colonial government thus successfully adjusted its immigration policy in accordance with the labour needs of the export industries. This willingness to use governmental powers to guarantee a cheap and available workforce was a strong inducement to private entrepreneurs to invest in British Malaya.

In a number of other ways the colonial government also assured British Malaya's economic development. The linking of the Straits Settlement dollar to sterling in 1904 provided the stability needed for currency exchange, while the introduction of banking and insurance facilities further assisted foreign capital to enter Malaya. In the ensuing years the government continued to maintain the confidence of European investors by establishing institutions of scientific research and technical training, by extending communication facilities, by building harbours and public utilities, and by providing a stable government. These measures were rewarded by a vast infusion of European capital, enterprise and management skills without which the rapid economic development of Malaya in the twentieth century would not have occurred.

A spectacular instance of the entry of European capital and expertise into Malaya's economy occurred in the rubber industry. Rubber estates had at first been developed by individual planters, usually those who had earlier experimented with other crops such as sugar and coffee. After the rubber boom in 1905 these planters sought assistance from British merchant firms already established in the Straits Settlements; the reputations of such firms enabled them to raise capital and float joint stock companies in London and Shanghai. European investors were willing to support these ventures because of the experience and expertise associated with prestigious companies like Guthries, Sime & Darby, and Harrisons & Crosfield. The merchant firms developed a system by which an agency house was responsible for supervising a number of companies and plantations. By thus concentrating management, vast amounts of capital could be committed to a new industry, and scarce management and administrative skills utilized to benefit all concerned. A manager and staff were appointed to oversee production in a particular estate, but technical and financial matters were left in the hands of the agency house with its expertise in large-scale operations. Each company could therefore enjoy a range of facilities at a fraction of the normal cost. In return, the agency houses, now responsible for exporting the rubber and importing consumer goods for the estates, benefited from the export–import trade and the economies achieved in large-scale operations.

Large European firms with substantial world-wide financial commitments were also a feature of the tin industry. As with rubber, the presence of a strong and sympathetic colonial government connected to the financial circles of London served to internationalize Malaya's tin industry. In 1913 the Europeans owned only a quarter of Malaya's tin mines, but by 1937 the proportion had grown to two-thirds. At first numerous groups were involved, but from the mid-1920s a process of consolidation began. Though about 80 separate European companies were still registered in 1937, as well as hundreds of incorporated Chinese concerns, many of the European businesses were financially linked. A third of the entire tin output, for example, was owned by Anglo-Oriental (Malaya) Ltd, a subsidiary of the London Tin Corporation. Controlled from abroad and managed by central agencies, the organization and administration of the European mines paralleled those of the rubber estates, although here international mining groups rather than agency houses ran the operation.

The tin industry

Although for centuries tin-mining by Malays had been able to satisfy the changing demands of India, China and Europe, production had been limited and carried out largely by a method known as *dulang*, the washing or panning of alluvial tin. It is estimated that until the middle of the nineteenth century Malay production reached only about 500 tonnes annually. A major development in the industry was the discovery of two large tin fields in Perak, one in Larut (1848) and another in Kinta (1880). By the end of that decade some 80 000 Chinese from China and the Straits Settlements were working in Perak as indentured labourers. The mining ventures in which they were involved were in the hands of Straits Chinese entrepreneurs, often underwritten by capital supplied by the European merchant firms in Singapore and Penang. During the first half of the nineteenth century the Chinese had already introduced small but significant innovations, such as the chain pump to keep tin mines free of water. However, with the discovery of extensive tin deposits, new mining techniques were developed that were patterned after Western tin-mining enterprises elsewhere. The steam engine and centrifugal pump, used in Perak as early as 1877, solved the problem of flooding in the mines and enabled operations to occur at greater depth than hitherto possible. Hydraulic sluicing and gravel pumping were two other extractive methods that came via Australia. These new techniques were readily adopted by Chinese miners, and by 1898 the FMS, with a total output of 40 000 tonnes, became the world's largest tin producer.

Although Europeans had participated in a minor way in the tin industry in Perak in the 1880s, the entry of major European capital occurred only with the introduction of the bucket dredge in 1912, a method of mining which had proved especially profitable in New Zealand. Dredges expanded mining operations because they were effective in swampy areas and also proved more profitable in extracting tin from ground with a lower ore content. Since this method of mining required large amounts of capital, developed technical knowledge and an extensive management capability, it could not be successfully employed unless a large area of tin-bearing ground was leased. The colonial government was well able to accommodate such needs, since the major tin areas were in Perak, Selangor and Pahang, all within the FMS. The government also provided the mining concerns with land surveys that contained information on tin areas and enabled leases to be accurately assigned. Because of the substantial capital expenditure required, only the large international mining companies had sufficient resources to make the bucket dredge method worth while. A principal source of finance and specialized skills was found in the Cornish tin industry, which was seeking new areas of exploitation after the depletion of Cornwall's tin fields in the late nineteenth century. In the early twentieth century an increased demand for tin in the canning industry also contributed to a rapid rise in Malaya's tin production.

Restraints were placed on the tin industry, however, by a slowing of world purchases. Between 1870 and 1900 consumption of tin trebled; between 1900 and 1930 it doubled; but between 1930 and 1960 it increased only slightly. The USA had earlier been a major market, but after the 1920s the American demand remained constant at around 2540 tonnes because of more economic use of tin and better recovery methods. Large fluctuations in world tin prices between the world wars led tin-producing nations to adopt the Tin Control Scheme, which aimed at restricting exports by quota. Established in March 1931, and reaffirmed in 1934 and 1937, this scheme had only limited success, and at the outbreak of the Second World War the Malayan tin industry was still facing difficulties.

Early plantation crops

During the nineteenth and early twentieth centuries several agricultural crops had been grown commercially in Malaya. These had been pioneered by Chinese planters, who favoured crops that would yield returns within a short time of planting, grow well in most localities, and require no specific skills or undue outlay of capital for equipment and processing. Large Chinese-owned gambier and pepper plantations under *kongsi* direction had developed in Johor, Melaka, Negeri Sembilan and Selangor, while tapioca was generally restricted to Melaka and adjacent areas of Negeri Sembilan and Johor. These Chinese plantations were more successful than any other commercial cultivation prior to the introduction of rubber, and during the nineteenth century the Chinese pattern of shifting agriculture affected at least 200 000 hectares. Around the turn of the century, however, Chinese interest in gambier, tapioca and pepper declined as prices fell and experiments were made in growing tea, coffee and rubber. The colonial government's attitude to Chinese agricultural practices was also instrumental in encouraging them to move away from traditional crops. Chinese plantations were considered to be inimical to the larger interests of Malaya because they led to soil exhaustion and a depletion of forests to supply firewood in numerous small factories. While moving to suppress this type of agriculture, the authorities also expressed a wish to see the land more permanently cultivated.

In colonial eyes, any hope of achieving this lay with a group of commercially oriented Europeans who had shown an interest in developing export crops which had been profitable elsewhere. Though early European plantations were experimental, since little was known about tropical conditions, they satisfied the government's desire for more stable agricultural entrepreneurs. Europeans had access to much greater capital than the Chinese planters and could employ an experienced labour force. At the same time, Europeans viewed their agricultural ventures as a long-term investment, and therefore wanted legal titles to their lands. The colonial government was not only willing to oblige, but actively encouraged European planters by importing pepper, cloves and nutmeg for the early plantations.

Of all the crops planted by Europeans, only sugar and coffee had some degree of success. Early Chinese efforts in growing sugarcane and the participation of experienced sugar planters from Mauritius assured the success of this crop as a commercial venture. Malayan sugar became a highly capitalized European-controlled industry and appeared to have a bright future. However, by 1905 sugar planting declined rapidly in Province Wellesley and Perak. In 1911 the total area planted in sugarcane in the FMS was concentrated in the Kerian district of Perak and consisted of only 8400 hectares. Two years later in Province Wellesley the area under sugar had fallen to a mere 12.4 hectares. A significant cause of the decline, particularly in the Kerian area, was a change in government policy towards agriculture. During the 1890s the colonial authority had decided to expand *padi* (wet rice) production by financing irrigation schemes, but unfortunately areas suited to such schemes coincided with lands planted in sugar. There were other reasons for the sugar industry's decline, but the *coup de grâce* was the increasing profitability of rubber as an export crop.

The only other form of commercial agriculture which proved to be moderately profitable was coffee. Large-scale coffee planting in Selangor, Negeri Sembilan, Perak and Johor in the last quarter of the nineteenth century was entirely a European effort, with a number of former coffee planters from Ceylon participating. As the first commercial crop which could be grown successfully in much of Malaya, coffee brought in capital and management personnel, and led to the importation of Tamil and Javanese labour. Since coffee plantations appeared to satisfy the official goal of establishing large and stable European agricultural enterprises, the government was eager to facilitate the industry's operations. Coffee planters received advantageous land terms and large planting loans which, combined with a favourable labour situation, encouraged capital investment. Consequently, proprietary estates were rapidly replaced by those owned by companies. Despite these advantages and the 1891–6 coffee boom, by the first decade of the twentieth century Europeans had largely abandoned coffee planting for rubber. But albeit short-lived, the efforts to develop a coffee industry in Malaya had generated new government measures, while European planters had gained specific knowledge of local conditions. Together these contributed to rubber's rapid and unprecedented success.

The rubber industry

The phenomenal rise of rubber as the pre-eminent export crop in Malaya is the more remarkable when one considers that at the end of the nineteenth century almost the total world production of natural rubber came from largely uncultivated plants in Brazil's Amazon basin. In 1820 world consumption of natural rubber was about 100 tonnes, but in the following decades demand rapidly grew because of a series of technical developments. Charles Goodyear's discovery of the vulcanization process in 1839, the growth of the electrical industry and especially the expanding uses of pneumatic tyres for bicycles, and later motor cars, in the late nineteenth and early twentieth century all contributed to the growth of the world market for natural rubber.

Malaya's involvement with rubber began when seeds of the rubber-producing tree, *Hevea brasiliensis*, which had been collected in Brazil in 1876, were sent to the Royal Botanical Gardens at Kew. Some successful germinations were taken to Ceylon and a few to Singapore, but subsequently died. Another consignment of seedlings was sent to Singapore the following year, and towards the end of 1877 nine of these were planted at the side of the Residency in Kuala Kangsar. Early experiments were unsystematic and intended principally for scientific observation, since in the 1880s European planters were far more interested in coffee. Planters were apprehensive about rubber for a range of reasons: it had never been grown on plantations, it was indigenous to another part of the world, its maturity period was long (six to eight years), its productive life was unknown, areas in Africa were also growing the tree, and above all the future of the market was uncertain. The individual who did most to encourage the growing of the rubber tree was H.N. Ridley, who arrived in Singapore in November 1888 to become the Director of the Botanical Gardens. Through his own experiments and personal persuasion he succeeded in having a number of trees planted on estates, and his enthusiasm for popularizing this new crop earned him the nicknames 'Mad Ridley' and 'Rubber Ridley'. Yet he was ultimately successful because continuing experiments helped develop new strains of rubber, and because these improvements coincided with an increase in rubber prices and the collapse of the coffee market.

Rubber was first planted commercially in Malaya in the mid-1890s on estates previously developed for other crops. A decline in coffee prices encouraged growers to experiment with rubber because of their ready access to capital, management personnel and a labour supply. But by the beginning of the twentieth century, interplanting of rubber became commonplace on almost all existing estates, and new land was increasingly used solely for this crop. The expansion of rubber seemed an ideal means of fulfilling the government's aim of long-term agriculture by Europeans, and from 1897 land regulations were introduced in the FMS specifically to support its cultivation.

The first rubber boom occurred in 1905–8 with the expansion of the motor car industry, and during this period the total area planted in rubber increased almost fivefold. By 1908 rubber was planted in every state of Malaya, occupying some 109 000 hectares, an area greater than that planted with any other previous crop. Government measures favourable to rubber planters in terms of land alienation, flow of capital and labour regulations established the bases for expansion. During this period numerous small rubber-planting companies were formed, floated mainly by the large merchant houses of Singapore, of which the most important were Guthries, and Harrisons & Crosfield.

Another rubber boom period occurred from 1909 to 1912, and European companies expended large sums to buy up Malay lands as well as old Chinese sugar, gambier and tapioca plantations where crops had been interplanted with rubber. Malay and Chinese smallholders also began to grow rubber with the hope of eventually selling their land to Europeans. In these years rubber acreage in the estates rose by 110 per cent, the number of rubber estates doubled, and the total area alienated for rubber on estates rose by about 291 000 hectares. By 1913 rubber in Malaya covered some 322 000 hectares, and three years later it had passed tin as Malaya's chief export earner, a position which it held until 1980.

The rubber boom was especially noticeable in the west coast states because here the infrastructure developed for the tin industry also came to benefit plantations. The absence of railway lines, an adequate road system, and suitable year-round ports in the east coast states deterred major European investment in rubber estates there – the same reasons that had convinced nineteenth-century European entrepreneurs to concentrate their activity along the west coast. But to non-European smallholders rubber seemed an ideal cash-crop, since its hardiness and adaptability to various types of soils and growing conditions meant it thrived almost anywhere in Malaya. Although a rubber tree could not be tapped until about its eighth year, it could be successfully interplanted with more rapidly maturing crops. Once the tree was ready to be tapped, its productive life was about 30 years. The smallholder was therefore assured a steady source of income from his rubber trees, which required little care and minimal cost in the preparation of the latex for market.

The extent of smallholder participation in the rubber industry only became apparent when the Stevenson Scheme came into effect in late 1922, setting a quota on rubber production that discriminated against native producers. As a result of a general rubber depression in 1920–1, most of the European companies involved in the industry were unable to cover their costs. The international Stevenson Scheme was primarily intended to protect the European rubber companies of Malaya, Borneo and the Netherlands East Indies from competition by native smallholders. One serious outcome of the scheme was its damage to American customers in the motor car industry, which was just coming out of the post-First World War depression. As a result, big companies in the United States decided to diversify their sources of rubber. Firestone opened rubber estates in Liberia, and Ford did the same in Brazil. Americans also made efforts to economize in the use of natural rubber, and a rubber-reclaiming industry was established.

The problems experienced by the industry remained unrelieved during the Depression of the early 1930s. In 1934 an International Rubber Regulation Agreement was signed among the rubber producers of Southeast Asia, which limited production and applied a fixed quota per country for an initial period of four years. Like the Stevenson Scheme, this new agreement principally hurt smallholders because it came at a time when they were expanding faster than the rubber estates. The estates easily switched to oil palm, just gaining popularity as an export crop, but smallholders lacked the capital and expertise to make such changes. However, the rubber industry survived, and by the outbreak of the Pacific War in 1941 new high-yielding trees, fertilizers, mechanization of estates and methods of preserving and concentrating latex appeared to ensure a prosperous future.

The palm oil industry

In the period when rubber dominated the agricultural export scene, a few estates with an eye to overseas markets began growing a new crop, oil palm (*Elaeis guineensis*). A native of West Africa, it had been introduced into the Peninsula in the 1850s but was mainly cultivated as an ornamental plant. Only in 1917 was the first plantation of oil palm begun as a commercial venture. Although palm oil was used in the manufacture of soap, candles, flux for the tin-plate industry, margarine, vegetable oils, grease, and fuel for internal combustion engines, there was little progress in the industry before the slump in rubber prices after the First World War forced planters to search for alternative crops. No large-scale development occurred until 1924, when three rubber companies in the Guthries group formed Oil Palms of Malaya Ltd. Their example was later followed by other firms. Because of the need for capital and special expertise, especially in the processing of the oil, the industry was confined to large plantations usually located near some rubber estate in order to take advantage of the existing infrastructure. Most oil palm estates were therefore developed along the west coast.

The oil palm, which in Africa grew naturally in riverine forests or fresh-water swamps, flourished in Malaya's tropical climate and readily adapted to a range of tropical soils. Without a pronounced dry season, Malaya was a place where it could be planted throughout the entire year. The attractiveness of palm oil in Malaya meant that the area under cultivation steadily increased. The production of 3350 tonnes in 1930, or 1 per cent of world output, rose to 58 300 tonnes in 1939 – 11 per cent of world output. This dramatic improvement in the industry was due mainly to technical improvements in cultivation, extraction of the oil, and the delicate task of transporting the finished product. At the outbreak of the Pacific War, oil palm plantations in Malaya covered some 36 000 hectares.

Padi *(wet-rice) farming*

The reshuffling of labour, reallocation of resources and encouragement to European investment by the colonial government was underwritten by its perception of Malays as essentially farmers for whom the production of *padi* was a major occupation. In 1932 an address by the high commissioner nicely captured the British vision of the appropriate place for Malays in the colonial economy:

> To my mind a picture of the ideal Malay homestead would be a small area of rice field, combined with a smaller area of *kampung* [village] land. On the latter should be planted fruit trees of suitable types. There should also be an area for vegetables and a certain stock of poultry should be kept.... Such a homestead would provide directly for the requirements of the smallholder and might give him some surplus for marketing beyond his own immediate needs.... The lesson of the past is, however, that money crops should on no account be allowed to supplant food crops[3]

In this conception Malays were small rice-growers who supplied their own basic needs with some surplus for resale in the domestic market. Like other 'Malay' institutions – kingship, custom, religion – the British saw rice-growing as a 'traditional' cultural component, and an occupation for which Malays were eminently suited. In their own best interests, these 'children of nature', as one official termed them, should be encouraged to remain on the land protected against exploitation by foreign Asians. In 1913, as the rubber boom was gaining force, the Malay Reservations Act was introduced. This empowered the FMS to set aside land for use by Malays, with particular encouragement to rice-growing, and made it illegal for them to sell their holdings to non-Malays.

The colonial vision, however, was not easy to apply to the Peninsula, where suitable ricelands were limited to the alluvial lowlands and river deltas of the northwest and northeast coastal plains. Historically, most Peninsular Malays had grown small amounts of rice for domestic use but much had also been imported. Chinese travellers in the Song period, for example, visiting a port believed to be in Terengganu, specifically noted that foreigners bartered rice for local products. In later years the same pattern was evident in the southern Peninsula, where Melaka was dependent on rice imports from Pegu and Java. Colonial aspirations did not change Malaya's geography, and during the colonial period 60 per cent of the cultivated area was in Perlis, Kedah, Penang, Province Wellesley and Perak, while 23 per cent was in the heavily Malay states of Kelantan and Terengganu.

Yet while the British hoped to reduce the amount of rice imported from Siam and Burma to feed Malaya's burgeoning population of foreign labourers, they never envisaged an economy that was self-sufficient in rice. Thus, although the government developed a massive irrigation scheme in the Kerian district as well as other smaller projects, it was largely Malay farmers who were responsible for the increase in rice acreage, notably in Kedah, where from the 1880s the aristocracy had taken a lead in encouraging *padi* farming. Elsewhere in the Peninsula the lack of colonial government initiatives was a marked contrast to the energy and research devoted to the development of tin and rubber. In the case of rice, the British were unwilling to convert large tracts of land to *padi* except in certain restricted areas, and only when imports were disrupted through war or drought were measures taken to increase local rice production. Towards the end of the First World War, for example, a Rice Lands Enactment was introduced to prevent the growing of rubber on areas allocated for rice, and in 1918 the Food Production Enactment set aside land specifically for the growing of food crops. These regulations effectively restricted most Malays to subsistence production and to residence in rural areas.

In their efforts to turn Malays into rice farmers, the British met persistent if low-level resistance, especially among those Malays who grew rice for domestic consumption and as a supplement to more profitable cash-crops such as gambier, pepper, coconut, rubber and (to a lesser extent) oil palm. Despite their goal of ensuring that Malays remained a 'settled peasantry', the British discouraged cash-cropping since they felt the activities of smallholders undercut and endangered the profitability of the large estates. But because rice cultivation was generally small-scale and seen as a 'Malay' occupation, farmers never received the kind of government support available to the tin and rubber industries. It is clear, furthermore, that the colonial perception of Malays as primarily farmers introduced serious problems into Malay society: land was often leased and credit was costly, thus leading to tenantry and indebtedness (often to Chinese or Indian moneylenders, but also to wealthier Malays). Favourable credit facilities were channelled principally to European firms involved with the extractive industries, and without access to credit at reasonable terms Malay farmers faced the ever-present threat of losing their land to a creditor or being evicted by a landlord. In any conflict of interest – whether in terms of funds, personnel or time – rice was always sacrificed to rubber and tin, the two pillars of British Malaya's economy.

In sum, the colonial government wished to promote long-term land development, and it was believed that this was best accomplished on the basis of a plantation industry funded by European capital. Rice production was necessary, but the plantation crops and the tin mines were to be the major export earners for British Malaya. Throughout the colonial period the growing numbers of workers in the plantations and mines and in the towns were fed through the import of rice rather than a domestic surplus. The low cost of rice imports made local production commercially unattractive, and so this largely Malay sector of the economy never became export-oriented. The most profitable aspect of the domestic rice industry was in the milling, procurement, distribution and sale of rice, which were in the hands of Chinese entrepreneurs rather than Malay producers.

Economic developments in North Borneo and Sarawak

From the late nineteenth century, especially with the appointment of W.C. Cowie as managing director (1894–1910), the economic policies of the North Borneo Company replicated developments on the Peninsula, albeit on a smaller scale. However, attempts to introduce such industries as sugar, tapioca, opium, silk, soya bean, orchids and pineapple, and to develop coal-mining, were unsuccessful. Coffee was hesitantly attempted and abandoned, while the initial success of gambier soon faded, and even pepper was displaced with the rise of the rubber industry. Prior to the twentieth century tobacco was the only imported crop to enjoy any commercial success, although this was short-lived. In 1884 a few bales sent to London were judged to be equal to the world's best, but by 1891 tariffs imposed by the American government to protect its own industry signalled tobacco's eventual decline in North Borneo. In the early years of the British North Borneo Company the financial main-stay was not therefore alien crops but the traditional trade in sea and jungle products. For example, swallows' nests for the unique Chinese delicacy, 'bird's nest soup', were systematically harvested under contract from caves along the coasts and offshore islands, and sent directly to Hong Kong. Other local products, such as rattans, gutta-percha and *damar* (tree resins), were gathered and shipped to Singapore, where they were processed for the world market.

Among the jungle products, it was North Borneo's abundant stock of timber, especially the much-desired family *dipterocarpaceae*, which attracted European attention. In February 1885 the first shipment of logs was sent to Australia, signalling the advent of what was to become a prosperous and controversial export industry. Logging grew substantially in the last decade of the nineteenth century, spurred by the demands for rail sleepers for the railway expansion under way in China. Access to virgin forest was also facilitated by the brief tobacco boom, which opened up interior rivers, encouraged some development in road transport, stimulated Chinese migration, and gave Europeans valuable local experience. Of the four concerns involved in the industry, the British Borneo Trading and Planting Company was by far the biggest. In 1920, however, with the financial assistance of Harrisons & Crosfield, a new giant was formed under the name British Borneo Timber Company. This new company obtained a monopoly for 25 years to log on state land, and provided the capital needed to expand the timber trade. By 1937 timber exports were estimated at 178 000 cubic metres, and Sandakan became one of the most important timber ports in the world. Though the European-dominated logging industry was generally hostile to shifting agriculturalists, it none the less expanded with very little regard for conservation. Helped by the Forestry Research Institute of Malaya, North Borneo's Forestry Department gained increasing expertise in timber culture and administration, but the measures they took could not prevent the generally indiscriminate logging of the jungle.

Although from 1921 timber became North Borneo's second most valuable export product, it was rubber which dominated the economic landscape. The rubber plant arrived in 1882, but, as in Malaya, some time passed before its acceptance as a viable commercial crop. Within a generation it became obvious that rubber had a secure future in light of the technical advances in transportation and communications. Investors were enticed to North Borneo by attractive land leases, low rents, exemption from export duties, and the availability of cheap Chinese and Javanese labour. The building of railways, initiated by Cowie and resumed in 1921, incurred heavy debts but opened up much of the west coast, where land adjoining the tracks was quickly acquired by Europeans and Chinese for development into estates. The building of roads for land transport also assumed greater priority. As a result of these factors, the area under rubber, which amounted to 1306 hectares in 1906, grew to 53 812 in 1940, with considerable smallholder involvement.

Sarawak's economic development was deliberately restricted by the personal philosophy of its White Rajas, who had pledged that they would preserve the indigenous way of life. It was this philosophy as much as a lack of finance, for example, which justified the preference for river transport and neglect of road building. By 1938 Sarawak had only 1094.4 kilometres of roads in the entire country, with less than 10 per cent of the all-weather type. Both James and Charles Brooke also used the monopoly system to assert control over the state's land and resources. Antimony, for instance, had been retained as a government monopoly, while income was also extracted from the Chinese community through farming out rights to sell opium and local wine (*arak*), and to run gambling dens and pawn shops. Charles Brooke was especially adamant that large-scale estates with their armies of coolie labourers should not be permitted in Sarawak, and laws preventing speculation and alienation of native land deterred European developers. At the beginning of the twentieth century Sarawak's revenue was derived principally from export duties on jungle products and from sago production, which had flourished through a partnership between Melanau producers and Chinese processors. Trade in both items benefited as sea links to Singapore improved, and by the end of the nineteenth century Sarawak supplied about half of the world market in sago.

Yet despite Brooke avowals of non-interference, their policies actively encouraged indigenous peoples to move from shifting cultivation to sedentary farming. As in North Borneo and Malaya, the attempts to introduce tobacco, sugarcane, tea and coffee as commercial crops were disappointing, although Chinese success in interplanting gambier and pepper helped make Sarawak second only to the Netherlands East Indies in pepper production. It was in this context that Charles Brooke, like his uncle, began to look favourably on Chinese migration in the hope that their skills as farmers could be transferred into rice-growing. His strongest move to encourage Chinese migration was government sponsorship for several hundred Christians from Foochow, and from 1900 these new arrivals began to settle along the lower reaches of the Rejang river. After a series of unsuccessful rice seasons, many turned to other crops such as pepper and rubber, often encroaching on Dayak or Melanau land. The so-called 'rubber fever' gripped the indigenous population as well, since rubber cultivation involved few skills, little capital outlay and could be readily incorporated into the existing economy of most interior groups. From the 1920s rubber became Sarawak's main agricultural export; as a result, Sarawak was still importing around 60 per cent of its rice requirements by 1940, while 97 000 hectares were under rubber cultivation, largely by smallholders.

It has also been argued that in practice the Brookes gave much greater encouragement to European commercial endeavour than they themselves acknowledged. At the forefront of most economic initiatives in Sarawak was the Borneo Company, the one Western commercial enterprise Charles Brooke had permitted. Its ventures had mixed success. Antimony and mercury mining in upper Sarawak was declining even by the mid-1880s, and, although gold flourished briefly, deposits were largely exhausted by the 1920s. Coal also proved a disappointment. None the less, until the outbreak of the Second World War the Company was able to make an acceptable profit without upsetting the White Rajas' conception of their role as guardians of local culture. Part of the reason was the revenue generated by the Company as marketing agent for Sarawak Oilfields, to which it gave a concession for oil production in Miri. Although Company officials had been aware of what locals called *minyak tanah* (earth oil) since the 1880s, the first shipment was not made until 1913. The mid-1920s saw some success, and until 1940 petroleum was Sarawak's chief foreign-exchange earner, although production levels never approached those reached across the border in Brunei. Furthermore, since finds were confined to the thinly populated Miri area and controlled by Sarawak Oilfields, the industry had little impact on the domestic economy centred on Kuching.

Logging was another matter, for the growing recognition of its potential value could not fail to impinge on the lives of many local people. The Brooke administration, which claimed sovereign rights over all land, certainly acknowledged that native cultivators (as opposed to nomadic hunter-gatherers) were entitled to land rights. Legally, however, this did not mean ownership, but rights to the use or rent of state land. A portent of more vociferous complaints was already evident in European criticism of the shifting cultivation traditionally practised by many interior groups. In this method of farming, trees and undergrowth were cleared and burned, with the ash providing nutrients for growing dry land rice and other crops. After several harvests, the land was left to regenerate for eight to ten years, while a new plot was cleared, and the cycle began again. Brooke administrators, who believed that the felling of 'primitive jungle' led to the loss of 'much good and valuable wood', considered that they could protect the forest by limiting access. However, during the 1920s and 30s the growing demand for written permits and legal documents as evidence of native title was often puzzling to indigenous groups, and ignored or undermined established traditions regarding communal land use. Government intrusion was also felt in the harvesting of jungle produce. Monopoly rights in the high-revenue wild rubber (*jelutong*) and wood oil (*cutch*) were farmed out to Western companies, destabilizing many of the old exchange connections and transforming Dayak collectors into paid workers. Overall, the Chinese middleman remained important, although here too the traditional economy was reshaped by the displacement of barter by coinage and by the debt–credit chain that stretched from Dayak longhouses to the heart of Singapore's commercial district.

Thus, despite avowals of non-interference, the very presence of Europeans both here and in North Borneo inevitably disturbed existing economic and social patterns. One must be careful not to overstate the case, but there are certain similarities in the commercial development of Sarawak and North Borneo, which were now peripheral players in the world-wide British trading empire. Both governments relied on European and Chinese capital to develop export-oriented industries such as oil and timber, and this brought closer connections with large companies already established in Singapore and Malaya. In turn, these enterprises depended heavily on wage labour. Indians, for the most part, were not attracted to Borneo, but large numbers of Chinese and Indonesians were employed, and indigenous groups were also recruited for short-term or seasonal employment. By 1907, for example, Chinese comprised more than 50 per cent of North Borneo's total labour force. As in Malaya, there was a clear tendency to allocate economic roles according to ethnicity; in particular, the first half of the twentieth century saw the entrenchment of Chinese in all aspects of economic life, especially as creditors. In Sarawak and North Borneo, governments also worked to exercise greater control over people and resources. Increasing interest in the commercial value of land and forests was accompanied by a hardening attitude towards swidden cultivators, and growing pressure on local people to become more settled. Inevitably, this brought greater competition between Chinese and indigenous smallholders for access to land. The reach of both governments was also steadily extending into the interior. Although communication infrastructures remained undeveloped, it was increasingly difficult to escape government demands for taxes and for corvée duties, such as porter services and the building of bridle paths. Perhaps official impositions were most keenly felt in 1934, when North Borneo and Sarawak became signatories to the International Rubber Regulation Agreement. The policing and punishments for illegal growing and tapping were a telling sign of the extent to which the economies of Sabah and Sarawak had become entangled in the global commercial system.

Education under the colonial government

The philosophy current in Britain at the beginning of the twentieth century dictated that some education should be available to all children, and in Malaya colonial officials certainly espoused this goal. But the government was generally content with a declaration of intent, and only small steps were taken towards the creation of an education system for all Malaya. Furthermore, early colonial policies towards education were fundamentally shaped by the identification of ethnicity with a specific economic role. In the colonial view, it would be sufficient for most children to receive a basic education in their own language that would prepare them to accept their allotted role in the colonial scheme. Put crudely, Europeans were to govern and administer, immigrant Chinese and Indians to labour in the extractive industries and commercial sector, and Malays to till the fields. The creation of the FMS in 1896 and the subsequent demand for English-educated personnel did lead to an expansion of English schools, but as always the British were guided by the practical needs of colonial society. Regardless of their ethnicity, only a privileged few gained access to English schools and hence to lucrative and prestigious positions in government or in European firms. Whether Chinese, Indian or Malay, the small group of socially and economically privileged students at these élite schools were bonded by a common educational experience that reinforced their status in relation to the vast majority of the population. As a result, it was only in English-medium schools that the educational experience cut across ethnic lines. Apart from efforts to expand teaching in Malay, until the 1920s the management of non-English-medium schools was largely relinquished to the respective ethnic communities.

Formal Indian education in Malaya was pioneered in the first half of the nineteenth century by missionaries who opened Tamil schools in Penang, Melaka and Singapore. These proved unsuccessful, and it was not until the 1870s that Tamil education in the Straits Settlements was revived. Although the colonial government established Tamil schools in Perak and Negeri Sembilan in 1900, the authorities obviously expected missionary societies and the management of coffee and rubber estates to accept responsibility for educating Indian children. Since the government had neither guidelines nor provision to enforce such education, the quality of the voluntary primary schools on estates varied considerably. Few rubber-growing companies were willing or able to hire a qualified teacher and to provide the books and equipment necessary to run a school. The 'teacher' was often the Indian labour recruiter (*kangani*), a clerk, or sometimes simply a literate labourer employed on the estate. Needless to say, such teachers had little or no training. While the medium of most schools was Tamil, there were also a few where the language of instruction was Telegu, Malayalam, Punjabi or Hindi. Textbooks were imported from India and provided some coverage of India's culture, history and geography, but they had nothing to say about Malaya and there was no effort to teach Malay. Whatever learning occurred during the brief period that an Indian estate child attended school was thus almost wholly India-orientated.

Other factors served to undermine the value of estate education. From the age of ten or twelve children could usually find employment in the rubber-tapping operation, and low wages for adult workers meant that families desperately needed this extra income. There was thus little incentive for children to prolong their school attendance. A reluctance to pursue further education was reinforced by the estate-owners themselves, who saw the advantages of retaining children on the premises to add to the workforce. Not until 1923, when a Labour Code was promulgated, were estates with ten or more children of school age required to provide education. However, there was no substantial change in the quality of instruction available and no serious attention was given to Indian education until 1937, when an official inspector of schools with a knowledge of Tamil was appointed to the Department of Education, and a scheme for training Tamil teachers was initiated.

Although in 1949 there were 26 government Tamil schools, as well as others run by missions and local residents, three-fifths of all Tamil school enrolments were still on plantations. The government's participation in Tamil education thus remained minimal, and no provision beyond primary school was deemed necessary because a basic knowledge of agriculture and handicrafts was considered sufficient for the needs of an Indian labourer. Parents in search of higher education for their children had no alternative to the English-medium schools, and here the fees were usually prohibitively high for a common labourer. Since English schools had always been envisaged as the preserve of the élite, the British saw no reason to make them affordable or freely available to ordinary children. The manner in which Indian education developed under colonial government thus perpetuated and in fact accentuated the existing divisions in Indian society, separating the middle and upper class, who were primarily urban and English-educated, from the rural and urban poor.

The Chinese in Malaya had long regarded functional literacy – the ability to recognize and use about 2000 Chinese characters – as essential for success. Even in 1794 Francis Light had been struck by the fact that Penang Chinese 'have everywhere people to teach their children, and sometimes they send males to China to complete their education'. As early as 1829 Singapore had both Cantonese and Hokkien schools, and other dialect groups in the Straits Settlements quickly followed; by 1884 it was reckoned that there were around 115 Chinese schools in Penang, Melaka and Singapore. While differing in size, facilities and quality, overseas Chinese schools were all patterned after those which Chinese migrants had known in their homeland, and were commonly established by a district or clan association, or sponsored by wealthy patrons. Fees varied, but were often set very low or in some cases waived altogether in order to make education accessible to the poor. However, it was not easy to meet the rigorous standards of a traditional Chinese education, since genuine scholars well acquainted with the Confucian classics were hard to find in a population of poor migrant labourers. Nor was there the same pool of young men who had failed official examinations and who in China provided a ready supply of teachers. Often the only qualification of so-called teachers was an ability to read and write fluently, while many also combined their teaching roles with those of professional geomancers and fortune-tellers. While there may have been some exposure to classical texts, simplified primers relating the lives of virtuous men provided the basic teaching material. Yet the eagerness with which Chinese boys crowded into often dilapidated and makeshift buildings testifies to parental belief in the necessity of education. Instruction may have involved simply rote-learning and recitation, but these schools played an important role in providing Chinese with rudimentary literacy and numeracy skills.

The willingness and the ability of the Chinese community to provide schools for a growing number of locally born children also relieved the British of any educational responsibility for Malaya's 'transient' Chinese population. However, because local Chinese schools were orientated to China, they were affected by political and intellectual trends in their homeland, especially towards the end of the nineteenth century. From around 1904 this became evident in the appearance of 'new style' schools, which included subjects such as geography and physics, and included English as a foreign language. The founding of schools for girls similarly reflected a greater stress on female education in China itself. The intellectual debates between reformers and revolutionaries in China were also followed closely by all overseas Chinese communities (*huaqiao*), since both sides sent representatives to the 'Southern Seas' to explain their programmes and obtain financial support. Education was a particular target. Under attack from reformers and revolutionaries alike, the Confucian classical tradition now appeared not merely politically bankrupt but associated with the foreign Manchu overlords of China. Chinese newspapers, established in the late nineteenth century, provided an important conduit for information about political developments, as the Republican Revolution in 1911 restored China's self-respect after almost a century of humiliation by Western powers. Growing involvement by the Kuomintang government in the education of *huaqiao* helped politicize Malaya's Chinese schools, fostering a new pride in China's accomplishments, and inculcating the idea of a common 'Chinese' identity. This changing mood was particularly pertinent to Baba and locally born Chinese, many of whom were caught up in a process of resinicization of home and family life that encouraged closer affiliations with more recent migrants. As one writer urged, 'We, Straits Chinese fathers, should encourage our girls in every possible way to give up the Malay language and revert to the Chinese tongue'.[4] Not only were *huaqiao* to be regarded as Chinese nationals, all overseas Chinese schools were deemed part of the Chinese educational system and were thus affected by its policies. In 1917, in an attempt to increase literacy in China and undermine the value of a classical education, China initiated the *baihua*, or written vernacular movement. Three years later China's minister of education mandated the introduction of a form of *baihua* known as *guoyu* (National Language), a compromise between northern and southern Mandarin, for use in primary teaching.

This development had important consequences for Malayan Chinese. Previously instruction had reflected the dialect of the particular Chinese community sponsoring the school, and this tended to perpetuate the cleavages that had been a source of conflict in the nineteenth century. The introduction of *guoyu* as the medium of instruction provided a unifying element, since the Chinese could now communicate with each other in a neutral language which also linked them to the new republican government of China. A critical element in this promotion of 'Chineseness' was the influx of teachers firmly convinced of the righteousness of the revolutionary changes in China and eager to proselytize among overseas Chinese communities. These highly motivated teachers brought with them inspiring nationalistic literature, including blatantly anti-foreign school texts with stories of revolutionary heroes and accounts of China's humiliation by Western nations, especially Japan and Britain.

In itself, the spread of education in the Chinese community was not unacceptable to the colonial government. What was disturbing was the growing recruitment of teachers from China and the involvement of Chinese students in political activities inspired by events in China. The colonial government's disquiet seemed to be justified because of the active role taken in anti-Japanese demonstrations by teachers and students from Chinese schools; in June 1919 the situation became so serious that martial law was imposed in the largely Chinese towns of Singapore and Penang. The nature and scale of such demonstrations forced a fundamental rethinking of British policy towards Chinese education, and inexorably drew the colonial government in Malaya towards a policy of intervention and a reluctant admission of the need for stricter controls. Despite strenuous Chinese opposition, in 1920 and 1921 the Registration of Schools Ordinance introduced new measures to ensure that all schools in Malaya were 'properly conducted'. But a confidential dispatch makes clear that the real target was Chinese schools, and the main purpose of the Ordinance was 'to prevent the teaching of undesirable political doctrines'.[5] More amendments followed: xenophobic elements in

Chinese texts were removed; China-born teachers were restricted; and more government officials were appointed to oversee Chinese education. The provision of federal grants to Chinese schools now entailed greater British control.

With these measures the British abandoned their *laissez-faire* policy towards Chinese education and in practice acknowledged that they were dealing with large numbers of Chinese who considered Malaya their home. In part, these new demographic patterns can be traced to changes within the economic sector. After the introduction of bucket dredges in the early twentieth century, it was no longer necessary for European tin-mining companies to employ large numbers of Chinese labourers. By 1937 as many as 70 per cent of Chinese males were working outside the tin industry, primarily in agricultural and commercial occupations. The increasing pattern of permanent Chinese settlements in the FMS and the growing perception of Malaya as a homeland in the early twentieth century was also reinforced by the growing numbers of Chinese women and children: in 1911 there had been only 215 women for every thousand males, but by 1931 the figure had doubled to 486. By this time, too, almost 30 per cent of Peninsular Chinese were locally born.

The British found, however, that registration and other controls did not eliminate political debates from Chinese schools. Indeed, from the late 1920s, Chinese schools in Malaya, North Borneo and Sarawak increasingly became the battleground of two separate ideologies: that of the government in power in China, the Kuomintang (KMT), and that of the opposition, the Chinese Communist Party (CCP). Like the reformers and revolutionaries who had previously vied for the support of the *huaqiao* communities, the KMT and CCP exerted their own pressure on Chinese education, a situation regarded as particularly dangerous in British eyes because of the introduction of Marxist-Leninist ideas. With the rapid rise of the CCP, the situation deteriorated further as ideology began to take precedence over all other considerations. The political activities in Chinese schools were threatening not merely because of their anti-British message, but also because they directly challenged the economic and social bases of the colonial state. Increasing surveillance during the regime of Sir Cecil Clementi (1929–34) may have forced schools to be more circumspect, but they did not remove the political influences coming from China.

Colonial debates about the most effective policy continued. Should primary education in Malay be used as a means of 'Malayanizing' the population? Could the government afford to convert Chinese schools to English medium? Tentative proposals in this direction were quickly rejected because of the prohibitive cost. In 1938 it was estimated that English schooling for children of all ethnic groups would cost around $16 million. In the event, it was decided that the best means was to work towards a reorientation of the existing structure. In 1935 the Education Department was empowered to introduce changes in Chinese education, to be financed by substantial subsidies. One major step was a teacher-training programme; another was the formal recognition of Mandarin as a medium of instruction. While these measures were an improvement over earlier colonial attitudes, the financial subsidies were inadequate and came too late to overcome a basic Chinese distrust towards British involvement after so many years of neglect.

Nor were the reforms successful in making the Chinese curriculum more 'Malayan' in content. Chinese parents, unenthusiastic about the stress on Malaya in the colonial government's curriculum, believed fervently that education about China was necessary so that their children would not be alienated from their cultural heritage. For them, an orientation towards China was valued precisely because it ensured the preservation of ancestral traditions in their new homeland. Tan Cheng Lock (1883–1960), a prominent Melaka Straits Chinese and the first 'Asian' to be appointed to the Straits Settlements Executive Council, advocated the promotion of a common 'Malayan' identity. Nonetheless, in 1934 he spoke for most Chinese when he argued against the idea of a 'homogeneous' society in which Malay characteristics would predominate. To avoid unwelcome interference, some Chinese schools rejected grants-in-aid, electing instead to receive financial support and school inspectors from the KMT government in China. In the Unfederated Malay States, which did not receive assistance until after the Second World War, local Chinese populations financed schools through donations, patronage, fund-raising campaigns, the imposition of 'taxes', and dues from pupils.

The growing number of such schools was a testimony to Chinese determination to bring education within the reach of all boys. In the Depression years, struggling schools closed, but quickly reopened when the economic situation improved. By 1938 there were over 1000 Chinese schools in the Straits Settlements and the FMS, which served 91 534 pupils and employed nearly 4000 teachers. But under British colonial rule Chinese-medium schools, like their Indian counterparts, did not provide the vehicle for further advancement. There was little demand from parents for Chinese schools beyond primary level, and in 1938 there were only 36 schools with secondary classes. For this reason, it was difficult to recruit locally born teachers. As one authority has recently stressed, neither local Chinese attitudes nor colonial policies encouraged the education of young Chinese who were 'Malayan in their thinking and outlook'.[6] Events such as the Japanese invasion of China in 1937 simply served to fan feelings of loyalty among Malayan Chinese which had been fostered by their school experiences.

As with the Chinese and Indians, the colonial education policy toward Malays reflected the British view of the Malay economic role. Despite the official stance that Malays were masters of their own lands, the extension of colonial control showed only too clearly the extent to which the Malay aristocracy had surrendered authority to the British 'Advisers'. Only the Malay sultans appeared to have maintained and in some cases even enhanced their prestige. By contrast, the numbers of Malay chiefs employed in the State Councils remained small, and the creation of posts such as native magistrate, judges and superintendents of penghulu was insufficient to absorb all the displaced Malay élite. If the latter were to be incorporated into the new governmental structure the British were creating, a fundamental change in their attitudes and skills was required. It was in the hope of instituting such changes that Malays of good background were first encouraged to attend British schools.

Stamford Raffles had earlier foreseen the need to educate 'the sons of the higher order of natives' and towards this end had established the Raffles Institution in Singapore in 1823. His vision, however, was not shared by his successors, and the school failed to live up to expectations. While some Malay princes attended mission schools in the Straits Settlements, two English schools that opened in Perak in 1878 and 1883 had little success in attracting well-born Malays or changing élite attitudes towards an English education. An important exception was Sultan Idris, who ascended the Perak throne in 1887. He had visited London as raja muda (heir apparent), and had been favourably impressed by England's strength and prosperity. This experience apparently convinced him that a modern English education held the key to Malay economic and social progress. Through his initiative a 'Raja Class' was formed in the palace at Perak's royal capital, Kuala Kangsar, in 1888. An arrangement with a British tutor lasted for only a little over a year, but the interest shown soon led to the establishment of the first government English school in Kuala Kangsar, which became known in 1927 as the Clifford School.

Following Perak's lead, the raja muda of Selangor requested British help to form a school for the young princes in his state. In December 1890 the new 'Raja School' of Selangor was inaugurated with an Oxford-trained English clergyman as tutor. The school, said the British Resident of Selangor, W.E. Maxwell, was intended to educate the 'sons of Rajas and Chiefs, whose hereditary influence we desire to be used to the advantage of the State'. Basically, Maxwell saw this education as a means by which Malay sons of rajas and chiefs could be employed as government clerks and other lower officials. The British could then benefit from a trained bureaucracy while 'conciliating' the Malay nobility by increasing their participation in the new governing apparatus. In addition to imparting a good knowledge of English, a principal aim of the school was to 'build character' as understood in Victorian England. The sense of fair play, loyalty, co-operation and class which characterized many English public schools was inculcated in Malay students, no strangers to hierarchy and privilege in their own society. With their traditional attitudes remoulded and reinforced by the British, a common bond bred of similar social backgrounds began to grow between colonial officials and the Malay ruling classes. The Raja School in Selangor closed in January 1894 but any interested Malay student could now study at the Victoria Institution in Kuala Lumpur, which had been established the previous year.

Despite the interest shown by the Perak and Selangor royal families in English education, as yet the openings in government service were insufficient to convince other Malays that English education had any practical value.

This situation changed in 1896 with the formation of the Federated Malay States. As a result, the four state civil services were combined to form the Malayan Civil Service (MCS), leading to an expansion of the administrative and specialist services officered by Europeans. The local clerical and technical staff, most of whom were Jaffna Tamils, Indians, Eurasians and Chinese, also expanded. This aroused some concern among those British officials who felt the government should do far more to fulfil its stated intention of educating the Malay ruling classes in the governing of their lands. Consequently, scholarship schemes were introduced to provide better access to English schools for Malays 'of good birth'. Through these schemes Malays were able to study at English schools where instruction was maintained at a high level, like the Penang Free School, Victoria Institution in Selangor, Taiping Central School (later the King Edward VII School) in Perak, and St Paul's School in Negeri Sembilan. An attempt was also made to include some of the ablest commoner boys from Malay vernacular schools in this programme.

Such measures were clearly inadequate. By the end of the century the numbers of English-educated Malays were still insufficient to fill the government's need for writers, clerks and interpreters. In 1899 Anglo-Malay Departments were added to the Victoria Institution and Kelang Anglo-Chinese School to supplement the scholarship scheme. These departments were to assist in easing boys into an English school by providing one part of their education in English and the other in Malay. On a small scale the scheme was successful, but any thought of extending English education generally to Malay commoners was rejected. Governor-General Frank Swettenham instead proposed that a Malay college be established 'where the best boys from the vernacular schools can be taught to become Malay teachers; and an Institute where a boy can obtain an industrial and technical education'. Swettenham still echoed the early British dual conception of their task regarding the Malays: conciliation of the Malay nobility and minimum interference with the Malay commoners. Greater employment of Malays in government was certainly desirable, but it should be limited to men of 'good birth'.

Concern at the small numbers of Malays in the civil service surfaced at the Second Durbar or Conference of Rulers, which was held in Kuala Lumpur in 1903. Of a Malay population of 310 000 in the FMS, only 2636 were employed by the government, and of these 1175 were policemen. While it had been the intention, if not the avowed policy, of the British eventually to fill the most important posts in state administrations with Malay rajas and chiefs, there was little evidence that this was being effectively implemented. The ruling classes in the FMS looked enviously towards Johor and the Siamese-controlled northern Malay states, where the aristocracy had retained substantial control over their own affairs. Demands by the Malay rulers at the Second Durbar for greater involvement in government, combined with British realization of the increasing costs of employing a disproportionate number of Europeans, succeeded in overcoming most objections to the creation of a Malay residential school for the training of Malay administrators.

In January 1905 the Malay College at Kuala Kangsar was opened. Although it had originally been conceived as a special institution to train Malay boys from royal and noble families for government service, R.J. Wilkinson, the federal inspector of schools, advocated the admission of some commoners. His idea was to cull the best Malays presently attending English schools in the FMS, whatever their rank. However, Wilkinson's removal from the Education Department in 1906 brought a change in policy. Only occasionally were commoners admitted to the college and they were from families closely associated with Malay nobility or royalty. With a total enrolment of around 140, the Malay College became an institution reserved for the traditional élite, being aptly termed 'the Eton of the East' because of its English public school image and the aristocratic backgrounds of its students. The observation of Muslim holidays, attendance at Koran classes and the requirement that students wear Malay dress helped recast the cricket, rugby, prefects and other trappings of the English public school system into a local environment. But while the college brought Malay boys from all over the Peninsula together, the few commoners selected to attend also found that the social distinctions so essential to aristocratic status were rigidly maintained.

The success of the Malay College in providing an English education for upper-class Malay boys forced the government to fulfil its promise of recruiting the better graduates into the administrative service. A scheme drawn up in 1908 and implemented in 1910 was intended specifically to absorb Malay College graduates into the newly created Malay Administrative Service (MAS). The wry Malay nickname for the College, 'Bab ud-Darajat', the Gateway to High Rank, seemed eminently appropriate.

The opening of the Malay College and the subsequent flow of English-trained Malays into government service were tangible evidence to Malay parents of all classes that English education did confer social and economic benefits. This realization was simultaneously reinforced by the expansion of European commercial enterprises requiring ever more English-educated clerks and other officials. Several Malay penghulu asked for English schools to be established in their villages, and others for English classes in the Malay vernacular schools. But British administrators were reluctant to expand the number of English schools, even if teachers had been available. English education continued to be exclusive, especially after 1924 when the British expressed their desire to correlate the numbers of pupils enrolled in English-medium government schools with openings in the civil service. During the 1930s, however, the expansion of government services like the Straits Medical Service, the Straits Settlements Civil Service and the Straits Legal Service created more opportunities for the employment of English-educated Asians, both non-Malays and Malays. In order to maintain the Malay presence, there was an increased admission into English schools of students who had completed four years of primary Malay education. As a result, in the FMS the Malay presence in English-medium schools rose from 9 per cent of all pupils in 1919 to 15 per cent by 1936. Nevertheless, in the same years Chinese pupils accounted for 48 per cent and 50 per cent of total enrolment, and the Indians 30 per cent and 28 per cent.

The colonial attitude towards English education for Malays was well illustrated in the largely agricultural and Malay state of Kelantan. An English school was not considered necessary here because there would be few opportunities for its graduates, and able students were therefore sent to boarding schools on the west coast. The existence of several small private schools points to the local demand for English education, but it was 1936 before a government English school for boys opened in Kota Baru, followed by another two years later for girls. The latter's primary purpose, however, was to train female pupils to be 'alert and quick-minded and suitable wives for Malay officers . . . rather than seek any high standard of technical education.'[7]

What distinguished English-medium from vernacular schools was the possibility for education beyond the primary level. In addition to the normal secondary education, English-educated students could obtain technical and trade skills following the establishment of the Federal Trade School in 1926, the Agricultural College at Serdang and a technical school in 1931. The lack of a university, however, reflected the British fear of creating 'a literary class with no employable skills', and in this regard Malay scholar-administrators like R.J. Wilkinson and R.O.W. Winstedt were particularly influential. In 1923, as director of education for the Straits Settlements and the FMS, Winstedt expressed a view shared by many of his colleagues: 'A university education for the few will not materially affect the difficult social problems of a community of mixed races or directly benefit the economic life of the many'. At the tertiary level, emphasis was therefore away from university training to more vocational courses which would provide students with 'useful' skills. The University of Malaya was not founded until 1949, and even then it was located in the overwhelmingly Chinese environment of Singapore.

A distinctive feature of English education in the Malay Peninsula was the mixed ethnic composition of the classes. Unlike the vernacular schools which catered almost exclusively to a particular ethnic group, Malays, Indians, Chinese, Eurasians and Europeans attended the same English-medium institutions (apart from those specifically reserved for Malays). The shared aspirations of the students, their largely élite origin and the conformity to certain ideals imposed by the English school system helped create a bond which to a considerable extent overcame differences in ethnicity and social background. In mission schools religion could also play a unifying role, though Malays tended to avoid such institutions because of their reluctance to be associated with any religion except Islam. But in the government English schools, a shared language and educational experience for the first time bridged the cultural and linguistic gaps that had separated Malaya's various ethnic groups. In relative terms, however, the percentage of Malays was still low, since these schools were located principally in the urban areas where the Chinese and Indians were concentrated. Girls were particularly disadvantaged: of the 44 English schools in the Straits Settlements and FMS in 1938, only 2 were open to girls. A select college for upper-class girls, which would be the equivalent of the Kuala Kangsar Malay College, was planned for the end of 1941, but never eventuated because of the Japanese Occupation.

Because the vast majority of the Malays lived in rural areas, the formal secular education they received, if any, was at the government Malay vernacular school. Envisaged as agriculturalists, they were provided with the skills necessary 'to carry out the work of their forefathers more efficiently'. Schools would become valuable socializing agents that would prepare Malays to accept their place in colonial society. As Swettenham put it:

> At present the large majority of Malay boys and girls have little or no opportunity of learning their own language, and if the Government undertakes to teach them this, the Koran, and something about figures and geography (especially of the Malay Peninsula and Archipelago), this knowledge and the habits of industry, punctuality and obedience that they will gain by regular attendance at school will be of material advantage to them and assist them to earn a livelihood in any vocation, while they will be likely to prove better citizens and more useful members of the community[8]

Until the early twentieth century the appeal of Malay vernacular schools was very limited. With the transfer of the Straits Settlements to the Colonial Office in 1867, attempts had been made to introduce education in Malay, but by 1882 almost all government schools had closed through lack of attendance. Governor Frederick Weld (1880–8) therefore made a concerted effort to revive the concept of vernacular schooling. Education expenditure was increased, and all teachers were required to be competent in teaching the Koran, literary Malay and simple arithmetic. These new criteria for teachers proved too demanding, and before long the British reluctantly approved the practice of using some of the older pupils as assistant teachers. These apprentices underwent a probationary teaching period of a year or two, and following satisfactory performance were transferred to a school of their own.

A more serious problem, and one less easily resolved, concerned attendance. Despite free instruction and government-provided books and slates, it was difficult for Malays to see the relevance of secular education. The value of studying the Koran was unquestioned, but the need to read and write Malay or to do arithmetic appeared of very limited use to a village Malay. Moreover, many parents required the help of children at home or in the fields. In 1891, for example, there were 12 Malay schools in Selangor with an enrolment of 543 pupils from a Malay population of about 27 000; on any given day, however, only around 370 were present. By the 1880s and early 1890s poor attendance figures finally convinced the British government to attempt the implementation of compulsory education. There were some successes; it was discovered that the newly introduced sport of soccer was so popular that a playing field could be an effective lure. In both Perak and Selangor the incorporation of Koran-reading classes into the curriculum was also an inducement for boys to enrol in the new government schools. Persuading village parents to educate their daughters proved far more difficult, but the 1880s saw the opening of a number of Malay schools for girls, offering Koranic instruction and training in household skills as well as basic literacy. On the whole, however, the numbers of Malay children attending school was low and formal education beyond one or two years was rare.

With the appointment of R.J. Wilkinson as the new federal inspector of schools in May 1903, Malay vernacular education took on a new significance. Wilkinson argued that the whole system of public instruction should be devoted to combating what he believed was a deterioration of Malay culture. Education, he believed, could lay the foundations for new attitudes that would enable Malays to deal with the modern age. As an amateur historian, Wilkinson saw the past as the period of Malay glory, and to preserve this heritage he introduced to the Malay school system the study of Malay literature printed in Rumi (the Malay language in Latin characters). Wilkinson feared that these classical tales, until then available only in Jawi (Malay written in Arabic characters), might remain unread if future generations were more comfortable with romanized Malay. He also hoped that studying Malay classics in Rumi would help to imbue Malays with a renewed appreciation of their heritage. In addition, these publications would be more accessible to other ethnic groups who knew Rumi but not Jawi, and thus foster common bonds based on an understanding of Malay culture. A major advance in textbook production came with the standardization of Malay spelling in 1904. The establishment of small school libraries was intended to allow the Malay community access to the new books, but also to make them available to other ethnic groups. In Wilkinson's views we can thus see some divergence from the official British stance that the Malay Peninsula belonged to the Malays and that the other ethnic groups were transient. His vision of Chinese and Indian children reading Malay classics implies some recognition that migrant communities were becoming a permanent part of the Malayan landscape. In this sense Wilkinson helped sow the seeds of an educational concept which was pursued with greater vigour and urgency by the independent government of Malaya after 1957.

In November 1906 the Education Departments of the Straits Settlements and the FMS were amalgamated and Wilkinson's post as federal inspector abolished. With Wilkinson's strong influence removed, Malay vernacular education was neglected until the appointment of R.O.W. Winstedt as assistant director of education (Malay), a new post approved by the Colonial Office. His tenure as assistant director between 1916 and 1921 and as director between 1924 and 1931 saw a revival in Malay vernacular education. A 'lady supervisor' was also appointed to supervise instruction of Malay girls, and by 1935 a total of 82 Malay-medium girls' schools had been established. While most initiatives were undertaken in the FMS, there were also significant developments in the Unfederated States; in Kelantan the first government Malay school had been opened in 1903, but between 1909 and 1917 the numbers increased to 17.

Expanding Malay education brought an urgent need for more teachers. A teachers' college had been set up in Melaka in 1900 and another in Perak in 1913, but they were clearly inadequate. A new era dawned in 1922 with the founding of the Malay-medium Sultan Idris Training College (SITC) in Tanjong Malim, Perak. The goal of the college was to provide a central teachers' college for the entire FMS system and to train 'all Malay teachers in gardening and elementary agriculture, so that they in turn may introduce scientific methods into the most remote villages'. The government belief that education should not encourage unattainable aspirations among ordinary Malays thus persisted. In the opinion of British administrators a more important aim was the preservation of Malay social structure and the modernization of Malay royalty, a goal which suited the aristocratic English-medium Malay College at Kuala Kangsar rather more than the Malay-medium SITC, where students were of commoner backgrounds. Despite its founders' efforts to encourage a practical agricultural education, virtually from its inception until the outbreak of the Second World War, the SITC stood as the centre of Malay literary activity and provided a platform for Malay spokesmen.

An important stimulant to this new role was the transfer in 1924 of the Malay Translation Bureau from Kuala Lumpur to the SITC. The bureau published textbooks for Malay schools and introduced a Malay Home Library Service in 1929. Its staff of Malay translators also produced a fortnightly newspaper and the *Majallah Guru*, a teachers' magazine, which served as a platform for debating current issues, especially the place of Malays in a changing society. Through their graduates and publications, the SITC and other training colleges disseminated a new awareness of the economic and social problems now confronting Malays. The role of teachers and the opening of new channels of communication are especially apparent in regard to women's issues. Advocates of reform within Islam, such as the editor and writer Sayyid Shaikh al-Hadi (1867–1934), were also outspoken in their support for female education. The same views were expressed by the members of the Union of Johor Women Teachers (Persekutuan Guru-Guru Perempuan Johor) through their monthly journal, *Bulan Melayu* (Malay Monthly, 1930–8). The message was especially pointed because in 1938 in the FMS and Straits Settlements, government Malay boys' schools outnumbered those for girls by more than five to one. The Malay Women's Training College, founded in Melaka in 1935 as the female counterpart of the SITC, concentrated on domestic skills and had no textbooks and no library.

The discussion of 'Malay' issues found another forum in the so-called Islamic *pondok* ('hut') schools, which flourished in all the Unfederated Malay States (UMS). The exception was Johor, where secular and religious education had been placed under the state Education Department, established in

1885. The term *pondok* was derived from the fact that pupils lived in 'huts' close to the place where their religious teacher taught, whether at his home or at a central mosque. Named after the area or the principal scholar, the school's ability to attract students was built on its reputation for religious learning and the environment it provided for the study of Islamic texts, both in Arabic and in Malay translations. Since the colonial presence was far less evident in the UMS than in the FMS, *pondok* schools were unchallenged by the educational developments occurring under British tutelage in the Federated States. During the nineteenth century the *pondok* network in the UMS provided a strong Islamic-based focus for the reaffirmation of Malay identity and unity against their Siamese overlord. After the transfer of the northern Malay states to Britain in 1909, the thrust of this Malay consciousness was directed towards the colonial regime.

The vitality with which Islam imbued the *pondok* schools is exemplified by the famous *ulama* (religious teacher), To' Kenali of Kelantan. Born in about 1868 to a farming family near Kota Baru, To' Kenali's first encounter with Islamic doctrine was at the central mosque, a well-known centre for religious scholarship. At 18 he went to Mecca and later Cairo, where he studied with several eminent religious teachers and was exposed to modernist Islamic ideas. In 1908 To' Kenali returned to Kelantan and began to teach, initially at his 'pondok To' Kenali' and later at the central mosque. So widespread was his reputation that at one point he had as many as 300 pupils from all over the Peninsula, Indonesia (especially Sumatra), Patani and Cambodia.

To' Kenali was characterized by his Socratic method of teaching and his willingness to discuss political issues, introducing his pupils to journals like *Al-Ahram*, *Qullaushai* and *Al-Muqattan*, which presented news on world events from an Islamic viewpoint. Whereas other *ulama* often avoided discussing secular matters, To' Kenali encouraged an examination of problems confronting not only Kelantan but Malay society in general. Several of his pupils, influenced by his knowledge of Islam and international affairs, went on to become religious teachers and writers as well as social critics. Like the products of government Malay vernacular schools in the FMS, former students of *pondok* schools in the UMS were at the forefront of Malay demands for reform within the British colonial system.

In Kelantan the formation of the Majlis Ugama dan Adat Isti'adat Melayu (Council of Religion and Malay Custom) in 1915 represents another important development. Two years later it launched its education programme with the founding of a modernist Islamic school, the Madrasah Muhammadiah, which eventually offered three language streams – English, Arabic and Malay. Though financial restraints prevented the Majlis from incorporating the *pondok* schools, the Madrasah itself prospered. Many of its students continued their education at the Malay College in Kuala Kangsar, at the Penang Free School (established 1816) or at the SITC. Kelantan's Madrasah Muhammadiah was a prime example of the type of education available in the modernist *madrasah* that were developing throughout Malaya and Singapore. In contrast to the more individualistic style of the *pondok* schools, *madrasah* were characterized by a set curriculum and an organizational structure more in keeping with the secular schools. Arabic was the medium of instruction, but every opportunity was provided for the learning of 'modern' subjects like English, mathematics and science. Indeed, the very impetus for the formation of *madrasah* schools was the desire to preserve the 'Islamic-ness' of the Malays. At a time when Malaya appeared to be succumbing in every respect to the British, *madrasah* teachers hoped to demonstrate to their pupils that Islam was not incompatible with change.

Madrasah also made attempts to combine religious learning and vocational training. One school in Perak, for example, offered courses which included commercial subjects, mathematics, history, English, business, and techniques for *padi*-planting and making soap and *kicap* (a type of soy sauce). None the less, their rationale and prime purpose remained religious training, a training which reinforced the belief that to be a Malay was to be a Muslim. By the very nature of their education, students in *pondok* schools and *madrasah* saw Islam as being more important in constituting 'Malayness' than did their contemporaries from the colonial government's vernacular schools. The continuing debate on the place of Islam in Malay identity was to gather force as graduates of the religious schools joined their counterparts from secular vernacular institutions to become the Malay-educated intelligentsia of the 1920s and 1930s.

Thus, with the exception of English-medium schools, the educational systems in Malaya all emphasized a distinct ethnic culture and history that helped preserve separate group identities. This development was not actively fostered by the British: on the contrary, it arose through colonial inactivity. From the beginning of their involvement, in the nineteenth century, the British regarded the Peninsula as naturally Malay. But although the influx of large numbers of Chinese and Indian labourers brought a radical demographic shift, by the outbreak of the Second World War British attitudes were only beginning to accommodate the new realities. The Chinese and Indians were long regarded as transitory labourers whose ultimate goal was to return home with their hard-earned wealth. The fact that the migrant communities lived apart from each other, conducting their own affairs like separate nations under a British overlord, aroused little concern. The Malay ruling classes were reconciled to the conception/deception that, directed by the British, alien Asian communities were needed to extract the riches from Malay soil for the ultimate welfare of the Malay community. Even though Malays comprised less than half the Peninsula's total population in 1921, the presence of these alien Asians was considered a temporary phenomenon. Their immediate needs should be satisfied but they did not need to be incorporated into any long-term planning. To some extent this view was encouraged by the extent of Chinese and Indian mobility: in 1921, for example, 191 043 Chinese arrived and 98 986 left, while in Penang there were 95 220 Indian arrivals and 55 481 departures. The British government thus felt justified in adopting a *laissez-faire* policy towards the education of Chinese and Indian children, and only later became actively involved in Chinese schools in response to direct and increasingly disruptive political influences from China.

Education in Sarawak and North Borneo

Although the Borneo states had become British protectorates in 1888, their educational development reflected the philosophies of their respective rulers, the British North Borneo Company and the Brooke family. In Sarawak a systematic approach to education was first introduced by Raja Charles Brooke. While he appreciated the values of a Western education, he wanted Sarawak to stand apart from British colonies like Malaya, where he felt local cultures had been suppressed by educational policies. To put his beliefs into practice, at the turn of the twentieth century Charles Brooke established a 'Government Lay School' in Kuching, where Malay boys were taught in Malay and Chinese boys in Mandarin. From 1904 to 1911 similar schools, and sometimes separate Chinese and Malay ones, were set up in many outstations. After 1912 the government withdrew from the field of Chinese education, since independent Chinese schools began to proliferate and others were opened by Christian missionaries. Although these independent schools received minimal government support, they were able to survive because the flourishing rubber industry made the imposition of fees viable. As on the Peninsula, Chinese schools played a critical role in reinforcing the sense of being Chinese and of belonging to a specific language group.

Government Malay schools continued to exist side by side with traditional Malay schools under religious teachers. True to his philosophy, Charles Brooke refused to 'tamper' with the lifestyle of the indigenous groups, particularly the Ibans, by subjecting them to Western education. Instead, he allowed missions to establish schools and provided them with an initial subsidy for a building as well as an annual grant. The Anglican Society for the Propagation of the Gospel was given charge of all Iban education in the Second Division, and the Roman Catholic Mission of the few schools in the Third Division.

A striking feature of government and mission efforts was the low enrolment of Iban and Dayak pupils. By 1936 the 2086 students in the 25 government schools for Malays and Muslim Melanaus included only six Ibans and one Land Dayak; the mission schools had a somewhat better record, with 339 Ibans and 296 Land Dayaks. By contrast, three-quarters of Sarawak's total school population of about 14 000 were Chinese attending independent Chinese and mission schools. In 1935, under the direction of C.D. Le Gros Clark, a report was compiled that proposed wide-ranging changes in the educational system. These included the appointment of a director of education and an Education Board composed of representatives from the missions and the people; an upgraded *Madrasah Melayu* to groom village schoolteachers and native officers for administration; and technical and agricultural instruction at the village level. But there was little support for the report's assumption that there should be a gradual transfer of the administration to local hands, and by 1941 the only results of the recommendations were a director of education and a Malay Teachers' College.

Education in North Borneo prior to 1909 was principally in the hands of missions, though there were a few Chinese and Muslim schools. In 1919, however, an Education Department was formed with inspectors of schools appointed for both the east and west coasts. The government also continued its grants to mission schools. The first government vernacular school was established at Jesselton (Kota Kinabalu) in 1915 to train sons of native chiefs in a three-year course given in Malay. But because there was no Koran study, most of the Muslim chiefs soon withdrew their sons, and only the Muruts of the interior continued to attend. To remedy this situation, in 1923 the government introduced instruction in the Koran and in English, both of which helped restore the school's popularity. Emulating colonial policy in Malaya, the North Borneo Company encouraged Malay education as an alternative to the English-medium and government-subsidized mission schools. However, by 1934 only eight Malay vernacular schools had been established, with an enrolment of around 400 pupils, virtually all boys who were Muslims or who came from homes sympathetic to Muslim culture.

Under Governor D.J. Jardine (1934–7) greater attention was given to Malay education, but since the Company sought the advice of R.O. Winstedt, it is not surprising that the curriculum was closely modelled on that of the FMS. As in Malaya, government vernacular schools were seen as providing basic education to equip boys to become better cultivators, and despite requests from local community leaders the teaching of English was not included. On the other hand, physical education was introduced so that pupils would have the 'strong and healthy bodies ... so essential to a cultivator'. Other 'useful' subjects were added to the basic curriculum of Malay language study: arithmetic, geography and hygiene, although the advantages of gardening and basketry for boys who were products of a long indigenous tradition of horticulture and basket-making are unclear. Female education, however, was accorded little attention. Muslim parents in particular were opposed to co-education, and the state of Company finances precluded separate schools for native girls.

Female attendance was higher in the English schools run by the missions, which also increased during this period. Block grants from the government helped ease their financial burdens without bringing interference in curriculum planning. In general, the mission schools reached a standard that enabled their students to pass the Cambridge University Syndic examination instituted in 1933. Within a few years the combined demands of Malay vernacular education and mission schools imposed such a financial strain on the government that it decided to channel most financial support to its own schools. The government of North Borneo was satisfied to leave Chinese vernacular education almost wholly to the Chinese communities, subject only to an annual inspection. By 1940 there was a total of 10 993 students enrolled in Malay vernacular, mission and Chinese schools throughout North Borneo; of these, however, only 1663 were registered with the 28 government schools.

Because of the complexity of local societies and languages, and the particular policies of the North Borneo and Sarawak governments, education for indigenous groups did not provide the same nurturing environment for cultural identity as did vernacular schools in Malaya. Malay and English speakers continued to dominate the government bureaucracies in both states, and the children from indigenous groups who did receive formal schooling were taught in an alien language. Enrolment in Malay-medium government schools or English mission schools certainly provided a path to advancement, but exposure to Islam and Christianity simply contributed to the many adjustments demanded by a changing environment.

Ethnicity and identity

Though often deeply divisive, the ideological debates which raged in China during the first decades of the twentieth century were rooted in a growing commitment to a Chinese nation rather than to a region, clan or language group. In Malaya, supporters of the KMT and CCP may have been bitterly opposed, but those who shared political beliefs found that a common sense of identity did bridge some of the differences which had previously cut through *huaqiao* society.

Despite new linkages, however, barriers of class remained. Social divisions were especially pronounced between vernacular-educated Chinese, often migrants, and those who had attended English schools, especially when the latter had been born in the Straits and were thus British subjects. This gap was widened during the economic Depression of 1931–3 when there was great unemployment among the working-class Chinese population, and when many Straits Chinese were anxious to demonstrate their loyalty to the colonial government by distancing themselves from more radical groups. The founding of the Malayan Communist Party in 1930, with its roots in Chinese immigrant society and the Chinese nationalist organizations of the 1920s, reflected this social and economic divide. From the early twentieth century rural Chinese squatter settlements had begun to spring up whenever there was a slump in tin prices, and their numbers were swelled again during the Depression when the industrial collapse in the West led to a catastrophic drop in the demand for rubber and tin. While the government paid for the repatriation of many labourers, those who remained and who had lost their jobs or were simply unable to exist on reduced wages were often drawn to the

MCP. Chinese settlers were encouraged to become involved in food cultivation, but the British were unwilling to convert Temporary Occupation Licences of potential mining land into permanent title. The tenure of Chinese squatters who had retreated to the jungle margins to eke out a living, in some cases intruding into Malay Reservations, was especially insecure. Such people were naturally receptive to the MCP message.

The divisions of caste, language, occupation, religion and social status made unity even more difficult among Malayan Indians. The effects of the independence movement in India and the views of leaders like M.K. Gandhi were belatedly felt in Malaya during the 1930s as middle-class and English-educated Indians tried to forge bonds with the largely Tamil estate workers. Bridge-building efforts, however, were adversely affected by the Depression, which hit estate labourers hard. The often cavalier attitude with which estate labourers were dismissed, and the abyss between them and wealthier urban Indians inevitably led to a sharpening of class-consciousness. In this climate, the opening of an upper-caste temple in Penang to Untouchables in 1935 was a real comment on new efforts to overcome centuries of prejudice. In 1936 the Central Indian Association of Malaya was formed to safeguard the interests of Indians, and the following year its leaders invited Jawaharlal Nehru to visit Malaya. During the 1930s there were several instances of labour militancy and strikes involving Indian workers as a new group of working-class Indian leaders began to emerge.

Within Malay society the 1920s and 30s were equally a period of ferment, which saw new articulations of what it meant to be 'Malay'. A sense that Malay culture was imperilled was undoubtedly enhanced by the growing presence of foreign Asians, and the revelation in 1931 that there were more Chinese (1 709 392) in British Malaya than Malays (1 644 173). The world-wide Depression of the 1930s, which exposed the vulnerability of Malaya's export economy, also exacerbated economic competition among the ethnic communities. This competition was least evident at the highest levels of Malay society, where the aristocratic élite was cushioned by the privileges extended to them by the British policy of conciliation. Malay rulers had a long history of co-operation with leading Chinese merchants, and in the colonial period these links between privileged Chinese and Malays were fostered by the common experience of an English education and their acceptance of their own social status. Chinese representation on the Federal Council and State Councils, albeit as Unofficial Members, also helped bring Chinese leaders and the Malay élite together in a wary but workable relation-ship. Even so, well-born and English-educated Malays were apprehensive at Chinese and Indian pressure to open up the civil service to non-Malays.

At the lower levels of government the undercurrent of ethnic distrust was far greater. The lack of English-educated Malays meant that by 1920 immigrant and locally born Indians and Chinese dominated clerical and technical ranks in all departments of the colonial administration. In a 1923 essay deploring the material and educational poverty of Malays, which 'enveloped them on all sides', the influential Malay intellectual Zaʿba (Zainal Abidin bin Ahmad, 1895–1973) foresaw a bleak future, when Malays would be left behind in the 'march of nations' and the 'race of progress'. At that time there were perhaps 700–800 Malays enrolled in English schools in the FMS; by 1933 this figure had increased to 2464. But while the 1920s saw a rise in the numbers of Malay commoners appointed to clerical and semi-technical positions in the civil service, unemployment during the Depression heightened the competition between Malays and non-Malays for these subordinate but desirable posts. Furthermore, there were also subtle divisions amongst English-educated Malays themselves. In the Unfederated States, Johor and Kedah had managed to ensure that local Malays were employed in preference to those from the FMS, but this was less possible in Kelantan and Terengganu, where graduates of English schools were few. When FMS Malays gained civil service posts in the east coast states, they were often regarded with as much resentment as non-Malays. By the same token, west coast officers sent to work in an isolated area like Ulu Pahang felt they had been effectively exiled. And threading through the privileged world of government employment was the ever-present distinction between Malays of good birth and those of commoner background. Malays relegated to subordinate positions were not necessarily willing to see the old links between ruler and subject as inviolable, or to accept that direction of the Malay community should automatically be entrusted to the ruling class.

Modernist Islamic leaders were also alert to these debates. As Arabic-educated Malay scholars returned from the Middle East, they reiterated the old message that the renovation of Islam was the only means by which Malays could respond effectively to colonialism and the economic dominance of non-Muslims. In the face of outspoken comments from locally born Indians and Chinese who regarded Malaya as their home, this message acquired a new relevance. In 1931, for example, Sayyid Shaikh al-Hadi's reformist journal *Al-Ikhwan* (The Brotherhood) published a Malay version of a speech by a Chinese member of the Straits Settlements Legislative Council. The headline read 'The Chinese say the Peninsula is their country, not that of the Malays.'[9] But in reinforcing the religion–race connection which had long distinguished Malays from other ethnic groups in the Peninsula, these modernizing Muslims placed discussions about the future of the Malay nation or *bangsa* within the framework of a larger Muslim community, the *'ummat*. Writings and teachings produced from this perspective were often critical of those co-operating with the colonial authorities, and the status differences that were embedded in the traditional *kerajaan*. Not surprisingly, reform-minded Muslims frequently met opposition from the more conservative Islamic hierarchy, of which the sultan was the formal head. Though the strength of Muslim reformism was in urban centres such as Penang and Singapore, reverberations were also felt in rural society as a new generation of *ulama* questioned the localization of Islamic practices and the privileges of the ruling class. Yet even in the reaffirmation of Malay identity, links to a wider *'ummat* opened up further debates about the extent to which Muslims of mixed ancestry should be considered 'Malay'. Stressing the inclusiveness of Malay-Islamic tradition, Za'ba argued strongly that Malay-Muslims, whether of Indian, Arab or Thai descent, were indeed part of the same culture.

Although the debates about what it meant to be 'Malay' received particular attention from a new intelligentsia that included Malay administrators, teachers and journalists, here too there was a range of viewpoints. The state Malay Associations that were formed from 1938 were committed to the preservation of Malay interests, but their loyalty was primarily oriented towards their specific state. Since well-born MAS officers were often appointed as presidents and secretaries, it is not surprising that the Malay Associations were generally noted for their conservative stance, and their anxiety to be differentiated from left-wing and Islamic modernist groups. Their major concern was to ensure that the Malay élite was accorded a greater role in public affairs, and that the Malay community at large was given more access to education and civil service positions. On the other hand, there was also an awareness of the need to appeal to the wider Malay population, to whom they appeared as natural leaders. One important initiative was the founding of the newspaper *Utusan Melayu* in 1939 by the Singapore Malay Association. While avoiding direct criticism of the colonial authorities, *Utusan Melayu*, like other Malay-language journals, periodically featured articles hostile to the encroachment of migrant groups into Malay life. The paper also tried to give space to all the state Associations, reflecting a recognition of the need for Peninsula-wide co-ordination. Accordingly, a Pan-Malayan Malay Congress was convened in Kuala Lumpur in August 1939, and another in Singapore in December 1940. The latter meeting was attended by eleven state Associations, including Sarawak and Brunei. They were unable, however, to reach agreement on how to constitute a pan-Malayan organization.

The same group of teachers, administrators and journalists also produced more radical Malays. Often graduates of the SITC who had been assigned to village schools, they were particularly conscious of the effects of the Depression, as rubber prices fell and indebted Malay smallholders struggled to survive. Although a number had also received some English education, in writing and in public addresses they were fervent advocates of the Malay language and of expanded educational opportunities for Malays. The more extreme were highly critical of the establishment, by which they meant not merely the British colonial government but the traditional ruling classes. In their view, the *kerajaan* mentality was incapable of instituting the far-reaching changes they considered necessary. In Sarawak, for example, the writings of an SITC graduate, Haji Muhammad Bujang, censored the alliance between local leaders and the Brooke regime and their lack of provision for the Malay future. Such individuals also called for a restoration of an older Malay community, a 'Greater Melayu' or 'Greater Indonesia' that pre-dated colonial boundaries and would rise above parochial state concerns. The rallying cry of *Hidup Bahasa, Hiduplah Bangsa!* (Long live the Language, Long Live

the Nation!) became an emotional focus around which to assert Malay interests. It was members of this group who in late 1938, under the leadership of
Ibrahim Yaacob (1911–79) and Burhanuddin Al-Helmy (1911–69), founded
the Kesatuan Melayu Muda (Young Malay Union), a nationalist organization
very similar to the left-wing youth groups springing up throughout the
Netherlands East Indies.

By the end of the 1930s British officials in Malaya had become deeply
concerned at the growth of radical ideas, especially those that threatened the
socioeconomic framework on which colonial government rested. The primary focus, however, was on the Chinese community, where it was only too
evident that the government's inaction in regard to education had been a
major contributor to the propagation of left-wing ideas. Anti-colonial May
Day rallies in 1940 and subsequent strikes promoted strong reaction by the
authorities, and by July more than 200 communist leaders in Singapore and
Malaya had been arrested. Ironically, just as the British finally recognized
the reality of permanent Chinese and Indian communities within Malaya,
and accepted the corresponding need to adjust their previous attitudes,
world-wide events overtook the country. The economic retraction caused by
the Depression followed by the outbreak of the Second World War in 1939
prevented the colonial government from reversing even slightly the divisive
trends in the Malay Peninsula to which their economic and educational
policies had directly contributed.

Colonial government and the Malay rulers

In the 1920s and 1930s arguments about Malaya's future, and the way in
which economic and political power would be allocated, took on an added
sharpness because of the so-called 'decentralization debate'. While the
majority of Malaya's inhabitants were unaware of the often-heated discussions between colonial officials, the controversy raised critical questions
about the rationale for supporting Malay rulers and maintaining state
boundaries. For the British, indirect rule had long been seen as indispensable to maintaining authority over the Malay population. Although some
officials reported a lessening of respect for the rulers in certain circles, the
prestige of sultans within their own states and their hold over rural Malays
was repeatedly made evident. But despite the historical and cultural traditions of individual states, arguments in favour of economic efficiency and
administrative rationalization resulted in the establishment of the Federated
Malay States in 1896 and the Federal Council in 1909. The practical effect of
these centralization efforts was to relegate the Malay sultan and his State
Council to 'traditional' Malay affairs, interpreted by the British as matters
dealing with Islam and Malay ceremonial. As early as 1903 a memorandum
from the Resident-General acknowledged that the relationship between

rulers and residents was the reverse of that laid down in the original Pangkor Treaty. Instead of the sultan administering with the advice of the Resident, it was the Resident who administered, seeking the sultan's advice only when he considered it necessary. The refusal of the UMS sultans to join the FMS was a telling comment on the value they placed on retaining traditional royal powers.

Though the loss of authority by Malay rulers had caused concern among some officials, it only became a subject of debate in the Federal Council in 1922 when the economic recession after the First World War led to a re-examination of policy. The call for greater administrative economy was also prompted by a feeling that the FMS, under the chief secretary, was over-centralized and unduly expensive. The obvious solution was to relinquish more governmental duties to the states, a policy which the rulers of the FMS themselves strongly favoured. Although British Residents in the FMS were always instructed to rule by persuasion, rulers had been dismayed at their own dwindling control over state affairs. They were also aware of the contrast with the UMS, where Advisers seemed more willing to consult the sultan and his council and were reluctant to override concerted Malay objections. The invidious comparison with their own position was a source of considerable resentment among FMS rulers, despite the more extensive wealth they had acquired through the new export industries. Indeed, on a visit to England in 1924 the sultan of Perak specifically asked the secretary of state for the colonies to transfer some of the federal government's powers back to FMS rulers.

The move towards decentralization gained momentum in 1925 when High Commissioner Sir Laurence Guillemard, with Colonial Office approval, announced his intention of abolishing the chief secretaryship. Its powers would then gradually devolve to the state councils, Residents, and federal heads of departments. Although the FMS sultans welcomed these suggestions, Guillemard's proposals were ultimately set aside because of pressure from European and Chinese business interests. In lobbying against decentralization, the latter raised the bogey of pre-Federation days. In their view, returning powers to the states could lead to a lack of support for export industries, and a consequent decline in confidence among the all-important capital investors overseas. They were also reluctant to see the abolition of the chief secretaryship, since they believed that Peninsular interests would then be subordinated to the colony of Singapore, the home base of the high commissioner. Guillemard bowed to these pressures by preserving the chief secretaryship and making only a few gestures towards decentralization. Increased financial responsibility was given to the State Councils, and four more members were added to the Federal Council. But an unfortunate consequence of Guillemard's proposals was an agreement signed with all four FMS sultans in 1927 by which they could be represented at Federal Council meetings by the Residents. As a result, they effectively relegated almost total powers over legislation to the British. Their official powers in government were limited to attaching their signatures to laws passed by the council and attending the Durbar, the annual meeting of rulers.

The question of decentralization again arose in 1931, when the export economy was reeling from the effects of the global Depression, and it again seemed that useful economies could be made by delegating more responsibility to the states. On this occasion decentralization found a champion in the High Commissioner, Sir Cecil Clementi, who argued that support for the rulers was essential to safeguard Malaya against the turbulence threatened by a 'modern democracy'. Furthermore, Clementi's African experience made him a vigorous proponent of indigenous rights, and he was convinced that the gradual extension of British control in the FMS was at variance with their treaties with the Malay sultans. In addition to proposals that were very similar to Guillemard's, Clementi also advocated the complete dissolution of the FMS as a prelude to a future Pan-Malayan Union which would encompass all the Peninsular states. But again questions were raised, especially about the treatment of Chinese and Indians under the rule of Malay sultans whom some elements in the Colonial Office saw as potentially 'autocratic'. In such circles it was even said that the Malay rulers were anachronistic in a Malaya where the future 'lay in the hands of Chinese and Indians'. As before, there was opposition from commercial interests in the FMS who were satisfied with the status quo and were wary of any new administrative structure. They were particularly apprehensive of subordination to Singapore, whose economic goals often diverged from those of the FMS. On the Malay side, while FMS rulers were enthusiastic about the prospect of enhanced powers, Clementi's idea of an eventual Pan-Malayan Union aroused protests from the UMS, where the sultans feared the same loss of authority they had witnessed among their fellow rulers in the FMS.

These debates foreshadowed the arguments that were to resurface after the Second World War when the proposal for a Malayan Union was revived. The central issue was plainly stated in 1932 by Sir Samuel Wilson, permanent under-secretary of state for the colonies. He recognized that from an economic point of view 'it would no doubt be advisable in a country the size of Malaya to have one central government administering the whole territory'. On the other hand, he saw the need for greater states' rights because the Malay sultans were clearly discontented with their rapidly diminishing authority. In arguing for decentralization, Wilson advocated a more gradual pace than hitherto, and reiterated the stand which had always adumbrated official pronouncements, whatever their practical outcome:

The maintenance of the position, authority and prestige of the Malay Rulers must always be a cardinal point in British policy: and the encouragement of indirect rule will probably prove the greatest safeguard against the political submersion of the Malays which would result from the development of popular government on Western lines. For in such a government the Malays would be hopelessly outnumbered by the other races owing to the great influx of immigrants that has taken place.[10]

The subsequent decision to work towards decentralization raised serious questions about the calibre and quality of state governments and the capacity of individual rulers. The dearth of Malays with adequate administrative training raised fears that the states would not have sufficient experienced personnel to deal with the new responsibilities that would result from the devolution of power. The choice was between 'a substantial amount of power conferred upon an enlarged and cosmopolitan state council, or a small amount of power conferred on the old type of state council'.[11] Clementi's decision in favour of the first alternative meant the State Councils were enlarged with additional Chinese, Indian and European members. Against this background it is hardly surprising that in all states the rulers became patrons for the new Malay Associations, which staunchly affirmed the inviolability of Malay rights.

Other developments reinforced the move towards increasing state powers, albeit under the British aegis. In 1935 the chief secretaryship was abolished and by 1939 the Departments of Agriculture, Education, Forestry, Medical Services, Mining and Public Works were largely under the direction of individual states. Legislative powers had been divided between the Federal and State Councils, although one clause gave the Federal Council the power to legislate on 'all projects of substantive law not otherwise enumerated which are intended to have force throughout the Federation', and on any other subject determined by the high commissioner 'to be within his competency'. The Federal Council also retained substantial financial control, despite decentralization measures. Each state received an annual block grant from the Federal Council, but the latter supervised its expenditure. The Federal Council still wielded considerable authority, of which the rulers were periodically reminded. In 1934, for example, the high commissioner directly intervened in the Selangor succession to oppose the sultan's choice as raja muda. Furthermore, even though the restoration of some powers to the sultans and the states was far more than a token gesture, the Colonial Office hoped that decentralization would ultimately lead to the incorporation of all Malay states into some kind of constitutional unity. Perhaps ironically, the steps the British had taken helped revive the loyalties attached to the traditional Malay *kerajaan* and to harden resistance to the idea of a dominating centre.

Such attitudes were, of course, particularly evident in the Unfederated Malay States (UMS). Like the FMS, they were 'juridically independent and practically dependent' on the British. However, there was one significant difference: the Malay environment of the UMS administrations was more pronounced, and the opinions of the sultans and their councils had considerable influence on the decisions of the British Advisers. As in the FMS, the political evolution of these states had been affected by economic factors. Johor had become a valuable hinterland for pioneering Chinese agriculturalists from Singapore who cleared virgin land to plant tapioca, pepper, gambier and, from 1910, rubber. Rail and road links between west coast states and

Singapore integrated Johor into the economy of this whole area. Chinese and Indian immigrants involved in the rubber industry added to those Chinese already engaged in agricultural pursuits. By 1931 Chinese and Indians comprised 52.3 per cent of Johor's population, making it the only Unfederated Malay State where Malays were not in the majority. The extensive agricultural and mining concerns which transformed Johor resembled those of the FMS, necessitating certain changes in the style of government. Unlike their FMS counterparts, however, Johor rulers and their Advisers were successful in negotiating a considerable degree of independence.

Of the four northern states which made up the rest of the UMS, Perlis was the smallest. With a population of less than 60 000, it remained basically a Malay rice-growing state highly dependent upon Kedah. In contrast to the situation in Selangor, the Colonial Office in 1937 avoided any direct intervention during questions over the ruler's succession. The larger neighbour of Perlis, Kedah, also enjoyed considerable Malay political control, especially after an agreement with the British in 1923 affirmed the ruler's suzerain rights and the place of Malay as the official language. Like Johor, Kedah was governed by capable leaders who were able to limit the degree of British influence and thus preserve the state's Malay character. Economic developments in Kedah likewise resembled those in Johor, as rail and road communication strengthened links to ports and towns along the west coast, and Chinese capital and labour flowed in from Singapore's northern counterpart, Penang. But despite the spread of European and Chinese rubber estates, economic changes in Kedah never reached the level experienced in Johor, and were confined primarily to the southern areas. Along the border with Siam and in Ulu Kedah were pockets of rural poverty and marginalized groups such as the mixed Malay–Thai Sam-Sam. The incidence of lawlessness and membership in secret brotherhoods in these areas can be interpreted not merely as criminal activity but as a response to the increasing gap between rich and poor. Although by 1930 the reorganization of the Kedah police force had led to a reduction in rural crime, the names of bandits are still invoked as folk heroes and champions of the disenfranchised.

Rural poverty was also evident in Kelantan and Terengganu, which were still the most inaccessible of the Malay states, with railway links to Kelantan being completed only in 1931 and to Terengganu a few years later. Monsoon winds and high seas also closed both states to shipping for several months each year. These difficulties, coupled with the historical lack of commercial interest in the east coast, discouraged large-scale capital investment. The pattern of *padi*-planting and small-scale sea and river fishing continued to characterize the economic patterns of their predominantly Malay populations at a time when the other Peninsular states were experiencing rapid economic and social changes wrought by the tin and rubber industries. In Kelantan, even after 30 years of British administration, the public sector and private commercial operations employed less than 2 per cent of the total population as wage-earners. This did not mean, however, that peasants did not feel the effects of new taxes, fees, duties, licences and fines imposed by the colonial government. The 1928 revolt in Terengganu can be seen as evidence of deep-felt frustrations, not only against the colonial regime but against the upper class who were its allies.

The divergent economic and political developments of the FMS, UMS and the Straits Settlements meant that by 1941 the colonial goal of creating some kind of greater administrative unity for British Malaya was still unfulfilled. Despite general agreement that a union for Malaya was ultimately desirable, established political and commercial interests distrusted any change. Those within the FMS did not want an expansion of their administrative unit, which they found sufficient for their purposes. They feared control by Singapore and the prospects of bearing the financial cost of assisting in the development of the poorer states of the UMS. UMS rulers were apprehensive that the introduction of foreign capital and labour would lead to a loss of sovereignty and Malay control. The Colony of the Straits Settlements saw little benefit in becoming a part of a union where it would lose its advantage of free trade. In theory many were in favour of a union, but the reality frightened the vested Malay, European and Chinese interests. There was thus little progress towards a unification of these separate political entities. Furthermore, although powerful and influential voices had begun to question the value of indirect rule, the constitutional relationship that bound rulers and the British together was highly resistant to change. In August 1941, four months before the Japanese invaded Malaya, the high commissioner reaffirmed Britain's intention to respect its treaties with the Malay sultans and to maintain the sultans' interests in their separate states.

Final years of Company and White Raja rule in Borneo

In both North Borneo and Sarawak the early twentieth century brought a noticeable change in governmental styles. The death in 1910 of W.C. Cowie, managing director of the British North Borneo Company, removed a strong hand from North Borneo's affairs; in Sarawak, the dominating Raja Charles Brooke died in 1917, to be replaced by his less assertive elder son, Vyner. In each case the passing of these giant personalities heralded the end of individualistic rule and of isolation from international economic and political forces. The growing engagement of the Borneo states with the world economy meant that they were increasingly affected by external influences. Technological and administrative advances introduced in British Malaya were soon brought to Borneo, albeit on a modified scale adapted to the local situation.

In North Borneo salaries and pension schemes were made more comparable with those of the British Colonial Service; new Departments of Education and Forestry were established, and in 1915, a Native Chiefs' Advisory Council. Closer links between the Colonial Office in London and the Company directors were forged through an arrangement by which the latter received all general directives and circulars to the Colonial Service, Acts of Parliament pertaining to the colonies, Orders in Council and Royal Proclamations. In North Borneo itself the administration tended to implement ideas and techniques introduced from Malaya and to rely on staff recruited from there. A Legislative Council was introduced in 1912 with seven official and four unofficial members to represent the Chinese community, business interests and planters on the east and west coasts. But the Native Chiefs' Council lay moribund for many years, and though revived in 1935 its recommendations were only influential when permitted by Company finances and general policy. There was no sustained effort to increase political participation among the indigenous peoples of North Borneo or to awaken any sense of common purpose. By 1941 the concerns of vested economic interests were still the prime factor in shaping government policy.

In Sarawak the Brooke government had operated on the principle of the allotted roles of the Malay as administrator, the Chinese as trader and cash-crop farmer and the Iban as police and soldier. Furthermore, while other indigenous groups such as the Bidayuh, Melanau, Kenyah and Kayan remained generally outside the scope of government policy, administrative attitudes always favoured the amalgamation of smaller groups into one of the larger categories. The Muslim Melanau, for example, were encouraged to become 'Malay', while the other non-Muslim indigenous peoples were often categorized with the Iban despite their obvious rejection of Iban values. On the other hand, this simple logic of the Sarawak rulers did nurture a sense of one Iban people, an ideal which eventually helped to overcome the reality of numerous distinctive and often rival groups.

In 1915, only two years before his death, Charles had decided to modify the authoritarian nature of Brooke government by introducing a new Committee of Administration, although this would be composed wholly of European officials. It was to operate alongside the old Supreme Council, composed of the Kuching Malay chiefs, which was now regarded as an anachronism. Three years earlier he had also organized a State Advisory Council in Britain to oversee Sarawak's finances. These measures were prompted in part by Charles's lack of confidence in the ability of his son and successor to maintain a stable government in Sarawak without help, and in part by the rapid economic and administrative changes in other British colonies. Sarawak could no longer avoid involvement in events beyond its borders, and Charles hoped his measures would assure the smooth transition of Sarawak into the twentieth century.

During the regime of the third White Raja, Vyner Brooke, these institutional innovations were neglected, and the Supreme Council no longer met after 1927. Nevertheless, Sarawak had become part of the world economy and was much more closely linked to the other British colonies than before. Administration became more bureaucratic and rationalized, with a written criminal code based on the Indian Penal Code introduced in 1923 and a Legal Department in 1928. More departments were created, municipal administration introduced in Kuching and Sibu, and a chief secretary appointed with a Secretariat in Kuching.

Many of these changes occurred in spite of Raja Vyner, who spent much of his time in England. Government in the 1930s was principally in the hands of the chief secretary, and executive power gradually began to be assumed by the Kuching bureaucracy. Although residents were told to regard the chief secretary as 'co-ordinator' and themselves as part of 'one united Sarawak',[12] the moves towards centralization evinced relatively little regard for the 'interests of the natives', the *raison d'être* of Brooke rule. The future of the White Rajas was itself in question, since Vyner had no son and was wary about the ambitions of his nephew, Anthony. These concerns, coupled with his anxiety to provide long-term financial security for his family, led him to think seriously of selling Sarawak to Britain or of having a British General Adviser appointed to govern in his absence. Significantly, even in the early 1930s Clementi was suggesting a 'federation of British Borneo'.

In July 1939 the British government suggested that a General Adviser be appointed to Sarawak, with the occasional secondment of officers from Malaya. One was indeed posted in early 1940, but his tenure was brief. On 24 September 1941, in the week celebrating the centenary of Brooke rule, Vyner proclaimed a Constitution which altered the regime's individualistic nature and remodelled the old Council Negeri and the Supreme Council so that they resembled the legislative and executive councils of the British colonies. The Constitution was approved by the British government, and by October 1941 Colonial Office plans for assuming control over Sarawak's internal affairs were well advanced. A British Resident was to be appointed whose powers were undoubtedly intended to equal those in Malaya. However, before any of these plans could be effectively implemented the Japanese invasion had begun.

During the first half of the twentieth century the success of Malaya's export economy was primarily due to direct governmental intervention that deliberately aimed to attract European capital and expertise. In the passage towards this goal the British allocated broad economic roles to each of Malaya's ethnic groups: as colonial masters, the Europeans provided the skilled personnel; the Chinese and Indians were labourers and entrepreneurs who would eventually return to their homelands; the Malays should be left to their 'traditional' occupations such as fishing and farming. This simplistic conception was modified by the need for local English-educated clerks and administrators to staff the expanding government bureaucracy and business enterprises, and by the government's commitment to 'conciliate' the Malay ruling classes through their involvement in the administration. Such considerations allowed a few privileged members to rise above the economic functions envisaged for their particular ethnic group.

Having drawn up this economic blueprint, the British could then fulfil their self-conceived role as 'civilized' rulers by providing a basic vernacular education for Malay children and by overseeing primary schooling in Chinese and Indian languages. It was considered unnecessary to offer higher levels since the government viewed education as a means of equipping the population with the tools appropriate for their assigned lot. The exception was the privileged upper strata across all ethnic groups who, through English-medium instruction, were also enabled to fill their specific role in colonial society.

For the directors of North Borneo's Chartered Company, the economic achievements of British Malaya provided the measure by which their own success was gauged. Though North Borneo never became more than a pale shadow of its larger neighbour, the fundamental attitudes regarding economic priorities, appropriate government and ethnic capabilities were common to both. And while the Brookes looked with disdain on the changes brought about by Malaya's mines and plantations, as time went on they too were forced to seek out ways of furthering state revenues and rationalizing government. In the end, however, the most significant element of each administration, whether in Borneo, Singapore or Malaya, was the underlying assumption that the British presence was in the best interests of local societies, and that the superior knowledge of colonial officials would work towards the good of all. By the 1920s a growing political awareness among all ethnic communities was already challenging such assumptions, which were irreversibly overturned by the outbreak of the Pacific War in 1941 and the Japanese conquest of Southeast Asia.

Negotiating a New Nation, 1942–69

At the outbreak of the Pacific War in 1941 the outlines of contemporary Malaysia, though certainly visible, were only lightly drawn. More than a generation after the creation of 'British Malaya', the kind of administrative unity colonial officials had envisaged remained elusive, and though closer connections with the Borneo states were contemplated, the form of any future affiliation was as yet unclear. Singapore's fall to the Japanese initiated a long and sometimes painful process which involved not merely the negotiation and defence of political boundaries, but decisions about the determinants of a national identity and the extent to which priorities should be shaped by ethnic considerations. Critical events – the Japanese conquest in 1942, the rejection of the Malayan Union in 1946, the Emergency, 1948–60, independence in 1957, the formation of Malaysia in 1963, and the ethnic riots of 1969 – can all be seen as steps in 'the making of Malaysia'. At no stage, however, was the outcome predictable; indeed, at times the very existence of the country seemed threatened by the succession of challenges which marked the end of British colonialism and the beginning of the experiment in nation-building.

Historiographical considerations

Although an increasing corpus of source material has encouraged historians to see the end of the Second World War and the declaration of Malaya's independence as important divisions in the nation's past, the Japanese Occupation is often regarded as an unpleasant interlude separating colonial times from the period leading to self-government. Perhaps the paucity of documentation, due to accidental and deliberate destruction of wartime records, may account for the Occupation's minor place in Malaysian historiography. Recent studies, however, have made possible a reappraisal of these wartime years. From 1945 the sources are so voluminous and so varied that they have encouraged a range of interpretations based on differing ideological and intellectual perceptions. As sensitive archival files are gradually released with the ending of the 30-year restriction, more material will become available to historians, enabling further reassessments of the postwar years. Equally important to the historian is an analysis of previous scholarship, particularly in the fields of anthropology and sociology. In detailing what were then contemporary customs and attitudes, earlier social science studies can now be treated as historical sources in their own right.

A major development in Malaysia during the last 20 years has been the flourishing of social histories and student exercises which focus on ordinary people. The increasing involvement of Malaysians in writing their own history has helped promote a shift from colonial concerns to historical treatments that lay greater stress on local perspectives, especially those of the Malays. At the same time, the ethnic considerations which weigh so heavy in Malaysian life are also evident in historiography, as each community seeks to make its voice heard in the nation's history and as individuals choose lines of enquiry in keeping with their own ethnic backgrounds.

The Japanese Occupation and the immediate postwar years

Japanese forces landed in southern Thailand and northern Malaya on 8 December 1941 and by the end of the month had established their control of both the Peninsula and the Borneo states. Within a few weeks, on 15 February 1942, the 'impregnable' island fortress of Singapore capitulated, followed in March by the Netherlands East Indies. With remarkable speed British rule in Malaya was replaced by that of the Japanese military. Singapore, now renamed Shonan, became the centre of a regional administration which incorporated the Straits Settlements and the FMS, and, until 1943, the Unfederated Malay States (UMS) and Sumatra.

A primary Japanese concern was to maintain a smooth-running administration in 'Malai' that would not require diversion of troops for peace-keeping operations. To this end the Peninsula was divided into provinces which largely followed state lines and which were placed under Japanese governors. The Malay sultans were retained as 'advisers' and representatives of the various communities appointed to advisory councils (*sanji kai*). The UMS were treated somewhat differently, notably after Thailand declared war on the United States and Great Britain in 1942. Although the Japanese retained full control over economic resources, Japan allowed its new ally to annex Kedah, Perlis, Kelantan and Terengganu in October 1943. The northern states remained under Thai suzerainty for the duration, and were thus spared some of the trauma of the war experience. Local Malays were alienated, however, by the insistence on Thai as the official language, and attempts to regulate social customs permitted by Islam, such as the prohibition of polygamy.

Few had regrets at the end of the war when Thailand's annexation of the northern states was declared invalid and they reverted to their prewar status.

Under the 37th Army, Japan established a separate military government over Sarawak, Brunei and North Borneo, which were divided into five prefectures, although the lack of personnel meant a heavy reliance on the prewar administrative structure. Malay native officers were retained to assist the Japanese, who were so pressed that in the early stages even European prisoners of war were required to help. Local members of the Brooke and Chartered Company civil services thus gained valuable experience in a variety of capacities. In Sarawak, for example, the Occupation provided new opportunities for Iban advancement as police and native officers. But because the Japanese focused on control of Borneo's coast and the restoration of the oil fields in Miri and Seria (Brunei) that had been destroyed by the retreating British, interior areas saw little fighting and were essentially left ungoverned.

The surrender to the Japanese dealt irreparable harm to British prestige, but the disillusionment and anger was particularly pronounced among the Chinese, especially in Singapore, where residents felt betrayed by Britain's inadequate defence of the city. Ironically, the Japanese achieved what had always eluded the British: for the first time Malaya came under an integrated government where the importance of the states and the rulers was much reduced. But the removal of the colonial umbrella also affected ethnic interactions. This was less evident in the Borneo states, even though the Chinese certainly experienced discrimination, and indigenous groups like the Iban were sometimes favoured over Malays. In Malaya, however, one of the most significant legacies of the Occupation was its effects on inter-ethnic relations. While perpetuating the pro-Malay policy of the British, the Japanese regarded the Chinese with intense suspicion because of their loyalty to the anti-Japanese movement at home.

During the Occupation the festering ethnic tensions of the prewar years were exacerbated by economic competition as groups and individuals struggled to provide for themselves and their families in the face of unemployment, food shortages, poverty, poor health and general uncertainty. Much of this privation can be attributed to a collapse in Malaya's export economy, even though the Japanese expected Malaya to be a major contributor to their war effort. The tin industry was already facing difficulties before the outbreak of hostilities, and the scorched-earth policy carried out by the retreating British forces destroyed much equipment. Japan could not absorb Malaya's tin capacity without a strong export market, and so production languished. Rubber plantations were neglected, and most of the output was sold domestically. Unemployed tin miners and rubber-estate workers became 'squatters', eking out a living by growing food on unoccupied land. Inevitably this brought Chinese in particular into closer contact and potential competition with rural Malays. From 1943 the Japanese emphasis on increased food production meant that restrictions on Malay reservation land were further ignored as communities of Chinese, Indians and Eurasians were resettled in agricultural areas.

A second area of tension can be traced to the unequal standing of Malays and Chinese in the eyes of the Japanese. In general, Malays were treated more favourably than the other ethnic groups, particularly in the administration. Many who already had some experience in the civil service were promoted to positions such as district officer, formerly held only by the British. Malay schools were accorded preferential treatment, and 721 out of the Peninsula's 885 Malay schools reopened in the twelve months after the invasion. Although there were certainly many cases of conscripted 'volunteers', the Malays recruited as vigilantes into the auxiliary police force (self-reliance corps or *Jikeidan*) and other paramilitary support units normally gained some access to privileges. They gained in organizational experience through Japanese-run conferences, language training and administrative education. Malay women were encouraged to form associations, and in 1944 they were admitted to the auxiliary forces. In contrast to Indonesia the Japanese gave little attention to Islam and only began to foster Malay nationalism from mid-1943 when the tide of war was turning against them.

In the evolution of a Malay sense of community, the Occupation is significant because the pan-Malayan organizations sponsored by the Japanese promoted the idea of a larger and more unified Malaya that reached beyond individual state loyalties. Moreover, Japanese approval of closer co-operation 'between Moslems residing in Sumatra and Malai' infused new life into old Malay linkages. Names such as Melaka and Hang Tuah provided potent symbols in the wartime literature produced on both sides of the Straits, and were frequently invoked as nationalist Malay writers exhorted their fellows to work towards greater unity through the preservation of *bahasa*, or Malay language, customs and tradition. As a poem published in the Japanese newspaper, *Sinaran Matahari*, put it, 'Through *bahasa* the race (*bangsa*) is successful. ... Through *bahasa* the *bangsa* is known'.[1] Perhaps significantly, little mention of the rulers emerges in these wartime expressions of Malayness. Although by 1944 the Japanese had restored to the sultans most prewar privileges, they were not accorded the same deference as in British colonial days. The weakened status of the traditional rulers in the Occupation, combined with Japanese encouragement of Malay nationalism, contributed to the growing importance of the new Malay élites who had arisen in the 1920s and 1930s.

The new vision of Malay society projected by left-wing nationalists had only limited appeal for rural Malays, still attached to a village environment and their traditional rulers. None the less, advocates of fundamental change in existing socioeconomic relationships gained greater prominence during the Occupation because of Japan's tendency to favour those less associated with the British regime. The more radicalized Malays were quick to seize the opportunities that opened up when they were appointed to lead youth movements and head publicity campaigns. Several also gained prominence in the Japanese-organized paramilitary youth group, PETA (Pembela Tanah

Air – Defenders of the Fatherland). But while hoping to use the Japanese to gain independence, Ibrahim Yaacob and the Kesatuan Melayu Muda (KMM) maintained ties to the traditional Malay élite and also secretly courted the Chinese-dominated Malayan Peoples Anti-Japanese Army (MPAJA).

Despite their ambitious plans, however, the radicals had little to offer potential allies because they lacked a strong power base and were geographically divided. Furthermore, the Japanese did not extend a promise of independence, since they eventually hoped to make Singapore a permanent colony and the Malay states a protectorate. Most pre-existing communal organizations were abolished, and even the KMM was dissolved in June 1942 because of Japanese fears that its pro-independence stance might endanger their long-term interests. Ibrahim nevertheless maintained his position as a Malay spokesman, and in July 1945 the Japanese finally agreed to promote a Malay nationalist movement based on the 'Greater Indonesia' concept. A new political organization, KRIS (Kesatuan Rakyat Indonesia Semenanjung – Union of Peninsular Indonesians, but later changed to Kekuatan Rakyat Indonesia Istimewa, meaning Supreme Strength of the Indonesian People) was formed under the leadership of Ibrahim and Burhanuddin Al-Helmy. Calling for the 'spirit of independence' to be built 'on the ruins of Melaka's fort', they hoped to see the Peninsula not only free from colonial rule but united with Indonesia. However, the unexpected surrender of the Japanese in August brought these plans to a premature end. Ibrahim, who had been a PETA leader, left for Jakarta to escape charges of collaboration.

In general, Indians were not treated as well as the Malays during the Occupation, and many of those who had served in the British army or police force were imprisoned. But although hundreds of Indian estate workers were forcibly conscripted for Japanese projects like the infamous Death Railway in Siam, they were never brutalized in the same way as the Chinese. The comparatively mild treatment accorded the Indians was doubtless attributable to the strength of the anti-colonial movement in India itself, and to the fact that the Japanese used Indian nationalism as a means of obtaining Malayan Indian co-operation. Leaders of the Central Indian Association became involved in the Indian Independence League, which was established in 1943 and was highly effective in reaching into the Indian community. In July Subhas Chandra Bose, a former president of the Indian National Congress who had been living in exile in Germany, arrived in Malaya. In October he proclaimed a Provisional Government of Free India (Azad Hind) and began recruiting civilian volunteers into the Indian National Army. The INA was notable because it even included a women's unit intended to supply soldiers, cooks, nurses and orderlies and general support to the main force. Though the Occupation was a significant period in the overall politicization of Indians, wealthier individuals were resentful of the constant demands for 'voluntary' contributions both by the Japanese and the Independence League. The dominant role of north Indians and the use of Hindi and English in communication also meant that the INA had limited appeal for

Malaya's Tamil and Muslim Indian populations. Even so, the participation of Malayan Indians in anti-British nationalist organizations was an important factor in softening the Japanese attitude towards the Indian community.

Of all Malaya's ethnic groups, the Chinese received the harshest treatment during the Occupation. China's long and bitter struggle to oust the Japanese invaders had been generously supported by funds from overseas Chinese, and there were many Kuomintang and Chinese Communist Party sympathizers in Singapore and Malaya who were strongly anti-Japanese. To root out these enemies, the Japanese systematically rounded up all the Chinese male population of Singapore in the first week of the Occupation and then followed the same procedures on the Peninsula. This special operation, known as *sook ching* (purification through suffering) involved the screening of Chinese neighbourhoods, followed by the detention or execution of any suspected of working against Japan. The numbers of those who died varied, but estimates range from 6000 to 40 000. While this mass punishment of the Chinese was never repeated, smaller but equally brutal atrocities were committed against the Chinese throughout the Occupation, and they were constantly squeezed for financial contributions to the war effort. Steps were also taken to eradicate communal institutions seen as contributing to Chinese resistance. Dialect and clan associations were disbanded, and a year after the invasion only 180 Chinese schools were functioning, as opposed to 1369 before the war; even these were required to operate in Japanese. Chinese schools were similarly closed in Borneo, and in Sarawak Chinese were required to deliver $2 000 000 as *sook ching* payment.

Ultimately, however, the Japanese were forced to rely on Chinese assistance because of their key role in the economy. While some prominent merchants were willing to work with the Japanese because of the profits possible in a wartime situation, others were placed in a situation where there was little choice. Albeit reluctantly, locally born Chinese, who were more emotionally distanced from the traumatic events in China, also proved more willing to work with the Japanese. By mid-1944 Japanese-sponsored clubs had even been formed in the Straits Settlements for Chinese to discuss problems in the economy. This type of collaboration, even when enforced, created deep rifts within the Chinese community, and undermined the standing of many wealthier businessmen who had previously acted as natural spokesmen. Such antagonism is understandable in light of the fact that although Indians and Malays were also involved in underground movements, the Chinese, especially the China-born, were the most committed to opposing the Japanese.

Formed in consultation with the British, the largely Chinese Malayan People's Anti-Japanese Army had begun resistance activities even before Singapore's fall. While resistance groups linked to the KMT maintained a separate existence, the MPAJA was dominated by the Malayan Communist Party (MCP). Following the Japanese invasion of China in 1937, the MCP had emerged as the champions of Malayan Chinese through its leadership of the anti-Japanese National Salvation Associations. It was thus in a strong position when the Japanese invaded, and in secret negotiations offered its full assistance to the colonial government. The expected British leadership of a combined operation did not eventuate, however, because the Japanese advanced far more rapidly than expected. Many young Chinese men, MCP sympathizers, fled to the jungle to escape the *sook ching* purges, which also forced the MCP to go underground. But within a year the highly effective Japanese intelligence had located and eliminated Singapore's entire Central Committee and almost all of the MCP Central Committee, except for Lai Tek, the secretary-general. In North Borneo the brutal suppression of a Chinese-led uprising in 1943 effectively ended organized resistance to the Japanese, but in Malaya the MCP survived and regrouped to play an effective role in the MPAJA's general resistance movement. Through its insistence on a shared cause and the inspiration provided by events in China, the MCP was highly successful in overcoming regional and dialect differences within the Chinese community.

Because the hard core of the MPAJA was provided by largely Chinese MCP members as well as a few left-wing Malay units, anti-Japanese resistance in the Occupation displays several features which came to characterize the later communist insurgency period. First, the MPAJA had a support unit in its civilian wing, the Anti-Japanese Union (renamed the Min Yuen during the insurgency) which helped provide supplies and recruits to the MPAJA. Second, the MPAJA developed an antagonistic attitude towards the police, who were largely Malays. Third, it cultivated close relations with Orang Asli groups in their shared jungle environment. Fourth, it combined a policy of friendship and intimidation to achieve its aims among the civilian population. And finally, it gained valuable experience in guerrilla warfare. It is also important to note that apart from its links with the Allied special forces, the MPAJA fought practically alone against the Japanese until the last few months of the war. It is not surprising that in 1945 members of the MCP saw themselves as the rightful victors because of their intense involvement in the MPAJA's wartime activities. Having achieved the immediate goal of defeating the Fascist powers in accordance with Communist International (Comintern) policy enunciated in 1941, they could now turn their attention to the attainment of a 'national revolution'. However, the violence that erupted following the Japanese surrender on 15 August and the British return on 3 September was a reminder of their failure to reach across ethnic lines.

In explaining the collapse of order in this postwar interregnum, historians have pointed to the unprecedented level of distrust and tension resulting from long-standing economic competition, the increasing presence of Chinese squatters in rural areas, the position of Malays as police and district officers, Malay resentment against MPAJA requisitions, and MPAJA reprisals against Malays who collaborated with the Japanese. As the war turned against Japan, the economic situation had grown more desperate and communal relations deteriorated even further. Malay attacks on Chinese settlements began in Johor as early as May 1945, forcing thousands of Chinese to flee to larger towns or settlements. The rumour-ridden environment in which the Japanese surrendered in mid-August made the situation worse, with many Malays convinced that a Chinese army was on the point of landing in Malaya. The demoralized and weakened Japanese, charged with upholding order until the British return, proved incapable of withstanding MPAJA attacks on their own positions or preventing the capture or execution of Malay police and district officials. This was in marked contrast to Borneo, where Japanese authorities were generally able to maintain control until the arrival of Australian forces in September. Even here, however, observers were struck by the new assurance of the Chinese, buoyed by China's emergence as a world power.

Chinese confidence was far more evident on the Peninsula, where the MPAJA was the only armed, well-organized group. It was thus able to move quickly to impose control over numerous areas, especially where there was a substantial Chinese population. Not surprisingly, large numbers of Malays believed that the Chinese were about to take over the country, for even after the British return MPAJA units were used in some areas to maintain order – a measure which Malays interpreted as preferential treatment for Chinese. Communal relations were also seriously damaged because the MPAJA/MCP used this opportunity to deal harshly with old enemies and those perceived as working with the Japanese or displaying 'capitalist' sympathies. Although some Chinese also suffered, the major MPAJA/MCP targets were Malays, especially those classed as 'collaborators'. Responding to what they saw as 'Chinese' aggression, Malays organized themselves under village secular and religious leaders and retaliated in kind.

Isolated clashes between Chinese and Malays had occurred periodically in previous decades, but never with such intensity. Though brought to a head by wartime conditions, this bloodshed can be seen as an outcome of simmering resentments that had their seedbed in colonial policies and attitudes. In a world which was indeed turned 'upside down', interethnic distrust was easily transformed into fear and hatred, as banditry, personal vendettas and group vengeance established their grim hold. It is not surprising that violence continued well after the British return, nor that as late as 1948 order had not been completely restored. The perpetuation of memories of a time when 'the knife and pistol reigned' had implications that were not lost on the people of Malaya.[2] While independence was a desirable goal, some were fearful that an independent Malayan government would be unable to restrain ethnic enmities once the mediating hand of the colonial power had been removed.

Across the Straits, Indonesia had already declared its independence in August 1945, and some Malays saw the end of the war as the logical moment to resuscitate the concept of a Greater Malaya. In the latter part of 1945, Malay leftist groups (including MCP as well as former KMM and KRIS members) established the Partai Kebangsaan Melayu Muda (PKMM). As well as self-government, political rights and social reforms, it stressed Malay unity and racial harmony. Urged on by its chairman, Dr Burhanuddin Al-Helmy, for whom Srivijaya, Melaka and Majapahit formed a historical continuum, the PKMM adopted the Indonesian flag as its banner and called for Malaya to become part of the Republic of Greater Indonesia.

Despite its support for racial co-operation, the potential appeal of the PKMM was largely limited to Malays, since Chinese were totally opposed to a future as a tiny minority in a Malay-Indonesian union. However, there were other groups who hoped that common political goals might be sufficient to overcome the wartime legacy of communal conflict. In December 1945 an organization with MCP affiliations, the Malayan Democratic Union, was formed in Singapore. Consisting principally of left-wing, English-educated, Malaya-born individuals, its goal was 'to create a real sense of loyalty to Malaya among all races by inspiring in the Malay a national loyalty over and above his natural loyalty to the Sultans...and by weaning the non-Malay races from their nostalgia for the homelands of their ancestors'.[3] Though laudable, this appeal could not counter the persisting fear that each ethnic community must be committed to the protection of its own interests.

The Malayan Union and the Federation of Malaya

British discussions about Malaya's postwar future had begun as early as 1942. Assuming an Allied victory, it was decided that Britain should resume control but that preparations would be made for self-government. Despite the fact that two Malay battalions had fought against the Japanese at Singapore, Britain's former pro-Malay attitude was undermined by the refusal of the sultans to evacuate, their alleged co-operation with the Japanese, and Malay involvement in Japanese-sponsored organizations like PETA. By contrast, the British believed that the Chinese and Indian communities had remained generally loyal to the colonial power. Some community leaders like Tan Cheng Lock had thrown in their lot with the British by evacuating to India, while the suffering and resistance of Chinese who remained in Malaya was a matter of record. British appreciation of the Chinese contribution to victory was made evident during an impressive ceremony held in Singapore in early 1946, when Lord Louis Mountbatten presented campaign medals to eight MPAJA leaders.

Changing colonial perceptions of their relationship with Malaya's different ethnic groups were of prime importance in shaping plans for self-government. In 1944 the British government adopted a scheme put forward by Edward Gent, the assistant permanent under-secretary for the colonies (and later high commissioner). According to this plan, the separate administrations of the FMS, UMS, Penang and Melaka would be incorporated into a Malayan Union, in which citizenship would be widened to include non-Malays. Although this was not the first time a unified British Malaya had been proposed, there was a sense of urgency because of the need for centralized direction to oversee postwar economic recovery as a prelude to self-government. As a signatory to the Atlantic Charter, which had laid down the right of nations to self-determination, Britain felt bound to declare its intention of returning independence to Malaya. De-colonization was also one of the principal tenets of American foreign policy, and Britain's self-interest argued against arousing criticism from its powerful ally. The Malayan Union, therefore, was presented as a necessary step towards the granting of independence to a united nation in which each group would have equal rights.

In formulating the Malayan Union proposal, Gent had paid little attention to representations made by various Malayan groups operating in exile, whose members generally favoured a federation that included Singapore. More influential were business interests in Malaya, which were traditionally apprehensive of Singapore's commercial hegemony. Furthermore, the liberal citizenship policy in the Union plans was bound to arouse suspicion among Malay leaders, fearful of being overrun by Singapore's large Chinese population. In any case the British government saw the value of retaining Singapore as a free port and as a naval base for its own strategic operations in the 'Far East'.

The future of the Borneo territories was more uncertain. Included in an earlier plan, they had been subsequently omitted because of the added complications they would present to an already difficult Union proposal. It was decided that they would more appropriately be administered together as British Borneo. Civil administration was restored to Sarawak in April 1946, when Vyner Brooke returned temporarily to rule the country, having earlier indicated his willingness to step down. But the situation in Sarawak was not easily resolved because certain members of the Brooke family and some senior Malay officials were opposed to any transfer of power. Other local Malays objected to the proposed arrangements, not because they wanted a continuation of the Brooke regime but because they hoped Sarawak would eventually become self-governing. Finally, an orchestrated vote in the Council Negeri narrowly approved the cession of Sarawak to the British Crown. In North Borneo, where Allied bombing and heavy fighting in 1945 had flattened Jesselton and Sandakan, and destroyed ports, roads, bridges and railway tracks, it was evident that the cost of postwar reconstruction would be well beyond the Chartered Company's economic and administrative resources. In July 1946 Labuan, North Borneo and Sarawak became Crown Colonies. Opposition within Sarawak never completely subsided, however, and in 1949 the British governor was assassinated by members of the Malay Youth Movement who had opposed Sarawak's inclusion in the new British Borneo. In a replay of events in Perak over 70 years earlier, four of the conspirators were hanged and seven given long prison sentences. The rifts in Sarawak Malay society created by the anti-cession movement took many years to heal.

Because of clear indications that the Borneo states would oppose further changes, it was thus considered safer to confine the Malayan Union to the Malay Peninsula. The first step was to obtain the agreement of the sultans, who had legally remained sovereign rulers over their respective states. In the autumn of 1944 the Colonial Office selected Sir Harold MacMichael to undertake a mission to Malaya when hostilities ended. His task was to secure new treaty arrangements that would change the constitutional position of the rulers in order for a Malayan Union to be legitimately created. On 3 September 1945, as the British were reoccupying Malaya, the Cabinet gave its final authorization to the new Malayan policy. MacMichael himself reached Malaya the following month.

Obtaining the signatures of the rulers required a combination of tact, cajolery and veiled threats. Although Sultan Ibrahim of Johor was relatively compliant, it seems that the other rulers and their Malay advisers did their best to delay or avoid signing the new treaties. They were fully aware, however, that their position was vulnerable, since discussions with British officials invariably raised the issue of collaboration during the Occupation; indeed, the Japanese-installed ruler of Selangor had already been temporarily deported to the Cocos Islands. By late December every sultan or regent had consented to the new terms. All previous treaties with the British concluded on basis of the sovereign rights of the Malay sultans were annulled, and the pretence that Residents and Advisers had been merely assisting the rulers to govern their lands was finally removed. The sultan of Kedah, who had only signed under extreme pressure, declared that 'this was the most distressing and painful moment of his entire life'.[4]

In late January 1946 the British revealed the Malayan Union Plan in a White Paper. The new Union would create a unitary state comprising the FMS, UMS, Penang and Melaka, which would be under a central government, a governor, and legislative and executive councils. The Malay sultans were to retain their positions but sovereignty would be transferred to the British Crown. All citizens of the new Malayan Union would have equal rights, including admission to the administrative civil service. Finally, Malayan citizenship was to be extended to all without discrimination as to race or creed.

Unfortunately for the British, the announcement of the Malayan Union was made during a period of considerable tension. The interim Military Administration was quite unable to live up to local expectations of a return to normalcy, and the inefficiency, corruption and insensitivity displayed by some of its personnel further undermined British standing. Food shortages, especially rice, inadequate wages and the high cost of living had triggered off a number of demonstrations and strikes, particularly among urban Chinese. Ethnic violence, often stemming from competition over land occupancy by Chinese squatters, had continued through 1945. Already bitter about what they regarded as a Chinese intrusion into rural areas, many Malays saw the Malayan Union as a harbinger of future Chinese dominance. In the subsequent outcry, any supporting Malay voices, as in the pro-Malayan Union PKMM, were simply drowned out. Spurred on by these protests and stung by criticism from their own subjects, the rulers were now willing to take a leadership role in opposition to the Malayan Union. Their resolve had been strengthened as they came to realize that a Malaya reconstituted according to the proposed formula would, in the words of the sultan of Perak, 'deprive [the] sultans of sovereign rights recognized by Great Britain and [the] world from time immemorial'.[5] Protesting at the manner in which MacMichael had obtained their signatures for the new treaties, the rulers rejected the Union plan and proposed sending a mission to London to seek its repeal. Meanwhile, influential retired British members of the Malayan Civil Service in England joined the campaign, with men like Swettenham, George Maxwell, Winstedt, Clementi and Guillemard writing to national newspapers and petitioning Downing Street.

Despite these developments, the British government pushed for an immediate implementation of the Malayan Union so that the British Military Administration, which had governed Malaya since the end of the Japanese Occupation, could be removed. But when the Malayan Union was inaugurated on 1 April 1946, the British were confronted by united, vehement and unforeseen Malay opposition. Under the leadership of the able chief minister of Johor, Datuk Onn bin Jaafar (1895–1962), a new force had emerged to channel and articulate Malay opinion. Though associated with left-wing, pro-Indonesia groups in prewar days, Datuk Onn had since distanced himself from radical views. In March 1946 he was instrumental in convening an All-Malaya Congress in Kuala Lumpur. Comprising 41 Malay associations (including the PKKM) and some 200 delegates, it adopted a resolution to form a new organization which would help galvanize nationwide Malay opposition to the Malayan Union.

In May the Pertubuhan Kebangsaan Melayu Bersatu (United Malays National Organization – UMNO) was established, with Datuk Onn as its first president. This was a highly significant event. For the first time Malays had been brought together in a political movement which was supported by virtually all the key components in Malay society, from aristocrats and civil servants to radicals and Islamic leaders. In a major pronouncement, the Congress declared the MacMichael treaties to be invalid and demanded the repeal of the Malayan Union. The 'remarkable' fact that women were also participating in protest rallies and political demonstrations, '[going] up on political platforms and making speeches' was persuasive evidence of the extent of Malay feeling. Gent himself warned London that 'organized and widespread non-cooperation and disorder on the part of the Malay people' was likely if the Malayan Union proposals were implemented.[6] Given their memories of the anti-colonial movement in India and the continuing anti-Dutch struggle in Indonesia, British officials could not ignore the groundswell of opposition to the Malayan Union,

Although the Chinese and Indian communities could see that the Malayan Union promised certain advantages, they also did not give it unqualified approval. When the Malayan Indian Congress (MIC) was formed in August 1946, its leadership initially supported the Malay position. However, resentful at its exclusion from UMNO–British negotiations, the MIC joined other parties advocating greater political rights for non-Malays. The Chinese approved the general tenor of the proposals, but were apprehensive that they would lose their Chinese nationality should they take on Malayan citizenship. In addition, left-wing groups of all ethnicities were critical because the Union proposal presented no specific arrangements for an elected government. Yet it is doubtful whether even united and outspoken support could have countered the strength of Malay opposition, which was so effective that the Malay Union was never promulgated. It was finally revoked in its entirety when a Federation of Malaya was declared on 1 February 1948.

The possibility of a Federation as an alternative to a Union had been raised by the rulers as early as March 1946, and from July the new arrangements were hammered out in a series of meetings between the rulers, British officials and UMNO leaders. After intense discussion, it was agreed that the Federation would uphold the sovereignty of the sultans, the individuality of the states, and Malay special privileges. A strong unitary central government was established with legislative powers, though the states were assured jurisdiction over a number of important fields. Citizenship was made more restrictive than in the Malayan Union proposals, requiring residence for at least 15 of the previous 25 years, a declaration of permanent settlement, and a certain competence in Malay or English. A high commissioner was appointed, rather than a governor, as a symbolic gesture that authority derived from the Malay sultans rather than the British Crown. The term 'Malayan' was not recognized in the final Federation document, while *Melayu* was clearly reserved for those individuals who habitually spoke Malay, who professed Islam, and conformed to Malay custom.

Although it is certainly possible to track UMNO compromises, Federation was widely regarded as a victory for more conservative Malay opinion. It was greeted with dismay by other ethnic groups, especially the Chinese, among whom less than 10 per cent would qualify for automatic citizenship. Malays who had hoped that independence would bring a reshaping of the social order were also disappointed, especially since the Federation Agreement did not grant immediate self-government. For a brief period the opposition to Federation provided the basis for a coalition of parties that reached across communal lines. In December 1946 a Pan-Malayan (subsequently All-Malay) Council of Joint Action (AMCJA) was organized in Singapore, led by the Malayan Democratic Union and other MCP-affiliated groups. The Malayan Indian Congress was also included. Two months later the AMCJA was joined by the Malay Pusat Tenaga Rakyat (Centre of People's Power, or PUTERA), an alliance of leftist Malays, both militant and moderate, notably the Malayan Nationalist Party (MNP, Partai Kebangsaan Melayu Malaya). The influential Straits Chinese leader, Tan Cheng Lock, whose earlier advocacy of Chinese interests had broadened to a concern for improved inter-ethnic relations, served as chairman of this new AMCJA–PUTERA alliance.

Submitted in March 1947, and later incorporated into a 'People's Constitution', the AMCJA–PUTERA agenda attempted to meet the principal concerns of both Malays and non-Malays. It called for a united Malaya that would incorporate Singapore; equal citizenship for all Malaya-born; elected state councils and constitutional monarchies; advancement of Malays; protection for Malay customs; and immediate self-government. Always tenuous, the AMCJA–PUTERA relationship ultimately broke down, partly because of difficulties in identifying a term that could incorporate all ethnic groups without conveying ideas of cultural hegemony. Malays saw the term 'Malayan' as applicable to non-Malays, rather than themselves, and in Chinese eyes *Melayu* could only be used as a substitute if it was divested of any religious implications.

Although the AMCJA–PUTERA partnership ended with the declaration of the Federation of Malaya, the MCP dialogue with left-wing Malay nationalists had aroused concern among UMNO leaders, and was watched carefully by the Security Service. The escalation of MCP activities and the declaration of a State of Emergency in June 1948 were followed by the arrest of PUTERA officials for subversive activities, and the MNP was banned two years later. Opponents of government policy thus faced formidable obstacles, for the authorities could call on a battery of legal and political ammunition to quash any activities considered 'seditious'. It is understandable that the new Federation, which underscored the exclusiveness of Melayu status, left many Chinese with a sense of betrayal, especially since they believed their loyalty to the British during the war had far exceeded that of any other group. Disenchanted, a significant number now saw their only hope for a just society in the promises of the MCP. The political and demographic shape of Malaya, contested for so many years, and apparently settled by the creation of a Federation, was now subject to another challenge.

The MCP and the Emergency

MCP leaders were aware that the interim between the Japanese surrender and the return of the British in September 1945 presented a real opportunity for seizing power, but had decided against such action. Not only were their forces small in number, but they were poorly equipped and ill prepared to oppose the returning British troops. There were also larger questions of strategy, since the Communist Parties in Britain and China and the secretary-general of the MCP, Lai Tek, had urged the adoption of a 'open and legal' struggle. Encouraged by British assurances that communists would be allowed participation in political planning for Malaya, the MCP postponed violent action in favour of 'peaceful agitation'. The arms collected during and immediately after the war were hidden in the jungle for the future struggle, and in December 1945 the MPAJA was disbanded. In its place the

MPAJA Ex-Comrades Association was created to maintain liaison with the former guerrillas.

The MCP's legal activities began with its inclusion in the governor's Advisory Council in Singapore in 1945 and its involvement with groups such as the Malayan Democratic Union and the Malayan Nationalist Party. Its greatest success was the establishment of the General Labour Unions (GLU), initially in Singapore, and later in all the Malayan states. Throughout 1945 and 1946 the GLU's organizational ability was convincingly demonstrated in widespread strikes and rallies, although there was certainly spontaneous protest action and unionization independent of the GLU. None the less, at the height of its power in early 1947, the Pan-Malayan GLU, renamed the Pan-Malayan Federation of Trade Unions (PMFTU), directly controlled 80–90 per cent of Malaya's unions. The ability of the GLU to force concessions from the government and employers was impressive: a strike by 12 000 railway workers in January 1946 lasted for two months, with the result that most of their demands were met.

The GLU's principal strength was among the Chinese, who provided a steady supply of committed party members, not only from a highly politicized workforce but also from Chinese schools. Reopened after the war, these schools provided a particularly fertile recruitment field for the MCP because many of their students, deprived of education during the Occupation, were now young adults in their late teens and early twenties. In addition, it was estimated that 50 per cent of the teachers in Chinese schools still came from China. But the Pan-Malayan GLU was also anxious to attract Indian workers, especially on the plantations. Its leadership was therefore tolerant of communal unions, while also appointing Indians to high-ranking positions on state and national committees. By 1946 almost all the Indian unions were brought under the PMFTU umbrella. None the less, despite the adverse economic climate, efforts to attract Malays were unsuccessful. Malays were rarely employed in unionized occupations, and were generally reluctant to become part of a Chinese-controlled organization.

In mid-1947, when rubber prices temporarily fell and wages were lowered by 20 per cent, there was a notable increase in the number of strikes. Pressured by employers to move more strongly against the trade unions, and confronted by increasing violence, especially against European planters, the government strengthened the already stringent laws controlling labour which had been introduced in 1940. Strikes and processions were declared illegal, and Chinese communist leaders arrested and deported. New measures were introduced requiring all unions to register, and imposing certain terms on the eligibility of union officials to hold office as a condition for registration. But what spelt the end to militant unionism was suppression of all labour and anti-colonial activities following the declaration of an Emergency in 1948.

Events leading to this decision can be traced directly to a change in MCP strategy. In March 1947 the secretary-general, Lai Tek, disappeared, and the MCP later revealed that he had been a double agent. Though this revelation brought suspicion and recriminations within the MCP, it discredited the moderate policy with which he had been associated and strengthened the faction which had long argued for an armed struggle. The new hard-line secretary-general, Chin Peng, believed that it was now time to seize power through an armed insurrection. At the MCP's Fourth Plenary Session it was decided to prepare for this struggle by moving all party activities underground, while trade unions were directed to lead the workers 'to the road of violent action'. Through the early months of 1947 there was a marked increase in communist propaganda and violence associated with industrial disputes, as well as attacks on mining and estate personnel. The European community mounted scathing attacks on the government and on the high commissioner, Sir Edward Gent, but officials continued to maintain that the situation was under control. Finally, when three European estate managers were among five people murdered on 16 June, the government took decisive action. Two days later a State of Emergency was declared throughout Malaya, and the following month membership of the MCP was declared illegal.

The MCP was caught off-guard by this move. Emergency Regulations empowered the government to arrest and detain without trial, so that by the end of 1948 a total of 1779 known communist sympathizers were held in detention, and hundreds of others had been deported. Although the MCP was still able to mount successful attacks on mining and estate personnel and government officials, it was evident by December that there would be no popular uprising, and that the armed struggle would be protracted. The MCP set aside its earlier strategy in favour of a retreat into the deep jungle where its main forces, numbering around 3000, could establish permanent bases. Supported by auxiliary forces of about 8000, the MCP was able to regroup, retrain and concentrate on developing strong popular support through the Min Yuen, or People's Movement. In the early stages these Min Yuen provided supplies, intelligence and auxiliary combat units, although they were to become more involved in fighting in later years when the MCP was under greater pressure. The Min Yuen was especially active in the Chinese squatter settlements which proliferated in Forest Reserves, Malay reservations, and on privately owned mining and agricultural estates. While Occupation conditions and the Japanese policy of encouraging food production on all available land was responsible for some of these settlements, the roots of many could be traced back to the Depression and even earlier as unemployed Chinese sought out their own sources of livelihood. Throughout the Occupation these settlements had provided the MPAJA with food, shelter and recruits. When the British civil government was re-established in Malaya, the MCP had championed the cause of the Chinese squatters against official efforts to evict them. In 1948 the problem of how Chinese families involved in agriculture could legally acquire land title was still unresolved. Through the mixture of gratitude and fear generated by their links with the MCP, these Chinese squatter settlements, especially in remote areas with little government authority, provided guerrilla fighters with their major source of support.

In the middle of 1949 communist activity exploded once again. This new offensive highlighted the difficulties faced by the government in trying to eliminate the sources of communist support in the local Chinese communities. Assuming it was dealing with a limited number of 'bandits' led by extremist agitators, the British initially believed that coercion and enforcement would be sufficient to restore order. The ineffectiveness of a policy that conceived of the problem as criminal rather than political was underscored by the poor organization and morale of the British-led police and military units. A fresh initiative was clearly needed, and this came in March 1950 when the government announced the appointment of Lieutenant-General Sir Harold Briggs as the new director of operations in the Emergency. For Briggs, the principal goal was the elimination of the Min Yuen and the communist main forces, the Malayan Races Liberation Army (MRLA). His plan was to establish complete security within populated areas in order to infuse local authorities with greater confidence. It was hoped that this confidence would lead to a flow of intelligence to the British, enabling them to destroy the Min Yuen and hence deprive the MRLA of any support. Without access to the Min Yuen for food, information or recruitment, the MRLA would be eventually forced to undertake bolder action and would be destroyed by the security forces fighting on their own grounds.

Implementation of the Briggs Plan was facilitated by wide-ranging security measures announced by the high commissioner, Sir Henry Gurney, in mid-December 1950. Malaya was now effectively placed on a war footing. Conscription for the military and police force was introduced, employment controlled, and special powers created to regulate society and destroy any communist guerrilla support. Armed with these measures, the government began the relocation of Chinese squatter communities from areas of strong Min Yuen presence. The rapidity of the resettlement programme was impressive. Prior to the arrival of Briggs, the total number of resettled people throughout Malaya was well under 7000; during May 1951, however, 23 000 people were moved in Perak alone. The communist guerrillas were all too aware of the devastating effect this would have on their activities, and they therefore stepped up their attacks on the resettlement areas. By the second half of 1951 guerrilla incidents had moved from individual terrorist acts to large-scale action involving about 30–50 men.

The expected outcome of the Briggs Plan was soon evident. The continuing isolation of the main body of guerrillas from their civilian sources of support forced them to turn to Indian labour lines and Malay villages in the homegrounds of the security forces. Intimidation and violence became far more common in dealing with the civilian population, and animosity towards them grew accordingly. The guerrillas also failed to prevent the resettlement of Chinese squatters, and by the beginning of 1952 the programme was four-fifths completed with some 400 000 settled in about 400 'New Villages'.

But though successful in terms of security issues, the resettlement programme had not adequately addressed the long-term issue of land title, which was to resurface in the post-Emergency years. At the same time, many Malays resented the funds being spent on New Village creation. Government measures, like the creation of the Rural and Industrial Development Authority (RIDA) in August 1950, were insufficient to assuage Malay grievances.

In 1951 the communists again rallied, striking a severe blow to the morale of the government and to those who had come to believe in the ability of the British to provide security. On 6 October the high commissioner, Sir Henry Gurney, was assassinated by a platoon of guerrillas on the long, narrow, one-way road leading up to the small resort of Fraser's Hill, about 105 kilometres outside Kuala Lumpur. The authorities had barely recovered from the shock when a month later the guerrillas inflicted the heaviest weekly casualties ever suffered by government forces. The retirement of Briggs in December, followed shortly by his death, and the departure in the same month of the commissioner of police, further contributed to the demoralization within the country. According to the author Graham Greene, who visited Malaya in early 1951, 'there was defeat in the mind'.

The MCP was unable to take advantage of the disarray in the government because it was undergoing severe internal strains over questions of leadership and interpretation of the Communist Party line. In October 1951 the MCP's Central Committee adopted a new programme of action that emphasized the subordination of military activities to political goals. Selective attacks were to be made principally for purposes of morale, propaganda and securing arms. The more important struggle, however, would be the awakening of the revolutionary awareness of the masses and the guerrilla units.

The MCP's new political initiative coincided with several developments that considerably strengthened the British hand. In June 1950, just after the introduction of the Briggs Plan, tensions in Korea had erupted into open war. The resulting conflict led to increased demand for both tin and rubber, long the pillars of the Malayan economy. In a climate where smallholders prospered along with the government and estate owners, the appeal of the MCP was much diminished. Secondly, when Lieutenant-General Sir Gerald Templer arrived in Malaya in early February 1952 as the new high commissioner he announced a new approach that would aim to capture the 'hearts and minds' of the general population. The resettlement of Chinese squatters into New Villages, enforcement of strict food controls, and more effective intelligence made it increasingly difficult for the communists to obtain support. Thirdly, in the wake of the British announcement of Malaya's impending independence came the forging of a political alliance in 1952 between UMNO and the recently formed Malayan Chinese Association (MCA).

The loss of momentum suffered by the MCP following the British announcement of their intention to grant independence to Malaya was heightened by Templer's other measures. Introduced in September 1953, the concept of 'White Areas' rewarded districts considered free of guerrilla influence by relaxing food restrictions and curfews. There was therefore an inducement for people to co-operate with the government so that their area could also be declared 'white'. Support for the communists was also undermined by the establishment of MCA branches in New Villages, and by the use of lower-echelon members to promote the image of the MCA as a party that could represent all Chinese. The government now had the expertise and the finance to begin developing a highly effective propaganda machine. By the time Templer left Malaya in July 1954, guerrilla numbers had markedly declined and their Min Yuen were largely dismantled. The government had also gained the upper hand in jungle fighting, as Orang Asli groups were weaned away from communist units. Orang Asli groups had been ignored by the colonial regime until this time, but from 1950 they had been placed under the more watchful eye of a federal Department of Aboriginal Affairs. During this period a number of laws aimed at the regulation of Orang Asli movement were introduced, many of which are still in force today.

Despite the fact that victory was now in sight, the Emergency years had left bitter memories. Many Chinese felt that they had again become scapegoats and victims in a quarrel that was not of their making, and had suffered simply because of their ethnic origins. Displaced and resettled squatters were frequently disappointed in the difference between the government's promises and what was actually delivered. On the other hand, Malay suspicions of the Chinese had been reinforced, and they had also been made aware of the extent to which they themselves had depended on British protection. Some felt resentful at the amount of money that had been injected into New Village facilities, often far better than those available in Malay *kampung*. For more radical Malays, the MCP challenge was evidence that basic questions about the future remained unanswered. As one nationalist poet put it, 'The country's defence in English hands/means the Emergency's not yet ended/ Foreign capital still protected/means the people continue to suffer.'[7]

Independence

In April 1949 the British Parliament made a commitment to Malaya's independence which was reaffirmed the following March by the prime minister. On Templer's arrival in 1952 he had publicly declared that his immediate objective was the formation of a united Malayan nation. Towards this goal and in the hope of undermining and eventually destroying the MCP, Templer introduced local elections, village councils and Chinese citizenship to over half the Chinese population; merged the War Council with the Executive Council; and enabled the Chinese for the first time to enter the Malayan Civil Service. In April 1954 he announced that an election for a majority of Federal Council seats would be held in 1955, thereby indicating that Malaya was drawing closer to independence. Towards the end of that year leaders of the major Malayan political parties were appointed by the government to the War Executive Council so that they would be able to view Emergency operation planning at first hand and contribute to the destruction of the MCP.

Political developments within Malaya itself had moved in an unexpected direction but one which pleased the British authorities. In February 1949 the MCA had been established, partially in response to UMNO's founding three years earlier. A guiding figure was Tan Cheng Lock, previously chairman of the AMCJA, who acted as MCA chairman until 1950. Tan's experience in the anti-Federation movement had convinced him that Chinese interests could only be protected by political involvement and by a 'Malayanization' of the Chinese community through which a working relationship with other communal organizations could develop. Respected by the British and an accepted leader of the Straits Chinese, Tan was sufficiently sinicized to be able to relate well to the commercial and social world of the China-born. Throughout his career he believed that Malayan Chinese should give their political loyalty to Malaya, but should still be able to maintain a distinct Chinese cultural heritage through a Chinese education. By drawing together prominent Straits and China-born figures, his leadership went some way towards mending the rifts that had developed between different Chinese social and political groupings.

Another important endorsement came from Datuk Onn, the UMNO president, who called for joint action between Malays and 'law-abiding' Chinese in the fight against communism. For a short time it seemed that the co-operation between Datuk Onn and Tan Cheng Lock might result in a truly multi-ethnic party. Datuk Onn, however, could not persuade UMNO to open the party to non-Malays, and his founding of the non-communal Independence of Malaya Party (IMP) in 1951 (and in 1954 the more pro-Malay Party Negara) was unable to obtain grass-roots support among Malays. At the same time, Tan Cheng Lock's proposal that his own party might accord non-Chinese voting and office-holding rights was also rejected by the MCA's General Assembly. The British viewed this institutionalization of communal politics with some misgiving, since they had stressed the need for a *united* Malayan nation – a policy that Datuk Onn's IMP seemed to answer. Yet in the Kuala Lumpur municipal elections of February 1952, the IMP gained only two of the twelve seats. The Selangor branches of the UMNO and the MCA, however, contested the elections as a united front and won nine seats. From this local initiative grew a coalition in which both parties retained their separate identities and political objectives, while acting as one body in determining the candidates and the party to contest a particular seat. Increasingly, this arrangement appeared to hold out the only hope for a workable independent Malayan government.

Between the end of 1952 and 1954, the UMNO–MCA Alliance won 226 of 268 municipal and town council seats. Though Alliance leaders were unsuccessful in persuading the British to bring forward the elections, a boycott of local, state and federal councils resulted in an assurance that the majority party in the Federal Council would be supported by the nominated members. Accepting political realities, the leadership of the Malayan Indian Congress also decided to work with UMNO after several years of opposition to the Federation Agreement. With elections scheduled for July 1955, the MIC's incorporation as a full-fledged partner in April further legitimized the Alliance, even though Indians formed only 3.9 per cent of the electorate. Through a carefully worded election manifesto and a strategic campaign that focused on the immediate objective of independence, the Alliance was able to deflect attention away from communal issues and present itself as the only viable candidate for government. In an overwhelming victory, Alliance candidates obtained 81 per cent of the vote and 51 of the 52 contested seats. It is worth remembering, however, that only 11.2 per cent of those registered to vote were Chinese; overall, only one in eight Chinese actually cast a ballot.

Well aware that many Chinese were still outside the emerging political structure, the Alliance leadership was ready to listen when the MCP, encouraged from London, decided to explore the possibility a 'peaceful co-existence' in an independent Malaya. In December 1955, in the government English school in Baling, Kedah, Chin Peng led three MCP leaders into a meeting that included Tunku Abdul Rahman, the new chief minister; Tan Cheng Lock, leader of the MCA; and David Marshall, chief minister of Singapore. But the talks revealed only too clearly that legal co-existence between the Communists and the Alliance was impossible. The Tunku insisted that MCP members would have to abandon the party's goals and activities if they were to be accepted back into Malayan society, while the MCP leaders refused to countenance an idea which they saw as tantamount to surrender. The collapse of the talks ended MCP hopes of reaching a political settlement.

The electoral dominance of the Alliance Party meant that its views were given prominence by the Reid Commission, which toured Malaya in 1956 as part of the process for drawing up a constitution for an independent Malaya. Nevertheless, the final document was not totally satisfactory even to Alliance members. Among the most controversial features of this Merdeka ('Independence') Constitution were those dealing with citizenship and the special privileges of Malays. UMNO had been asked to agree to a document which would provide for a single nationality, and which would allow all persons in Malaya to qualify as citizens either by birth (*jus soli*) or by fulfilling requirements of residence and language, and by taking an oath of loyalty. UMNO's final acceptance of this provision was only obtained in return for a guarantee of Malay privileges. In the new Constitution the paramount ruler (yang dipertuan agung) was given the responsibility for safeguarding the special position of the Malays, as well as the 'legitimate interests' of the other communities. The latter clause reflects the Commission's dilemma of attempting to satisfy Malay demands while preserving the original principle of a single nationality with equal citizenship. The Merdeka Constitution also provided for a paramount ruler to be chosen by the Conference of Rulers (Durbar) on the basis of seniority for a term of five years; a parliament composed of a wholly elected House of Representatives (Dewan Rakyat) and an appointed Senate (Dewan Negara); an allocation of power designated in subjects under a Federal List, State List and Concurrent List; and a guarantee of civil rights and of judicial review. On 15 August 1957 the Legislative Council ratified the Constitution, and on 31 August the independence of the Federation of Malaya was proclaimed.

By this time the government was secure in the knowledge that the war against the communists was being won. The programme of psychological warfare, food denial and the relentless pressure of security forces contributed to the disintegration of guerrilla organization and the lowering of MCP morale. In 1958 over 500 guerrillas surrendered, and major incidents were reduced to one a month. The Malayan Races Liberation Army ended its existence as an organized military unit, and the few remaining guerrillas retreated to the Thai border or to inaccessible jungle areas. By the end of the year, the communist armed threat to Malaya was deemed to have ceased and the State of Emergency was officially ended on 31 July 1960. The Alliance government, which had won another impressive victory in the second federal elections in 1959, could now devote its full attention to the creation of a united Malayan nation. The depth of the divisions resulting from British and Japanese colonial rule and the extent to which they had been exacerbated by the communist insurgency made this a daunting task.

The Alliance

When British rule ended in 1957, the new Federation of Malaya inherited a number of features from the colonial past which represented a mixed blessing. On the one hand, the economy appeared healthy with 85 per cent of the total gross export earnings coming from rubber and tin, though fears were already being expressed at their disproportionate strength in the export sector. Although the government's eventual victory over the MCP had not yet been achieved, the threat of a communist takeover had effectively disappeared. On the other hand, the State of Emergency, which was declared to deal with the danger, had made all too apparent the serious ethnic divisions bequeathed by colonial policies and the Japanese Occupation. This legacy meant that the most important political parties in the newly autonomous Malaya were destined to be communally based, drawing support from their claims to represent the interests of individual ethnic groups. In a situation where the ever-present threat of communal violence could not be ignored, the Alliance coalition held out the concept of consensus government by which each ethnic group could be represented and its leaders seek workable solutions to social and economic problems.

The dominant group within the Alliance was UMNO, where Datuk Onn had been replaced as president by the popular Tunku Abdul Rahman, whose credentials as a defender of Malay interests were unquestioned. UMNO's initial success was due to its ability to harness Malay opinion in the fight against the Malayan Union. This had been accomplished through Malays in government service who exploited the various state administrative structures for political mobilization. At the district level, Malay officials and a great cohort of Malay teachers worked with the penghulu, the village heads, to arouse the villagers to action. A woman's branch of UMNO was formed in 1949, and numbers of Malay women (usually the wives of UMNO members) were drawn into politics, although it was understood that their role was to support male activities. Through activating and expanding a structure inherited from colonial times, UMNO was able to call on all levels of Malay leadership and emerge as a mass political party.

Although Datuk Onn had envisaged that UMNO might eventually evolve into a multi-ethnic party, such hopes quickly faded in the face of the need to retain Malay loyalty. While the majority of Malays supported UMNO, there were other more radical organizations which vied for Malay allegiance. Despite attracting some support among recent migrants from Java and Sumatra, their slogans were meaningless or alienating for villagers who were wary of earlier associations with Indonesian nationalism and with Chinese-dominated parties. One group which was more successful in its challenge to UMNO, however, was Parti Islam Sa-Tanah Melayu [-Malaysia] (PAS, or the Pan-Malay [later Malaysian] Islamic Party). As part of UMNO, it had been earlier known as the All-Malaya Islamic Association, but it later adopted the name PAS in order to contest the 1955 federal elections as a separate political party. The PAS emphasis on Islam as the basis of a Malay-dominated society and demands for the preservation of Malay privileges were by no means new. However, they struck a particularly responsive chord in the northern states, home to a high percentage of Malays and with relatively low economic development. In these areas PAS became UMNO's natural rival in the contest to obtain Malay votes. In 1955 PAS gained the only seat not won by the Alliance, hence earning their lone parliamentarian the dubious distinction of being known as 'Mr Opposition'. A stronger PAS showing in Kedah, Kelantan and Terengganu in subsequent years has been attributed to an ability to recruit the 'sub-élite' of teachers and pupils in *pondok* schools and thus disseminate its ideas among Malay villagers. By the 1959 federal elections, under the experienced leadership of Dr Burhanuddin Al-Helmy, PAS had made considerable inroads into UMNO's support among Malays.

The MCA, the second major party in the Alliance, believed that the protection of Chinese concerns could best be achieved through accommodation with UMNO. By maintaining access to the highest echelons of government, the MCA hoped to convince the Chinese community that it was best placed to defend their interests. At first the MCA primarily expressed the views of a small Western-educated business and professional Chinese class. However, although they were largely locally born, most spoke some Chinese dialect and could thus also reach out to Chinese guilds, clan associations and trade unions. The MCA president, Tan Cheng Lock, developed a working relationship with the leaders of the other ethnic groups in the Alliance. Their shared educational experience in English schools gave these men common interests which facilitated accommodation and compromise in government. By dispensing patronage to the MCA's Chinese-speaking state leaders, the English-speaking MCA élite was able to reach the lower levels of Chinese society.

By 1958, however, Tan's health was fading and, as the MCA sought to expand its political following, other individuals – the products of Chinese education – began to play a more active part in MCA politics. More radical, and with strong communal roots, they were far more representative of the concerns of the majority of the Chinese than were the MCA's English-educated leaders. When the ability of the MCA to operate within the Alliance appeared threatened by the demands of this new faction, the old guard suspended the instigators. While sympathetic to some of the communal demands made by the party's radical wing, the MCA leadership remained convinced that their position in the Alliance depended on the maintenance of good relations with UMNO. A third faction, which emerged in 1957 around Dr Lim Chong Eu, obtained the support of young left-wing Western-educated intellectuals in the cities of Kuala Lumpur, Penang and Ipoh. Small in number, it was none the less a highly motivated and effective group, and in 1958 Lim was voted president of the MCA over Tan Cheng Lock. Although Lim assured Tunku Abdul Rahman that the MCA would continue to co-operate with UMNO, the close personal friendship between Tan and the Tunku, a major factor in the smooth relationship between the two parties, was now absent.

As the 1959 federal elections drew near, the new MCA leadership fought hard to retain the favourable treatment the MCA had received in 1955. In that election, the MCA had been allocated slightly less than half the positions on the Alliance ticket, even though the Chinese then made up 11.2 per cent of the total electorate. Because of the new citizenship laws the Chinese electorate in 1959 had increased to 35.6 per cent of the total, but the Alliance National Council had informally agreed on only 28 places for the MCA. Lim, pressing for 40 positions and urging that Mandarin be recognized as an official language, presented MCA demands in a manner that was tantamount to an ultimatum. The Tunku replied by announcing that UMNO would contest the election without the MCA. Unwilling to risk an election alone, the MCA leadership hastily reconsidered and succeeded in having the MCA retained within the Alliance. The price, however, was high. The extreme communal faction within the MCA lost influence, Lim resigned as president, and only MCA members acceptable to the Tunku appeared on the Alliance ticket for the 1959 elections. As a result of this 'July crisis' the Alliance became a much more unified body, clearly responsive to the Tunku's leadership. Even though the Tunku recognized the economic importance of the Chinese community and was therefore willing to pursue a softer line in terms of Malay special rights, the MCA's claim to be the advocate of Chinese interests had been significantly undermined. In particular, many Chinese were dismayed by MCA support for Alliance measures which appeared to be directed against Chinese education. A substantial number of Chinese now began to look elsewhere for the leadership that they believed essential to prevent their total submergence by the Malays.

The third and weakest member of the Alliance was the Malayan Indian Congress (MIC). In the early years the MIC was clearly disadvantaged by the small Indian electorate, and in the 1955 elections the MIC was allotted only two seats, whereas the MCA had fifteen and UMNO thirty-five. A number of factors undermined its bargaining position. In the first place, endorsement of the merger by MIC delegates had been half-hearted at best, and some considered that the vote was so unrepresentative it should be declared null and void. More significantly, the MIC had yet to prove that it could galvanize the full support of the Indian community, whose cultural and ethnic fragmentation had been accentuated by events such as the partition of Pakistan from India in 1947. The MIC had been largely ineffective in overcoming the rifts between recent Indian migrants and those who were locally born. Its electoral strength was also weak among the Jawi Peranakan, who had long been associated with Malay nationalism, and who often felt stronger connections with UMNO than with the Hindu-dominated MIC. In addition, Indian trade unionists and the educated Hindu élite frequently supported non-communal parties rather than the MIC. Nor had the MIC been able to establish enduring links with the mass of Indian labourers, especially after 1950 as Tamil nationalism became more pronounced. While Tamils were never able to dominate Malayan Indian society, despite their numbers, the Tamil press was vociferous in criticizing the UMNO–MCA merger and the MIC's lacklustre performance in championing Indian interests. The MIC was also perceived as lax in addressing citizenship questions and ineffective in advocating Tamil education and obtaining better conditions for Indian plantation workers. At best it was regarded as simply 'tagging along' with UMNO and the MCA, and, at worst, accused of sacrificing Indian interests to achieve the government's goals.

As with the relations between the other two members, the ability of the MIC to operate within the Alliance in these early years was largely due to a close personal bond between the Tunku and V.T. Sambanthan, MIC president from 1954 until 1973, a Perak-born estate owner who had been educated in both Tamil and English. When the activities of more radical communally minded members of the MIC threatened to jeopardize relations with UMNO, they were removed from the party. Though the old leadership re-established control over the MIC from 1958, its bargaining power remained hampered by the small size of the Indian electorate, which in 1959 was only 7.4 per cent of the total.

By the time of the 1959 federal elections the Alliance, registered in 1958 as a political party independent of its constituent members, was centralized and responding as one to the directions of Tunku Abdul Rahman. None the less, the Alliance had only become a viable political vehicle because of compromises which had been reached by the three parties on the sensitive issues of education, citizenship and Malay special privileges. In 1956, on the eve of Malaya's independence, a Committee headed by Abdul Razak bin Datuk Hussein, minister of education and later prime minister, issued the following statement, capturing precisely the UMNO-dominated Alliance view of education's role in the new nation: 'We cannot overemphasize our conviction that the introduction of syllabuses common to all schools in the Federation is the crucial requirement of education policy in Malaya. It is an essential element in the development of a united Malayan nation'.[8] The Committee argued that the separate educational systems which had developed under British colonial rule were largely responsible for the divergent and distinct outlooks on Malaya as a homeland. If the new nation were to survive and flourish, its leaders would need to act on the premise that the entire population could develop an allegiance to Malaya as a nation, and that this could be fostered by inculcating common ideals and aspirations. Another reason for extending government control over education and curriculum content was the fact that the MCP had long used Chinese schools as a recruiting ground. The Razak Report accordingly recommended limiting access to the school system for mature students.

The resulting Education Ordinance of March 1957 was an example of the sensitivities involved in reaching political compromises. Both MCA and MIC leaders accepted the principle that Malay, as the national language, should be accorded primacy; for its part, UMNO recognized Chinese and Indian concerns that vernacular education be preserved. Under the new educational system, primary National Schools (Sekolah Kebangsaan) would be conducted in Malay; government-supported National-Type Schools (Jenis Kebangsaan) could use English, Mandarin or Tamil as the medium of instruction, although the study of Malay was required. The Ordinance also established the first national Malay-medium secondary schools, evidence of the government's determination to help Malays acquire modern skills beyond the primary level. Secondary schools in other languages were permitted, but although they received partial government support, their status was left ambiguous. The MCA and MIC leadership worked hard to reassure their constituencies that the new regulations would be implemented gradually and that they would be able to negotiate a permanent place for vernacular education. Although the Ordinance was passed unanimously by the Federal Legislature, where only one seat was held by a non-Alliance party, local MCA and MIC branches were less enthusiastic. Like militant Chinese and Tamils, many of the rank and file suspected that the UMNO-dominated Alliance ultimately planned to eliminate vernacular education completely.

A second area of compromise concerned citizenship, which the MCA and MIC had always wanted to be based on the principle of *jus soli*, whereby all those born in Malaya would automatically become citizens. UMNO agreed to this in return for an agreement from its Alliance partners to an educational policy where Malay would be compulsory and a common 'Malayan curriculum' devised for all schools of whatever language medium. The third area concerned the highly sensitive issue of Malay special rights. By endorsing Alliance statements which asserted the position of Malays as 'sons/daughters of the soil' (Bumiputera), the MCA and MIC accepted the existing four-to-one ratio of Malays to non-Malays in the Malayan Civil Service, the status of the sultans, and the adoption of Malay as the national language. In return for these concessions, the UMNO assured the other two parties that liberal economic policies would be pursued to enable non-Malays to engage in economic activities without fear of confiscation or discriminatory taxation.

The Alliance therefore assumed, perhaps unjustifiably, but nevertheless effectively, the role of representing the interests of Malaya's three major ethnic groups. While the more communally minded politicians probably accurately reflected the dominant thinking of their particular ethnic communities, the Alliance held the reins of power because of the political pragmatism of its leaders and their ability to submerge their differences during elections. Similar educational and social backgrounds among the principal leaders contributed significantly to their ability to effect practical solutions to problems. Their methods were often individualistic in nature, involving a widespread use of personal persuasion in dealing with foreign and local financial interests, the bureaucracy and local state power structures. As the Tunku remarked: 'There are no water-tight compartments in our policies. In my party we are right and centre and left according to what is needed and what we think best.'[9] No other rival political group could amass sufficient seats to challenge the united Alliance, which therefore claimed a mandate to mould a new society from the various competing and frequently antagonistic groups.

The formation of Malaysia

The attainment of independence in 1957, while a significant goal in itself, raised further questions about the shape of the new nation. While the Alliance had succeeded in establishing a *modus vivendi* among the three major ethnic groups, this could obviously be only a short-term solution to the problem of creating a viable and acceptable government. The Alliance leaders agreed that their ultimate aim should be the creation of a new Malayan citizen whose loyalties would be to the nation, and not to any particular communal group. Such a goal appeared formidable, even to the most optimistic. It was something of a surprise, therefore, when Prime Minister Tunku Abdul

Rahman announced in 1961 the idea of an expanded Malaya that would include Singapore, North Borneo, Brunei and Sarawak.

The idea of extending political boundaries beyond the Peninsula was not itself new, having been broached on a number of previous occasions by the British and by various local groups seeking a 'Greater Indonesia' or 'Greater Malaysia'. One author has even suggested that the initiative for the 1961 plan had come from the British government.[10] Whatever the origins of this plan, political observers were puzzled by the willingness of the Alliance government to incorporate Singapore into the proposed union. Malaya had firmly rejected earlier suggestions to the same effect because of fears that Singapore's predominantly Chinese population would upset the ethnic 'balance' and that Singapore's economic interests would clash with those of Malaya. There was also a belief that Malayan politics might become radicalized through contact with Singapore's strong left-wing groups. But by 1961 political circumstances in Singapore had given the Malayan government cause to reconsider its attitude towards union.

Since the introduction of elections in 1948, Singapore's politics had become increasingly dominated by the communists and other radical groups. These groups, however, had been kept under control by the colonial administration. Even when Singapore was given internal self-government in 1958, the British retained the responsibility of maintaining internal security and defence. This transitional Constitution was to expire in 1963 and it was expected that Singapore would then demand and obtain full independence with total charge of its own affairs. With memories of the Emergency so recent, such prospects were regarded with some apprehension in Malaya. In conversations with certain UMNO officers, Tunku Abdul Rahman openly expressed his concern that an independent Singapore might be controlled by communists, who would then use their independent base to aid their compatriots in Malaya. One way of preventing this was to incorporate Singapore into some federation with Malaya where more moderate forces could counteract the left-wing elements in Singapore. In addition to the concern for national security, the Tunku saw a federation of Malaya and Singapore as desirable in advancing their 'mutual economy', which was too closely tied to be left to the political vagaries of separate and possibly hostile governments. Fears among UMNO members that Singapore's inclusion would lead to Malays being overwhelmed by Chinese were allayed by the proposal that North Borneo and Sarawak also join the federation to restore the ethnic balance. Malay leaders saw the indigenous groups in North Borneo and Sarawak as sharing a single ethnicity with the Malays, so that the term 'Bumiputera' could be used to refer to all indigenous peoples in Malaysia. While their common appellation did not prevent friction arising later over the allocation of resources between Malays and other Bumiputera, at the time the argument did serve its political purpose in convincing sceptical UMNO members to approve Singapore's entry into the proposed federation.

The government in Singapore at the time of the Malaysia Federation proposal was the People's Action Party (PAP) under the leadership of a young lawyer, Lee Kuan Yew. The PAP had come to power in 1959 on an election platform calling for Singapore autonomy within some form of union with Malaya. In August 1961 Lee met Tunku Abdul Rahman to draw up a preliminary agreement for merger. This agreement reflected Lee's success in obtaining specific concessions essential for eliminating some of the more serious objections to union. Singapore would maintain its free port status, a major concession to the business community who feared tariff barriers being erected to protect Malaya's export-orientated economy. It would also be given special autonomy in education and labour policies as well as a large proportion of its revenues for expenditure in those areas, thereby appeasing those Singaporeans who feared a loss of control over Chinese schools and Chinese-dominated labour unions. Because the concessions would give Singapore a degree of political and financial independence, it was agreed that Singapore's representation in the Federal House of Representatives would be limited to 15 seats, three or four less than would have been allocated proportionate to its population. The merger was strongly opposed by the Barisan Sosialis (Socialist Front) and the United Peoples' Party, but it received a resounding 71.7 per cent approval vote in a referendum.

The Borneo territories were more resistant to the idea of a 'Mighty Malaysia', even though British colonials had previously discussed the idea of uniting Sarawak, North Borneo and Brunei as a prelude to inclusion in a larger Malayan Federation. In fact, the ground had already been prepared by policies put in place following the cession of North Borneo and Sarawak to the British Crown. As full colonies, the two were subject to a similar administration which lessened the differences between them and tightened the economic links with Malaya. A common currency, the Malaysian *ringgit*, was adopted; the revenue and tax base was widened; investment was encouraged, especially in the timber industry; and attempts were made to encourage sedentary farming and irrigated rice in preference to shifting cultivation. But in other areas such as administrative experience the disparity between Borneo and the Peninsula was still marked. Although the creation of advisory councils and local authorities had provided a valuable apprenticeship period, in 1957 most service posts in Borneo were still held by British officers, some of whom had been trained during the prewar regimes. This is hardly surprising, given the small pool of local candidates. In 1962 about half Sarawak's school-age population had never received any formal education. Political involvement at the time of the Tunku's proposal was also undeveloped, and in North Borneo there were no political parties at all.

Not surprisingly, the notion that the three Borneo states should join Malaya and Singapore in a new Federation was initially rejected outright by local leaders, some of whom had hoped for separate independence. Donald Stephens, a Kadazandusun leader from North Borneo, expressed a common view when he remarked that joining 'Malaysia' would inevitably lead to domination by Peninsular Malays. Although a United Front was formed in July 1961 to provide the basis for Borneo resistance, the persuasive powers of the Tunku and Lee Kuan Yew soon began to make an impression. Brunei remained unenthusiastic, but in January 1962 the governments of Sarawak and North Borneo each urged their people to support Malaysia. Critical in gaining the approval of these two states was the agreement of Malaya and Singapore to certain conditions, foremost among which were:

1. Sarawak and North Borneo would be given authority over immigration, including that of Malaysian citizens from other states.
2. Malay would be recognized as the national language, but English would continue as a medium of instruction and as the official language for state government until the State Legislature decided otherwise.
3. Islam would be the official religion but other religions could be propagated.
4. Indigenous peoples of these two states would enjoy special privileges similar to those the Malays enjoyed in Malaya.
5. Financial arrangements would be made to guarantee federal funds for economic development.
6. A separate federal public service for the two states would be created, and expatriate officers could be retained until sufficient trained local officers became available.

Through 1962 the fine details were worked out in meetings of an Intergovernmental Committee, which included representation from Britain, Malaya, North Borneo and Sarawak. In North Borneo (to be renamed Sabah), the formation of a grand coalition of newly established political parties, the Sabah Alliance, was a clear endorsement of the Malaysia concept, as was the Pro-Malaysia Sarawak Alliance. Both won decisively in the 1963 state elections.

Brunei, the fourth state invited by Malaya to join the Federation, was very conscious that its days of greatness lay in the past. The steady loss of territory to Sarawak and North Borneo during the nineteenth century had only been forestalled when the British government appointed a Resident in 1906. Ruling over the remnants of a once extensive and powerful kingdom, the sultan of Brunei continued to exercise autocratic powers over his subjects, supported by substantial oil revenues. The first steps towards a constitutional monarchy appeared to come in 1959, when the sultan promulgated a new Constitution, and in the elections held in 1962. For some, however, progress towards democratic government was too slow. Local leaders like A.M. Azahari, president of Brunei's Partai Rakyat (People's Party), were also fearful that the sultan might choose to join Malaysia and thus end the dream of a Greater Brunei which would reclaim control over North Borneo and Sarawak. Azahari and his supporters received secret financial and material assistance from both Indonesia and the Philippines because of their hostility to the idea of a Malaysian Federation. The so-called Brunei Revolt on the night of 7 December 1962 was quickly suppressed by British troops, though Azahari, who was then in Manila, escaped capture. In the midst of this drama, the sultan of Brunei became disenchanted with certain financial and constitutional aspects of the Malaysia proposal that would have weakened his position. The prospect of sharing his kingdom's substantial oil revenues was not appealing, and he also felt he was entitled to a more senior position among the hierarchy of Peninsular rulers in line for the revolving post of yang dipertuan agung or paramount ruler. Considering he was being asking to concede too much, the sultan finally declined the invitation to become part of the new Malaysia.

In the week following the outbreak of the Brunei Revolt, Indonesia officially proclaimed its support for Azahari and his rebels. Not long afterwards, in January 1963, President Sukarno announced a policy of 'Konfrontasi' (Confrontation) against Malaya. Yet despite Indonesia's attacks on Malayan fishing boats and repeated violations of Malaya's air space, the Alliance government felt no great cause for alarm. Malaya had a defence agreement with Great Britain and knew that it could call on Commonwealth troops for support, as it eventually did. Indonesia's threats to bring economic pressure on Malaya never eventuated because of the mutual disadvantages such action would incur, although its diplomatic campaign did arouse some concern. Directed especially at the Afro-Asian Third World nations, this campaign sought to isolate Malaya and bring about the collapse of the Malaysia Federation scheme. But even here Indonesia's 'Confrontation' scheme ultimately proved ineffectual.

In early 1962 President Macapagal of the Philippines also voiced opposition to the Malaysia Federation on the grounds that the inclusion of North Borneo could not be legally upheld. According to Philippine claims, the original 1878 transfer of the territory of North Borneo from the sultanate of Sulu (now part of the Philippines) was in the form of a lease rather than a sale. This had been demonstrated by subsequent regular annual payments from the Company to the Sulu sultan. Initially, the Malayan government regarded the Philippine claims as having been motivated by domestic political considerations. It adopted a conciliatory attitude but never intended to relinquish Sabah nor allow this claim to interfere in the formation of Malaysia. As the Philippines became more belligerently insistent, Malaya eventually made clear its determination to proceed with the plan of including North Borneo in the proposed Federation.

Because of steadily deteriorating relations between Malaya and its two neighbours, the three heads of government met in Manila in July–August 1963. Both Indonesia and the Philippines declared their willingness to recognize Malaysia, 'provided the support of the people of the Borneo Territories is ascertained by an independent and impartial authority, the Secretary-General of the United Nations or his representative'. But they later repudiated a UN survey demonstrating that North Borneo and

Sarawak wished to become part of Malaysia, and severed diplomatic relations with the new Federation of Malaysia when it was officially inaugurated on 16 September 1963. Indonesia conducted a 'crush Malaysia' campaign, and attacks along the borders of Sarawak and Sabah from Indonesian Borneo (Kalimantan) increased in number and severity. Indiscriminate bombing and terrorist acts were also carried out by saboteurs landed or dropped secretly into Malaya and Singapore.

Indonesia's hostile activities were successfully contained by Malaysian and Commonwealth forces, and Malaysia at no time felt endangered by its much larger and more populous neighbour. Relations between the two countries improved after September 1965, when the communists were ousted from all positions of influence in the Indonesian government. In August 1966 a peace agreement was signed between the two nations formally ending 'Confrontation' and indicating Malaysia's intention to have Sabah and Sarawak decide in an election whether they still wished to become part of Malaysia. In contrast to Indonesian actions, the battle over Philippine claims to Sabah was conducted on a diplomatic level. The election of President Marcos in mid-1965 raised hopes in Kuala Lumpur that some agreement could be reached, since he seemed less concerned to pursue Philippine claims. Initially, domestic political pressure prevented him from any disavowal of this policy, but by June 1966 the Philippines had extended recognition to Malaysia.

At the beginning of the twenty-first century the opposition of Indonesia and the Philippines to the formation of Malaysia seems to lie in the very distant past. In 1967 all three became founding members of the Association of Southeast Asians Nations (ASEAN), which today includes the ten countries of the region (except for newly independent Timor) and is one of the planks of Malaysian foreign policy. However, this period has its own significance in the 'nation-building' process. The open conflict with Indonesia and the strong opposition from the Philippines fostered a stronger sense of what it was to be Malay and now Malaysian. Until the declaration of 'Konfrontasi', many Malays had seen Sukarno as the leader of a greater Malaysia. The events of these years, however, contributed to the creation of a historical memory by drawing Malays into a national entity that went beyond identification with state or *kerajaan*. The Occupation, the immediate postwar years, the Emergency, and now the violence of 'Confrontation' became incorporated into a national historical drama with the Malays as the principal protagonists. The departure of Singapore from the Federation became another episode in that unfolding story.

Maintaining the unity of the Federation

Even before 'Confrontation' and the Philippine claim to Sabah had been resolved, the strains of welding a Federation of Malaysia from very disparate states were already evident. On 9 August 1965 the Malaysian House of Representatives (Dewan Rakyat) passed a Constitutional Amendment Bill enabling Singapore to secede from the Federation. From the very inception of the Federation proposal, Singapore had posed a problem. The basic reason for Malaya's decision to include Singapore was the widely held view that a left-leaning Singapore outside Malaysia was more dangerous than one within it. But shortly after the formation of the Federation, the wisdom of this view was challenged. In the Singapore elections of September 1963 and the Malaysian elections of 1964 the Singapore-based PAP did battle with the Malayan Alliance. The PAP concentrated on undermining the MCA's claims to speak for the Chinese, although it assiduously avoided any attack on UMNO. The latter, too, was circumspect and refrained from portraying the PAP as a threat. None the less, in the political heat engendered in these elections, communal tensions rose and in Singapore serious interethnic clashes occurred. Both the PAP and the Alliance won handily in their respective strongholds. In Singapore in the September 1963 elections the PAP gained 37 of the 51 elected seats in the Singapore Legislative Assembly. Across the causeway, in the 1964 Malaysian federal elections, the Alliance government won 123 of the 159 seats in the Dewan Rakyat, undoubtedly helped by the Alliance call for national solidarity in face of external threats.

As the political struggle between the PAP and the Malayan Alliance intensified, Singaporeans came to regard various economic and political measures taken by the Malaysian government as detrimental to their interests and as Alliance attempts to dislodge the PAP from power. In September 1964 discussions were held by the leaders of both parties to consider a coalition government, but the Alliance rejected any such arrangement. It was then that the PAP decided to fight for a 'Malaysian Malaysia' as opposed to a 'Malay Malaysia', which it claimed was being imposed by the UMNO-dominated Alliance government. In order to challenge its formidable opponent, the PAP organized an alliance of its own which comprised a number of opposition parties throughout Malaysia under the banner of the Malaysian Solidarity Convention. The heavily Chinese composition of this new political union made the struggle appear increasingly as one between non-Malays and Malays. As the media on both sides of the causeway focused on the significance of the new alignments, the expression of communal sentiments grew more blatant and ethnic riots broke out in Singapore. In the Dewan Rakyat itself debates were acrimonious, but the new coalition appeared determined to persevere on its chosen course, despite the growing danger of open conflict.

The threat of communal violence was apparently the crucial factor in the government's decision to separate Singapore from the Federation of Malaysia. In the Dewan Rakyat Tunku Abdul Rahman explained that the communal issue concerned him most 'because the peace and happiness of the people in this country depend on goodwill and understanding of the various races for one another. Without it this nation will break up with consequential disaster'. While the Alliance government had preserved the unity of the Malaysian Federation in the face of diplomatic and military pressures from Indonesia and the Philippines, it succumbed to the threat of violence among its own people. It therefore agreed to Singapore's secession, despite protests from Singapore's leaders.

With the secession, the attention of the Alliance government was no longer diverted by draining political battles with the PAP, and it could resume the urgent task of promoting a genuine unity among the Federation's remaining members. Of particular concern was the inclusion of Sabah and Sarawak, where the pace of development and the nature of local society were very different from the Peninsular states, despite colonial connections. To compensate for such differences, and to ensure the entry of these states to the Federation, the Alliance government had agreed to allow the Borneo states greater autonomy and a longer time-frame for integration. None the less, Kuala Lumpur was unwilling to tolerate any attempts to undermine the newly created union. When Sabah's chief minister Donald Stephens championed the cause of the indigenous peoples of Sabah, especially his own numerically dominant Kadazandusuns, he brought down the ire of the central government. The latter saw him as exercising a degree of state autonomy in a manner that bordered on separatism. As a result, Stephens was eased out of office and replaced as chief minister in 1967 by Datu (later Tun) Mustapha, a Muslim Sulu chief. In Sarawak, too, the chief minister, Stephen Kalong Ningkan from Sarawak's largest group, the Ibans, fought to preserve concessions granted to the state by the Malayan government prior to Federation. But he suffered a fate similar to that of his Sabah counterpart and was replaced as chief minister in 1966 by another Iban, Tawi Sli, who was more amenable to directives from Kuala Lumpur.

Under the leadership of Tunku Abdul Rahman the Federation had survived an Indonesian Confrontation, a Philippine claim to Sabah, a Singapore secession and a Bornean assertion of state autonomy. But the ability of the Alliance government to overcome these threats could only temporarily divert attention from the ever-present problems of ethnicity within Malaysian society itself. The solution, argued the government, must be to plan for the future and mould a new Malaysian citizen whose loyalty would be to the nation instead of a particular state or ethnic group. Few then would have disagreed in seeing this goal as the only guarantee of Malaysia's survival. It was the interpretation of what should constitute the 'new Malaysian' which became the contentious issue. Although barely acknowledged at the time, the inclusion of Sabah and Sarawak made this question far more complex. The categories of Malay, Chinese, Indian and 'lain-lain' ('Others') which had shaped perceptions of society and governance on the Peninsula were hardly workable in the Borneo states, where language and identity were multi-layered, and where the idea of 'non-interference' in traditional life had permitted considerable cultural autonomy among different groups. Even defining what it meant to be 'indigenous' in Sarawak resulted in a semiotic conundrum. According to the 1947 census, it included all those 'who recognize

allegiance to no other foreign territory, who regard Sarawak as their homeland, who believe themselves to be a part of the territory and who are now
regarded as native by their fellow men'.[11] Undeterred by such complicating
factors, the UMNO-dominated Alliance government decided that the basis
for creating a future citizenry would be Malaya's traditional culture and
heritage, meaning Malay language and culture. Non-Malays, however, argued
that a more appropriate path was to work towards a Malaysian identity that
would reflect the country's multi-ethnic background.

Growing ethnic tensions

The national language question was a crucial aspect of what quickly became
a highly emotional debate. When the Merdeka (Independence) Constitution
was promulgated in 1957 it included a provision that after ten years Malay
would be the sole official language. The establishment of the Dewan Bahasa
dan Pustaka (Literary and Language Agency) in 1956 was intended to
encourage this development by creating Malay terminology in such fields as
commerce, higher education, technology and science. Co-operation between
the Indonesians and Malaysians in the late 1960s and the 1970s resulted in
some standardization of terminology and the adoption in 1972 of a uniform
system of spelling in their basically common languages. These steps, it was
hoped, would answer critics and effectively demonstrate that Malay would
be able to cope as a national language in a modernized society. A National
Language Bill was passed on 3 March 1967, representing the kind of compromise that had come to be associated with the Alliance government. Malay
was recognized as the national language, but English could be used in an official capacity, and teaching and learning other languages would be permitted.
But as with all previous Alliance compromises, the more communally
minded elements of each ethnic group were dissatisfied. Once again, this
debate set Malays and Chinese at odds.

For their part, Malays argued that only with a widespread and official
use of the Malay language would they be able to keep pace and share in the
benefits of the rapid economic development of their country. There was also
an underlying concern that without protection Malay might be swamped by
English and Chinese. Since the days of Melaka, Malays had regarded language (*bahasa*) and the customs and attitudes it subsumed as a fundamental
component of their identity. Despite local variations in dialect and custom,
and the strength of state loyalties, *bahasa* was seen as the essential element
that drew Malays together. The view that Malay should be the official national
language found new champions during the 1950s with the emergence of a
new generation of Malay writers, editors and journalists, like the Singapore-
based and Indonesia-inspired group Angkatan Sasterawan 50 ('Literary
Generation of 1950'). Circulated via newspapers and magazines, the 'ASAS

50' writers popularized a new genre of literature in which social commentary was at the forefront. For many Malay villagers, struggling on the edge of subsistence as rubber prices declined, stories of the inequities between 'poor Malays' and 'rich Chinese' reawakened deep-seated fears of Chinese economic dominance. In this context debates about *bahasa* were not simply about language or even the primacy of the Malays: they concerned the very survival of Malay culture.

Believing that *bahasa jiwa bangsa* (language is the soul of the nation), nationalistic Malays found very little room for compromise with those Chinese who felt that maintenance of their mother-tongue and education in the Chinese language was not merely economically useful, but a crucial cultural component. For generations Malayan Chinese had maintained the schools by which knowledge about their ancestral home was passed on to their children. It is not hard to see why many Chinese firmly believed that the loss of their language would inevitably lead to a disintegration of the Chinese heritage. At the same time, the official Alliance view was clear: an integrated language and educational policy was a key instrument in forging an integrated and united society that would be assimilated to Malay cultural traditions. As an Alliance member, the MCA was obliged to work towards compromise with its partners, and it was these compromises which convinced Chinese that in any disagreement their interests would be overridden by those of the Malays.

These fears appeared to be confirmed with the passing of the Education Act of 1961. Implementing the recommendations of the Rahman Talib Report of 1960, it laid down that Chinese-medium secondary education in National-type schools was to be abolished. In order to receive full government aid as National-Type Secondary Schools, Chinese schools were required to convert to teaching in English. If they continued to teach in Chinese, they would forfeit government aid. The sometimes agonizing decisions which set principle against pragmatism divided the Chinese community and sometimes Chinese families, but by the end of 1961, a total of 54 out of 70 high schools had accepted the government's conditions. In 1965 the government announced further far-reaching changes in educational policy. First, the Primary Six exam was abolished, allowing anyone who completed primary grades to enter the Lower Secondary Schools (Forms 1, 2, 3). Secondly, Cambridge School Certificate and Higher School Certificate exams to determine entry into the University of Malaya would no longer be exclusively in English but would also be conducted in Malay.

While these measures sent important signals to non-Malay communities, the continued existence of English-medium schools was indicative of the government's ambivalence towards English education. The decision-makers in the Alliance were themselves English-medium graduates, and their own experience had convinced them that it was in these schools that integration of pupils of various ethnic groups was most easily achieved. The leaders of the different ethnic groups realized that it was their common educational experience which had made meaningful dialogue possible and which had underwritten the compromises they had made. It was also generally recognized that the prestigious English-medium schools, then considered the best in the country, were the training ground for the future élite. For the present, therefore, English was permitted as a medium of instruction in National-type Schools. When the University of Malaya was established in 1949 it was set up in Singapore, and although it moved to Kuala Lumpur in 1963 it was essentially an English-speaking campus. Not until 1967 was a Malaysian history course offered in Malay. To many Malays it seemed that the persistence of English was both a denial and a denigration of the status of Malay as the national language.

In North Borneo and Sarawak the retention of English for at least ten years and the slower introduction of Malay had been a condition of entry into the Federation, and therefore made the language issue less contentious. It was not until September 1973 that Sabah made the national language (*Bahasa Kebangsaan*), i.e. Malay, the only official medium of communication. Sarawak decided in March 1974 to retain officially both Malay and English until 1980, when English would be dropped. A greater concern was actual availability of schooling. Even though increased resources went some way towards satisfying a growing demand for education, town dwellers were inevitably privileged. It was not financially feasible to establish schools in remote areas of the interior, and the subsistence lifestyle of many groups meant low retention rates in the few rural schools that were established. Lack of access to education reflected not only ethnic inequalities, but also gender disparities. In 1932 the earliest Sarawak Malay novel, *Melati Sarawak* (Sarawak Jasmine), had urged the education of Malay women, yet by 1948 girls comprised less than a quarter of the school population, and they were mostly Chinese. Some improvements came in 1955, when a new system of government aid provided substantial capital grants for new school buildings and helped regularize teachers' salaries. The establishment of boarding schools in inland centres and continuing missionary work also helped bring education within the reach of many children. But the fact that so many different cultural groups were involved meant the language question was far less politically charged than on the Peninsula. Here, issues regarding language and education became increasingly explosive during the 1960s because they reached deep into the heart of the ethnic communities.

Once again, Malay concerns were most clearly articulated by writers and journalists, members of the small but influential Malay middle class. While literary competitions and access to a range of publishers injected fresh energy into Malay writing, it is evident that much of its stimulus stemmed from the feeling that independence had not brought Malays the better life they had expected. It was increasingly clear that Chinese entrepreneurs had flourished under the government's *laissez-faire* policies, and that the income disparity between Malays and Chinese had worsened. Rural areas, where most Malays still lived, remained poor, village youths were leaving for the cities, governments appeared unresponsive, class privilege seemed entrenched, Islam was not honoured, Malays lacked access to higher education, and the position of Malay culture and language was contested. These issues became the focus for much of the Malay writing of the 1960s, resulting in novels that were relentless in their depiction of the harshness of rural life, the economic hold of the Chinese and the moral corruption of political leadership. In 1961 PENA, the National Writers Association, was founded on the assumption that Malay language and literature would stand as the foundation of Malaysia's national culture. As in the past, several writers among this new generation were teachers, and teachers also made up about half of the delegates to the UMNO general assembly.

While many non-Malays felt that the government's policies regarding language and education were simply an attempt to secure the schools as one more area for Malay special privileges, the Chinese were particularly resentful. Here too teachers had played a major role in the campaign to preserve instruction in Chinese. In 1961 the citizenship of the leader of the United Chinese School Teachers' Association was even revoked because his comments were considered so inflammatory. The Chinese-language press also fanned the fears of total submersion by the Malays, and to an increasing number of Chinese it seemed that their culture was being sacrificed at the altar of national unity. Many despaired of the MCA's ability to ensure the preservation of Chinese interests, despite its membership in the governing coalition. Though less vociferous in regard to the language issue, Indians similarly felt that the MIC had been an ineffectual lobbyist, especially in regard to the problem of Indian 'non-citizens': in 1969, for example, 20 per cent of Indians who fulfilled residential qualifications were still without Malaysian citizenship.

Economic developments

It could well be argued that the early leaders of Malaya/Malaysia were given time to deal with many of the problems that faced their new nation because they inherited an export economy that was the envy of Southeast Asia. Through co-operation between the colonial government and European and Chinese business interests, an economy dependent on subsistence agriculture and regional trade had been transformed into one which dominated world production of valuable commodities, notably rubber, tin and palm oil. While the revenues of North Borneo and Sarawak were still small by Malaya's standards, the post-colonial regimes continued to subscribe to the economic priorities bequeathed by the pre-independence period.

In the First (1956–60) and Second (1961–5) Malayan Plans, the government's main objectives were to achieve economic growth and to eliminate economic disparity among the ethnic groups. While development would be accorded priority, it would always be tempered by considerations of ethnicity in order to ensure that prosperity was spread more evenly through the population. A third objective was greater employment opportunities, presumably through high economic development. The First Malaysia Plan (1966–70) also stressed these three main objectives, according them the same order of priority. The goal of economic growth continued to receive greatest attention because it was believed to be the key to achieving the other two. Industrialization and manufacturing, however, received little attention, and the Pioneer Industries Ordinance of 1958, intended to introduce import-substitution industrialization, had only a limited effect because the domestic market was so small. But while the stress remained on primary production, growth prospects were by no means assured because of challenges to the two pillars of Malaysia's economy: rubber and tin.

The rubber industry had recovered quickly after the war, and by 1946 Malaya's production was already up to 410 000 tonnes, only about 100 000 tonnes less than in 1941. By 1948 production was at 708 000 tonnes, some 150 000 tonnes more than the previous record in 1940. However, it faced stiff competition from the synthetic rubber industry, which had made significant advances in technology, packaging and marketing techniques. Synthetic rubber production had rapidly expanded in the United States during the war years, reaching 950 000 tonnes per annum by 1944. But although demand declined, natural rubber could still command a ready market. High-tear strength, resilience and properties of abrasion resistance and heat dissipation made natural rubber preferable to synthetic rubber for certain products such as aeroplane and heavy-duty truck tyres, parts of ordinary car tyres, and numerous mechanical goods.

Despite the difficulties faced by planters during the Malayan Emergency (1948–60), rubber production generally continued at a high level. In 1951 around a fifth of Malaya's economically active labour force was working on rubber estates, and at independence rubber was still the country's chief export earner, accounting for 85 per cent of British Malaya's gross export earnings. In part at least the industry's profitability was due to its success in curtailing wage rises while avoiding prolonged strikes. This in turn was possible because the National Union of Plantation Workers, formed in 1954, promoted a more conciliatory approach to labour relations. None the less, rubber was no longer as attractive to European investors as it had been in the early decades of the twentieth century, and the subdivision of estates was already evident. A parallel story was evident in North Borneo and Sarawak, where rubber moved from boom periods prior to the First World War to slumps and restrictions in the 1920s and 1930s, and from disaster during the Japanese Occupation to modest profits in the postwar years. One difference, however, was the slower rate of recovery and adaptation after 1946. Only through government pressure did the industry finally modernize to reach the standards set on the Peninsula.

While the rubber industry survived, revenues from tin-mining were seriously threatened because of a growing world-wide economy in its use, better recovery techniques and the effects of prewar restrictions on production. The Occupation years had exacted a further toll, and in subsequent years the Malayan tin industry experienced continuing difficulties as tin prices fluctuated and controls were again imposed to limit output. By the time Malaya became independent in 1957, tin as an export commodity was a poor second to rubber.

Government planners were fully aware of the implications of these trends, and economic diversification was therefore an important component in the first three development plans. One of the major successes was the palm oil industry. Like rubber and tin, palm oil had suffered during the Occupation, but by 1948 production was four-fifths that of the prewar figure. By the mid-1950s palm oil was well established as an export commodity, with plantations covering some 50 000 hectares spread over 63 estates. Within a decade, aided by a large influx of capital after the Second World War, a sophisticated research programme and a buoyant overseas market, Malaysia had become the world's largest producer of palm oil.

Iron ores and manufacturing also contributed to growing export earnings. With the reconstruction in Japan in the immediate postwar years, timber was in great demand, benefiting Malaya and particularly North Borneo. A number of new companies were allowed to enter the once exclusive domain of the British Borneo Timber Company, considerably increasing the area being logged. By 1961 timber had passed rubber as the major export earner in the state, earning $102.8 million to rubber's $41.2 million. Although copra, manila hemp (abaca) and cocoa rose in importance as commercial crops, rubber and timber remained the chief revenue earners. In 1960 primary commodities accounted for just over 80 per cent of total exports, with rubber contributing the largest share at 55.5 per cent, followed by tin 14 per cent, timber (sawlogs and sawn timber) 5.4 per cent, petroleum 4 per cent, and palm oil 1.7 per cent.

Notwithstanding the country's impressive economic growth, problems of unemployment and poverty persisted, particularly in the rural areas. Returning to a Kelantan fishing village in 1963 after more than twenty years, the anthropologist Rosemary Firth noted that while children no longer suffered from yaws, items such as condensed milk, sugar and manufactured cigarettes remained a luxury.[12] When the government discussed 'rural poverty', it was largely seen as a Malay problem, which could be addressed by land development and the creation of facilities such as roads, schools, clinics, irrigation, and so on. To this end a number of specific projects were developed or extended, notably the Federal Land Development Authority (FELDA), the Federal Land Consolidation and Rehabilitation Authority (FELCRA), and the Rubber Industry Smallholders Development Authority (RISDA). RISDA was able to provide funds to rubber smallholders through a tax on replanting, which would help finance the propagation of higher-yielding and more disease-resistant rubber trees. In FELDA schemes between 1600 and 2000 hectares were cleared and planted by contractors, then divided into plots of between 3.2 and 4 hectares to be allocated to mainly rural Malay settlers. The latter received fertilizer and a subsistence allowance based on daily work on approved economic activity. Land development costs, charged against the settler's loan account, were to be repaid over 10–15 years to allow sufficient time for crops to mature. Some of the largest FELDA schemes were the Jengka Triangle Project, covering some 132 000 hectares in Pahang; the Johor Tenggara Project, with 148 500 hectares; and the Pahang Tenggara Project, involving one million hectares.

Although FELDA was an ambitious and costly undertaking, between 1956 and 1973 only about 174 000 people of a total rural population of about 7 065 000 were resettled on FELDA lands, and the numbers of those who drew benefits from the scheme were thus very limited. Furthermore, some Malays were already objecting to their relegation to the agricultural sector. In 1965 and again in 1968 UMNO had convened an Bumiputera Economic Congress to address complaints that Malays were insufficiently represented in commerce and industry. In 1967 Shahnon Ahmad's fictional but highly influential novel *Menteri* ('Minister') even foresaw a future in which Chinese controlled the country while Malays had been driven into the jungle.

The perception of Malays as the rural poor had been reinforced because many of the New Villages, where more than 500 000 Chinese squatters had been resettled, had expanded into sizeable towns. By 1957 as much as 73 per cent of the Chinese population were living in urban areas of 1000 people or more. Even so, some New Villages lacked basic facilities, and as 'urban' areas they were bypassed when funds were diverted to rural development programmes. In its early years the MCA had worked to establish a support base in the New Villages, but this rapidly eroded in the face of limited financial help from the government, deficiencies in amenities, and rising unemployment. Not surprisingly, disenchanted New Villagers, almost all Chinese, were disinclined to see the MCA as their defender. For its part, the MIC had always faced problems in generating support from Indian labourers, and its attempt to stand as an advocate for poor workers became more difficult in the 1960s. When many estates were subdivided after local businessmen bought up estates from Europeans, thousands of mostly Indian plantation workers lost their jobs.[13]

These developments meant that in the campaign preceding the 1969 federal elections there was a sizeable pool of Chinese and Indians who felt their interests had not been served by the Alliance government. There was thus widespread response to the promises of a new party formed in Penang in April 1968, the Gerakan Rakyat Malaysia (Malaysian People's Movement). A minority voice among Malaysian leaders had always spoken in favour of political parties based on philosophy and policy rather than race. The Gerakan represented a revived effort to create a non-communal party, as had been attempted by groups like the Malayan Democratic Union immediately after the war. Gerakan's leadership was a multi-ethnic mix of trade unionists, professionals and university lecturers who campaigned on the slogan of 'equality, justice and equal opportunity for all'. Because many of its members were Chinese, Malays came to view Gerakan as Chinese rather than non-communal.

Another political party which benefited from Chinese and Indian dissatisfaction with the Alliance was the Democratic Action Party (DAP), the old Singapore-based PAP now reconstituted as a Malaysian party to contest elections in the Peninsula. Arguing for ethnic equality and cultural pluralism, it wanted an end to Malay special privileges and a commitment to true equality in education, whether in the language medium of Malay, English, Chinese or Indian. The People's Progressive Party (PPP), with its strength among the Chinese and Indian communities in Perak, also capitalized on dissatisfaction at what were regarded as the pro-Malay policies of the Alliance government. But memories of decades of perceived injustices and discrimination were felt in all communities, among Malays and non-Malays alike, and in May 1969 the long-suppressed anger and disappointment exploded into ethnic violence.

Ethnic disturbances of May 1969 and Emergency Government

The ostensible cause of this communal conflict was the federal elections of 10 May 1969. Fought on the highly emotional issues of education and language, the pre-election campaign exposed deep and abiding concerns among all communities regarding their situation within the new Malaysian nation. Although public discussion had sometimes been intense, the Alliance leaders had hitherto been largely successful in conveying the message that compromise would ensure fair treatment for all ethnic groups. By 1969, however, a disillusioned electorate was ready to make plain its grievances at the polls, as each ethnic group sought to preserve its interests against the encroachment of others. In the wake of a tireless campaign mounted by Chinese opposition parties supporting non-Malay rights, the volatility of the public mood became all too evident. Held in a Kuala Lumpur suburb the day before the elections, the funeral procession of a young (allegedly communist) Chinese man killed by the police became the magnet for a huge demonstration of around 10 000 people.

The election results, which started to come in on 11 May, simply ignited smouldering ethnic tensions. Although the Alliance retained a majority in the Dewan Rakyat, its seats fell to 66 from the 1964 figure of 89, and its popular vote had declined from the 1964 total of 58.4 per cent to 48.5 per cent. Of equal concern were Alliance losses in the state assemblies, and the failure of the coalition to deliver communal votes as it had done in the past. In some electorates with Malay majorities a DAP or Gerakan Chinese candidate won because the Malay vote was split between UMNO and PAS. More seriously, the Chinese vote deserted the MCA, which held only 13 of 33 contested seats, while the election of Indian candidates standing for non-communal parties showed all too plainly the lack of Indian confidence in the Alliance. In

Selangor and Perak, two economically vital states with large Chinese constituencies, the Alliance had failed to obtain a majority. The Gerakan, DAP and PPP together won a total of 25 seats and PAS 12 seats, thus depriving the Alliance government of the two-thirds majority which had previously enabled it to obtain constitutional amendments with ease.

On 12 May jubilant Gerakan and DAP supporters took to the streets of Kuala Lumpur in a victory celebration, taunting Malays and predicting future Chinese successes. A counter-rally by UMNO supporters the following day quickly deteriorated into unprecedented and uncontrolled ethnic violence. On 14 May a State of Emergency was declared and the Constitution suspended. Elections scheduled for the Borneo states were postponed. All administrative powers were centralized in a National Operations Council headed by the deputy prime minister, Abdul Razak. After four days of bloody fighting order was finally restored to the city, but for two months incidents of communal violence persisted. Officially, 196 people died and 409 were injured, but the numbers were certainly higher, with most of the victims being Chinese. The homes and property of about 6000 residents of Kuala Lumpur, again primarily Chinese, were destroyed. The Malay leadership in the Alliance attributed Malay violence to the opposition's unrestrained attacks on Malay privileges, although this claim was vehemently rejected. Militant Malay groups even called for the Tunku's resignation, claiming his attitude towards the other ethnic communities was too accommodating. These groups were only subdued when the government threatened severe retaliatory action. One of the government's most outspoken critics was a relatively junior member of parliament from Kedah, Dr Mahathir Mohamad, who had lost his seat in the elections because of declining Chinese support for the Alliance. His claim that the Tunku had been too conciliatory led to his expulsion from UMNO.

As in the immediate postwar years, the riots of 1969 painfully revealed how strong were the undercurrents of distrust running through the various ethnic communities. Indeed, the government warned that if further political excesses continued it would not be safe to return to a parliamentary-style democracy. Once again the old question was raised, but this time with a far greater sense of urgency: how was a united and enduring Malaysia to be forged? The Emergency Government moved quickly, and one of its first steps was the creation in July of a Department of National Unity to formulate a national ideology and new social and economic programmes. On 31 August 1970, Malaysia's Independence Day, the new ideology Rukunegara ('Articles of Faith of the State') was formally proclaimed:

> Our nation, Malaysia, being dedicated to achieving a greater unity of all her peoples; to maintaining a democratic way of life; to creating a just society in which the wealth of the nation shall be equitably shared; to ensuring a liberal approach to her rich and diverse cultural traditions; to building a progressive society which shall be orientated to modern science and technology.

We, her people, pledge our united efforts to attain those ends guided by these principles:

Belief in God
Loyalty to King and Country
Sanctity of the Constitution
Rule of Law
Good Behaviour and Morality

The government also took steps to control publications which it felt had inflamed communal feeling. Speeches or writing considered likely to incite ethnic hostility were banned. One of the censored works was a trenchant analysis of the reasons behind Malay poverty, entitled *The Malay Dilemma* by the unrepentant Dr Mahathir Mohamad. The government could still invoke the security apparatus inherited from the Emergency, but now the definition of sedition was expanded to include any criticism of special Malay rights or the privileges of Malay royalty. The former ambivalence towards English-medium education shifted sharply. The minister of education, Datuk Patinggi Abdul Rahman Yakab, later to become chief minister of Sarawak, announced a specific timetable for the introduction of Malay in English-medium schools. Beginning in 1970, all subjects in Form 1 would be taught in Malay except for lessons in English, Tamil and Chinese. The next year Form 2 would follow suit, and so on until the conversion of Form 6 in 1982.

Because parliament was suspended, a National Consultative Council (NCC) had been formed in January 1970 to 'establish positive and practical guidelines for inter-racial co-operation and social integration for the growth of a Malaysian national identity'. This body comprised representatives from ministers of the National Operations Council, state governments, political parties, Sabah, Sarawak, religious groups, professional bodies, the public services, trade unions, employers' associations, the press, teachers and minority groups. The government hoped that if discussions were closed to the media, a body representing all segments of society might be able to determine where mistakes had been made and reach a consensus (*muafakat*) on what should now be done. This *muafakat* government was not intended to replace the Dewan Rakyat, but it was hoped that a frank analysis of such issues as the New Economic Policy, the Rukunegara, the National Language and Malay special privileges might go some way towards resolving the explosive problems within Malaysian society. Yet when the Dewan Rakyat reconvened on 23 February 1971 it was very apparent that, important though consensus and national ideology might be, the battle for unity would be won or lost in the economic and social restructuring of the nation. It was to this problem that the government thus directed its greatest energies.

Between 1942 and 1969 a generation of Malaysians experienced a series of traumatic events that cast a long shadow over the nation's development. To a considerable extent, therefore, the emergence of this new nation can be written as a simple history of survival. Although plans for the independence of Malaya were not derailed, the Japanese Occupation and postwar violence had exposed deep ethnic divisions and bequeathed a storehouse of bitter memories. The Malay rejection of the Malayan Union and the non-Malay response to Federation proposals were a further reminder of underlying fears about cultural survival felt by all ethnic groups. The outbreak of the communist insurrection made prospects for the survival of a political unit that had been essentially created by Britain seem especially remote. Yet while a final victory over the communists had not been achieved by 1957 when Malaya became independent, the communist threat had all but disappeared. Most observers saw the formation of a political coalition by the leaders of the major ethnic groups as a major achievement. Indeed, despite the departure of Singapore, and the ill-will of its neighbours, Malaysia emerged in seeming defiance of the odds. None the less, beneath this surface history of negotiation, compromise and survival were festering ethnic antagonisms which always had the potential to erupt into violence. The events of May 1969 impelled the Malaysian government towards radical and controversial measures which, it was hoped, would resolve the communal problems that represented the primary threat to the nation's future.

Restructuring Malaysia, 1969–2000

Virtually all recent accounts of Malaysia's post-independence history treat 1969 as a watershed that marks the beginning of a new era in the country's political, economic and social development. At the beginning of the twenty-first century the sight of young Malaysians ice-skating in a shopping mall built where Chinese tin-miners once toiled encapsulates the often breath-taking changes which have occurred since the inception of the New Economic Policy (NEP) in 1970. For almost a generation, debates over the impact of these changes have provided the stuff of academic discussions on Malaysia, and because there are so many contending voices these discussions are likely to continue well into the future. At this stage it is certainly possible to formu-late some assessment of the social effects of post-1969 policies on Malaysian society, but only the passage of time will provide the perspective necessary for historical evaluations and judgements.

Contemporary Malaysia: sources and historiographical problems

In writing about the very recent past, a historian is confronted with different historiographical problems from those relating to earlier periods. Obviously one issue is the sheer bulk and almost infinite variety of material; one Malay-sian scholar working on post-1973 Peninsular Malaysia, for example, identi-fied more than 1000 titles, published and unpublished, dealing with various aspects of the NEP.[1] A range of specialized studies by political scientists, soci-ologists, anthropologists, economists, educationalists, ethnomusicologists and so on deal in detail with many aspects of Malaysian society. The growing use of the Internet has added yet another source of information, particularly on politically sensitive issues. Because so much information is available on so many subjects, a historian must make decisions about which events or topics should be discussed, realizing that those issues selected may ultimately prove of minor importance, while others mentioned only in passing may prove to be critical. In drawing on the research of others, a historian is also required to balance or assess competing analyses, even in relation to 'hard' data like statistics, where expert evaluations may be based on different readings of the same 'facts' or on different figures altogether. Ultimately, it is the individual historian's perception of the past and the identification of significant themes that determines how particular studies select and interpret contemporary developments.

Economic and social restructuring under the New Economic Policy

The ethnic disturbances of May 1969 and the now vociferous Malay demand for a greater share of the country's wealth forced the Malaysian government to fundamentally rethink its economic policies. Malayanizing the economy had been a goal of the three five-year plans introduced between 1956 and 1970, but there had been little progress in eliminating the pre-independence pattern of foreign and local Chinese ownership of the corporate sector. This fact had been a source of considerable resentment among the new cohort of educated and urbanized Malays who were products of affirmative action measures introduced in the 1960s. Since many were influential members of UMNO or well-placed officials, their pressure on the government to take stronger action was highly effective. In 1965, when the first Bumiputera Economic Congress was held to promote Malay capitalism, and during a second meeting in 1968, resolutions were passed urging greater state support for Malay commerce. In 1965 the government responded by creating the first Malay commercial bank, the Bank Bumiputera, to create easier credit facilities for Malays, and a year later formed the Majlis Amanah Rakyat (MARA – Council of Trust for Indigenous People). In the First Malaysia Plan (1966–70), a special allocation had also been made to promote Malay economic development. None of these measures, however, had adequately addressed the issue of Malay poverty.

Viewed against the background of the ethnic riots, the statistics were disquieting. In 1970 the incomes of some 49.3 per cent of all households in Peninsular Malaysia (791 600) were below the poverty line, estimated then at M$33 per capita monthly. Of these, about 75 per cent were Malays. It was patently obvious that the goal of eliminating economic disparity between the major ethnic groups had simply not been achieved. Malays were also poorly represented in most sectors of the modern economy, being visible primarily in teaching and government service, and at the lower professional and technical levels. Under the leadership of Tun Abdul Razak, who succeeded Tunku Abdul Rahman as prime minister in 1970 and led the government until 1976, a vigorous new economic initiative was launched. Characterized by strong government intervention, this initiative addressed the highly charged question of maintaining economic growth while ensuring that more resources and more opportunities became available to Malays. The result was enshrined in the New Economic Policy (NEP). More than any other measure, the NEP has been responsible for the immense changes that have occurred in Malaysia over the past 30 years.

Implemented through four five-year plans from 1971 to 1990, the NEP had two principal objectives: firstly, a reduction and eventual eradication of poverty, irrespective of race; and secondly, a restructuring of society so that identification of race with economic function would be reduced and ultimately eliminated. The first objective was to be achieved by facilitating access to land, physical capital, training and public amenities for the economically underprivileged. The second would be brought about by reducing the dependence of Malays and other indigenous groups on subsistence agriculture, and by increasing their share of the country's wealth through greater ownership of the corporate sector. The government assured non-Malays that restructuring would occur through sustained economic growth, not through redistribution of existing resources, so that 'no particular group experiences any loss or feels any sense of deprivation in the process'. To many, however, it seemed that attainment of these goals was simply impossible.

Objective One: the eradication of poverty

The campaign to reduce poverty yielded only slow results. Despite increased expenditure on development projects, as well as subsidies for rice and rubber cultivators, rural Malay poverty persisted. Development programmes were the target of criticism from those who argued that the enormous outlay benefited only a portion of the rural population, and that the areas of greatest poverty in the northern Malay states were largely excluded. Kelantan, together with its neighbour Terengganu and tiny Perlis, remained the poorest states in Malaysia. The disparity was particularly pronounced when the small numbers of people receiving assistance were compared to the cost of direct subsidies and the indirect burden to society of higher prices and increased taxes. It was difficult for the landless and sharecroppers to derive any benefit from land development programmes, and government training and income-generating projects often did not reach the very poor. High rates of tenancy combined with smaller landholdings militated against any rapid rise in farm incomes, especially given the expenses involved with the introduction of double-cropping and high yielding rice varieties.

Rural indebtedness thus continued to take its toll. Malay rubber smallholders often did not participate in the RISDA programme, the main beneficiaries of which were wealthier Malay villagers whose land titles were secure and who had access to alternative sources of income while cash-crops matured. In some cases poverty eradication programmes enabled well-connected local politicians to act as patrons whose sponsorship had to be courted. As in the colonial period, it is possible to track a story of persistent low-level rural protest that has occasionally found expression in more violent demonstrations and clashes with civil authorities. In the mid-1970s, for example, many smallholders were hard hit by a fall in rubber prices. In 1974 angry demonstrations broke out in the Kedah districts of Baling and Sik as thousands of Malay farmers marched to demand government action. In the cities a new generation of Malay university students from rural areas also mounted demonstrations, drawing in various Islamic youth organizations, including ABIM (Angkatan Belia Islam Malaysia) led by its chairman Anwar Ibrahim. The government moved quickly to contain this protest (Anwar himself was held in detention for two years), but it was a sharp reminder of continuing Malay frustrations.

Although the new education minister, Dr Mahathir Mohamad (readmitted to UMNO in 1971) was sharply critical of student involvement in rural Malay protest, the question of poverty was addressed with a new energy after he succeeded as prime minister in 1981. Known for his strong stand on Malay ethnic issues, he was obviously impatient with the lack of progress in attaining NEP goals. In 1984 the government announced the formation of the National Agricultural Policy (NAP), which sought to revitalize the agricultural sector through greater efficiency in land use and support services. By the end of 1988 land development spearheaded by FELDA and at least five similar bodies had settled some 224 700 people on more than 2 072 290 hectares of cleared and planted lands. Between 1986 and 1990 the NAP brought 782 179 new hectares into production, rehabilitated another 116 000 hectares, and opened a further 802 000 hectares of new land through public sector agencies, with some participation of the private sector. An additional 342 000 hectares were added through the In Situ Agricultural Development Programmes (IADP), which employed an integrated approach of new technologies, infrastructure and services to increase productivity and income, particularly among the two groups with the highest incidence of rural poverty: rubber smallholders and wet-rice farmers. During this period the official figures relating to rural poverty did give grounds for optimism. In Peninsular Malaysia the percentage of poor rural households dropped from 58.7 in 1970 to 19.3 in 1989, although income levels in the northern states continued to be disproportionately lower. The statistics, however, may be misleading because the indexes used to measure poverty are not always adjusted in terms of inflation, nor do they take into account fluctuations in prices of some agricultural produce.

To some extent, the growing signs of prosperity in many Malay villages following the introduction of the NEP could be traced to the new opportunities for rural dwellers to participate in the modernizing sectors of the economy. Migration of the young to urban areas and growing numbers of women employed in factories located in free trade zones and industrial estates further contributed to an increase in rural household income. The post-1969 period thus saw a continuing narrowing of the gap between urban and rural household incomes, and a lowering of the incidence of poverty in Peninsular

Malaysia from 49.3 per cent in 1970 to 15.0 per cent in 1989. In Baling, for instance, which had been the site of Malay protests in 1974, there was a noticeable rise in prosperity by the end of the 1980s, with over half the families now owning television sets, and a fifth a refrigerator. More significantly, the consumption of protein such as fish and meat had also increased. Nevertheless, certain occupational groups continued to be disadvantaged. Figures from 1987 show that the incomes of around half the *padi* farmers and two-fifths of rubber and coconut smallholders still fell below the poverty line. There was also a marked territorial distribution of wealth. Terengganu, Kedah and Kelantan, the most rural and most Malay of the Peninsular states, had the highest percentages classified as poor at 31.2 per cent, 30 per cent and 29.9 per cent, respectively.

The Third Malaysia Plan (1976–80) is noteworthy because it acknowledged the poverty of non-Malay groups such as Chinese New Village residents, Indian plantation workers, and Orang Asli, and their need for improved access to education, health services and amenities. The government was clearly concerned at growing signs of discontent among some poor Chinese, aggravated by the physical neglect of the New Villages and the difficulties residents still faced in obtaining permanent land title. This discontent had been manifested since 1968 in a resurgence of communist activity in a number of areas. In Kinta, security forces clashed with guerrillas apparently supported by Chinese New Villagers, while Thai and Malaysian Chinese villages provided bases for communist action along the Thai border. The terrorist incident rate in 1974–5 reached its highest peak since 1958, and although more funds were allocated to alleviate the lot of poor Chinese, in 1982 it was estimated that around 2300 guerrillas were still active. However, a Thai-brokered peace agreement with the MCP in 1989 was seen as a positive step towards reconciliation.

Another disadvantaged group consisted of former plantation workers, who were mostly Tamil. In the wake of the 1969 riots the policy of limiting employment to Malaysian citizens was applied more strictly to the private sector, and as a result around 60 000 Indian plantation workers lost their jobs. Although many took advantage of free repatriation, others drifted to urban areas to find work. Here they faced bleak prospects, since as non-citizens they were ineligible for government benefits. Even those whose papers were in order were unlikely to find employment in the plantations, now retrenching in order to survive. By 1973 most rubber was being produced on smallholdings, and large estates held only 35 per cent of all rubber acreage. Other groups, such as Indonesian migrants and Orang Asli, were being employed on the estates as cheap non-unionized labourers. Those Indians who remained on the estates were disadvantaged because plantations were considered to lie outside government responsibility, thus excluding them from rural development schemes. Furthermore, because plantation Tamil schools were located on private property, they received only partial government assistance. Poorly equipped, with low teaching standards and a high drop-out rate, they offered few opportunities for Indian children to break out of the cycle of poverty. These problems were exacerbated as more plantations were converted to factories, golf courses and housing developments. Failure rates among Indian high school pupils remain high, and Indians currently comprise only around 4 per cent of university students.

The new emphasis on rural development directed the spotlight towards a group previously overlooked in considerations of rural poverty – the Orang Asli. As dams, logging, road building and land clearance projects extended into what had once been remote jungle areas, displaced Orang Asli were pressured to 'regroup' in permanent settlement sites. The intention was to have them within reach of government medical and educational facilities, and to encourage them to move away from shifting agriculture and 'nomadic habits', officially condemned as destructive to the jungle environment. But because the resettlement project was based on the FELDA model, it was structured by assumptions which were relevant to sedentary Malays but not to the semi-nomadic Orang Asli. The sale of jungle products in local markets had been an important source of income for the Orang Asli, but access to the forests was becoming increasingly restricted by the government's new emphasis on modernization and development, and by the extension of logging activities. Many Orang Asli either became farmers by default, or hired themselves out as contract labourers. It is ironic that at the very time the government was attempting to bring Malays out of the small-scale farming sector, it was encouraging Orang Asli to grow commodities like rubber, the future of which was increasingly doubtful.

As the end of the NEP drew closer, sympathetic observers were already deploring the transformation of the Orang Asli into a rural proletariat, with the accompanying poverty, poor nutrition and consequent ill-health. In 1995 Orang Asli women were found to be the most malnourished adult group in Peninsular Malaysia, and stunted growth was evident in 40 to 80 per cent of Orang Asli children.[2] Orang Asli are also less likely to have access to education. Around 90 per cent do not complete Form Five of primary school, mainly because they feel so estranged from the system. Though the Orang Asli have sunk to the bottom of Malaysia's economic pile, their needs are rarely accorded priority in poverty eradication programmes. Orang Asli themselves have noted that they are commonly excluded from state-sponsored tourism projects located in their areas, even though they are theoretically well placed to benefit from eco-tourism.

The development projects initiated by the NEP also raised questions about the condition of Borneo's rural populations. In Sarawak a major concern was the growing strength of the largely Chinese Sarawak Communist Organization (SCO). Because more Sarawak Chinese were engaged in agriculture than in any other occupation, they were generally much poorer than Peninsular Chinese. During the late 1960s, in a situation similar to that along the Malaysian–Thai border, the lack of land tenure, youth unemployment and limited access to Malaysian citizenship fuelled Sarawak Chinese support for the SCO. In some cases, Iban – heavily rural, economically disadvantaged and often politically ignored – also co-operated with the communists, partly because of coercion and partly because of the SCO's agricultural extension programmes. By the early 1970s insurgency in Sarawak was a matter of grave concern as attacks on civilians and security forces escalated. In a renewed anti-communist campaign, the federal government therefore introduced a series of operations designed to assert its authority over rural Chinese and to prevent SCO intimidation of Iban communities. An important step was the state's assumption of control over local schools, which had often been targeted by the SCO. Patrols and military operations were increased, and between 1970 and 1975 an estimated 3725 individuals were arrested. Support for the communists began to fall away as a result of government efforts to address Chinese grievances, and an improvement in the Chinese standard of living. In 1976, for example, 14 per cent of Chinese fell below the poverty line; by 1982 this had dropped to 8.5 per cent. The success of government policies was affirmed in October 1990 when a peace agreement was signed with the SCO leaders, and the few remaining members surrendered.

The improvement in the Chinese economic position, however, was in sharp contrast to the persistent poverty of many indigenous peoples in the Borneo states during the NEP years, despite official rhetoric. Particularly contentious has been the impact of government policies on the lives of indigenous peoples, especially forest dwellers and semi-nomadic farmers. The importance of the logging industry, and the heavy reliance of Sabah and Sarawak on timber revenues has meant a hardening of opposition to 'slash and burn' methods of shifting agriculture. The decline in forest areas, and limitations on use have adversely affected shifting cultivators, whose farming cycle depends on access to extensive jungle tracts so that previously cultivated land can rejuvenate in order for the next burning to produce crop nutrients. Despite arguments to the contrary, the authorities have categorized this method of farming as backward and harmful to the environment. In its campaign to address rural poverty the government hopes to change traditional farming practices and transform shifting agriculturalists into sedentary farmers.

In Sarawak the Land Consolidation and Rehabilitation Authority and its Sabah counterpart, the Rural Development Corporation, aim to encourage the transition by assisting subsistence farmers and cash-crop smallholders. These schemes involve estates of rubber, oil palm, cocoa and tea, with farmers operating as smallholders or wage labourers, and include such facilities as roads, housing, community amenities and processing plant. The Department of Agriculture also maintains a programme intended to encourage more sedentary cultivation as well as crop diversification. Assistance is offered to farmers to switch from dry to wet-rice cultivation, and to plant higher-yielding rubber seedlings or establish pepper gardens; and to fishermen to diversify into coconut cultivation as another source of income. Information and assistance are also provided for the introduction of new crops, livestock and aquaculture.

Enclave projects of rubber and oil palm have been developed along the lines of the FELDA schemes on the Peninsula. Criteria are laid down for settler selection, and each household is given a specific amount of land for cash-crops, and a smaller amount for fruit and vegetables. Houses, schools, clinics, roads, piped water, and a centralized processing plant for the cash-crop have been provided. Learning from failed rubber estate schemes in the 1960s, often abandoned by indigenous groups, the new oil palm ventures do not involve settler-owned plants. Instead, the government has retained ownership of the oil palms and merely hired local people as wage labourers. Most are from poor farm families, young and mobile workers whose parents often continue to practise shifting cultivation. Indeed, younger people generally are more likely to relocate and take jobs in the modernizing economic sector, whether in government, the service industry, the agricultural estates, logging, or the oil and natural gas industries. But even for their parents, lifestyle changes have become increasingly necessary as widespread deforestation caused by logging makes forest-collecting more difficult and as government schemes promote the resettlement of indigenous populations into nucleated villages. Pressure on land also makes shifting agriculture less efficient because of premature clearing of forest cover and hence poorer preparation of the soils for crops. The decline in shifting agriculture has been accompanied by a corresponding demise of traditions dealing with the spirits of the land and the forests, of ancestor worship and fertility, and their replacement with new gods, whether of Islam or the popular Christian evangelical movement known as the Sidang Injil Borneo (Borneo Evangelical Mission).

Helped by sizeable revenues from timber and petroleum extraction, NEP initiatives made some progress in Sabah and Sarawak, where there was an overall decline in poverty. However, even though the economies of Sabah and Sarawak grew faster than Peninsular Malaysia under the NEP, and government services were considerably improved, the per capita GDP deteriorated in relative terms and both states had higher unemployment rates than the Peninsula in 1985. Despite an overall decline in poverty levels in East Malaysia, the figures were still relatively high. In 1976 Sabah recorded 58.3 per cent at the poverty level and a decline to 34.3 per cent in 1989; Sarawak's figures were 56.5 per cent in 1976 and 34.3 per cent in 1989. As always in Malaysia, the statistics must be read against the ethnic grid, since they mask the great discrepancy between Chinese households and those of the indigenous communities. In 1990 just 4 per cent of Chinese households were classified as poor, in stark contrast to 29 per cent of households in the indigenous communities of Sarawak and a high 41 per cent in Sabah.

As a new generation of educated women rises to the fore, more attention is also being given to questions of gender in relation to poverty. Women are still more likely than men to lack education and fall below the poverty line, and the numbers of elderly women without family or adequate financial support will almost certainly become more evident in the future. With the advent of the new century around 13 per cent of the Malaysian population is expected to be over 60 years of age, and a majority of this group will be women. Furthermore, all ethnic groups have seen an increasing tendency towards female-headed households, since divorce is on the rise, and it is currently estimated that there are about 670 000 single mothers in the country as a whole. Unfortunately, women who are the family's sole earner are far less likely than men to gain access to credit, loans and other forms of government assistance. Muslim women are further disadvantaged because of delays in the *syariah* courts which are responsible for approving divorce applications and maintenance claims for Muslims. Enforcement of decisions is complicated because *syariah* court jurisdiction is limited to state boundaries, and there are practical difficulties of seeking redress from husbands who move to another state. Divorced or abandoned Orang Asli women may also find little support in the court system, which does not recognize customary marriages unless they are officially registered.

Another rising and neglected group are the urban poor, many of whom are squatters from rural areas. Indeed, it could be argued that the rural to urban migration has effectively meant a transfer of poverty to towns and cities, and that the emphasis on rural development has tended to ignore the plight of poor city-dwellers. In 1985, for example, less than 2 per cent of 2402 studies on Malaysian poverty were conducted in urban areas. During the 1970s over 68 per cent of migrants from the countryside were Malays, but initiatives to improve their welfare were not introduced until the Third Malaysia Plan (1976–80).

The problem has been exacerbated by the increasing numbers of foreign workers in urban centres. In a manner reminiscent of colonial attitudes, the Malaysian government was relatively accommodating towards the entry of foreign workers because of the growing demand for labour from the early 1970s. As more Malaysians sought employment in better-paying sectors it was necessary to import labour to fill positions which Malaysians found less attractive. Between 1991 and 1995 around 1.2 million jobs were created, and from June 1992 to June 1995 a total of 615 720 foreign workers were granted work permits, and those of another 300 072 extended. Mainly from Indonesia, Bangladesh, Thailand and the Philippines, they were concentrated in the Federal Territory, Johor, Selangor and Sabah, where they were employed in factories, plantations, on construction sites and, with so many Malaysian women moving into the workforce, as household help.

Most legal foreign workers have some kind of education. The majority have completed secondary school, and about 14 per cent of this group are university graduates. There are also large numbers of illegal migrants. Police records indicate that between January and September 1994 as many as 886 000 people entered the country without legal papers, and during an amnesty period in 1996 some 240 804 workers registered in less than four months. This may have been only the tip of the iceberg, for it has been estimated that foreign workers, both legal and illegal, represented about 9 per cent of the population by 1999. This has an important if hidden effect on the economy because illegal migrants, who are usually uneducated and poor, are willing to work at very low rates, especially in areas such as construction. The high poverty figure in Sabah, for example, is thought to be due to the numbers of Indonesian and Filipino migrants.

Of all the Southeast Asian countries, Malaysia has the most severe problem of illegal foreign workers and overstayers. Without access to sources of government assistance, they remain extremely vulnerable to economic downturn, and quickly become part of the growing mass of urban poor. With little recourse in exploitative situations, some inevitably become involved in crime, prostitution, and drug trafficking, all increasing in Malaysia's urban centres. In Sabah, the granting of identity cards to large numbers of Indonesian and Filipino workers has been a major source of resentment among Kadazundusun groups. During any recession, when Malaysian citizens feel pressed, foreign workers often find themselves singled out as scapegoats. Many were forcibly repatriated after the economic crisis in 1997, and there are disturbing allegations of abuse of migrants at Malaysian detention camps. Foreign workers are viewed as transient labour necessary in times of economic growth but a burden in less prosperous times.

At the close of the twentieth century the squatter shacks huddled in the shadow of Kuala Lumpur's giant buildings serve as a reminder of groups untouched by Malaysia's prosperity. In the Seventh Malaysia Plan (1996–2000) the government allocated M$610 million (US$160 million) in nine programmes for the hard-core poor, defined as those families with a monthly income of less than M$230 (US$60) a month. In 1997 some 58 000 households on the Peninsula fell into this category, the highest number (16 800) being in Kelantan; the figure for the Borneo states was 9300. The government agencies FELDA and RISDA instituted a programme in June 1999 which distributed a monthly stipend of M$250 (US$65) to the heads of 22 000 of the country's poorest households who were unemployed because of age or disability.[3] While Objective One of the NEP has not yet been accomplished, at the beginning of the twenty-first century substantial economic growth has helped to lower the poverty levels for most Malaysians.

Objective Two: removing the association of ethnicity with economic function

The second major goal of the NEP was the removal of the association of ethnicity and occupation. Crucial to the achievement of this objective was a restructuring of education for Malays. Against a colonial legacy that saw a basic vernacular education as sufficient, the government has placed primary emphasis on training Malays so that they can move into spheres formerly dominated by other ethnic groups. The number of universities has increased dramatically, together with technical institutes such as the MARA Institute of Technology. For Malays in particular the introduction of Malay-medium education has created options formerly closed to them because of lack of access to English schooling. The last 30 years have seen Malays in large numbers abandon agriculture in favour of employment in the secondary and tertiary sectors. By 1982 the new education policy launched during the NEP had achieved the transition from English to Malay in all national primary and secondary schools, and from 1983 this gradually occurred in the universities as well. Although Mahathir relented in 1993 to allow English instruction in the sciences, medicine and technology at universities, all other courses are taught in Malay. In conjunction with the affirmative action which enables far more Malays to enter tertiary institutions than previously, these new education policies have produced the Malay personnel who have been essential in the radical restructuring of Malaysian society.

In stark contrast to the nineteenth century, when the British had to cajole Malay boys to enter schools by building soccer fields, today's youth are well aware of the opportunities offered by education, particularly in technology. In the professional fields, at the start of the NEP in 1970 there were only 40 accountants, 79 doctors and 33 engineers who were Malay. By 1997 the figures had changed dramatically to 1766 accountants, 4508 doctors and 11 481 engineers.[4] A similar impressive change in the fortunes of the Malays is evident in the numbers in higher education. In 1953 only 90 of the 954 students enrolled in the University of Malaya were Malay. By 1970 there had been some improvement, but in the whole country there were only five Malay students pursuing a degree in technical courses, 384 in sciences, and 2695 in arts. But by 1997 a remarkable transformation had occurred. Official figures showed that in tertiary institutions 12 608 Malays were enrolled in technical courses, 16 148 in sciences and 43 616 in arts. The magnitude of this development can only be properly appreciated if one recalls that until 1956 there was not a single Malay secondary school in the entire country.

The progress made in women's education, especially among the Malays, has been particularly impressive. In 1994 women made up 49.5 per cent of the enrolment in universities, and by 1999 well over half Malaysia's university students were female. Although still clustered in non-science and non-technical areas, women were moving increasingly into fields once the preserve of men, such as medicine, dentistry, accountancy and university teaching. The Islamic revival, with its greater stress on the proprieties of male–female interaction, fostered a demand for women doctors, and by 1988 as many as 25 per cent of doctors were women. The entry of women into the workforce is evident across all sectors, but has been very pronounced in government service, which in the past was a preferred area for males. Higher pay rates and expanding opportunities in other sectors of the economy have led to a movement of men away from traditional areas of employment. For example, fewer men have been recruited into the civil service over the last ten years, which is now around 40 per cent female, with 40 000 more women employed in 1999 than in 1990. Women also represent the largest group among primary and secondary school teachers. Not everyone is pleased with this trend, however, and some trace disciplinary problems in schools to the feminization of the teaching profession.[5]

The government's affirmative action policy on education in favour of the Malays has been an extremely contentious issue among the Chinese. Between 1980 and 1985 Malay students made up about 65 per cent of the total enrolment in Malaysian universities, as against 27 per cent Chinese and 6 per cent Indian. During the 1970s and 1980s the revival of the Chinese Education Movement and the pressure for a Chinese-language university reflected a growing Chinese resentment fed by the persisting belief that Chinese rights were being denied. Fortunately for the government, this potentially explosive situation was largely defused by Malaysia's spectacular growth rate, averaging between 6 and 7 per cent in the 1970s, bolstered by the discovery late in the decade of vast gas and oil supplies off Terengganu and Sarawak. Although ethnic tensions resurfaced during the recession in 1985–7, opposition to the government's pro-Malay policies was muted by another exceptional decade when the growth rate averaged between 8 and 9 per cent. In the 20 years of rapid industrialization during the NEP between 1971 and 1990, the GDP trebled and the poverty rate in Peninsular Malaysia was reduced from 49.3 per cent to 15 per cent.

In these two decades of industrial growth, Malaysia succeeded in its aim of retaining foreign investment while increasing Malaysian, particularly Bumiputera (which on the Peninsula meant almost exclusively Malay), ownership in the corporate sector. To achieve this, the government became involved in the creation of three types of corporate bodies: departmental enterprises providing essential services; statutory bodies such as the Majlis Amanah Rakyat (MARA – Council of Trust for Indigenous People), the Perbadanan Nasional Berhad (PERNAS – National Corporation Ltd) and Petroliam Nasional Bhd (PETRONAS – National Petroleum Ltd.); and state economic development corporations (SEDCs). In the 1970s PERNAS was the most important and effective in the government's intensive efforts to achieve Malay participation in commerce and industry. One government measure introduced to promote Bumiputera interests in the economy was the Industrial Co-ordination Act of 1975, which imposed administrative controls in the manufacturing sector. It gave the government the authority to ensure that the manufacturing sector complied with the NEP objectives of ethnic redistribution of ownership and employment.

In addition to assisting Malay entrepreneurs to enter a mainly foreign and local-Chinese dominated business world, these large enterprises have engaged in business ventures with the intention of eventually relinquishing control to Malay private groups. The new government bodies also contributed to the NEP goal of increasing Malay ownership in the corporate sector by purchasing shares on behalf of the Malays through the Amanah Saham Nasional (National Unit Trust, founded in January 1981) run by the Permodalan Nasional Berhad (National Equity Corporation). Amanah Saham Wanita (Women's Unit Trust), the brainchild of Wanita UMNO, was launched in 1998 and by December had about 70 000 unit-holders with total investments of M$70 million (US$18 million). Malay women have traditionally played a prominent role in petty trading and marketing, but in today's world the female Malay entrepreneur is also no rarity.

To retain Malay ownership and prevent individuals from disposing of their units to outsiders, as has occurred in the past, units can only be sold back to the Trust. Malay equity ownership in the country rose from 1.5 per cent in 1969 to 20.3 per cent in 1990, with the percentage of individual Malay ownership rising from 39 per cent of the total in 1983 to 68 per cent in 1990. The increase in Malay ownership has not come at the expense of the local Chinese, as the latter had feared, but of foreign holdings. Foreign ownership of the modern sector of the economy fell from 61.7 per cent in 1970 to 25.1 per cent in 1990. During the 1970s and early 1980s majority holdings in all sectors of the economy shifted from foreign to Malaysian control. Malay share of corporate equity rose from 2.4 per cent in 1970 to 20.3 per cent in 1990, though only 8.2 per cent of this was held by private investors and the rest by public enterprises and trust agencies. There are experts who believe that the Malay share is underestimated and that it is much closer to 30 per cent equity, which was the target of the NEP.[6]

Mahathir's economic nationalism was manifested in several new programmes. In 1980, as minister of trade and industry, he foreshadowed future policies when he established the Heavy Industry Corporation of Malaysia (HICOM, later renamed HICOM Holdings) to replace a manufacturing sector reliant on processing imported materials and assembling foreign-made components. The intent was to form joint ventures with foreign corporations in the creation of heavy industry, and to promote technology transfer and the training of a skilled labour force. Among the most well-known of HICOM's efforts was the Perusahaan Otomobil Nasional (National Automobile Industry), which produced the Proton Saga in a joint venture with Mitsubishi. The project faced difficulties at first, but a change in management and rise in export sales finally made the car profitable in 1990. A second national car, the Kancil, was created through a joint venture with Daihatsu, and a third was being contemplated in 1999 with Ford. Another high-profile heavy industry project was the Bakun Dam in Sarawak, which aroused world-wide criticism because it would displace a number of indigenous groups from their lands. Suspended during the economic recession of the 1980s and again in August 1997 because of the currency crisis, the project has also been plagued by serious problems with the private developers. Work was resumed in June 1999, but the government has had to inject funding into the project and to scale back its original plans.

When Mahathir became prime minister in 1982, he invited as advisers a group of influential business people who had benefited from the NEP policies in the late 1970s and early 1980s. It was they who convinced Mahathir to transfer assets from the state to the private sector. The appointment of Daim Zainuddin as minister of finance in 1984 confirmed this new direction of the government. Privatization was seen by Mahathir as a means to implement the NEP while reducing the strain on government resources due to direct intervention. It was also considered a way to wean Malays away from a 'subsidy mentality'. In 1981 government expenditure had reached a peak of 19.7 per cent of GDP, and by 1983 there was a slowing of the economy and a growing external debt. Although government investment was scaled down, public enterprises increased their capital expenditure, stimulated to a great extent by the new emphasis on the development of heavy industry. Privatization, therefore, promised to bring financial benefits both in terms of sale proceeds and in capital expenditure. Major targets of privatization were transportation (among which was the Proton in 1995), utilities and communications. By 1995 some 50 entities a year were being privatized, reaping a financial windfall of US$10 billion and a savings in capital expenditure of about US$30 billion. This new policy of privatization was in sharp contrast to the previous interventionist stance, and allowed the private sector to generate growth and employment with minimal government involvement.

The impact of earlier intervention policies can be clearly seen in relation to Malay employment. The government had initially depended on voluntary compliance by industry and commerce in order to achieve a 30 per cent Malay workforce in the corporate sector. But the lack of progress towards this goal led to an amendment in 1971 to the Investment Incentives Act, known as the Labour Utilization Relief, extending the period of exemption from corporate tax for any firm employing a certain number of Malay workers. Even this, however, was considered inadequate, and in 1975 the Industrial Co-ordination Act came into force which no longer relied on incentives for change. It now required firms to employ 30 per cent Malays at every level or risk revocation of their licences. One of the major obstacles to the implementation of this policy was the fear among non-Malays that the increase in Malay employment would come at their expense. They saw the discriminatory practices in hiring, issuance of licences, and the allocation of distribution agencies and bank credit as undermining their own positions. Moreover, they despaired of being able to compete against state-supported enterprises with access to enormous resources. From 1976 to 1985 there was a capital flight of some US$2 billion, half of which was Chinese-owned.[7]

In response to these government measures, the Malayan (later Malaysian) Chinese Association (MCA) formed the Multi-Purpose Holdings Bhd (MPHB) in 1975 to combine the funds of small family businesses, voluntary associations and clans in order to compete effectively in the new economic environment. The MCA sought to reassure its Malay political partners in UMNO that the MPHB was not intended to derail the measures to increase Malay ownership of the economy. In the early 1980s the MPHB had become one of the largest companies in Malaysia, but a series of confrontations with Malay enterprises began the slide in its fortunes. Internal conflict over its leadership, poor investment decisions, corruption, and resistance from Malay politicians and the government led to its demise by the end of the NEP.

The failure of the MPHB made Chinese business leaders much more alert to the kind of strategies required for achievement in the new investment environment of the NEP and the post-NEP era. The new Chinese business success stories represented by such conglomerates as Berjaya, Kamunting, Malayan United Industries and Hong Leong, demonstrate the necessity of a close integration of Chinese and Malay capital, the latter involving a mix of state, UMNO and private funds. Crucial to the success of such co-operation is the support of the state's regulatory and financial bodies, which the Malay capitalist partners can facilitate. These new Chinese businesses are therefore complementing rather than competing with Bumiputera businesses. The result has been the rise of new Bumiputera ventures and increased Bumiputera investment in the economy, both of which had been primary aims of the NEP. The new co-operation between local Chinese and Bumiputera business tycoons highlights their common capitalist rather than their ethnic backgrounds.

Toward the close of the NEP, Malay equity ownership had risen dramatically from 1.5 per cent in 1969 to 20.3 per cent by 1990, while Chinese equity ownership also rose from 27.2 per cent in 1970 to 44.9 per cent in 1990. All groups shared in this prosperity, and the rise in Malay and Chinese ownership of the corporate sector had come at the expense of foreign holdings, as had been predicted. These developments were translated to the ballot box. In the elections of 1974, 1978, 1982 and 1990 the opposition DAP's share of the Chinese vote was larger than that of either MCA or Gerakan, but its 1995 and particularly the 1999 electoral losses point to the Chinese community's general willingness to accept the politics of accommodation. MCA-sponsored projects like the founding of Tunku Abdul Rahman College, which provided places for many Chinese unable to enter universities, also released much of the pressure on Chinese families.

One significant development during the years of the NEP has been the expansion of the middle class, which by 1990 made up almost a third of the workforce. What has been particularly striking is the increase in the Malay component, largely as a result of preferential recruitment in the public sector and government pressure on private enterprises to employ Malays. In 1970, when the NEP was introduced, the proportion of the Malay workforce employed in middle-class occupations (professional, technical, administrative, managerial, clerical, sales) was only 13 per cent. By 1990 the number had risen to 27 per cent, an impressive increase though still far less than the proportion of Malays in the population (60 per cent). Malays also came to constitute about 22 per cent of workers in 1993, up from only 7.8 per cent in 1970, and 33.5 per cent of agricultural labourers, substantially down from 65.2 per cent for the same period. One area where greater employment of Malays has occurred is in the manufacturing sector, which rose from 11.4 per cent of total employment in 1970 to 19.5 per cent in 1990. While Malays still formed the largest component in the agricultural sector, their increased participation in other sectors of the economy is an indication that, at least for the Malays, the NEP has succeeded in eliminating the association of economic function with ethnic group.

From agriculture to manufacturing

In 1970 the five major primary commodities – rubber, tin, timber, palm and petroleum – contributed a total of 78.4 per cent of total exports. Ten years later the same five commodities contributed only 32.8 per cent of total exports, and the individual percentages had declined dramatically. Rubber had lost its pre-eminence to petroleum, and tin ranked only fifth in percentage of total exports.[8] While the timber industry remained the main source of revenue in the Borneo states, on the Peninsula the largest export earner was manufactured goods. The latter had contributed only 11.9 per cent of total exports in 1970 but an impressive 58.8 per cent in 1990. Behind this shift is the fact that the government's plans for social restructuring were absolutely dependent on the continuing success of the manufacturing sector.

The Second Malaysia Plan (1971–5) acknowledged that primary industry would not provide a solution, and that an expanded secondary industry base was required. It was thus decided that Pahang, Johor, Terengganu and Kelantan, and to a lesser extent Kedah, Perak and Negeri Sembilan, would focus on new agricultural and land development; the Borneo states, Pahang, Kelantan, Johor, Terengganu and Perak on forestry; and west coast Peninsular states on manufacturing. During this period Malaysia's economic growth of 7.4 per cent per annum was somewhat higher than the original target and compared extremely well with other countries. The Third Malaysia Plan (1976–80) emphasized manufacturing tied to an urban growth-centre strategy. This strategy was based on the belief that there was a critical urban population size, above 30–50 000 people, which would accelerate general industrial activity. By adopting this urban-industrial strategy the government hoped to spread urban development more evenly throughout the country, and incentives were provided to encourage movement of industries. Thus a new interrelated urban system on the east coast of the Peninsula was created, and the existing network on the west coast was extended northward to the poorer states.

The Fourth Malaysia Plan (1981–5) continued the policies of the two previous five-year plans, with its principal thrust being to develop the infrastructure linking the towns with the rural areas and to create corridors of urban development, particularly on the east coast. This represented a shift in industrial policy, from a focus on labour-intensive initiatives to industrialization based on capital and technology, coupled with an allocation of economic functions to specific regions. Penang was assigned high technology; Perak mining and manufacturing; Perlis and Kedah agriculture, manufacturing and services; Selangor, the Federal Territory (Kuala Lumpur), Negeri

Sembilan and Melaka industrialization; Johor agriculture and industrialization; Pahang forestry, agriculture and some manufacturing; and Terengganu petroleum, gas and associated heavy industry. The PAS-dominated state of Kelantan did not figure prominently in the Plans, partly because of political reasons and partly because its leaders had specified that Kelantan was to be an agriculturally based economy.

A significant development in the Third and subsequent Malaysia Plans has been the greater attention accorded to female employment and a recognition of women's contribution to the economy. Initially this was probably simply a show of support for the United Nations Women's Decade (1975–85), but the full chapter in the Sixth Malaysia Plan (1990–5) points to the government's realization of female economic potential. Although the primary role of women is still seen as that of wife and mother, their entry into the workforce has been striking, especially in manufacturing industries such as electronics, textiles and clothing. As this sector expanded from the 1970s, multinational corporations were particularly receptive to employing women, not merely because they were perceived as dextrous and compliant, but because their willingness to accept relatively low wages helped improve productivity. Malay rural women provided a ready pool for recruitment because mechanization had reduced or eliminated many traditional female tasks in rice-growing. Again, the figures are revealing. In 1957 female employment in manufacturing was around 22 500, or 17 per cent of the total; by 1980 it had reached 39.5 per cent and in 1995 was reckoned at 43.4 per cent. Observers have been careful to point out, however, that factory jobs that have drawn in so many women are characterized by tedium, long hours, low wages and poor career prospects. Furthermore, women may not be able to acquire the new technological skills necessary to maintain their jobs as industrial work becomes more sophisticated. They are also more likely to be laid off during periods of recession, as occurred during the mid-1980s, when a downturn in the international market for export products such as computer components led to a large-scale retrenchment of factory workers.

It was in fact this economic recession, coupled with some disappointment in the achievements of earlier Plans, that resulted in a shift of approach in the Fifth Malaysia Plan (1986–90). The emphasis moved away from states to six newly created regions – four on the Peninsula and two in Sabah and Sarawak – to encourage joint industrial development within the regions and the creation of secondary growth centres in conjunction with the private sector. It was argued that the poorer states would not only benefit from greater resources and economies of scale, but the problem of industries spread too thinly through the country would be eliminated. It was also hoped that the new policy would discourage interregional migration and prevent the flight of young, better educated and hence more productive labour to attractive areas of employment in Kuala Lumpur and the Kelang valley. Furthermore, regional focus would promote rural urbanization and help modernize rural settlements, and thus contribute to the eradication of poverty, one of the NEP's primary goals. The Industrial Master Plan of 1986–9 reflected this line of thinking. It sought to accelerate the growth of manufacturing, maximize the efficient exploitation of natural resources, and establish the foundations for Bumiputera participation in an advanced industrial society. Because of the constraints of investment resources, the IMP proposed the idea of 'corridor development' for the Peninsula, with a western corridor linking the existing industrial and manufacturing complexes from Penang in the north to Johor Baru in the south; and a much smaller eastern corridor joining Kota Baru, Terengganu and Kuantan. This proposal encouraged the use of existing infrastructure to develop the areas in the corridors between the major centres.

By 1990 an important shift in the contribution of two of the largest sectors to the nation's Gross Domestic Product had occurred. At the start of the NEP in 1970, agriculture contributed 31 per cent of GDP but only 19 per cent by 1990; manufacturing, by contrast, rose from 13 per cent in 1970 to 44 per cent of GDP in 1990. Equally impressive was the increase in Bumiputera employment in the manufacturing sector from 28.9 per cent in 1970 to 49.1 per cent in 1990.

National Development Policy and 'Vision 2020'

Notwithstanding substantial progress towards meeting planning goals, ethnic and economic disparities were still very much part of Malaysian life when the NEP ended in 1990. Accordingly, the Economic Planning Unit of the Prime Minister's Department formulated the Second Outline Perspective Plan that became the basis for the National Development Policy (NDP). The NDP continued the NEP's emphasis on balanced development, stable growth, ethnic harmony and the removal of social and economic inequalities in society. Despite the progress made in the NEP, the government admitted that it had failed to create competent Bumiputera entrepreneurs in sufficient numbers. Under the NDP greater attention was to be placed on quality, with more stringent requirements for Bumiputera candidates in business posts, as well as for the products and services they delivered. However, since more private shareholdings were also encouraged, there were associated problems. Private holdings tended to be accumulated by certain groups, such as Malay royal families and UMNO leaders, and shares allocated to other Bumiputera were usually sold for a quick profit.

A far more serious problem facing the NDP is what government critics have labelled 'crony capitalism', whereby private sector business people gain excessive financial benefits because of their personal links with government leaders. The involvement of political parties in business has also widened the opportunities for politicians to dispense patronage. Certain individuals have amassed immense fortunes during the restructuring of the economy because they have enjoyed the favour of the prime minister or the leaders of UMNO, the leading party of the governing Barisan Nasional coalition (see below). Preferential treatment of political favourites is not a new feature in Malaysian politics, but in the current situation it has reached alarming proportions, and even within UMNO there are objections to the extent to which politics is controlled by access to money. By 1992 there were about 1150 state and federal enterprises, all enjoying government protection and resources. With excellent prospects for dominating strategic segments of the economy, these enterprises have formed a lucrative source of crony capitalist activity and widened the gap between the lower and middle classes and the very wealthy. In many cases smaller entrepreneurs, both Malays and non-Malays, are dependent on the 'super-Bumis' to gain access to lucrative con-tracts, especially in construction. Without adequate controls, critics believe, such activities will be a major stumbling block to any meaningful achievement of NEP-NDP goals.

The dominance of manufacturing in the export sector has continued in the NDP. In 1998, at the midway point of the Seventh Malaysia Plan (1996–2000), manufacturing accounted for 34.4 per cent of GDP. Statistics for the first four months of 1999 showed that the top five export earners were elec-trical and electronic products; palm oil and palm-based products; apparel and clothing; liquefied natural gas; and crude petroleum. Significantly, elec-trical and electronic products accounted for 57.1 per cent of total export earnings. This has reinforced the government's conviction that the future economic prosperity of Malaysia no longer rests on the export of primary products but on the fruits of high technology. Towards this goal the govern-ment has created yet another ambitious project known as the Multimedia Super Corridor (MSC) as part of the effort to modernize society and create a skilled professional labour force. A sum of M$100 (US$26 million) was alloc-ated in the Seventh Malaysia Plan for the MSC Research and Development Grant Scheme to establish collaboration among world-class research and development centres, universities and public research institutions in the country.

Conceived as a super high technology park, the MSC is intended to enable Malaysians to participate in and benefit from the global information revolution. It comprises a 15×50 kilometre zone extending south of Kuala Lumpur, equipped with the latest and fastest communication links and served by the large and efficient new Kuala Lumpur International Airport at Sepang. One sector within the corridor, known as Technology Centre One, was established earlier as an 'incubator' of the project. The city of Cyberjaya, some 40 kilometres south of Kuala Lumpur, will provide the nerve centre for the infrastructure and facilities to support the multimedia industry. Mahathir has taken a very strong personal interest in this project, and it is no coincidence that in June 1999 the Prime Minister's Department was the first government office to move from Kuala Lumpur to the new administrative capital of Putrajaya, located next to Cyberjaya.

Recognizing the enormous gap still existing between Malaysia and the more technologically advanced nations, the government is hoping through various inducements to attract well-established overseas high-tech companies willing to transfer some of their skills to Malaysians. Among the incentives offered are a waiver from local ownership requirements, the right to bid for infrastructure projects for the MSC, and freedom to employ skilled foreign workers. For example, only 48 hours is needed to obtain a work permit for a qualified foreign engineer. Firms will also be exempt from customs for ten years or given 100 per cent investment tax allowance, and they will not be subject to the currency restrictions imposed in September 1998. To qualify for invitation to become part of the MSC, firms have to be primary providers and users of multimedia services and products, be employers of large numbers of trained personnel, and, for foreign firms, seek to transfer technology to Malaysia. By December 1998 some 198 companies had been given MSC status, of which 88 were local. While the government's commitment to the MSC is impressive, private investment in Malaysian technology companies is limited primarily because of the relative novelty of these enterprises.

By the end of 1998 it was estimated that there were 87 000 workers involved in information technology, of whom 28 000 were technical staff and 8000 engineers. Without more trained Malaysians the ambitious projects currently under way will clearly falter, and the government is relying on both private and public universities to supply the necessary skilled workers. It has encouraged, for example, the founding of a private university, appropriately named Multimedia University, located within the MSC itself. The first intake of 1300 students to the new university was in 1998, and another 600 were welcomed with great ceremony by the minister of education, Datuk Seri Najib Abdul Razak, in June 1999. Owned by the privatized Telecom Malaysia, the Multimedia University is a twin campus of the Melaka-based Telecom University. In 1999 it comprised four faculties: Creative Multimedia, Engineering, Management, and Information Technology. Its joint ventures in research and development with firms in the MSC is an example of the type of co-operation that the government hopes will enable Malaysia to benefit economically from its transformation into a high-tech society.

The new emphasis on information technology is part of an ongoing reassessment to make education relevant to the changing needs of the country. The growth in private, often English-medium, colleges has been in response to a growing demand for higher education among Chinese students, especially those denied entry to public universities because of quotas. Many prefer an English-medium education because it is seen as enhancing prospects of employment and further education abroad. Indeed, in pronouncements which some interpret as undermining the status of Malay as the national language, government leaders have repeatedly stressed that command of English is necessary for economic advancement. In the 1980s more opportunities became available in 'twinning' arrangements with foreign institutions. Malaysian students would spend the first two years studying with a branch of that institution in Malaysia, and then complete the final two years at the home campus. In a recent development, Monash University in Melbourne established an entire four-year branch campus in a suburb of Kuala Lumpur, offering a limited course of study taught by lecturers either on secondment from the home institution or hired in Malaysia itself.

The strong emphasis on education and on the development of the MSC are part of a larger conception known as 'Vision 2020', which was first introduced in 1991 by Prime Minister Mahathir at the inaugural meeting of the Malaysian Business Council. Its principal aim is to achieve first world status by the year 2020 by raising the average income of Malaysians to the same level as in highly industrialized states. Unlike the NEP, which had produced a number of five-year plans with precise goals, Vision 2020 is more an exhortation to Malaysians to work harder and double the GDP every ten years from 1990 to 2020. In 1991, when Malaysia had enjoyed a decade of phenomenal growth, the Vision appeared potentially attainable. But in late 1997 the currency crisis struck Malaysia and severely set back its economic programme. The rapidly falling value of the Malaysian *ringgit* and the danger of major business failures led to a government decision to impose currency controls in September 1998. This move went against the policies of the International Monetary Fund and made Malaysia unpopular with the international financial community. By mid-1999, however, the economy had emerged from the worst of the crisis. Although some commentators have argued that the level of debt was far higher than revealed by official figures, government economists cautiously declared an end to the recession.

There are, none the less, likely to be repercussions, even after currency controls are lifted, since fear of further government intervention will probably make foreign institutions and investors more careful about committing to Malaysia. The influence of political considerations in the framing of economic policy remains a source of concern in overseas financial circles. In particular, the controversy surrounding the treatment of the former deputy minister Anwar Ibrahim has raised disturbing questions about leadership succession and future political stability in Malaysia. Foreign perceptions of Malaysia's weakened judicial system and absence of legal transparency may also stem the flow of investment capital to the country at a time when it is most needed to fund the ambitious Multimedia Super Corridor project. With low and even negative growth during the crisis, the prime minister himself has expressed doubt that the goal of first world status by 2020 will now be achievable.

Environmental costs of development

For the casual visitor the modernization of Malaysia is indeed impressive: commuter trains link the outlying towns to Kuala Lumpur, and a light railway system has made access to the various parts of the city easy and pleasant. The new Multimedia Super Corridor has created another pocket of development to the south of Kuala Lumpur, while outside the cities miles of planted oil palms and rubber trees border the major highways. But Malaysia's strong economic position has come at a cost to the environment, although in general there has been very little outcry from the public. The reason, according to one perceptive comment, is that '[p]ride of achievement and impatience for more, rather than alarm over the shape of the future, remain dominant almost throughout national society and among all ethnic groups'.[9] In Kuala Lumpur in mid-1999 massive buildings rise along major railways and high-ways, while vacant land scraped bare of any vegetation awaits yet further development. Indeed, it is now difficult to imagine that much of the Penin-sula was once covered with thick jungle. The scale of deforestation in Malay-sia in recent times has been compared to Central America, the Amazon basin, and the 'great ages of clearance' in medieval Europe and early-modern America, but it has occurred on a greater scale and at a far greater speed. Only in a few inaccessible areas and in the Taman Nagara (National Park) in Pahang has the lowland forest been left undisturbed.

In the Kelang valley and the Federal Territory of Kuala Lumpur the ravaging of the landscape has been caused largely by the massive demand for housing in a sector which is now home to about 3 million people. For housing development, the tree cover is usually levelled with heavy machinery, because it is more cost effective to do so, even though much of the land could be left undeveloped for longer periods. In heavy rainfall the cleared land is subject to erosion and landslips, contributing to the polluting of rivers. Des-pite the passing of the Environmental Quality Act in 1974 and the Sewage and Industrial Effluent Regulations in 1979, there has not been any dramatic improvement in the situation. The Second Outline Prospective Plan recognizes the importance of protecting the environment, but once again the problem is ineffective implementation. In June 1999, of the 31 rivers throughout Malaysia monitored by the Department of the Environment, 6 were classified as polluted, 16 were moderately polluted, and only 9 were 'clean'. Although international attention has focused on the forests rather than rivers and oceans, the use of explosives and poison by Malaysian fishermen is a major threat to fishing grounds and has seriously damaged offshore coral reefs. Albeit belatedly, official campaigns have been launched to educate the public about the long-term harm of such practices.

In the cities, motor vehicle emissions remain a major pollutant, particu-larly in greater Kuala Lumpur, where there is a motor vehicle for every three or four people. Despite the introduction of the light rail system and the com-muter trains, traffic in downtown Kuala Lumpur and in every major town in the Kelang valley makes cross-town travel during peak hours a nightmare. Leaded petrol is still being used, and exhaust fumes create a haze of low-altitude pollution. Kuala Lumpur is particularly vulnerable because the ranges of hills on two sides trap air and thus exacerbate the already poor ventilation caused by local atmospheric conditions. Emission controls have been only weakly enforced, and pollution control devices for factories are still rare. Smoke from forest fires in Sumatra and Borneo, in 1994 and subsequent years, merely highlighted the seriousness of the pollution problem in Malaysia.

Malaysia's active Green movement is led by such groups as the Sahabat Alam Malaysia (Malaysian Friends of the Earth), the Malayan Nature Society and the Consumers Association of Penang, and their criticism of developmental policies has been a recurring irritation to government. The environmental protection movement suffered a setback during a spate of political arrests in 1987, when a number of its leaders were gaoled for short periods. Publications by its members have also been more rigidly controlled following their vehement defence of indigenous groups threatened by logging in Sarawak. In this particular case the government reacted swiftly and ruthlessly because several powerful political figures had interests in these logging ventures. Since then environmental activists have adopted a different tactic by avoiding direct attacks on the government and suggesting instead workable and environmentally friendly solutions.

In October 1996 an international consortium was formed to construct the hydroelectric Bakun Dam in Sarawak. The area to be flooded was estimated to be the size of Singapore, and arrangements were therefore made to relocate all animals and some 10 000 people, including the indigenous Penan. Despite domestic and international protests, the project went ahead but was plagued by problems and doubts about its financial viability. The government called an indefinite halt to the project when the currency crisis hit in late 1997. By mid-1999 the economy appeared to be back on track, and so the government resumed construction, but with a far more modest goal. No longer would it be expected to provide electricity to the Peninsula, in addition to Sarawak and Sabah, and the amount of power generated would be reduced from an estimated capacity of 2400 megawatt to 500 megawatt. A group of non-governmental organizations (NGOs) calling itself 'Coalition of Concerned NGOs on Bakun' then proposed that the government institute a study to implement energy-saving measures and to ensure that current power stations operate at full efficiency as alternatives to Bakun. They argued that Malaysia had to optimize use of its renewable energy sources, and that hydroelectric dams were not renewable. The government's scaling down of the project may have been a result of financial constraints, but arguments from NGOs couched in terms of economic development may also have had an impact.

While the government's suspicion of NGOs is a response to their outspoken opposition to many of its development policies and political tactics, it is not necessary for this relationship to be one of confrontation. If environmental groups can persuade the electorate that responsible environmental protection need not threaten commercial development and hence jobs, then there may be greater implementation of environmental safeguards by both the government and the ordinary person. One unintended ally of the Greens may be tourism, particularly eco-tourism. The tourism industry has invested considerable energy in advertising the unique features of the Malaysian landscape and in emphasizing the 'pristine' jungles and unique peoples of Sarawak and Sabah. Perhaps an alliance of the environmental groups and the tourism industry could convince the government that eco-tourism would provide a far more stable and long-term source of revenue for Malaysia than a steadily declining timber industry with rapidly diminishing forest reserves.

The environmentalist movement highlights what may be a significant development in promoting a greater sense of civic rights and responsibilities among Malaysians – the emergence of a nascent 'civil society' in the form of non-government organizations operating in the political and social space between the family and formal state agencies. This development is of particular importance in Malaysia, where the print and broadcast media are largely controlled by political interests connected to the ruling coalition, and where successive colonial and independent governments have bequeathed a corpus of restrictive legislation which limits the expression of dissent through the established political system. In this situation, NGOs can provide a training ground and serve as foci for activism in a wide range of areas, while their publications and websites can become a means of linking people of diverse backgrounds but common interests. It is NGO groups, whose members are often drawn from the burgeoning middle class which has enjoyed the fruits of Malaysia's social and economic transformation, that have been most active in defence of those neglected by the NEP-NDP.

The shape of politics post-1969

Whatever the degree of success, the bold measures of the NEP would have been difficult to implement had it not been for UMNO's power in the governing coalition. This dominance enabled UMNO to use its two-thirds majority in parliament to achieve its goals through legislative means, thus providing a legal justification for action. When considered necessary, the executive branch of the government was willing to call upon the enforcement agencies of the state to remove any obstacles to its programmes. Constitutional amendments were passed by the Dewan Rakyat after the resumption of parliamentary rule in February 1971. According to the government, these were aimed at removing 'sensitive issues from the realm of public discussions so as to allow the smooth functioning of parliamentary democracy; and to redress the racial imbalance in certain sectors of the nation's life and thereby promote national unity'. Any public discussion, even by parliamentary members, of topics dealing with the power and status of the Malay rulers, Malay special privileges, citizenship, Malay as the national language and the status of Islam as the official religion was now considered seditious. The amendments also reserved a quota of places within institutions of higher learning for Bumiputeras as one means of redressing the ethnic imbalance in the professions. The intention was to reserve places for Malays and the indigenous people of the Peninsula and Sabah and Sarawak in certain areas of study, but especially in the fields of engineering, medicine and the sciences. Most importantly, by constitutional amendments restricting discussion of 'sensitive issues', the government was able to pursue its policies with greater freedom. The media and even parliament, instead of being critics of government actions, became the instruments of endorsement and consensus. The entire structure of the Malaysian state, from the law courts to the police and the army, was being mobilized to carry out the government's wishes.

One significant result of the 1969 ethnic disturbances was a questioning of the effectiveness of the Alliance partnership of UMNO, MCA and MIC, which had successfully governed Malaya/Malaysia since independence. During these years the easy comradeship among the English-educated leaders of the Alliance parties meant that the more dominant UMNO continued to treat its two weaker partners with respect. The myth of equality of the three was maintained by genuine efforts to meet the varying demands of the different ethnic groups. But by 1969 it was already evident that the MCA and the MIC were losing credibility as representatives of the Chinese and Indian communities. The success of the opposition parties in amassing an unexpectedly large number of votes and their proclamation of a 'victory' in the 1969 elections forced UMNO to rethink its political strategy. To prevent any future ethnic strife, it was decided that the political base of the Alliance needed to be widened to enable debate and resolution to occur within the government and not in society itself. Thus in 1970 the Barisan Nasional (National Front) was formed, consisting of the Alliance members and other political parties, with UMNO as the dominant partner.

UMNO's dominance in Barisan was enhanced in part because the initial aim of including the major political players in a single governmental party was not achieved. The main Chinese opposition party, the DAP, which had traditionally accounted for around half of the Chinese votes, remained outside the coalition. Since the DAP was regarded widely as the political voice for the Chinese, the bargaining power of the MCA and the largely Chinese Gerakan within Barisan was greatly weakened. PAS, the principal Malay opposition party, did join Barisan in 1973 but was expelled in 1977. Thus, although Barisan comprised 14 parties in the year 2000, UMNO had become even stronger than it was in the Alliance. The MIC continued to be the only major party of the Indians, but it had very little bargaining power because Indians did not constitute a majority in any constituency, and because the MIC never truly represented the interests of all Indians. The enlargement of the Barisan has further diluted MIC influence, which was also weakened by leadership disputes in the 1980s. A breakaway group, the All-Malaysian Indian Progressive Front, was formed in mid-1990, and was relatively successful in mobilizing support, primarily among poor and working-class Indians. None the less, as the 50th anniversary of independence approaches, many Indians still feel marginalized, and it is not surprising that their interests are often addressed by NGOs rather than political parties.

The political situation in Sabah and Sarawak is far more complex than on the Peninsula because of the unique circumstances of their historical development and their range of ethnicities. In the 1991 census Sarawak had a total population of 1.7 million people, of whom 29.5 per cent were Iban, 27.7 per cent Chinese, and 21.0 per cent Malay. Since 1970 Sarawak has been governed by varying coalitions dominated by Muslim Malay-Melanau parties. To counter the political grouping of the Muslim Melanau and Malays, the concept of 'Dayakism' has been promoted by the Ibans (formerly 'Sea Dayaks'), the Selako and the Bidayuh (formerly 'Land Dayaks'). When the newly formed Parti Bansa Dayak Sarawak (PBDS – Party of the Sarawak Dayak Nation) did well in the elections in 1983, it was invited to become a member of Barisan. Although later withdrawing from Barisan at the state level, PBDS retained its membership in the national coalition. The major parties in the state Barisan are the Parti Pesaka Bumiputera Bersatu (United Bumiputera Pesaka Party, which emerged from a merger of a Muslim and non-Muslim indigenous party), the Iban-based Sarawak National Party, and the Chinese-based Sarawak United People's Party. As one might expect, patron–client relationships are a primary consideration in political formation in Sarawak.

A similar observation could be made of Sabah, which has also been characterized by alignments between political parties and ethnic and religious affiliation. Of a total population of 1.8 million in Sabah in 1991, the non-Muslim/Christian Kadazandusun comprised 18.4 per cent, followed by the Chinese with 11.7 per cent, and the Muslim Bajau with 11.4 per cent. Non-Malaysian citizens, principally Indonesian and Filipinos, comprise the largest group or 24.9 per cent of the population. Political parties have formed around Muslim Bumiputera, non-Muslim Bumiputera, and non-Bumiputera (Chinese) groups. From the late 1960s it was dominated by the Muslim-based United Sabah National Organization (USNO) under the leadership of Tun Mustapha. Sabah's wealth from the timber industry and its distance from Kuala Lumpur enabled Tun Mustapha to rule the state as his personal fiefdom. He alienated many groups by his declaration of Islam as the state religion, his aggressive programme of Malayization, and his authoritarian style. When he flouted Kuala Lumpur and continued to support separatist rebels in the southern Philippines, Mustapha finally fell from favour. Encouraged by the federal leadership, dissidents from USNO formed a new party, Berjaya (Bersatu Rakyat Jelata Sabah, or the United People's Party of Sabah), and Tun Mustapha was effectively locked out of power when Berjaya won the state elections in 1976. Berjaya, like USNO, was basically a Kadazandusun party but with multi-ethnic support that included wealthy Chinese business leaders. Both parties had joined Barisan, but at the state level Berjaya formed the government with USNO in opposition.

During the decade of Berjaya rule, Sabah witnessed a repetition of the corruption and mismanagement that had characterized the previous government of Tun Mustapha. A new Kadazandusun-based party, Parti Bersatu Sabah (PBS – United Sabah Party), was formed by Berjaya dissidents to contest the 1985 state elections. Despite Mahathir's open support of Berjaya, PBS won the elections by attracting votes from both Kadazandusun and Chinese, many of whom were Christian. PBS accepted the invitation to join the Barisan in 1986, but relations were always strained and it withdrew in 1990. Although PBS won a narrow victory in 1994, the defection of several members led to parliamentary dissolution and the formation of a new government by an UMNO-led alliance. In the 1995 federal elections which were won by Barisan, PBS took all eight seats it contested, but this was less than half the total 19 seats at stake. To assure the continuance of Barisan control in Sabah, the federal government allocated an additional M$2.25 billion (US$500 million) to the state in the Mid-Term Review of the Seventh Malaysia Plan in 1998. Just prior to the state elections in March 1999, there was a further allocation of M$50 million (US$13 million) to be distributed to 48 state constituencies in Sabah for 'development purposes'. The message to the Sabah voters was clear, and when Barisan won all 24 seats it contested in the election the federal government provided a further M$230 million (US$60.5 million) to the state in soft loans.

Since its formation, the Barisan Nasional has been able to win consistently more than two-thirds of the seats in parliament, thus allowing it the luxury of amending the Constitution at will to suit its purpose. It gained 88 per cent of the seats in 1974, 85 per cent in 1978, 86 per cent in 1982, 84 per cent in 1986, 71 per cent in 1990, 84 per cent in 1995 and 76 per cent in 1999. Between 1978 and 1995 UMNO accounted for 64–74 per cent of Barisan seats in the Peninsula, and between 53 and 56 per cent of the total number of seats in parliament. Although it suffered some losses in 1999, UMNO's continued dominance can be attributed to a number of factors: first, the steady rise of the numbers of Malays in the population, reaching close to 60 per cent in the 1990s; second, favourable constituency boundaries so that in 1995 Malays formed the majority in 101 of a total 144 constituencies; and third, UMNO's effective patronage system, machinery and tactics.

For Mahathir the maintenance of a two-thirds majority marks a symbolic divide. Addressing the 53rd UMNO General Assembly in June 1999, he cited the dangers posed by the new coalition headed by the Parti KeADILan Nasional (National Justice Party) because it could 'weaken and affect UMNO's struggle and reduce the BN [Barisan Nasional] two-thirds majority *which is vital to the country's stability and development*'. Though acknowledging the role of the other parties in the Barisan, Mahathir stated bluntly that 'UMNO is the backbone, the very bulwark of the Barisan National.'[10] As president of UMNO he already wielded considerable power in the political process, but he further strengthened his position as prime minister by undermining two important institutional safeguards against the power of the

executive branch. He removed the right of the head of state, the yang dipertuan agung, to veto any legislation, and he replaced high court judges to
assure a judiciary responsive to his demands. As we have seen, debates over
the role of the traditional rulers within the *kerajaan* (the term still used for
government) have a long history in Malaysian society, and impatience and at
times hostility are nothing new. Under Mahathir, however, the old tensions
were vented in ways that were unprecedented and irreversible. As members
of the Malay aristocracy asserted their claims to traditional perquisites and
intervened to obtain commercial privileges for themselves and their (often
Chinese) clients, they incurred the resentment of a newly ambitious generation of Malay commoners. In 1990, for the first time, the position of the
Malay rulers was debated in UMNO's General Assembly and in 1993 the
immunity of Malay sultans to criminal offences was removed.

Because of UMNO's dominance in government, internal divisions
within the party became in fact a struggle for the exercise of national power,
and reflected larger debates in the Malay community. UMNO's unity was
seriously threatened on two occasions. The first was in 1987 when UMNO
was split between supporters of Prime Minister Mahathir, and those who
sided with the former Deputy Prime Minister Musa Hitam and Tengku
Razaleigh Hamzah. Although these two had been ambitious rivals with hopes
of succeeding or toppling Mahathir, they had set aside their differences in
a common cause. In a close election within UMNO, the challengers were
defeated, and Mahathir moved quickly to thwart the possibility of widening
opposition to his regime. In October of that year the Internal Security Act
was invoked to arrest and detain over 100 people, including politicians and
leaders of dissident groups. The following year Mahathir's UMNO opponents resorted to litigation, alleging that there had been irregularities in the
voting. Deciding in favour of the challengers, the High Court declared
UMNO an illegal organization and froze its assets. Mahathir and his supporters renamed their organization UMNO Baru ('New UMNO') and regained
UMNO's assets, while the challengers adopted the name Semangat '46
('Spirit of '46', 1946 being the year UMNO was founded). Many Malays were
disturbed by Mahathir's treatment of the sultans, while other government
measures, such as the replacement of judges critical of Mahathir's use of
executive power, and the imposition of much stricter press controls also
aroused public concern.

These developments coincided with a controversial education policy
introduced by the then minister for education, Anwar Ibrahim. It placed
non-Mandarin speaking Chinese as principals and administrators in Chinese-
type national schools, thus arousing strong opposition from the Chinese
community. Hoping to tap the deepening sense of unease which was evident
in both Malay and non-Malay communities, Semangat '46 entered into a
coalition with the DAP and PAS. In the 1990 election Semangat '46 won 8
seats and 15.1 per cent of the votes, and together with PAS won all of the state
and parliamentary seats in Kelantan. It proved impossible, however, to

sustain this level of support, and in the 1995 elections its share of the vote declined to 10.2 per cent of the votes, which translated to only 6 seats. Although popular feeling against Mahathir was initially high, it was contained by the economic recovery. In 1996 Tengku Razaleigh disbanded the party, and he and his followers rejoined UMNO (the 'Baru' was dropped), while Musa abandoned further efforts to gain high office.

The second threat to UMNO's dominance came in June 1998 when then Deputy Prime Minister Anwar Ibrahim was deposed and accused of sodomy. His arrest, beating and incarceration shocked Malaysians and the outside world, accustomed to perceiving Malaysia as a stable parliamentary democracy. It also exposed the extent to which government measures over the previous 20 years had emasculated the legal system. Encouraged by supporters, Anwar's wife, Dr Wan Azizah Wan Ismail, assumed the leadership of a movement that developed into the Parti KeADILan Nasional. As in 1987 the formation of this new party divided the UMNO membership, and once again led to the rise of a new coalition, the Barisan Alternatif (Alternative Front), consisting of KeADILan, PAS, DAP and Parti Rakyat Malaysia. The strong support for KeADILan reflected not only Anwar's popularity, but also the dissatisfaction with an authoritarian style of government which had silenced dissenting voices while tolerating the political and financial excesses of political favourites.

In mid-1999 Barisan held 163 of the 192 parliamentary seats, and thus the opposition needed to win 65 seats to deny Barisan a two-thirds majority. In the November 1999 elections, Barisan succeeded in retaining its two-thirds majority, despite losing 18 seats to the Barisan Alternatif. PAS showed considerable strength in the northern Malay states, retaining Kelantan and winning Terengganu. Although KeADILan appeared to have fared worse than expected, with only five seats, an analysis of the elections showed strong support among Malay voters, with many of the seats lost by very narrow margins. The casualties among the government members included four cabinet ministers and six deputy ministers. Government losses were particularly severe in the so-called Malay heartland in the north. In the state elections, Barisan was a big loser, retaining only 281 of 350 seats won in the 1990 elections. With a considerably reduced majority, many Barisan seats became marginal.

In a sharp reversal of previous practice, however, Chinese voters gave their overwhelming support to the government. Many had benefited from the years of prosperity under Mahathir, while others were swayed by government propaganda that a DAP–PAS coalition did not bode well for the Chinese in Malaysia. The decision by the Chinese voters to vote for Barisan left the DAP the major losers. Not only was the DAP soundly defeated in the Chinese stronghold of Penang, but its leaders, Lim Kit Siang and Karpal Singh, lost their seats in the process. The strong multi-ethnic support for Barisan in Johor, Sabah and Sarawak could be interpreted as a 'Malaysianization' of politics in these states, though whether this portends a trend in the rest of the country is yet to be demonstrated. The inability of the Barisan Alternatif to deny the government its two-thirds majority was a disappointment since many believed that revelations of abuse in high places and the humiliating treatment of former Deputy Prime Minister Anwar Ibrahim would be reflected in a strong anti-government vote. Although the government was returned with a two-thirds majority, the defection of Malay voters from Barisan was of some concern to UMNO.

A review of the 1999 elections reveals that the Barisan Alternatif was a fragile coalition held together by the strong emotions surrounding the harsh treatment of the former deputy prime minister. Although PAS had indicated a willingness to defer its goal of an Islamic state, it remained a fundamental plank in the party's platform, and will always pose a problem in any alliance with non-Muslim parties, particularly with the DAP. Some non-Muslims also remember that Anwar himself had been a vehement proponent of Malay interests, while it is not at all clear that his supporters would take a firm stand against cronyism. However, if the KeADILan movement survives, it may provide the foundations for renewed attempts to create a truly non-communal party in Malaysia. Senior politicians and activists from all ethnic groups have joined the new party, and the chairperson of the Gagasan Demokrasi Rakyat (Movement for People's Democracy), Chua Tian Chong, was elected one of its vice-presidents. Chandra Muzaffar, a well-known social activist who has been vocal in his criticisms of the government, was another of KeADILan's vice-presidents.

Another significant development was support for KeADILan from women's organizations representing different ethnic and religious constituencies. The Pembangunan Wanita Kolektif (Women's Development Collective), a secretariat comprising some 34 groups involved with issues relevant to the Agenda Wanita Untuk Perubahan (Women's Agenda for Change), was formed in June 1998. Among its members are Sisters in Islam, Wanita Jemaah Islam Malaysia (Malaysian Reform Assembly of Women) and the Selangor Chinese Union (Women's Branch). The figure of Wan Azizah as the head of KeADILan has given a further boost to the rise of the female vote in Malaysian politics. This is significant because although the Constitution guarantees equal citizenship rights, there is no reference to gender, and some have argued that the state endorses a gender ideology which subordinates women. While all the major parties have formed women's branches, they have been generally seen as supportive but essentially subordinate political auxiliaries.

In recent years political leaders have become more aware of the potential of the female vote. In 1989 the government formulated a National Policy on Women which laid down that they should be integrated into all sectors of development, and in 1997 this was followed by the Women's Development Action Plan. In the elections of November 1999 a total of 61 women were among the candidates for 587 parliamentary and state seats, and 44 were successful. In the Dewan Rakyat, female membership has increased from

2.9 per cent in 1959 to 10 per cent (20 of 193 seats). Although more women were successful at the federal level, they are less visible in the states, especially in Terengganu, Kelantan and Kedah, where Islamic influence is stronger (PAS does not field women candidates). With the rising number of educated women, there is some evidence of impatience with their limited political role and lack of access to positions of authority. Only two women, for example, are cabinet ministers. According to some estimates, another 25 per cent increase in female representation at the national level is needed for any meaningful political participation to occur. At present, women who succeed in politics are not necessarily advocates for women's interests, since female members of Barisan parties are such a minority, and outspoken criticism of government policies is not welcomed. It is not easy to galvanize joint action across the coalition on matters such as child support and protection against domestic abuse, while the gap between educated leaders and the female electorate is a formidable barrier to building any kind of grass-roots movement. In poor areas of the country where many women are struggling to feed their families, it is difficult to generate support for issues discussed in distant cities.

In the larger picture, the political hegemony of UMNO is a reminder that any challenge to Barisan would be a formidable undertaking. Certain institutional factors cited above, as well as the growing authoritarianism of the government as a result of Mahathir's undermining of the power of the yang dipertuan agung (paramount ruler) and the judiciary, are major obstacles to any challengers. Moreover, the period of the NEP-NDP has improved the lot of many Malays, as well as many lower- and middle-class Chinese and Indians, making them much more ready to support the existing government. On the other hand, this may also point to a greater potential for the evolution of non-communal parties. Although ethnic identity will continue to be important in Malaysia, sectarian appeals may lose their potency as political weapons, as class interests become increasingly more relevant. As in the past, however, religious affiliations and the old Melayu-Muslim links remain a complicating factor.

The Islamic factor

Islam has gained greater prominence in public life since the beginning of the NEP. For 500 years Islam has been central to Malay identity, being periodically reshaped by reformist influences generated from the Islamic heartlands. In the 1970s Malays responded to a world-wide resurgence of Islam and found a new certainty and solace in religion at a time of considerable social and economic change. Commonly termed *dakwah* (literally, 'call'), the reform movement sought to energize Malay Muslims and to inject a new religiosity into all aspects of the nation's life. In practice, however, the stress on Muslim versus non-Muslim and the call for an Islamic state created barriers between Malays and non-Malays, and to some extent among Muslims themselves.

The electoral success of PAS testified to the appeal of these ideas among Malays, and has forced UMNO to adopt a much stronger Islamic stance in order to counter the argument that it is essentially secular. The impulse to accord Islam a greater visibility in Malaysian society gathered force after Mahathir became prime minister in 1981. Soon after taking office he sponsored a seminar on the subject, 'The Concept of Development in Islam', and in 1984 officially announced a policy of Islamization – 'the inculcation of Islamic values' – in government. Greater emphasis was placed on Islamic-related projects, and the media were encouraged to make adjustments in coverage to reflect this new shift. There was an immediate outcry at the increase in Islamic programmes on television and radio, and other religions called for equal time. In refusing to grant this request, Mahathir defended the policy 'since Islam is the national and official religion and every citizen should learn its values'.[11] Mosques and other Islamic religious halls proliferated throughout the country, though attention often focused on such show-pieces as the M\$126-million mosque in Shah Alam. There were also policy shifts in education, where religious knowledge became a school examination subject, and in economic strategy, where balance between economic and spiritual development was encouraged. The declaration that Malaysia's economic system would be remodelled to conform to Islam was followed by the establishment of such institutions as the Islamic Bank and the Islamic Economic Foundation.

In dealing with Islamic law Mahathir has found it necessary to tread a very fine line, so that he may be seen as a proponent of Islam while allaying fears of religious hegemony among the country's substantial non-Muslim population. The strong Islamic stance adopted by PAS has forced the government to strive to appear equally staunch Muslims and protectors of the Malay heritage. Enforcement of Islamic prohibitions during the fasting month has increased, a special foundation to co-ordinate all *dakwah* activities has been established, and public pronouncements by Mahathir and other high officials stressing the government's deference to Islam have become commonplace.

The government has been careful to monitor extreme statements by Muslim radicals, particularly after PAS regained control of government in Kelantan in 1990. The PAS government has tried to bring Islamic principles into practice through the introduction of *hudu* or Islamic criminal law (later blocked by the federal government). By condemning Kelantan's PAS government for its 'extreme' measures, the government has sought to reassure the non-Muslim population that it would safeguard the right to practise non-Muslim religions. At the same time the government has continued to emphasize that UMNO is the country's largest Islamic party, and that its modernist interpretation is closer to the true spirit of Islam than that of their political rivals in PAS. This is a politically astute stance since Malaysia's Muslim population has become more obviously devout. Believers flock to the numerous mosques and *suraus* (prayer houses) springing up all over the country. Malay women, who have traditionally worn the *baju kurung*, a loose skirt and long-sleeved overblouse, have now adopted the headcovering, either the *telekung* (Islamic prayer shawl) or a smaller and more decorative version; men are seen increasingly with the white skull cap to indicate that they have made the pilgrimage to Mekka and Medina.

While PAS has always aimed for the introduction of an Islamic state, it is by no means alone. ABIM, the Islamic youth movement, has shared this objective since its inception in 1971, as have the 'Islamic Republic' groups among university students. The latter are much more outspoken on the need to bring the people and the government to a 'proper' understanding of Islam. Groups such as ABIM, the Ulama Association of Malaysia, PAS, and Muslim students and intellectuals in the universities have spearheaded calls for an Islamic state. Government fear that *dakwah* activities may provoke confrontation with the country's substantial non-Muslim population has led to a restriction of certain activities and the highly publicized suppression of the fundamentalist *Darul Arqam* group. In its role as a mediating Islamic voice, the government has been able to win the support not only of non-Muslims but also of many moderate Muslims.

In foreign affairs, too, a change in direction is apparent. Mahathir declared in 1983 that the Non-Aligned Nations and the Commonwealth would no longer be as important to Malaysia as the Islamic bloc. This policy shift was evident in Malaysia's support of the struggle of Muslim groups around the world, including the *Mujahideen* in Afghanistan, the Palestinians in Israel, the Arakanese in Myanmar, the Chechens in Russia, and the Bosnians and the Kosovars in Yugoslavia. But Islam forms only one facet of the 'New Malay' who is to lead the country into first world status by 2020.

'The *Melayu Baru* (New Malay)'

Midway through the NEP a reporter described the ideal Malaysian who would emerge in 1990 as

> a Malay who sees his position as secure in a country where migrant Chinese appear (falsely) to be the economic overlords; a Chinese who sees his acquisitive talents are not unfairly circumscribed by political manipulations; an Indian who sees his minority status as not exploited because he is defenceless; a Dayak [Iban] or Kadazan who sees his distance from Kuala Lumpur as no reason to be neglected.[12]

The year 1990 has come and gone, and while this ideal Malaysian has yet to emerge, there has been progress towards this goal, primarily because of the spectacular economic growth in Malaysia over the course of the NEP (1971–90).

Malays would agree that the NEP was necessary to enable many of them to break out of the low-income subsistence agricultural sector to which they had been consigned by the British, and to gain a proportionate share of the country's wealth. In addition, they believe that they are the primary indigenous inhabitants of the land and have the right and privilege to determine the standard language, culture and priorities in their own society. A number of striking changes that have occurred in Malaysian society since the introduction of the NEP bear witness to the sincerity of this belief.

The Malay language has now become the major vehicle of communication in the country and is heard widely in the streets, in the shops, in offices, in the media, in the schools, and even in the universities, which were once bastions of English-speakers. No longer can Malays be regarded as primarily rural inhabitants as they now comprise close to half the urban population. A large and ever-growing Malay middle class is evident everywhere, setting standards of behaviour, language and aspirations for the modern Malay. They frequent the expensive shops in shopping malls, eat in upmarket restaurants, and holiday abroad, as would any middle-class individual in Western society. Malays themselves express justifiable pride in the country's accomplishments, where they can enjoy many of the benefits to be found in other advanced societies. While there are still many Malays who live in a rural environment where income levels are among the lowest in the country, government incentives offer an opportunity for upward mobility. As Malays become increasingly urbanized, the idea of 'going home to the village' has assumed a nostalgic quality that invokes ideas of core Malay cultural values. It is noteworthy that a favourite holiday destination for Malays is Kelantan, still regarded as the most Malay of all the Malaysian states.

The increasing number of urban and middle-class Malays, the beneficiaries of the NEP education policies, have emerged as a new and self-confident status group, who enjoy opportunities that were simply unavailable to their parents. The state's contribution to this social restructuring is undeniable, but Prime Minister Mahathir remains insistent that Malays must become independent of government assistance. Alternatively scolding, harrying and cajoling, he has urged them to become 'Melayu Baru' (New Malays) who can compete successfully in the larger commercial world by relying on their own skills rather than on government patronage. Under the NDP, quotas and special privileges for Malays have been downplayed, and the emphasis is instead on the acquisition of modern technological skills. Towards this end Mahathir has made the creation of the Multimedia Super Corridor his special project, and has encouraged the nation to become more involved in the new information technology. Television talk-back shows discuss the value of being technologically informed, and even leaders of UMNO are encouraged to develop some understanding of this new development.

In the first years of its existence, the NEP aroused strong opposition among non-Malays. Although poverty was to be eradicated among all groups, both the Chinese and Indian communities believed that the goal of reallocating a certain amount of the country's wealth and corporate ownership to the Malays could only be achieved at their expense. Statistics have shown, however, that the increase in Malay ownership of the corporate sector came through the retraction of foreign rather than Chinese or Indian holdings. In fact, all ethnic groups experienced an overall rise in income which has in turn been reflected in Malaysia's growing middle class. While traditionally the DAP is thought to have attracted an estimated half of the Chinese vote, the November 1999 election results demonstrated that many Chinese see little reason to reject a government which has brought them benefits. For the Indians, the MIC is viewed as the only viable link to those in power with access to resources. Even the previously much maligned government policy of making Malay the sole standard of instruction in schools and universities has not resulted in an unfair advantage for the Malays. For the most part Chinese and Indians have learned to cope successfully, and some exceptionally well, in Malay. On the other hand, affirmative action in favour of Malays for university places has indeed resulted in hardship for non-Malays. This policy has been a bitter pill for communities which have traditionally regarded education as a prerequisite to advancement and a mark of social status. Some can afford to send their children abroad for university education, but most have been forced to seek alternative places in private institutions. In recent years an increase in the number of private colleges, twinning institutions, and even Malaysian campuses of foreign universities have helped to lessen criticism of the pro-Malay university policy.

Nearly 40 years have passed since Sarawak and Sabah became part of Malaysia in 1963. While certain conditions for entry were conceded to ease their transition into the Federation, Sarawak and Sabah have continued to maintain their uniqueness. Wealth from the timber industry has enabled both to avoid financial dependence on Kuala Lumpur, although revenues have been declining with the steady depletion of forests. Each state sees a future in the development of tourism, not only for foreign but also for domestic visitors. Both Borneo states have achieved a fair degree of autonomy, even limiting the length of stay and requiring passports of Peninsular Malaysians wishing to visit. Incorporated into the larger ethnicity of 'Bumiputera', identifying them as indigenous to the land, the various ethnic groups of Sabah and Sarawak have still been able to maintain many aspects of their own identities.

In the early years of the Federation, both states tended to support local chauvinistic politicians who exercised considerable freedom from Kuala Lumpur. But through the use of coercion and patronage the central government has been able to undermine these challenges and to assure the victory of parties and individuals meeting the approval of UMNO. The establishment of federal universities in both Sarawak and Sabah in the late 1990s is another example of the gradual incorporation of these states into a unified system for the whole country. Even though 'Kadazandusun' and Iban are now taught in local schools, the official language of administration remains Malay. Given

Borneo's highly pluralistic religious and linguistic environment, it remains to be seen how far local attitudes towards 'Malaysia' are affected by the increasing influence of Peninsular interests, the declining status of vernacular languages, the prominence given to Islam as a national religion, and the homogenizing tendencies of Bumiputera categorization.

In this context, it is important to note that the replacement of the NEP by the NDP signalled a significant shift in the government's thinking regarding Malay privileges. While there is no talk of amending the Constitution that safeguards these privileges, Mahathir has urged the creation of a 'Melayu Baru' armed with the necessary skills to face the competitive global environment of the twenty-first century and secure in a culture which is 'appropriate to the times'. Proponents of the *Melayu Baru* concept have presented themselves as heirs of early Malay modernists, but in this reincarnation almost a century later, Malay language and culture are less heavily weighted and are intended to incorporate not merely Malays but a larger 'Bangsa Malaysia (Malaysian nationality)' identity. It is encouraging that more Malays, like other Malaysians, have begun to accept the notion that the 'national culture' should represent elements of all the country's different communities, and that this diversity may be a key element in an emerging national identity. Whereas the NEP was born of ethnic violence and communal politics, the NDP was inaugurated in a period of economic prosperity and increasing political centralization. Shared by many who have benefited from federal programmes over the last three decades of the twentieth century, the government's optimism for the future is captured in its influential media campaign and the new millennium slogan of 'Malaysia Boleh!' (Malaysia Can [Do It]!).

Conclusion: Some Themes in Malaysian History

un through the long span of Malaysian history. One of ...enness to external influences, an attribute undoubt-...g and persistent contact with the outside world. From ...mmunities living in what is now Malaysia were witness ...raffic which linked India, the Middle East and Europe ...apan, Korea and China on the other. Taking advant-...ourable location and access to desired products, local societies became active participants in this international trade, an involvement that led to the emergence of several successful entrepôts. The most impressive of these early maritime kingdoms was Srivijaya, whose traditions were continued in an almost unbroken line to Melaka, Johor and Riau. Such places were noted not only for their flourishing commerce but also for their patronage of religion, the medium for many of the intellectual trends in the Straits and beyond. This area, then, was never a backwater, but was exposed to a continuing progression of ideas from abroad, the most suitable of which were adopted and adapted by the local population to suit their own needs.

Indigenous societies initially accepted the European arrival in the sixteenth century in the same spirit with which they had greeted earlier influences and made pragmatic assessments of potential advantages to be gained from closer connections. The Dutch East India Company, for example, was seen by smaller states less as a trading partner than as a source of protection against threats from larger neighbours. At the same time, rulers and chiefs were also ready to respond to a changing and growing world market. By the mid-nineteenth century several had reorganized traditional patterns of collecting and redistributing resources in order to take advantage of the increased demands for raw materials from Europe's industrializing nations. This response was especially noteworthy in Johor, but was also reflected in economic co-operation between Europeans and/or Chinese and Malay chiefs in other states. A broad historical perspective provides some grounds for the assertion that, given time and their own methods, communities along the

337

Straits and in Borneo would have adjusted to and profited by these new external influences as successfully as they had before.

A major difference with the past, however, was the rate of change which characterized the nineteenth century. The rapid technological advances and the insatiable demands of industrial Europe, first for raw materials and later for lands to colonize, soon overtook the Malays. The formidable union of new economic forces and political power in the industrialized West, which confidently viewed the whole world as a field of exploitation, impatiently swept aside any real or perceived hindrance. Insistent on the superiority of Western 'civilization', European imperialists were determined to assert their supremacy through a reshaping of economic relations. It was this implacable determination that impelled many societies in Asia, Africa and Oceania to question the wisdom of a closer association with the West. Debates in the Islamic world, of which Malaya was a part, were infused with an added intensity because of the long history of rivalry with Christian Europe.

This legacy is reflected in local attitudes and adumbrated in policies formulated by the governments of Malaya/Malaysia since independence in 1957. Still present is the admirable resilience and genius for adaptation to changed circumstances which has been the hallmark of indigenous populations for more than 2000 years. Equally evident, however, is the fear of being overwhelmed by the West's cultural and economic voracity. In the late twentieth century, Malaysia's confidence in dealing with the outside world is fully apparent as it embraces the concept of 'globalization'. Receptivity to external ideas has acquired new conduits through expanded education, international travel, and vastly improved access to information via the Internet. Yet the rapid pace of change and the singlemindedness with which the government has pursued its 'development' goals have aroused concern and at times vehement objections from an increasingly alert populace linked via the Internet to like-minded individuals throughout the globe. For any new government initiatives to succeed in the future will involve greater attention to the concerns of a sophisticated and highly informed public.

From this perspective, another theme in Malaysia's history has been the evolving relationship between those who hold power and the people they govern. According to Malay legend, the ruler–subject relationship was underwritten by a contract between the ancestor of all Malay kings and the representative of Malay commoners. In return for unquestioning loyalty, rulers would respect the rights of those under them. Even if rulers were guilty of crimes against their subjects, the latter should not rebel but let Almighty God mete out a just punishment. Despite its remarkably pervasive influence in Malay society, this idealized relationship also cloaked underlying tensions as rulers sought to win over the loyalty of independent princes and chiefs with strong ties of allegiance to their own followers. Since force alone could not ensure compliance with royal commands, a more compelling rationale for obedience was required. Thus was created the royal traditions of divine descent that affirmed kingly authority and depicted treason (*derhaka*) as a heinous crime punishable by the forces of majesty (*timpa daulat*).

Historically, the questioning of a ruler's special claims was particularly evident in the rivalry between a Malay sultan and his ministers and chiefs. Although individuals attributed with extraordinary powers occasionally arose from among the ordinary people, dissatisfied subjects most commonly sought alternative leaders among those of high rank. Changes in leadership, however, did not undermine the existing Malay political ethos on which the government (*kerajaan*) rested. Only in the late nineteenth and twentieth centuries was there a true challenge to this ethos and a demand for greater social equality. In post-independence times the electoral process has produced a new leadership, no longer based on birth and royal traditions but on qualities which the public has identified as necessary for governing a modern society. Nevertheless, the contemporary call for greater transparency and accountability in political life harks back to an earlier age when Malays sought guarantees of just rule from their kings in return for promises of unswerving loyalty.

A third and related theme is the ongoing struggle by the centre to restrain centrifugal tendencies in outlying territories. These centrifugal forces can be partly explained by geography, for several of the states in Peninsular Malaysia are separated from their neighbours by mountain ranges and dense jungles. Early 'empires' which developed in the region exercised only a very loose form of authority over their tributaries, a pattern which was repeated within the kingdoms themselves. The ruler and his capital were normally sited at the estuary of the major river, leaving the interior largely free of central control. Individual areas developed independently under their own leaders and were linked loosely to the ruler's capital through the occasional affirmation of allegiance and acknowledgement of subservience. Not until the late nineteenth century was there any attempt to establish a unified bureaucracy linking all outlying territories to a centre. With the influx of Chinese and Indian migrants in the nineteenth and twentieth centuries, the likelihood of separate development occurring in certain urban centres, such as Singapore, created another possibility for fragmentation. The inclusion of Sabah and Sarawak within Malaysia contributed still further to centrifugal tendencies since they were physically and, to a considerable extent, culturally separated from the Peninsula.

One effective counter to centrifugal forces has been the important role played by the centre as the principal reception and redistribution point for goods and ideas. Many outlying areas in the past submitted to the loss of a degree of sovereignty in exchange for these benefits and for the added inducements of prestige acquired through association with a major centre and assurance of protection against enemies. At times force was used by the centre to maintain its economic dominance, but what sustained the unity was the centre's ability to continue assuring specific benefits to its subordinate states. There were, nonetheless, areas that were never totally responsive to

339

the centre. In the Srivijayan period it was Kedah and north Sumatra; in Melaka times it was Kedah and east coast Sumatra; and since the formation of the Malaysian Federation it has been such states as Sabah, Sarawak, Singapore, Kelantan and more recently Terengganu. The forces of fragmentation in Malaysia have at times been so great that both the centre and its subsidiaries have been forced to reconsider the arguments for maintaining the status quo. When the benefits no longer appeared to outweigh the disadvantages, a severance of ties between centre and periphery occurred, as happened in Singapore's expulsion from the Federation in 1965. This secession made Malaysia's leaders more determined to preserve the unity of the remaining states of the Federation. Towards this end government policy has aimed at creating a united people through language, formal education and even the arts.

Yet in the year 2000 regionalism remains a significant point of identity, especially in Sabah and Sarawak. Having had a different historical trajectory from the Peninsula, these Bornean states were accorded guarantees to safeguard certain established practices when they entered the Malaysian Federation in 1963. While they have become far more integrated into the federation system of governance, their large indigenous population and highly complex political allegiances continue to make them unique in the Federation. The northeastern Peninsular states of Kelantan and Terengganu form another area with an intense regional pride. In defiance of the centre, the people of these two states rejected government parties in 1999 in favour of PAS, thus reaffirming their claim to be the heartland of both Islamic and Malay values.

Despite the physical separation between the Peninsula and Borneo, the effectiveness of modern communications means that geographic distance is less a factor in regionalism than the perception of central neglect. Centre–periphery tensions will no doubt continue, but secession will not be the central issue; instead, it will be the demand for greater sharing in the making of national policy and a more equitable redistribution of wealth. Whatever their grievances, it appears that all regions are firmly committed to the idea of Malaysia.

A fourth theme which emerges in Malaysian history is the changing conception of what constitutes 'Melayu' or Malay. It has been suggested that the initial use of 'Malay' as an exclusive term may have occurred during the early history of Melaka, though the name first appeared in Srivijaya in southeast Sumatra some time in the seventh century. In the Melaka period things Malay became the ultimate measure of refinement and acceptability. As the local population gradually assimilated the language and culture of the newcomers, Malay retained its exclusive connotation, but was invoked to distinguish a now-famous Melaka from other areas in the Malay-Indonesian archipelago that were emulating its language, style and customs. To be truly Malay was to be a Melakan, a definition expanded in the mid-fifteenth century to include Islam. With the passing of time understandings of Malayness broadened and became more regionally inclusive, but Islam remained a vital component. When the northern Malay Peninsula was threatened by the Thais, the Malay association was employed to underscore the identity of a people based not only on language and customs but also on religion. The perceived threat of cultural absorption into a Thai-Buddhist nation gave greater urgency to the need to safeguard Malay sovereignty in order to ensure the survival of a distinctively Malay way of life.

Under colonial rule the term 'Malay' was formalized by the British to distinguish the Malay-speaking Muslims residing in the Peninsula and off-shore islands as well as Borneo from the large immigrant groups of Indians and Chinese. Migrant Indonesians who spoke Malay or Indonesian and were Muslims became incorporated into the Malay category because the colonial power viewed local society in terms of broad ethnic divisions. In the interwar period the anti-foreign attitudes of some Malays led to an expansion of the definition of 'Malay' to include all the indigenous peoples of the Indonesian-Malay archipelago. Generally, however, the colonial government's categor-ization of Malay was retained until discussions preceding the independence of Malaya in 1957, when it was suggested that 'Melayu' be used to designate all those who wished to become citizens of the new nation. The suggestion was considered but rejected and the Constitution confirmed colonial practice by defining a Malay as 'one who speaks the Malay language, professes Islam and habitually follows Malay customs'.

Despite this precise description, Muslim immigrants from Indonesia and the southern Philippines experienced little difficulty in taking on a new Malay identity. By the second generation, their children had become 'pure' Malay and part of the favoured ethnicity. In the days when the threat of being outnumbered by other ethnic groups haunted Malay society, Indone-sian immigration was seen as necessary to maintain an ethnic balance. But the expulsion of Singapore from the Federation of Malaysia in 1965 and the high Malay birthrate means that in the year 2000 Malays make up almost 60 per cent of the population. As more Malays have begun to compete for government resources, earlier tolerance for immigrant groups has diminished. The currency crisis of late 1997 revealed the darker side of Malay national-ism, as many Indonesians and Filipinos were forcibly repatriated because of the slowdown in the economy. Today, Malay identity is highly prized as a privilege which some believe should not be extended to others simply because they fulfil the minimum requirements listed in the Constitution. Others view the issue in a positive light by citing the contributions of many 'Malays' whose parents or grandparents originated outside the Peninsula.

After the formation of Malaysia, the inclusion of large numbers of indi-genous groups from Sabah and Sarawak necessitated a revision of the old ethnic categories. Although for political purposes the Bornean peoples had been classified with the Malays of the Peninsula, they remained an anomaly since most were clearly not Malay in language, religion or culture. To overcome this difficulty the term 'Bumiputera', 'sons of the soil', was created to refer to the Peninsular Orang Asli, the indigenous peoples of Sabah and Sarawak, and Malays. In practical administrative calculations regarding employment, education and economic quotas, the Bumiputera category virtually replaced that of Malay. Yet distinctions within the Bumiputera category persist. On the Peninsula, Malay Bumiputera are clearly favoured over Orang Asli Bumiputera; in Sabah and Sarawak, Bornean Bumiputera take precedence over Bumiputera from the Peninsula. In Borneo the situation is further complicated by the religious issue. The dominant Iban in Sarawak and the Kadazandusun in Sabah are generally Christian, and some of them feel that the central government favours Muslim Bumiputera such as the Malay/Melanau. In addition, smaller Bumiputera groups have been forced to regroup into larger entities in order to compete successfully for federal resources. This has resulted in the formation in Malaysia of new composite ethnicities such as the 'Dayak', the 'Orang Ulu' and 'Orang Asli' from a number of related but separate ethnic groupings. The increased emphasis on the economic implications of being 'Malay' has made other groups in the country re-examine their ethnic identity in view of their access to resources.

The attempt to incorporate migrant groups into a larger society is another recognizable theme in the history of Malaysia. In the process of creating a 'new Malaysian', the government is not embarking on a novel idea, but is attempting to reactivate methods used in centuries past. The founders of Melaka successfully established their language and culture as the basis of a new society composed of immigrant and local Malays, Orang Asli and Orang Laut. Subsequent centuries saw the Minangkabau, Bugis, Javanese and various other Indonesian groups conform to the standards of Malay society. What contributed to the ready absorption of these latter groups has been their basic similarity of lifestyle with the Malays, and their common religion. Such commonalities did not exist between Malays and Chinese and Indians, who differed physically, culturally and frequently in religious belief. Nonetheless, the process of incorporation was successful in early times mainly because the newcomers arrived in small numbers and elected to adapt to their new environment. For example, the Baba and Jawi Peranakan groups arose through marriages between local women and Chinese or Indian men. Both communities readily accepted Malay authority and played an important role as cultural brokers between immigrant and local societies.

This situation was radically changed by the policies of the colonial government, which resulted in such large and self-sufficient migrant communities that the older pattern of absorption into local society now only rarely occurred. In addition, the vast majority of Chinese and Indian immigrants lived in areas that were governed by the British or by individuals associated with Britain. In colonial societies so efficiently compartmentalized, the Chinese and Indians understandably regarded Malays and other indigenous groups as standing basically in the same relation as themselves to the colonial authority. Each was assigned a role, which was performed according to British prescriptions. The latter carried on the charade of sharing rule, but the migrant societies did not distinguish between legalities and actualities. For them it was the British who were the true rulers of the lands in which they resided.

It was these attitudes so naturally acquired in 'British Malaya', Sarawak and North Borneo that proved a major obstacle to the creation of a united people in independent Malaya/Malaysia. At the end of the Second World War the British authorities proceeded to prepare for an independence in which all groups would be regarded as equal citizens. But such a course of action aroused the anger of many Malays who saw Malaya as their homeland and argued that the British had merely served as 'advisers'. They were supported by influential former British colonial officials, who believed that their government should honour past agreements which acknowledged the sovereignty of Malay rulers. The protests against the Malayan Union helped galvanize Malays into action as one people, and it was this unprecedented unity which led to the creation of UMNO, soon to become the pre-eminent political voice of the Malay people.

The Federation arrangements not only restored Malays to their former positions of authority, but were based on an assumption that the Chinese and Indians should accept the Malays as rightful rulers. Fortunately for the young nation, there were Malay leaders who acknowledged the vast changes in Malayan society and the folly of advocating a style of government that ignored the rights and needs of the migrant communities. Yet the basic question remained: How were such substantial minorities to become combined into a new 'Malaysian' identity? What should this identity be? These questions were debated with emotion but remained unresolved until the tragic events of May 1969. The ethnic violence shocked the nation and made apparent the need for some resolution of these questions. The post-1969 Malaysian governments have therefore felt it necessary to create a 'new Malaysian' whose identity, espoused in the Rukunegara, is based on Malay language and culture but incorporates aspects of the migrant cultures.

Throughout Malaysian history migrant groups have come to the Peninsula and have become part of the established society. Though the situation of the Chinese, Indian, Indonesian and Filipino communities in Malaysia today differs in scale and complexity from earlier migrant groups, the present Malaysian government believes that they can be integrated into a basically Malay society. It is towards this goal that Malaysia's leaders attempted to restructure society by formulating a series of elaborate development plans known as the New Economic Policy. By target date 1990 the government had made good progress but had not yet achieved its goals. The ten-year National Development Policy was basically an 'extension' of the major social and economic restructuring which began with the NEP in 1970. Despite minor setbacks and concern at the methods and the direction of the Mahathir government, at the start of the new millennium a longer perspective permits grounds for optimism. Much will depend on the degree to which the government is willing to permit a larger number of players to take active roles in the national drama, and to respect the contribution that they can make.

These, then, are some themes which have recurred throughout Malaysia's long and varied history. Though we have tried to be sensitive to the role of non-majority groups in the evolution of Malaysian history, it is not easy to escape a centrist perspective. This vantage point needs to be balanced by other views from the 'margins' if the full mosaic of Malaysia's rich past is to be surveyed and appreciated. None the less, we hope that the themes we have identified will contribute to a better understanding of Malaysia's past. We also hope that they may prove instructive to Malaysia's young adults, whose attitudes and outlook will help determine their country's future as it moves into the twenty-first century.

Notes

Introduction: The Environment and Peoples of Malaysia

1. A 1998 estimate of 107 411 was listed at the Orang Asli Museum in Gombak in June 1999. However, some doubt has been expressed as to whether the figures of the Department of Orang Asli Affairs represent an accurate count.

Chapter 1: The Heritage of the Past

1. Paul Wheatley, *The Golden Khersonese* (Kuala Lumpur, 1961), p. 273. Colonel James Low (1791–1852) was the civil officer of Province Wellesley between 1827 and 1837.
2. Peter Bellwood, 'Cultural and Biological Differentiation in Peninsular Malaysia: The Last 10,000 Years', *Asian Perspectives*, 32, 1 (1993), p. 53.
3. For further discussion, see Geoffrey Benjamin, 'Ethnohistorical Perspectives on Kelantan's History', in Nik Hassan Shuhaimi bin Nik Abd. Rahman (ed.) *Kelantan Zaman Awal: Kajian Arkeology dan Sejarah di Malaysia* (Kota Bahru, Kelantan, 1987), pp. 108–25 and 'Issues in the Ethnohistory of Pahang', in Nik Hassan Shuhaimi bin Nik Abd. Rahman, Mohamed Mokhtar Abu Bakar, Ahmad Hakimi Khairrudin and Jazamuddin Bahruddin (eds), *Pembangunan Arkeology Pelancongan Negeri Pahang* (Kuantan, 1997), pp. 92–3.
4. F.L. Dunn, *Rain-Forest Collectors and Traders: A Study of Resource Utilization in Modern and Ancient Malaya* (MBRAS Monograph no. 5, Kuala Lumpur, 1975), pp. 78–103. The Temuan, numbering around 9000, are found mainly in Selangor and Negeri Sembilan. The settlement studied by Dunn was within a day's reach of Kuala Lumpur.
5. F. Hirth and W.W. Rockhill (eds), *Chau Ju-Kua on the Chinese and Arab Trade* (St Petersburg, 1914; reprinted Amsterdam, 1966), p. 32.
6. Hinduism, which grew out of a much earlier brahmanical religion in India, began to assume identifiable features about the first century of the Christian era. In maritime Southeast Asia ideas associated with Hinduism often merged with Buddhism, which had originated in India during the sixth century BCE. The involvement of rulers and courts in the sponsoring of temples and religious ritual in India meant that there was a close link between religion and the legitimization of royal authority.

7. Hirth and Rockhill, *Chau Ju-Kua on the Chinese and Arab Trade*, pp. 105–6.
8. Wheatley, *The Golden Khersonese*, p. 28.
9. Ibid., p. 254.
10. O.W. Wolters, *Early Indonesian Commerce: A Study of the Origins of Srivijaya* (Ithaca, New York, 1967), p. 15.
11. Paul Wheatley, *Impressions of the Malay Peninsula in Ancient Times* (Singapore, 1964), p. 85.
12. Hirth and Rockhill, *Chau Ju-Kua*, p. 23.
13. Wolters, *Early Indonesian Commerce*, p. 187.
14. J.G. de Casparis, *Prasasti Indonesia: Selected Inscriptions from the Seventh to the Ninth Century AD*, vol. 2 (Bandung, 1956), p. 41.
15. G.R. Tibbetts, *A Study of the Arabic Texts Containing Material on South-East Asia* (Leiden, 1979), pp. 43, 182; Wheatley, *The Golden Khersonese*, p. 199.
16. Teuku Iskandar, *Kesusasteraan Klasik Melayu Sepanjang Abad* (Brunei, 1995), pp. 23–7; O.W. Wolters, *History, Culture and Region* (Singapore/Ithaca, New York, 1999), pp. 23–4.
17. Herman Kulke, 'Kedatuan Srivijaya – Empire or Kraton of Srivijaya? A Reassessment of the Epigraphical Evidence,' *BEFEO*, 80, 1 (1993), pp. 162, 176.
18. Wheatley, *The Golden Khersonese*, pp. 38, 57, 68, 84, 91; Hirth and Rockhill, *Chau Ju-Kua*, p. 31.
19. Wheatley, *The Golden Khersonese*, p. 82.
20. Wheatley, *The Golden Khersonese*, p. 200.
21. Ibid., p. 80.
22. Hirth and Rockhill, *Chau Ju-Kua*, pp. 155 ff.
23. C.C. Brown, '*Sejarah Melayu* or Malay Annals', *JMBRAS*, 25, 2 and 3 (1952), p. 12.
24. O.W. Wolters, *The Fall of Srivijaya* (Ithaca and London, 1970), chapter 4.

Chapter 2: Melake and its Heirs

1. H. Kern (ed.), *Het Itinerario van Jan Huygen van Linschoten, 1579–1582* (The Hague, 1955), p. 80.
2. Armando Cortesão (ed.), *The Suma Oriental of Tomé Pires* (London, 1944), vol. 2, pp. 241–6.
3. Cortesão, *Suma Oriental*, vol. 2, p. 246.
4. The *Hikayat Hang Tuah* is an epic of incidents in the life of the Malay hero, Hang Tuah, which probably existed in oral form long before it was written down during the seventeenth century. The first definite reference to a text occurs in 1736. A romanized edition is Kasim Ahmad, *Hikayat Hang Tuah* (Kuala Lumpur, 1964).
5. *DaÀsia de João de Barros*, Década Segunda, Parte Segunda (Lisbon, 1973), pp. 7–9.
6. C.C. Brown, '*Sejarah Melayu* or Malay Annals', *JMBRAS*, 25, 2 and 3 (1952), p. 134.
7. The term *sufi* was first applied to Muslim ascetics who wore coarse garments of wool (*suf*). Through various means Sufis aim to attain a more direct communion with Allah and thus, they felt, a high level of spiritual experience. A *tariqa* (Malay *tarikat*) provided a group relationship whereby a teacher could guide a student through progressive levels of Sufi worship.
8. Mark Dion, 'Sumatra Through Portuguese Eyes: Excerpts from João de Barros *Decadas da Asia*', *Indonesia*, 9 April (1970), p. 143.

9. Cited in Barbara Watson Andaya, *Perak, the Abode of Grace: A Study of an Eighteenth-Century Malay State* (Kuala Lumpur, 1979), pp. 20–1, 186.

10. Syed Muhammad Naguib Al-Attas, *The Oldest Known Malay Manuscript: A 16th Century Malay Translation of the 'Aqā'id of al-Nasafī* (Kuala Lumpur, 1988), pp. 57, 62.

11. D.K. Wyatt, *The Crystal Sands: The Chronicles of Nagara Sri Dharramaraja*, Cornell University Southeast Asia Program Data Paper no. 98 (Ithaca, New York 1975). Three nineteenth-century recensions of this chronicle are extant, though it probably dates from the seventeenth and eighteenth centuries and was subsequently recopied and adapted.

12. 'Drums of sovereignty', the *nobat*, consists of drums and wind instruments that are played at the installation of the ruler. To accept a *nobat* from a ruler is to accept his overlordship, and an acknowledgement that sovereignty derives from that particular ruler.

13. 'Phongsawadan Muang Trangganu', in *Prachum Phongsawadan* (Collected Chronicles) (Bangkok, 1963), vol. 2, part 2, p. 301. This text was kindly translated for the authors by Orrawin Hemasilpin. See also D.K. Wyatt, 'Nineteenth-Century Kelantan: A Thai View', in W.R. Roff (ed.), *Kelantan: Religion, Society and Politics in a Malay State* (Kuala Lumpur, 1974), pp. 1–22.

14. J.E. Heeres, *Bouwstoffen voor de Geschiedenis der Nederlanders in den Maleischen Archipel*, vol. III (The Hague, 1895), p. iv.

15. Paul Wheatley, *The Golden Khersonese* (Kuala Lumpur, 1961), p. 311.

Chapter 3: The Demise of the Malay Entrepôt State, 1699–1819

1. 'Phongsawadan Muang Trangganu', in *Prachum Phongsawadan* (Collected Chronicles) (Bangkok, 1963), vol. 2, part 2, p. 299. This text was kindly translated for the authors by Orrawin Hemasilpin.

2. Raja Ali Haji, *Tuhfat al-Nafis* (*The Precious Gift*), ed. and trans. Virginia Matheson and Barbara Watson Andaya (Kuala Lumpur, 1982), p. 43.

3. SSR G34/6 Light to Shore, 23 Jan. 1794 (FWCP, Aug. 1794), fols. 128–30 (British Library, Oriental and India Office Collection, London).

4. *Dagh-Register Gehouden in't Casteel Batavia . . .* (Batavia, 1887 etc.), 1682, p. 68.

5. Mohd Yusof Md. Nor (ed.), *Salasilah Melayu dan Bugis* (Petaling Jaya, 1984), p. 67. This text has been tentatively attributed to Raja Ali Haji of Riau. If his authorship is accepted, it would have been written in the mid-nineteenth century.

6. VOC 2630, Gov. de Laver's Report on Melaka, 27 Dec. 1743, fol. 73. The KA numbers of the first edition have been altered to comply with the new numbering system applied to the VOC material deposited in the Algemeen Rijksarchief, The Hague.

7. A. Teeuw and D.K. Wyatt (eds.), *Hikayat Patani: The Story of Patani* (The Hague, 1970), vol. 1, p. 201. The *Hikayat Patani* probably dates from the early eighteenth century.

8. Raja Ali Haji, *Tuhfat al-Nafis*, pp. 359, 373.

9. Jennifer Cushman and A.C. Milner, 'Eighteenth and Nineteenth Century Chinese Accounts of the Malay Peninsula', *JMBRAS*, 52, 1 (1979), p. 24.

10. As note 3 above.

11. Although eighteenth-century Dutch sources mention Rembau 'with its nine *negeri* (settlements)', there is no evidence of the nature of these divisions and it may have been simply a notional figure.
12. SFR G35/15 King of Kedah to Governor of Madras (FSGCP, 25 June 1772), fols. 101–2 (British Library, Oriental and India Office Collection, London).
13. VOC 3157 (third section), Gov. of Melaka to Batavia, 13 Oct. 1765, fol. 65.
14. R. Bonney, *Kedah, 1771–1821: The Search for Security and Independence* (Kuala Lumpur, 1971), p. 170.
15. Reinout Vos, *Gentle Janus, Merchant Prince: The VOC and the Tightrope of Diplomacy in the Malay World, 1740–1800* (Leiden, 1993), p. 178.
16. Bonney, *Kedah, 1771–1821*, p. 79, fn. 4.
17. Bonney, *Kedah, 1771–1821*, pp. 180–1.
18. Ibid.
19. Cushman and Milner, 'Eighteenth and Nineteenth Century Chinese Accounts', p. 32.
20. A.H. Hill (ed.) *Hikayat Abdullah* (Kuala Lumpur, 1970), p. 272.
21. Cushman and Milner, 'Eighteenth and Nineteenth Century Chinese Accounts', p. 52.
22. Hill, *Hikayat Abdullah*, pp. 158–9, 162.
23. Hill, *Hikayat Abdullah*, p. 63.

Chapter 4: 'A New World is Created', 1819–74

1. A.H. Hill (ed.) *Hikayat Abdullah* (Kuala Lumpur, 1970), pp. 64, 126.
2. Asa Briggs, *The Age of Improvement, 1783–1867* (New York, 1959), p. 3.
3. Estimates of the Peninsula's Malay population in the 1830s vary from around 200 000 to 425 000.
4. VOC 3967, Secret, King of Terengganu to Gov. of Malacca, 6 October 1791, Algemeen Rijksarchief, The Hague.
5. The heads of the more important Siamese provinces as well as the Malay vassal rulers were given the title *phraya*, loosely translated as 'governor', and second highest of the five grades of conferred nobility in Siam. For praiseworthy service a *phraya* could be promoted to *chao phraya*.
6. SSR F5, King of Perak to Gov. of Penang, 10 Sept., 1826, fol. 7, British Library, Oriental and India Office Collection, London.
7. Nureeyan Saleh, *Lagu Dodoi Melayu Patani* (Kuala Lumpur, 1999), pp. 138–43.
8. Kassim Ahmad (ed.), *Kisah Pelayaran Abdullah* (Kuala Lumpur, 1970), p. 54; Hill, *Hikayat Abdullah*, p. 301. *Joget Melayu* is a Malay dance performed by two people keeping in step. Skill is judged by one partner's ability to copy the other's steps exactly.
9. *Hikayat Panglima Nikosa: The Story of Panglima Nikosa*, trans. and ed. Philip L. Thomas and R.H.W. Reece (Kuching, 1983), p. 43.
10. Raja Ali Haji, *Tuhfat al-Nafis (The Precious Gift)*, ed. and trans. Virginia Matheson and Barbara Watson Andaya (Kuala Lumpur, 1982), p. 271.
11. C.M. Turnbull, *A History of Singapore, 1819–1976* (Kuala Lumpur, 1977), p. 37.
12. SSR G34/6, Light to Shore, 25 Jan. 1794 (FWCP, 1 Aug. 1794), fol. 120.

13. C.M. Turnbull, *The Straits Settlements, 1826–67: Indian Presidency to Crown Colony* (Singapore, 1972), p. 292.
14. Khoo Kay Kim, *The Western Malay States, 1850–1873: The Effects of Commercial Development on Malay Politics* (Kuala Lumpur, 1972), pp. 123–4.
15. Turnbull, *The Straits Settlements*, p. 301.
16. Eunice Thio, 'British Policy Towards Johor: From Advice to Control', *JMBRAS*, 40, 1 (1967), p. 3.
17. Carl Trocki, *Prince of Pirates: The Temenggongs and the Development of Johor and Singapore, 1784–1885* (Singapore, 1979), p. 204.
18. Barbara Watson Andaya and Virginia Matheson, 'Islamic Thought and Malay Tradition', in Anthony Reid and David Marr (eds), *Perceptions of the Past in Southeast Asia* (Singapore, 1979), p. 123.
19. C.M. Turnbull, 'Origins of British Control in the Malay States before Colonial Rule', in John Bastin and R. Roolvink (eds), *Malayan and Indonesian Studies: Essays Presented to Sir Richard Winstedt on his Eighty-Fifth Birthday* (Oxford, 1964), p. 174.

Chapter 5: The Making of 'British' Malaya, 1874–1919

1. J.M. Gullick, 'The Tampin Succession', *JMBRAS*, 49, 2 (1976), p. 3.
2. P.L. Burns (ed.), *The Journals of J.W.W. Birch* (Kuala Lumpur, 1976), p. 178.
3. P.L. Burns (ed.), 'Annexation in the Malay States: The Jervois Papers,' *JMBRAS*, 72, 1 (1999), pp. 9, 26. The comment was made by the private secretary of Jervois, presumably reflecting the governor's views.
4. W. Linehan, 'A History of Pahang', *JMBRAS*, 14, 2 (1936), p. 121.
5. Eunice Thio, *British Policy in the Malay Peninsula, 1880–1910*, vol. 1, *The Southern and Central States* (Singapore, 1969), p. 91.
6. Emily Sadka, *The Protected Malay States, 1874–1895* (Kuala Lumpur, 1968), p. 105.
7. Frank Swettenham, *British Malaya* (London, 1906), p. 282.
8. Sadka, *The Protected Malay States*, p. 17.
9. Frank Swettenham, *Malay Sketches* (London and New York, 1913), pp. 2–3.
10. Burns, 'Annexation in the Malay States', p. 29.
11. R. Emerson, *Malaysia: A Study in Direct and Indirect Rule* (New York, 1937); reprinted Kuala Lumpur, 1964, p. 503.
12. Amin Sweeney, *Reputations Live On: An Early Malay Autobiography* (Berkeley, 1980), p. 87.
13. Sir George Maxwell, cited in Colin E.R. Abraham, *Divide and Rule: The Roots of Race Relations in Malaysia* (Kuala Lumpur, 1997), p. 176.
14. Dr Uri Tadmor has suggested this is from Mon *sam* (mixed) via Thai *pasom*. Personal communication, 29 June 1999.
15. Emerson, *Malaysia*, p. 137.
16. Colin N. Crisswell, *Raja Charles Brooke* (Kuala Lumpur, 1978), p. 160.
17. Nicholas Tarling, 'Britain and Sarawak in the Twentieth Century', *JMBRAS*, 43, 2 (1970), p. 28.
18. Ian Black, 'The Ending of Brunei Rule in Sabah', *JMBRAS*, 41, 2 (1968), p. 187.
19. Ibid., p. 185.
20. Callistus Fernandez, 'The Rundum Rebellion of 1915 Reconsidered', *The Sarawak Museum Journal*, 53 (December 1998), p. 129.

21. Nicholas Tarling, *Britain, the Brookes and Brunei* (Kuala Lumpur, 1971), p. 518.
22. Sharom Ahmad, 'The Political Structure of the State of Kedah, 1879–1905', *JSEAS*, 1, 2 (1970), p. 125.
23. J. De Vere Allen, 'The Elephant and the Mousedeer – A New Version: Anglo-Kedah Relations, 1905–1915', *JMBRAS*, 41, 1 (1968), p. 94.
24. Keith Sinclair, 'The British Advance in Johore, 1885–1914', *JMBRAS*, 40, 1 (1965), p. 100.

Chapter 6: The Functioning of a Colonial Society, 1919–41

1. J.M. Gullick, *A History of Selangor (1766–1939)* (MBRAS Monograph no. 28, Kuala Lumpur, 1998), p. 2.
2. P.J. Drake, 'The Economic Development of British Malaya to 1914: An Essay on Historiography with some Questions for Historians', *JSEAS*, 10, 2 (1979), p. 274.
3. Shaharil Talib, *History of Kelantan, 1890–1940* (MBRAS Monograph no. 21, Kuala Lumpur, 1995), fn. 87, pp. 146–7.
4. Tan Chee Beng, *The Baba of Melaka* (Kuala Lumpur, 1988), p. 59.
5. Tan Liok Ee, *The Politics of Chinese Education in Malaya, 1945–1961* (Kuala Lumpur, 1997), p. 20.
6. Ibid., p. 24.
7. Talib, *History of Kelantan*, p. 141.
8. Rex Stevenson, *Cultivators and Administrators: British Educational Policy towards the Malays, 1875–1906* (Kuala Lumpur, 1975), pp. 57–8.
9. 'Orang Cina Mengaku Semanjong Negeri-nya dan kata-nya Bukan Negeri Melayu.' Cited in W.R. Roff, *The Origins of Malay Nationalism* (Kuala Lumpur, 1967) p. 209.
10. L.A. Mills, *British Rule in Eastern Asia: A Study of Contemporary Government and EconomicDevelopment in British Malaya and Hong Kong* (London, 1942), p. 60.
11. Ibid., pp. 63–4.
12. Robert Pringle, *Rajahs and Rebels: The Ibans of Sarawak under Brooke Rule, 1841–1941* (Ithaca, New York, 1970), pp. 335–6.

Chapter 7: Negotiating a New Nation, 1942–69

1. Ahmad Kamal Abdullah, Hashim Awang, Ramli Isin, Sahlan Mohd Saman and Zakaria Ariffin, *History of Modern Malay Literature*, vol. 2 (Kuala Lumpur, 1992), pp. 10–11. The poem is *Bahasa dan Bangsa*, by Muhammad Hassan Abdul Wahab.
2. Cheah Boon Kheng, *Red Star over Malaya: Resistance and Social Conflict During and After the Japanese Occupation of Malaya, 1941–1946* (Singapore, 1983), p. 173.
3. Cheah Boon Kheng, *The Masked Comrades: A Study of the Communist United Front in Malaya, 1945–48* (Singapore, 1979), p. 5.
4. Simon C. Smith, *British Relations with the Malay Rulers: From Decentralization to Malayan Independence, 1930–1957* (Kuala Lumpur, 1995), p. 62.
5. Ibid., p. 67.

6. Virginia H. Dancz, *Women and Party Politics in Malaysia* (Kuala Lumpur, 1987), p. 85; Smith, *British Relations with the Malay Rulers*, p. 66.
7. Ahmad Kamal Abdullah *et al.*, *History of Modern Malay Literature*, p. 55. The poem is *Darurat* (Emergency), by Dahlia M.A.
8. F.H.K. Wong and Gwee Yee Hean, *Perspectives: The Development of Education in Malaysia and Singapore* (Singapore, 1972), p. 31.
9. D.K. Mauzy and R.S. Milne, *Politics and Government in Malaysia* (Vancouver, 1978), p. 131.
10. Stanley S. Bedlington, *Malaysia and Singapore: The Building of New States* (Ithaca, New York, 1978), pp. 103–4.
11. Ooi Keat Gin, *Of Free Trade and Native Interests: The Brookes and the Economic Development of Sarawak, 1841–1941* (Kuala Lumpur, 1997), p. 10.
12. Rosemary Firth, *Housekeeping among Malay Peasants* (London, 1966), pp. 171, 178.
13. In 1963 Indians made up 51.59 per cent of the membership of the National Union of Plantation Workers, Malays comprised 28.2 per cent and Chinese 19.29 per cent.

Chapter 8: Restructuring Malaysia, 1969–2000

1. Shamsul A.B., *From British to Bumiputera Rule: Local Politics and Rural Development in Peninsular Malaysia* (Singapore, 1986), p. 134, fn. 31.
2. A. Baer, *Health, Disease, and Survival: A Biomedical and Genetic Analysis of the* Orang Asli *of Malaysia* (Subang Jaya, Malaysia, 1999), p. 4.
3. *New Straits Times*, 22 June 1999; *New Straits Times*, 23 June 1999.
4. Malay architects numbered only 4.3 per cent in 1970 but 15.6 per cent in 1990; the number of Malay engineers went from 7.3 to 34.8 per cent of the total; doctors from 3.7 to 27.8 per cent; and accountants from 6.8 to 11.2 per cent.
5. *New Straits Times*, 5 July 1999, p. 1.
6. Peter Searle, *The Riddle of Malaysian Capitalism: Rent-seekers or Real Capitalists?* (Sydney and Honolulu, 1999), pp. 67–8.
7. Edmund Terence Gomez, *Chinese Business in Malaysia: Accumulation, Ascendance, Accommodation* (Honolulu, 1999), p. 70.
8. The 1970 figures are rubber 33.4 per cent; tin 19.5 per cent; timber 16.5 per cent; palm oil 5.1 per cent; petroleum 3.9 per cent. In 1990 these were petroleum 11.6 per cent of total exports; timber with 9 per cent; palm oil 5.5 per cent; rubber 3.8 per cent; tin 1.1 per cent.
9. Harold Brookfield, 'Change and the Environment', in Harold Brookfield (ed.), *Transformation with Industrialization in Peninsular Malaysia* (Kuala Lumpur, 1994), p. 269.
10. Italics added. *New Straits Times*, 19 June 1999, pp. 6, 18.
11. Hussin Mutalib, *Islam in Malaysia: From Revivalism to Islamic State* (Singapore, 1993), p. 31.
12. *Far Eastern Economic Review*, 22 August 1980, p. 40.

Further Reading

Note: Please refer to the List of Abbreviations at the front of the book.

The literature on Malaysia in both English and Malay has grown massively in the last twenty years, and the following represents only a selected list of largely English works. Readers are referred to the specialist bibliographies provided by most academic authors.

Introduction: The Environment and Peoples of Malaysia

A new 15-volume *Encyclopedia of Malaysia* in the process of publication (Kuala Lumpur, 1998–) provides an attractive and authoritative illustrated overview of all aspects of Malaysia's geography, culture and history. Edited by specialists, it will cover Languages and Literature, Religions, Peoples, the Performing Arts and Crafts and other visual arts.

Two books by Jonathan Rigg, *Southeast Asia: A Region in Transition* (London, 1991) and *Southeast Asia: The Human Landscape of Modernization and Development* (London and New York, 1997), incorporate geographical descriptions with contemporary socioeconomic analysis, and place Malaysia into a regional framework. A specialist geographical description of Peninsular Malaysia is Ooi Jin Bee, *Peninsular Malaysia* (New York and London, 1976). Several essays in a recent volume, Amarjit Kaur and Ian Metcalfe (eds), *The Shaping of Malaysia* (London and New York, 1999), provide geographical and botanical details, as well as a political and historical overview. A demographic coverage is Richard Leete, *Malaysia's Demographic Transition: Rapid Development, Culture and Politics* (Kuala Lumpur, 1996). For linguistic history, see Asmah Haji Omar, *The Malay Peoples of Malaysia and their Languages* (Kuala Lumpur, 1983) and James Collins, *Malay World Language: A Short History* (Kuala Lumpur, 1998).

There are numerous anthropological studies of specific Orang Asli groups, and a guide to this literature is J.A. Corfield, *A Comprehensive Bibliography of Literature Relating to the Orang Asli of West Malaysia* (Working Paper no. 61, Centre of Southeast Asian Studies, Monash University, Australia, 1990). A recent and rather depressing view is

Razha Rashid (ed.), *Indigenous Minorities of Peninsular Malaysia: Selected Issues and Ethnographies* (Kuala Lumpur, 1995). Although somewhat dated, Iskandar Carey, *Orang Asli: The Aboriginal Tribes of Peninsular Malaysia* (Kuala Lumpur and London, 1976), is still cited. The most useful work on Borneo is Victor King, *The Peoples of Borneo* (London, 1993). Comprehensive bibliographies on Sarawak groups published by the Institute of East Asian Studies of the Universiti Malaysia Sarawak are *Bibliography of the Malay, Melanau and Kedayan Communities in Sarawak; Bibliography on the Orang Ulu Communities in Sarawak*; and *Bibliography on the Iban and Bidayuh Communities in Sarawak* (Kota Samarahan, Sarawak: 1999 [?]).

Several studies of Malay society were written before modernizing forces began to make an impact. R.O. Winstedt, *The Malays: A Cultural History* (Singapore, 1947) and N.J. Ryan, *The Cultural Heritage of Malaya* (Kuala Lumpur, 1971) recall a world that has not completely disappeared. For readers of Malay, Ismail Hussein *et al.*, *Tamaddun Melayu* (Malay Culture) (Kuala Lumpur, 1993–5) is a comprehensive five-volume collection of essays. For the background to the Chinese, Victor Purcell, *The Chinese in Malaya* (London 1948; reprinted 1967), remains a standard work, despite the dated approach. Sinnappah Arasaratnam's *Indians in Malaysia and Singapore* (Kuala Lumpur, 1979) still provides the most concise overview of the Indian community.

There are various histories in English available, some of which will withstand the test of time. The colonial viewpoint is nicely captured in R.O. Winstedt, *A History of Malaya*, revised edition (Singapore, 1962), and R.J. Wilkinson, *A History of the Peninsular Malays* (Singapore, 1923), is also an important early source. Wang Gungwu (ed.) *Malaysia: A Survey* (Melbourne, 1964), is an older but still useful collection of essays on different aspects of Malaysia's history, edited by a leading Malaysian historian. C.M. Turnbull, *A Short History of Malaysia, Singapore and Brunei* (Singapore, 1981), gives more attention to Brunei and Singapore than the present work. There is a formidable number of books on the contemporary scene, but Harold Crouch, *Government and Society in Malaysia* (Ithaca and London, 1996), is both authoritative and well written.

Chapter 1: The Heritage of the Past

An excellent introduction to the prehistory of the region that incorporates earlier research and lays out current theories and debates is Peter Bellwood's *Prehistory of the Indo-Malaysian Archipelago* (revised edition, Honolulu, 1997). Two articles provide useful overviews of recent finds: Adi Haji Taha, 'Recent Archaeological Discoveries in Peninsular Malaysia (1991–1993)', *JMBRAS*, 66, 1 (1993), pp. 67–84, and Nik Hassan Shuhaimi Nik Abdul Rahman and Kamaruddin bin Zakaria, 'Recent Archaeological Discoveries in Kedah', *JMBRAS*, 66, 2 (1993), pp. 73–80. Volume IV of the new illustrated 15-volume *Encyclopaedia of Malaysia*, edited by Nik Hassan Shuhaimi Nik Abdul Rahman (Singapore, 1998), deals with early history and presents in a readable form much information hitherto available only in academic journals. A summary of the debates regarding migration is in Peter Bellwood, 'Cultural and Biological Differentiation in Peninsular Malaysia: The Last 10,000 Years', *Asian Perspectives*, 32, 1 (1993), p. 53.

Further Reading

A useful survey of jungle collecting, which attempts to relate anthropological research to the archaeological record, is F.L. Dunn, *Rain-Forest Collectors and Traders: A Study of Resource Utilization in Modern and Ancient Malaya* (MBRAS Monograph no. 5, Kuala Lumpur, 1975). A discussion of commercial centres on the Peninsula is found in Leong Sau Heng, 'Collecting Centres, Feeder Points and Entrepôts in the Malay Peninsula, c.1000 BC–AD 1400', in J. Kathirithamby-Wells and John Villiers (eds), *The Southeast Asian Port and Polity: Rise and Demise* (Singapore, 1990), pp. 17–38. Geoffrey Benjamin, 'Ethnohistorical Perspectives on Kelantan's History', in Nik Hassan Shuhaimi bin Nik Abd. Rahman (ed.), *Kelantan Zaman Awal: Kajian Arkeology dan Sejarah di Malaysia* (Kota Bahru, Kelantan, 1987), pp. 108–25, places Orang Asli within the local origin argument.

Srivijaya has spawned considerable research. A transliteration of early inscriptions is in J.G. de Casparis, *Prasasti Indonesia: Selected Inscriptions from the Seventh to the Ninth Century AD*, vol. 2 (Bandung, 1956). A basic monograph is O.W. Wolters, *Early Indonesian Commerce: A Study of the Origins of Srivijaya* (Ithaca, New York, 1967). A good reference is *A Bibliography for Sriwijayan Studies* (École Française del'Extrême Orient, Jakarta, 1989) by Pierre-Yves Manguin, who has been closely involved with archaeological excavations. The details of the debates on Srivijaya and the relevant French articles have been translated in *Srivijaya: History, Region and Languages of an Early Malay Polity. Collected Studies by Georges Coedès and Louis Charles Damais* (MBRAS Monograph no. 20, Kuala Lumpur, 1992). O.W. Wolters reviews the academic debates in 'Studying Srivijaya', *JMBRAS*, 52, 2 (1979), pp. 1–32; on recent archaeological work, see Pierre-Yves Manguin, 'Le programme de fouilles sur les sites de Sriwijaya', *BEFEO*, 79, 1 (1992), pp. 272–7, and 'Palembang and Sriwijaya: An Early Malay Harbour-City Rediscovered', *JMBRAS*, 66, 1 (1993), pp. 23–46. Another reassessment is Herman Kulke, 'Kedatuan Srivijaya – Empire or Kraton of Srivijaya? A Reassessment of the Epigraphical Evidence', *BEFEO*, 80, 1 (1993), pp. 159–80.

A second monograph by O.W. Wolters, *The Fall of Srivijaya in Malay History* (Ithaca, New York and London, 1970), is a controversial but stimulating reconstruction of the connection between Srivijaya and Melaka based on Armando Cortesão, *The Suma Oriental of Tomé Pires* (London, 1944), primary Chinese dynastic and travel records, and the *Sejarah Melayu*, the Melaka court text (ed. C.C. Brown, '*Sejarah Melayu* or Malay Annals', *JMBRAS*, 25, 2 and 3, 1952). A new romanization, with several useful articles attached, is Cheah Boon Kheng (ed.), *Sejarah Melayu: The Malay Annals* (MBRAS Monograph no. 18, Kuala Lumpur, 1998).

The Minangkabau–Melayu association is explored in Jane Drakard, *A Kingdom of Words: Language and Power in Sumatra* (Kuala Lumpur, 1999).

Chapter 2: Melaka and its Heirs

The two indispensable works for the history of the Malay region during the fifteenth and sixteenth century are the Malay court history, the so-called *Sejarah Melayu*, translated into English by C.C. Brown as '*Sejarah Melayu* or Malay Annals', *JMBRAS*, 25, 2 and 3 (1952) and the work by the sixteenth-century Portuguese apothecary, Tomé Pires, translated into English by Armando Cortesão, *The Suma Oriental of Tomé Pires* (London, 1944).

A detailed account of the trade patterns in the Malay-Indonesian archipelago from the fifteenth to the early seventeenth centuries is found in M.A.P. Meilink-Roelofsz, *Asian Trade and European Influence in the Indonesian Archipelago between 1500 and about 1630* (The Hague, 1962). C.R. Boxer's *The Portuguese Seaborne Empire, 1415–1825* (London, 1969) and *The Dutch Seaborne Empire, 1600–1800* (London, 1965) provide a readable and broad perspective of Portuguese and Dutch activities, not only in Asia but in other parts of the world.

Paul Wheatley and Kernial S. Sandhu (eds), *Melaka: The Transformation of a Malay Capital ca. 1400–1800* (Kuala Lumpur, 1983), 2 vols, follows Melaka's history from early times; Muhammad Yusoff Hashim, *The Malay Sultanate of Melaka* (Kuala Lumpur, 1992) exploits all Malay and English sources relating to Melaka. J.V. Mills (ed. and trans.), *Eredia's Description of Melaka, Meridional India and Cathay* MBRAS reprint no. 14, (1997), is a lively contemporary description. A useful survey which makes full use of Portuguese sources is Luis Filipe Ferreira Reis Thomaz, 'The Malay Sultanate of Melaka', in Anthony Reid (ed.), *Southeast Asia in the Early Modern Period: Trade, Power and Belief* (Ithaca, 1993), pp. 69–90. There are several texts of the Melaka legal codes, which provided a model for those of several other Malay states. A detailed study is Liaw Yock Fong, *Undang-Undang Melaka* (The Hague, 1976). Virginia Matheson, 'Concepts of Malay Ethos in Indigenous Malay Writings', *JSEAS*, 10, 2 (1979), pp. 351–72, examines the use of the term 'Melayu' in early Malay writings. The possible influence of Sufi ideas is discussed in A.C. Milner, 'Islam and Malay Kingship', *Journal of the Royal Asiatic Society* (1981), pp. 46–70.

On the story of the efforts of the descendants of Melaka's royal house to establish a kingdom on the Johor river, and their conflicts with the Portuguese, see I.A. MacGregor, C.A. Gibson-Hill and G. de G. Sieveking, 'Papers on Johore Lama and the Portuguese in Malaya, 1511–1641', *JMBRAS*, 28, 2 (1955). Leonard Y. Andaya, *The Kingdom of Johor, 1641–1728* (Kuala Lumpur, 1975), discusses the Melaka period and an analysis of events in the Malay world in the seventeenth and early eighteenth centuries. An account of the sixteenth- and seventeenth-century events in Perak, Kedah and Aceh can be found in Barbara Watson Andaya, *Perak, the Abode of Grace: A Study of an Eighteenth Century Malay State* (Kuala Lumpur, 1979). Denys Lombard's *Le Sultanat d'Atjeh au temps d'Iskandar Muda, 1607–1636* (Paris, 1967) is a study of Aceh under its greatest ruler and its expansion on both sides of the Straits of Melaka in the early seventeenth century. Another view of seventeenth-century events from the Sumatra perspective is Barbara Watson Andaya, *To Live as Brothers: Southeast Sumatra in the Seventeenth and Eighteenth Centuries* (Honolulu, 1993).

There are also studies of the history, literature, and customs of a number of Malay states written by Malaya's scholar-administrators. An early scholarly work is W.J. Linehan, 'A History of Pahang', *JMBRAS*, 14, 2 (May 1936). Two of the most prolific of these administrators were R.J. Wilkinson and R.O. Winstedt. Among Wilkinson's long list of works are *A History of the Peninsular Malays* (Singapore, 1923); 'The Melaka Sultanate', *JMBRAS*, 13, 2 (1935); and, in collaboration with Winstedt, 'A History of Perak', *JMBRAS*, 12, 1 (1934). Winstedt was even more productive than Wilkinson, and among some of his studies are *A History of Malaya*, revised edition (Singapore, 1962); 'The Early Rulers of Perak, Pahang and Aceh', *JMBRAS*, 10,1 (1932); 'A History of Johore (1365–1895 AD)', *JMBRAS*, 10, 3 (1932); 'A History of Negeri Sembilan', *JMBRAS*, 12, 3 (1934); 'A History of Selangor', *JMBRAS*, 12, 3 (1934); and 'Notes on the History of Kedah', *JMBRAS*, 14, 3 (1936). See Lim Huck Tee and D.E.K. Wijasuriya (eds), *Index Malaysiana* (Kuala Lumpur, 1970) for a listing of works by Wilkinson and Winstedt and other scholars like W.E. Maxwell that were published in the *JSBRAS* and *JMBRAS*.

For a discussion of the political nature of certain Malay states, see the articles in Anthony Reid and Lance Castles (eds), *Pre-Colonial State Systems in Southeast Asia* (MBRAS Monograph no. 6, Kuala Lumpur, 1975). A brief but competent discussion of the history and society of Brunei is given in D.E. Brown, *Brunei: The Structure and History of a Bornean Malay Sultanate*, Monograph of the *Brunei Museum Journal*, vol. 2, 2 (1970). For early relations between the southern Philippines and North Borneo, see Cesar Adib Majul, *Muslims in the Philippines* (Quezon City, 1973).

Material on early Thai–Malay relations can be found in Charnvit Kasetsiri, *The Rise of Ayudhya: A History of Siam in the Fourteenth and Fifteenth Centuries* (Kuala Lumpur, 1976). It is especially valuable in its discussion of the various types of vassals subject to Ayudhya and its manner of dealing with them. D. K. Wyatt's *The Crystal Sands: The Chronicles of Nagara Sri Dharramaraja* (Cornell University Southeast Asia Program Data Paper no. 98, Ithaca, New York, 1975), is a useful study of the influence of Ligor (Nagara Sri Dharramaraja-Nakhon Sithammarat), Ayudhya's southern provincial capital, on the northern Malay states. For an understanding of Patani's ambiguous position between the Thai and Malay worlds, see A. Teeuw and D.K. Wyatt (eds), *Hikayat Patani: The Story of Patani* (The Hague, 1970), 2 vols. The early chapters of Kobkua Suwannathat-Pian, *Thai–Malay Relations: Traditional Intra-Regional Relations from the Seventeenth to the Early Twentieth Centuries* (Kuala Lumpur, 1988), are also useful in explaining the framework for the Thai–Malay relationship.

Chapter 3: The Demise of the Malay Entrêpot State, 1699–1819

There are a number of relevant Malay texts for the eighteenth century but unfortunately few of these have been published, and still fewer translated into English or historically annotated. The nineteenth-century work, *Tuhfat al-Nafis (The Precious Gift)* by Raja Ali Haji, deals with Bugis, Malay and Minangkabau relations. It has been translated and annotated by Virginia Matheson and Barbara Watson Andaya (Kuala Lumpur, 1982). Another text attributed to Raja Ali Haji, *Salasilah Melayu dan Bugis*, has been edited by Mohd Yusof Mohd Nor (Petaling Jaya, 1984). E.U. Kratz's romanization and German translation of the Malay court notebook from Johor, *Peringatan Sejarah Negeri Johor* (Wiesbaden, 1973), listing events of note from 1677 to 1750, is a valuable example of the genre. It is very similar to a Bugis-influenced work, the so-called *Hikayat Negeri Johor*, which goes on to describe events in Riau and Selangor until the beginning of the nineteenth century. This has been romanized and edited by Ismail Husain, MBRAS reprint no. 6 (1979), pp. 183–240. The important work known as the *Hikayat Siak* has recently become available through a romanization by Muhammad Yusuf Hashim (Kuala Lumpur, 1992). The *Misa Melayu*, an eighteenth-century court chronicle from Perak, was first edited and romanized by Richard Winstedt, and has since been reprinted (Kuala Lumpur, 1962). A later text from Kedah, *Al-Tarikh Salasilah Negeri Kedah* (Kuala Lumpur, 1968) was compiled in 1928 by the court archivist and, despite its relatively recent date, contains many fascinating legends relating to the eighteenth century. A well-annotated Malay work relating to the late eighteenth and early nineteenth century is the *Hikayat Abdullah*, ed. A.H. Hill

(Kuala Lumpur, 1970), which gives a personal but perceptive view of Singapore and Melaka society at the beginning of the nineteenth century.

There are several studies of the economic policies of the Dutch East India Company, but the most readable on the Company's role as a whole, setting it in the context of events in Asia and Europe, is C.R. Boxer, *The Dutch Seaborne Empire, 1600–1800* (London, 1965). Holden Furber, *Rival Empires of Trade in the Orient, 1600–1800* (Minneapolis, 1977), compares the VOC with its rivals, the other European trading companies. Nicholas Tarling, *Anglo-Dutch Rivalry in the Malay World, 1780–1824* (Brisbane, 1962), describes Dutch and British conflicts and relates these to events in Europe and the Malay areas. An overview of the eighteenth century, based on Dutch sources, is Dianne Lewis, *Jan Compagnie in the Straits of Malacca, 1641–1795* (Athens, Ohio, 1995). Reinout Vos, *Gentle Janus, Merchant Prince: The VOC and the Tightrope of Diplomacy in the Malay World, 1740–1800* (Leiden, 1993), provides a detailed picture of Johor politics in the eighteenth century, but sees a more symbiotic Dutch–Malay relationship than that represented here.

A detailed study of Johor, attempting to balance European and Malay material, and bringing together information on the Orang Laut and Bugis, is Leonard Y. Andaya, *The Kingdom of Johor, 1641–1728* (Kuala Lumpur, 1975). Barbara Watson Andaya, *Perak, the Abode of Grace: A Study of an Eighteenth-Century Malay State* (Kuala Lumpur, 1979), incorporates European and Malay material relating to Perak, and also covers events in Kedah, Selangor and the wider Malay world as they impinged on Perak. The history of Kedah from 1770 based on English sources is covered by R. Bonney, *Kedah, 1771–1821: The Search for Security and Independence* (Kuala Lumpur, 1971). A. Teeuw and D.K. Wyatt, *Hikayat Patani: The Story of Patani* (The Hague, 1970), 2 vols, contains a brief summary of what is known of Patani's history in the eighteenth century. On Siak, see Timothy Barnard, 'Multiple Centers of Authority: Society and the Environment in Siak and Eastern Sumatra, 1674–1827' (PhD Thesis, University of Hawai'i, 1998). Mubin Sheppard, 'A Short History of Trengganu', *JMBRAS*, 22, 3 (1949), pp. 1–74, depends heavily on the *Tuhfat al-Nafis*. Anker Rentse, 'History of Kelantan', *JMBRAS*, 12, 2 (1934), pp. 44–62, gives a short account of Kelantan's history incorporating material from H. Marriott, 'A Fragment of the History of Trengganu and Kelantan', *JSBRAS* 72 (May, 1916), pp. 3–23, a translation of part of a Malay text now lost. The first chapter of Carl Trocki, *Prince of Pirates: The Temenggongs and the Development of Johor and Singapore, 1784–1885* (Singapore, 1979), deals with the background to the founding of Singapore, which is the specific focus of C.M. Turnbull, *A History of Singapore, 1819–1975* (Kuala Lumpur, 1977). Khoo Kay Kim, *The Western Malay States, 1850–1873: The Effects of Commercial Development on Malay Politics* (Kuala Lumpur, 1972), provides a useful survey of the western Malay states in the first decades of the nineteenth century.

The material relating to Brunei, Sabah and Sarawak in this period is very limited. For an important study of Iban oral literature, see Benedict Sandin, *The Sea Dayaks of Borneo before White Rajah Rule* (London, 1967). The first chapters of Robert Pringle, *Rajahs and Rebels: The Ibans of Sarawak under Brooke Rule, 1841–1941* (Ithaca, New York, 1970), discuss Iban migration into present-day Sarawak and also contain an excellent geographical description. Nicholas Tarling, *Britain, the Brookes and Brunei* (Kuala Lumpur, 1971), brings together the relevant English material for the eighteenth and early nineteenth century. James Francis Warren, *The Sulu Zone, 1768–1898: The Dynamics of External Trade, Slavery and Ethnicity in the Transformation of a Southeast Asian Maritime State* (Singapore, 1981), draws on Spanish, Dutch and

English archives to see Borneo's northwest coast in terms of its relationship to the Sulu sultanate.

A translation of an eighteenth-century Chinese account of the Malay Peninsula which casts light on trading contacts with China in this period is included in Jennifer W. Cushman and A. C. Milner, 'Eighteenth and Nineteenth Century Chinese Accounts of the Malay Peninsula', *JMBRAS*, 52,1 (1979), pp. 1–56.

Chapter 4: A New World is Created, 1819–74

The founding of Singapore and the development of the Straits Settlements in the nineteenth century are well covered in L.A. Mills, 'British Malaya, 1824–67', *JMBRAS*, 33, 3 (1960); Nicholas Tarling, *Anglo-Dutch Rivalry in the Malay World, 1780–1824* (Brisbane, 1962); C.M. Turnbull, *The Straits Settlements, 1826–67* (Kuala Lumpur, 1972); C.M. Turnbull, *A History of Singapore, 1819–1975* (Kuala Lumpur, 1977). Wong Lin Ken, 'The Trade of Singapore, 1819–69', *JMBRAS*, 33, 4 (1960), gives a survey of Singapore's trade, with useful tables. Lesley M. Potter, 'A Forest Product out of Control: Gutta Percha in Indonesia and the Wider Malay World, 1845–1915', in *Paper Landscapes: Exploration in the Environmental History of Indonesia*, eds Peter Boomgaard, Freek Columbijn and David Henley (Leiden, 1997), is a case study of the impact of the gutta percha frenzy. All contain extensive bibliographies.

British involvement with the Malay states and the events leading up to intervention are analysed in C.D. Cowan, *Nineteenth Century Malaya: The Origins of British Political Control* (London, 1961), and C.N. Parkinson, *British Intervention in Malaya, 1867–77* (Singapore, 1960). Nicholas Tarling, *British Policy in the Malay Peninsula and Archipelago, 1824–71* (Kuala Lumpur, 1969) and *Piracy and Politics in the Malay World: A Study of British Imperialism in the 19th Century* (Melbourne, 1963), deal in some detail with British relations with neighbouring Malay areas. Khoo Kay Kim, *The Western Malay States, 1850–1873* (Kuala Lumpur, 1972), discusses the commercial links between the Straits Settlements and the Malay states before formal British intervention. Emrys Chew, 'The Naning War, 1831–1832: Colonial Authority and Malay Resistance in the Early Period of British Expansion', *Modern Asian Studies*, 32, 2 (May 1998), pp. 351–87, argues for early British interest in the extension of control into the Peninsula. J.M. Gullick's classic, *The Indigenous Political Systems of Western Malaya* (London, 1958), presents an analysis of the Malay political system immediately prior to intervention. This can be read together with A.C. Milner, *Kerajaan: Malay Political Culture on the Eve of Colonial Rule* (Tucson, Arizona, 1982), which adopts a more textually based approach, especially in explaining the dynamics of the civil war in Pahang in 1856–63.

Several good histories of individual states have built on early studies by individual British scholars, notably W. Linehan, R.O. Winstedt and R.J. Wilkinson. J.M. Gullick, *A History of Selangor (1766–1939)* (MBRAS Monograph no. 28, Kuala Lumpur, 1998), uses primarily English sources, with a focus on the latter half of the nineteenth century. The footnote annotations provide a useful guide to relevant literature. Aruna Gopinath, *Pahang 1880–1933: A Political History* (MBRAS Monograph no. 18, Kuala Lumpur, 1993), surveys earlier work on Pahang. C. Skinner, *The Civil War in Kelantan in 1839* (MBRAS Monograph no. 2, Kuala Lumpur, 1965), can be used in conjunction with Shaharil Talib, *History of Kelantan* (MBRAS Monograph no. 21, Kuala Lumpur, 1995). An account of the civil war in early nineteenth-century Kelantan is in C. Skinner, *The Civil War in Kelantan in 1839* (MBRAS Monograph no. 2, Kuala Lumpur, 1965). M. C. Sheppard, 'A Short History of Trengganu', *JMBRAS*, 22, 2 (1949), remains the most accessible account of Terengganu's history in the early nineteenth century. For Johor, see especially Carl Trocki, *Prince of Pirates: The Temenggongs and the Development of Johor and Singapore, 1784–1885* (Singapore, 1979). See also the readings for Chapter 5.

Thai relations with the northern states have received increasing attention. Kobkua Suwannathat-Pian, *Thai–Malay Relations: Traditional Intra-Regional Relations from the Seventeenth to the Early Twentieth Centuries* (Kuala Lumpur, 1988), provides an important perspective using Thai archival sources. Ibrahim Syukri, *History of the Malay Kingdom of Patani* (Athens, Ohio, 1985), is a translation of a bitterly anti-Siamese work.

Sarawak has spawned a large body of literature, the emphasis in recent years being more on economic and environmental topics. An early, less academic but valuable, biography of James Brooke is Emily Hahn, *James Brooke of Sarawak* (London, 1953); the most recent is Nicholas Tarling, *'The Burthen, the Risk and the Glory': The Life of Sir James Brooke* (Kuala Lumpur, 1982), which includes a good bibliography. On Brooke's relationships with the Bidayuh, see J.H. Walker, 'James Brooke and the Bidayuh: Some Ritual Dimensions of Dependency and Resistance in Nineteenth Century Sarawak', *Modern Asian Studies*, 32, 1 (February 1998), pp. 91–116. The only full study of Charles Brooke is Colin N. Crisswell, *Rajah Charles Brooke* (Kuala Lumpur, 1978). The best book on nineteenth-century Sarawak is still Robert Pringle, *Rajahs and Rebels: The Ibans of Sarawak under Brooke Rule, 1841–1941* (Ithaca, New York, 1970), which, although focusing on the Iban–Brooke relationship, covers numerous other topics. Benedict Sandin, *The Sea Dayaks of Borneo before White Raja Rule* (London, 1967), has incorporated much of the oral material of the Ibans. Hugh Low, *Sarawak: Its Inhabitants and Productions* (London, 1848), and Spenser St John, *Life in the Forests of the Far East* (London, 1862), 2 vols, are interesting contemporary accounts. The development of Kuching itself is traced by Craig Lockard, *From Kampung to City: A Social History of Kuching, Malaysia, 1820–1970* (Athens, Ohio, 1987). For the relationship between Brunei, North Borneo and Sarawak, see the suggested Further Reading for Chapter 5.

The literature on Chinese migration is extensive. First published in 1947, Victor Purcell, *The Chinese in Malaya* (Kuala Lumpur, 1967), remains a classic. An important study of early Chinese mining organizations is Wang Tai Peng, *The Origins of Chinese Kongsi* (Kuala Lumpur, 1994). Carl Trocki, *Opium and Empire: Chinese Society in Colonial Singapore, 1800–1910* (Ithaca and London, 1990), develops his earlier work on Johor to argue for an economic and class-based perspective. A contemporary account is J. Vaughan, *The Manners and Customs of the Chinese of the Straits Settlements* (Singapore, 1879; reprinted Kuala Lumpur, 1971). An exhaustive study of the secret societies is W.L. Blythe, *The Impact of Chinese Secret Societies in Malaya* (London, 1969). Chinese commercial agriculture is discussed in James C. Jackson, *Planters and Speculators: Chinese and European Enterprise in Malaya, 1786–1921* (Kuala Lumpur, 1968), while Wong Lin Ken, *The Malayan Tin Industry to 1914* (Tucson, 1965), provides detailed information on Chinese tin mining in the nineteenth century.

There are several contemporary Malay texts. A. H. Hill (ed. and trans.), *Hikayat Abdullah* (The Story of Abdullah) (Kuala Lumpur, 1970), contains perceptive contemporary material, as does Abdullah's *Kisah Pelayaran Abdullah* (The Story of Abdullah's Voyages), ed. Kassim Ahmad (Kuala Lumpur, 1970), which describes his journey to the east coast of the Peninsula. It is available in an English translation in A. E. Coope, *The Voyages of Abdullah* (Kuala Lumpur, 1967). Abdullah's son Ibrahim was employed by Maharaja Abu Bakar of Johor and also wrote an account of several trips on official business. It has been edited and translated by Amin Sweeney and Nigel Phillips, *The Voyages of Mohamed Ibrahim Munshi* (Kuala Lumpur, 1975). Amin Sweeney (trans.), *Reputations Live On: An Early Malay Autobiography* (Berkeley and Los Angeles, 1980), is a valuable contemporary account by another of Johor's Malay officials. Raja Ali Haji, *Tuhfat al-Nafis (The Precious Gift)* remains an important source, especially concerning developments in Islam. It has been translated and edited by Virginia Matheson and Barbara Watson Andaya (Kuala Lumpur, 1982). Mohd Taib Osman, 'Hikayat Sri Kelantan' (MA thesis, University of Malaya, 1961), a romanization of a manuscript dated 1914 in the Royal Asiatic Society's collection, throws considerable light on many aspects of Kelantan history, especially in the nineteenth century. *Hikayat Panglima Nikosa: The Story of Panglima Nikosa*, trans. and ed. Philip L. Thomas and R.H.W. Reece (Kuching, 1983), a Malay text from Sarawak, provides an example of how traditional literary forms could be used for didactic purposes.

Numerous contemporary sources in English have been published, several of which contain transcripts of official documents since lost. The most important are: John Anderson, *Political and Commercial Considerations Relative to the Malayan Peninsula, etc.* (Penang, 1824; reprinted *JMBRAS*, 35, 4 (1962)); P.J. Begbie, *The Malayan Peninsula* (Madras, 1834; reprinted Kuala Lumpur, 1967); J. Cameron, *Our Tropical Possessions in Malayan India* (London, 1865; reprinted Kuala Lumpur, 1965); T.J. Newbold, *Political and Statistical Accounts of the British Settlements in the Straits of Malacca* (London, 1839; reprinted Kuala Lumpur, 1971), 2 vols; G.W. Earl, *The Eastern Seas* (London, 1837; reprinted Kuala Lumpur, 1971). *The Journal of the Indian Archipelago and Eastern Asia*, ed. J.R. Logan (1847–59), 12 vols, contains many invaluable descriptions of contemporary customs and local history.

Chapter 5: The Making of 'British' Malaya, 1874–1919

The literature on the first half of colonial rule is extensive and the bibliographies of works cited below should also be consulted. British colonial policy in Malaya in its imperial setting is discussed by W.D. McIntyre, *The Imperial Frontier in the Tropics, 1865–75* (London and New York, 1967). For an overall picture of the British advance, see the classic by Rupert Emerson, *Malaysia: A Study in Direct and Indirect Rule* (New York, 1937; reprinted Kuala Lumpur, 1964). Political expansion after 1874 is covered in the last chapters of C.D. Cowan, *Nineteenth Century Malaya: The Origins of British Political Control* (London, 1961). The first 20 years of colonial rule in the FMS is analysed in Emily Sadka, *The Protected Malay States, 1874–1895* (Kuala Lumpur, 1968). The British response to the 'turbulent frontier' is traced by Eunice Thio, *British Policy in the Malay Peninsula, 1886–1901*, vol. 1, *The Southern and Central States* (Singapore, 1969). Chai Hon Chan, *The Development of British Malaya, 1896–1909* (Kuala Lumpur, 1967) covers the same period but adds further detail on social measures using material obtained from annual reports.

Singapore's history during the late nineteenth century is well covered in C.M. Turnbull, *A History of Singapore, 1819–1975* (Kuala Lumpur, 1977). Two books by Jim Warren, *Rickshaw Coolie: A People's History of Singapore (1880–1940)* (Singapore, 1986) and *Ah Ku and Karayuki-San – Prostitution in Singapore 1870–1940* (Singapore, 1993), are an important contribution to the social history of the region.

The FMS is well studied. Joget Singh Sandhu, *Administration in the Federated Malay States, 1896–1920* (Kuala Lumpur, 1980), analyses the priorities of the colonial administration and its effect on the indigenous population. Two very readable books by J.M. Gullick contain a wealth of information and display his masterful knowledge of the archival material: *Malay Society in the Late Nineteenth Century: The Beginnings of Change* (Singapore, 1987), which includes an appendix of useful brief biographies, and *Rulers and Residents: Influence and Power in the Malay States, 1870–1920* (Singapore, 1992).

Relevant readings on individual states are listed for Chapter 4. Although most studies of the FMS rely heavily on material from the west coast, Aruna Gopinath's *Pahang, 1880–1933* provides a valuable corrective and a detailed study of the Pahang uprising. This can be read in conjunction with R.G. Cant, *A Historical Geography of Pahang* (MBRAS Monograph no. 4, Kuala Lumpur, 1973), which gives a geographer's view of the effects of British intervention on local society.

There are a number of studies on the UMS. A useful collection of essays on Kelantan is W.R. Roff (ed.), *Kelantan: Religion, Society and Politics in a Malay State* (Kuala Lumpur, 1974). Shaharil Talib, *History of Kelantan, 1890–1940* (MBRAS Monograph no. 21, Kuala Lumpur, 1995), looks closely at the impact of Western economic and political intervention. Clive Kessler, *Islam and Politics in a Malay State: Kelantan, 1838–1969* (Ithaca, New York and London, 1978), gives a background synthesizing nineteenth-century material. The most complete study of late nineteenth-century Terengganu society and the 1928 uprising is Shaharil Talib, *After its Own Image: The Trengganu Experience, 1881–1941* (Kuala Lumpur, 1984). See further Heather Sutherland, 'The Taming of the Trengganu Elite', in Ruth McVey (ed.), *Southeast Asian Transitions: Approaches through Social History* (New Haven and London, 1978), and J. de Vere Allen, 'The Ancient Regime in Trengganu, 1909–1919', *JMBRAS*, 41, 1 (1968), pp. 23–53. W.A. Graham, *Kelantan: A State of the Malay Peninsula* (Glasgow, 1907), is a contemporary description by the first Adviser. For Kedah see Sharom Ahmad, *Kedah: Tradition and Change in a Malay State: A Study of the Economic and Political Development, 1878–1923* (MBRAS Monograph no. 12, Kuala Lumpur, 1984). For Johor in this period, see Christopher Gray, 'Johore 1910–1941: Studies in the Colonial Process' (PhD Thesis, Yale University, 1978). Amin Sweeney, *Reputations Live On: An Early Malay Autobiography* (Berkeley, 1980), looks at the development of Johor through the eyes of one of Johor's chief ministers. Two recent publications on Johor by Malaysian scholars are Shaharom Husain, *Sejarah Johor, Kaitannya dengan Negeri Melayu Selangor, Darul Ehsan* (Kuala Lumpur, 1995), and Rahiman Abd. Aziz, *Pembaratan Pemerintahan Johor, 1800–1945: Suatu Analisis Sosiologi Sejarah* (Kuala Lumpur, 1997).

W.R. Roff's classic, *The Origins of Malay Nationalism* (New Haven and Kuala Lumpur, 1967), provides important information on intellectual movements in Malay society, while the early sections of Lim Teck Ghee, *Peasants and their Agricultural Economy in Colonial Malaya, 1874–1941* (Kuala Lumpur, 1977), discuss the effects of colonial rule on the Malay peasant in the Protected States. Hendrik J. Maier, *In the Center of Authority: The Malay Hikayat Merong Mahawangsa* (Ithaca, New York, 1988), is a perceptive analysis of the development of British understanding of Malay society and their approach to Malay textual studies. A.C. Milner,

The Invention of Politics in Colonial Malaya (Cambridge, 1994), is a mature and insightful reconsideration of the evolution of differences in Malay political thinking still evident today.

For the Chinese, see the bibliography for Chapter 4. To this can be added Yen Ching-hwang, *A Social History of the Chinese in Singapore and Malaya, 1800–1911* (Kuala Lumpur, 1986), and Loh Kok Wah, *Beyond the Tin Mines: Coolies, Squatters and New Villages in the Kinta Valley, Malaysia, 1880–1980* (Singapore, 1988), a sympathetic case study of the problems faced by poor rural Chinese. Jürgen Rudolph, *Reconstructing Identities: A Social History of the Babas in Singapore* (Boulder, Colorado, 1998), traces a continuing reconstruction of Baba identity within the larger social and economic environment. Kernial Singh Sandhu, *Indians in Malaya: Immigration and Settlement, 1786–1957* (Cambridge, 1969), deals in detail with Indian migration; a briefer overview is in Sinnappah Arasaratnam, *Indians in Malaysia and Singapore* (Kuala Lumpur, 1979). The large collection of essays edited by K.S. Sandhu and A. Mani, *Indian Communities in Southeast Asia* (Singapore, 1993), contain a number of contributions that bring the Indian story up to date. See also the Further Reading for Chapter 6.

British colonial society is described in a lively manner in John Butcher, *The British in Malaya, 1880–1941: The Social History of a European Community in Colonial Southeast Asia* (Kuala Lumpur, 1979). A selection of contemporary sketches about life in Malaya from the colonial viewpoint is W.R. Roff, *Stories by Sir Hugh Clifford* (Kuala Lumpur, 1966), and *Stories and Sketches by Sir Frank Swettenham* (Kuala Lumpur, 1967). D.J.M. Tate, *The Lake Club, 1890–1990* (Kuala Lumpur, 1990), provides numerous insights into colonial life. An excellent analysis of changing attitudes towards race is Charles Hirschman, 'The Making of Race in Colonial Malaya: Political Economy and Racial Ideology', *Sociological Forum*, 1, 2 (1986), pp. 330–61.

There are numerous contemporary commentators, and the journals of individual residents are particularly useful. See particularly P.L. Burns (ed.), *The Journals of J.W.W. Birch* (Kuala Lumpur, 1976); P.L. Burns and C. D. Cowan, *Swettenham's Malayan Journals, 1874–76* (Kuala Lumpur, 1975); Peter Burns, 'Annexation in the Malay States: The Jervois Papers', *JMBRAS*, 72, 1 (1999), pp. 1–95 ; Emily Sadka, 'The Journal of Sir Hugh Low, Perak 1877', *JMBRAS*, 27, 4 (1954); J.M. Gullick, 'Selangor, 1876–1882: The Bloomfield Douglas Diary', *JMBRAS*, 48, 2 (1975); Peter Wicks (ed.), *Journal of a Mission to Pahang, January 15 to April 11, 1887, by Hugh Clifford* (Honolulu, 1978).

Books of reminiscences and travel supply other interesting details. Isabella Bird, *The Golden Chersonese and the Way Thither* (New York, 1883; reprinted Kuala Lumpur, 1967), should be read in conjunction with Emily Innes, *The Golden Chersonese with the Gilding Off* (London, 1885), 2 vols. J.F. McNair, *Perak and the Malays: 'Sarong and Kris'* (London, 1878), is by a participant in the Perak campaign following the murder of Birch.

Kobkua Suwannathat-Pian, *Thai–Malay Relations: Traditional Intra-Regional Relations from the Seventeenth to the Early Twentieth Centuries* (Kuala Lumpur, 1988), provides an important perspective using Malay material as well as British and Thai archival sources.

Nicholas Tarling, *Britain, the Brookes and Brunei* (Kuala Lumpur, 1971) and *Sulu and Sabah: A Study of British Policy towards the Philippines and North Borneo from the Late Eighteenth Century* (Kuala Lumpur, 1978), discusses the emergence of the Borneo territories in relation to changing British imperial policies. L.R. Wright, *The Origins of British Borneo* (Hong Kong, 1970), covers the late nineteenth century, with a somewhat different interpretation from Tarling. An economic study is Ooi Keat Gin,

Of Free Trade and Native Interests: The Brookes and the Economic Development of Sarawak, 1841–1941 (Kuala Lumpur, 1997). The works cited in the Further Reading for Chapter 4 are also relevant for this period.

The material on Sabah, while not as extensive as that for Sarawak, is increasing. An early publication is Owen Rutter, *British North Borneo* (London, 1922), which gives an uncritical but informative account of the early development of North Borneo. The most recent interpretative history for this period is Ian Black, *A Gambling Style of Government: The Establishment of Chartered Company Rule in Sabah, 1878–1905* (Kuala Lumpur, 1983), although the older K.G. Tregonning, *A History of Modern Sabah: North Borneo, 1881–1963* (Singapore, 1965), is still useful for an overall view. Callistus Fernandez, 'The Rundum Rebellion of 1915 Reconsidered', *Sarawak Museum Journal*, 53 (December 1998), pp. 109–36, has brought together local memories and archival sources. James Warren, *The North Borneo Chartered Company's Administration of the Bajau, 1878–1909*, Center for International Studies, Ohio University (Athens, Ohio, 1971), provides disturbing evidence of the dislocating effects of Company policies on the Bajau.

Chapter 6: The Functioning of a Colonial Society, 1919–41

There are a number of excellent studies on British rule in Malaya in the twentieth century. Colonial administration is the subject of a penetrating analysis by R. Emerson in *Malaysia: A Study in Direct and Indirect Rule* (New York, 1937; reprinted Kuala Lumpur, 1964). Its critical view of the intent of British policy became the inspiration to a new generation of scholars writing about the post-independence period in Southeast Asia. Other studies of British rule are L.A. Mills, *British Rule in Eastern Asia: A Study of Contemporary Government and Economic Development in British Malaya and Hong Kong* (London, 1942); Virginia Thompson, *Postmortem on Malaya* (New York, 1943); and Jagjit Singh Sidhu, *Administration in the Federated Malay States* (Kuala Lumpur and New York, 1980). An important study of the impact of British rule on the Malays is W.R. Roff's *The Origins of Malay Nationalism* (New Haven and Kuala Lumpur, 1967). Simon C. Smith, *British Relations with the Malay Ruler: From Decentralization to Malayan Independence, 1930–1957* (Kuala Lumpur, 1995), is of particular relevance to the debates on decentralization.

For accounts of colonial rule in the Borneo states, see the readings on Sarawak listed for Chapter 4 and also K. G. Tregonning, *A History of Modern Sabah: North Borneo, 1881–1963* (Singapore, 1965), and Nicholas Tarling, *Sulu and Sabah: A Study of British Policy towards the Philippines and North Borneo from the Late Eighteenth Century* (Kuala Lumpur, 1978). Robert Pringle, *Rajahs and Rebels: The Ibans of Sarawak under Brooke Rule, 1841–1941* (Ithaca, New York, 1970), is an excellent study of Brooke rule and its impact on indigenous society. Steven Runciman, *The White Rajahs* (Cambridge, 1960), presents a more personal look at the Brookes themselves. Robert Reece, *The Name of Brooke: The End of White Rajah Rule in Sarawak* (Kuala Lumpur, 1982), deals with events leading up to the cession. A Borneo view of Chinese migration is John M. Chin, *The Sarawak Chinese* (Kuala Lumpur, 1981). Daniel Chew's more recent *Chinese Pioneers on the Sarawak Frontier, 1841–1941* (Singapore, 1990) focuses on Chinese settlement outside Kuching. A parallel reading for North Borneo is Danny Wong Tze-Ken, 'Chinese

Migration to Sabah before the Second World War', *Archipel*, 58 (1999), pp. 131–58. Craig Lockard, *From Kampung to City: A Social History of Kuching, Malaysia, 1820–1970* (Athens, Ohio, 1987) is a detailed study of Kuching's socio-ethnic development. Ooi Keat Gin, *Of Free Trade and Native Interests: The Brookes and the Economic Development of Sarawak, 1841–1941* (Kuala Lumpur, 1997), is an economic study of Sarawak. Amarjit Kaur, *Economic Change in East Malaysia: Sabah and Sarawak since 1850* (London and Basingstoke, 1998), is a valuable comparative study by an economic historian.

On the economic development of British Malaya, an indispensable study is G.C. Allen and A.G. Donnithorne's *Western Enterprise in Indonesia and Malaya: A Study in Economic Development* (London, 1957), which describes the manner in which government and Western capital co-operated in the development of Malaya's economy. A more general study which traces the development of Malaya's economy from the early tin-mining days to the post-independence period is P.P. Courtenay, *A Geography of Trade and Development in Malaya* (London, 1972). The first European and Chinese ventures into agricultural export commodities is the subject of James C. Jackson, *Planters and Speculators: Chinese and European Enterprises in Malaya, 1786–1921* (Kuala Lumpur, 1968). A valuable analysis of the effects of colonial policy on Malay farmers is Lim Teck Ghee, *Peasants and their Agricultural Economy in Colonial Malaya, 1874–1941* (Kuala Lumpur, 1977). There are several studies on tin for this period, the most impressive being Wong Lin Ken, *The Malayan Tin Industry to 1914* (Tucson, 1965). For the tin industry after 1914, see Yip Yat Hoong, *The Development of the Tin Mining Industry of Malaya* (Kuala Lumpur/Singapore, 1969). For rubber, the classic work is P.T. Bauer, *The Rubber Industry: A Study in Competition and Monopoly* (London/New York, 1948). John Drabble, *Rubber in Malaya, 1876–1922: The Genesis of the Industry* (Kuala Lumpur, 1973), and the sequel, *Malayan Rubber: The Interwar Years* (Basingstoke, Hampshire, 1991), bring the picture up to the modern period. The development of oil palm has not been so extensively researched, but see Harcharan Singh Khera, *The Oil Palm Industry in West Malaysia: An Economic Study* (Kuala Lumpur, 1976). A case study of a female-dominated industry is Maznah Mohamad, *The Malay Handloom Weavers: A Study of the Rise and Decline of Traditional Manufacture* (Singapore, 1996). A history of communications is Amarjit Kaur, *Bridge and Barrier: Transports and Communications in Colonial Malaya, 1870–1959* (Singapore, 1985). The history of health care is treated by Leonore Manderson in *Sickness and the State: Health and Illness in Colonial Malaya, 1870–1940* (Cambridge and Melbourne, 1996).

A well-written study of education of Malays both in English- and Malay-medium schools is Rex Stevenson, *Cultivators and Administrators: British Educational Policy towards the Malays, 1875–1906* (Kuala Lumpur, 1975). A detailed examination of Chinese-medium education is Tan Liok Ee, *The Politics of Chinese Education in Malaya, 1945–1961* (Kuala Lumpur, 1997). Indian education, which was basically Tamil-medium, is discussed in K. S. Sandhu, *Indians in Malaya: Immigration and Settlement, 1786–1957* (Cambridge, 1969), and in S. Arasaratnam, *Indians in Malaysia and Singapore* (Kuala Lumpur, 1979). For a general discussion of all of these 'systems' of education and their impact on the unity of Malayan society under British rule, see Phillip Fook Seng Loh, *Seeds of Separatism: Educational Policy in Malaya, 1874–1940* (Kuala Lumpur, 1975). Islamic education, especially in the northern Malay states, has been little studied. Relevant material can be found in Khoo Kay Kim, *Malay Society: Transformation & Democratisation* (Petaling Jaya, 1991); Abdullah al-Qari bin Haji Salleh, 'To Kenali: His Life and Influence', in W. Roff (ed.), *Kelantan* (Kuala Lumpur, 1974), pp. 87–106; and Abdullah Alwi Haji Hassan, 'The Development of Islamic Education in Kelantan', in Khoo Kay Kim (ed.), *Tamadun Islam di Malaysia* (Kuala Lumpur, 1980), pp. 190–228. Leonore Manderson, 'The Development and Direction of Female Education it Peninsular Malaysia', *JMBRAS*, 51, 2 (1978), provides a useful overview, with statistics. Alijah Gordon (ed.), *The Real Cry of Syed Shaykh al-Hady* (Kuala Lumpur, 1999), is an intriguing biography with translations of work by this militant reformist. For Sarawak, Ooi Keat Gin, *World Beyond the Rivers: Education in Sarawak from Brooke Rule to Colonial Office Administration, 1841–1963* (Hull, 1996), is a comprehensive study; Sabah awaits further research, but see Sabibah Osman, 'The Role of Governor Jardine in Improving the Welfare of the Indigenous People of Sabah, 1934–37', *JSEAS*, 20, 2 (1989), pp. 196–215.

On the civil service, Khasnor Johan, *The Emergence of the Modern Malay Administrative Elite* (Singapore, 1984) can be compared with Robert Heussler, *British Rule in Malaya – the Malayan Civil Service and its Predecessors, 1874–1942* (Oxford, 1981). Naimah S. Talib, *Administrators and their Service: The Sarawak Administrative Service under the Brooke Rajahs and British Colonial Rule* (Kuala Lumpur, 1999), identifies features that make Sarawak distinctive from other colonies.

There are several useful volumes on Indians and plantation labour. See the Further Reading for Chapter 5, and also M.R. Stenson, *Industrial Conflict in Malaya: Prelude to the Communist Revolt of 1948* (London, 1970) and *Class, Race and Colonialism in West Malaysia* (St Lucia, Queensland, 1980). Two more recent books are Selvakumaran Ramachandran, *Indian Plantation Labour in Malaysia* (Kuala Lumpur, 1994), and P. Ramasamy, *Plantation Labour, Unions, Capital and the State in Peninsula Malaysia* (Kuala Lumpur, 1993). An important study of the Peranakan is Helen Fujimoto, *The South Indian Muslim Community and the Evolution of the Jawi Peranakan in Penang up to 1948* (Tokyo, 1989).

An insightful addition to the Chinese readings listed for Chapter 4 is Francis Loh Kok Wah, *Beyond the Tin Mines: Coolies, Squatters, and New Villagers in the Kinta Valley, Malaysia, c.1880–1980* (Singapore, 1988).

Histories of the underprivileged are also more numerous than previously. Donald M. Nonini, *British Colonial Rule and the Resistance of the Malay Peasantry, 1900–1957* (New Haven, 1992), examines Malay attitudes towards British rice-growing policies. Cheah Boon Kheng, *The Peasant Robbers of Kedah, 1900–1929: Historical and Folk Perceptions* (Kuala Lumpur, 1988), looks at the significance of lawlessness along the Siam–Kedah border. The essays in Peter J. Rimmer and Lisa M. Allen (eds.), *The Underside of Malaysian History: Pullers, Prostitutes, Plantation Workers . . .* (Singapore, 1990), are particularly rich in economic detail on working conditions of migrant communities in the FMS.

Several writers have treated developments in Malay historiography. See, for example, A.J. Stockwell, 'The Historiography of Malaysia: Recent Writings in English on the History of the Area since 1874', *Journal of Imperial and Commonwealth History*, 5 (1976), pp. 82–111; Khoo Kay Kim, 'Local Historians and the Writing of Malaysian History in the Twentieth Century', in Anthony Reid and David Marr (eds), *Perceptions of the Past in Southeast Asia* (Singapore, 1979), and 'Malaysian Historiography: A Further Look', *Kajian Malaysia*, 10, 1 (1992), pp. 37–62; Cheah Boon Kheng, 'Writing Indigenous History in Malaysia', *Crossroads*, 10, 2 (1996), pp. 33–82. Virginia Matheson Hooker, *Social Change Through the Novel in Malay* (Sydney and Honolulu, 2000) explores literature as a historical source.

Chapter 7: Negotiating a New Nation, 1942–69

There are now more studies on the Japanese Occupation. Personal accounts are found in Chin Kee Onn, *Malaya Upside Down* (Singapore, 1946), which describes the life of a civilian in Perak under the Japanese. It can be read with Sylvia Kathigasu, *No Dram of Mercy* (Singapore, 1983), and Agnes Keith, *Three Came Home* (Boston, 1947), the prison-camp memoirs of a European woman. F. Spencer Chapman, *The Jungle is Neutral* (London, 1949), describes anti-Japanese resistance in the jungles of Malaya by a British army officer who remained behind when the Japanese invaded the Peninsula. Tom Harrisson, *The World Within* (London, 1959), is an account of the author's experiences after being parachuted into Borneo during the Second World War.

P. Elphick, *Singapore, the Pregnable City: A Study in Deception, Discord and Desertion* (London, 1995), uses archival material only recently opened to provide more depressing information regarding the military debacle surrounding Singapore's fall. Two books, Paul Kratoska (ed.), *Malaya and Singapore During the Japanese Occupation* (Singapore, 1995), and Paul Kratoska, *The Japanese Occupation of Malaya, 1941–1945* (London, 1997), have made available new material regarding the effects of the Occupation on the lives of ordinary people.

Race relations and communal politics during the war are the focus of Cheah Boon Kheng's compelling *Red Star over Malaya: Resistance and Social Conflict During and After the Japanese Occupation of Malaya, 1941–1946* (Singapore, 1983). Ooi Keat Gin, *Rising Sun over Borneo: The Japanese Period in Sarawak, 1941–45* (London, 1999), can be read in conjunction with his *Japanese Empire in the Tropics: Selected Documents and Reports of the Japanese Period in Sarawak, Northwest Borneo, 1941–45* (Athens, Ohio, 1999), 2 vols, a compilation of official papers and reports, private letters and memoirs that offer a revealing view of wartime experiences.

There have been several important books on the Malayan Union and the events leading to independence. Earlier works are J. de Vere Allen, *The Malayan Union* (New Haven, 1967); A.J. Stockwell, *British Policy and Malay Politics During the Malayan Union Experiment, 1942–1948* (MBRAS Monograph no. 8, Kuala Lumpur, 1979); Mohamed Noordin Sopiee, *From Malayan Union to Singapore Separation* (Kuala Lumpur, 1974). The opening of archival material has enabled Albert Lau to re-examine the period in *The Malayan Union Controversy, 1942–1948* (Singapore, 1991). Firdaus Haji Abdullah, *Radical Malay Politics: Its Origins and Early Development* (Petaling Jaya, 1985), considers political divisions within Malay society in the postwar years. Ariffin Omar, *Bangsa Melayu: Malay Concepts of Democracy and Community, 1945–1950* (Kuala Lumpur, 1993), examines the events surrounding the Malayan Union and Federation debates, giving particular attention to left-wing groups. Tim Harper, *The End of Empire and the Making of Malaya* (Cambridge, 1999), is a detailed study of the social and political climate in the pre-independence period, focusing specifically on debates within the different ethnic communities.

The communist insurrection in Malaya between 1948 and 1960 has been discussed in a number of detailed studies. The origins are examined in M.R. Stenson, *Repression and Revolt: The Origins of the 1948 Communist Insurrection in Malaya and Singapore* (Ohio, 1969) and *Industrial Conflict in Malaya: Prelude to the Communist Revolt in 1948* (Kuala Lumpur, 1970). Military accounts are Richard Clutterbuck, *The Long War: The Emergency in Malaya, 1948–1960* (London, 1967), and *Riot and Revolution in Singapore and Malaya, 1945–1963* (London, 1973); and E. O'Ballance, *The Communist Insurgent War, 1948–1960* (London, 1966), is a military account of the conflict.

A. Short, *The Communist Insurrection in Malaya, 1948–1960* (London, 1975), is a study of the insurrection which began as an official government history and therefore contains considerable previously highly classified material. Han Su-yin, *And the Rain My Drink* (London, 1956), is a novel about life in the Emergency and particularly in a New Village. Richard Stubbs, *Hearts and Minds in Guerilla Warfare: The Malayan Emergency, 1948–1960* (Singapore, 1989), analyses the reasons for the ultimate British success. John D. Leary, *Violence and the Dream People: The* Orang Asli *in the Malayan Emergency, 1946–1960* (Athens, Ohio, 1995), is a sympathetic description of the ways in which Orang Asli groups responded to pressures from both sides.

Politics in post-independence Malaya are discussed in several excellent books. See especially G.P. Means, *Malaysian Politics* (London, 2nd edn, 1976), and R.S. Milne and Diane K. Mauzy, *Politics and Government in Malaysia* (Vancouver, 1978). Other general works on the politics and the political process in Malaysia are M.E. Osborne, *Singapore and Malaysia* (Ithaca, New York, 1964), and Stanley S. Bedlington, *Malaysia and Singapore: The Building of New States* (Ithaca, New York, 1978). The latter is especially interesting with regard to Sabah, which the author knew intimately after seven years in the British colonial service. On the ethnic aspects of politics in Malaysia, see K.J. Ratnam, *Communalism and the Political Process in Malaya* (Kuala Lumpur, 1965), R.K. Vasil, *Politics in a Plural Society* (Singapore, 1971), and Cynthia Enloe's stimulating *Multi-Ethnic Politics: The Case of Malaysia* (Berkeley, 1970). Karl von Vorys, *Democracy without Consensus: Communalism and Political Stability in Malaysia* (Princeton, 1975), attempts to demonstrate the viability of the democracy created by Malaya/Malaysia's leaders, based not on a national integrated community but a discrete communal one. John Funston, *Malay Politics in Malaysia: A Study of UMNO and PAS* (Kuala Lumpur and Singapore, 1980), discusses the evolution of these two Malay political parties, which represent two differing approaches to Malaysia's future, in the pre- and post-1969 period.

On the Borneo states, R.H.W. Reece, *The Name of Brooke: The End of White Raja Rule in Sarawak* (Kuala Lumpur, 1982), provides a detailed coverage of postwar negotiations. The reaction of Sabah and Sarawak to the Malaysia Federation is discussed in R. S. Milne and K. J. Ratnam, *Malaysia, New States in a New Nation: Political Development of Sarawak and Sabah in Malaysia* (London, 1974); M.C. Roff, *The Politics of Belonging: Political Change in Sabah and Sarawak* (Kuala Lumpur, 1974); J.P. Ongkili, *The Borneo Response to Malaysia* (Singapore, 1967); J. P. Ongkili, *Modernization in East Malaysia, 1960–1970* (Kuala Lumpur, 1972); and Michael Leigh, *The Rising Moon: Political Change in Sarawak* (Sydney, 1974). A recent economic study is Amarjit Kaur, *Economic Change in East Malaysia: Sabah and Sarawak since 1850* (London and Basingstoke, 1998).

Several books look specifically at ethnic groups; see, for example, Peter Searle, *Politics in Sarawak, 1970–1976: The Iban Perspective* (Kuala Lumpur, 1983); Sanib Said, *Malay Politics in Sarawak, 1946–1966* (Singapore, 1985), which examines the roots of Sarawak Malay opposition to the formation of Malaysia. On Sabah, Edwin Lee, *The Towkays of Sabah: Chinese Leadership and Indigenous Challenge in the Last Phase of British Rule* (Singapore, 1976), traces the ability of the Chinese business community to exploit the patronage system.

On the economy of postwar Malaya, a readable study is David Lim, *Economic Growth and Development in West Malaysia, 1947–1970* (Kuala Lumpur, 1973). A concise and penetrating analysis of the interrelationship among inequality, economic development and ethnicity in Malaysia is Donald R. Snodgrass, *Inequality and Economic Development in Malaysia* (Kuala Lumpur, 1980). Other books on Malaya's economy are R. Ma and You Poh Seng, *The Economy of Malaysia and Singapore* (Singapore, 1966), and P.J. Drake, *Financial Development in Malaya and Singapore* (Canberra, 1969). J.M. Gullick, *Malaysia: Economic Expansion and National Unity* (London and Boulder, Colorado, 1981), is a very competent study of key topics such as education, the economy, the political scene and social change. The second edition of Rosemary Firth's pioneering *Housekeeping among Malay Peasants* (London, 1966), discusses the domestic economy of a Kelantan village revisited after more than twenty years. See also the Further Reading for Chapter 6.

For a straightforward account of educational policy and the changing curricula in Malaya/Malaysia's schools see Francis H. K. Wong and Gwee Yee Hean, *Perspectives: The Development of Education in Malaysia and Singapore* (Singapore, 1972). Cynthia Enloe, *Multi-Ethnic Politics, op. cit.*, examines educational policy in the wider perspective of multi-ethnic politics.

On the Federation of Malaysia, see W. A. Hanna, *The Formation of Malaysia: New Factor in World Politics* (New York, 1964); T. E. Smith, *The Background to Malaysia* (London, 1963); M. E. Osborne, *Singapore and Malaysia, op. cit*; Nancy Fletcher's *The Separation of Singapore from Malaysia* (Ithaca, New York, 1969); and Robert A. Andersen, 'The Separation of Singapore from Malaysia: A Study in Political Involution' (PhD Thesis, American University, Washington, DC, 1973). The story of the opposition to the Malaysia Federation from the Philippines and Indonesia can be found in J.A.C. Mackie, *Konfrontasi – The Indonesia–Malaysia Disbute, 1963–1966* (Kuala Lumpur, 1974).

Several studies focus on ethnic communities in the postwar period. On Indians, see Rajeswary Ampalavanar, *The Indian Minority and Political Change in Malaysia, 1945–1957* (Kuala Lumpur, 1981). Ravindra K. Jain, *South Indians on the Plantation Frontier in Malaya* (New Haven, 1970), written as an anthropological study, is relevant for the early years of independence. A wide-ranging collection of essays on Indians is K.S. Sandhu and A. Mani (eds), *Indian Communities in Southeast Asia* (Singapore, 1993).

On the Chinese, see Heng Pek Koon, *Chinese Politics in Malaysia: A History of the Malaysian Chinese Association* (Singapore, 1988), which uses previously untapped material, including MCA papers. Tan Liok Ee, *The Politics of Chinese Education in Malaya, 1945–1961* (Kuala Lumpur, 1997), is a meticulously researched account of this important topic that brings much new data to light. Francis Loh Kok Wah, *Beyond the Tin Mines: Coolies, Squatters and New Villagers in the Kinta Valley, Malaysia, c.1880–1908* (Singapore, 1988), is a sympathetic case study of Chinese squatters in one area of Perak.

On the 1969 ethnic disturbances and post-1969 events, the works by von Vorys (1975), Means (1976), Milne and Mauzy (1978) and Bedlington (1978), cited above, are helpful. For a more detailed account of May 1969, see the official report published by the National Operations Council, *The May 13th Tragedy* (Kuala Lumpur, 1969), which describes the background of the riots, the riots themselves, and then discusses the future direction of the nation. Goh Cheng Teik, *The May Thirteenth Incident and Democracy in Malaysia* (Kuala Lumpur, 1971), provides a political analysis of the reasons for the outbreak of violence; Mahathir bin Mohamad, *The Malay Dilemma* (Singapore, 1970), attempts to see a deeper cultural basis for the disharmony between the Chinese and Malays in the society. Two other studies of the event are J. Slimming, *Malaysia: Death of a Democracy* (London, 1969), and Felix Gagliano, *Communal Violence in Malaysia, 1969: The Political Aftermath* (Athens, Ohio, 1970). Richard Clutterbuck, *Conflict and Violence in Singapore and Malaysia, 1945–83* (Boulder, Colorado, 1983), provides additional analysis, and sets the events of 1969 against the historical background.

Chapter 8: Restructuring Malaysia, 1969–2000

The literature on Malaysia's political and economic development over the last 30 years is voluminous, and only a selection of relevant work can be cited here. Earlier studies of the government's efforts to achieve its economic and social goals through various development plans are the focus of B.A.R. Mokhzani and Khoo Siew Mun (eds), *Poverty in Malaysia* (Kuala Lumpur, 1977), which includes essays by Malaysian scholars discussing various aspects of the Second Malaysia Plan; the contributions in James C. Jackson and Martin Rudner (eds), *Issues in Malaysian Development* (Singapore, 1979), are largely by foreign scholars mainly based in Australia. More recent, but equally critical of the progress in eradicating poverty and removing inequalities in society, are Jomo K.S., *A Question of Class: Capital, the State and Uneven Development* (Singapore, 1986) and *Growth and Structural Change in the Malaysian Economy* (Basingstoke, 1990). The essays in Joel S. Kahn and Frances Loh Kok Wah (eds), *Fragmented Vision: Culture and Politics in Contemporary Malaysia* (Sydney, 1992), provide insightful comments on the contemporary economic background. Two case studies examining the effects of the NEP are Shamsul A.B., *From British to Bumiputera Rule: Local Politics and Rural Development in Peninsular Malaysia* (Singapore, 1986), which focuses on a Malay village in Selangor, and Patrick Guinness, *On the Margin of Capitalism: People and Development in Mukim Plentory, Johor* (Singapore, 1992). Zawawi Ibrahim, *The Malay Labourer: By the Window of Capitalism* (Singapore, 1998), looks at Malay plantation workers in Terengganu. Ishak Shari, 'Rural Development and Rural Poverty in Malaysia: The Experience during the New Economic Policy (1971–1990) Period', in Jamilah Ariffin (ed.), *Poverty amidst Plenty: Research Findings and the Gender Dimension in Malaysia* (Petaling Jaya, 1994), pp. 25–67, gives an excellent analysis of the problems of the government's rural development programme, particularly among the rubber smallholders and the rice farmers who constitute the largest percentage of the rural poor. Other essays in this volume give particular attention to poor women, often ignored in the statistics. Victor T. King and Michael J. G. Parnwell (eds), *Margins and Minorities: The Peripheral Areas and Peoples of Malaysia* (Hull, 1990), focus on peoples and areas who have been marginalized by government development policies.

Harold Brookfield (ed.), *Transformation with Industrialization in Peninsular Malaysia* (Kuala Lumpur, 1994), is an excellent collection of articles on Malaysia's transformation into an industrialized society and the political and environmental consequences of this development. Another recent study is Rokizah Alavi, *Industrialization in Peninsular Malaysia* (London, 1996). Edmund Terence Gomez and Jomo K.S., *Malaysia's Political Economy: Politics, Patronage and Profits* (Cambridge, 1997), examines the manner in which party politics have influenced public policy and the economy, and the links between a growing authoritarian style of government and the rise of crony capitalism. Jomo K.S., *Malaysia's Economy in the Nineties* (Petaling Jaya, 1994) is a collection of essays assessing the economy from different perspectives, including agricultural development, manufacturing, technology transfer and privatization. A clear discussion of the political and economic developments in Malaysia since the introduction of the NEP can be found in Peter Searle, *The Riddle of Malaysian Capitalism: Rent Seekers or Real Capitalists* (Honolulu, 1999). James V. Jesudason, *Ethnicity and the Economy: The State: Chinese Business and Multinationals in Malaysia* (Singapore, 1989), written after the 1987 economic crisis, argues that the government would have been better advised to give more attention to the needs of Chinese and foreign business groups. A more recent study of Chinese business survival is Edmund Terence Gomez, *Chinese Business in Malaysia: Accumulation, Ascendance, Accommodation* (Honolulu, 1999). Wee Chong Hui, *Sabah and Sarawak in the Malaysian Economy* (Kuala Lumpur, 1995), argues that that Sabah and Sarawak are slowly losing the special advantages negotiated when they joined the Federation.

The political scene during the NEP years has been exhaustively discussed in Gordon P. Means, *Malaysian Politics: The Second Generation* (Kuala Lumpur, 1991). Harold Crouch, *Government and Society in Malaysia* (Ithaca/London, 1996), is a well-written and thoughtful analysis of NEP politics and the impact on Malaysian society. R.S. Milne and Diane K. Mauzy, *Malaysian Politics under Mahathir* (London/New York, 1999), give an account of Mahathir's influence on the course of politics in Malaysia since his accession to power in 1981, and can be read together with Khoo Boo Teik, *Paradoxes of Mahathirism: An Intellectual Biography of Mahathir Mohamad* (Kuala Lumpur, 1995). The complexities of Chinese politics are discussed in Heng Pek Hoon, *Chinese Politics in Malaysia: A History of the Malaysian Chinese Association* (Singapore, 1988); a Sarawak perspective is Chin Ung-Ho, *Chinese Politics in Sarawak: A Study of the Sarawak United Peoples Party* (Kuala Lumpur, 1996).

The literature on women and development in Malaysia is expanding. Two collections of essays on specific topics are Cecilia Ng (ed.), *Positioning Women in Malaysia: Class and Gender in an Industrializing State* (London and Basingstoke, 1999), and Jamilah Ariffin (ed.), *Women & Development in Malaysia* (Kuala Lumpur, 1992). For women in industry, see Aihwa Ong's influential, *Spirits of Resistance and Capitalist Discipline: Factory Women in Malaysia* (Albany, New York, 1987), and Merete Lie and Ragnhild Lund, *Renegotiating Local Values: Working Women and Foreign Industry in Malaysia* (Surrey, 1996). An examination of Malay women in the context of a national culture is Wazir Abdul Karim, *Women and Culture: Between Malay Adat and Islam* (Colorado, 1992). There are a few studies of women in political life: see the pioneering monograph by Leonore Manderson, *Women, Politics and Change: The Kaum Ibu UMNO, Malaysia, 1945–1972* (Kuala Lumpur, 1980); Virginia Dancz, *Women and Party Politics in Peninsular Malaysia* (Singapore, 1987); Rashila Ramli, 'Democratisation in Malaysia: Towards Gender Parity in Political Participation', *Akademika*, 53 (July 1998), pp. 61–76. Michael Peletz, *A Share of the Harvest: Kinship, Property and Social History among the Malays of Rembau* (Berkeley, 1988) and *Reason and Passion: Representations of Gender in a Malay Society* (Berkeley, 1996), examines the adaptation of matrilineal Minangkabau traditions to a modernizing Malay environment.

Selvakumaran Ramachandran, *Indian Plantation Labour in Malaysia* (Kuala Lumpur, 1994), discusses the extent to which Indian plantation workers have been relegated to a marginalized existence. Another contemporary study is P. Ramasamy, *Plantation Labour, Unions, Capital, and the State in Peninsular Malaysia* (Kuala Lumpur and New York, 1994). A valuable collection of essays on Indians in contemporary Malaysia is K.S. Sandhu and A. Mani, *Indian Communities in Southeast Asia* (Singapore, 1993).

Richard Leete, *Malaysia's Demographic Transition: Rapid Development, Culture, and Politics* (Kuala Lumpur, 1996), provides a clear discussion of population trends in both Peninsular and the Borneo states together with helpful statistics. Muhammad Ikmal Said and Zahid Emby (eds), *Malaysia: Critical Perspectives. Essays in Honour of Syed Husin Ali* (Kuala Lumpur, 1996), is a provocative collection of essays in Malay and English which focuses especially on issues connected with class, and other socio-political issues. Patricia Sloane, *Islam, Modernity and Entrepreneurship among the Malays* (London, 1999), is a lively and insightful commentary on the attitudes of a new generation of Malay entrepreneurs. Ahm Zehadul Karim, Moha Asri Abdullah and Mohd Isa Haji Bakar, *Foreign Workers in Malaysia: Issues and Implications* (Kuala Lumpur, 1999), amasses considerable data to present a case against the use of foreign labour.

There is a growing corpus of books and articles on the Orang Asli, many related to environmental issues. Razha Rashid (ed.), *Indigenous Minorities of Peninsular Malaysia: Selected Issues and Ethnographies* (Kuala Lumpur, 1995), gives a grim picture of the effects of development which is supported by most of the literature. See further Robert Knox Dentan, Kirk Endicott, Alberto G. Gomes and M.B. Hooker, *Malaysia and the 'Original People': A Case Study of the Impact of Development on Indigenous Peoples* (Needham Heights, Massachusetts, 1997); Lim Hin Fui, *Orang Asli, Forest and Development* (Kuala Lumpur, 1997). Another collection by well-known authorities is Robert L. Winzeler (ed.), *Indigenous Peoples and the State: Politics, Land and Ethnicity in the Malayan Peninsula and Borneo* (New Haven, 1997)

The environment has also received considerable attention, especially in relation to Sabah and Sarawak. A recent study which focuses on the NEP period is Fadzilah Majid Cooke, *The Challenge of Sustainable Forests: Forest Resource Policy in Malaysia, 1970–1995* (Honolulu, 1999). Mark Cleary and Peter Eaton, *Borneo: Change and Development* (Singapore, 1992), place contemporary issues in Sarawak and Sabah in both a historical and Borneo-wide framework.

The literature on Islam available in Malay is extensive. Among publications in English, Judith Nagata, *The Reflowering of Malaysian Islam* (Vancouver, 1984), is a thoughtful examination of the *dakwah* movement which can be read in conjunction with Chandra Muzaffar, *Islamic Resurgence in Malaysia* (Petaling Jaya, 1987). Another study which also examines the ideas of revivalism and the Islamic state in the Malaysian context is Hussin Mutalib, *Islam in Malaysia: From Revivalism to Islamic State* (Singapore, 1993). His chapter 2 is especially useful in discussing the growing strength of Islam in Malaysia since 1969.

Glossary

adat	customs and traditions
anak raja	royal offspring
Baba	people of Chinese-Malay descent
bahasa	from Sanskrit: literally 'language', but often used in the past to refer to the whole range of acceptable behaviour among Malays
bendahara	principal officer in a Malay kingdom, often likened to a prime minister
bukit	hill
Bumiputera	'sons of the soil'; a term employed by the Malaysian government to refer to Malays and all other indigenous groups in the country
bunga mas dan perak	'gold and silver flowers', which evolved into bejewelled ornamental trees accompanied by valuable gifts, sent regularly as tribute from vassal states to the Thai court
chao phraya	high-ranking Thai title bestowed on vassal rulers and governors
daeng	a Bugis title of nobility
dakwah	to 'call' or 'invite', i.e. the duty of Muslims to call all mankind to Islam; in Malaysia the term is associated with a fundamentalist Islamic revival movement
dato, datuk	a title often associated with a great non-royal chief; in modern Malaysia the term 'Datuk' is conferred in recognition of outstanding service to the nation

daulat	Arabic loan word, often translated as 'sovereignty' but which traditionally referred to the special spiritual forces surrounding Malay kingship
derhaka	Sanskrit loan word, meaning treason to the lawful authority, thus most often equated with treason to the ruler
Dewan Negara	the Senate, the Upper House of Malaysia's Parliament
Dewan Rakyat	the House of Representatives, the Lower House of Malaysia's Parliament
Durbar	Conference of Rulers, referring to the periodical meeting of the rulers of the Malay states
hikayat	narrative, story, tale in prose
hui	Chinese society
huaqiao	overseas Chinese
Jawi Peranakan	locally born Muslims of mixed Indian/Malay or Arab/Malay descent
kampung	a village; a compound of houses usually under the authority of an important individual
kerajaan	literally, 'the state of having a raja', government
kongsi	Chinese business co-operative
kuala	estuary
laksamana	an important official whose principal duty was to be in charge of the ruler's fleet, hence often equated with an admiral
Madrasah	a Modernist Islamic school
menteri	minister in government administration
menteri besar	chief minister
monthon	Thai provincial administrative unit; 'circle'
mukim	administrative district around a common mosque

Glossary

Nan Yang	'Southern Ocean', a term used in Chinese imperial records to refer generally to the Southeast Asian region
negeri	settlement, state, country
nipa	thatch palm, *Nipa fruticana*
Orang Asli	indigenous groups living on the Malay Peninsula, excluding ethnic Malays
Orang Kaya	literally 'rich man', but a term applied more commonly for nobility; sometimes used to refer to a district chief
Orang Laut	sea and riverine peoples
padi	wet-rice agriculture
penghulu	headman; head of a village; district head
perahu	Malay boat without deck
pikul	a measure of weight, about 62.5 kilogrammes
pondok schools	'hut' schools, referring to the past practice of pupils erecting huts for accommodation during the period they studied with an Islamic teacher; traditional Islamic education
prathesaraj	Thai vassal of semi-independent status
pulau	island
raja muda	heir-apparent, but in the kingdom of Johor this title was appropriated by the Bugis in the early eighteenth century for their leader, who often directed affairs of the kingdom on behalf of the Malay ruler
Rukunegara	Articles of Faith of the State
singkeh	literally 'new man'; a recent Chinese immigrant
suku	clan; among Minangkabaus in the Malay Peninsula, this term refers to a number of uterine families (*perut*); also used to refer to Orang Laut tribes
sungai	river

syahbandar	harbour master, a post which gained in importance as international trade grew in Malay kingdoms
syariah	Islamic law, in contradistinction to *adat*, which is law based on customs and traditions
temenggung	Malay minister in charge of defence, justice and palace affairs
tengku, tunku	title for Malay princes
thesaphiban	a reorganization of Siamese provinces into circles (*monthon*), instituted in the 1890s
ulama	religious teacher
ulu	upriver
umat or *ummat*	the world community of Muslims
yang dipertuan agung	paramount ruler
yang dipertuan besar	'great king': a title given to Malay and Minangkabau rulers
yang dipertuan muda (*yamtuan muda* in Johor)	'young king': title of the raja muda, or heir-apparent, in Malay states, but in Johor bestowed on the Bugis leader

Index